FREEDOM'S ODYSSEY

African American History Essays from *Phylon*

Edited by

ALEXA BENSON HENDERSON AND JANICE SUMLER-EDMOND

Clark Atlanta University Press
Atlanta, Georgia

For Lucy Clemmons Grigsby (1916-1999),

a student research assistant to W. E. B. DuBois

and for forty-four years associate editor of *Phylon*

and

For our husbands,

Steven Edmond and William A. Henderson

Acknowledgments

We are delighted that *Freedom's Odyssey* was selected as the inaugural publication of the newly established Clark Atlanta University Press. We acknowledge our indebtedness to the scholars whose insightful work provides the foundation for this volume, and we express our appreciation to Charles Duncan, editor of the CAU Press, for providing his expertise throughout the course of this project. Our appreciation goes to Clark Atlanta University and the Editorial Board of *Phylon* for permission to republish the essays, and also to Toni O'Neal Mosley and the staff of University Relations for the cover design. We thank also Title III administrator Elton Hugee and his staff for support of this publication. We extend our gratitude to President Thomas W. Cole, Jr., for his commitment to the CAU Press and to *Phylon*, an important aspect of the DuBois legacy. Finally, our deepest gratitude is reserved for our husbands, Steven Edmond and Bill Henderson.

ALEXA BENSON HENDERSON
JANICE SUMLER-EDMOND

Freedom, too, the long-sought, we still seek—

the freedom of life and limb, the freedom to work

and think, the freedom to love and aspire.

W. E. B. DuBois
The Souls of Black Folk

FREEDOM'S ODYSSEY

Contents

Editors' Introduction

Shout, O Children!
Shout, you're free!
For God has bought your liberty!

W. E. B. DuBois
The Souls of Black Folk

In many ways *Freedom's Odyssey* is a tribute to the monumental legacy of William E. B. DuBois—legendary scholar, social activist, and distinguished professor at Atlanta University. During a lifetime of nearly a century, DuBois made immense intellectual and political contributions to the historical struggles of peoples of African descent. In hundreds of books, articles, essays, and speeches, DuBois passionately decried racism and vigorously championed freedom and equality for African Americans and other oppressed minorities. He also founded and edited a number of magazines and journals including, most notably, *The Crisis*, the official organ of the NAACP, through which DuBois spread his racial philosophy, and *Phylon*, a quarterly journal he founded in 1940 at Atlanta University to present scholarly research on the race problem.

In *Phylon: A Review of Race and Culture* DuBois created a powerful vehicle for education and scholarship. Initially proposing the establishment of a scholarly journal early in the century, DuBois underscored the need to combat racism by dispelling the ignorance and prejudices that relegated blacks to second-class citizenship through scientific, reliable studies of the African American experience. His return to Atlanta University in 1933 to resume an academic career as head of the Sociology Department, following an intervening stint with the NAACP in New York, provided the opportunity to establish the long-waited scholarly journal. Beginning with its initial publication in 1940 and continuing through 1988, *Phylon* served as a significant medium for scholars conducting research on race and racism as international phenomena and for promoting the rich cultural life of black peoples throughout the African diaspora.

During its nearly fifty years of continuous publication, articles on African American history constituted one of the most frequent and significant topic areas addressed in *Phylon*—cumulatively, nearly 200 articles. *Freedom's Odyssey* contains twenty-nine essays on African American history selected from this important body of research. The essays address significant aspects of the African American odyssey to achieve full freedom, including the interminable battles to overcome enslavement and racial oppression. The excellent scholarship comprising this volume covers topics including African enslavement and abolition, Reconstruction issues of education and peonage, Westward migration, Jim Crow separation and inequality, twentieth-century race and organizational leadership, and the modern civil rights movements. The articles, including all their critical apparatus, have been reprinted in the form in which they originally appeared.

Freedom's Odyssey is intended both as a monographic reference work and homage to the *Phylon* and DuBois legacy as well as a work of contemporary pedagogical significance. Toward that end, *Freedom's Odyssey* is designed to be suitable for graduate and undergraduate courses in African American history, United States history, African American studies, and historiography. While the essays collectively provide a broad framework for the study of the African American experience, each entry individually chronicles a significant aspect of the racial dilemma in America. Organized chronologically and thematically, the anthology explores the odyssey of Africans in America from the horrors of the middle passage to the modern civil rights strategies of Dr. Martin Luther King, Jr. and others. Each essay is preceded by a contextual introduction by the editors, positioning the essay in the study of African American history and diasporic scholarship. The editors' objectives include contributing to the debate on race and racial issues while introducing a new generation of students to *Phylon*, a significant component of the DuBois legacy.

Freedom's Odyssey is divided into five parts, each focusing on an aspect of the African American struggle for freedom. In Part One, "Freedom Denied," the essays examine the brutality of the slave system and the myriad ways enslaved Africans expressed their unceasing desire for freedom. In the lead essay, Janet Cornelius examines the insatiable desire for literacy and the enduring belief in its liberating potential that characterized the black population. Cornelius emphasizes the resourcefulness of enslaved Africans in acquiring literacy and in using the resulting skills to achieve mobility, improve communication within their community, and expand opportunities for escaping slavery's tyrannical grasp. Clarence L. Mohr, describing the unenviable lot of enslaved blacks in Oglethorpe County, Georgia, demonstrates the powerful currents for violence and unrest that existed under slavery and under the tightening of controls that followed rumors of uprisings by blacks. The essays by Lorenzo J. Greene and Marion D. de B. Kilson address the rebellious acts of enslaved Africans, including uprisings aboard slave ships bound for the New World and the range of attempts to thwart slavery that varied from individual negligence in work to mass slave revolts. Concluding this section, the essay by John Herbert Roper and Lolita G. Brockington examines a racial theme that dominated Euro-American political debate for three hundred years, namely that blacks could never rise above a servile class.

Part Two, "Freedom Beckons," consists of four essays devoted to abolitionists and their proposals to improve the status of blacks in the United States, both enslaved and free. The Declaration of Independence served as the mainspring of arguments against slavery as a basic violation of human rights. The Declaration also provided sound philosophical arguments to propel African Americans toward full freedom and citizenship. The essays selected show that, in the ordeal of moving toward freedom, the viewpoints of African Americans and their antislavery supporters varied from firmly held opinions that the United States represented the best hope for realizing first-class citizenship to the equally strong convictions in some quarters that colonization was a desirable, even necessary, measure to accompany emancipation.

In these essays, the writers explore the divergent sentiment on the issues of antislavery and manumission. John L. Rury, examining the New York Manumission Society created in 1785, describes the work of an early organization established for the emancipation and protection of blacks and emphasizes the developing institutional framework of a free black community in the 1790s. The essay by Bruce Rosen examines the issues of abolition and colonization, clarifying the opposition of many blacks to colonization and their condemnation of the early schemes to remove free blacks to Africa or elsewhere. Conversely, Howard Bell shows that as discontent increased among blacks in the early 1850s, some, earlier opposed to colonization, began embracing emigration strategies. Finally, Tyrone Tillery analyzes the perspectives of two preeminent, but warring, proponents of immediate emancipation: Frederick Douglass and William Lloyd Garrison. Despite the forceful voices of these and other proponents, resistance to antislavery arguments hardened as civil war loomed on the horizon and freedom for blacks remained unrealized.

The six essays in Part Three, "Freedom's People," portray African Americans exercising their newly won rights of citizenship. Blacks championed crucial issues such as universal tax-supported education, widespread economic advancement, and the elective franchise. African Americans envisioned the dawning of a new era of freedom with a semblance of opportunity for all. According to Edward F. Sweat's essay, African American delegates to the South Carolina constitutional convention of 1868 believed that education provided knowledge and that knowledge provided citizen power. Thus, the creation of a public education system remained high on their legislative agenda. August Meier's essay demonstrates that for many African Americans the sophisticated use of the ballot box to advance the race took precedence over loyalty to the Republican party. Economic advancement also figured prominently in the Reconstruction era, as demonstrated in William Holmes' essay on the Colored Farmer's Alliance, one important cooperative venture.

Regrettably, the nation's preoccupation with race and the invidious effects of racism in every aspect of American life clouded black optimism about the future. Philip Foner's essay explains how racist attitudes prevented significant black participation in the Centennial celebration of 1876. Similarly, Billy Higgins' essay discusses how the combination of white racism and a downturn in the economy led to the mass exodus of blacks to Kansas and Indiana in 1879. N. Gordon Carper's essay analyzes how the national acceptance of a "white over black" status quo fostered an exploitive peonage system, entrapping hundreds of African Americans in the South. During this same era, racial antipathy sometimes erupted into violent massacres, creating roadblocks to African American freedom.

Part Four, "Freedom Delayed," chronicles the widespread racial separation and inequality of the Jim Crow era and the varied African American responses to those obstacles. During segregation, for example, black community activists labored to ensure quality education for their children. Similarly, many African Americans joined forces to press toward greater integration of blacks into the military. Arthur O. White's essay examines how one Northern black community used judicial process and civil rights legislation to effect change, while Hal S. Chase's essay traces the creation of the Fort Des Moines Training Camp for Colored Officers during World War I. According to Daniel F. Littlefield, Jr., and Lonnie E. Underhill, the search for a black promised land led some visionary African Americans to promote settlement in the Oklahoma territory, and black townships in Oklahoma formed one response to the national agenda of racism and suppression of black citizenship rights.

Beyond issues of community development and organization in the West and elsewhere, the essays by Bill Weaver, Oscar Page, and Richard M. Dalfiume discuss the black press and the NAACP's respective roles in attacking segregation in the military, in higher education, and in professional sports. The essay by Brenda Gayle Plummer provides clear evidence that as African Americans protested segregation within the nation, they also matured in their awareness of closely related international issues. When the United States occupied the black island nation of Haiti, many African Americans opposed the racist and imperialist aspects of the mission. Collectively, the essays in Part Four demonstrate that, through a variety of strategies, African Americans struggled to realize the inherent freedom that accompanies first-class citizenship. Although that elusive freedom was effectively delayed during the Jim Crow era, ultimately, it could not be denied.

The essays in Part Five, "Freedom's Champions," explore African American leadership and organizational efforts to achieve full freedom. In seeking solutions to problems of the color line, identified by DuBois as the central problem of the twentieth century, the individuals and organizations discussed worked vigorously to improve conditions for African Americans. Booker T. Washington was for several decades a central and imposing figure, acclaimed by many as the most significant and influential black leader of his era. Willard Gatewood's essay examines Washington and racial prejudices through the 1911 Ulrich Affair, a much publicized event arising from a physical attack upon Washington by a white New Yorker. The activities of Ida B. Wells, militant newspaperwoman and crusading foe of lynching in the South, are explored in the essay by David M. Tucker. Bernard Eisenberg's analysis of the NAACP under the leadership of the first African American Executive Secretary, James Weldon Johnson, gives specific attention to its role in championing the cause of the urban black laborer.

Several of these essays probe dilemmas confronting black Americans in the post-World War I era. The 1932 presidential election provides the setting for Charles H. Martin's essay, in which he explores the political and economic issues facing African American leadership during the Great Depression. Focusing on Walter White's historic visit to the British war front during World War II, Thomas Hachey's essay provides insight into the treatment of African Americans in the armed forces and the efforts to accelerate military desegregation. The emergence of the Federal Bureau of Investigation as a modern governmental agency is treated by Kenneth O'Reilly, who examines how African American leaders lobbied for a bureau that would protect civil rights, although bureau administrators had different priorities. Finally, James A. Colaiaco's essay underscores the successful strategy of nonviolent direct action employed by Martin Luther King, Jr., and the value of mass demonstrations in exposing the evils of American racism. As skillful and pragmatic champions of freedom, these and other black leaders demonstrated, as King wrote in the 1963 "Letter from Birmingham Jail," that "freedom is never voluntarily given by the oppressor; it must be demanded by the oppressed."

ALEXA BENSON HENDERSON AND JANICE SUMLER-EDMOND

Part One

FREEDOM DENIED: ENSLAVED AFRICANS

Blacks, by insisting on their humanity and on their adult-hood, had refused to live unprotesting in a slave world. Whites heard the shrillness of the protest but consciously did not hear its deeper resonance; in the end whites refused to hear blacks at all. At critical junctures . . . society could not body forth a definition of Africans or Afro-Americans that permitted blacks any freedom; to be here, the blacks must be other than free.

Roper and Brockington,
Slave Revolt, Slave Debate: A Comparison

"We Slipped and Learned to Read": Slave Accounts of the Literacy Process, 1830-1865

Janet Cornelius

All over the South, proscriptions against literacy for blacks existed in both law and custom. A body of repressive measures, generally known as the "Black Codes" provided the legal context for systematic control of all aspects of the lives of enslaved Africans, including prohibitions against their learning to read and write. Fearing that literate blacks would undermine the established social order, whites enacted harsh penalties for any slave engaging in this activity. Despite the dangers that existed in learning to read and write, enslaved blacks frequently aspired to basic literacy.

Janet Cornelius's essay provides insight into the literacy process within the slave community in the face of legal and social prohibitions. Using the slave narratives collected by the Federal Writers Project of the Works Progress Administration in the 1930s, along with autobiographies, interviews, and other sources by nineteenth-century black writers, the author reveals a good deal about the individuals seeking to learn, as well as the people, both blacks and whites, providing instruction to African Americans. This essay is an excellent resource for understanding the motivations of African Americans in their pursuit of literacy and their belief in its promise as a path to mobility and increased self-worth.

DESPITE THE DANGERS AND DIFFICULTIES, thousands of slaves learned to read and write in the antebellum South. Few left traces of their accomplishments, but 272 ex-slaves who told how they learned to read and write during slavery provide insight into the literacy process within the slave community. For slaves, literacy was a two-edged sword: owners offered literacy to increase their control, but resourceful slaves seized the opportunity to expand their own powers. Slaves who learned to read and write gained privacy, leisure time, and mobility. A few wrote their own passes and escaped from slavery. Literate slaves also taught others and served as conduits for information within a slave communication network. Some were able to capitalize on their skills in literacy as a starting point for leadership careers after slavery ended.

Historians of education have drawn a distinction between "Bible literacy," whose prime motive was the conservation of piety, and "liberating literacy," which facilitates diversity and mobility.[1] The majority of owners who taught slaves were concerned with Bible literacy, and connected their instruction with Christian worship and catechization. The traditional nature of this teaching is shown by the number of slaveowners who gave slaves religion-associated instruction in reading but not in writing, a practice which recalled the early Protestant insistence that even the poor and powerless should be able to read the word of God for themselves, but that teaching them to write would threaten the social order.[2]

The religious context for learning was as important for slaves as it was for owners; most slaves who learned to read on their own initiative did so in a religious context, demonstrating that Christian teachings and opportunities could have liberating as well as conservative results. Reading the Bible for oneself enabled a slave to undercut a master's attempt to restrict Christian teaching to carefully selected Biblical passages. Knowing how to read gave slaves opportunities to assume religious leadership within the slave community, where reading and preaching were closely associated.[3]

The present study compiles and measures evidence from former slaves on specific aspects of the literacy process: which slaves learned to read and write, what levels of literacy they attained, who taught them, the context in which this teaching and learning took place, and why slaves were taught or taught themselves. Two sources for evidence by former slaves who learned to read and write were used to examine literacy in the slave community. Most evidence was taken from the slave narratives gathered by the Federal Writers Project of the Works Progress Administration, as edited by George Rawick and published under the title *The American Slave: A Composite Autobiography*, in its original 19 volumes and the 12-volume Supplement 1, and in the Virginia interviews published separately as *Weevils in the Wheat: Interviews with Virginia Ex-Slaves*.[4] A reading and analysis of all the 3,428 responses by ex-slaves questioned by the Federal Writers Project interviewers as compiled in these volumes pinpointed just over 5 percent (179) who mentioned having learned to read and write as slaves.[5] In addition to the evidence from the Writers Project interviews, 93 ex-slave accounts were taken from a variety of other sources, including autobiographies and narratives by former slaves; interviews with former slaves by nineteenth century black writers; life histories told by ex-slaves who had fled to Canada or were seeking help on the Underground Railroad; and cyclopedias compiled by black editors listing prominent black Americans, for which they submitted their own autobiographies.[6] Only two of these narratives and autobiographies, taken largely from ex-slaves in the public sphere, were written by women. However, the Federal Writers Project interviewees who learned to read and write included 67 women out of the 179 blacks interviewed for the Project who mentioned acquiring skills in literacy while they were slaves.

These two kinds of sources encompassed a broad time frame and extensive regional coverage. Since the Federal Writers Project interviews took place more than seventy years after the end of slavery, the majority of ex-slaves who talked about their experiences were small children during slavery. This was less true for the other slaves in the study. Most of the Writers Project former slaves learned to read after 1855, while two-thirds of the other ex-slaves learned to read before that date. The two kinds of ex-slave sources also represent literate slaves in different regions of the South. The Writers Project was weighted towards the Old South and the New South frontier states. The Border South states are more strongly represented in the other ex-slave sources. The Old South is most heavily represented overall.

Accounts by former slaves used in this study illustrate the reasons why the extent of literacy among slaves is almost impossible to measure. According to these accounts, neither slaves nor slaveowners and other whites who taught them could proclaim their activities safely. Patrols, mobs, and social ostracism faced owners who taught their slaves. One former slave even recalled whispered rumors that her master had been poisoned because he taught his slaves to read and write and allowed them to save enough money to buy land at the end of the Civil War.[7] Slaves themselves believed they faced terrible punishments if whites discovered they could read and write. A common punishment for slaves who had attained more skills, according to blacks who were slaves as children in South Carolina, Georgia, Texas, and Mississippi, was amputation, as described by Doc Daniel Dowdy, a slave in Madison County, Georgia: "The first time you was caught trying to read or write, you was whipped with a cow-hide, the next time with a cat-o-nine-tails and the third time they cut the first jint offen your forefinger." Another Georgia ex-slave carried the story horrifyingly further: "If they caught you trying to write they would cut your finger off and if they caught you again they would cut your head off."[8] None of the 272 slaves in this study actually suffered any such punishments as they learned to read and write, but some had personal knowledge that such atrocities had occurred. Henry Nix's uncle stole a book and was trying to learn to read and write with it, so "Marse Jasper had the white doctor take off my Uncle's fo'finger right down to de 'fust jint" as a "sign fo de res uv 'em." Lizzie Williams told of "one woman named Nancy durin' de war what could read and 'rite. When her master, Oliver Perry, found dis out he made her pull off naked, whipped her and den slapped hot irons to her all over. Believe me dat nigger didn't want to read and 'rite no more." Joseph Booker's father, Albert, was charged with "spoiling the good niggers" by teaching them to read and was whipped to death when Joseph was three years old.[9]

Few such demonstrations were necessary to effectively stifle the desire to read among most slaves, and to establish a mythology about the dangers of reading and writing. That former slaves remembered the atrocity stories so well from their childhood suggests that they had been tempted to learn to read, and that their parents feared that they might take advantage of an opportunity to do so. It also might give rise to speculation that the children themselves did not know how many people in a single plantation community might actually possess reading and writing skills, since the knowledge of this possession led to so much danger. The recollection of Campbell Davis, thirteen years old when slavery ended, that "us git some book larnin' mongst ourselves, round de quarters, and have our own preacher," may therefore have been true within many slave communities without the knowledge of the children. As Sarah Fitzpatrick observed from her experiences as a house servant in Alabama, many slaves could read but "de ke' dat up deir sleeve, dey played dumb lack de couldn't read a bit till after surrender."[10]

Slaves who learned to read and write were a select group. Slaves who could read included a higher percentage of urban and house slaves than was true for the slave population as a whole. While the urban population of slaves in the southern United States in the immediate antebellum period is estimated at less than 4 percent,[11] at least 16.5 percent of the former slaves who could read and write described themselves as urban. House slaves were also highly represented among the slaves who learned to read: three-fourths of the former slaves who specified their tasks during slavery described domestic duties.[12] A mitigating factor might be taken into account in observing the high number of house slaves, though: the majority of slaves studied were young children when they began to acquire the skills of reading. Young children often did house duties before they reached an age when they worked in the fields:

(N=212)   Slaves who read before age 12 . . . . 150 (70.8 percent)

Slaves who read at age 12 or over   62 (29.2 percent)

Nevertheless, the former slaves who learned to read and write had more opportunities for learning than other slaves. Their careers after slavery provide another indication of the exceptional nature of the former slaves who learned to read and write. A large number held leadership positions in the ministry, government, and education.

Almost one-third of the slaves learned to read but not to write. However, given the lack of tools and the special dangers involved in writing, it is noteworthy that the majority of former slaves did learn to write as well as to read.

Teachers of slaves were tabulated in two ways: those who were most responsible for initiating learning (only one person was counted per slave) and those who participated in teaching slaves (more than one could be mentioned by the same slave). When the initiators of learning are compiled, the two sources of former slave evidence vary greatly. Two-thirds of the Writers Project former slaves credited whites with providing the initiative and the means for their learning to read, while well over half the ex-slaves in the other sources gave themselves the credit for initiating and obtaining their learning. Some of this disparity is due to the ways in which evidence was gathered. Living in poverty and dependent for their basic needs on the good will of others, most of the Writers Project interviewees consisted of those ex-slaves most easily found by the predominantly white interviewers. Dependent ex-slaves, hoping that the interviewers could help them collect their old-age pensions, could have inflated the helping role played by the "kind" white master or mistress.

The slaves who wrote their own autobiographies and narratives, on the other hand, were the more perceptive and gifted members of the black community, as well as the relatively more fortunate, and had more control over the information they sought to give. Those former slaves who wrote narratives for a Northern antebellum audience had good reason to minimize any role by Southern whites in their achievements. Those who wrote autobiographies after slavery understandably may have remembered their own roles more sharply and precisely than the part played by others, including whites, who may have contributed to their learning.[13] Fewer owner-taught slaves assumed leadership careers after slavery. "Stealing" their own learning and obtaining subsequent leadership positions suggests that certain talented slaves acted effectively upon their belief in the "liberating" quality of literacy.

Counting all who participated in teaching slaves to read or write, 203 whites taught or helped to teach the 272 ex-slaves. Highlighting the closed character of the plantation system, at least three-fourths of these whites were slaveowners, their children, or teachers they hired. Twice as many mistresses as masters taught. Teaching was an acceptable female function; some women inherited this task as part of household management. Charity Jones' mistress taught her to read and write, along with learning to card bats and spin, weave cloth, sew, and sweep. Close association in the house between white and black women sometimes included opportunities for reading. Jane Pyatt recalled that "when I was a slave, I worked in the house with my mistress, and I was able to learn lots from her. . . . although it was against the law to teach a slave, my mistress taught me my alphabets." Betty Ivery's mistress taught her to read after the day's work was done, "long after dark."[14]

Former slaves mentioned children more than any other group of whites as their teachers. Most were the adolescent daughters and sons of slaveowners or the younger playmates of slaves. Slave children often learned while accompanying their white playmates to and from school, or during studying time at night. White children taught their slave playmates secretly or without conscious violation of law or custom. Sometimes white children were more tacitly or openly encouraged by white adults, who may have allowed their children to dare to do what they could not. Henry Bruce, for example, learned from the white boy he accompanied to and from school. When the boy's aunt found out and complained, Henry's owner seemed not to care about it and did nothing to stop it; in fact, he corrected Henry's spelling. Solomon, the black overseer on a large plantation, took his little mistress Liza to school. She taught him to read, and "as she growed up she kept learning more and Solomon had married and Miss Liza would go down to his cabin every night and teach him [and his wife] some more." When his master caught Solomon with a Bible in his lap and found out Liza had taught him, he was pleased and amused and even had Solomon show off by reading the Bible to some of his friends. He was able to parade Solomon's accomplishment since he had not been personally responsible for it.[15]

White teachers hired by slaveowners also participated in the teaching of the slaves. Louis Watkin's owner, for example, employed a white tutor who came on Sunday afternoons to his Tennessee plantation and taught slaves to read, write and figure. In Georgia, Neal Upson's master built a little one-room schoolhouse in the back yard of the main house, where a white teacher taught the slave children reading and writing. Harrison Beckett characterized his teacher on a large Texas plantation as a "broke-down white man," who taught "de chillen reading and writing, and manners and behaviour, too. . . . Slaves paid other whites in the cities to help them. Occasionally men or women came to the plantations on their own volition to teach slaves. Ellen Cragin remembered an old white man who used to come to teach her father in rural Mississippi. The old man cautioned the slave family not to tell the other whites what he was doing: "If you do [tell], they will kill me."[16]

Former slaves mentioned themselves as their own teachers more often than they named other blacks. Typically, Elijah P. Marrs explained that "very early in life I took up the ideal that I wanted to learn to read and write. . . . I availed myself of every opportunity, daily I carried my book in my pocket, and every chance that offered would be learning my A,B,Cs." Many slaves credited their parents with a role in their learning. Determined mothers taught their children, sent them to schools when available, or paid others to teach them. Fathers also figured as teachers, even when they did not live with their families. Anderson Whitted's father, for example, lived fourteen miles away from him, but was allowed to use a horse to visit him and taught Anderson to read on his biweekly visits.[17]

Brothers and sisters also taught one another. The children in Henry Bruce's family shared the knowledge learned from their white playmates: "The older one would teach the younger, and while mother had no education at all, she used to make the younger study the lessons given by the older sister or brother, and in that way we all learned to read and some to write." Other family members served as teachers. Ann Stokes' cousin taught her the alphabet "in the middle ob a field unnerneath a 'simmon tree." Grandmothers, central family figures, were mentioned as teachers. Maria Parham's grandmother, "Old Lady Patsy," took care of all the sick and also taught Maria to read. Henrietta Murray's grandmother taught a Sunday school class on her Choctaw County, Mississippi, plantation and, according to Henrietta, "taught us all we knowed."[18]

Other blacks mentioned as teachers included those who shared their knowledge of reading and writing beyond their family group. These included a slave in Tennessee who would make figures and letters on a wooden pad to teach the slave boys how to read and write, and Solomon, free and "ginger cake color," who made his living carrying his slate and book from plantation to plantation in Georgia, teaching slaves "for little what they could slip him along." Teaching was hazardous for the health of the black teacher and also a terrific responsibility. Enoch Golden, known to the slaves as a "double-headed nigger" because he could read and write and "knowed so much," was said to have confessed on his deathbed that he "been the death o' many a nigger 'cause he taught so many to read and write."[19]

Slaves seldom identified specific reasons why whites taught them to read and write.[20] Only the religious context of much of the teaching by whites stands out clearly as a motivation. Often teaching was casual and depended upon the slave's proximity to the house or to white playmates or upon the whims of owners. Some slaves became the pets of the white family as tiny children and family members thought it "cute" to see them learning the alphabet and trying to read. "Bunny" Bond's owners dressed her up and let her go to school with the white children when she was five, then laughed when she fell asleep and wanted to go home. Robert McKinley's owner gave the little boy to his favorite daughter, Jane Alice, as a present; she was very fond of little Bob so she taught him to read and write.[21]

A few slaveowners obviously taught their slaves because they believed in the intrinsic value of education. Robert Laird's Mississippi owner had his slaves taught how to read and write simply because "he didn't want us not to know nothin." The owner of Robert Cheatham's mother in Kentucky tried to carry on a family tradition from Virginia, telling his slaves, "You colored boys and girls must learn to read and write, no matter what powers object . . . your parents and your grandparents were taught to read and write when they belonged to my forefathers and you young negroes have to learn as much."[22]

Sometimes whites taught for pragmatic reasons. Washington Curry's father was a doctor, and Curry recalled that "there were so many folks that came to see the doctor and wanted to leave numbers and addresses that he had to have someone to 'tend to that and he taught my father to read and write so that he could do it." Adeline Willis' mistress taught her the letters on the newspapers and what they spelled so she could bring the papers the whites wanted. Simpson Campbell's "Marse Bill" taught some of his slaves reading and writing so he could use them "booking cotton in the field and such like."[23]

Religion, however, was mentioned by former slaves more often than any other context in which teaching by whites took place. On the plantation and in cities, according to ex-slave accounts, owners built churches and schoolhouses and hired teachers or conducted worship and Sunday schools themselves, where they perpetuated the original function of the Sunday school as the inculcator of literacy as well as religion. Squire Dowd's mistress taught such a class on a North Carolina plantation; so did Mollie Mittchell's and Easter Jones' owners on plantations in Georgia. Near Birmingham, Alabama, Andrew Goodman's "Marse Bob" built his slaves a church, where a nearby slave, "a man of good learnin," preached to them on Sundays;

then on Sunday afternoons, Marse Bob taught them how to read and write, telling his slaves "we ought to get all the learnin' we could."[24]

These owners felt their slaves should be able to read the Bible, but many hoped to shield their slaves from the liberating aspects of literacy. One measure of the conservative nature of "Bible literacy" is the level of learning attained by ex-slaves under white religiously inspired teaching. Whites who taught slaves in a religious context taught reading only and not writing more frequently than other whites. Owners expressed sentiments about the virtue of reading but not of writing. Henry Bruce's owner was "glad his Negroes could read, especially the Bible, but he was opposed to their being taught writing," and Bruce did not learn to write until after slavery ended. Elijah Marrs' owner said that he wanted all the slave boys to learn how to read the Bible, but that it was against the laws of the state of Kentucky to write (though this was untrue). Marrs said, "we had to steal that portion of our education."[25]

Slave-initiated learning took place in a different context than that of white-initiated learning; slaves depended more on opportunity and desire. Therefore, urban slaves and household slaves were in particularly favorable positions to obtain their own learning. Many domestic workers were taught to read by whites, but more than a third of the household slaves taught themselves or tricked others into teaching them. Belle Caruthers' duties, for example, were to fan her mistress and to nurse the baby: "The baby had alphabet blocks to play with and I learned my letters while she learned hers." Moses Slaughter's mother, the housekeeper, would say to the owner's daughter, "Come here, Emily, Mamma will keep your place for you," and while little Emily read, "Mamma Emalina" followed each line until she too was a fluent reader and could teach her own children.[26]

In the cities, alert apprentices like teenage Noah Davis, bound out to learn boot and shoe-making in Fredericksburg, made the most of their chances. Davis saw his employer write the names of his customers on the lining of the boots and shoes which he gave out to be made; Davis imitated him, and could soon write his name. Benjamin Holmes, apprentice tailor in Charleston, studied all the signs and all the names on the doors where he carried bundles and asked people to tell him a word or two at a time. By the time he was twelve, he found he could read newspapers. Frederick Douglass made friends with white boys he met in the Baltimore streets and converted those he could into teachers by exchanging bread from his house for lessons. He learned to write by watching ship's carpenters write their letters for shipping lumber, and by copying lessons secretly from the master's son's books when the family was out of the house.[27]

Whether in urban or rural areas, slaves created innovative solutions to the problems of tools for reading and writing and finding
the time and place to use them. Slaves "borrowed" books from their
owners, or bought them with their treasured small savings if the
purchase did not arouse suspicion.[28] They made their own writing
materials and used planks to write on, or practiced writing in sand.[29]
Slaves used weekends or Sundays to learn to read and write; many
studied at night. Ex-slaves told Fisk University interviewers that they
slipped old wooden planks into the house, and they would light them
and sit down at night and read from the light of the fire. W. E.
Northcross had been warned by his master that if he were caught
with a book he would be hung by the white men of his Alabama
community, so Northcross carried some old boards into his house to
make a light by which to read secretly. This was a hazardous undertaking, as he recalled: "I would shut the doors, put one end of a
board into the fire, and proceed to study; but whenever I heard the
dogs barking I would throw my book under the bed and peep and
listen to see what was up. If no one was near I would crawl under the
bed, get my book, come out, lie flat on my stomach, and proceed to
study until the dogs would again disturb me." Former slaves were
proud of conquering opposition to their learning. Jenny Proctor tri-
umphantly told how her community of several hundred slaves under
a particularly oppressive regime rose to the challenge of restrictions
against books: "Dey say we git smarter den dey was if we learn anything, but we slips around and gits hold of dat Webster's old blue
back speller and we hides it 'til way in de night and den we lights a
little pine torch and studies dat spellin' book. We learn it too. . . ."[30]

Given the very real dangers involved in learning to read and
write, what lay behind slaves' "insatiable craving for some knowledge
of books," as Lucius Holsey put it? Some former slaves attributed
their high valuation of reading and writing skills to their owners' resistance. Their desire to learn, along with their belief that such skills
could greatly expand their world, was augmented by the fact that
these skills were withheld. Henry Morehead's owners objected to his
attending night school in Louisville, because school "would only
teach him rascality." Morehead resented the use of that word, and his
owners' resistance persuaded him to use his own money and time for
school. Frederick Douglass claimed that he owed as much to the bitter opposition of his master, as to the kindly aid of his mistress, in
learning to read: "I acknowledge the benefit of both."[31]

Slaves were aware of the promise of literacy as a path to mobility and increased self-worth. Claims about literacy's intrinsic and practical value, espoused by educational reformers in England and the

northern United States had an impact even in the South. An interesting interpretation of this message came from a poor white boy who assured the enslaved Thomas Jones that "a man who had learning would always find friends, and get along in the world without having to work hard, while those who had no learning would have no friends and be compelled to work very hard for a poor living all their days." Lucius Holsey, who was the son of his master and who identified in many ways with the white world, "felt that constitutionally he was created the equal of any person here on earth and that, given a chance, he could rise to the height of any man," and that books were the path to proving his worth as a human being.[32]

Former slaves who learned on their own initiative mentioned the religious context for their learning more than any other factor. Since many of the former slaves who wrote their own narratives and autobiographies were ministers, many attributed their desire for learning to their religious aspirations. One-third of the Federal Writers Project interviewees whose learning was slave-initiated also specified a religious context for their learning to read and write.

To many slaves, the religious context for learning provided a chance for leadership; the ministry was the chief outlet for such ambition, and the literate preacher served as a leader of the black community both during and after slavery. Preachers recalled that they first wanted to learn to read after their conversion and their desire to preach. Peter Randolph's account of his conversion was typical: "After receiving this revelation from the Lord, I became impressed that I was called of God to preach to the other slaves . . . but then I could not read the Bible, and I thought I could never preach unless I learned to read the Bible. . . ."[33] The ability to read and write also obtained other advantages for slaves, including privacy. Sarah Fitzpatrick pointed out that if a slave wanted to court a girl and could not write, his master had to write his love letter for him, so "anytime you writ a note white folks had to know whut it said."[34]

Slave narratives reinforce the connection between reading and preaching. Rhiner Gardner recalled that "if there chanced to be among the slaves a man of their own race who could read and write, he generally preached and would, at times and places unknown to the master, call his fellow slaves together and hold religious services with them." On many plantations, such as that near Beaufort, South Carolina, where Melvin Smith was enslaved, "the preacher was the onliest one that could read the Bible." Former slaves recalled their belief that "white people taught their niggers what Bible they wanted them to know" only, and saw the literate black preacher as their key to unlocking the Bible's power. The preacher's high status is exemplified by Byrd Day, whose fellow slaves valued his ability to read and write so highly that they bought him a Bible so he could read to them, and they farmed his patch of ground for him so that he could spend his nights studying the Bible.[35]

The preacher and the religious authority often became teacher too. Slaves learned to read and write in Sunday schools operated by black preachers and teachers. When Frederick Douglass was hired out to a Maryland farm, he began a Sunday school and "devoted my Sundays to teaching these my loved fellow-slaves how to read." At one time his class numbered over forty pupils of all ages. Austin Butler, Virginia Harris' preacher on a Louisiana plantation, tried to teach other slaves the alphabet during Sunday school, since "he was a man with learning." In Tennessee, James Southall recalled that "all our cullud preachers could read de Bible," and that they taught any slaves who wanted to learn.[36]

Slaves who learned to read and write were exceptional people who used their skills in literacy in exceptional ways. Some gained mobility: in Mary Colbert's Athens, Georgia, slave community those slaves who could read and write were usually chosen to travel with their master, so that if anything happened to him they could write home. At least five of the former slaves in this study used their ability to write to escape from slavery, including James Fisher, who wrote passes which got him safely across the border from Tennessee.[37]

Literate slaves also helped other slaves. Milla Granson, for example, learned to read and write in Kentucky, was moved to Natchez, and established a midnight school there, where she taught hundreds of fellow slaves to read. Slaves who could read were often furnished with newspapers stolen or purchased by other slaves, and former slaves recalled the roles played by literate slaves in the spread of the news of the war and the coming of freedom. In Georgia, for example, Minnie Davis' mother stole newspapers during the war and kept the other slaves posted as to the war's progress. Cora Gillam's uncle was jailed until the Union soldiers came because he "had a newspaper with latest war news and gathered a crowd of fellow Mississippi slaves to read them when peace was coming."[38]

After slavery, many of the blacks who learned reading and writing skills as slaves used their learning in public leadership positions, including famous "men of mark" like Frederick Douglass and "women of mark" like Susie King Taylor; founders and presidents of black colleges such as Isaac Lane and Isaac Burgan; scholars and writers like W. S. Scarborough and N. W. Harlee; and businessmen like Edward Walker of Windsor, Ontario. Government office holders included Blanche K. Bruce, U.S. Senator from Mississippi, and Isaiah

Montgomery, who with his family founded the black colony of Mound Bayou, Mississippi. Forty-five of the former slaves became ministers either during or after slavery: they served congregations or traveled circuits, assumed bishoprics or other positions in church hierarchies, or became missionaries, like Thomas Johnson, evangelist to Africa and the British Isles. Literate slaves opened schools immediately after the war, including Sally Johnson, taught by her owners at the academy where she served as a nurse, and Celia Singleton, who taught her own school in Georgia two years after freedom.[39]

Some of these community leaders were taught by whites, but the connection between slaves who seized learning for themselves and their subsequent public leadership careers suggests that the belief by slaves in the liberating aspects of literacy as a form of resistance was not unfounded.

TABLE 1
DECADE OF BIRTH OF EX-SLAVES BY SOURCE

Decade of Birth	Federal Writers Project Interviewees		Other Ex-Slaves	
	N	Percentage	N	Percentage
1800-1830	11	6.1	41	44.1
1831-1840	39	21.8	19	20.4
1841-1850	66	36.9	16	17.2
1851-1859	63	35.2	17	18.3
Totals	179	100.0	93	100.0

TABLE 2
DECADE WHEN LEARNED TO READ BY SOURCE

Decade When Learned to Read	Federal Writers Project Interviewees		Other Ex-Slaves	
	N	Percentage	N	Percentage
1820-1835	1	0.8	23	27.4
1836-1845	9	7.0	18	21.4
1846-1855	33	25.8	15	17.9
1856-1865	85	66.4	28	33.3
Totals	128	100.0	84	100.0

TABLE 3

REGIONAL LOCATION OF SLAVES WHEN THEY LEARNED TO READ BY SOURCE

Region	Federal Writers Project Interviewees		Other Ex-Slaves	
	N	Percentage	N	Percentage
Border South (Ky., Tenn., Mo., Md., Del., D.C.)	27	15.1	33	35.5
Old South (Va., N. Car., S. Car., Ga.)	68	38.0	43	46.3
New South (Miss., La., Ark., Fla., Ala., Tex.)	84	45.0	14	15.1
Totals	179	100.0	90	100.0

TABLE 4

POST SLAVERY CAREERS OF EX-SLAVES BY SOURCE

Careers	Federal Writers Project Interviewees		Other Ex-Slaves	
	N	Percentage	N	Percentage
Leadership (Ministry, education, govt.)	27	15.1	64	68.8
Other (Skilled trades, domestic, farm or day labor)	21	11.7	3	3.2
Careers after slavery not specified	131	73.2	26	28.0
Totals	179	100.0	93	100.0

TABLE 5

LEVELS OF LITERACY ATTAINED WHILE SLAVES BY SOURCE

Level of Literacy	Federal Writers Project Interviewees		Other Ex-Slaves	
	N	Percentage	N	Percentage
Learned "letters" (Knowledge of alphabet to some spelling)	30	16.8	5	5.4
Learned to read but not to write	40	22.3	34	36.6
Learned to read and write	94	52.5	45	48.3
Learned to read, write, cipher, some grammar	15	8.4	9	9.7
Totals	179	100.0	93	100.0

TABLE 6

OWNER VS. SLAVE-INITIATED LEARNING BY SOURCE

Initiators of Learning	Federal Writers Project Interviewees		Other Ex-Slaves	
	N	Percentage	N	Percentage
Owners	144	81.3	33	35.5
Slaves	33	18.7	60	64.5
Totals	177	100.0	93	100.0

TABLE 7

CONTEXTS FOR OWNER-INITIATED TEACHING
BY EX-SLAVE SOURCE

Context	Federal Writers Project Interviewees		Other Ex-Slaves	
	N	Percentage	N	Percentage
Owner-initiated teaching in a religious context*	63	43.7	13	39.4
Owner-initiated teaching in context other than religious	5	3.5	2	6.1
Owner-initiated teaching in unspecified context	76	52.8	18	54.5
Totals	144	100.0	33	100.0

*Criteria for religious context for owner-initiated teaching:

1. Owner or agent taught slaves to read as part of religious instruction or Sunday school.

2. Owner or agent taught slaves to read the Bible.

3. Owner insisted on or encouraged religious worship as well as reading and writing by slaves in one or more of the following ways:

   a. Provided church on premises

   b. Encouraged slaves to hold their own services

   c. Paid black or white preacher for them

   d. Accompanied them to church in nearby town or city

   e. Held daily worship service or Bible reading

TABLE 8
CONTEXTS FOR SLAVE-INITIATED TEACHING
BY EX-SLAVE SOURCE

Context	Federal Writers Project Interviewees		Other Ex-Slaves	
	N	Percentage	N	Percentage
Slave-initiated teaching in a religious context*	11	33.3	25	41.7
Slave-initiated teaching in context other than religious	2	6.1	8	13.3
Slave-initiated teaching in unspecified context	20	60.6	27	45.0
Totals	33	100.0	60	100.0

*Criteria for religious context for slave-initiated teaching:
  1. Slave was taught by slave preacher or teacher as part of religious instruction or Sunday school.
  2. Slave stated that he/she decided to learn in order to read the Bible and/or preach the Gospel.

Notes

[1] Kenneth A. Lockridge attributes the initial rise of mass literacy in the Atlantic world to "intense Protestantism," whose primary purpose was "pious conformity." Lockridge, *Literacy in Colonial New England: An Enquiry into the Social Context of Literacy in the Early Modern West* (New York, 1974), pp. 98-100. Harvey Graff notes that the early 19th century American public school movement fostered traditional Protestant morality; its architects were clergymen, its publicists were the religious press, and its major goals included the inculcation of morality. Graff, *The Literacy Myth: Literacy and Social Structure in the Nineteenth Century City* (New York, 1979), pp. 28, 314-15. For a definition of the "liberating" aspects of literacy, see Graff, p. 20 and Lawrence A. Cremin, *Traditions of American Education* (New York, 1977), pp. 32-5.

[2] For the teaching of reading but not writing in religious education in 17th century Sweden, see Daniel P. Resnick and Lauren B. Resnick, "The Nature of Literacy: An Historical Exploration," *Harvard Educational Review*, 47 (August 1977): 374. For a similar practice in late 18th and early 19th century England, see Michael Sanderson, "Literacy and Social Mobility in the Industrial Revolution in England," *Past & Present* 56 (August 1972): 81; John McLeish, *Evangelical Religion and Popular Education: A Modern Interpretation* (London, 1969), p. 95; Philip McCann, "Popular Education, Socialization, and Social Control: Spitalfields, 1812-1824," and Simon Frith, "Socialization and Rational Schooling: Elementary Education in Leeds before 1870," both in *Popular Education and Socialization in the Nineteenth Century*, ed. Philip McCann (London 1977), pp. 11-12, 81-2.

[3] Northern observers during and immediately after the war noted that the former slaves considered learning to read almost a religious act. One Northerner on the Sea Islands described black children reciting the alphabet over a grave at a funeral in ritualistic style, and numerous missionaries commented upon the freed slaves' great desire to read the Bible. Lawrence W. Levine, *Black Culture and Black Consciousness: Afro-American Folk Thought from Slavery to Freedom* (Oxford, 1977) p. 156; *The American Missionary* (Magazine), V:11, p. 257.

⁴ Charles L. Perdue, Jr., Thomas E. Barden, and Robert K. Phillips, eds., *Weevils in the Wheat: Interviews with Virginia Ex-Slaves* (Charlottesville, 1976); George L. Rawick, ed., *The American Slave: A Composite Autobiography*, 19 vols. (Westport, Conn., 1972); Supplement, Series 1, 12 vols. (Westport, Conn., 1977). Supplement cited in notes is Series 1; Series 2 (Westport, Conn., 1979) is used for text correction only and is thus cited in notes.

⁵ For purposes of tabulating slaves who learned to read and write, I have read all the narratives and used those accounts of former slaves who told of learning or being taught their "letters," or to "read" or to "read and write." Only those former slaves who were personally taught, or whose close relative such as a mother or father or a specific acquaintance were taught were tabulated; accounts of slaves who reminisced that "all the slaves were taught to read and write" were not included in the tabulations of the 272 slaves in this study.

⁶ Octavia V. Rogers Albert, *The House of Bondage or, Charlotte and Other Slaves* (New York, 1890; reprint ed., 1972); Sam Aleckson, *Before the War, and After the Union: An Autobiography* (Boston, 1929); *Aunt Sally; or, The Cross the Way of Freedom* (Cincinnati, 1858); John W. Blassingame, *Slave Testimony: Two Centuries of Letters, Speeches, Interviews, and Autobiographies* (Baton Rouge, 1977); Charles Octavius Boothe, *The Cyclopedia of the Colored Baptists of Alabama: Their Leaders and Their Work* (Birmingham, 1895); Levi Branham, *My Life and Travels* (Dalton, Georgia, 1929); Hallie Q. Brown, *Homespun Heroines and Other Women of Distinction* (Xenia, Ohio, 1926); Henry Clay Bruce, *The New Man. Twenty-Nine Years a Slave, Twenty-Nine Years a Free Man* (York, Pa., 1895; reprint ed., 1969); Edward R. Carter, *Biographical Sketches of our Pulpit* (Atlanta, 1888; reprint ed., 1968); Daniel W. Culp, ed., *Twentieth Century Negro Literature* (Naperville, Il., 1902; reprint ed., 1969); Noah Davis, *A Narrative of the Life of Rev. Noah Davis, a Colored Man, Written by Himself, at the Age of 54* (Baltimore, 1859); Frederick Douglass, *Narrative of the Life of Frederick Douglass* (Boston, 1845); Benjamin Drew, *The Refugee: or the Narratives of Fugitive Slaves in Canada Related by Themselves* (Boston, 1856); Orville Elder and Samuel Hall, *The Life of Samuel Hall, Washington, Iowa: A Slave for Forty-Seven Years* (Washington, Ia., 1912); Elisha Green, *Life of the Rev. Elisha W. Green* (Maysville, Ky., 1888); Laura Haviland, *A Woman's Life-Work* (Chicago, 1887); Lucius Holsey, *Autobiography, Sermons, Addresses, and Essays* (Atlanta, 1898); Louis Hughes, *Thirty Years a Slave* (Milwaukee, 1897); Thomas L. Johnson, *Twenty-Eight Years a Slave*, 7th ed. (Bournemouth, England, 1909); Thomas Jones, *The Experience of Thomas Jones, Who was a Slave for Forty-Three Years* (Boston, 1862); Isaac Lane, *The Autobiography of Bishop Isaac Lane* (Nashville, 1916); Elijah P. Marrs, *Life and History of the Rev. Elijah P. Marrs* (Louisville, Ky., 1885; reprint ed. 1969); A. W. Pegues, *Our Baptist Ministers and Schools* (Springfield, Ma. 1892); Gustavus D. Pike, *The Jubilee Singers and their Campaign for Twenty Thousand Dollars* (Boston, 1873); Peter Randolph, *Sketches of Slave Life* (Boston, 1893); William J. Simmons, *Men of Mark: Eminent, Progressive and Rising* (Cleveland, Ohio, 1887; reprint ed., 1968); William Still, *The Underground Rail Road* (Philadelphia, 1872); Susie King Taylor, *Reminiscences of My Life in Camp* (Boston, 1902; reprint ed., 1968); Alexander Wayman, *Cyclopedia of African Methodism* (Baltimore, 1882).

⁷ Rawick, ed., *The American Slave*, Alabama, VI, pp. 212-14; Texas, V (3), p. 121. Contrary to popular belief, there were few specific laws against owners teaching their slaves. By the 1850s, the legal codes of only four Southern states—North and South Carolina, Georgia, and Virginia—prohibited the teaching of individual slaves to read and write, and Virginia's law did not ban owners from teaching their own slaves. North Carolina, *Revised Statutes*, 1837, pp. 209, 578; 1854, pp. 218-19; George M. Stroud, *A Sketch of the Laws Relating to Slavery* (Philadelphia, 1856), pp. 58-63; *Code of the State of Georgia* (Atlanta, 1861), pp. 1878-879); *Digest of the Laws of Georgia* (Philadelphia, 1831),

pp. 316-17; *Code of Virginia,* 1849, pp. 747-48. Alabama had passed a law in 1832 prohibiting the teaching of slaves or free blacks, and it had appeared in the *Digest of the Laws of Alabama* in 1843, p. 543, but is not in the *Code of the State of Alabama,* 1852. Similarly, Louisiana's law fining or imprisoning "all persons who shall teach any slave" to read or write, passed in 1830, appeared in a digest of its laws published in 1841, but did not form part of its 1856 revised Black Code, though other provisions of the same act did (*Louisiana Digest of Laws,* 1841, pp. 521-22; *Louisiana Revised Statutes,* 1856, p. 54.) Mississippi revised its slave code in 1831 to prohibit blacks from exercising functions of ministers unless on the premises of a slaveowner with his permission, but did not ban teaching of slaves to read. *(Code of Mississippi,* 1798-1848, p. 534.) Other states, including Maryland and Missouri, banned public assemblages of blacks for religious or educational purposes, but did not penalize individuals teaching individual slaves or free blacks to read or write. *(Maryland Code,* 1860, p. 462; *Missouri Laws,* 1847, pp. 103-104; *Missouri Revised Statutes,* 1856). Moreover, slaveowners tended to disregard any laws which seemed to interfere with their management of their own slaves, preferring to think of their plantations as kingdoms in themselves, where each planter "exercises in his own person, all the high functions of an unlimited monarch," to quote Whitemarsh Seabrook in his *Essay on the Management of Slaves* (Charleston, 1834), p. 15.

⁸ Rawick, ed., Oklahoma and Mississippi, VII, pp. 78-9; Georgia, XIII (4), p. 305.

⁹ Rawick, ed., Georgia, XIII (3), p. 144; Mississippi, Supplement, X (5), p. 2337; A. W. Pegues, *Our Baptist Ministers and Schools,* pp. 62-3.

¹⁰ Rawick, ed., Texas, IV (1), p. 286; Blassingame, *Slave Testimony,* p. 643.

¹¹ Claudia Dale Goldin, *Urban Slavery in the American South, 1820-1860: A Quantitative History* (Chicago, 1976), p. 12. House slaves, or slaves engaged in domestic tasks such as cooks, housemaids, gardeners, stewards, and coachmen, are estimated by Robert Fogel and Stanley Engerman to have comprised 7.4 percent of male workers and about 20 percent of women workers. Fogel and Engerman, *Time on the Cross: The Economics of American Negro Slavery,* 2 vols. (Boston, 1974), 2: 37-43.

¹² Census interviewers in most countries ask respondents whether they can read or write; no tests or other ways to measure "functional literacy" have yet been agreed upon. See Harvey Graff, "Literacy Past and Present: Critical Approaches in the Literacy-Society Relationship," *Interchange* 9, No. 2 (1978), pp. 8-9. Resnick and Resnick, p. 371, note that expectations in literacy range from the ability to write one's name to "the ability to read a complex text with literary allusions and metaphoric expression and not only to interpret this text but to relate it sensibly to other texts."

¹³ While legitimate concerns are felt about the validity of both kinds of sources used in this study—each group is select rather than representative, and former slaves in each group were addressing a particular audience for particular purposes—the two kinds of sources present the researcher with a body of testimony about slave life which cannot be obtained elsewhere, and so have been used extensively in studies of slavery and the slave community. For discussions of the strengths and weaknesses of each kind of source and comparisons of their validity, see David Thomas Bailey, "A Divided Prism: Two Sources of Black Testimony on Slavery," *Journal of Southern History,* 46 (August 1980): 381-404; Blassingame, *Slave Testimony,* pp. xxxii-lxii; William L. Van Deburg, *The Slave Drivers: Black Agricultural Labor Supervisors in the Antebellum South* (Westport, Conn., 1979), pp. 77-94; Paul Escott, *Slavery Remembered: A Record of Twentieth Century Slave Narratives* (Chapel Hill, 1979), pp. 3-17; Thomas Webber, *Deep Like the Rivers: Education in the Slave Quarter Community* (New York, 1978), p. 26.

¹⁴ Rawick, ed., Mississippi, Suppl., VIII (3), pp. 1195-1196; Perdue, ed., p. 234; Rawick, ed., Oklahoma, Suppl., XII, pp. 354-56.

[15] Henry Bruce, *The New Man*, pp. 25-6; Rawick, ed., Oklahoma, Suppl., XII, pp. 298-300.

[16] Rawick, ed., Indiana, Suppl. 2, II (1), p. 224; Arkansas, VIII (2), p. 44.

[17] Elijah P. Marrs, *Life and History*, p. 11; *Aunt Sally*, pp. 74-5; Thomas Johnson, *Twenty-Eight Years a Slave*, p. 5; William J. Simmons, *Men of Mark*, p. 235.

[18] Bruce, p. 45; Rawick, ed., Missouri, XI, p. 333; Mississippi, Suppl. IX (4), pp. 1674, 1610.

[19] Levi Branham, *My Life and Travels*, p. 10; Rawick, ed., Arkansas, VIII (2), p. 20; Georgia, XIII (3), p. 212.

[20] Evidence for white motivations for teaching slaves has been limited in this study to accounts by former slaves. For white accounts of teaching slaves to read, see Moncure D. Conway, *Autobiography, Memories and Experiences of M. D. Conway*, 2 vols. (Boston, 1904; reprint ed. 1979), I:5-7; Susan Dabney Smedes, *Memorials of a Southern Planter* (Baltimore, 1888), pp. 79-80; Nehemiah Adams, *A South-Side View of Slavery* (Boston, 1854), pp. 56-7; Frederika Bremer, *Homes of the New World*, 2 vols. (New York, 1853), I:499; Mary Chestnut, *A Diary from Dixie* (New York, 1929), pp. 292-93. For connections between the Southern white mission to evangelize slaves and slaveowners who taught their slaves to read the Bible, see Janet Cornelius, "God's Schoolmasters: Southern Evangelists to the Slaves, 1830-1860" (unpublished Ph.D. dissertation, U. of Illinois, 1977), pp. 263-87; Milton Sernett, *Black Religion and American Evangelicalism* (Metuchen, N.J., 1975); Albert Raboteau *Slave Religion* (New York, 1978), pp. 209-318. Southern churchmen proclaimed that the literacy law was constantly being violated, and was practically a "dead letter," thereby encouraging owners to follow their own consciences. Petitions on Slavery, South Carolina State Archives, Columbia; *Biblical Recorder*, Nov. 9, 1844; James Henley Thornwell, *A Sermon Preached* . . . (Charleston, 1850), p. 47; Richard Fuller and Francis Wayland, *Domestic Slavery Considered as a Scriptural Institution* (New York, 1845), p. 160; William E. Clebsch, ed., *Journals of the Protestant Episcopal Church in the Confederate States of America* (Austin, Tex., 1962), pp. 10-12.

[21] Rawick, ed., Arkansas, IX (3), p. 311, Arkansas, VIII (1), pp. 197-98; Indiana, VI, p. 131.

[22] Rawick, ed., Mississippi, Suppl. VIII (3), p. 1292; Indiana, Suppl., V, p. 45.

[23] Rawick, ed., Arkansas, VIII (2), p. 84; Georgia, XIII (4), p. 163; Texas, Suppl. 2, III (2), p. 612.

[24] Rawick, ed., North Carolina, XIV (1), p. 268; Georgia, XIII (3), p. 134; Georgia, Suppl., IV (2), p. 350; Texas, Suppl. 2, V (4), p. 1522.

[25] Bruce, pp. 25-6; Marrs, p. 15.

[26] Perdue, ed., p. 187; Rawick, ed., Indiana, Suppl., V, p. 48; Mississippi, VII (2), p. 365; Indiana, Suppl., V, p. 197.

[27] Noah Davis, *Narrative of the Life of Rev. Noah Davis*, p. 17; Gustavus D. Pike, *The Jubilee Singers*, pp. 57-8; Frederick Douglass, *Narrative of the Life of Frederick Douglass*, pp. 58-9.

[28] Slaves named Webster's speller more often than any other book as the tool for their initiation into reading. Distributed in millions of copies, its use was a tribute to the persistance of the nineteenth century student, since it was a small book with small print and few illustrations or other enticements to attract a beginning reader. While more secular than earlier spellers had been, the "blue back" still emphasized religious precepts and spiritual and moral virtues along with its syllabic exercises. Noah Webster, *The Elementary Spelling Book* (Cincinnati, 1843), esp. pp. 26, 29, 69.

[29] Rawick, ed., Mississippi, Suppl., IX (4), pp. 1664-665; Thomas Jones, p. 15; Lucius H. Holsey, *Autobiography*, pp. 16-18; Blassingame, *Slave Testimony*, p. 131; Rawick, ed., Arkansas, X (6), p. 332; Arkansas, XI (7), p. 185; Drew, *The Refugee*, p. 97; Blassingame, *Slave Testimony*, p. 45; Rawick, ed., South Carolina, II (2), p. 50.

[30] Rawick, ed., Fisk University, *Unwritten History of Slavery*, XVIII, p. 57; Alabama, VI, pp. 300-02; Texas, V (3), p. 213.

[31] Holsey, p. 16; Drew, pp. 180-81; Douglass, p. 65.

[32] Thomas Jones, p. 14; Holsey, pp. 16-18.

[33] Peter Randolph, *Sketches of Slave Life*, pp. 10-11.

[34] John B. Cade, "Out of the Mouths of Ex-Slaves," *Journal of Negro History* 20 (January 1935): 330; Rawick, ed., Georgia, XIII (3), p. 291; Arkansas, X (6), p. 190; Charles Octavius Boothe, *Cyclopedia of the Colored Baptists of Alabama*, pp. 69-70.

[35] Douglass, p. 70; Rawick, ed., Mississippi, Suppl., VIII (3), p. 940; Oklahoma, VII, p. 308.

[36] Rawick, ed., Georgia, XII (1), p. 220. Blassingame, pp. 234, 237. At least 55 out of 625 runaway slaves (8.8 percent) who sought assistance from William Still on the Underground Railroad in the 1850s knew how to read and write, as did 15.1 percent of the runaways to Canada questioned by Benjamin Drew in 1855. Since neither Still nor Drew was particularly interested in whether the fugitives they interviewed had learned to read or write during slavery, the proportion of literate slaves among these fugitives may have been much higher. William Still, *The Underground Rail Road*, Benjamin Drew, *The Refugee, op. cit.*

[37] Blassingame, *Slave Testimony*, p. 643.

[38] Laura Haviland, *A Woman's Life-Work* (Chicago, 1887), pp. 300-01; Rawick, ed., Georgia, XII (1), p. 257; Arkansas, IX (3), pp. 28-9.

[39] Douglass, *op. cit.*; Taylor, *op. cit.*; Isaac Lane, *The Autobiography of Bishop Isaac Lane*, Simmons, *Men of Mark*, pp. 1087, 411-12; Daniel W. Culp, ed., *Twentieth Century Negro Literature*, p. 279; Bruce, *op. cit.*; Rawick, ed., Mississippi, Suppl., IX (4), pp. 1538-539; Thomas Johnson, pp. 50 ff.; Rawick, ed., Fisk Interviews, XVIII, p. 226; Georgia, XIII (3), p. 270.

Slavery in Oglethorpe County, Georgia, 1773-1865

CLARENCE L. MOHR

The population of enslaved Africans in the Southern states, particularly in the lower South, increased rapidly in the early decades of the 1800s, and, in some areas, exceeded the white population. The rapid growth and rumors of uprisings created widespread apprehension on the part of whites in these communities. Although stringent laws governed every aspect of black life and ensured effective enforcement, slaveholders enjoyed considerable latitude in meting out punishment for infractions of the laws. In Georgia's Oglethorpe County, as in many other Georgia counties and in other states, the actual treatment of enslaved Africans was determined largely by individual owners and the general attitude of the local white community.

Clarence Mohr uses court records and other sources to describe the slave regime from the early 1770s until the end of the Civil War. Through descriptions of acts and behaviors by both blacks and whites in Oglethorpe County, he shows that enslaved Africans were subjected to numerous restrictions and repressive measures; that they generally lacked legal protection; and that they frequently encountered mob and other violence. Despite a relatively calm social exterior, characterized by the absence of major uprisings and efficiency in the enforcement of the Black Codes, these oppressive conditions prevailed in Oglethorpe County throughout the era and were barely modified with the end of chattel slavery.

WHEN GEORGIA LEFT the Union in January, 1861, slavery was a time-honored institution in Oglethorpe County. Located in the eastern section of the Georgia Piedmont, the Oglethorpe region had known slavery since late colonial times, although initially on a very modest scale. Slaves were brought into the area almost as soon as the Creeks and Cherokees moved out in 1773, but at the end of the American Revolution their numbers were still small.[1] When land hungry immigrants began pouring into the region during the 1780s, they were encouraged by liberal headright laws to bring along their

TABLE 1

SLAVEHOLDINGS IN OGLETHORPE COUNTY AS COMPILED FROM MANUSCRIPT TAX DIGESTS*

Year	Number of Slaves Owned						Largest Holding	Average Holding	Total Owners	Total Slaves	Total Whites
	1-3	4-9	10-19	20-49	50-99	Over 99					
1795	215	114	60	10	0	0	26	5.01	395	1,980	
1800	275	163	69	17	0	0	31	5.32	521	2,788	6,691
1805	295	234	79	22	1	0	76	5.7	631	3,598	
1810	316	262	139	37	3	0	73	7.07	757	5,255	6,862
1815	286	230	138	50	5	0	77	7.73	709	5,457	
1820	280	258	130	82	8	0	77	8.5	758	6,444	6,863
1830	233	233	151	98	10	1	108	10.15	726	7,369	5,619
1835	219	203	142	89	12	0	80	10.2	658	6,689	
1850	183	153	131	103	17	0	90	12.1	587	7,111	4,382
1860	165	151	112	96	16	1	130	12.2	541	6,589	4,014

*Most of the data in the above table was compiled originally in U. B. Phillips, "The Origin and Growth of the Southern Black Belts," *American Historical Review*, XI (July, 1906), 798-816. The present author has compiled the data for 1830, and corrected minor errors in Phillips's figures. White population statistics are taken from published U. S. Census reports.

human chattels.[2] At first slaveholdings were limited in both size and number, and no real planter class existed for several decades. Yet as early as 1795, the county contained nearly 2,000 blacks and some 395 individual slaveowners (see Table 1).

After 1800, cotton rapidly displaced tobacco as a staple crop, greatly increasing the demand for black labor. Between 1800 and 1810, Oglethorpe's slave population nearly doubled, and by 1820, blacks outnumbered whites.[3] During the later antebellum period, the number of slaves leveled off at about 7,000, while slave ownership was slowly concentrated into fewer and fewer hands. By 1860, the average size of slaveholdings had risen to 12.2, but there were fewer owners than at any time since 1805. Negroes constituted roughly two thirds of the country's total population.[4]

As Oglethorpe's white residents rallied to the standard of the embryonic Southern Confederacy, they were doubtless keenly aware of the high proportion of slaves within their county. During the campaign and election of 1860, rumors of slave insurrections had swept the South, causing widespread fear and panic.[5] That these rumors were not without effect in Oglethorpe County is clearly demonstrated by the erratic behavior of some local whites. In late April, for example, a veteran overseer on one of Oglethorpe's largest plantations reported that he had shot at and wounded a slave named Calvin, for a minor infraction of rules. Calvin's only real offense was breaking a wagon while hauling fodder, but when the overseer attempted to "correct" him, he became frightened and ran away. The overseer fired one warning shot, and when Calvin refused to stop, fired a second time. The second shot struck home and Calvin was soon recaptured, leaving the overseer with some difficult explaining to do.[6]

In June of the same year, a group of Oglethorpe whites resorted to mob violence against a Negro accused of murdering one William Green. The Negro managed to escape on Saturday evening, after stabbing Green eighteen times, but was captured on Sunday, and the next morning was summarily burned at the stake by "a number of citizens who had investigated the case. . . ."[7] Some three months later, the danger of a slave rebellion was discussed candidly by a newspaper editor in the nearby town of Athens, located only sixteen miles from the Oglethorpe County seat. The editor urged his readers:

> . . . to be watchful upon our negro population, and especially upon itinerant pedlers, teachers and other strolling vagabonds. We think there is no danger if there is watchfulness; but we think it is the duty of every man to practice the greatest vigilance. A successful insurrection is impossible; but great evil may be accomplished and val-

uable lives may be lost before the fact of an outbreak can be made
known.[8]

In what may have been an oblique reference to the mob action in
Oglethorpe, all citizens were cautioned to "carefully guard against
hasty judgement of any who may excite suspicion, either black or
white." The editor felt strongly that "Lynch law should be resorted to
in no case" and regretted that it had "been done in several cases
recently."[9]

If Oglethorpe slaveowners were apprehensive about their bondsmen, such fears were not totally groundless. On paper, the slave system was designed to implement a rigid system of safeguards and
controls, but scholars have long recognized that Southern slave codes
were enforced haphazardly.[10] Punishment and discipline were left
largely up to individual masters, with the result that some slaves enjoyed much more freedom than others. In Oglethorpe County this
was often the case, and throughout the ante-bellum period, many
laws were bypassed or ignored.

The pass system, for example, was intended to confine slaves to
their home plantations, but it was seldom applied rigorously. Negroes
seem always to have enjoyed considerable freedom of movement, and
enforcement of patrol laws was often so lax as to be nearly nonexis-
tent. In one of their numerous presentments on this subject, the
Oglethorpe grand jury complained in 1810 that patrol laws "have
been so little attended to that they appear to be nearly forgotten."[11]
More than a decade later, the "total neglect" of these laws remained
"an evil of dangerous consequences," and as late as 1845, grand jurors deplored the fact that slaves were permitted "to go at large when
and where they please either day or night without any restraint
whatever."[12]

The county seat at Lexington was the scene of frequent Sunday
gatherings of idle whites and Negroes, who congregated at various
stores to gamble and consume "ardent spirits."[13] The fact that slaves
could easily obtain alcoholic beverages caused deep concern among
many Oglethorpe residents, and in 1824, an extra tax was proposed
for taverns because they tended to produce "habits of disorder, insubordination & dishonesty" among local blacks. For unknown reasons, this tax was never passed, and up to the Civil War, court
records remain cluttered with indictments for illegally selling liquor
to slaves.[14]

Commerce between whites and Negroes was not limited solely
to liquor traffic, however, and some bondsmen were themselves part-
time entrepreneurs. Slaves frequently sold corn, cotton, or other farm
produce without permission from their owners, in clear violation of

state law.[15] In addition to being illegal, this practice was frowned upon because it caused "dissatisfaction" among slaves who were not allowed such liberties, and more importantly, because it furnished "a ready means to Negroes who are disposed to pilfer of distributing their stolen plunder."[16] Between 1800 and 1861, the legal offense of "trading with a slave" produced numerous accusations, albeit few indictments or convictions.[17] In spite of occasional ten-dollar fines, there is little evidence that slave commerce was ever significantly reduced.

Another area in which slave codes were sometimes disregarded was that of manumission. While Oglethorpe County was never a haven for free Negroes (there were only 21 in 1860), a few slaves were granted freedom by last will and testament.[18] Such acts were usually void unless legalized by the state legislature, and this seldom occurred.[19] In 1830, however, a judge ruled in Oglethorpe Superior Court that a local planter, James Bradley, could liberate his slaves, provided they were sent to the colony of Liberia in Africa.[20] Some forty-six of Bradley's Negroes ultimately made the trip, departing from Norfolk, Virginia, in May, 1832, aboard the ship *Jupiter*.[21] Another Oglethorpe resident who favored colonization was Richard Hoff. Following the Bradley precedent, he sent fifty slaves to Sinou, Liberia, in December, 1853, aboard the brig *General Pierce*.[22] In addition to paying $3,000 for their passage, he gave them an extra $2,500 at the time of their departure.[23] Less than three years later, Hoff manumitted another fifty-three slaves, and sent them to Africa aboard the *Mary Caroline Stevens*.[24]

Although the attitudes of Hoff and Bradley were not shared by most Oglethorpe residents, their actions provide a striking illustration of the latitude which individual masters enjoyed in dealing with their bondsmen. The results of this latitude, however, were not always beneficial to Negroes. Many of the most repressive aspects of the Oglethorpe slave regime may be traced, directly or indirectly, to the status of Negroes as chattel property and consequent lack of legal protection. In the absence of legal restraints, the treatment of slaves was determined largely by the temperament of each master, in conjunction with the general attitudes of the white community. Since these attitudes ranged, at any given time, from paternalism to paranoia, slaves were constantly in a precarious situation.

Theoretically, the Georgia Penal Code provided bondsmen with ample safeguards against physical mistreatment, but in actual practice these provisions meant little.[25] Prosecution of whites for crimes against Negroes was rare, and the reluctance of juries to return indictments or convictions was almost universal. A typical exercise in futility took place in Oglethorpe Superior Court in October, 1847, when the state charged that a group of twelve white men:

> . . . did unlawfully beat, whip and wound, with sticks, poles, whips and cowhides, a certain negro man slave named Charles, the property of Samuel Lumpkin . . . without sufficient cause or provocation being first given by said slave. . . .[26]

In this case, as in most others throughout the period, grand jurors refused to return an indictment.[27]

Nowhere was the slave's lack of legal protection more evident than in the realm of sexual behavior. Negro women were virtually at the mercy of unscrupulous masters, and miscegenation was an inescapable fact of life. The county's local churches were the institutions most directly concerned with improper moral conduct, but they were often reluctant to intervene in such delicate matters. In 1818, for example, the miscegenation issue produced heated exchanges in one Oglethorpe congregation, and the members were accused of placing "too much Confidence in Negroes, to the wounding of the Church. . . ." The church refused to take action, however, and the dispute was not resolved until five months later, when the accused white member voluntarily withdrew.[28] About a decade later, a member of the Clouds Creek Baptist Church was charged by his granddaughter with being the "reputed father" of her slave's bastard child. After a brief investigation, the church declared the charge "not gospelly supported" and dismissed the case.[29] In 1823, the County Line Baptist Church was forced to confront the miscegenation problem directly, when a female church member declared in a notarized statement that she had seen:

> . . . Benjm. Rhoades & a negroe woman . . . down together by a pen and as she beleaves at an unchristianlike action & . . . her mother . . . saw the same [and] charged her perticular never to tell it.[30]

On the basis of this explicit testimony, Rhoades was excommunicated.

Such interracial adultery not only disrupted Oglethorpe churches, but also caused untold anguish in the ranks of local white, Southern womanhood. In an era when divorces were far from common, petitions of aggrieved wives and mothers speak passionately of the damaging effects of such relationships upon normal family life. Petitioning for a divorce in 1852, Oglethorpe resident Susan Potts charged her husband Napolean B. Potts with "habitual intoxication" as well as "cruel and barbarous treatment," and further asserted:

. . . that on the nineteenth day of April[,] eighteen hundred & fifty two & on diverse other days . . . the said Potts has been guilty of illicit & adulterous intercouse with diverse persons & that he drove your petitioner from her home, by threats of actual violence, because she mildly remonstrated with him for committing the last charged offense in her presence & that with a negress.[31]

In 1855, one Sarah A. Culbreath, the defendant in a divorce case, stated that her husband was not entitled to a divorce because he had forced her to abandon him by "cruel & inhuman & unprovoked treatment. . . ." She further charged that he was "often to be found in a state of beastly intoxication" which rendered him "furious & uncontrolable & dangerous to any one with whom he meets, unless possessing greater physical strength." The husband's greatest offense, however, was having sexual intercourse with a "negro wench" who belonged to a prominent citizen of the county.[32] Less than two years later, it was stated that Henry P. Hoff of Oglethorpe County had:

left and abandoned . . . his wife and has sought the company of and associated and connected himself with one of his own Slaves[,] a negro woman named Ellen—with whom he has had on diverse days and time . . . carnal and sexual intercourse . . . has committed frequent acts of adultery with the said negro woman . . . and thereby broke his Solemn marriage obligation. . . .[33]

Other examples could be cited, but those given above illustrate only too well the disastrous results of miscegenation for both slaveholders and slaves.[34] One can only speculate as to the extent of sexual contacts between the races, but the unlimited character of the master's prerogative made prevention of such behavior nearly impossible.

The same circumstances which rendered slave women vulnerable to sexual misconduct acted as a powerful deterrent to the stability of the family life of Negroes. Although many slaves adhered to *de facto* marital arrangements, such relationships were never recognized by Georgia law.[35] In most local churches, "adultery" was considered a sin for blacks as well as whites,[36] but policy in this area was always subject to pragmatic modification. Since slave husbands and wives might be sold to different owners or otherwise separated, white church members were often presented with something of a moral dilemma. This problem arose in Oglethorpe County during 1830, when the Millstone Church was asked to decide what should be done with the slave Coleman, who "had taken a second wife[,] his former one being removed out of his reach. . . ."[37] The question was referred to the church's regional governing body, the Sarepta Baptist Association,

which advised its member churches to "consider the circumstances
well and if [slaves are]sepperated by force, to let them stay in the
Church if they have or should take another companion."[38] Acting
upon this advice, the Millstone Church restored to membership two
blacks who had taken second "companions," but refused to sanction
the marriage of Coleman and finally excommunicated him at a special meeting held in January of 1831.[39]

The breakup of Negro families was probably most often the result of financial necessity, and even in times of economic crisis, some
Oglethorpe planters were more willing to part with land than with
slaves.[40] In addition, there were always masters who, for reasons of
both kindness and expediency, took cognizance of the Negro's conju-
gal ties. Yet humanitarianism was a luxury which few slaveholders
could afford, since the reuniting of slave families was often a costly
business. This fact was forcefully brought home to David Crenshaw
Barrow, one of Oglethorpe's largest planters, when he attempted to
obtain the wife and child of his slave Tom. Upon inquiring about the
possibility of a purchase, Barrow learned that the owner had come to
prize Tom's wife very highly, and did not "wish to sell her at any
price." But, it appeared that "Matilda [Tom's wife] . . . wished to go
with her husband" and "under such circumstances" the owner con-
sented to sell mother and child for $1,600—an offer which probably
did not strike Barrow as overly magnanimous.[41] Similar financial obstacles were doubtless encountered by other masters seeking to unite
slave families, and there were many slaveholders who possessed
neither the money nor the inclination for philanthropic gestures.
Available evidence indicates that most Oglethorpe blacks were bought
and sold on a purely pragmatic basis, with little or no regard for family ties.[42]

TABLE 2

'FAIR MARKET VALUE' OF OGLETHORPE COUNTY SLAVES
AS ESTIMATED BY INFERIOR COURT JUSTICES IN
JANUARY, 1865

	Age			
	2-6 yrs.	6-12 yrs.	12-16 yrs.	16-25 yrs.
Males	$ 600	$ 800	$1600	$3000
Females	600	800	1600	2000
	25-35 yrs.	35-45 yrs.	45-55 yrs.	55-65 yrs.
Males	$3000	$2000	$ 600	00
Females	2000	1600	400	00

Although Oglethorpe slaves enjoyed few civil rights, they were
not totally excluded from the legal process. Throughout most of the

ante-bellum period, Negroes charged with serious crimes were subject to trial by county inferior courts.[43] Records of these trials for Oglethorpe County have apparently been lost, but there is considerable evidence that they did take place, and that punishment was often swift and severe.[44] After 1850, jurisdiction of capital offenses committed by slaves was transferred to the superior court, and slave trials were recorded along with regular legal business.[45] The only slave to be tried in Oglethorpe Superior Court prior to the Civil War was the Negro man Willis, charged with the murder of his fellow bondsman Adam. Willis was found guilty of involuntary manslaughter and sentenced to receive thirty lashes "upon his naked body or limbs" for three successive days. Punishment was to be administered by the county sheriff, who was cautioned not to lose sight of "feelings of mercy & humanity."[46]

The financial interest of the owner, if nothing else, demanded that slave trials be conducted with reasonable impartiality and thoroughness. Both before and after 1850, witnesses were formally subpoenaed, written testimony taken, and the slaves' guilt or innocence decided by a twelve man jury.[47] On balance, however, the scales of justice were weighted against the Negroes, for while they were subject to prosecution, they were denied the right to initiate legal action. If the law sometimes protected them against the summary punishment of the masters or the white community, it more often abandoned them to that very fate. Then, as in later times, legal statutes were made and administered by white men, and the blacks were consigned to the role of spectators, not participants.

Any balanced treatment of the Oglethorpe slave regime must take into account the thoughts, feelings and reactions of the slaves themselves. It is, of course, impossible to say with any degree of certainty, how the "average" slave reacted to his environment, but there is little question that the lot of most bondsmen was unenviable at best. Professor Stanley M. Elkins has used the analogy of the Nazi concentration camp to suggest that many Southern slaves were "Samboized" or "infantilized" into near total acceptance of their own helplessness before the overwhelming power of the white community.[48] While such an argument admits of numerous exceptions, the Oglethorpe experience tends, in some ways, to confirm its partial validity. Indeed, the nature of the master-slave relationship made it almost inevitable that chattel servitude would produce a long term impact on the character of at least some local Negroes.

One of the most revealing contemporary accounts of the behavior of Oglethorpe blacks is provided by the ante-bellum author and critic Joseph B. Cobb. Born in Oglethorpe County in 1819, Cobb spent much of his early life on his uncle's "Mount Airy" plantation, which adjoined the estate of Georgia senator William H. Crawford, a few miles west of the county seat. After attending the University of Georgia and studying law, Cobb moved to Mississippi where he soon became a prominent author and highly respected member of the planter class.[49] In his book *Mississippi Scenes*, published in 1851, Cobb tells of his close boyhood acquaintance with a group of five native Africans, most of whom lived on the nearby Crawford plantation.[50] In discussing the character and temperament of these Africans, he provides an unwitting commentary on the effects of the Oglethorpe slave system upon the Negro personality.

The habits and dispositions of Africans, according to Cobb, "were as unlike those of our native negroes as it is possible to conceive, when it is considered that they are the same race." Whereas local blacks were characterized by "merry heartedness and vivacity," Africans remained always "exclusive and somewhat unapproachable." Because of their haughty and dignified bearing, the Africans were "treated with marked respect by all other negroes for miles and miles around." On quiet Sunday afternoons, Oglethorpe slaves would listen with "staring eyes, open mouths and peculiarly respectful attitudes" to stories of "fierce wars" which had raged in the Africans' homeland. The greatest differences between the two groups, however, lay in their respective attitudes towards white authority. Native Africans were generally good workers who required little punishment or coercion. But when disputes occasionally arose with a master or overseer, the Africans stood their ground doggedly, "like the Roman or British soldier" and refused to give in or run away "regardless of consequences." If worst came to worst, they would be openly defiant and often fought with "determined courage, unhappily for them!" Native born Negroes, on the other hand, almost never offered open resistance, and were easily frightened by newly employed overseers. In spite of their apparent docility, whipping was sometimes necessary for local blacks, since they were "generally indolent and careless if . . . allowed to think that whipping will not be resorted to."[51]

Cobb's Sambo-like image of Oglethorpe slaves, while undoubtedly valid within limits, fails to stand the test of full historical scrutiny. Repressive though slavery may have been, there were always black people in Oglethorpe County whose spirit was unbroken and whose will to resist remained intact. If slaves often appeared fawning or servile, they were in many cases simply acting out their expected role.[52] Masters learned, through hard experience, to watch closely the bondsmen who spoke "in a low tone of voice" but had "good sense" and took the first available opportunity to head north and pose as a free man.[53]

This distinction between role playing and reality is crucial to any interpretation of the slave experience, since the entire "Samboization" argument turns upon the question of whether or not slaves internalized their surface patterns of behavior, thus giving reality to the Sambo stereotype.[54] Any generalizations in this area must rest upon tenuous assumptions and incomplete data, but there can be little question that many Oglethorpe blacks were relatively unaffected by psychological intimidation. As critics of the Sambo thesis have pointed out, slaves lived in two separate worlds, one black and one white. If the slaves' personality was defined through their reaction to "significant others," then blacks as well as whites must be included in this latter category.[55] The attempts of Negroes to gain status among their fellow bondsmen could, and often did, lead to open conflicts with their masters or the white community.

An excellent illustration is provided by the slave Aleck, who was employed in a carriage factory near Bairdstown in southeastern Oglethorpe County. In November, 1851, the carriage works were destroyed by a fire which many people felt had been deliberately set. The story from this point is best related in the words of a Bairdstown resident, George W. Neal:

> The whole community as if with one mind[,] fixed their suspicions on Aleck[,] more probably from his character than from any circumstances which they knew at the time. He had given himself altogether too much license heretofore and had become a source of annoyance to the community here and was closely watched by everyone[,] and he had found that he had to pursue a different course or he would be punished every time he transgressed. He had been chastized 3 times since he returned from your [*i.e.*, David C. Barrow's] house. After he returned I gave him his orders which were that he should on no account be found on Mr. Cone's premises. I ascertained that he had been there and gave him 50 lashes not breaking the skin. The Sunday morning before the fire Mr. B. W. Williams whipped him . . . without taking off his shirt for throwing rocks against the store. The day but one before the fire Mr. Graham whipped him slightly for stealing some beef which he had laid out to dry. As I said before[,] I think he had found that he could not do as he had done here and out of revenge . . . he did the mischief that has been done. Mr. French has told me since the fire that when he bought Aleck that he was run from (Columbus I think) for setting fire to a building. . . . The night before the fire [at Bairdstown] he was . . . in the shop where the fire originated and was heard to say that 'this would be a nice warm place by the stove for him to

sleep this winter'[;] one of the other negroes replied, 'You can't do that thing'[,] this was heard by a white person. Now it has occurred to me that he removed the lock from its place to show that he could do that thing. There are plenty of rumors that he has told negroes that he means to give Bairdstown Hell. . . .I have not written this so much the purpose of convincing you of Aleck's guilt[,] but as an apology for the abrupt and unceremonious manner of our sending him home and I honestly believe it would not have been safe for him to have remained here.[56]

Aleck's behavior was perhaps exceptional, but in no sense unique. Resistance to white authority was fairly widespread among Oglethorpe blacks, although open defiance led inevitably to reprisals. Three cryptic entries from the diary of a local planter are illustrative:

May 24 "Luck ran away from Jack & came to me after dinner."
May 25 "Heard to day Luck had resisted Jack & negroes[,] cut Pomp on the arm & made his escape from all."
May 26 "Took Luck home to Jack[,] Whipped him & put him under martial law."[57]

In most cases, slave resistance was less dramatic in nature and took such forms as stealing or destroying property. Significantly, food and clothing were common objects of theft, but in some cases malice, rather than necessity, seems to have been the slaves' principal motive.[58] A determined campaign of sabotage by Negroes could have serious consequences if allowed to continue, and at least one Oglethorpe planter was brought to the brink of despair by such activity. Writing in 1855, this planter gave a lengthy account of his efforts to feed his slaves, but sadly concluded that:

. . . my Negroes are in every difficulty in the neighbourhood & convey the Idea they are not bountifully fed. If so, I can't help it. I am at my best. But they have stolen it—they have stolen a good deal—how much I don't know[.] They have torn up rock under pining & taken off locks & spoilege keys & procurred false keys &c. But I am at a loss to know what to do. I am unable to know what disposition they have made of it—some we find in their possession.[59]

Another indication of discontent among local Negroes was their tendency to avoid work by "lying out" or running away. Oglethorpe blacks were habitually restless, and when the federal census taker made his rounds in 1860, he reported that some 236 of them were "Fugitives from the State."[60] Accurate statistics are not available for the earlier ante-bellum period, although local church records indicate that the problem was always fairly common.[61] During the 1850s, one large planter used dogs to pursue runaways, but continued to be plagued by frequent absconders.[62]

In sum, it was manifestly clear on the eve of the Civil War that beneath the generally calm exterior of the Oglethorpe slave regime ran powerful currents of violence and unrest. True enough, most county residents did not envision an impending racial bloodbath in 1861 (or in 1865 for that matter), but thoughtful slaveowners found little in the past behavior of Negroes to inspire overwhelming confidence. Even in peacetime, rumors of slave rebellions were not uncommon, and memories of the 1860 insurrection panic were still fresh as local planters made ready to march off to war. The county's first two military units, known as the "Gilmer Blues" and the "Oglethorpe Rifles," were formed during the wave of patriotic fervor which swept the South early in the War. With a combined total of nearly 150 officers and men they departed for active service in May, 1861.[63] Some four months later, a third company, the Tom Cobb Infantry, left the county after obtaining 85 volunteers.[64] Many new recruits soon joined these companies, and before the year was out Oglethorpe County had given nearly a third of its adult white male population to the Confederate cause.[65]

No one knew for sure how local slaves would act while their masters were absent, but the wisest policy seemed to be one of watchfulness and caution. One of Oglethorpe's largest slaveowners was advised by a friend to stay out of the army in 1861, because "prudence & patriotism as a citizen and rebel, suggest, that you ought to look well to domestic dangers, and not expose your plantation to the risk of disturbances by your absence."[66] In spite of such warnings, however, the problem of slave control did not seem critical to most county residents during these early months. For many people, both white and black, the War remained little more than a remote conflict somewhere in Virginia, and life at home went on much as usual.

The first indication of a change in attitude came early in 1862. Oglethorpe citizens now began to realize that the War would be a "bitter and protracted struggle," which would demand their "utmost efforts . . . to carry it on to a favorable termination."[67] The martial fervor of the previous year had all but vanished, and when attempts were made to raise a fourth military company in early March, very few recruits could be obtained.[68] With the passage of the first conscription act on April 16, the realities of war came forcefully to the home front. Like their fellow Georgians in other parts of the state, Oglethorpe residents bitterly resented the conscript law and opposed it openly.[69] Resistance came to a head in May, when a judge in Oglethorpe Superior Court declared the conscription act unconstitutional and ordered an illiterate petitioner to be released.[70] A few months later the local Confederate "sub-Enrolling officer" was actually thrown into jail by this same judge, for failing to obey a writ of *habeas corpus*.[71]

All these developments had a sobering effect on public opinion, and nowhere was this more evident than in changed attitudes towards Negroes. In many parts of the South, feelings of uneasiness and uncertainty regarding the conduct of slaves tended to diminish as the war continued,[72] but in Oglethorpe County the reverse seems to have been true. Comparatively little attention was paid to Negroes in 1861, and the behavior of most slaves offered no cause for alarm. As conscription gained momentum in 1862, however, blacks showed increasing signs of restlessness, and attempts were made to implement stricter law enforcement.

On May 19, the slave Ned was indicted in superior court for "Assaulting a free White person with intent to murder & with a weapon likely to produce death." Ned's court-appointed attorney initially entered a plea of innocence, but changed the plea to guilty upon hearing the evidence. Ned was sentenced to be hanged on June 27.[73] On May 20, the slave Arthur was indicted for murder, and through his attorney entered a plea of not guilty. He was subsequently convicted of voluntary manslaughter, a crime which did not carry a mandatory death penalty. The court decided that Arthur's punishment would consist of fifty stripes "on the bare back," half to be inflicted on May 24 and half on June 4. On June 7, Arthur would be branded on the cheek with the letter M, and then returned to his owner.[74] The manner of administering this punishment was specified in a detailed set of instructions which seem to have been primarily aimed at restraining local authorities. The stripes were to be inflicted:

> . . . with hickory rods of the size usuallly used for chastising slaves[,]
> to be well laid on the bare back but not to cut the skin[,] and not
> to inflict more than five stripes with the same rod and each rod to
> be well trimed. [It is] Further ordered that the letter M to be
> branded on the cheak shall not exceed the size or cover a space on
> the cheak larger than one square inch and the breadth of the lines
> of the letter M shall not exceed one-tenth of an inch. The branding
> iron [is] to be only moderately heated and applied only long
> enough to make the mark distinct & permanent but not to burn
> through the skin.[75]

The ability of white society to close ranks was further demonstrated a few months later, when one James W. Martin informed the members of a local Baptist church of a "difficulty" which had arisen between himself and a slave belonging to another church member. Martin asserted that he had shot and killed the slave in question after the Negro became recalcitrant and "refused to obey & resisted." Upon hearing the details of the incident, the congregation took a vote and "unanimously sustained" Martin in his actions.[76]

In spite of these initial efforts to subject bondsmen to tighter controls, there is considerable evidence that slave unrest continued. As the War entered its third year, conscription was making heavy inroads in Oglethorpe County, and even large planters were feeling the pinch of decreased manpower. Temporary relief had been provided in October, 1862, when overseers of twenty or more slaves were exempted from the draft; but the so-called "twenty nigger law" proved so unpopular that on May 1, 1863, it was modified and made applicable to most plantations.[77] Reactions to this change came swiftly from Oglethorpe planter David C. Barrow, who declared on May 3 that the new conscription act was a "most unfortunate piece of legislation" which would leave his own as well as neighboring plantations in "a very exposed condition."[78] The picture of Oglethorpe County presented by Barrow on this occasion does little to substantiate the legend of Southern confidence in the "loyal slave":

> I have two plantations in Oglethorpe County . . . , one on Little River, and for miles up and down that River there are but two effective overseers, mine & Col. Fulton's, and both these will be taken now. There are other overseers on the plantation adjoining[,] but they are old or crippled men, and are not effective for police duty, and there are hundreds of negroes within the scope I refer to. In the District [in] which my other Oglethorpe plantation is situated, there are not men enough left liable to militia duty to provide Gov.[ernor] Brown with officers, and there are hundreds of negroes in it. There were at the beginning of the war, more negro men in the district than white, and now there are a good many to one. I do think some efficient men should be left.[79]

By 1863, most Oglethorpe planters were concentrating on the production of food crops, especially corn,[80] and this was a strong arguing point for the retention of local overseers. Under the best of circumstances the overseer's task was not an easy one, and there is little question that many Negroes gave their labor less willingly in 1863 than in 1860. Writing in late December, Oglethorpe resident James H. McWhorter complained that without strict supervision his Negroes would raise only enough food to feed themselves. He considered the assignment of old or inexperienced men as overseers to be nothing less than "absurd," and declared himself ready to give up if the gov-

ernment persisted in this policy.[81] But the government did persist,
and before the War was over, Oglethorpe County had yielded, if
sometimes grudgingly, more than 750 of her native sons.[82] The few
able bodied white men who remained at home during the latter
stages of the conflict found that strict policing of slaves was increasingly necessary, but also increasingly difficult.

Whatever the wishes of local planters may have been, there
seems little question that blacks met with fewer and fewer restrictions
as the War went on. In many cases, slaves were slow to take advantage
of lax discipline, but this did not mean that they were indifferent to
the basic issue at stake in the sectional struggle—their freedom.
Throughout most of the War, Oglethorpe County was far removed
from actual combat, so bondsmen could do little except wait passively
while their fate was decided on distant battlefields. With the Sherman
invasion in 1864, however, Negroes glimpsed a distant ray of hope as
rumors of impending Yankee raids began to sweep the Georgia
upcountry.[83]

In early August, Union troops actually entered neighboring
Clarke County, but were quickly repulsed by local defenders.[84] Slaves
were impressed to work on defenses in the nearby town of Athens,
and when Atlanta fell in September, concern over federal military action increased among slaveholders.[85] One large planter became so apprehensive over possible Yankee invasion that he considered sending
his bondsmen to another part of the state, or even hiring them out
to work on government fortifications at Macon.[86] The reaction of the
slaves themselves to invasion rumors was summed up graphically by a
worried overseer, writing in early October.

> . . . I can tell you that most any of the negroes will go to the Yankee
> if they can get a half a chance. I can see a wide difference in them
> [now, and] what they were three months ago[;] it is time for every
> man to keep his eyes open[.] I watch them closer than I ever did
> [before]. . . .[87]

In spite of this overseer's concern, the Yankees did not come in
1864, and the anticipated mass defections never took place. County
residents ushered in the new year with a week long round of parties
and "frolics," trying to forget, at least temporarily, the sadness and
privations of war.[88] Many people doubtless realized that the days of
the Confederacy were numbered, but few would admit it publicly.
Slave prices remained high, due more to inflated currency than real
public optimism, and as late as January, 1865, the market value of a
prime field hand was officially estimated at $3,000.[89] As Confederate
military fortunes plummeted in the early spring, one abortive attempt

was made to organize a regiment of Negro troops in Oglethorpe County.[90] Before the scheme could be executed, however, units of the Thirteenth Tennessee Cavalry stormed into the county seat in hot pursuit of Jefferson Davis, and the War was over.[91]

If the end of the War meant defeat for white Southerners, it did not mean victory for black ones. In actual fact, the abolition of chattel slavery did nothing to change the attitudes of ex-slaveowners, and very little to improve the lot of former slaves. During the brief interlude of military occupation, Oglethorpe Negroes voted freely and glimpsed momentarily the promise of full political equality. By 1868, however, the old regime had fully recovered; and blacks were forcefully driven from polling places by special duty sheriffs, among whom was Oglethorpe planter James Monroe Smith, later to become notorious for his use (and abuse) of convict labor.[92] Fifteen years after Appomattox, many local Negroes still remained on the plantations of their former masters, sharecroppers in name but little more than "free slaves" in fact.[93] Booker Washington never needed to urge Oglethorpe blacks to cast down their buckets where they were; they had no other choice.

Notes

[1] For details of the founding and early settlement of Oglethorpe County, see Clarence L. Mohr, "Oglethorpe County, Georgia During the Formative Period, 1773-1830" (Unpublished master's thesis, University of Georgia, 1970) chaps. I, II; see also E. Merton Coulter, *Old Petersburg and the Broad River Valley of Georgia* (Athens, 1965), pp. 1-21; Alex M. Hitz, "The Earliest Settlements in Wilkes County," *Georgia Historical Quarterly*, XL (September, 1956), 260-80; Grace G. Davidson, comp., *Early Records of Georgia, Wilkes County* (2 vols., Macon, 1932), I, 4-29.

[2] For the specific provisions of Georgia's postwar land laws see Robert and George Watkins (eds.), *A Digest of the Laws of the State of Georgia. From its Establishment as a British Province down to the Year 1798, Inclusive, and the Principal Acts of 1799* . . . .(Philadelphia, 1800), pp. 258-59, 290-95; Allen D. Candler and Lucian Lamar Knight (eds.), *The Colonel Records of the State of Georgia.* (26 vols., Atlanta, 1904-1916) (Volumes 27-36 in manuscript at Georgia Department of Archives and History, Atlanta), XIX, Part 2, 434-41. For a succinct resumé of these laws see Coulter, *op. cit.*, p. 7.

[3] *Census for 1820* [Book I of the Fourth Census] (Washington, 1821), p. 28.

[4] *Population of the United States in 1860; Compiled From the Original Returns of the Eighth Census, Under the Direction of the Secretary of the Interior* . . . [Book I of the Eighth Census](Washington, 1864), pp. 61, 65, 69 (hereinafter cited *Eighth Census*).

[5] Clement Eaton, *A History of the Southern Confederacy,* New York, 1965), pp. 14-15; Clement Eaton, *Freedom of Thought in the Old South* (Durham, 1940), pp. 102-03.

[6] Jas. A Spratlin to Col. D. C. Barrow, April 27, 1860, Colonel David Crenshaw Barrow Papers, University of Georgia Library (hereinafter cited Barrow Mss.).

[7] *Southern Banner* (Athens, Georgia), June 14, 1860, quoted in Ulrich B. Phillips, *American Negro Slavery* (Baton Rouge, 1966), p. 511. This was not the only such incident in 1860. In August a Negro accused of murdering a white man was burned at the stake by twelve executioners at station number 11 on the Southwestern Railroad. In apparent

mockery of the legal process, the group posted bond before taking the prisoner from official custody and later returned his ashes to the sheriff. See Savannah *Republican,* August 13, 1860, pp. 1, 5, quoting Augusta *Dispatch.*

[8] *Southern Banner,* September 13, 1860, pp. 3, 2. Slavery in Athens during the Civil War era is treated in a balanced, if somewhat abbreviated, manner in Kenneth Coleman, *Confederate Athens* (Athens, 1967), pp. 15-16, 21, 52-53, 156-59, 169. For a more lengthy but regrettably opinionated account see E. Merton Coulter, "Slavery and Freedom in Athens, Georgia, 1860-1866," *Georgia Historical Quarterly,* XLIX (September, 1965), 264-93.

[9] *Southern Banner,* September 13, 1860, pp. 3, 2.

[10] Phillips, *op. cit.,* pp. 501-05; Kenneth M. Stampp, *The Peculiar Institution Slavery in the Ante-Bellum South* (New York, 1956), pp. 207, 228-29.

[11] Oglethorpe County Superior Court Minutes, 1794-1812 (Original in manuscript at the county courthouse, Lexington, Georgia [Microcopy, State Archives, Atlanta, Georgia. Unless otherwise stated, all subsequent citations of county records will refer to microcopies.]) no page numbers, minutes of September, 1810 (hereinafter cited Sup. Ct. Min.).

[12] Sup. Ct. Min., 1820-1823, minutes of October 26, 1822; Sup. Ct. Min., 1842-1849, p. 151.

[13] Sup. Ct. Min., 1812-1819, minutes of March 25, 1818; Sup. Ct. Min., 1820-1823, minutes of October 19, 1821; Sup. Ct. Min., 1823-1829, minutes of June 1, 1824, October 19, 1826.

[14] Sup. Ct. Min., 1842-1849, pp. 267, 294-95, 355; Sup. Ct. Min., 1847-1853, pp. 177-78, 193-94, 360. A prime offender during the 1840s was George W. Maxey, who was charged with seven counts of this offense in less than one year.

[15] Ralph Betts Flanders, *Plantation Slavery in Georgia* (reprint edition, Cos Cob, 1967), p. 237.

[16] Sup. Cit. Min., 1858-1862, p. 58.

[17] See, for example, Sup. Ct. Min., 1794-1812, minutes of September, 1810; Sup. Ct. Min., 1820-1823, minutes of October 18, 1820, April 22, 1823; Sup. Ct. Min., 1823-1829, minutes of April 16, 1827, October 24, 1828; Sup. Ct. Min., 1847-1853, pp. 142-43, 180-81; Oglethorpe County Equity and Appeals, Book B, 1854-1866, p. 606.

[18] For examples of attempted manumission or lesser rewards given to slaves in wills see Oglethorpe County Will Book A, pp. 61-62, 81-82, 84-85, 105-06; Will Book B, pp. 19-24, 76-78, 84-85, 112-13, 114.

[19] Flanders, *op. cit.,* pp. 248-51. In the year 1800, the legislature set free a Negro boy belonging to Joseph Thomas of Oglethorpe County. See *Acts of the General Assembly of the State of Georgia, Passed at Louisville in November and December, 1800* (Louisville, 1801), pp. 6-7.

[20] The decision referred to came in the landmark case of *Jordan vs. Heirs of Bradley.* For details and background see Will Book C, p. 42; G. M. Dudley, *Reports of decisions made by the judges of the superior courts of law and chancery of the State of Georgia* (New York, 1837), p. 170; Flanders, *op. cit.,* pp. 250-51. The judge who rendered this decision was a strong supporter of the American Colonization Society who wanted to insure that black immigration to Africa would not be thwarted by a strict interpretation of Georgia law. See *African Repository and Colonial Journal,* VII (July, 1831), 144.

[21] *African Repository,* VIII (May, 1832), 94.

[22] *Ibid.,* XXX (February, 1854), p. 56.

[23] *Thirty-Seventh Annual Report of the American Colonization Society, with the Proceedings of the Board of Directors and of the Society; and the Addresses Delivered at the Annual Meeting January 17, 1854* (Washington, 1854), p. 7.

[24] *African Repository,* XXXIII (January, 1857), 24-25; *Forty-First Annual Report of the American Colonization Society, with the Proceedings of the Board of Directors and of the Society: January 19, 1858* (Washington, 1858), p. 13.

[25] Flanders, *op. cit.,* pp. 240-42.

[26] Sup. Ct. Min., 1843-1847, pp. 452-53.

[27] For other examples of white men accused of crimes against slaves, see Sup. Ct. Min., 1800-1808, minutes of September 24, 1802, March 24, 1803; Sup. Ct. Min., 1812-1819, minutes of March 10, 1818, March 9, 1819; Sup. Ct. Min., 1820-1823, minutes of October 23, 1822, October 23, 1823; Sup. Ct. Min., 1823-1829, minutes of October 24, 1828. These accusations ranged in seriousness from "assault" to "murder." The only conviction came in 1823, for the former offense, and brought a fine of ten dollars.

[28] Minutes of Millstone Baptist Church, 1788-1842 (Microcopy, State Archives, Atlanta, Ga.) no page numbers, minutes of October 31, 1818, January 2, 1819, February 5, 1819. (hereinafter cited Min. Millstone Ch.)

[29] Minutes of the Baptist Church at Clouds Creek, 1826-1856 (Microcopy, State Archives, Atlanta, Ga.) pp. 47-48 (hereinafter cited, Min. Clouds Creek Ch.)

[30] Minutes of County Line Baptist Church, 1807-1915 (Microcopy, State Archives, Atlanta, Ga.) no page numbers, minutes of September 5, 1823 (hereinafter cited, Min. County Line Ch.)

[31] Equity and Appeals, Book A, 1846-1856, pp. 311-12.

[32] *Ibid.,* pp. 459-60. The prominent stature of the individuals involved is indicated by the fact that the name of the slave in question, as well as that of her owner, was purposely omitted in the official records.

[33] Equity and Appeals, Book B, 1854-1866, p. 171.

[34] For other examples of miscegenation see Sup. Ct. Min., 1840-1843, pp. 341-42. The son of a former Lexington hotel keeper asserts that during a ten-year period of that town's early history "there was only one child born whose father could claim any kindred with the African race. . . ." This statement is probably a gross exaggeration. See George W. Paschal, *Ninety-Four Years Agnes Paschal* (Washington, 1871), pp. 62, 65-67. For a broader treatment of the miscegenation problem in the South as a whole, see James Hugo Johnston, *Race Relations in Virginia & Miscegenation in the South 1776-1860* (Amherst, 1970).

[35] Flanders, *op. cit.,* p. 172.

[36] For instances of slaves being excommunicated or otherwise disciplined for committing "adultery," see Min. Millstone Ch., September 5, 1829; October 1, 1859, November 5, 1859, February 4, 1860, October 6, 1860, November 3, 1860; Min. County Line Ch., February 3, 1816, August 31, 1822, July 11, 1830; Min. Clouds Creek Ch., pp. 33-36, 52-53, 55, 59, 60, 63, 69-70, 71-73, 75, 88.

[37] Min. Millstone Ch., September 4, 1830.

[38] Minutes of the Sarepta Baptist Association, 1800-1867 (Microcopy, State Archives, Atlanta, Ga.) p. 122.

[39] Min. Millstone Ch., November 6, 1830, January 11, 1831.

[40] In 1844, for example, the Oglethorpe planter George Lumpkin offered to dispose of a 2,500 acre tract of land for a moderate price, explaining that he needed to raise $4,000 and would "rather sell land than Negroes." Geo[rge] Lumpkin to Middleton Pope, January 23, 1844 in Barrow Mss.

[41] W. R. Wright to [David C. Barrow?], December 4, 1856 in Barrow Mss.

[42] The author bases this statement upon an examination of county will books for the ante-bellum period. While slaves were sometimes willed to a single individual or allowed to choose their new owners, they were most often treated simply as a portion of the chattel property in an estate and disposed of accordingly.

[43] Flanders, *op. cit.*, 234.

[44] In 1823, for example, Sheriff Britton Stamps was paid $13.25 for "the trial and hanging of Shadrick, a negro the property of George Hudspeth" and two years later the sheriff received a lesser amount for "executing [the] negro man Daniel," who belonged to John Gilmer. See Inf. Ct. Min., 1822-1823, minutes of January 21, 1823, June 23, 1825. This was certainly true in nearby Baldwin County where some of these records have survived.

[45] Flanders, *op. cit.*, p. 235. Prior to 1850, records of slave trials were kept separately from other court proceedings, which may account for their frequent loss.

[46] Sup. Ct. Min., 1847-1853, pp. 194-95.

[47] That slave trials were not mere perfunctory affairs is clearly indicated by the trial of Daniel (mentioned above), for which a total of eleven witnesses were subpoenaed. See *supra* n. 44. For the procedure followed in slave trials in Elbert County, Georgia, which adjoins Oglethorpe on the north, see E. Merton Coulter, "Four Slave Trials in Elbert County, Georgia" in *Georgia Historical Quarterly*, XLI (September, 1957), 237-46.

[48] Stanley M. Elkins, *Slavery, A Problem in American Institutional and Intellectual Life* (New York, 1963), pp. 81-139, 223-30, *passim.*

[49] For biographical data on Cobb see *American Whig Review*, XIII (February, 1851), 131-33; Tommy W. Rogers, "Joseph B. Cobb: Antebellum Humorist and Critic" in *Mississippi Quarterly*, XXII (Spring, 1969), 131-46; George T. Buckley, "Joseph B. Cobb; Mississippi Essayist and Critic" in *American Literature*, X (May, 1938), 166-78. See also Cobb's obituary in Athens (Ga.) *Southern Watchman*, October 7, 1858, p. 3, 1, quoting *Tombigby Press*.

[50] Joseph B. Cobb, *Mississippi Scenes: Or, Sketches of Southern and Western Life and Adventure, Humorous, Satirical and Descriptive, Including the Legend of Black Creek* (Philadelphia, 1851), p. 173.

[51] *Ibid.*, pp. 173-75. For a more lengthy treatment of Cobb's views on slave personality see Clarence L. Mohr, "Samboization: A Case Study," in [Washington State University]*Research Studies*, XXXVIII (June, 1970), 152-54.

[52] Stampp, *op. cit.*, p. 379. Elkins has recently received sharp criticism for his failure to adequately distinguish between acting and reality in slave behavior. See, for example, Roy Simon Bryce-Laporte, "The American Slave Plantation and Our Heritage of Communal Deprivation" in *American Behavioral Scientist*, XII (March-April, 1969), 6.

[53] *Augusta Chronicle*, August 19, 1809, pp. 3, 4. Billy, the slave in question, was owned by the Lexington merchant John Gresham, who had purchased him in Southampton County, Virginia—later to be the scene of the famous Nat Turner Rebellion. In 1809, Billy was already a notorious runaway, well-known in Smithfield and Norfolk, Virginia, and even in Baltimore, Maryland.

[54] Elkins, *op. cit.*, p. 125, *passim.*

[55] Mary Agnes Lewis, "Slavery and Personality: A Further Comment" in *American Quarterly*, XIX (Spring, 1967), 114-21; see also Eugene D. Genovese, "Rebelliousness and Docility in the Negro Slave: A Critique of the Elkins Thesis" in *Civil War History*, XIII (December, 1967) 293-314.

[56] Geo[rge] W. Neal to David C. Barrow, December 10, 1851 in Barrow Mss. After the Bairdstown fire, Aleck continued to be recalcitrant and ran away early in 1852. See pocket diary of David C. Barrow for 1851, entries of December 6, December 8; Barrow Diary for 1852, entries of January 7, January 9, both in Barrow Mss.

[57] Barrow diary for 1851, entries of May 24-26 in Barrow Mss.

[58] For examples of slaves accused of stealing see *ibid.*, entries of May 17, June 9; Min. Millstone Ch., May 29, 1830, August 5, 1859, September 3, 1859; Min. County Line Ch., August 6, 1814; Min. Clouds Creek Ch., June 13, 1829. Numerous other examples

could be cited. Those given above are chosen because they provide specific details about the nature of the type of articles stolen.

59 Geo[rge] Lumpkin to [?], July 29, 1855 in Barrow Mss. The present author has made minor corrections in grammar and punctuation in the above quotation for the sake of clarity.

60 Manuscript U. S. Census Returns for Oglethorpe County, Georgia, 1860, Schedule 2, Slave Inhabitants (Microcopy No. T-7, Roll 33, University of Georgia Library), pp. 43-89.

61 See, for example, Min. Clouds Creek Ch., pp. 34-35, 37-38, 50, 77-79, *passim.*

62 Barrow diary for 1851, entry of June 9; *ibid.* for 1852, entries of March 17, 18, 23. In 1860, six of the slaves on Barrow' Syls Fork plantation were listed as fugitives. See Manuscript Oglethorpe County Census Returns for 1860, Schedule 2, Slave Inhabitants, p. 52.

63 Lillian Henderson (comp.), *Roster of the Confederate Soldiers of Georgia 1861-1865* (6 vols., Hapeville, Ga., 1960), I, 825-33, 986-93; Gussie Reese (comp.), *This They Remembered[:] The history of the four companies and those in other companies, who went from Oglethorpe County to serve in The War Between the States* (Washington, Ga., [1965?], pp. 1-3, 41-43.

64 Henderson, *op. cit.,* IV, 157-165; Reese, *op. cit.* pp. 71-73.

65 In 1860, Oglethorpe County contained some 964 white males between the ages of 15 and 50. By the end of 1861, at least 285 Oglethorpe residents had joined the Confederate Army, most of whom undoubtedly fell within this age group. See *Eighth Census,* p. 60; Henderson, *op. cit.,* I, 825-33, 986-93, IV, 157-66.

66 William McKinley to David C. Barrow, November 1, 1861, quoted in E. Merton Coulter, *Lost Generation: The Life and Death of James Barrow, C.S.A.* (Tuscaloosa, 1956), p. 40.

67 Reese, *op. cit.,* p. 118, quoting *Oglethorpe Echo,* July 29, 1885.

68 *Ibid.,* p. 119. The company referred to was the "Echols Artillery," which departed for Griffin, Georgia on March 18, 1862 with "about thirty" recruits.

69 T. Conn Bryan, *Confederate Georgia* (Athens, 1953), pp. 85-90; Albert B. Moore, *Conscription and Conflict in the Confederacy* (New York, 1924), pp. 255-79.

70 Sup. Ct. Min., 1858-1862. pp. 419-21. In November, 1862, the Georgia Supreme Court unanimously upheld the constitutionality of the conscription act, and Judge Thomas, who had presided in the Oglethorpe case, agreed to abide by its ruling. See Bryan, *op. cit.,* p. 87; *Southern Confederacy* (Atlanta), December 21, 1862, pp. 3, 4.

71 Moore, *op. cit.,* p. 183, n. 51; *Southern Confederacy,* December 21, 1862, pp. 3, 4.

72 Bell Irwin Wiley, *Southern Negroes, 1861-1865* (New Haven, 1965), p. 38.

73 Sup. Ct. Min., 1858-1862, pp. 407-08, 414.

74 *Ibid.,* pp. 409, 414-16.

75 *Ibid.,* p. 416.

76 Min. Millstone Ch. 1858-1864, minutes of July 5, 1862.

77 *The War of the Rebellion: A Compilation of the Official Records of the Union and Confederate Armies* (128 vols., Washington, 1880-1901), Series 4, II, 160-62, 690-91 (hereinafter cited O.R.); Moore, op. cit., p. 73.

78 David C. Barrow to Col. W[illiam] M. Browne, May 3, 1863 in Barrow Mss.

79 *Ibid.*

80 In 1862, the Georgia legislature had made it illegal for any person to plant more than three acres of cotton for each hand. In May, 1863, David C. Barrows reported that the entire southeastern part of Oglethorpe County was planted in corn, and asserted that he had reduced his own cotton acreage drastically, and now grew only enough for home use. See Bryan, *op. cit.,* p. 121; David C. Barrow to William M. Browne, May 3, 1863 in Barrow Mss.

[81] James H. McWhorter to David C. Barrow December 29, 1863 in Barrow Mss.

[82] Henderson, *op. cit.*, I, 825-33, 986-93, Iv, 157-66; Reese, *op. cit.*, pp. 1-3, 41-43, 71-73, 189-90.

[83] For a discussion of invasion rumors in the Oglethorpe region see, Coleman, *op. cit.*, pp. 164-65, 168-70.

[84] *Ibid.*, pp. 170-71.

[85] *Ibid.*, pp. 169, 172-74.

[86] David C. Barrow to Howell Cobb, September 8, 1864 in Howell Cobb Papers, University of Georgia Library, Athens, Georgia.

[87] Baker Daniel to David C. Barrow, October 6, 1864 in Barrow Mss.

[88] Ionia[?] Upson to "Miss Sawyer," January 11, 1865 in Barrow Mss.

[89] Inf. Ct. Min., 1863-1869, p. 175.

[90] William M. Browne to David C. Barrow, March 26, 1865; Pope Barrow to David C. Barrow, March 26, 1865; James H. McWhorter to David C. Barrow; March 29, 1865; same to same, April 8, 1865; John A. Cobb to David C. Barrow, April 15, 1865 in Barrow Mss.

[91] The Thirteenth Tennessee Cavalry was dispatched to Lexington from Athens on the afternoon of May 4, 1865. See O. R., Series 1, XLIX, Part 1, 548-549.

[92] Ellis Merton Coulter, *James Monroe Smith Georgia Planter Before Death and After* (Athens, 1961), p. 94.

[93] For the story of the transformation of one Oglethorpe County plantation after the War see [David C. Barrow, Jr.], "A Georgia Plantation" in *Scribner's Monthly*, XXI (April, 1881), 830-36.

Mutiny on the Slave Ships

Lorenzo J. Greene

For many Africans, enslavement began in Africa when they were captured and placed on ships bound for the Americas. The voyage from Africa, popularly known as the Middle Passage, was a horrific nightmare, endured for months under the tyranny of white traders concerned only for the profits to be made from the sordid business of trafficking in human cargo. Subjected to such wretched conditions and unbearable suffering, the captured Africans frequently struck blows for freedom in courageous attempts to return home or die trying.

Lorenzo Greene's essay focuses on uprisings aboard American vessels, particularly ships owned by traders from the Puritan colonies of New England. Highlighting the period before the American Revolution and the legal abolition of the slave trade, Greene directs his attention to eighteenth-century insurrections on vessels such as the Hope *(1764) and the* Jolly Bachelor *(1742), while urging the reader to link the mutinies of these African captives to the later struggles for freedom of enslaved blacks such as Nat Turner, Denmark Vesey, and others. This article, published in 1944, helps to document the epic tragedy for Africans that ensued from the notorious triangular slave trade and depicts some of the rebellions that preceded the now well-known* Amistad *mutiny of 1839.*

THE EXCELLENT STUDY OF *American Negro Slave Revolts* by Herbert Aptheker was one of the earliest works to revise the carefully nutured notion of the Negro's natural docility to slavery.[1] In his scholarly volume, however, Mr. Aptheker confines his attention to slave insurrections upon American soil. Yet, these outbreaks were but the second act in this tragic drama of the Negro's continuous struggle for freedom. The first act—the bloody uprising of the slaves on board the ships bringing them to America—is yet to be written. In the following pages an attempt will be made to portray some of the battles for freedom waged by Negroes on New England slave ships—battles which lay outside the scope of Mr. Aptheker's volume.

In the more than three hundred and fifty years of the slave trade to America, ships of every nationality participating in the traffic—Spanish, French, Dutch, Portuguese, English, and American—

were scenes of desperate attempts by the slaves to regain their liberty.[2]

Of the American ships involved in these insurrections those from New England suffered most. This is not surprising, for the Puritan colonies in the eighteenth century were the greatest slave-trading communities in America. From Boston, Salem, and Charlestowne in Massachusetts; from Newport, Providence, and Bristol in Rhode Island; and from New London and Hartford, Connecticut, swift, sturdy ships took rum, bar iron, and trinkets to Africa. There the captains bartered their goods for Negroes whom they carried to the West Indies or to the plantation colonies of the South and sold for rum, molasses, sugar, cocoa, or bills of exchange. The molasses and sugar were brought to New England, distilled into rum, thence transported to Africa for more slaves. Thus developed the notorious triangular slave trade, with New England, Africa, and the West Indies as its chief focal points.

The profits from the slave trade were almost incredible. Seldom has there been a more lucrative commerce than the traffic in Negroes. In 1699, it was reported that ten shillings in English goods would buy a slave in Madagascar,[3] and early in the eighteenth century the choicest West Coast slaves sold in America for £3 or £4.[4] These slaves and others costing £5 in rum or bar iron were sold in the West Indies and in the plantation colonies at prices ranging from £30 to £88 sterling.[5] In 1746, Joseph Manest of London made a profit of £11,200 on a cargo of slaves that cost £1800. With gross profits sometimes as high as sixteen hundred percent,[6] the slave trade easily became the most lucrative commerce of the seventeenth and eighteenth centuries.[7] Before the American Revolution it was regarded as the mainstay of New England's prosperity.[8]

Puritan exploitation of this profitable commerce bred a wealthy merchant class whose names include some of the most prominent families in American history. George Cabot of Salem; Samuel and Cornelius Waldo, Andrew and Peter Fanueil of Boston; James Brown and his four sons of Providence; and George Champlin, William Ellery and Caleb Gardner of Newport were only a few of the well-known merchants whose fortunes rested upon the slave trade.[9]

Interested in obtaining the greatest possible returns from their slaving activities, these merchants contrived in every way to cut the overhead cost of slave voyages. Small ships, generally ranging between forty and sixty tons were found most practical for the trade. All of them were undermanned, with crews numbering from six to eighteen hands, including the captain and cabin boy. Cheating, kidnapping, and other sharp practices were freely indulged in.

Every possible precaution was taken to prevent the slaves from revolting. Slave ships were generously equipped with pistols, muskets, cutlasses, knives, and even cannon. Guards were posted at all times to insure against the crew's being taken by surprise. The vessels were also carefully searched to make sure that no pieces of iron, wood, or other weapons were within reach of the slaves.[10] Merchants regularly instructed their captains to transact their business on the African Coast with the utmost dispatch, and to be constantly on the alert against slave insurrection which might reduce or even wipe out entirely the profits of the entire voyage.[11] The admonition of Samuel Waldo to Captain Samuel Rhodes, prior to the latter's sailing for Africa in 1734 is typical: "For your safety as well as mine," he wrote, "You'll have the needful guard over your Slaves, and put not too much Confidence in the Women nor Children lest they happen to be Instrumental to your being surprised which may be fatall."[12]

In attempting to follow these instructions, the captain and crew of slave vessels made the existence of the blacks almost unbearable. In fact, the very measures taken to protect the profits of the merchants by preventing uprisings reacted to drive the Negroes into mutiny. Herded aboard ship, the slaves were crammed into the hot stuffy holds between decks. In these compartments only three feet, three inches high, it was impossible for the slaves to sit erect. Male slaves were chained together by twos; female slaves were unfettered but were separated from the men by partitions. To augment the carrying capacity of the ship, the Negroes were forced to lie spoon-fashion, each Negro fitting into the curve of the other's body. As the slaves lay naked on the rough planks, the rolling of the ship frequently rubbed the flesh off prominent parts of their bodies, leaving them writhing in "blood and mucous." When the hatches were closed and battened down at night, or when storms or attack from hostile vessels made it necessary to close the gratings and air ports, many of the slaves died of suffocation. Food and water often ran low or even ran out, causing indescribable torment and sometimes death from thirst and hunger. Loathsome diseases—yaws, syphilis, fevers, opthalmia, dropsy, seasickness, and the dreaded white and bloody fluxes—added to the misery and mortality of the slaves on the terrible Middle Passage. Sailors, making their daily rounds in the stinking holds, frequently unshackled dead slaves from the living and threw their bodies to the sharks that followed in the wake of the vessel.[13]

The terrible suffering of the Negroes on these vessels the Puritans justified on the high ground that slavery was an act of mercy by which the slaves could be brought to salvation.[14] Unless the heathen were acquainted with the Gospel, eternal misery would be his lot in the after life.[15] Therefore, any suffering that the slaves might experience either on the slave ship or in slavery was more than compensated for by their "fortunate delivery from a life of idolatry and savagery." For this reason, a slave-trading Rhode Island elder could piously rejoice, as he beheld his slave vessel coming into port, that "an overruling Providence had been pleased to bring to this land of freedom another cargo of benighted heathen to enjoy the blessings of a Gospel dispensation."[16]

The reaction of the Negroes to their condition aboard the slave ships showed that they did not generally share the conviction of those who would lead them into salvation through slavery. Driven to desperation by their wretchedness, the slaves seized every opportunity to escape enslavement or to end their suffering. Many refused to eat and were sometimes forced to do so, after having their teeth broken or their lips seared by hot coals. Others committed suicide. But the most dramatic protests were the frenzied mass efforts of the Negroes to win their freedom through violence. Biding their time, they frequently rose up against their captors in determined attempts to kill the crew, seize the vessel, and return to Africa. In this bloody but circumscribed theatre of action, the revolting slaves were generally at a disadvantage. The crew, although outnumbered by the Negroes, was fully armed, organized, disciplined, and under authoritative leadership. The crew also had the advantage of strategic position for it controlled the decks and superstructure of the ship. On the other hand, the slaves were unorganized, undisciplined, and united only in their insatiable desire for liberty. They were unarmed, shackled and weakened by confinement. Pieces of iron, wood, and their chains were their only weapons. Moreover, in the event of an uprising, they could easily be dispatched by the gunfire of the crew as they climbed on deck. But these "bozal" or raw Negroes feared neither their captors nor death, and in spite of the slender possibilities of success, struck time and again in maniacal fury for their freedom. Sometimes the slaves gained their objective. More frequently the firearms of the crew prevailed, and after desperate struggles the slaves were repulsed, but only after casualties had been inflicted on both sides.

Ships of all the slave trading communities of New England experienced these insurrections.[17] Carroll tells of a successful slave insurrection aboard a New Hampshire vessel commanded by Captain John Majors of Portsmouth. The Negroes revolted, killed the entire crew, and seized both the schooner and its cargo.[18] On October 5, 1764, came a report from Charleston, South Carolina, telling of the death of Captain Millar of the ship *Adventure*. When Millar and all but one of his crew died of illness off the coast of Africa, two white men assumed control of his ship. "While the vessel lay at anchor with her slaves," continued the report, "the natives came off, barbarously murdered the white men and plundered the whole cargo except for two slaves."[19] In 1764, a Boston Court listened to a tale of mutiny, murder, and Negro insurrection from William Preest of the slave ship *Hope*, belonging to Messrs. Forseys of New London, Connecticut. Preest was charged with murdering his skipper, Captain Goold, as the *Hope* lay at anchor on the Senegal River in Africa. According to Preest's testimony, the chief mate then assumed command and later took on a cargo of slaves. En route from Africa to the West Indies, the Negroes mutinied. In the ensuing struggle two members of the crew and eight slaves were killed. The ship put into Porto Rico, where the Spanish authorities, charging that it was illicitly trading with their possessions, confiscated both vessel and slaves.[20] In the same year conflicting reports filtered into Connecticut concerning Captain Faggott, master of a brig owned by the Forseys of New London. One version said that Faggott had been killed when his slaves revolted at Goree off the Coast of Africa.[21] According to the second report, the slaves freed themselves of their chains and attacked the ship at night, killing the captain and two members of the crew.[22]

Because of the much larger slave trade of Massachusetts, insurrections on board her ships were more numerous. On January 28, 1731, an English newspaper reported that Captain Jump of the Massachusetts schooner *William* and all but three of his crew had been killed in a slave uprising off the coast of Africa.[23] Two years later (1733), Captain Moore of a Massachusetts slaver reported that at midnight on June 17 his ship was attacked by natives on the Gambia River. The battle, Moore related, lasted till dawn. When the wind and tide finally drove the ship close to the shore, the natives tried to board her, but were finally driven off after a hard fight during which one member of the crew was killed.[24] In 1761 slaves aboard the Boston ship *Thomas*, commanded by Thomas Day, revolted, broke through the hatches, and set upon the crew. Only after the leader had been killed and others wounded was the insurrection put down.[25] A more celebrated case was that of the *Jolly Bachelor*, a slave ship belonging to Peter Fanueil, his brother-in-law, John Jones, and Captain Cutler of Boston. While taking on slaves in the Sierra Leone River in March 1742, the vessel, according to George Burchall, was attacked and captured by the natives. In the fight Captain Cutler and two of his men were killed. The Negroes stripped the vessel of its rigging and sails, freed the slaves in the hold, then abandoned the ship. One month later, Burchall and others refitted the vessel, appointed one

Charles Wickham master and brought it into Newport. There the vessel was libelled and sold for £2924. Two-thirds of this amount went to the Fanueil and Jones families; one-third to Burchall.[26]

In April 1789 another uprising occurred aboard the schooner *Felicity*. Thirteen days out from Africa the slaves revolted, killed Captain William Fairfield, and wounded several of the crew. Three of the slaves were killed. The captain's son, who, either during or after the struggle, scalded himself with hot chocolate, sent his mother the following report of the uprising:

> Honour'd Parent: I take this Opportunity to write unto you to let know of a very bad accident that Happen'd on our late passage from Cape Mount, on the Coast of Africa, bound to Cayenne. We sail'd from Cape Mount the 13th of March with 35 Slaves On bord; the 26th day of March the Slaves Rised upon us, at half past seven, my Sir father and all hands being Forehead [forward] Except the man at below and myself. Three of the Slaves took Possession of the Caben, and two upon the quarter Deck, them in the Caben took Possession of the fier Arms and them on the quarter Deck with the Ax and Cutlash and other Weapons, them in the Caben handed up Pistels to them on the quarter Deck. One of them fired and killed my honoured Sir and still we strove for to subdue them, and then we got on the quarter Deck and killed two of them. One that was in the Caben was Comeing out at the Caben Windows in order to get on Deck and we Discovered him and Knock'd him overboard. Two being in the Caben we confined the Caben Doors so that they should not kill us, then three men went forhead and got the three that was down their and brought them aft. And their being a Doctor on bord [a] Passenger that Could speak the tongue he sent one of the boys down and Brought up some fier arms and Powder and then we cal'd them up and one Came up and Cal'd the other and he Came up. We put them in Irons and Chained them and then the Doctor Dres'd the Peoples Wounds they being Slightly Wounded. Then it was one o'clock they buried my honoured Parent,. . . I scalt myself with hot Chocolate but now am able to walk again . . . We have sold part of the Slaves and I hope to be home soon.[27]

Ships from Rhode Island, the leading slave-trading colony, suffered most frequently from these uprisings. One of the worst insurrections was attended with complete success for the slaves. On June 1, 1730, Captain George Scott in the sloop *Little George* sailed from the Guinea Coast with a cargo of ninety-six slaves, thirty-five of whom were men. Six days later, the slaves slipped out of their shackles, and at four-thirty in the morning, attacked the ship. Breaking through the bulkhead, they gained the deck, where they were confronted by the watch of three men. These the slaves quickly dispatched and pitched overboard. Terrified, the Captain, three men, and a boy sought refuge in the cabin below, where the slaves promptly imprisoned them. One of the sailors attempted to fashion a bomb by filling two bottles with gunpowder to be thrown among the slaves. This strategem was thwarted by a Negro, who dropped an axe on the bottle just as the sailor lighted the fuse. The explosion set fire to a keg of powder, blew open the cabin door, raised the deck, discharged all except one musket, and seriously injured both the captain and bombmaker. Determined to wipe out the crew, the slaves loaded one of the carriage guns and fired it down the scuttle where the sailors were imprisoned. According to the captain, the blast "blew the Scuttle all to pieces" but no one was injured. For several days the slaves controlled the ship, while the captain and the remainder of the crew, armed with muskets, defended themselves below. Sometime later, the cabin boy, impelled by hunger, ventured upon deck, whereupon the slaves promptly clapped him in irons. Finally, the Negroes guided the ship into the Sierra Leone River and ran it aground on a bar. After removing all the women and children, they abandoned the ship. Later they returned with other natives in an attempt to kill the crew, but the latter successfully defended themselves with firearms. At the first favorable opportunity the captain and the rest of the crew came upon deck, lowered a boat and started down the river. Weak from hunger, they were finally rescued, after having subsisted for nine days on raw rice.[28]

Equally as disastrous was the experience of Captain Bear, master of a Rhode Island slaver. On December 4, 1753, he had stored on board his ship at Coast Castle, Africa, a number of slaves and a quantity of gold dust. Without warning, the slaves rebelled, killing the captain and all the crew except two mates, who escaped by leaping overboard and swimming ashore. The ultimate fate of both vessels and Negroes is not known.[29] In 1753, according to Captain David Lindsay, the slaves aboard a Rhode Island ship commanded by Captain Hamblett revolted, causing him to lose his best Negroes.[30] Nicholas Owen, an Englishman serving aboard a Rhode Island vessel, told of a calamity which befell a ship from that colony between 1746 and 1757. The ship had anchored off Banana Island, where the captain and five of the crew went ashore. There they were captured by Negroes, who later took and plundered the ship.[31] Twelve years later Captain T. Rogers, master of a vessel belonging to Messrs. Samuel and William Vernon of Newport, was carrying a cargo of slaves from Barbados to St. Christopher in the West Indies. On the way, the slaves rose up and attempted to seize the ship. In suppressing the revolt, Rogers is said to have lost eleven male slaves. A second report said that thirteen slaves jumped overboard, one was killed, and several wounded.[32]

Far more disastrous was the voyage of Captain Hopkins, who commanded a ship belonging to the Brown brothers of Newport. In 1765, he sailed from Africa to Antigua with a cargo of slaves. On the way, sickness so depleted the crew that the captain impressed some of the slaves to help man the ship. But the Negroes, seizing the opportunity to gain their freedom, released some of their fellows and fell upon the crew. After a bloody struggle, the crew, outnumbered, but armed with muskets, put down the rebellion after they had killed, wounded, or forced to jump overboard eighty of the slaves.[33] In the same year, a report stated that the entire crew of a Bristol (Rhode Island) vessel had been killed by the slaves off the African coast. The only white survivor was a Mr. Dunfield who escaped by being out in a boat when the uprising took place.[34]

Eleven years later, the slaves aboard the Rhode Island ship *Thames*, taking advantage of the carelessness of the Chief Officer,[35] made a desperate effort to gain their freedom as the ship lay off the Guinea Coast. Armed only with staves and chunks of wood, the Negroes fell upon the crew who sought refuge behind a barricade on the deck. After a desperate but futile forty minute struggle to surmount the barricade, all the men slaves jumped overboard. In this manner between thirty-three and thirty-six[36] of the most valuable slaves were drowned. Six slaves were picked up by townspeople who charged Captain Clarke eleven ounces of gold dust for their return. In his letter to John Fletcher of London, dated December 15, 1776, Dr. John Bell, a physician on board the *Thames*, graphically described the insurrection:

> . . . As Capt. Clarke has Observed to you the Voyage has been attended with nothing but losses and disappointments, so to complete the whole on Friday the 8th inst., we had the misfortune to lose 36 of the best slaves we had by an insurrection. This unluckly affair happened when there was only the Boatswain, Carpenter, 3 white people and myself on board. . . . We had 160 Slaves on board and were that day lett out of the Deck Chains in order to wash. About 2 o'clock they began by siesing upon the Boatswain but he soon got disengaged . . . after receiving a wound in the Breast and one under his chin. . . . They Continued to threw Staves, billets of wood etc., and in endeavoring to get down the Barricade, or over it for upward of 40 Minutes, when finding they could not effect it, all the Fantee and most of the Accra men Slaves jumped overboard. It was thought that the slaves intended to get abaft of the ship but the current was so strong they could not reach the vessel. When all was

settled we found 32 Men and boys w't 2 women a mising, the best Slaves we had.[37]

The women slaves did not join the attack, Bell asserted, only because the spontaneity of the uprising had not given the men time to notify them. Had they also been involved, the doctor assured his superior, "Your property here at this time would have been but small."[38]

A marked decrease occurred in the number of slave insurrections on New England ships during the last quarter of the eighteenth century. The American Revolution ruined the slave trade,[39] and all the principal slaving states—Rhode Island (1784), Connecticut (1784), and Massachusetts (1787)—abolished the slave trade.[40] Prohibition of the traffic, however, only increased the profits from a successful voyage; therefore many Puritan merchants continued to engage illicitly in the slave trade. Evidence of the clandestine exploitation of the traffic in Negroes is revealed in continued reports of slave insurrections aboard New England vessels. Seven years after Connecticut abolished the slave trade (1791), Captain William Wignall of New London lost his life when his slaves revolted off the Coast of Africa.[41] Two years after Massachusetts proscribed the trade, the insurrection of slaves aboard the *Felicity*, previously noted, took place.[42] In 1795, a bloody encounter occurred between insurgent slaves and the crew of a Boston ship off the Coast of Africa. The Negroes, forty in number, attacked the crew, killed a common seaman, the first and second mates, and the captain and seized control of the ship. The vessel drifted ashore near the mouth of the River Nunez where, after a bloody battle lasting almost seven hours, another trader recaptured the ship.[43]

Because a larger number of Rhode Island merchants continued to carry on an illicit trade in Negroes, slave uprisings aboard their vessels were more frequent. In the year following Rhode Island's prohibition of the traffic, complete disaster overtook one of its vessels. In 1785, the ship left Newport for Africa. Twelve months later it was found by an English ship, drifting helplessly upon the high seas. Her sails were gone, and upon her decks crouched fifteen emaciated slaves. Whether the crew had died of illness, or whether the Negroes had risen up, slain the captain and crew, and then attempted to steer the ship back to Africa will never be known.[44] In 1793 or 1794, several slaves lost their lives in a futile attempt to seize the *Nancy*, commanded by Captain Cook.[45] Only the timely warning of a Negro cabin boy probably saved the *Mary* from total disaster in 1796. Some of the slaves, having freed themselves from their leg irons while in the hold, planned to attack the crew with them when they came on deck. Although the sailors were forewarned, the slaves fought savagely. Only after two of them had been drowned, one shot dead, a sick slave trampled to death and four Negroes wounded was the uprising put down.[46]

As late as 1807, Captain Joshua Vial, the Rhode Island master of the ship *Nancy*, belonging to John Phillip and John Gardner of Charleston, South Carolina, reported several slave uprisings on his vessel. During one of these attacks three slaves were killed and one jumped overboard. Another outbreak occurred when a slave attempted to seize Vial as "he was pouring molasses in his victuals." Immediately the slaves attacked the crew and a furious struggle followed. However, the firearms of the crew prevailed and the slaves were driven below, but only after one Negro had jumped overboard and several had been wounded. These uprisings so unnerved the sailors that several days later when four members of the crew were disabled by illness, the captain reported that a sailor on night watch, imagining that the Negroes were about to revolt again, shot and killed one of them and on the next night stabbed another.[47]

The foregoing insurrections portray but a single scene in the first act of a mighty drama for freedom, in which African slaves were the principal actors and the New England slave ships the stage. To complete the act, it is necessary to set forth similar struggles aboard other American vessels and the ships of all the other nationalities which participated in the trade. Thus would be told the epic tragedy of battles for freedom fought by millions of blacks on thousands of ships over a span of three and a half centuries. Such a work would make an heroic prelude for the second act in the drama—the Negro's struggle for liberty on American soil—and overthrow completely the fiction that the Negro tamely submitted to enslavement.

Notes

[1] Herbert Aptheker, *American Negro Slave Revolts,* Columbia University *Studies in History, Economics, and Public Law,* No. 5 (Columbia University Press, N.Y., 1943). Less satisfactory studies are Joseph C. Carroll's *Slave Insurrections in the United States, 1800-1865* (Chapman and Grimes, Boston, 1938); Harvey Wish, "Slave Insurrections Before 1861," *Journal of Negro History,* XX, No. 3, April, 1937.

[2] For excellent first-hand accounts of these insurrections, see the incomparable volumes of Elizabeth Donnan, *Documents Illustrative of the History of the Slave Trade to America,* 4 vols. (Carnegie Institution of Washington, 1930-1935); Nicholas Owen, *Journal of a Slave Trader, 1746-1757,* ed. Eveline Martin (London, 1930); George Dow, *Slave Ships and Slaving* (Salem, 1927).

[3] Charles Johnson, *A General History of Pyrates* (1715), cited in Donnan, III, 440n.

[4] Donnan, *op. cit.,* III, 58.

[5] *Ibid.,* 141n., 196, 267.

[6] *Ibid.,* III, 141.

[7] *Ibid.,* II, 405.

⁸ See "A Statement of the Massachusetts Trade and Fisheries," *Conn. Historical Society Collections*, XVIII, 262-273; *Rhode Island Colonial Records*, VI, 378-383.

⁹ Lorenzo J. Greene, *The Negro in Colonial New England, 1620-1776*, Columbia University *Studies in History, Economics, and Public Law*, No. 494 (Columbia University Press, N.Y., 1942), pp. 27-28.

¹⁰ Wish, *op. cit.*, p. 301.

¹¹ Greene, op. cit., p. 45.

¹² *Ibid.*

¹³ For examples, see Dow, *Slave Ships and Slaving*, chs. vii, ix-xi and *passim*; Thomas Buxton, *The African Slave Trade* (London, 1840), ch. ii; Owen, *op. cit.*, chs. i-iii; best of all are the indispensable volumes of Donnan, *op. cit.*, I-IV, *passim*.

¹⁴ George Champlin Mason, "The African Slave Trade in Colonial Times," *American Historical Record*, I, No. 1 (Philadelphia, 1873), 312.

¹⁵ *Massachusetts Historical Society Collections*, Fifth Series III, 384.

¹⁶ Mason, *et supra*; cited in Greene, *op. cit.*, p. 62.

¹⁷ Donnan cites many first-hand accounts of uprisings aboard New England slave vessels. Those cited hereinafter are taken almost wholly from Volume III, dealing with the New England slave trade.

¹⁸ *Op. cit.*, p. 20.

¹⁹ Donnan, *op. cit.*, III, 207. The ship belonged either to Rhode Island or to New London, Connecticut. *Ibid.*

²⁰ *Ibid.*, p. 71.

²¹ *Ibid.*, p. 2.

²² This ship also is said to have gone to Puerto Rico where the Spaniards confiscated it ostensibly for illicitly trading with their possessions. *Ibid.*, p. 71n.

²³ *Read's Weekly Journal and British Gazette*, Jan. 1731; cited in Donnan, III, 37n.

²⁴ Donnan, *op. cit.*, III, 41.

²⁵ *Ibid.*

²⁶ For interesting and conflicting accounts of the *Jolly Bachelor*, see William B. Weeden, "Early African Slave Trade in New England," American Antiquarian Society, *Proceedings*, 1887-1888, New Series, V (Worcester, 1889), 123-128; for first-hand account of principals involved, *cf.* Donnan, *op. cit.*, III, 52-65.

²⁷ Donnan, III, 82-83.

²⁸ See *Ibid.*, pp. 118-121, for Captain Scott's story.

²⁹ *Ibid.*, p. 51n.

³⁰ *Ibid.*, p. 201. Another account says that twelve blacks were killed and that the ship was bound for Antigua from Barbadoes.

³¹ *Op. cit.*, pp. 37-38.

³² Mason, *op. cit.*, p. 339.

³³ Donnan, III, 213.

³⁴ *Ibid.*, p. 209n.

³⁵ According to the ship's captain, Peleg Clarke, the Chief Officer not only failed to chain the Negroes while on deck, but had further weakened the crew by going ashore and taking several officers with him. *Ibid.*, p. 331.

³⁶ Captain Clark placed the loss at thirty-three; Dr. Bell, at thirty-six. *Ibid.*, pp. 331, 323.

³⁷ *Ibid.*, p. 323.

³⁸ *Ibid.*

³⁹ William E. B. DuBois, "The Suppression of the African Slave Trade to the United States of America, 1808-1870," *Harvard Historical Studies*, No. 1 (New York, 1896), p. 5; Donnan, III, 315-319.

[40] *Acts and Resolves of Rhode Island, May 1771-Oct. 1775* (Facsimile Reprints), V, 48-50; *Acts and Laws of the State of Connecticut* (Printed by Timothy Greene, New London, n.d.), p. 234; *Acts and Laws of Massachusetts, 1786-1787* (Reprint, Boston, 1893), pp. 615-16.

[41] *Salem Gazette*, September 13, 1791.

[42] See above.

[43] Donnan, III, 101.

[44] *Ibid.*, p. 341n.

[45] *Ibid.*, p. 359n.

[46] *Ibid.*, pp. 374-5.

[47] Dow, *op. cit.*, p. 399; for documents, see Donnan, III, 396, 401.

Towards Freedom: An Analysis of Slave Revolts in the United States

MARION D. DE B. KILSON

The brutality and inhumanity of slavery stimulated pro-test and resistance by enslaved Africans throughout the slave period. While resistance took a number of forms, ranging from negligence in work and destruction of property to self-mutila-tion and escape, the form of resistance most disturbing to the white community were the slave revolts. The revolts began as early as the inception of the slave system in the United States and continued until its abolition in 1865. While most revolts were unsuccessful, their goals varied from freedom for individ-ual participants to overthrow of the institution of slavery and the creation of a black state.

In Marion D. de B. Kilson's essay the documented slave uprisings are categorized into three types. Proceeding from anal-ysis of broad trends and salient characteristics observable in each of the prototypes, Kilson delineates differences in purpose, territorial extent, leadership, participants, and preconditions associated with each type. The data show, too, that retaliatory and repressive measures generally followed uprisings of all types, as the worst fears of whites were realized when blacks and their supporters dared to challenge the power of the slavocracy.

THROUGHOUT THE HISTORY of slavery in the United States there occurred a variety of more or less subtle expressions of opposition to the slave system by the enslaved. Opposition took many forms, rang-ing from individual attempts to thwart the system through negligence in work to mass endeavors to overthrow the system. One class of op-position to the status of servitude is represented by slave revolts, which may be defined minimally as attempts to achieve freedom by groups of slaves. Although the data on slave revolts are fragmentary, three types may be distinguished on the basis of sixty-five cases meet-ing this minimal definition. These are Systematic or Rational Revolts, Unsystematic or Vandalistic Revolts, and Situational or Opportunistic Revolts. The analysis of the characteristics of each of these types of

TABLE 1
TYPE I REVOLTS[1]

REVOLT	FORM	AIM:		SYSTEMATIC CHARACTERISTICS:					AREA	PARTICIPANTS:	
					PLAN:						
		ESTABLISH NEGRO STATE	TAKE CITY	MONTHS PREPARATION	FOR RETREAT	TO SPARE GROUPS	TO ALLOCATE TASKS			LEADER	INSURGENTS
Md. 1739	C	X		SEVERAL	X				1co		200
N.Y. 1712	R			3			X		1ci		25-30
Va. 1663	C			SEVERAL					1co		WI,S
Va. 1722	C	X							3co	3S	
Va. 1792	C		X	SEVERAL			X		4co		600+
Va. 1793	C			4					1ci		
Va. 1800[2]	C	X	X	6		X	X		4co	1S	c.7,000
Va. 1816	C		X						3co	1W	
S.C. 1720	C		X								"LARGE"
S.C. 1816	C		X	8					1ci		
S.C. 1822[3]	C	X	X	7			X		80mi	1F	c.7,000
Ga. 1810	C			1			X		2co		
Ga. 1819	C								1ci	S	
Ga. 1841	C		X								S,W
La. 1837	C		X			X	X		1co		F,S
La. 1840	C								7co		400+S 4W
La. 1853	C								1ci	1S 1W	2,500S 100W

KEY:
C:CONSPIRACY   CI:CITY   S:SLAVE
R:ACTUAL REVOLT   CO:COUNTY   W:WHITE
X:VARIABLE PRESENT   MI:MILES   WI:INDENTURED WHITE
    F:FREE NEGRO

[1] UNLESS OTHERWISE NOTED THE DATA CONTAINED IN THIS AND SUBSEQUENT TABLES ARE BASED UPON MATERIAL DERIVED FROM APTHEKER, *op. cit.*
[2] Gabriel Prosser's Revolt.
[3] Denmark Vesey's Revolt.

revolt, of their distribution in time and space, of their leadership, and of their repercussions is the concern of this paper.

The three types of slave revolt differ in form, purpose, salient attributes, territorial extent, and participants. Variable aspects of these categories are expressed in Tables 1, 2, and 3. While each table summarizes the available evidence on revolts of a particular type, further elaboration of the content and implications of these categories is necessary.

The Type I or Systematic Revolt, of which the prototypes are the conspiracies of Gabriel Prosser and Denmark Vesey, is oriented towards overthrowing the slave system itself and establishing a Negro state. It is characterized, therefore, by careful planning and organization which necessitate a considerable period of preparation. Careful planning is evidenced by the means decided upon to realize the establishment of the Negro state. Both Prosser and Vesey planned initially to gain control of a city and thereafter to extend their operations into the surrounding area. Such a plan involves the systematic allocation of tasks to various groups and individuals and the calculation of the numbers of insurgents upon whom reliance could be placed. Further evidence of the rational conception of these uprisings is found in the facts that Gabriel Prosser intended to spare certain sympathetic groups of whites and hoped for aid from poor whites and Indians, and that Vesey hoped to have external aid from the West Indies and Africa to maintain his state after its establishment.[1] One corollary of such systematic planning is a long period of preparation which, in turn, increases the likelihood of discovery by the slavocracy; it is not surprising, therefore, that of the seventeen Type I Revolts[2] which have been distinguished, only one went beyond the planning phase. A second corollary of such rational planning is that it is likely to involve the recruitment of a large number of insurgents from a number of counties.

Two aspects of Type I Revolts merit further comment: the urban factor and armed conflict with the slavocracy. The urban factor is significant in 71 percent of the Type I Revolts, five of them occurring within an urban complex and seven others initially oriented towards gaining control of a city. The urban factor appears to have been significant as a source both of more cosmopolitan ideas and of greater role differentiation for Negroes. This does not imply that Type I Revolts are necessarily urban inspired. While Vesey was a resident of Charleston, South Carolina, Prosser lived six miles outside of Richmond, Virginia. Moreover, 29 percent of the Type I Revolts were not urban oriented. Thus the urban factor seems to facilitate rather than

TABLE 2
TYPE II REVOLTS

REVOLT	FORM	AIM:	UNSYSTEMATIC CHARACTERISTICS:		AREA	PARTICIPANTS:	
		DESTRUCTION PROPERTY AND/OR SLAVE HOLDERS	LACK PREPARATION	GATHERING RECRUITS		LEADER	INSURGENTS
N.Y. 1708	R	x			1TO		"SMALL"
VA. 1687	C	x			1CO		
VA. 1691	R	x			1CO	S	
VA. 1792	R	x		x	1CO		900
VA. 1831[1]	R	x	x	x	1CO	S	70
N.C. 1776	C	x			3CO	1S 1W	
S.C. 1711	R	x				S	"SEVERAL"
S.C. 1730	C		x		1CI		
S.C. 1740	R		x	x			150-200
GA. 1774	R	x	x		1CO		10[2]
LA. 1730	C	x			1CI		
LA. 1795	C	x	x		1CI		
LA. 1811	R	x		x	2CO	F	400-500
MISS. 1835	C	x			1CO	W	

KEY:
C:CONSPIRACY   CI:CITY   F:FREE NEGRO
R:ACTUAL REVOLT   CO:COUNTY   S:SLAVE
X:VARIABLE PRESENT   TO:TOWN   W:WHITE

[1] TURNER'S REVOLT.
[2] Carroll, *op. cit.*, p. 38.

to determine the development of Type I revolts. The second noteworthy aspect of Type I Revolts is that while the achievement of their ultimate goals necessitates armed conflict with members of the slavocracy potentially leading to bloodshed and property destruction, this is a secondary phenomenon rather than a primary goal.

By contrast, the Type II or Vandalistic Revolt, of which the prototype is Nat Turner's insurrection, represents a haphazard expression of opposition to the slave system aimed at the destruction of slave holders and their property. It lacks systematic preparation but may be either of lengthy or of virtually spontaneous conception. Its unsystematic character and potential spontaneity imply both that it has a greater likelihood of reaching the activist stage[3] than Type I Revolts and that reliance upon the gathering of recruits as the revolt gains momentum is of more importance than in the Type I Revolt. For example, deciding one Sunday afternoon to begin his long contemplated revolt that night, Turner set out with a handful of fellow insurgents whose numbers swelled to seventy during the course of the rising.[4] A further implication of the unsystematic nature of the Type II Revolt is that it tends to be localized within a single county and to be a rural rather than an urban-oriented phenomenon.[5] Moreover, lacking any well-defined goals beyond the immediate destruction of the life and property of the slaveholder, the Type II Revolt implies the insurgents' unconscious acceptance of ultimate capitulation to the power of the slavocracy.[6]

The Type III or Opportunistic Revolt aims at escape from servitude. It is characterized by a group of slaves attempting to escape either to a non-slave area or from removal to areas of more oppressive servitude. It tends, therefore, to be situationally determined. Given the realistic opportunity to escape to a free area by land or sea, the group attempts to realize this objective. Thus like the Type I Revolt it is rationally conceived, and like the Type II Revolt it may be virtually spontaneous.[7] Significantly, the only successful slave revolt of which there is evidence falls into the Type III category.[8]

Slave revolts of all three types occurred throughout the slave period and in all the slave regions of the United States. The distribution of types of slave revolts in time and space is summarized in Table 4. If the slave period is divided into Pre-1776 or Colonial, 1776-1800 or Revolutionary, 1801-1829 or Old South Slave, and 1830-1860 or Deep South Slave periods, a number of broad trends are observable. In the Colonial period, slave revolts occurred in Northern colonies as well as in Southern colonies; in the Southern colonies they developed primarily in Virginia and South Carolina. In the Revolutionary period with the disappearance of the slave system from the North and its extension in the South, slave revolts necessarily originated only in Southern states, primarily in Virginia, South Carolina, and Louisiana. During the predominance of slavery in the Old South, slave revolts mainly occurred there and in border states. As the New South pattern was entrenched in the final period of slavery, slave revolts took place there as well as in other parts of the slave region.[9]

A noteworthy aspect of the distribution of slave revolts is the concentration of types of slave revolts in time. Type I Revolts occur fairly consistently throughout the slave period with slight peaks in the Colonial and Old South periods. Type II Revolts are a predominantly Colonial phenomenon (56 percent), while Type III are concentrated in the New South Period (58 percent). The predominance of Type III Revolts in the last period of slavery may be attributed to the increasingly oppressive character of slavery during this time, particularly in the New South, which made any other type of revolt virtually impracticable.

Finally, it should be mentioned that slave revolts were not evenly distributed spatially over the slave region. They were concentrated within three main areas: Virginia (25 percent), Louisiana (15 percent), and South Carolina (15.5 percent). Further, despite variations in time, within these states revolts clustered in a few counties. In Virginia revolts tended to recur in the coastal tobacco counties; Gabriel Prosser's revolt, however, encompassed the inland counties of Henrico, Louisa, Hanover, Chesterfield, and Caroline,[10] some of which were involved in another Type I Revolt in 1816. The following tabulation summarizes the agricultural situation in the eighteen insurrection counties of Virginia in 1860:

Eighteen Revolt Counties (12 percent) of Virginia-1860[11]

	percent of State total
Crop: Tobacco	14
Slaves	24
Slave holders	25
Holdings (acres)	
300-499	0
1,000+	15
200-299	50
3-9	13
1-3	24

TABLE 3

TYPE III REVOLTS

REVOLT	FORM	AIM:				ARMED	PARTICIPANTS:	
		ESCAPE:					LEADER	INSURGENTS
		TO FREE STATE	FROM SALE SOUTH	OUTSIDE USA	TO INDIANS			
PENN. 1734[1]	C				x			
MD. 1845	R	x				x		75
KY. 1829	R		x					90
KY. 1848	R	x				x	1W	75
MO. 1836	C			x				
MO. 1850	R	x				x	1S	30
VA. 1799	R		x					
S.C. 1826	R				x			
GA. 1849	C			x				300
GA.-MD. 1826	R		x					29
LA. 1840	C			x			1S	
TEXAS 1851	R			x				

KEY:
C:CONSPIRACY
R:ACTUAL REVOLT
X:VARIABLE PRESENT
S:SLAVE
W:WHITE

[1]JOSHUA COFFIN, *An Account of Some of the Principal Slave Insurrections* (New York, 1860), p. 14.

The slave revolt counties of Virginia were primarily tobacco plantation counties. In tobacco culture "the great properties were usually divided . . . into several plantations for more convenient operation."[12] Thus slavery under this system was less oppressive than in the Mississippi Delta region of the New South period.

With one exception the slave revolts of South Carolina were restricted to Charleston County. The principal plantation crop was rice, which involved larger plantation units and a greater number of slaves than tobacco, a task system of production, and frequently absentee landlordism.[13] The following tabulation summarizes the agricultural picture in the two insurrection counties of South Carolina in 1860:

Two Revolt Counties (7 percent) of South Carolina-1860[14]

	percent of State total
Crop: rice	63
Slave holders	11
1,000+	100
500-999	43
1-3	19
Slaves	14
Holdings(acres)	
1,000+	8
3-9	17

Considering the patently oppressive nature of the slave system associated with rice culture, it does not seem accidental that slave insurrections should have taken place predominantly in Charleston County with its major urban complex.

Although a few slave revolts in Louisiana occurred in the vicinity of New Orleans, most of the revolts recurred in counties bordering the Mississippi River north and west of Baton Rouge. Although there was considerable agricultural diversification in these counties, they were primarily sugar producers. Like rice, sugar production involved large numbers of robust adult slaves.[15] The general agricultural set-up in the insurrection counties of Louisiana in 1860 is summarized in the following tabulation:

Ten Revolt Counties (21 percent) of Louisiana-1860[16]

	percent of State total
Crops:	
rice	15
cotton	16
cane sugar	41
Slave holders	38
500-999	25
300-499	35
1-3	23
Slaves	30
Holdings(acres)	
1,000+	25
3-9	33

Among the factors which may have facilitated the development of these up-river revolts are proximity to a great communication network, agricultural diversification, and a fairly high proportion of small holdings.

Thus the pattern of a real clustering of slave revolts irrespective of temporal variations suggests that aside from the immediate catalysts which might induce a particular slave revolt, certain socio-economic variables facilitated their occurrence and recurrence in certain areas. Fundamentally, these socio-economic factors imply an alleviation of the condition of slavery due either to the type of plantation system itself or to access to external sources of communication as inherent in propinquity to an urban center or a transportation network. These constitute a few of the factors which are considered necessary preconditions for slave revolts.

Other more immediate factors also seem to constitute preconditions for slave revolts. These may include rapid population fluctuations often leading to a significantly higher proportion of Negroes in an area[17] and revolutionary ideas current in the wider society of the time.[18] In my view, none of these possible preconditions constitute sufficient cause for the development of a slave revolt. Rather there must be a catalyst in the form of an individual or individuals.

This catalyst may arise from within or without the slave system. The leaders of slave revolts have been drawn from the social categories of free Negro, slave, and white. The type of revolt does not appear to be determined by the social type of the catalyst. Vesey (Type I) was a free Negro, Prosser (Type I) and Turner (Type II) were slaves, Boxley (Type I) and Doyle (Type III) were whites.[19] Nevertheless, Boxley is probably exceptional, as the ultimate aim of a Type I Revolt would be unlikely to appeal to many whites.

Although very little data on Negro leaders of slave revolts are available, the three leaders of the most famous revolts furnish suggestions of relevant social and personality variables. Each of these men had had opportunities which the ordinary field hand would never have experienced. Vesey had traveled extensively as a slave; as a freedman he was an urban artisan; he was literate and aware of the Haitian success and the Missouri debate.[20] Both Prosser and Turner were slaves. Gabriel Prosser was a blacksmith and probably literate.[21] Turner was literate, had been a slave overseer, enjoyed making inventive experiments, and may have been a Baptist preacher.[22] Thus all three leaders had had opportunities to play more than one social role and had had access to a variety of ideas.

TABLE 4

DISTRIBUTION OF SLAVE REVOLTS

TYPE	PRE-1776	1776-1800	1801-1829	1830-1860	TOTAL
I	PERCENT	PERCENT	PERCENT	PERCENT	PERCENT
N.Y.	1.5	0.0	0.0	0.0	
MD.	1.5	0.0	0.0	0.0	
VA.	3.0	4.5	1.5	0.0	
S.C.	1.5	0.0	3.0	0.0	
GA.	0.0	0.0	3.0	1.5	
LA.	0.0	0.0	0.0	4.5	
	8.0	4.5	8.0	6.0	26.5
II	PERCENT	PERCENT	PERCENT	PERCENT	PERCENT
N.Y.	1.5	0.0	0.0	0.0	
VA.	3.0	1.5	0.0	1.5	
N.C.	0.0	1.5	0.0	0.0	
S.C.	4.5	0.0	0.0	0.0	
GA.	1.5	0.0	0.0	0.0	
LA.	1.5	1.5	1.5	0.0	
MISS.	0.0	0.0	0.0	1.5	
	12.0	4.5	1.5	3.0	21.5
"?"	PERCENT	PERCENT	PERCENT	PERCENT	PERCENT
N.J.	1.5	0.0	0.0	0.0	
MD.	0.0	0.0	1.5	0.0	
D.C.	0.0	0.0	0.0	1.5	
KY.	0.0	0.0	1.5	1.5	
TENN.	0.0	0.0	0.0	1.5	
N.C.	0.0	0.0	1.5	1.5	
S.C.	1.5	0.0	1.5	1.5	
GA.	0.0	0.0	0.0	1.5	
LA.	0.0	0.0	1.5	4.5	
TEXAS	0.0	0.0	0.0	1.5	
VA.	6.0	0.0	1.5	0.0	
	9.0	0.0	9.0	15.0	33.0
III	PERCENT	PERCENT	PERCENT	PERCENT	PERCENT
PENN.	1.5	0.0	0.0	0.0	
MD.	0.0	0.0	0.0	1.5	
KY.	0.0	0.0	1.5	1.5	
MO.	0.0	0.0	0.0	3.0	
VA.	0.0	1.5	0.0	0.0	
S.C.	1.5	0.0	0.0	0.0	
LA.	0.0	0.0	0.0	1.5	
GA.	0.0	0.0	0.0	1.5	
GA.-MD.	0.0	0.0	1.5	0.0	
TEXAS	0.0	0.0	0.0	1.5	
	3.0	2.0	3.0	11.0	19.0
TOTAL	32.0%	11.0%	22.0%	35.0%	100.0%

The personality of Negro leaders also appears to be a significant variable. The three major leaders were clearly charismatic individuals. They were imbued with a sense of personal destiny and considered themselves to be divinely inspired and sanctioned in their endeavors.[23] It seems likely that such charisma and egotism would be essential for any Negro leader to dare to challenge the power of the slavocracy. There is, however, an important personality difference between these leaders which appears to be linked to the type of revolt inspired by them. Neither Vesey nor Prosser was so self-absorbed that he could not formulate a rational plan and assign specific duties to assistants. The techniques which Vesey employed for binding the

masses to his endeavor are particularly fascinating: among his lieutenants were a "sorcerer" whose charms were considered to make their
wearers inviolable and a blind preacher who was believed to possess
second-sight.[24] Vesey clearly understood the importance of psychological as well as technological preparation for the success of his scheme.
Turner, on the other hand, seems to have been so self-absorbed that
it is unlikely that he could have formulated and executed a consistent
plan. Thus, there appears to be two personality types represented by
these three leaders; the one in which rationality has precedence over
egotistical emotionalism, and its converse. This distinction is borne
out by the conduct of the men following their capture: Vesey and
Prosser revealed very little about their intentions and maintained
themselves stoically until their deaths; Turner met his fate no less cou-
rageously but after a lengthy and effusive confession. How many Vesey-Prosser and how many Turner personality types led slave revolts is
unknown. It is hypothesized that only a Vesey-Prosser type could lead
a Type I Revolt, though Types II and III might have been led by either personality type.[25]

The final aspect of slave revolts to be discussed is their repercussions both within the area of the revolt and in other areas. As
shown in Table 5, throughout the slavery period the slavocracy reacted in a similar way to slave revolts. In its reactions it distinguished
between Type III Revolts and the other types of revolt, but not between Type I and Type II revolts.[26] Thus Type III revolts always resulted in reprisals only against the immediate offenders. This is
understandable as the situational and limited nature of this type of
revolt was clear. Consequently, it was a phenomenon with which the
slavocracy could deal in a relatively rational manner.

The reaction of the slavocracy to the Type I and Type II Revolts
followed a different but consistent pattern.[27] A slave revolt resulted in
a three-step syndrome within the area of revolt. There was an initial
period of panic in which vengeance was wrought not only upon
known insurgents but often upon innocent Negroes. During this period of mob panic and activity, aggression might also be vented upon
white moderates within the area and upon outsiders who were disliked but not directly involved with the revolt. This period was followed by one in which increased armed oppression was used to
enforce the threatened slave system. This second period was followed
by one in which legislative measures were taken to prevent similar
outbreaks. During the legislative debates ameliorative measures such
as colonization schemes and proposals to reduce the oppressive character of the slave system were frequently discussed but rarely enacted.

TABLE 5
REPERCUSSIONS OF SLAVE REVOLTS WITHIN THE AREA AND IN OTHER AREAS

Revolt	Within the Area:										In Other Areas:				
	Panic and Vengeance against:				Repressive Measures:			Ameliorative Measures:			Revolt Rumors	Slave Unrest	Repressive Measures:		Ameliorative Measures:
	Insurgents	Other Negroes	White Moderates	Outsiders	Increased Armed Oppressions	Legislation Against Slaves	Free Negro	Increased Emancipation Sentiment	Improved Conditions	Colonization Schemes			Legislation Against Slaves	Free Negro	Anti-Slavery Sentiment
TYPE I Pre-1776 Va. 1663	X														
NY 1712	X	X				X									
Md. 1739	X														
1776-1800 Va. 1792	X	X				X									
Va. 1800*	X	X			X	X	X			X	S.C.	Va.	X	X	
1801-1829 Va. 1816	X	?													
Ga. 1819	X														
SC. 1822*	X				X	X	X					no			North
1830-1860 La. 1837	X	?			X										
Ga. 1841	X														
TYPE II Pre-1776 Va. 1687	X					X									
NY 1708	X					X									
La. 1730	X														
SC 1740	X					X			X						
1776-1800 NC 1776	X	X													
Va. 1792	X	X													
La. 1795	X	?													
1801-1829 La. 1811	X	?													
1830-1860 Va. 1831*	X	X	X		X	X	X	X			X	X	X	X	North
Miss. '35*	X	X	X	X											
TYPE "?" Pre-1776 Va. 1723	X					X	X								
Va. 1730	X														
1801-1829 SC 1829	X				X										
1830-1860 Ga. 1835	X														
NC 1835	X														
La. 1840	X	X													
La. 1856	X	X													
TYPE III 1801-1829 Ky. 1829	X														
1830-1860 Mo. 1836	X														
Md. 1845	X														
Ky. 1848	X											X			
Mo. 1850															X

*—see footnote 27.

The upshot of the legislative period was invariably the harshening of repressive laws against both slaves and free Negroes.

Another aspect of the reaction of the slavocracy to a major slave revolt was the spread of the three-step syndrome, either partially or completely, to other slave areas not affected by the revolt. In part these measures may have been justified, for there is evidence that occasionally slaves in other areas were stimulated to emulate the attempts of the initial insurgents.

Nevertheless, both within the initial area of revolt and in other areas, the actual threat to the slavocracy was never great enough to invoke the exaggerated penalties which it envoked.[28] Yet indubitably the psychological threat makes this pattern comprehensible: a slave revolt whatever its form expresses the realization of the worst fears of the slavocracy and assaults its security at its most vulnerable point. These fears must be suppressed at all costs although the repressive measures taken were perceived by the slavocracy to lead to even greater threats to the system, for the members of the slavocracy assumed that an ill-treated slave was more likely to revolt than a well-treated one.

The data presented in this analysis support a rather different conclusion from that of the slavocracy as to the effect of their measures. This conclusion has been vividly expressed by Frederick Douglass and has been stated more systematically by Davies and Elkins.[29] In *My Bondage* Douglass wrote: " 'Beat and cuff your slave, keep him hungry and spiritless, and he will follow the chain of his master like a dog; but feed and clothe him well,—work him moderately—surround him with physical comfort,—and dreams of freedom intrude.' "[30] As has been noted in the preceding analysis, slave revolts tended to cluster in less oppressive slave areas and the catalyst for a revolt was an individual who had had opportunities to play multiple roles.[31] On the other hand, given the high rate of betrayal of conspiracies by oppressed individuals who identified themselves more closely with the master than the slave, the adverse impact upon most slaves of the repressive measures of the slavocracy, and the absolute power of the slavocracy, one can but conclude that slave revolts in the United States were doomed to failure.

Notes

[1] Herbert Aptheker, *American Negro Slave Revolts* (New York, 1943), pp. 101-02, 220, 225; 272, 98, 269. Joseph Cephas Carroll, *Slave Insurrections in the United States 1800-1865* (Boston, 1938), p. 50.

[2] Table 1 summarizes the evidence for Type I Revolts.

[3] Of the fourteen Type II Revolts, 59 percent succeeded in achieving this stage.

[4] Aptheker, *op. cit.*, pp. 297-98.

[5] Table 2 summarizes the data on Type II Revolts.

[6] The characterization of Type I and Type II Revolts has been based primarily on an analysis of their prototypes. Despite necessarily fragmentary evidence, it was decided to classify 28 other revolts as Type I or Type II. There are, however, 22 other conspiracies on which data are insufficient to classify as either Type I or Type II, but on which there is some useful information; they have been placed in a residual category: "?." The following conspiracies fall into Type "?": Ark.-La. 1856; D.C. 1838; Ky. 1810, 1838; La. 1812, 1835, 1856; N.C. 1825, 1835; S.C. 1713, 1829, 1835; Ga. 1835; Md. 1805; N.J. 1772; Tenn. 1856; Texas 1856; Va. 1709, 1710, 1723, 1730, 1810.

[7] Table 3 summarizes the data on Type III Revolts.

[8] Texas 1851. Aptheker, *op. cit.*, p. 343.

[9] For relative and absolute shifts in the Negro population of various states see United States Bureau of the Census, *Negro Population 1790-1915* (Washington, 1918), pp. 51, 57.

[10] Aptheker, *op. cit.*, p. 226.

[11] United States Census Office, *Agriculture of the United States in 1860* (Washington, 1864), pp. 155, 159, 163, 218-19, 243-45.

[12] Ulrich Bonnell Phillips, *American Negro Slavery* (New York, 1952), p. 84.

[13] *Ibid.*, pp. 89, 228, 250, 258.

[14] United States Census Office, *op. cit.*, pp. 129, 214, 237.

[15] Phillips, *op. cit.*, pp. 164-67, 245.

[16] United States Census Office, *op. cit.*, pp. 67, 69, 202, 230.

[17] E.g., Turner's revolt and Mississippi Revolt of 1835; Aptheker, *op. cit.*, pp. 293, 325.

[18] E.g., the influence of the Missouri debate on Vesey: Aptheker, *op. cit.*, p. 270; the importance of David Walker's Appeal for Turner: Carroll, *op. cit.*, p. 121.

[19] Aptheker, *op. cit.*, pp. 255-56, 338. See Tables 1, 2 and 3.

[20] Carroll, *op. cit.*, pp. 83, 85; Aptheker, *op. cit.*, p. 270.

[21] Cf. Carroll, *op. cit.*, p. 48 and T. W. Higginson, "Gabriel's Defeat," *Atlantic Monthly* X (1862), 338. Aptheker, *op. cit.*, p. 220.

[22] William Sydney Drewry, *The Southampton Insurrection* (Washington, 1900), p. 28; Carroll, *op. cit.*, p. 131. Cf. *ibid*, p. 130 and John W. Cromwell, "The Aftermath of Nat Turner's Insurrection," *Journal of Negro History* V (1920), 209.

[23] E.g., Turner: Carroll, *op. cit.*, pp. 130-31; Gabriel: *ibid*, p. 149; Vesey: *ibid*, p. 87.

[24] *Ibid*, pp. 91-93.

[25] Evidence from two Type I Revolts supports this hypothesis: Georgia 1819, Maryland 1739: *Aptheker, op. cit.*, pp. 191, 263.

[26] See Table 5 for summary of data.

[27] This analysis is based on the four reactions for which we have sufficient data: the revolts of Turner, Prosser, and Vesey and the Mississippi Revolt of 1835. See Aptheker, *op. cit.*, pp. 226, 228, 271, 275, 300, 305; Carroll, *op. cit.*, pp. 57-60, 107-09, 138-39, 166, 176; Cromwell, *op. cit.*, pp. 212, 214-15, 221, 225, 231; Drewry, *op. cit.*, p. 85; E. Franklin Frazier, *The Negro in the United States* (New York, 1957), p. 87; Higginson, *op. cit.*, pp. 341-44; Edwin A. Miles, "The Mississippi Slave Insurrection Scare of 1835," *Journal of Negro History*, XLII (1957), 49, 52-55.

[28] This fact was recognized by some contemporary observers. For example, less than ten days after Turner's bloody revolt, General Epps wrote the Governor of Virginia that local fear was exaggerated and that at no time were more than twenty men needed to put down the rebellion. Quoted in Drewry, *op. cit.*, p. 88.

[29] James C. Davies, "Toward a Theory of Revolution," *American Sociological Review*, XXVII (1962), 6; Stanley M. Elkins, *Slavery* (Chicago, 1959).

[30] Quoted in Kenneth M. Stampp, *The Peculiar Institution* (New York, 1956), p. 89.

[31] For the implications of multiple role-playing see Elkins, *op. cit.*, pp. 112 ff, 137-38.

Slave Revolt, Slave Debate: A Comparison

JOHN HERBERT ROPER AND LOLITA G. BROCKINGTON

In the 1550s, following rebellions by blacks in Central Mexico, Dominican Bishop Bartolome de Las Casas and secular humanist Juan Gines de Sepulveda argued issues of human enslavement. This debate, turning on Bishop de Las Casas' concern for the abuses of Indians by the Spanish conquerors in Mexico, established most of the defenses for and against slavery that prevailed from the sixteenth to the late nineteenth century. Nearly three hundred years later, in the 1830s, the Virginia House of Delegates echoed the same set of ideas and attitudes about slavery in the aftermath of the uprising led by Nat Turner.

The authors of this study argue that contemporary accounts do not reveal in a holistic way how the slave uprisings and slave debates link together to reflect the similarities of black slavery in different times and different places in the New World. Comparing the responses of whites to slave revolts in Mexico and Virginia, John Roper and Lolita Brockington assert that the subsequent debates in both locales produced a watershed in race relations and resulted in further harshening of the repressive laws against both enslaved and free blacks. In linking the two events, separated by time, place, culture, and context, this essay offers a compelling perspective on racism in the American hemisphere.

VALLADOLID IS A SPIRITUAL ENTITY, a monument to ghosts who maintain a palpable presence in American race relations. There in Central Spain in 1550, the Spanish Crown halted for the nonce its aggressive policies of expansion based on colonial labor, halted the machinery of slavery long enough to consider its meaning. Fray Bartolome de Las Casas, a Dominican brother, reported to his king, Charles V, a catalogue of abuses of slave subjects in Mexico. That catalogue became the first chapter in the "Black Legend" of Spanish colonial misrule of the Indians. Las Casas, the man of the Church, received an equally compelling argument from Juan Gines de Sepulveda, a secular representative of the humanities. Between the two disputants was established an intellectual force field which held in its suspension most of the ideas and attitudes for and against slavery which were voiced from the sixteenth to the late nineteenth century.

Richmond, Virginia—like Valladolid—is a ghostly place, no less a monument to hemispheric race relations. There, almost three hundred years later, was another debate, this one in the wake of the major slave uprising in North American history. True, the venerable House of Delegates witnessed no grand ethical debate between Thomistic Catholic concern for the disadvantaged and neo-Aristotlean secular humanism. No one matched the forensic eloquence, the tools of logic, or even the sheer knowledge of Las Casas or Sepulveda. Nevertheless, the Virginia debates on slavery culminating in 1832 fully equalled the depth of passion and the breadth of concern found at the Valladolid confrontations of 1550. Again, the expansion of a labor system halted for a compelling moment while the same sets of ideas and attitudes appeared, clashed, and found resolution.

Both of these chapters from the book of race relations—the Latin debates and the Virginia slave uprising—have received extensive attention from historians. Yet, in a curious way, neither story has been told in full, neither story has been linked up from its prerevolutionary start through its revolt, through its postrevolutionary debates, to its resultant societal adjustments. Both stories, then, for all their exposure, have been incomplete in the telling; moreover, the two have never been considered in relation to each other, as components of a holistic racial story. Taken as such, the two episodes become variations on a theme, the theme being the realization that black slavery, regardless of its location in time and place, had more similarities than dissimilarities within the different forms that it took in the New World.

Obviously, the two events were separated by the thick walls of time and place, of culture and context, of conscience and consciousness. Yet, for all that, the two dramatic debates were run through by lines of parallel. In the worlds of the mind and the soul, there is a remarkable affinity of nineteenth century Virginians for sixteenth century Latin. Moreover, that moral and mental affinity found expression in the physical world of slavery and race relations as that world developed in Mexico and in Virginia after the debates.

For one thing, the abstract followed the real, in Aristotlean terms: both debates came on the heels of major slave uprisings in America. For all the idealism of the antislavery and the proslavery sides, they expressed themselves in reaction to a material "real" event, *i.e.*, Nat Turner's revolt in Southampton, Virginia, of August 1831 and a conspiracy of a major revolt by blacks in central Mexico and subsequent numerous slave revolts and uprisings following that event in 1537. Both uprisings served to wake up the trans-Atlantic white cultures which, until the revolts, largely employed a slave system with little regard for the meaning of that system.

For the Spanish colonial possessions, and especially for New Spain in America, Negro slavery began tenuously, almost unacknowledged by the institutions of Church or state in the early decades of the sixteenth century. Perhaps this kind of beginning, this shadow labor force, has accounted for the present-day lack of historiographical acknowledgment of black slavery in New Spain. In point of fact, however, colonial administrators early on recognized the inadequacy of Indian labor for the wealth of the mines or for the wealth of the soil. An intricately woven web of factors—disease, maltreatment, declining birth rates, rebellions—impeded any plans for using Indian labor on an extensive scale. Instead, New Spain maintained the labor patterns for the New World: failing with Indian labor, the colony turned to the huge pool of captured black labor available in the African markets. In this case the colony's transition from red to black labor was especially complex, with significant variations by region and by role. Yet, by the middle of the seventeenth century, New Spain's black labor force had grown beyond the proportions of any mere shadow: over 120,000 Africans had come to the colony by slave ship and there were at least 20,000 African slaves in the Valley of Mexico alone. Despite these numbers, Spanish policy in these decades turned on the axis of Indian labor, Indian rights, Indian status as subjects of the Crown; the great pronouncements on treatment of slave labor that emanated from Isabella and later from Charles V were all concerned with Indian, not African slavery.[1]

There were two more compelling reasons for using black slave labor, albeit these latter were tacit assessments seldom voiced: racist color-coding and labor skills. The story of Spanish attitudes toward black people has not been completed; but the Spanish world did attach negative weight to the color black and consequently to black men and women. These attitudes were less severe in application than those of the English; in fact, the experiences with racial and cultural mixing which began even before the lengthy Moorish stay on the Iberian peninsula (732-1492) had given a pronounced "dark" cast to Spanish color valuation. Where Englishmen of the Elizabethan era defined *miscegenation* in pejorative terms, their Spanish contemporaries used *mestizaje* (technically the same word) with positive connotations. For all that, nevertheless, the Spanish considered the sub-Sahara "pure-black" Africans to be bad: un-Christian, evil, lascivious, sinful, death-related, ignorant, bestial, viz., "deserving" of the degradation wrought by servitude.[2]

The other compelling reason for black slavery sprang from more positive attributes of African culture and physiology. Simply put, African men and women adapted themselves better than did Indians to European-directed agriculture and to European people. None of this implied the old romantic notion that the Indians were *sauvage*, Rousseau's "natural" men unable to live outside of freedom while the Negroes were subservient and "happier" enslaved. What happened, strictly in labor terms, was that the African farming techniques resembled what Europeans wanted on large-scale New World plantations. And what happened in the vastly more complicated physiologic story was that Africans coped more successfully with the new human environment that now included white men. For one example, the "sickling cell" which has caused such suffering among blacks was a Janus-faced trait: its "smiling" side granted resistance to such New World diseases as malaria. In addition, Africans largely resisted the European strains of diseases which they faced in the Western hemisphere. By contrast, the Indian contact with European illness produced a sad tale of decimation, a large part of the reason for the phenomenal drop in Indian population in the first century of Spanish conquest.[3] Of course, such factors were seldom expressed in words *per se*: voicing such positive evaluations would give the lie to the European code of black/white, bad/good, failure/success. Still, the very reliance on African labor was proof of the pudding: African skills and traits made African slavery a desideratum in America.

In the Valley of Mexico some 20,000 to 50,000 black slaves performed services on the farm, in the mines, and in the urban economy. Fully as many mixed-blood (black and Indian, or *pardo*, and black and white, or *Afro-mestico*) slaves worked in the mines and ranches around the Valley and in the City of Mexico. Yet, for all the value of such African and Afro-mestico stoop-labor, these people occupied an anomalous position in the semi-feudal societal structure of New Spain. Clearly at the bottom of the great Chain of Being which defined society, Africans were still subjects of crown and Church, still possessors of certain entitlements as Christians, and as loyal servants of the King and Queen. Royal officials did little to clarify the African role in Mexico until forced to make definitive decisions by a rebellion by blacks in 1537.

On November 24 of that year, the colony faced its first large-scale, organized rebellion. According to the viceroy, Antonio de Mendoza, black slaves had named one of their number king and had plotted to assassinate all Spanish officials. Negroes in Mexico City and in the nearby mining settlements were to coordinate the campaigns of this rebellion. It failed aborning as Mendoza learned of the plans and executed the self-styled king and a good number of his entourage. Perhaps the viceroy overreacted to rumor, but David M. Davidson, a close student of Mexican slavery, has found good reasons to take Mendoza at his word, and by extension, to accept as valid history the story of the sable king and his rebellion.[4] At any rate, the most interesting aspect of the event lay in the response of whites to the threat of rebellion: from Mendoza down, whites in the Valley of Mexico took seriously the energy and will of blacks to revolt. Whatever present-day historians have felt about the "king," contemporary Spanish officials were quite sure of his reality.

Southside Virginia in the Age of Andrew Jackson was hardly an exact equivalent of the Valley of Mexico in the sixteenth century. Where the latter was a young colony, Virginia by 1831 had grown through colonial maturity and had earned its independence from the Old World in concert with other upstart British colonial possessions. Along the way to its nineteenth century status as state in a republic, Virginia had undergone experiences that transformed it in other ways: there was no centripetal church, no king, no nobility, no regular army, no neofeudal social structure. But there was the peculiar institution of slavery and that institution was clearly a black one.

Virginia slavery evolved by stages, a growth process still continuing in 1831. Always there was racism, an assumption of the "superiority" of whites over blacks, a recognition that the considerable labor required by the New World economy would not be the province of white men but of "colored." Still, those assumptions did not have to develop *a fortiori* into black slavery. Like the Spanish, British Americans had tried to use Indian labor in the Virginia "Plantation"; and, like the Spanish in Mexico, the British in the Chesapeake decimated the indigenous population, simultaneously removing competitors for land and also depleting the ranks of labor.[5]

With the red labor pool drained, colonial Virginians vacillated between full-scale African slavery and a white tenantry system whereby the poor and the unemployed of the British Isles would work off *indentiture,* paying for oceanic passage and protection in the New World with five to seven years of involuntary labor. Of course, the indentured whites were rambunctuous labor who, once within the forests, were indistinguishable from other, free white colonial citizens beholden to no indentiture. The indenture system worked poorly and by the 1650s had destroyed itself, being replaced by black, full-time, hereditary slavery. It is important to realize that very few blacks ever served indenture; they seem to have come on the scene strictly as slaves.[6]

Even these developments did not have to produce the full-blown slave system which dominated the entire South by the middle of the nineteenth century. As the decades rolled by after the failure of the indenture system, Virginians built a fairly diversified economy with a steel foundry in Richmond, some small-scale industry such as forestry and naval stores, considerable urban and rural small-crafts business, and a thriving maritime commerce. Withal, there was opportunity for free labor in Virginia, small-scale, independent, self-sustenant growers of wheat, corn, potatoes, barley, beans and other such crops which were decidedly not slave-oriented. Especially in the Shenandoah Valley west of the established tidewater, there were white folk opposed to slavery. These people, hardly liberal and in fact quite racist in their assumptions, resisted slavery for two interrelated reasons: the threat posed by full-scale slave labor industry to the independence of the modest operation of free farmers, and the threat to a large white majority population posed by the introduction of large numbers of blacks, whether those new arrivals came as slaves or as free people.

Once it was assumed that Eli Whitney's famed cotton gin committed the South in 1794 to full-scale black slavery. Certainly his gin, by making short-staple cotton profitable, opened up entire areas of the Upper South—areas such as the Shenandoah Valley—which were previously unsuited to slave labor. But it took more than an industrial development to commit white Southerners to black slavery. In point of fact, a full generation after Whitney's gin, the Shenandoah Valley was still the purview of free labor: the famed McCormick reaper and plows were developed over two generations by Robert McCormick and his son Cyrus; these new farm machines were conceived in the valley and first offered for use on the wheat fields there. Other students have demonstrated the vitality of the Midwest-Upper South trade through the conduit of the Mississippi River. It was, then, not essentially the economics of cotton gin production which moved Virginians to a hard-line, "positive" defense of slavery in the Jacksonian era.[7] Essentially, it was Nat Turner, preacher, mystic, revolutionary, charismatic, "privileged" slave of "kind master" Joseph Travis. Nat Turner created the positive defense of slavery as much as did any material conditions of an economic system or as did any finely spun logic from John C. Calhoun or George Fitzhugh. What Nat Turner did in August of 1831 was to wake up the whites of Virginia to the fact that no white could elude responsibility for slavery. By butchering some fifty-seven people, including women and children, even and especially including non-slaveholders, Nat Turner forced into racial consciousness the facts of slavery, the institution: any and all whites were responsible, any and all were in some sense beneficiaries, any and all were guilty. And any and all could meet death at the hands of rebellious slaves.[8]

Like his Mexican predecessor of a thousand miles and three centuries away, Nat Turner inspired debate. And the outcome of both debates was the same: a greater number and a greater degree of restrictions and repressions of blacks.

Spanish debate began fitfully, reflecting the lag in information traveling from New World to Old. Viceroy Mendoza acted quickly, imposing Draconian penalties on the rebels: he had them drawn and quartered publicly. As soon as he could, Mendoza got word to Charles V of this rebellion and of other slave unrest and he informed the Emperor of his own plans to tighten the bonds on the slaves. Meanwhile, the viceroy, the *cabildo* of Mexico City, and the major officers in the area garrisoned the capital city, intending to make it impervious to assault by other black rebels. Of course, these officials realized at the time that such action would be effective only for the nonce.[9]

For the long run, Mendoza and colonial administrators wanted departure from the Thomistic structure of the Spanish slave code, *Las siete partidas*. This code, in typical medieval Catholic fashion, considered any slave a potential Christian, *ergo*, servant of the king and hence eligible for the limited rights of peasants in the Iberian feudal system. Slaves could win freedom by marrying a free person, by saving a virgin, by other such "positive" actions; in addition, slaves could gain freedom from "negative" action by the master; the Church was to buy slaves from malevolent masters; slaves denied the privilege of marriage in the Church were to be freed.[10] As to these "kind" or "loose" rules in *Las siete partidas*, Mendoza complained of the number of slaves using them to gain freedom. Plainly put, colonizers intended to keep the vast majority of Afro-Americans in slavery. Most importantly, their labor in thralldom already was producing sizable profits for the colony and for the empire at a pace and on a scale hard to match in the free labor operation. In addition, colonists were fearful of large numbers of freed Negroes; such inferiors were safer under the controls of slavery.

Charles V did not immediately satisfy his colonial forces. At the time of the revolts, from 1537 to 1542, Charles paid much attention to the eloquent pleas for justice to slaves. Most of these pleas came from the great Dominican, Bartolome de Las Casas, who had already served in missions from Hispaniola in the Caribbean to Chiapas on the peninsula. This theologian took seriously Thomistic injunctions to convert pagans, which included the red pagans of the New World

and, by extension, those black pagans of Africa to the true God or
who had once been exposed and had since forgotten the revelations.
Such people were not truly infidels who should be punished by slavery and Las Casas argued for viewing the Indians of the New World
as ignorant of God, not as consciously evil. Furthermore, Las Casas
worried, with good reason, that there would soon be precious few Indians left in the Americas for the Church or anybody else to deal
with. These complaints and calls for justice Las Casas made both in
person and in his publication, *A Very Brief Account of the Destruction of
the Indies.* Initially, Charles responded favorably to Las Casas, issuing
the 1542 "New Laws" designed to keep slavery an *encomienda,* i.e., a
temporary system of tutelage and not one of permanent bondage.
Moreover, Charles wanted the ameliorative *Las siete partidas* enforced
on slaveowners by inspections and by reports of those inspections
from officials of the Church.[11]

Yet, royal policy created no real discomfort for slaveowners. Colonial labor was a hardship in general in the sixteenth century and
New Spain with its productive mines and bounteous fields was no exception. For one thing, within the "kindest" construction of Catholic
labor codes, the work was still arduous, dangerous, and abusive of
body and spirit, so that many perished in their "temporary" or tute-
lary status within the encomienda. For another thing, the slaveowners
obfuscated, misled, and even outright lied to the visiting clergy who
had huge areas of space to investigate with little time to do so. Finally, and most important, Spanish officials also made an early distinction by color: as the New Laws went into effect in the 1540s, so
too did Mexican restrictions on blacks, restrictions which limited privilege and mobility for blacks.[12] By practice, then, the "positive" New
Laws were protecting the rapidly disappearing red labor. Meanwhile,
black labor was simultaneously working harder and losing rights of
protection.

This Hispanic racism is the other side of the great campaign for
human dignity and justice led by Las Casas. By 1550, the Domincan
found himself at Valladolid, debating the Church's case for decent
treatment of the king's subjects in the New World across the ocean.
That grand debate signalled the culmination of at least three years of
combat in print between Juan Gines de Sepulveda and Las Casas.
Sepulveda demanded and received a chance for public encounter
with his antagonist before the best minds of the universities of Alcala
and Salamanca. It is interesting that the major points of debate about
black slavery are all in these Valladolid speeches, but that the
speeches concern Indians, not blacks. In point of sad fact, Las Casas
himself at that time owned black slaves. There is a vital aspect of ra-

cial perception at work which caused black slaves to disappear from the debate. These arguments turned on the controversy of the just war: St. Thomas Aquinas had said that war was justified if fought against the unjust infidel, *viz.*, those who knew of God but willingly refused to follow him. This point was crucial: Africans were not victims of war in this sense, just or unjust; they were merely bought and transported from another continent not claimed as a colony by the Crown. Thus, blacks, who would come to be the essential characters in the story of New World slavery, were curiously, and deleteriously, beside the point in these Valladolid debates. Here was an early, poignant case of the invisibility of blacks which novelist Ralph Ellison has lamented in our day: neither the "liberals" nor the "conservatives" see blacks except in subservient roles exactly at this time of public confrontation over roles of subservience.[13]

In the debates, Las Casas reiterated his main Thomistic argument: wars of conquest against the unsinning ignorant were unjust, hence title to such land and labor gained unjustly was invalid, hence further conquest in the Indies must cease. Sepulveda countered by citing the unjust or "rude" nature of the Indians and the injustice of their resistance to the Crown's prerogatives: Pope Alexander VI, in the Treaty of Tordesillas, 1494, after all, awarded the New World to the Catholic monarchs of Spain and Portugal. In reply, Las Casas reaffirmed the Treaty of Tordesillas but he called on the Spanish to convert the Indians to Christianity, after which conversion they would willingly become subjects of the Crown. This was not and never has been the way of the world of empire, but Las Casas won his point with the theologians. In a decision difficult for a secular age to fathom, Charles V accepted clerical advice and halted conquest of the Indies until judges could determine if such conquest would or would not proceed from just cause.

The process of the "public inquiry" itself was a controlled spectacle: a body of fourteen judges listened alternately to the arguments of Las Casas and of Sepulveda. Las Casas' argument, in vintage Thomistic schoolman style, went on for hundreds of manuscript pages of Latin, which he delivered for five days. Not surprisingly, the judges asked for and got an independent summation of both cases which they took home for solitary and autonomous study until the second stage of the hearings held in the spring of 1551. The exact decisions of this congregation are not available, obscured by the fact that both Las Casas and Sepulveda claimed victory in the wake of the judges' indecisive and unwritten ruling. Since, in fact, wars of conquest certainly continued under Charles and under his successor, Phillip II, it is obvious that Sepulveda won the battles on the front of empire-making. Key points which he established for future defenders of slavery were that the idolatrous, the rude, and the weak all needed the protection of slavery under masters who were Christian, gentle, and strong. This description of rudeness with its concomitants of primitiveness, simplicity, unintelligence, cruelty, self-destruction, childishness, and disorientation, was vital to Sepulveda and to proslavery forces after him. Borrowing from Aristotle, Sepulveda claimed that some men were by nature inferior and hence born to be ruled. Las Casas—like all Thomists deeply indebted to Aristotlean hierarchy—accepted that argument on principle but tried to disprove the particulars by example after example of positive Indian traits. What Las Casas did by this logical stratagem was to give powerful weapons to those who would enslave on the basis of color. Those who felt Africans to be inferior by color alone—which was most of sixteenth, seventeenth, eighteenth, and nineteenth century Western civilization— had from Las Casas and the debates at Valladolid "just" cause for enslaving "rude" Africans.[14]

Afro-Mexicans were thus doubly victimized: out of sight while human rights were under discussion, all too visible where the needs of an economic system fell into line with Aristotlean hierarchy, religious duty, and color prejudice. Blacks in Mexico remained untouched during Charles' curious moratorium: obviously, Negro slaves kept toiling away during the years when no new Indians were to be added to the ranks of slavery. And, with the debate resolved—for the purposes of New World colonization—on the side of the devils, Negro slaves worked that much harder in a newly legitimatized slave system. The result was a very tight, closed system of slavery which bore little resemblance to the kindly words of comfort and succor in *Las siete partidas* or in the dreams of justice borne by Las Casas.

It should be noted that Las Casas resolved, in part, a personal dilemma by freeing his own black slaves in the decade after Valladolid. What is significant is not his racism—by any standards mild for his day—but the peculiar way racism served and was served by the perceived needs of Church, empire, philosophy, law, and "nature." Moreover, black activism, militant and defiant, helped to force the great debate at Valladolid which, in the long run of history, was only one battle in a protracted war of hundreds of years. The oppression of Mexican slavery was thus called into being as a "logical" racist answer to an African question: what manner of man am I, slave or free? The answer—thou art slave, rude one—would find an echo in a very Protestant, liberal, Southern United States in the nineteenth century.

Nat Turner, by attacking in the dog days of summer, posed almost as many problems for the government of the Commonwealth of

Virginia as Afro-Mexican rebels had posed for the Empire of Spain. Where Charles V had to rely on the long months of ocean voyage to receive word from the New World, Governor John B. Floyd and the House of Delegates in Richmond had to delay official action until December and the next session of the General Assembly. Of course, local authorities moved immediately to quash the hopes of blacks for freedom, much as had Mendoza and the Spanish arms three centuries before. Moreover, every level of United States government moved in accord with the white slaveowning Virginians: the United States Navy detached sailors from the ship *Natchez* to chase down and to capture slaves and rebels, as did the United States Army, which lent soldiers from Fortress Monroe. Such action was largely symbolic, as Governor Floyd acknowledged, "all necessity for their cooperation had ceased, before they reached their point of destination." But, as pure symbols, the behavior of the federal military in so quickly leaping to the assistance of slavery is noteworthy, the more so because it occasioned so little comment.[15]

The odds which Nat Turner and his *banditti* faced were longest right at home in Southampton County. The terrain offered possible refuge to the east and south in the Great Dismal Swamp and the sparsely populated, dense woods all over Southside Virginia. Unfortunately for the rebellion, however, its "troops" were largely unfamiliar with land past their own homes, they received very little of the hoped for spontaneous enlistments from sympathetic slaves, and they received far more resistance from whites of all rank than they had expected. This resistance, in its very size, speed, and shape, verified what Turner had believed anyway: it was all white against all black. What Nat Turner miscalculated was the potential for cohesion and common effort among blacks, which he greatly overrated. Or, perhaps Nat Turner miscalculated nothing and was in fact attempting a desperate symbolic action. From this perspective, his motives and tactics—though they have inspired scholarly controversy in their own right—were less significant than the response of whites to them. This response, from the regular state militia under William H. Broadnas to the *ex oficio* squads of planters and nonslaveholding whites throughout the South, was quick and brutal: down with the dangerous black rebels, all of them.[16]

Even so, such reaction, while certainly militaristic and racist to the core, was not of necessity a proslavery reaction, at least not across the board in the Old Dominion. It was, instead, the predictable response of a white people who had feared such behavior by blacks for decades. Virginia in general had always been ambivalent about slavery; and her most famous son, Thomas Jefferson, in particular, had warned in 1820 that slave rebellion would come inevitably, when it came sounding "like a fire bell in the night." Much of this fear of slave rebellion, in Jefferson and in lesser Virginians, turned on the axis of anti-black sentiment; but, whatever it turned on, fear of slave rebellion produced genuine and forceful sentiment of antislavery, sentiment which impelled action. This was especially so in the Shenandoah Valley and the nonslaveholding West.[17]

A common hope voiced around the Upper South and the Midwest was that slavery would end, with the Negroes transported back to West Africa, or at least not permitted to move east of the tidewater littoral. Hence over a hundred of the nation's one hundred forty-three antislavery societies existed across the Upper South; and, hence, Virginians were particularly active in the American Colonization Society, whose plan was to free slaves and then to transport them to Liberia. The Midwestern expression of such antislavery negrophobia was evinced in the laws and the practice that restricted entry of free blacks to most towns and discriminated viciously against those who did enter. In large part the Illini, the Hoosiers, the Buckeyes of the heartland states of Illinois, Indiana, and Ohio who made these laws were old-time Virginians who had migrated westward almost in a straight line from the coast.[18]

The debates in Virginia after Nat Turner were thus more complicated than is often supposed. It was not merely antislavery versus proslavery and certainly not negrophobia versus negrophilia; rather, it included a wide range of attitudes on race and on slavery. Still, parliamentary debate, when it comes time to vote, does tend to break down complex issues into opposite poles, and that polarization happened here, too. Two obvious choices of action were to abolish slavery altogether or to tighten slave regulations; the former would end future revolt by destroying outright the institution which could cause the revolt, while the latter would impose considerable police responsibility on many non-slaveholders as well as greatly restricting the freedom of the master class itself. The nature of parliamentary procedure imposed an immediacy on the decisions: if one did not vote definitively to end slavery now, then the alternative of tighter slavery would triumph, which very triumph could well prevent any peaceful dissolution of slavery. In that sense, Nat Turner produced a watershed for race relations all over the South: vote to rid the Chesapeake of the institution or vote to make it work. Whichever way the legislature went, the cumulative force of subsequent legislation and the years of "tradition" in following that chosen path would make it very difficult for later generations to reconsider the issues as they stood so starkly in Richmond in the winter of 1831 and 1832.

Governor Floyd opened the session with his own ringing call to make slavery work. He would place strict controls on slaves, such as denying them the chance to learn to read or write and limiting their freedom of movement; he would severely restrict the rights of freedmen, with an end in mind of forcing all freed blacks out of Virginia; he would enlist the aid of all white men in an expanded militia and a patrol system to observe slave behavior on all plantations; and he would largely stifle debate or even talk about slavery by imposing censorship on antislavery activities, all of which he read as inspirations to Nat Turner and his ilk.[19]

A society as open as the United States in the Age of Jackson was a great threat to slavery, as Floyd rightly reckoned. Such an open society would ever bedevil localities committed to slavery, as Floyd raised the spectre of outside agitation as the precipitor of Southern troubles. "From the documents, which I herewith lay before you, there is too much reason [not] to believe those plans of treason, insurrection and murder, have been designed, planned and matured by unrestricted fanatics in some of the neighboring States, who find facilities in distributing their views and plans amongst our population, either through the post office, or by agents sent for that purpose throughout our territory," said Floyd. Thus, he wrote to state governors, especially at the North, requesting help in silencing the voices of antislavery. And, failing to receive such help, Floyd and other Southern governors thought to close the ears of their own people to the voices of antislavery, shutting off public debate, banning from the mails "unorthodox" literature, and keeping close watch on the Negro population. This last measure meant that blacks would have to be observed ceaselessly in all aspects of their lives, especially when on Sunday they turned to the Lord: unsupervised black preachers had been "the most active among ourselves, in stirring up the spirit of revolt;" *ergo*, the seemingly innocuous religious services must now be conducted by white ministers.[20]

This program was Draconian, sounding more like sixteenth century New Spain in the wake of its slave revolts than nineteenth century Virginia. Yet, in a way, Floyd demonstrated a basic unhappy truth: slavery functioned best in a closed society and if one sincerely wanted slavery with its attendant benefits, then one had to close and seal off the community as much as possible. Such a closed system posed an unconscionable threat to whites of the West, who correctly perceived the fragility of their own freedom in a slave state. To counter Floyd's proposals, Elias Preston introduced a resolution to consider a bill to end slavery in the commonwealth. Preston, from Hampshire in present-day West Virginia, drew strong support from like-minded Westerners who spoke for long days against the slavery which would bind them as surely as it bound the blacks of tidewater Virginia and the lower South.[21]

Nevertheless, the persistent problem of invisibility for blacks returned to complicate the debates. Nineteenth century Virginians, like their predecessors in New Spain, could not really see blacks outside their highly visible state of slavery. What was to be done with blacks once freed since few Southerners of any ideological camp wanted free blacks in their midst? The colonization experiment was obviously failing, sending only a few thousand blacks back to Africa despite the eloquent persuasion led by Supreme Court Justice John Marshall and Presidents Jefferson and James Madison. This vexing problem—what to do with the freed blacks—was a factor in the votes of several key Westerners who voted against Preston's bill. Linn Banks, Speaker of the House, was one such, a representative of Madison County who voted to perpetrate an institution of little importance to his locality. Representatives James G. Bryce of Frederick, Allen Wilson of Cumberland, Archibald Bryce of Goochland, William N. Patterson of Buckingham, Robert Campbell of Bedford, Rice W. Wood of Albemarle, Wylie Woods and Samule Hale of Frankling, George Stillman of Fluvana, all Westerners, all voted against Preston's resolutions. With their votes, the resolutions could have passed, 67-66 instead of failing, 58-73.[22]

As at Valladolid in another world, the moment had passed. With Preston's band defeated, slavery was more secure than ever. Eventually, Floyd's program of fortification for the institution became a reality. Where once there had been over a hundred antislavery societies, there were now, legally, none; where once there had been a Jeffersonian spirit of unlimited debate there was now a taboo subject, freedom for the Negro; where once the economy had been diversifying itself with free industry, now cash crop slavery came to dominate. These and other developments caused Virginia, ever the leader of the South, to resemble more closely the Lower South, which had scarcely worried once over its peculiar institution. Not surprisingly, Virginia lost its prominence as it lost its distinctiveness, the torch of Southern leadership passing to the hands of South Carolina after 1831.

After the Richmond debates, North Carolina and Tennessee both considered what to do with the peculiar institution. North Carolina, in 1835, basically followed Virginia's lead in voting to restrict black and Indian freedmen while creating a harsher slave world. On the other hand, the North Carolinians sweetened the pill of slave patrols and censorship by offering greater rights for all whites: there was universal male suffrage and most property restrictions for holding office were removed. Soon, in 1836, Tennessee followed suit, coupling greater "Jacksonian" privileges for the white males of all classes with greater limits on "coloreds" and on slaves. By 1837, then, the Upper South was as committed to slavery as the Lower South. Curiously, however, many historians have examined the constitutional conventions in North Carolina and in Tennessee as examples of growing participatory democracy, proof that the Jacksonian era brought substantive reform all over the country. In fact, what the constitutional conventions did was to affirm a decision made at Richmond: to sacrifice much of white freedom to ensure black slavery.[23]

The challenge of these revolts and the nature of the response of whites to each illuminated a problem in perception common to these otherwise disparate cultures: blacks were of a "rude" class of mankind and hence always slightly beyond antislavery legislation. The tiny opening in Las Casas' otherwise tight argument in 1550 had become a gaping hole by 1831. Blacks, by insisting on their humanity and on their adulthood, had refused to live unprotesting in a slave world. Whites heard the shrillness of the protest but consciously did not hear its deeper resonances; in the end whites refused to hear blacks at all, relying solely on the visual image of Sambo shuffling and smiling.

It could have been different: for a moment, Charles V had halted his mighty engines of colonization; for a moment, the Virginia Assembly paused to reconsider the expansion of slavery. For whatever motives, Charles halted, however briefly, at the very height of his imperial power; and, in the same way, Virginians halted—though only for a blink—as cotton slavery entered its period of economic "take-off." But, at these two critical junctures, neither society could body forth a definition of Africans or of Afro-Americans that permitted the blacks any freedom: to be here, the blacks must be other than free. That failure of definition resulted in the death of one kind of society that could ask a few questions of itself, and it produced on its ashes a Latin and a Southern society, each of which closed itself off from such questioning and thus paid a heavy toll in arrested cultural growth.

Notes

[1] Gonzalo Aguirre Beltran, *La poblacion negra de Mexico, 1519-1810* (Mexico, D.F.: Edicion Fuente Cultural, 1946).

[2] Ronald Sanders, *Lost Tribes and Promised Lands: the Origins of American Racism* (Boston, 1978); C. R. Boxer, *The Church Militant and Iberian Expansion, 1440-1770* (Baltimore, 1978); *cf.* the classic study of color-coding in Elizabethan England in Winthrop D. Jordan, *White Over Black: American Attitudes Toward the Negro, 1550-1812* (Chapel Hill, 1968).

[3] Peter Wood, *Black Majority: Negroes in Colonial South Carolina from 1670 through the Stono Rebellion* (New York, 1974) describes fully the sickling cell.

[4] David M. Davidson, "Negro Slave Control and Resistance in Colonial Mexico, 1519-1650," *Hispanic American Historical Review*, 46 (Summer 1966): 236-53.

[5] Jordan, op. cit.; Edmund Sears Morgan, *American Slavery, American Freedom: the Ordeal of Colonial Virginia* (New York, 1975).

[6] Wesley Frank Craven, *White, Red, and Black: the Seventeenth Century Virginian* (Charlottesville, 1971).

[7] Gerald Mortimer Capers, Jr., *The Biography of a River Town: Memphis: Its Heroic Age* (Chapel Hill, 1939); Robert H. Starobin, *Industrial Slavery in the Old South* (New York, 1970).

[8] Henry Irving Tragle, *The Southhampton Slave Revolt of 1831, a Compilation of Source Material* (Amherst, 1971).

[9] Davidson, op. cit.; Lolita Gutierrez Brockington, "Labor, the Tehuantepee Hacienda, 1588-1688; 100 Years of African, Indian and European Race Relations" (Unpublished doctoral dissertation, University of North Carolina, 1982).

[10] Frank Tannenbaum, *Slave and Citizen, the Negro in the Americas* (New York, 1946).

[11] Lewis Hanke, *The Spanish Struggle for Justice in the Conquest of America* (Philadelphia, 1949), pp. 111-32.

[12] Davidson, op. cit.; Brockington, *op. cit.*

[13] Hanke, op. cit.; Ralph Ellison, *Invisible Man* (New York, 1952).

[14] Ibid.

[15] Virginia House of Delegates, *Journal*, 1832. (hereinafter, *Journal*).

[16] Ibid.; Tragle, op. cit.

[17] Thomas Jefferson, *The Writings of Thomas Jefferson*, ed., Paul Leicester Ford, 10 vols. (New York, 1899), 10: 157-58. Thomas Jefferson, *Papers of Thomas Jefferson*, ed. Julian Parks Boyd et al., 17 vols. to date (Princeton: University, 1950-).

[18] Dwight Lowell Dumond, *Antislavery Origins of the Civil War in the United States* (Ann Arbor, 1939); Leon Litwack, *North of Slavery; the Negro in the Free States, 1790-1860,* (Chicago, 1961). Jacques Voegeli, *Free but Not Equal; the Midwest and the Negro during the Civil War*, Eugene M. Berwanger, *The Frontier Against Slavery: Western Anti-Negro Prejudice and the Slavery Extension Controversy* (Urbana, 1967).

[19] "Governor's Message, 1832," in *Journal*.

[20] "Governor's Message and Documents, 1832," in *Journal*.

[21] "Bills and Resolutions, 1832," in *Journal*; see also petitions from Ladies of the County of Augusta, free Negroes, Quakers, and other antislavery people in "Governor's Message and Documents, 1832" in *Journal*.

[22] See vote tabulations by county in "Bills, January, 1832," in *Journal*.

[23] North Carolina, General Assembly, *Journal*, 1832; Tennessee, General Assembly, *Journal*, 1836; Cf. Hugh Talmadge Lefler and Alfred Ray Newsome, *The History of a Southern State: North Carolina* (Chapel Hill, 1973); Arthur Meier Schlesinger, Jr., *The Age of Jackson* (Boston, 1945), 322 and passim.

Part Two

FREEDOM BECKONS: ABOLITION, COLONIZATION, AND EMIGRATION

The privilege of freedom acted to stimulate [Frederick] Douglass' awareness of becoming his own man. In his words, "you may hurl a man so low, beneath the level of his kind, that he loses all just ideas of his natural position; but elevate him a little and the clear conception of rights rises to life and power, and leads him onward."

Tillery,
The Inevitability of the Douglass-Garrison Conflict

Philanthropy, Self Help, and Social Control: The New York Manumission Society and Free Blacks, 1785-1810

JOHN L. RURY

The ideals promulgated by the American Revolution precipitated a sharp attack on slavery as a basic violation of human rights. By the war's end forces were set in motion that changed the status of many blacks in the North. In New York, the human rights argument together with the growing unprofitability of slavery as the supply of inexpensive white labor increased, led to the manumission of a large number of African Americans. For the city's white elite, a growing presence of black residents raised concerns about social stability and led to the establishment of the New York Manumission Society in 1785.

John Rury's study examines the efforts of the Manumission Society to influence the development of the free black community in New York. This group, along with similar manumission and antislavery societies, sought to define standards of conduct for the black population and to circumscribe their behavior along lines acceptable to elite whites. The article suggests that these attempts were not wholly successful. The emergence of free black institutions, such as churches and mutual aid societies, presaged the development of an independent black leadership in New York and the growth of a culturally distinctive black community.

THE AMERICAN REVOLUTION was accompanied by a wave of liberal sentiments in North America associated with the doctrines of human rights and innate equality. One of the consequences of the war's ideological backwash was a host of efforts, most of them in the North, to effect a gradual abolition of slavery.[1] It was in this context that the first movement to end slavery appeared in American history. Comprised largely of small, elite groups of whites based in cities, this "old" antislavery movement has been noted by historians for its largely conservative nature and its attachment to the doctrine of "gradual emancipation," whereby slavery was to be ended by freeing slave children when they reached adulthood.[2] But the early anti-slavery societies did a good deal more than agitate against slavery on philosophical and legal grounds. They also established themselves as the political and moral guardians of local free black populations. This entailed protecting blacks from a host of calamities, most notably the threat of being kidnapped and sold in the South; but it also meant observing their behavior to guarantee that it fell within guidelines deemed acceptable. In short, the old antislavery societies functioned as moral custodians for urban black communities across the Northeast.

This article will examine the manner in which one such group, the New York Manumission Society, attempted to monitor and influence the behavior of free blacks in the decades following the Revolution. The Manumission Society was among the largest and most important antislavery groups in this period, and its approaches to problems in the black community were often emulated elsewhere. Perhaps more importantly, however, the Society represented a substantial element of New York's mercantile and professional elite, men of great means and influence in the community at large. To a great extent, in that case, it was the white community's principal agency for dealing with a growing black minority in New York.

What follows is an effort to identify the chief characteristics of the Manumission Society's relationship to New York's black community in these years, and to assess its impact upon free blacks. Little is known about the influences which shaped the early stages of black community development in the North. It is possible that white philanthropy had an important effect on blacks in New York and other cities as they set out to define a world outlook all their own. There is evidence, on the other hand, of resistance of blacks to such designs. If so, this may have been the beginning of a long tradition of paternalistic efforts at control in black-white relations throughout American history, and determination of blacks to remain independent.

From Slavery to Freedom in Old New York

In the years following the Revolution, New York's community leadership faced the task of restoring social and economic order to a city which had changed considerably in the course of the war. One of the most striking developments was the appearance of a rather large free black population. The war had worked in a number of ways to help slaves acquire their freedom. In 1779 the British, hoping to incite slave revolts, offered liberty to any blacks who escaped and crossed their lines. Alarmed by the high desertion rate among the blacks, the Americans countered by offering them freedom for loyal service during the war. New York State provided for the manumission of blacks who served for three years in the militia or national army.

Whether they escaped or served with the Americans, blacks in New York used the Revolution to reduce slavery to a shadow of its colonial strength.[3]

A great surge of liberal sentiment and rapidly changing economic conditions helped maintain this trend after the war. From the beginning, the ideals of the Revolution had precipitated a sharp attack on slavery as a basic violation of human rights. A significant jump in the number of manumissions after 1774 reflected slaveholders' receptivity to such appeals. It became commonplace for slaves to bargain for their freedom when approached by prospective buyers, creating a sort of indentured servitude in lieu of slavery.[4] These arrangements were encouraged, no doubt, by the rising expense of maintaining slaves in eighteenth century New York. This was especially true in the latter half of the century, when the labor market began to expand and wages dropped. The city's white population expanded quickly in this period, reflecting a high birth rate and influx from other colonies. Following the Revolution this trend was exaggerated by the arrival of Irish, French and German immigrants. As the supply of inexpensive free labor increased and forced wages downward, slavery became unprofitable.[5]

Within twenty-five years of the Revolution the number of blacks in New York, both free and slave, tripled. This growth was largely a function of individual manumissions and migration to the city, although a considerable number of fugitive slaves came to New York in these years as well. Runaways gravitated to urban areas where they merged easily with the free blacks. By the end of the first decade of the nineteenth century the city's free black population outnumbered its slaves by nearly three to one.[6] But the free blacks' position was neither secure nor enviable. Growth of the free black population was accompanied by proliferating conditions of poverty and its attendant problems of crime, sickness and "immoral" behavior. Free blacks often lived in makeshift tenements interspersed among the residences of more affluent whites. Most were ill prepared for skilled employment and all were subject to severe discrimination when seeking any sort of work, however menial.[7] Their growing presence was a problem for the city's leadership as unprecedented numbers of manumitted slaves failed to be effectively absorbed into the social and economic mainstream. The task of resolving this problem fell to the newly formed Manumission Society.

The Manumission Society and Free Blacks

The New York Society for the Manumission of Slaves and protection of such of them as had been or wanted to be liberated was es-

tablished in January, 1785. Generally known simply as the
Manumission Society, the group was formed for two stated purposes:
first, to agitate for passage of antislavery legislation in New York
(there was an abolition bill then in the Assembly); and second, to
protect manumitted slaves from kidnappers and others who might exploit them.[8] Though small at first, the Society counted some of New
York's most prominent citizens in its ranks: Alexander Hamilton (to
be the first Secretary of the Treasury), John Murry, Jr. (a leading
merchant and a director of the Bank of New York), Congressman Eg-
bert Benson, Matthew Clarkson (a prominent Federalist), and Me-
lancton Smith (a lawyer and leading Clintonian). John Jay, eventually
to become the first Chief Justice of the U.S. Supreme Court, was selected as the Society's first president. Constituted as such, the Society
clearly represented the city's social and political elite, men who felt
their charge was to serve the community at large and see that social
stability and order were maintained.[9] Just a short time after its establishment, the Society turned its attention from the plight of slaves
and victims of racism to the behavior of New York's free black
population.

At its third meeting, in May, 1785, the Manumission Society ordered its standing committee to "Keep a watchful eye over the conduct of such Negroes as have been or may be liberated; and . . . to
prevent them from running into immorality or sinking into idleness."[10] The Society's minutes failed to specify just what immoral behavior entailed in its view, or why "idleness" was a problem to be
especially watchful of among blacks. Three years later, however, a
special committee was charged with devising means of influencing
free blacks to improve their behavior. In particular, blacks were to be
cautioned "against admitting slaves or servants into their homes, receiving or purchasing anything from them, against fiddling, dancing
or any other noisy entertainment in their houses, whereby the tran-
quility of the neighborhood be disturbed." No mention was made of
criminal behavior as a problem. Rather, the good men of the Manumission Society wished free blacks to conduct themselves with deportment and restraint. They dictated the social and economic groups
free blacks ought to associate with, and what sorts of behavior were
unacceptable even in their own homes.[11] Here the Society's interest
went beyond emancipation and the protection of blacks to directing
them to behave in a manner congruent with the expectations of the
city's social and political elite.

Apparently this matter was a source of great concern to the
Manumission Society. A number of means were discussed to compel
blacks to heed the society's advice. One was the establishment of a

registry of all free blacks in the city, to better keep track of their individual behavior. The Society's committee suggested that such a record would pressure blacks "to the end that they may be more sensible of their own privileges and may inform others of the disadvantages those labor under, from whom the Society's patronage is withheld." This remark conveys the frustration that some of the Society's members felt with the black community, but it also reveals something of the manner in which they viewed free blacks' problems.

By 1778 the Manumission Society saw itself extending "privileges" to the city's free black population rather than guaranteeing their basic human rights. More explicitly, the committee recommended "that the Negroes . . . be informed that the benefits to be derived from this society are not to be extended to any except such as maintain good characters and sobriety and honesty and peaceable living."[12] By threatening to withhold the "benefits" of their patronage (which may have included legal assistance) from unacceptable segments of the black population, members of the Society hoped to force these blacks toward compliance. Even though the register was never established, perhaps because of the time and expense it would have entailed, the committee's report and recommendation are revealing of the attitude of Society members toward the poor and consequently largely unenfranchised minority they had dedicated themselves to defend.

This sort of concern with the moral standing of free blacks remained characteristic of the old antislavery movement well past the opening decade of the nineteenth century. When societies from different cities came together for conventions they regularly exchanged reports on the behavior of free blacks in their locales. This was justified by the argument that bad behavior on the part of blacks hurt the emancipation cause, and buttressed the arguments of slaveholders that blacks were unfit for freedom.[13] Yet the standards of moral conduct demanded by the Manumission Society and similar groups was high indeed. And at least some of the Society's members were prepared to consider ways of compelling blacks to conform to their expectations. This suggests that something more than a good-natured interest in advancing emancipation was at play here. As late as 1808 the Society complained of the "looseness of manners and depravity of conduct" of the city's free blacks, and appointed a committee to devise a plan for "reformation among that part of the African race who are dissolute in their morals, keep houses of ill fame and are otherwise pursuing conduct injurious to themselves and others."[14] The Society, along with similar groups across the Northeast, was dedicated to the task of molding the black population to meet standards of conduct appropriate to the sort of community the city's elites envisioned.

Education for Social Control

Among the Manumission Society's earliest objectives was the development of a black community leadership which could take responsibility for the moral conduct of the city's free black population at large. To this end the Society took a hand in the early institutional development of New York's black community. Its most ambitious project in this regard was the establishment of the New York African Free School, which was intended to train a group of young blacks to assume positions of moral leadership in their community. The African Free School also provided Society members with a convenient avenue of contact with a certain segment of the black population. By and large, the Society's decision to establish a school was a major element of its program for influencing the city's black community.

In February 1786, the Manumission Society's standing committee suggested that "a committee be appointed to report a plan for establishing a free school in this city for the education of Negro children."[15] Nearly two years later, in November 1787, the African Free School opened its doors. From the beginning the school played an important role in realizing the Society's objectives. It was intended for the education of free black and slave children "in hopes that by an early attention to their morals they may be kept from vicious courses and qualified for usefulness in life."[16] Education was associated with the issue of freedom for blacks and with the Manumission Society's efforts to affect gradual emancipation across the state. The school's object was the education of blacks seemingly ill equipped for the ordeal of freedom and the responsibilities and Christian obligations of a well-defined social order. The Society felt that slavery often left blacks with an incomplete cultural identity, and easy prey for the immorality and criminal tendencies they associated with the class position of the former slaves. Manumitted slaves, it was felt, constituted an alien and undesirable social group, which only needed a proper education to prove acceptable. In 1788 the Society reported that

> . . . the importance of arresting youth in their advances toward the slippery paths of vice has induced us to go beyond our present abilities . . . if the rising generation were permitted to inherit the vices their parents acquired in slavery or to learn similar ones themselves through a want of proper education led us to think such a supplement to our original institution indispensably necessary.[17]

As Carl Kaestle has noted, the stated purpose of the African Free School was to intervene between black parents and their children, to rescue the latter from the low morality and poor behavior of the former.[18] If black children were to learn to behave properly, they would have to do so under the supervision of the Manumission Society. Moral education remained the essential purpose of the African Free School throughout its initial twenty-five years. Rules concerning matters of appearance, conduct to and from school, behavior in class, as well as respect for property and "our Great Maker's awful name" were rigidly enforced.[19] If they learned nothing else, the students at this school would have a clear understanding of the moral expectations they faced upon graduation.

Although the school was limited to boys at first, the addition of a girl's class in 1783 boosted enrollment to about a hundred.[20] In 1896 the school became one of the very first in the state to receive public funds for elementary education, putting it on a firm footing financially.[21] By 1805 the Manumission Society looked upon the African Free School as one of its most successful endeavors, and emphasized its role in inculcating proper morals and standards of behavior. The school became a model for other antislavery groups around the Northeast to admire and copy for their own educational efforts.[22]

From the beginning, moral responsibility and "fitness" were the major criteria for admission to the African Free School. The school's early growth was limited by the Manumission Society's policy of visiting the homes of prospective students to check their moral standing.[23] This policy also enabled Society members to make the school a key point of contact with the city's black community. Reports from the American Convention of Abolition Societies (the principal national meeting of old antislavery societies, known simply as the American Convention), were read there to groups of blacks, most of whom had children in the school.[24] Occasionally the Society called meetings of free blacks at the school, to address their attention to matters of impropriety in the black community. In January, 1798, for instance, a circular from the American Convention on the conduct of free blacks was the topic of such a meeting. "The address was read and explained by paragraphs, and the importance of their strict adherence to the advice contained therein was strongly urged" on the blacks present.[25] In 1808 the Society invited "a number of the most serious and influential characters" in the black community to discuss "the disorderly and riotous conduct of some of their colour in different parts of this city." Manumission Society members urged these black leaders to see that such outbursts did not occur again.[26] With this the purposes of the African Free School went beyond the training of a new moral leadership for the black community. It became a mechanism for identifying and manipulating black leaders to effect changes that the Society saw as desirable.

In the African Free School the Society hoped it had established an institution around which the black community could be developed along acceptable lines. The school became a focal point of moral admonition for both children and adults. The object, of course, was identification of a group of blacks who would take moral responsibility for the entire black community, in a fashion consistent with Manumission Society expectations. The record of the black community's early development, however, suggests that these efforts were not wholly successful.

Black Community Responses

The institutional framework of a free black community in New York began taking shape in the 1790s and the opening decade of the nineteenth century. Although evidence is sketchy, it is possible to discern the relationship of many of these early black institutions to the Manumission Society's purposes of moral conformity and moderation. Not surprisingly, many early black organizations reflected purposes or stated principles which were altogether consistent with those of the Society. On the other hand, there is evidence that blacks did not always look upon white paternalism in a positive light. In at least one instance (and almost certainly others), black community leaders rebuffed the Society's efforts to circumscribe their behavior. This and other evidence suggests that at least some members of New York's black community recognized the value of independence from the domination of elite whites.

The earliest signs of the black community's institutional development revolved around religion. In 1796 the Methodist Episcopal Church granted a group of free blacks permission to hold independent meetings, laying the foundation for what eventually became the African Methodist Episcopal Zion Church (A.M.E. Zion).[27] This group apparently grew rapidly, for within a year it was considering means of erecting a church and forming its own religious society. The Manumission Society was approached for counsel and support in 1798, but refused to become involved in what was clearly a denominational matter. Manumission Society members were pleased, however, with independent efforts of blacks to form a congregation. With the development of an active leadership and distinct community institutions such as a church, in their view, the necessity of their concern for the black community's moral development diminished.[28]

Aside from schools, the first two decades of black community development in New York was limited to churches and mutual aid societies.[29] Churches were important for their early contribution to independent community organization and the heavy emphasis they placed on piety and morality, particularly appropriate for early nineteenth century society. The black church was a center of community interaction, a source of considerable informal education, and a powerful moral force in the early years of community life. The original A.M.E. Zion congregation was joined by the Abyssinian Baptist Church in 1809 and the Asbury Church, an A.M.E. splinter group, in 1813. A New York congregation of Bishop Richard Allen's Philadelphia-based A.M.E. Bethel Church was organized in 1820. Even though some blacks used the early church as a means of adjusting to urban life, as a "buffer against the pressures and prejudices of the outside community," the number of communicants was relatively small. As with other areas of free black institutional development, early participation in the church was limited to those who had time and motivation to play an active role in community affairs.[30] The extent of early church influence, therefore, apparently did not extend much beyond the same group of blacks that dealt with the Manumission Society.

The principal secular agents of independent black community formation in early nineteenth century New York were mutual aid societies. Effectively beginning in 1809 with the New York African Society for Mutual Relief, these organizations were often little more than small-scale insurance cooperatives. Members paid dues toward their support in illness and care for their immediate families in cases of death. Following the initial success of the African Society for Mutual Relief, a number of similar organizations appeared in New York and Brooklyn, some of which lasted well beyond the antebellum period.[31] Even though these early cooperatives were rather narrow in scope and of limited effectiveness, they marked an important stage in the development of a distinct black leadership. Membership in a mutual aid society, particularly the African Society for Mutual Relief, was an early sign of distinction among blacks. These organizations provided a forum for emerging black community leaders, who arranged meetings, presented addresses and discussed the issues of the day. The older and larger groups became concerned with a wide range of interests, extending from education and cultural development to economic opportunity.[32]

The early black leadership was typically careful to promote principles in keeping with the morality of the day. The African Society for Mutual Relief, for instance, stood "above all things" for order and propriety, forbidding "the idea of its members becoming beggars . . . ."[33] Similarly, the African Marine Fund stressed the importance of good moral behavior for all its members. As with most other mu-

tual aid societies, such conduct was criteria for admission into the organization.[34] The early mutual aid societies, however, were also
guardians of the self-respect of blacks in an age of widespread belief
in African inferiority. Achievements of blacks in literature and science, the work of Phyllis Wheatly and Benjamin Banneker, were in-
voked to provide a measure of black potential.[35] These organizations
helped develop a distinct black identity in the face of popular
prejudice and genteel paternalism. While maintaining deference to
the prevailing value structure, the community leadership slowly faced
the necessity of developing its own cultural verities.

Education was widely regarded as important for the development of the potentials of blacks throughout the early period of community formation. Many blacks were gratified by the work of the
Manumission Society and saw the African Free School as an important means to a better future. In 1811, for instance, a black school
teacher urged blacks not to forget the Society and "the happy success
of the African Free School in the illumination of our minds."[36] In
1810 the African Marine Fund outlined plans to establish a school for
"poor African children whose parents are unable to educate them."[37]
A similar plan was proposed by "the Society among the Free People
of Colour in New York City" in 1812.[38] Support for education was
widespread and pointed to an underlying belief in its power to ame-
liorate unfavorable conditions.

There is also evidence, however, that some members of the
black community did not view the Manumission Society's efforts in
the same light. There were a number of private schools in New York
run by blacks in this period. The Manumission Society reported three
such schools in 1803, each of which required tuition enrollment.[39] In
1812 it reported the same number, although it is unclear whether
they were the same schools.[40] The appearance of these schools suggests that the African Free School did not entirely meet the black
community's educational needs. It may have been because the Society's school was inaccessible to some parts of the city. But perhaps
private black schools opened because some community members objected to the Society's purposes in education. A black teacher, John
Teasman, was dismissed from the African Free School in 1809, and
opened up a school of his own shortly afterward.[41] Although the reasons for Teasman's departure are not known, the very fact of his conducting his own school suggest that not all of New York's black
community was satisfied with the Manumission Society's efforts in the
field of education. Black private schools continued to appear intermittently through the opening decades of the nineteenth century.[42]
Though little is known about them, their existence indicates that self-

help—apart from philanthropy—was a strong theme in early black community development.

As indicated earlier, the Manumission Society devoted a good deal of its attention to seeing that free blacks improved their behavior along lines acceptable to elite whites. There is evidence, however, that by the end of the first decade of the nineteenth century the Society's admonitions in this regard were not always heeded. In 1809 free blacks in New York had planned an elaborate celebration for the day on which the slave trade was to be finally outlawed in the United States. Clearly worried that such a celebration would cause some free blacks to exhibit moral excesses, the Society counseled a group of black leaders that their proposed party was "improper, in as much as it tended to injure themselves and cause reflections to be made on this society." But the black leaders disagreed. According to the Society's Minutes, the city's free blacks had invested a great deal in preparing for the celebration and "could not think of relinquishing their proposed method of celebrating the day." They went ahead with their plan, regardless of the Society's concerns.[43] This time, apparently, independent-minded black leaders refused to follow the moral leadership represented by the Society and its elite membership.

Even though such important free black institutions as the churches and the mutual aid societies represented the same moral purposes as the Manumission Society (and the city's white elite), there is evidence of a growing independence on the part of community leaders. The persistence of private black schools indicated that some black families were willing to pay tuition rather than send their children to the African Free School, which was supervised by well-to-do whites. And although most black leaders probably agreed with the Society on issues of propriety and good conduct, they felt the abolition of the slave trade was worthy of an extraordinary celebration. The emergence of a visible independent black leadership in New York during these years presaged the development of the activist community leaders that started *Freedom's Journal* and helped launch the abolitionist movement in decades to come.[44] This was a process over which the old abolitionists could exercise little control.

The gradualist antislavery societies that formed in the wake of the American Revolution were comprised of men concerned with the social and moral condition of their communities. They represented the status quo, a social order where propriety and order were defined by elites and served their interests. These men worked to protect the interests of free blacks and agitated against slavery (albeit with respect for the "property" slaves represented). But they also monitored the behavior of free blacks carefully, and made reform of the conduct of the blacks guided by their own ideas of propriety and moral soundness an important area of their work.[45] While it is not altogether clear just what impact the Manumission Society and other such groups had upon free blacks, early black institutions reflected moral and social purposes consistent with those of elite whites. Yet black leaders also exhibited an independence of mind which anticipated the development of a distinctive black American identity in the decades to come.

Notes

[1] For an overview of this process, see Duncan J. MacLeod, *Slavery, Race and the American Revolution* (London, 1974), passim.

[2] For discussion of the old abolitionist movement, see Alice D. Adams, *The Neglected Period of Anti-Slavery in America* (Glouchester, Mass., 1905), passim; and Arthur Zilversmith, *The First Emancipation: The Abolition of Slavery in the North* (Chicago, 1967), passim.

[3] Edgar J. McManus, *A History of Negro Slavery in New York* (Syracuse, 1966), pp. 154 and 159.

[4] Ibid, pp. 152-54; and MacLeod, op. cit., *Revolution*, pp. 14-28.

[5] Sidney Pomerantz, *New York, An American City, 1785-1803* (New York, 1938), p. 201; McManus, op cit., p. 172.

[6] McManus, pp. 114-15; also see McManus' more comprehensive work, *Black Bondage in the North* (Syracuse, 1973), p. 111; and Rhonda C. Freeman, "The Free Negro in New York City in the Era Before the Civil War" (Unpublished Ph.D. dissertation, Columbia University, 1966), pp. 6-9.

[7] Freeman, op cit., pp 215-20; also see Arnet G. Linday, "The Economic Condition of Negroes in New York Prior to 1861," *Journal of Negro History* 6 (April, 1921): 193; and Leon Litwack, *North of Slavery: The Negro in the Free States, 1790-1860* (Chicago, 1961), p. 64.

[8] The best general discussion of the Manumission Society can be found in Thomas R. Moseley, "A History of the New York Manumission Society, 1785-1849" (Unpublished Ph.D. dissertation, New York University, 1963), passim. The Society's own statement of its purposes can be found in the New York Manumission Society Papers, housed in the New York Historical Society, Vol. 6, p. 4 (hereafter cited as New York Manumission Society Papers, Volume Number, page number).

[9] Moseley, op cit., p. 36; Pomerantz, op cit., p. 221; and Zilversmith, op cit., p. 19.

[10] New York Manumission Society Papers, Vol. 6 p. 24.

[11] Ibid., p. 100

[12] Ibid.

[13] Zilversmith, op. cit., p. 223.

[14] New York Manumission Society Papers, Vol. 2, pp. 171-81.

[15] Ibid., Vol. 6, p. 40.

[16] Ibid., p. 87.

[17] Ibid., p. 97.

[18] Carl F. Kaestle, *Pillars of the Republic: Common Schools and American Society, 1790-1860* (New York, 1983), p. 25.

[19] New York Manumission Society Papers, Vol. 6, p. 96.

[20] Ibid., p. 165.

[21] Ibid., p. 239; and New York Manumission Society Papers, Vol. 9, p. 81.

22 The American Convention of Abolition Societies, *Minutes and Proceedings, 1805* (Philadelphia, 1805) pp. 7-8.

23 New York Manumission Society Papers, Vol. 6, p. 23. The school's first Board of Trustees was "of opinion that it will be advisable to have a few children well trained at first that those who are admitted afterward may with greater ease be made orderly and regular." See Papers, Vol. 6, p. 85.

24 Ibid, pp. 241-46.

25 New York Manumission Society Papers, Vol. 9, p. 2.

26 Ibid., p. 181.

27 Christopher Rush, *A Short Account of the Rise and Progress of the African Methodist Episcopal Church in America* (New York, 1843), pp. 9-10; and Freeman, op. cit., p. 380.

28 New York Manumission Society Papers, Vol. 9, p. 10; and the American Convention of Abolition Societies, *Minutes and Proceedings, 1798* (Philadelphia, 1798), pp. 30 and 39.

29 Daniel Perlman, "The Free Negro in New York City, His Status and His Group Organizations, 1800-1850" (Unpublished M.A. thesis, City College of New York, 1966) p. 99.

30 Freeman, op. cit., pp. 375-76, 382, 386, 400 and 413.

31 Perlman, op. cit., pp. 59-62.

32 John T. Zville, *Historical Sketch of the New York African Society for Mutual Relief* (New York, 1892) p. 6; and Perlman, op. cit., p. 63.

33 William Hamilton, *An Address to the New York African Society for Mutual Relief. Delivered in the Universalist Church, January 2, 1809* (New York, 1809), p. 6.

34 *Constitution of the African Marine Fund for the Relief of Distressed Orphans and Poor Members of this Fund* (New York, 1810), p 5.

35 Hamilton, op. cit., p. 8, also see John Teasman, *An Address Delivered in the African Episcopal Church, On the 25th Day of March, 1811. Before the New York African Society for Mutual Relief, Being the First Anniversary of Its Incorporation* (New York, 1811), pp. 9-10.

36 Teasman, op. cit. p. 7.

37 *Constitution of the African Marine Fund*, p. 5.

38 New York Manumission Society Papers, Vol. 9, p. 308.

39 The American Convention of Abolition Societies, *Minutes and Proceedings, 1803* (Philadelphia, 1803), p. 6.

40 New York Manumission Society Papers, Vol. 9, p. 288.

41 Ibid, p. 214; also see Teasman, op. cit., p. 4.

42 Freeman, op. cit., p. 363.

43 New York Manumission Society Papers, Vol. 2, pp. 223-31.

44 For discussion of the development of black community institutions after 1820, see John L. Rury, "The New York African Free School, 1827-1836: Conflict Over Community Control of Black Education." *Phylon* 44 (September 1983): 187-98.

45 In this regard the Manumission Society anticipated a host of other philanthropic aid programs in the nineteenth century. See Raymond Mohl, *Poverty in New York, 1783-1825* (New York, 1972), passim, for discussion of these developments. Memberships of the Manumission Society and several of these later philanthropic organizations overlapped.

Abolition and Colonization: The Years of Conflict, 1829-1834

BRUCE ROSEN

The rise of militant abolitionism in the United States was heralded by the publication of David Walker's Appeal, *the beginning of William Lloyd Garrison's newspaper* The Liberator, *and Nat Turner's insurrection. Occurring between 1829 and 1832, these events helped to intensify slave debates and to increase the polarization on issues of abolitionism and colonization. In the early 1820s, the prevailing point of view among many individuals interested in the plight of blacks held that the United States was for whites only. Freedom for blacks was acceptable if they were removed to Africa or some other locale outside the United States. Founded in 1816, the American Colonization Society served as a primary vehicle for promoting gradual emancipation and colonization with slavery safely protected in the American social order.*

Bruce Rosen's study focuses on the American Colonization Society, depicting its expansion into the Southern slave states in the 1820s and the growing divergence of attitudes about slavery within the organization. The writer draws from a number of sources to show the growing militancy of Northern abolitionists and the increasingly defensive posture of Southerners as they sought to repress debate on the subject of slavery. The Prudence Crandall affair in 1833 in Canterbury, Connecticut, is highlighted as a confrontation between colonizationists and abolitionists that preceded the decline of the American Colonization Society.

DURING THE PERIOD from 1829 to 1834, a noticeable shift in sentiment regarding the amelioration of the plight of Negroes in the United States occurred. Prior to the late 1820s the most common position for whites concerned with the problem of Negroes in the social order was one of support for colonization. The position of the colonization groups was broad enough to permit either a liberal or conservative stance on slavery. Supporters of colonization could, if they wished, maintain the theory of the social, political, and intellectual inferiority of Negroes while at the same time supporting some potential improvement in the status of free Negroes through transportation to colonies in Africa.

With the rise of a more militant abolitionism, particularly as exemplified by William Lloyd Garrison in his outspoken newspaper *The Liberator,* whites were forced to side either for or against freedom for all enslaved Negroes. This polarization led to the virtual destruction of the American Colonization Society in the South, and reduced it to little more than a debating society in the North.

The American Colonization Society was founded in December of 1816 in Washington, D.C., with Henry Clay presiding in the absence of Judge Bushrod Washington.[1] Although Clay addressed the opening remarks to the meeting, the moving forces behind it were the Reverend Robert Finley of New Jersey, later president of the University of Georgia; Elias Caldwell, Clerk of the Supreme Court of the United States, and Francis Scott Key. It was Key who persuaded Washington, whose primary claim to fame was his prestigious family name, to endorse colonization. It was Key too who persuaded Clay to attend the organizational meeting of the Society. Although best known as the composer of our national anthem, Key was an attorney in Georgetown and the brother-in-law of Roger B. Taney.[2]

At the organizational meeting it rapidly became clear that whatever noble motives might have been in the minds of some of the founders, they would have to compromise with the realities of political life in a slaveholding society. John Randolph of Roanoke, a close friend of Key, and one never known for his reticence, made it clear that he would support the efforts of colonization only in order to rid the country of free Negroes whom he saw as troublemakers and a danger to the security of the slave system.[3] But it was the redoubtable Clay who most effectively set forth the premises upon which the American Colonization Society was to be formed. It was, Clay pointed out, "the object of the . . . meeting to be to consider of the propriety and practicability of colonizing the free blacks. . . ."[4] And, in support of Randolph, Clay made clear that,

> It was not proposed to deliberate upon, or consider at all, any question of emancipation, or that was connected with the abolition of slavery.[5]

It was upon such understanding that Clay had attended and that Southern and Western support of the Society could be expected. If the colonization scheme were not limited to free Negroes and interfered with the institution of slavery, it could not expect, according to Clay, the support of the South and West.[6]

Just ten years later, on January 20, 1827, at the annual meeting of the American Colonization Society in Washington, Clay delivered an address setting forth the philosophy of the Society. Regarding emancipation, he said that

> . . . [The American Colonization Society] entertains no purpose, on its own means, to attempt emancipation, partial or general; that it knows the general government has no constitutional powers to achieve such an object; that it believes that the States, and the States only, which tolerate slavery, can accomplish the work of emancipation; and that it ought to be left to them exclusively, absolutely, and voluntarily to decide the question.[7]

Clay went on to explain that the sole purpose of the colonization scheme was to hold the Negro population stable while the white population increased, thus continuously decreasing the percentage of Negroes in the general population.[8]

The first president of the Society was Bushrod Washington, and among the thirteen Vice-Presidents who signed its constitution were such influential figures as William Crawford, Henry Clay, John Taylor, and Andrew Jackson.[9]

Because the Society did not elect to interfere with the institution of slavery, emphasizing instead the removal of free Negroes from the United States, it received substantial Southern support. Legislatures in Georgia, Maryland, and Tennessee endorsed the Society, and by 1826 over 75 percent of the auxiliary local societies were to be found in slave states.[10] Among the Presidents of the Society were Southerners such as James Madison, James Monroe, Henry Clay, and John Marshall.[11] In Georgia there were, during the first fifteen years of the American Colonization Society, eight different auxiliaries: two in Augusta and one each in Jackson County, Waynesboro, Putnam County, Baldwin County, Eatonton, and Milledgeville.[12] Virginia in the same period had a total of forty-one different auxiliaries,[13] and in 1826 that state provided a legislative appropriation to help with the work of colonization.[14]

Not all of the Southern states looked with such favor on the colonization forces. After 1822 South Carolina no longer had any American Colonization Society auxiliaries, and prior to 1830 neither Mississippi nor Louisiana had auxiliary chapters.[15] It is no coincidence that the year of the last recorded colonization auxiliary in South Carolina is the same year as the Denmark Vesey conspiracy. By 1825 South Carolina had become virtually paranoid on the question of Negroes and slavery. South Carolinians opposed not only more radical proposals of the abolitionists but even the most moderate proposals such as those of the American Colonization Society.[16] During the late 1820s in that state attempts were made to repress open debate on the subject of slavery.[17]

In general, however, the Society was supported throughout the South during the 1820s. Support seems to have been engendered by the philosophy of the Society as set out by Henry Clay and others to the effect that the United States was a white man's country and Negroes should not mingle with whites. Among many members of the Society it appears to have been an article of faith that slavery was a fit circumstance for Negroes in this country, but that freedom was a condition best enjoyed in Africa.[18] Unfortunately for the Society, the majority of free Negroes did not share these views.

The opposition of free Negroes to the colonization scheme was intense. Until 1830 only one influential free Negro, John B. Russwurm, supported the colonization scheme; and as he wrote to R. R. Gurley, the Secretary of the Society, he was subject to violent antagonism from " 'the most influential of our people.' "[19] Meetings of Negroes throughout the North condemned the colonization plan, feeling that it would increase the price of slaves and remove free Negroes, the one body of true friends the slave might count on.[20]

In the first fourteen years of its existence the Society sent fewer than 1,500 colonists to Liberia; but even this figure does not tell how many of these were slaves manumitted for the sole purpose of colonization in Africa,[21] although it has been estimated that of the Negroes sent out by the Society between 1820 and 1833 about two thirds had been manumitted on the condition that they become colonists.[22]

Prior to 1830, abolitionist activity was fragmented and abolitionists often allied themselves with the American Colonization Society. Most of the leading abolitionists were in fact at one time or another members of the Society. Theodore Weld, Arthur Tappan, Benjamin Lundy, Gerrit Smith, and James G. Birney were all associated with it.[23] Even William Lloyd Garrison, on the Fourth of July, 1829, spoke at the Park Street Church in Boston on behalf of the colonization movement.[24] In his speech he concluded by saying

> I call upon our citizens to assist in establishing auxiliary colonization societies in every State, county and town. I implore their direct and liberal patronage to the parent society.[25]

In the main, the period from 1808, following the passage of the Slave Trade Act, to 1830 rightly deserves the characterization of the "period of stagnation."[26] What antislavery sentiment existed in the South was often a function of the density of the slave population. For example, in the Virginia Slavery Debate of 1832, the debate split generally along geographic lines. Westerners who held few slaves and less political power supported abolition; Easterners, representing the entrenched interests and the political power as well as the slaveholding interests, were opposed. A motion which suggested the expediency of the legislature enacting legislation for the abolition of slavery was finally defeated 73 to 58.[27]

As late as 1827, Southern antislavery societies outnumbered those in the North; but for the most part they were in Quaker areas or in Eastern Tennessee.[28] In the slaveholding areas of the South the decade of the twenties had worked substantial changes in the thinking of slave owners. Until the early 1820s most slave owners were apologetic about the institution and defended its existence as a necessary evil. W. S. Jenkins sums it up nicely when he says,

> The apathetic and apologetic attitude of slaveholders in this period was in striking contrast to the aggressive and even belligerent utterances in defense of their institution during the later decades.[29]

This "defense" took the form of the "positive good" theory of slavery, and led during the 1820s and 1830s to the South consistently overreacting to the innocuous attacks of the abolitionists. At least one scholar has recently suggested that the "frenzied response . . . [was] a measure of the guilt and fear which made Negro slavery a profoundly disturbing institution . . . ."[30]

The constant fear of insurrection and the awareness that abolitionists might contribute to slave revolts also contributed to the failure of this group to make any significant headway in slaveholding areas of the South. South Carolina still remembered that there was supposed to have been some relationship between Denmark Vesey and the free Negroes of San Domingo. It could not have escaped the notice of older residents of Charleston who knew of the revolts on that island when Negro seamen from there were allowed the freedom of the streets.[31]

After the mid-1820s it became clear that in the slaveholding areas of the South there was little or no likelihood of developing a successful abolitionist movement. The growing militancy of the Northern abolitionists and the outspoken antislavery writings of men like Benjamin Lundy, William Lloyd Garrison, and David Walker combined to force the South into a more defensive posture.

In September 1829, a free-born Negro from North Carolina, recently moved to Boston, published *Walker's Appeal*. In the *Appeal* David Walker called for slaves to show their manhood by standing up to their masters:

> . . . they want us for their slaves, and think nothing of murdering us in order to subject us to that wretched condition—therefore, if there is an *attempt* made by us, kill or be killed. Now, I ask you had

you not rather be killed than to be a slave to a tyrant who takes the
life of your mother, wife, and dear little children?[32]

Walker's Appeal had a profound and terrifying effect on the South. By
1830 newspapers in South Carolina were avoiding all public debate
regarding slavery. In Charleston, the papers would not even discuss
slave conspiracies.[33] Laws were passed by state legislatures to keep the
Appeal out of the hands of slaves. Laws regarding the teaching of
reading and writing to slaves were passed or stiffened.[34] Most damn-
ing of all was the attempt, particularly in South Carolina, to repress
open debate on the subject of slavery during the late 1820s and early
1830s.[35] It would be an understatement to say that the times were not
conducive to the abolition movement in the South. Yet during the
1820s in the South one man, Benjamin Lundy, stands out as the
voice of abolition.

Benjamin Lundy, a Quaker and a dedicated abolitionist, was to
be the mentor for perhaps the best known abolitionist of his time,
William Lloyd Garrison. Beginning in 1822, Lundy published *The Genius of Universal Emancipation* in Greeneville, Tennessee. Although
often attacked, Lundy's paper was to survive the decade of the 1820s.
Merton Dillon, in his biography of the abolitionist editor ascribes the
survival of *The Genius* to the fact that before 1830 slaveholders were
not fully aware of the potential danger of the abolition movement.[36]
In October 1824 Lundy and his paper moved to Baltimore where on
January 9, 1827, he was brutally assaulted by Austin Woolfolk, "perhaps the dean of Maryland slave traders." In court, Woolfolk pleaded
guilty, but charged Lundy with extreme provocation. Woolfolk was finally found guilty but was fined only one dollar and costs.[37] In March
of 1828, Lundy met with William Lloyd Garrison in Boston, and in
September of the following year Garrison was in Baltimore working
with Lundy on *The Genius*.[38] Of their relationship, Dillon says, "Garrison was captivated by the older man's dedication and the clarity with
which he communicated his moral vision. Garrison sought a cause;
Lundy had found one."[39] Never, Garrison once wrote of Lundy, "was
moral sublimity of character better illustrated."[40]

Despite the efforts of Lundy and other dedicated abolitionists,
the center for abolitionist thought was moving North. Soon it was to
be centered in Boston where Garrison was to publish *The Liberator.*
"The opponents of slavery [in the South] had either emigrated or
been intimidated or had begun to listen to the hollow music of that
respectable siren, the American Colonization Society."[41] By 1829 the
battle between the abolitionists and the colonizationists had been
joined—the battleground, New England.

By the time Garrison joined Lundy on *The Genius,* his conviction of the need for immediate and universal emancipation of slaves
had become fully established. Since Lundy did not share Garrison's
views on how to implement the abolitionist struggle, even when he
shared the younger man's convictions of the necessity of the struggle,
an accommodation was worked out. Lundy told Garrison, "thee may
put thy initials to thy articles, and I will put my initials to mine, and
each will bear his own burdens."[42] Thus, Garrison, in his first statement in *The Genius* was able to set forth his position over his own
name.

In this first statement, the new editor, while not condemning
the American Colonization Society, accused it of being "exceedingly
dilatory and uncertain" and indicated that his position on slavery was
"that the slaves are entitled to immediate and complete emancipation: consequently, to hold them longer in bondage is both tyrannical and unnecessary."[43]

Garrison and Lundy were in many ways quite unlike. Despite
his acerbic pen, Lundy was a careful craftsman capable of separating
editorial comment from fact. Garrison was a political pamphleteer
and propagandist, lacking in true reportorial instinct.[44] Garrison was
a powerful and moving speaker. Samuel J. May, no mean orator in
his own right, on hearing the young abolitionist wrote, "Never before
was I so affected by the speech of man."[45] Lundy, on the other hand,
"was not a good public speaker. His voice was too feeble, his utterance too rapid . . . his infirmity of deafness rendered it difficult to
engage with him in protracted conversation."[46] In 1830 Lundy was
forty-one years old and a widower with five children. "A slight, stoop-
shouldered, brittle man with thinning red hair,"[47] he had only nine
years to live and would never see the outcome of the great battle to
which he had lent his pen. Garrison, fifteen years younger, unmar-
ried, balding, with steel-rimmed spectacles from behind which his
piercing eyes held the persons to whom he was speaking, would live
through the Civil War and Reconstruction, surviving Lundy by 40
years. Yet despite their differences they remained close friends, and
"ever cherished for each other the kindliest feelings and mutual personal regard."[48] With the dissolution of the partnership because of
the economic failure of *The Genius,* Garrison relocated his base of
operations in Boston and on January 1, 1831, the first edition of *The
Liberator* made its appearance. In his address to the public Garrison
set forth the credo of the paper which was, in fact, his own personal
statement with regard to slavery and emancipation.

> I am aware, that many object to the severity of my language;
> but is there not cause for severity? I *will* be as harsh as truth, and as

uncompromising as justice. On this subject I do not wish to think, or speak, or write, with moderation. No! no! Tell a man whose house is on fire to give a moderate alarm; tell him to moderately rescue his wife from the hands of the ravisher; tell the mother to gradually extricate her babe from the fire unto which it has fallen; but urge me not to use moderation in a cause like the present. I am in earnest—I will not equivocate—I will not excuse—I will not retreat a single inch—AND I WILL BE HEARD.[49]

What he said in that first issue was not new, but the ringing tone set a standard for future issues of the paper.

In actual fact, the paper had only a small circulation and this largely among Negroes. There has been, because of this, a tendency to play down the importance of Garrison and *The Liberator* in the abolition movement. As John Thomas points out in his prize-winning biography of Garrison, the success of *The Liberator* lay in the frequency with which it was quoted, rebutted, requoted, and re-rebutted.[50] As one looks through the pages of the antislavery newspaper it appears as if Garrison is waging a war of words with several Southern newspaper editors at once.

A certain amount of notoriety accrued to the young editor and his paper when Nat Turner and his band of revolutionaries swept across the quiet countryside of Southampton County, Virginia, in August of 1831. Turner and his little band killed sixty-one whites before their day's work was ended but the aftermath was equally gruesome. A witch hunt swept across the Southampton County area, leaving in its wake over one hundred Negroes dead and others beaten. Many of the Negroes were subjected to maiming and torture before their deaths. Seventeen of the fifty-three Negroes arraigned for the rebellion were eventually executed.[51]

In the second issue of *The Liberator,* Garrison had published a poem which was to receive widespread circulation. It said, in part

> Though distant be the hour, yet come it must—
>   Oh! hasten it, *in mercy,* righteous Heaven!
> When Afric's sons, uprising from the dust,
>   Shall stand erect—their galling fetters riven;
> When from his throne Oppression shall be driven,
>   An exiled monster, powerless through all time;
> When freedom—glorious freedom shall be given
>   To every race, complexion, caste, and clime,
> And nature's sable hue shall cease to be a crime!
>
> Wo if it comes with storm, and blood, and fire,
>   When midnight darkness veils the earth and sky!
> Wo to the innocent babe—the guilty sire—

Mother and daughter—friends of kindred tie!
Stranger and citizen alike shall die!
Red-handed Slaughter his revenge shall feed,
And Havoc yell his ominous death-cry,
And wild Despair in vain for mercy plead—
While Hell itself shall shrink, and sicken at the deed![52]

In the minds of Southerners, there was no question but that the second stanza was a call to rebellion. Garrison, on the other hand, was to indicate that he saw it as prophecy rather than as a call to arms.[53] Thus, the two interpretations tended to reinforce Garrison and the South, each in the opinion of the other. While there can be little question that the second stanza is a bloody and descriptive passage, it is useful to read the last stanza of the poem.

Not by the sword shall your deliverance be;
Not by the shedding of your masters' blood,
Not by rebellion—or foul treachery,
Upspringing suddenly, like swelling flood:
Revenge and rapine ne'er did bring forth good.
GOD'S *time is best!*—nor will it long delay:
Even now your barren cause begins to bud,
And glorious shall the fruit be!—Watch and pray,
For, lo! the kindling dawn, that ushers in the day![54]

This is certainly a rejection of the principle of violence. While the paper may not have called for violence, it was certainly inflammatory, and while this distinction may have soothed Garrison's conscience, it is, at best, a rather thin line of separation. After the Nat Turner uprising, many cities and counties passed ordinances to keep *The Liberator* out of the hands of free Negroes and slaves. The Georgia Legislature passed a bill which was no more than an open invitation to kidnap the editor of *The Liberator* and which authorized ". . . the sum of five thousand dollars be . . . paid to any person or persons who shall arrest, bring to trial and prosecute to conviction, under the laws of this State, the editor or publisher of . . . the *Liberator*."[55]

Even while the furor arising over the Nat Turner rebellion occupied Garrison, he was increasing his attack on colonization. From the second issue of the paper onward, one could hardly pick up a copy of *The Liberator* without seeing some denunciation of the American Colonization Society or the colonization movement. The tone of the criticism gradually became more and more bitter. At first, Garrison seems to have been content to call those who supported the colonization movement "well-meaning but deluded."[56]

Within six weeks Garrison was referring to "the imbecility, heartlessness and timidity of this association. . . ."[57] As his attack grew more intense, friends remonstrated with him to at least modify his attacks. Samuel J. May, arguing that the colonization scheme was "introductory to more efficient measures," told him that, "I cannot go along with you in your opposition to the Colonization Society," and accused him of having "gone too far," of using language "too severe," and of being "too indiscriminate" in his censures.[58] May remained a member, albeit lukewarm, of the American Colonization Society until the Prudence Crandall affair drove him from the Society. Henry Benson, after seeing Garrison in September 1831, wrote to Reverend May, "Mr. Garrison says he shall write to you soon, and has no doubt that, as you are such an unprejudiced man, he shall soon make you a convert to his views of the Colonization Society."[59]

The difference between the abolitionists who opposed colonization and the colonizationists was not limited to their differing philosophies on the place and role of Negroes; it extended to the tone with which these attitudes were expressed. It was here that the abolitionists had a distinct advantage.

Early in 1832, the Reverend Simeon S. Jocelyn wrote to the Reverend R. R. Gurley, secretary of the American Colonization Society, raising three questions related to principles of the Society. All three dealt with the legal rights of free Negroes transported without their consent, and were outgrowths of the debates then going on in Virginia.[60] When Gurley refused to print the letter in the *African Repository,* Jocelyn sent it to *The Liberator,* where it appeared in its entirety on March 17, 1832. In the issue of *The Liberator,* dated March 24, Gurley's response to the Jocelyn letter is printed, in which Gurley writes,

> The general style of the letter is anything but conciliatory. I think there is a great want of the *suaviter in mode,* without which it is impossible to bring most minds to a practical acknowledgment of the truth. The general impression of Southern men who might read your letter, would be that you had little, very little respect for the principles, and very little confidence in the moral feelings of the South.[61]

Garrison, of course, could not let the exchange in the pages of his newspaper pass without editorial comment. He began by accusing Gurley of writing "any thing but a direct, manly, straightforward reply to the momentous letter of the Rev. Mr. Jocelyn." After poisoning the wells, he went on to say,

> . . . He [Gurley] would have him [Jocelyn] discourse on the subject of slavery with as much *sang froid* as if the victims of it were indeed beasts, destitute of souls, and scarcely worthy of the generous sympathy of our nature. Why, it seems to us that an American who can *calmly* reflect upon the brutal degredation of two millions of his

countrymen—who can listen to the clanking of their chains and their agonizing groans, without dissolving in tears, or feeling every muscle swell to its utmost tensions with indignation—who can see them deprived of all their just rights and of all the means of knowledge, and of the fruits of their toil, and driven about like cattle, and bought and sold at the expense of the holiest relations of life, without lifting up his voice in tones of remonstrance louder than thunder—must have nerves of steel and a heart of adamant. This is not a subject for calm analysis or frigid contemplation: moderation on such a theme were criminal.[62]

While Gurley may have corresponded with Jocelyn and even have had his letters published in *The Liberator,* he did not respond to the attacks of Garrison or of the other abolitionists in his own vehicle, the *African Repository.* It was not, in fact, until November 1832, under the continuous prodding of Joshua N. Danforth, that Gurley addressed himself to Garrison's attack on the colonization movement.[63] But once again the response of the colonizationists to the abolitionist crusade was too little and too late.

The year 1832 saw the publication of Garrison's most forceful attack on the colonization movement. Garrison's *Thoughts on American Colonization* is an impassioned diatribe the nature of which can be inferred from the various sections of the pamphlet.

Section I.	The American Colonization Society is Pledged Not to Oppose the System of Slavery.
Section II.	The American Colonization Society Apologises for Slavery and Slaveholders.
Section III.	The American Colonization Society Recognises Slaves as Property.
Section IV.	The American Colonization Society Increases the Value of Slaves.
Section V.	The American Colonization Society is the Enemy of Immediate Abolition.
Section VI.	The American Colonization Society is Nourished by Fear and Selfishness.
Section VII.	The American Colonization Society Aims at the Utter expulsion of the Blacks.
Section VIII.	The American Colonization Society is the Disparager of the Free Blacks.
Section IX.	The American Colonization Society Denies the Possibility of Elevating the Blacks in This Country.
Section X.	The American Colonization Society Deceives and Misleads the Nation.[64]

To support the arguments outlined in the titles of his sections, Garrison quoted the *African Repository. Thoughts* also includes a second part made up of statements by Negro groups and by individuals opposed to colonization.

When Gurley finally responded, his response was predictable. He quietly and calmly pointed out that Garrison had used, as his primary source, the *African Repository* rather than the official statements of the Managers of the American Colonization Society. Further, he suggested that Garrison was guilty of unfairness by quoting out of context and pointed out that "by the same process, we could exhibit Mr. Garrison and his opinions in no enviable light. . . ."[65] He accused Garrison of turning some from the "sober scheme of the Society, to follow the delusive but blazing lights [of abolition]."[66] And Gurley concluded by hoping that "experience and reflection will . . . give soberness to the views of Mr. Garrison."[67]

It is true that Garrison, in a number of spots, quoted out of context; but it is equally true that in the vast majority of instances he accurately represented what was written in the *African Repository.* While he did not quote from the official pronouncements of the Managers of the Society, and was indeed guilty of the sin of omission, the *African Repository* was the official publication of the society and reflected the views of the members and most of the officers.

Gurley's response had been the cue for which Garrison had waited, and Garrison's reply was swift and harsh. In a December number of *The Liberator,* the editor called Gurley's defense of the society, "flimsy and irrelevant." He accused Gurley of taking over six months to respond after he had been presented with a copy of the *Thoughts.*[68] The tone of the reply by Gurley was far less temperate in January of 1833 than it had been the preceding November. Once again Gurley accused the editor of *The Liberator* of misquoting not only from the *African Repository* in the *Thoughts,* but in *The Liberator's* response to Gurley's criticism of November 1832.[69] After 1833, Gurley and Garrison simply represented the leadership of the two outstanding groups attempting to come to grips with the questions raised by the presence of Negroes in the American social order. The real fight was being fought by their followers. Too late, Gurley realized that with the publication of the *Thoughts* and the continued growth of abolitionist thought the colonization movement was beginning to lose its appeal to whites as well as Negroes. As long as Garrison's following had consisted primarily of blacks, he offered no real challenge to the American Colonization Society; by 1833 more and more whites were beginning to flock to the abolitionist banner.

Garrison's anti-colonization crusade was reinforced when, in 1833, he found his first martyr.[70] It is an interesting sidelight to history that with the exception of contemporary writers, the Prudence Crandall case has not been treated as a confrontation between the colonizationists and the abolitionists.[71] Yet the leaders on both sides of the question of the right of Prudence Crandall to have a school for Negro girls represented these opposing philosophies.

In January 1833, Garrison received a letter from Prudence Crandall asking his opinion of her plan to change her boarding school in Canterbury, Connecticut, from one for white girls to one for Negroes.[72] Writing in 1869, Prudence Crandall Philleo recalled the events leading up to her first attempt to contact the editor of *The Liberator.*

The reason for changing my school of white pupils for a school of colored pupils is as follows. I had a nice colored girl . . . as help in my family and her intended husband regularly received *The Liberator.* The girl took the paper from the office and loaned it [to] me. In that the condition of the colored people both Slaves and free were . . . truthfully portrayed. The double dealing and manifest deception of the colonization society were faithfully exposed, and the Question of Immediate Emancipation of the millions of Slaves in the United States boldly advocated. Having been taught from early childhood the sin of Slavery my Sympathies were greatly arroused [*sic.*] Sarah Harris a respectable young woman and a member of the church . . . called often to see her friend. . . . In some of her calls I ascertained that she wished to attend my school. . . . I allowed her to enter as one of my pupils. By this act I gave great offence.[73]

The impact of the Quaker school teacher's decision was immediate and swept through the town like wildfire. She was first visited by the wife of an Episcopal minister and was informed that if she "continued that colored girl in . . . [her] school that it could not be sustained."[74] To this Prudence replied "that it might sink then, for I should not turn her out."[75] It became apparent that many of the parents would not return their children to the school, and with the enrollment dwindling Prudence decided "that if it were possible I would teach colored girls exclusively."[76] On January 29, Prudence was in Boston and there she met with Garrison.[77] Garrison must have approved her plan because shortly thereafter she closed her school to white enrollment and advertised in *The Liberator* on March 2, 1833, the opening, in April, of her school "for the reception of young Ladies and little Misses of color."[78] Among her references were listed some of the most outstanding names in the abolitionist movement: Arthur Tappan, Theodore Wright, Samuel Cornish, George Bourne,

James Forten, S. J. May, Simeon S. Jocelyn, William Lloyd Garrison, Arnold Buffum, and George Benson.[79] The reaction to the advertisement was immediate. Meetings of the inhabitants of Canterbury were called and a committee was appointed to call on Prudence Crandall. One member of the committee told her "that by putting her design into execution, she would bring disgrace and ruin upon them all."[80] She was further warned that "the blacks of that town . . . would begin to look up and claim an equality with those who came to her school and her scholars would claim an equality with the whites. . . ."[81] This, the committee went on to point out, would be dangerous since it would mean that life and property would be in danger and "the value of property would be greatly depreciated."[82]

A public meeting was called for March 9 in Canterbury, and Samuel J. May and Arnold Buffum attended on behalf of Prudence Crandall. May was to act as her attorney and she promised to be bound by whatever agreements he might make. The three agreed that a reasonable compromise might be reached whereby her opponents would take her house, stop molesting her, and allow her some time to procure a new house, and she would move the school to a more secluded part of the town.[83]

On the night immediately preceding the town meeting, Garrison had written to George Benson, "if possible, Miss C. must be sustained at all hazards. If we suffer the school to be put down . . . other places will partake of the panic."[84] On March 12 Henry E. Benson wrote to Garrison describing the meeting of March 9 as "disgraceful proceedings."[85] A number of speeches were given and a series of resolutions laid before the meeting, but the major attack on both the school and its teacher came from Andrew T. Judson.

Judson found the very thought of "a school of nigger girls so near him . . . insupportable."[86] On the school, and on its teacher, he "vented himself in a strain of reckless hostility . . . and declared his determination to thwart the enterprise."[87] When May and Buffum tried to respond they were silenced, insulted, and even threatened with physical violence.[88] It was only after the meeting that May and Buffum were able to make themselves heard and then only briefly, for the trustees of the building asked them to leave so that the building could be closed.[89] Shortly thereafter, an article appeared in the *Norwich Republican* which was highly critical of the role of these two men and accused them of using highly charged language and reprehensible conduct.[90] The article was signed "A Friend of the Colonization Cause." On March 22 a formal petition was sent describing the events in Canterbury. Addressed to the American Colonization Society, the petition attacked Garrison and Buffum in particular and the whole abolitionist movement in general. The first signature on the petition was that of Andrew T. Judson.[91] Thus, Prudence Crandall and her school in Canterbury, Connecticut, became the vortex around which the abolitionist-colonizationist controversy swirled.

Eventually Prudence was arrested and brought to trial under a provision passed by the State Legislature forbidding the teaching of blacks who did not reside in a community without the consent in writing of the majority of the civil authority.[92] But by this time there was no real effort to run a school. The maintenance of Prudence Crandall's establishment was largely a matter of principle and an attempt to goad the citizens of Canterbury who were associated with the American Colonization Society to more and more provocative activities. All this provided grist for *The Liberator's* mill. But it could not have been easy for Prudence. Writing to Simeon Jocelyn, she indicated that the citizens of the village had met and "resolved that they would not sell anything to me or my family."[93] By April 17, 1833, the school was down to two boarders and one day scholar. "Disappointment," she wrote Reverend Jocelyn, "seems yet to be my lot."[94]

The opposition was more than Prudence had considered possible. Yet she stuck it out. She was arrested and brought to trial. Her first trial ended in a hung jury. She was retried and convicted but her case was appealed to the Court of Errors where it was quashed on technical grounds.[95]

Finally, after her house had been set afire, her well polluted, and threats made on her life, Prudence closed her school. By then she had married a Baptist minister, the Reverend Calvin Philleo, and shortly thereafter left Connecticut. But the damage had been done. After the attacks in *The Liberator,* Garrison's *Thoughts,* and the episode of the Canterbury School, the American Colonization Society would never regain the enthusiastic support it had enjoyed prior to 1830.

By 1834 the American Colonization Society had lost most of its appeal, both North and South. In the South it was considered too radical and in the North too conservative. The inability, or unwillingness, of the Society to come to grips with the criticism of the abolitionists and their insistence on behaving like gentlemen despite the ungentlemanly attacks of their opponents put them at a distinct disadvantage. Further, the Society had a fully formulated and functioning program while the abolitionists were, in the main, only preaching—thus, the Society could be attacked on specific grounds, a much more difficult task when dealing with the abolitionists, who were both capable of and willing to change their ground.

Finally, it would be difficult indeed to conceive of a scheme more likely to win supporters to the abolitionist cause than the Prudence Crandall case. The hard-hearted attacks on a single woman trying to run a school for Negro girls would have melted the hearts of the most adamant men in Canterbury itself had the school been located, and the events occurred, anywhere than in their community.

From 1832 onward, the finances of the American Colonization Society show a steady decline until 1838 when it was totally restructured.[96] In terms of its stated objective, colonization, it was never again to achieve the high point reached in 1832 when 796 persons immigrated to Liberia.[97] John L. Thomas, in his biography of Garrison, has correctly summed up the great abolitionist-colonizationist controversy from 1829 to 1834, when he writes, "In 1832, standing at the crossroads of reform, Northern opponents of slavery read Garrison's signpost and chose the road that led to emancipation."[98]

Notes

[1] *The Papers of Henry Clay,* ed. James F. Hopkins (3 vols.: Lexington, Kentucky. 1961), II, 264.

[2] P. J. Staudenraus, *The African Colonization Movement, 1816-1865* (New York, 1961), pp. 25-27.

[3] *Ibid.,* p. 29.

[4] The Papers of Henry Clay, II, 264.

[5] *Ibid.*

[6] *Ibid.*

[7] *Works of Henry Clay,* ed. by Calvin Colton (6 vols.; Henry Clay Publishing Company, 1897), V. 331.

[8] *Ibid.,* p. 333.

[9] Staudenraus, *op.cit.,* p. 30.

[10] Charles S. Sydnor, *The Development of Southern Sectionalism, 1819-1848* (Baton Rouge, 1948), pp. 96-97.

[11] Ruth Scarborough, *The Opposition to Slavery in Georgia Prior to 1860* (Nashville, Tennessee, 1933), p. 194.

[12] *Ibid.,* pp. 197-200.

[13] Alice Dana Adams, *The Neglected Period of Anti-Slavery in America,* Radcliffe College Monographs, No. 14 (Boston, 1908), p. 106.

[14] Theodore M. Whitfield, *Slavery Agitation in Virginia, 1829-1832* (Baltimore, 1930). p. 13.

[15] Adams, *loc. cit.*

[16] William W. Freehling, *Prelude to Civil War* (New York, 1966), pp. 124-25.

[17] *Ibid.,* p. 82.

[18] Staudenraus, *op. cit.,* p. viii.

[19] Benjamin Quarles, *Black Abolitionists* (New York, 1969), p. 7.

[20] *Ibid.,* p. 6.

[21] Staudenraus, *op. cit.,* p. 251.

[22] Carter G. Woodson and Charles H. Wesley, *The Negro in Our History* (11th ed.; Washington: Associated Publishers, 1966), p. 293.

[23] Henry H. Simms, *Emotion at High Tide* (Richmond, Virginia, 1960), p. 8.

[24] Wendell P. Garrison and Francis J. Garrison, *William Lloyd Garrison* (4 vols., New York, 1885-89), I, 124.

[25] *Ibid.*, p. 137.

[26] Adams, *op. cit.*, p. 2.

[27] Sydnor, *op. cit.*, p. 228. For a more detailed discussion including a list of delegates, their votes and slaveholdings classified by section and area represented, see Joseph C. Robert, *The Road from Monticello*, Historical Papers of the Trinity College Historical Society, Series XXIV (Durham, 1941).

[28] George Dangerfield, *The Awakening of American Nationalism* (New York, 1965), p. 103.

[29] William S. Jenkins, *Pro-Slavery Thought in the Old South* (Chapel Hill, 1935), p. 48.

[30] Freehling. *op. cit.*, p. 49.

[31] *Ibid.*, p. 112.

[32] David Walker, *Walker's Appeal, in Walker's Appeal & Garnet's Address*, ed. by William Loren Katz (New York, 1969), p. 37.

[33] Freehling, *op.cit.*, pp. 82-83.

[34] Sydnor, *op. cit.*, p. 223.

[35] Freehling, *loc. cit.*

[36] Merton L. Dillon, *Benjamin Lundy and the Struggle for Negro Freedom* (Urbana, 1966), p. 54.

[37] *Ibid.*, pp. 118-19.

[38] *Ibid.*, p. 144.

[39] *Ibid.*, pp. 132-33.

[40] Garrison, *op. cit.*, p. 93.

[41] Dangerfield, *loc. cit.*

[42] Garrison, *op. cit.*, p. 140.

[43] *Ibid.*, p. 143.

[44] John L. Thomas, *The Liberator* (Boston, 1963), pp. 109-110.

[45] Samuel J. May, *Recollections of our Antislavery Conflict* (Boston, 1869), p. 19.

[46] *The Liberator* (Boston), September 20, 1839.

[47] Thomas, *loc. cit.*, p. 75.

[48] *Genius of Universal Emancipation* (Baltimore), January 25, 1830, quoted in Dillon, *op. cit.*, p. 158.

[49] *The Liberator* (Boston), January 1, 1831.

[50] Thomas, *op. cit.*, pp. 131-32.

[51] Woodson, *op. cit.*, p. 183.

[52] *The Liberator* (Boston), January 8, 1831.

[53] Garrison, *op. cit.*, p. 230.

[54] *The Liberator* (Boston), January 8, 1831. It is interesting to note that in his definitive biography of Garrison, Thomas quotes only part of the first, and all of the second stanza. Thomas, *op. cit.*, pp. 133-34, implying that it is a call to violence.

[55] Quoted in Garrison, *op. cit.*, p. 247.

[56] *The Liberator* (Boston), February 12, 1831.

[57] *Ibid.*, March 24, 1831.

[58] Quoted in Garrison, *op. cit.*, pp. 261-62.

[59] *Ibid.*, 261-62 fn.

[60] *The Liberator* (Boston), March 17, 1832.

[61] *Ibid.*, March 24, 1832.

[62] *Ibid.*

[63] Staudenraus, *op. cit.*, pp. 202-203.

[64] William Lloyd Garrison, *Thoughts on African Colonization* (Boston: Garrison and Knapp, 1832).

[65] *African Repository* (Washington), November, 1832, p. 273.

[66] *Ibid.*, p. 275.

[67] *Ibid.*, p. 277.

[68] *African Repository* (Washington), January, 1833, pp. 346-47.

[69] *Ibid.*

[70] Thomas, *op. cit.*, p. 190.

[71] See, for example, Alfred Thruston Child, Jr., "Prudence Crandall and the Canterbury Experiment," *Bulletin of Friends' Historical Association*, XXII (Spring, 1933), 35-55, and Edwin W. Small and Miriam R. Small, "Prudence Crandall, Champion of Negro Education," *New England Quarterly* (December, 1944), 506-29.

[72] Garrison, *op. cit.*, pp. 315-16.

[73] Prudence Crandall Philleo to Ellen Larned, May 15, 1869. Ellen Larned Collection, Connecticut State Library, Hartford, Connecticut.

[74] *Ibid.*

[75] *Ibid.*

[76] *Ibid.*

[77] Garrison, *op. cit.*, p. 317.

[78] *The Liberator* (Boston), March 2, 1833.

[79] *Ibid.*

[80]   George W. Benson to William Lloyd Garrison, March 5, 1833, in *The Liberator* (Boston), March 9, 1833.

[81] *Ibid.*

[82] *Ibid.*

[83] May, *op. cit.*, p. 44.

[84] William Lloyd Garrison to George W. Benson, March 8, 1833. Quoted in Garrison, *op. cit.*, p. 320.

[85] Henry E. Benson to William Lloyd Garrison, March 12, 1833. Quoted in *The Liberator* (Boston), March 16, 1833.

[86] May, *op. cit.*, p. 45.

[87] *Ibid.*

[88] Ibid., pp. 45-46.

[89] *Ibid.*

[90] *Norwich Republican*, quoted in *Liberator* (Boston) April 6, 1833.

[91] *The Liberator* (Boston), April 6, 1833.

[92] May, *op. cit.*, p. 52.

[93] Prudence Crandall to Simeon Jocelyn, April 9, 1833, Manuscript Collection, Connecticut College Library.

[94] Prudence Crandall to Simeon Jocelyn, April 17, 1833, Manuscript Collection, Connecticut College Library.

[95] May, *op. cit.*, pp. 66-70.

[96] Staudenraus, *op. cit.*, p. 237.

[97] *Ibid.*, p. 251.

[98] Thomas, *op. cit.*, p. 154.

The Negro Emigration Movement, 1849-1854: A Phase of Negro Nationalism

HOWARD H. BELL

As early as the 1770s, individuals and organizations advanced schemes to deport free blacks from the United States and to establish colonies in Africa or elsewhere. Among African Americans, there was resistance to colonization and the number of blacks that migrated before 1830 remained small. The enactment of the Fugitive Slave Law and other proscriptive edicts in the mid-1800s revived interest in emigration among a growing number of free blacks. Black leaders—some of whom had either been silent on the issue or distinctly anticolonizationist in sympathy—began championing emigration as a legitimate way for African Americans to obtain freedom, dignity, and economic opportunity. Emigrationist sentiment climaxed with a plan devised by Martin Delany and approved by proponents at the National Emigration Convention of 1854.

Howard Bell's study traces the growing support for emigration among the increasingly discontented free blacks. He draws from contemporary press accounts and proceedings of state and national assemblies to describe the emigrationists' philosophy and program as well as the arguments and actions of opposing groups. The motivating spirit for emigration, described as a phase of nationalism, grew out of the unwillingness of African Americans to remain submissive to white domination, as well as their desire for economic security and independence.

DURING THE FIRST HALF of the nineteenth century free Negroes in the United States had become increasingly discontent with their lot. Through many channels they had endeavored not only to provide for the individual self-expression which they lacked but also to achieve full citizenship within the nation. As these goals continued to be unattainable, Negro leaders began to think more and more in terms of self-government. If protest and petition and political affiliation with the whites proved ineffective, then they must seek their fulfillment through the development of a unity based upon mutual interests. The hopes of the Negro had been raised by the Free Soil Party movement in 1848 only to be dashed by the enactment of the stringent Fugitive Slave Law of 1850. Increasingly proscriptive laws were being enacted in the South, while Negroes were becoming less welcome in the North. Where then might the Negro turn? Some saw the answer in a kind of racial self-government within the United States. Others, weary of the struggle for equality in America, saw the answer in emigration and the formation of a new nation where the Negro would be sovereign. This emphasis on emigration and Negro sovereignty can best be described as a kind of Negro nationalism and that nationalism was one of the dominant forces affecting the free Negroes in the decade before the Civil War.

The idea of emigration was not new to the Negro community. They had practiced it intermittently for over thirty years, but Negro leaders had not been consistent in their attitude toward the practice. Generally, the conservative and established leaders had opposed it. By 1845, however, a change was becoming apparent in the Negro's attitude toward emigration, and after that date, sons of prominent anticolonizationist leaders were often found, temporarily at least, seeking their fortunes in Liberia or Haiti or the British West Indies, or California. Visiting Liberia in 1846, William C. Cornish, son of Samuel E. Cornish, minimized the disadvantages of the climate and spoke highly of the government there.[1] Two years later Robert Douglass, son of a prominent Philadelphia minister, was in Jamaica, but found it economically inexpedient to stay long.[2] George B. Vashon, son of John B. Vashon of Pittsburgh, spent over two years in Haiti as a youth and he remembered the experience with some degree of nostalgia many years later.[3]

By 1847 the National Negro Convention at Troy, New York, was ready to listen respectfully to a plan for a commercial venture involving Negroes of Jamaica, the United States, and Africa. The proposition called for the development of a company owned and operated by people of African descent. It would exchange its own products in its own triangle trade from Jamaica to the United States to Africa.[4] This practical interest in activities closely related to emigration is noteworthy because here for the first time a national assembly of Negro leaders gave careful consideration to an African project. And in the following months there is evidence of a growing interest in emigration.

By August 1848 A. M. Sumner of Ohio was seeking passage to Africa. He believed that a sizable minority of American Negroes were seriously considering emigrating, but he was not convinced that Africa was the place to go. He intended publishing the truth about what he found, "should I live to return."[5] In September of the same year, S. S. Ball, representing Illinois Negroes, returned from Liberia, and he seems to have been favorably impressed with what he found there. Delegations returning from Africa were also reported for the states of Ohio and Kentucky.[6]

This new interest in Africa was influenced in part by the Liberian declaration of independence (1847). A Negro nation had thereby replaced the suspect American Colonization Society as chief authority in the Anglo-African settlement. Thenceforth, Liberia, like Haiti and Canada, was to be considered worthy of the respect of the American Negroes. It should not be assumed that Liberian independence was responsible for the new ideas concerning emigration. The birth of the republic fitted into and encouraged a trend that was already well under way.

Up to this time, few outstanding Negro leaders had favored emigration, but for the next fifteen years there was to be no dearth of champions of this cause. Among these new champions was Henry Highland Garnet. Educated at Oneida Institute, advocate of the political action as opposed to dependence upon moral suasion, Garnet had devoted most of his efforts during the 1840s to promoting the Liberty Party and to battling down the strongholds of the "slavocracy." Emigration to him had been strictly taboo. But by January 1849 he was publicly recognizing emigration as a legitimate means to wealth and power, and he was even willing to accept the work of the American Colonization Society insofar as it had benefited Africa.[7] A few weeks later he was urging that those dubious about advancement in America should emigrate. He supported no particular area: California, Mexico, Central America, and Liberia were all satisfactory.[8]

Martin R. Delany, editor of *The Mystery* during the 1840s, had been anticolonizationist in sympathy, but by 1849 he too was glad to see an independent Negro nation in Africa.[9] As late as 1851, however, Delany was still clinging to the belief that the American Negro should not be lured away to lands beyond the bounds of the United States, not even to Canada.[10] But in the spring of 1852 he was to come forth with a fully developed plan for a colored empire in the Caribbean area;[11] and for a decade and more thereafter he devoted his chief efforts to encouraging Negro emigration and Negro nationalism, which, in his estimation, went hand in hand. It was not until he turned in his emigration schemes for an officer's uniform in the Union Army that he was once more reconciled, temporarily at least, to living in the land of his birth. Meantime, he, like Garnet, had spent some of those years as an emigrant.

Two other men who had been active in Liberty Party circles during the 1840s transferred their activities to foreign soil in 1851. Unlike Garnet and Delany, however, they did not return to the United States for any significant length of time. Samuel R. Ward, edi-

tor of the *National Watchman*, and later of *The Impartial Citizen*, emigrated to Canada, where he established a third newspaper, *The
Provincial Freeman*. Later in the decade he moved to Jamaica, where
he died shortly before the opening of the American Civil War.[12]
Henry Bibb, poorly educated but a man of ability and of commanding bearing, preceded Ward to Canada by a few months and established the *Voice of the Fugitive*, which he edited to the time of his
death in 1854.[13] Ward and Bibb were fugitive slaves, and the Fugitive
Slave Law of 1850 has been credited with driving them beyond the
borders of the United States. But the law was not wholly responsible
since rapidly growing Negro settlements in Canada were a challenge
to men accustomed to making their living by pen and voice.

Opportunity beckoned also from England where at one time in
the early 1850s the roster of American Negro leaders included Garnet, Alexander Crummell, James W. C. Pennington, William Wells
Brown, and Ellen and William Craft.[14] Ostensibly they were there for
purely antislavery purposes, or to avoid the Fugitive Slave Law. In
most cases, however, the retreat to Europe was socially and financially
remunerative. As the period of special recognition for Negro speakers drew to a close in America, England was anxious to hear what
they had to say. The welcome accorded there and the growing difficulty of Negro leaders in securing satisfactory appointments in
America were not conducive to keeping able and amibitious speakers
at home.

And while Negro leaders bivouacked on British soil, the average
American Negro was not unaffected by the new interest in distant
places. California, long considered by Garrisonian abolitionists and by
many Negroes to be as undesirable for emigration as any other region, was reported, by 1855, to be the home of nearly five thousand
Negroes.[15] A Cincinnati meeting, under the chairmanship of E. P.
Walker, went on record as favoring emigration to Africa;[16] and newspapers reported the lectures of S. S. Ball at Springfield, Illinois, and
St. Louis, Missouri, to be favorable also.[17] Meantime, a city and
county convention at Philadelphia recorded a favorable opinion of
colonization of "Queen Victoria's Dominions."[18]

With this manifest interest in emigration, the old-line leaders
were hard-pressed in their efforts to hold the Negro community
steady. Frederick Douglass, chief spokesman for the stay-at-homes,
noted the upsurge of feeling in favor of emigration but countered it
with nothing more than the traditional protests which had been
voiced for many years.[19] In a private communication, however, he
stated:

I really fear that some whose presence in this country is necessary to the elevation of the Colored people will leave us—while the degraded and worthless will remain behind—to help bind us to our present debasement.[20]

It was inevitable that the renewed interest in emigration should be reflected in state and national assemblies. Those interested in preserving the *status quo* in New York were challenged on more than one occasion by Lewis H. Putnam who was accused of working with the American Colonization Society in an attempt to persuade free Negroes to accept expatriation to Africa. By the autumn of 1851 he and his colleagues seem to have been responsible for an organization known as the United African Republic Emigration Society.[21] On October 6, 1851, Putnam was denounced at a public meeting in New York; and a report on emigration to Liberia was refused a hearing.[22] But the emigrationists were not to be deterred. While championing Negro nationalism, they sought also to discredit those wishing to keep the Negro in America. They charged that the stay-at-homes opposed emigration "for the purpose of keeping full churches and schoolhouses, a plenty of patients, waiters, and other assistants."[23] To accomplish this end the ministers and teachers and doctors and restauranteurs, in the eyes of the emigrationists, would misrepresent the facts about advantages to be gained by leaving the United States.

Within a few months Putnam was accused of having gained Governor Washington Hunt's ear with a plea that state funds be diverted to his colonization scheme.[24] This move, and the Governor's favorable comment in his annual message,[25] created consternation among the Negro leaders bent on staying in America. On the morning that the Governor's message was made public, the Committee of Thirteen, a kind of Negro vigilante organization representing New York and Brooklyn, issued a call for a state convention to meet at Albany, January 20, 1852.[26] They also called a metropolitan area meeting for January 13, which, when assembled, listened to addresses by John J. Zuille, James McCune Smith, Samuel E. Cornish, and George Downing.[27] These men, representing the teaching, medical, ministerial, and business professions respectively, were outstanding examples of the very class that Putnam and his associates had accused of seeking to thwart the interests of the Negroes of the nation in order to safeguard their own positions of leadership.

The "state convention," called on such short notice for January 20, 1852, consisted largely of the New York delegation. They were received by Governor Hunt who accepted their address in a friendly manner. He was reported to have been favorably impressed by their arguments that the Negroes did not wish to leave their brethren in

bondage and that the colonization scheme was a fraud.[28] But the
Committee of Thirteen did not stop with the appeal to the Governor.
To the people of the state they issued an educational and propagandistic address, replete with statistical data. In this they sought to
correct alleged misconceptions of the accomplishments and ambitions of the Negro.[29]

Despite the efforts of the Committee of Thirteen, Putnam and
the new emigration society secured funds, probably through an arrangement with some of the established colonization societies. It sent
out an agent, one Abraham Cauldwell, who wrote enthusiastic and
colorful reports, with promises of houses and farming tools to settlers
who would come to Liberia: "Send me axes and I will cause the wil-
derness to bow before them and the desert to blossom as the rose,
and the sons and daughters of Africa to shout."[30] Cauldwell's second
report indicated that nine houses were already awaiting occupants
and alleged that two hours of labor per day would be as fruitful as a
whole day's work in the United States.[31] But Putnam found few who
cared to accept the invitation, and by 1853 he was again trying to
persuade various states to send their Negro population to Africa. In
so doing he ran afoul of the biting pen of James McCune Smith who
contended Putnam's god was his belly and that he would stoop to
any level to satisfy it: "He bows down before a 'ragout' with oriental
obeisance, and counts it canonized in that it will minister to that organ." Smith insisted that Putnam could enjoy the ill-gotten fruits of
his labors even while listening to the protests of free Negroes being
deprived of their homes because of his machinations.[32]

While Putnam held the center of the stage in New York, Maryland Negroes, in July 1852 were examining the problem of emigration in the state convention at Baltimore. Some residents of
Baltimore felt that the convention delegates had been selected in
such a way that decisions reached would not reflect the opinion of
the colored people generally but only that of a group already looking
to Africa. Under these circumstances, certain Balitmore Negroes set
about intimidating the delegates.[33] Although police protection was
provided, some violence ensued.[34] In fact, pressure on the convention
became so great that several representatives dropped out on the second day,[35] and by the third day even the president was "indisposed"
and had to be replaced.[36]

The chief problem before the Maryland convention was that of
emigration, and, as represented in the colonizationist press, the trend
was toward Liberia. This bent toward Liberia, if it did exist, was mate-
rially modified before the convention was over. In the end, the assembly stood for emigration, with some preference for Liberia, but with

provision for investigation of, and education on, other suitable localities. Furthermore, it was held that pending emigration the time
should not be wasted but should be utilized in securing a better
training and education at home.[37]

In Ohio where the Negro was more likely to consider emigration to Canada or the Caribbean Sea area, the forces of emigration
and Negro nationalism were strong enough by 1849 to command extensive consideration in the state convention at Columbus. An attempt to condemn emigration in the traditional manner was
answered by David Jenkins, who looked forward to the eventual emigration of all colored people. He was ably supported by John Mercer
Langston, young, well-educated, and later to become active in Republican circles, who held that he loved his freedom more than his country and that he would be happy to see the emigration of Negroes and
the establishment of a Negro nation.[38]

Eventually the matter was entrusted to a committee comprised
of Langston, W. H. Burnham, and J. L. Watson of Cleveland. Langston and Burnham agreed on a resolution calling for the Negro to
remain in the United States until the slaves were freed and then at
pleasure to withdraw from the country and form a separate nation.
But Watson, once a slave, held fast to the traditional stand against
emigration for any reason, and his minority report was approved by
the majority of the convention.[39]

Three years later (1852) Negroes met in state convention at
Cincinnati and once more grappled with the probem. Again a majority of the committee on emigration recommended leaving the country, and again a minority report presented the opposite view.[40] John
M. Langston, still an ardent advocate of emigration, spoke of the
"natural repellancy" between the races, and paradoxically, of the fear
of loss of identity if Negroes were to remain in the United States.[41]
But able speeches by Langston and others were not enough to swing
the convention in favor of emigration; the emigrationists lost by a
four-to-one ratio.[42] This decision appears to have been reasonably
representative of Negro opinion in Ohio, for only a year later Frederick Douglass, perhaps the most influential anti-emigrationist leader of
the time, estimated that one out of every four Ohio Negroes favored
emigration.[43]

The convention of 1852 was well received in Cincinnati, with at
least two of the local papers agreeing that emphasis on emigration
was well placed.[44] But the report in one of the Cleveland papers,
probably written by William H. Day, who had not yet embraced the
cause, sought to minimize the importance given to the subject on the
convention floor.[45] By 1852, however, it was impossible to disregard

an issue so much in the Negro mind, and as late as October and November there were still repercussions in the abolitionist press on the Ohio State Convention held at Cincinnati in January.[46]

Meantime Canada had continued to be the haven of refuge for many slaves fleeing from bondage and for free Negroes who had grown weary of their second-class status in the United States. Negroes of Trenton, New Jersey, held a series of meetings in 1851 with a view to the purchase of land in Canada for settlement purposes.[47] Maryland Negroes had long been interested in Canada,[48] and there was a report that in one brief period settlers had arrived in Canada from Ohio, Vermont, Pennsylvania, and the District of Columbia.[49] Henry Bibb, voicing a common opinion on the advantages of emigration, stated that "it is useless, therefore, for such of the leading colored men in the states as have been looked up to for advice, to resist the current of feeling which is prompting so many to seek to better their condition."[50] Bibb himself was serving the cause of emigration effectively through the columns of his newspaper, and only a few months after establishing the *Voice of the Fugitive* he was printing a call for a North American Convention to meet at Toronto. Included in the call was an invitation to Negroes of the United States to come to Canada.[51]

When assembled on September 9, 1851, the Toronto convention considered a plan presented by James T. Holly of Vermont, later prominent in the Haitian emigration movement. Holly's plan envisaged a North American and West Indian Federal Agricultural Union, with provision for the cooperative purchase and distribution of land in the areas listed in the title. Land thus acquired could be sold on easy terms or for cash as the needs of the individual settler might dictate.[52]

A second Canadian convention, which met at Amherstburgh in 1853, also invited United States Negroes to cross the border to a land of freedom.[53] They held that the American Negro owned no loyalty to the United States; that if emigration did not take place, revolution would; that if Canada were not an acceptable haven, than Haiti beckoned.[54]

By that time (1853) a climax was approaching. Emigrationist feeling had been pronounced since 1849, and it was motivated variously by a desire for economic opportunity or for adventure or for personal safety or for social advantage. Whatever the explicit motive, the feeling was often accompanied also by a strong desire to be rid of a second-class citizenship; and almost as often it was accompanied by a kind of Negro nationalism which refused to accept plans presented by whites for emigration or colonization of Negroes but which encouraged plans for emigration and establishment of new homes and perhaps new governments under Negro leadership. Under these circumstances those leaders who were anxious to keep the Negro community stable faced strong opposition. They were influenced, moreover, by the same abuses which had led their opponents to seek relief in emigration; they sought the same fulfillment of the desire for recognition and for self-expression; they felt the same stirrings of Negro nationalism. But they offered a different solution.

Meeting in national conclave at Rochester, New York, immediately following the Canadian convention of 1853, these established leaders of Negro society made plans for setting up a Negro National Council with supervisory authority over a Negro national college, a Negro national arbitration committee, a Negro national consumers' union, a Negro national trade and labor office, and a Negro national library and propaganda headquarters.[55] National organization on the home front—from food supply to propaganda and from education to semi-judicial decisions—was the answer of the traditional leaders to the challenge of the emigrationists. In their effort to keep the Negro community stable they had themselves resorted to a kind of Negro nationalism. They had created what one of their opponents described as "an informal national organization of a denationalized people, whereby an organic, though premature and sickly birth was given to the idea of national independence."[56]

The emigrationists, momentarily checked by the action of the stay-at-homes, were quick to regain the initiative. They issued a call for a national emigration convention to meet at Cleveland, Ohio, in August 1854. Those opposed to emigrating from the United States were not invited; even supporters of the American Colonization Society with its emphasis on Africa were warned that they would not be welcome. The convention was to be devoted solely to developing plans for emigrating to Canada, the West Indies, or Central America[57]—areas close enough to encourage run-away slaves to seek safety in their midst. For the present, emigration to more distant places must be postponed.

The largest single delegation came from Pittsburgh, Pennsylvania. Michigan and Ohio were well represented; and a half dozen other states, as well as Canada, also sent delegates.[58] Officers of the convention included William C. Monroe, president, and several vice-presidents among whom were the Right Reverend William Paul Quinn and Mrs. Mary Bibb, wife of Henry Bibb, recently deceased. Martin R. Delany headed the strategic business committee.[59]

This assembly had been called with the understanding that those opposed to emigration would not have a hearing. However,

John M. Langston, no longer an advocate of emigration, was invited to speak. "In a lengthy and rhetorical speech, replete with classic elegance," he stated his opposition. Such defection could not be tolerated, and H. F. Douglass replied with "withering sarcasm."[60] He accused Langston of inconsistency; he championed emigration; and he held for Negro nationalism. He maintained that the emigrationist was interested, not in the individual, but in the group; that Langston and his kind were selfish for staying at home. He denounced his own American citizenship and stated that he would gladly fight against the nation in order to secure the future of the race.[61] The public scorn which had been heaped on the Negro emigrationists in the 1830s had come full circle in the National Emigration Convention of 1854.

The philosophy of the emigrationists was embodied in a lengthy report, "Political Destiny of the Colored Race," read by Martin R. Delany and accepted by the convention. It denied both the citizenship and the freedom of the American Negro and contended that freedom existed only where a racial group constituted a majority; it approved emigration to the Caribbean area via Canada as a way station; and it warned that the rights withheld by a majority were never freely given but must be seized. On the other hand, the emigrationists were far from being convinced that they would have to deal forever with white supremacy: "The white races are but one-third of the population of the globe—or one of them to two of us—and it cannot much longer continue, that two-thirds will passively submit to the universal domination of this one-third."[62]

The convention approved of Delany's plan first published in 1852 which called for temporary emigration to Canada en route to the Caribbean and a Negro empire, or rather, an empire of the colored peoples in the tropical areas of the Western Hemisphere.[63] They were well satisfied with what they had started. They claimed credit for being the first colored organization in the nation to develop a satisfactory plan for the uplift of the race.[64] They spoke of their work as "equal to the duration of a season, and of vastly more importance than [that of] any other similar body of colored people ever assembled in the United States."[65] The spoke with pride of their heritage from Africa and they looked forward to the time and place of redemption from their semi-bondage beyond United States boundaries. One sympathetic editor caught the motivating spirit of the movement for emigration—and for Negro nationalism—when he wrote:

> It is a gallant faith (and not without data to rest upon) which prompts the manly declaration, 'I believe it to be the destiny of the Negro to develope a higher order of civilization and Christianity,

than the world has yet seen.' When any considerable number of black men come to a true and sublime faith in such a destiny, their lives will soon begin to compel the world to award them some praise.[66]

In final analysis, the National Emigration Convention and the whole emigration movement represented minority action in 1854. But that minority was strong enough to command wide respect. The established leaders were hard pressed in the middle 1850s to keep their fellows interested in remaining in the United States. The old order was fighting a defensive action against the newer concept of emigration and the establishment of a new nation beyond the bounds of the United States.

Notes

[1] *The African Repository and Colonial Journal,* October, 1846, pp. 303-4. Organ of the American Colonization Society. Hereafter cited as *African Repository.*

[2] *The North Star,* June 2, 1848. Edited and published by Frederick Douglass. The name of the paper was later changed to *Frederick Douglass' Paper,* and in 1860 the weekly gave way to a monthly edition.

[3] *Douglass' Monthly,* October, 1862, pp. 727-28.

[4] *Proceedings of the National Convention of Colored People, and Their Friends, Held in Troy, N[ew] Y[ork] on 6th, 7th, 8th, and 9th October, 1847* (Troy, N[ew] Y[ork]: J. C. Kneeland & C[ompany], 1847), pp. 21-25.

[5] *African Repository,* August, 1848, pp. 243-44.

[6] *Ibid.,* pp. 261-63.

[7] *The North Star,* January 26, 1849.

[8] *Ibid.,* March 2, 1849.

[9] *Ibid.*

[10] *Voice of the Fugitive,* September 24, 1851. Edited and published by the fugitive slave, Henry Bibb, in Canada.

[11] Martin R. Delany, *The Condition, Elevation, and Destiny of the Colored People of the United States, Politically Considered* (Philadelphia: printed by King and Baird, 1852). Hereafter cited as Delany, *Condition, Elevation, and Destiny.*

[12] See *ibid.,* p. 112 for notice of Ward's move to Canada. Ward's death in Jamaica is recorded in Carter G. Woodson, *The History of the Negro Church* (Washington, D. C.: The Associated Publishers [c. 1921]), p. 183.

[13] Bibb was dead by August 1854, when his widow, Mrs. Mary Bibb, participated in the national emigration convention at Cleveland. See *Proceedings of the National Emigration Convention of Colored People; Held at Cleveland, Ohio, on Thursday, Friday and Saturday, the 24th, 25th and 26th of August, 1854. With a Reference Page of Contents* (Pittsburgh: A. A. Anderson, 1854), pp. 7-8. Hereafter cited as *National Emigration Convention, 1854.*

[14] *Frederick Douglass' Paper,* July 13, 1851.

[15] *Proceedings of the First State Convention of the Colored Citizens of the State of California, Held at Sacramento Nov[ember] 20th[,] 21st and 22d, in the Colored Methodist Church* (Sacramento: *Democratic State Journal,* 1855), p. 18.

[16] *African Repository,* July, 1850, p. 219.

[17] *The Impartial Citizen,* September 27, 1851. Edited and published by Samuel R. Ward at Boston and elsewhere before Ward went to Canada.

[18] *The Pennsylvania Freeman,* May 2, 1850.

[19] *Frederick Douglass' Paper*, July 31, 1851.

[20] Frederick Douglass to Gerrit Smith, January 21, 1851, in Gerrit Smith Miller Collection.

[21] *African Repository*, November, 1851, pp. 322-24; *New York Colonization Journal*, December, 1851, p. [2]. The name of the society seems later to have been changed to The Liberia Agricultural and Emigrating Association. However, some confusion exists in the whole matter since there was mention of the Liberia Agricultural Association as early as March, 1851. For this last reference see the *National Anti-Slavery Standard*, March 27, 1851.

[22] *Frederick Douglass' Paper*, November 13, 1851.

[23] *African Repository*, January, 1852, pp. 4-8.

[24] *National Anti-Slavery Standard*, January 22, 1852.

[25] *New York Colonization Journal*, January, 1852, p. 2.

[26] *Frederick Douglass' Paper*, January 15, 22, 1852.

[27] *New York Herald*, January 15, 1852; *National Anti-Slavery Standard*, January 22, 1852.

[28] *The Liberator*, March 5, 1852; *National Anti-Slavery Standard*, January 29, 1852; *Frederick Douglass' Paper*, February 12, 1852.

[29] *The Pennsylvania Freeman*, February 26, 1852; *New York Herald*, January 29, 1852.

[30] *African Repository*, August, 1852, pp. 234-37.

[31] *New York Daily Tribune*, December 1, 1852.

[32] *Ibid.*

[33] *The (Baltimore) Sun*, July 27, 28, 29, 1852.

[34] *Ibid.*, July 27, 1852.

[35] *Ibid.*, July 28, 1852.

[36] *Ibid.*, July 29, 1852.

[37] *Ibid.*

[38] *Minutes and Address of the State Convention of the Colored Citizens of Ohio, Convened at Columbus, January 10th, 11th, 12th, and 13th, 1849* (Oberlin: J. M. Fitch, 1849), pp. 7-8.

[39] *Ibid.*, pp. 11, 13.

[40] *Proceedings of the Convention of the Colored Freemen of Ohio, Held in Cincinnati, January 14, 15, 16, 17 and 19* [1852] (Cincinnati: Dumas and Lawyer, 1852), p. 9. Hereafter cited as *Negro State Convention, Ohio*, 1852.

[41] *Daily Cincinnati Gazette*, January 15, 19, 1852.

[42] *Negro State Convention, Ohio*, 1852, p. 2.

[43] *Frederick Douglass' Paper*, October 28, 1853.

[44] *Cincinnati Daily Nonpareil*, January 16, 1852; *Daily Cincinnati Gazette*, January 15, 1852.

[45] *Morning Daily True Democrat* (Cleveland), January 24, 1852.

[46] *The Liberator*, October 22, 1852; *Frederick Douglass' Paper*, October 22, 1852.

[47] *Voice of the Fugitive*, April 9, 1851.

[48] *The Liberator*, August 20, 1852.

[49] *Voice of the Fugitive*, June 17, 1852.

[50] *Ibid.*

[51] *Ibid.*, July 30, 1851; *The Pennsylvania Freeman*, August 28, 1851.

[52] *Voice of the Fugitive*, December 3, 1851; *The Pennsylvania Freemen*, October 23, 1851; *National Anti-Slavery Standard*, October 2, 1851.

[53] *Minutes and Proceedings of the General Convention for the Improvement of the Colored Inhabitants of Canada, Held by Adjournments in Amherstburgh, C[anada] W[est] June 16th and 17th, 1853* (Windsor, C[anada] W[est]: Bibb and Holly, 1853), pp. 7-11.

[54] *Ibid.*, pp. 11-16.

[55] *Proceedings of the Colored National Convention, Held in Rochester, July 6th, 7th and 8th, 1853* (Rochester: printed at the office of *Frederick Douglass' Paper*, 1853).

[56] [M. T. Newsome (comp.)], *Arguments, Pro and Con, on the Call for a National Emigration Convention, to be held in Cleveland, Ohio, August 1854, by Frederick Douglass, W. J. Watkins, and James M. Whitfield. With a Short Appendix of the Statistics of Canada West, West Indies, Central and South America* (Detroit: George E. Pomeroy and Company, [1854]), pp. 3-4.

[57] *Ibid.*, pp. [5]-7.

[58] *National Emigration Convention, 1854,* pp. 16-18.

[59] *Cleveland Morning Leader,* August 25, 1854; *The Daily Cleveland Herald,* August 25, 1854.

[60] *National Emigration Convention, 1854,* p. 13.

[61] [H. F. Douglass], *Speech of H. Ford Douglass, in Reply to Mr. J. M. Langston before the Emigration Convention, at Cleveland, Ohio, Delivered on the Evening of the 27th of August, 1854* (Chicago, William H. Worell, 1854), pp. [3]-14.

[62] *National Emigration Convention, 1854,* pp. 33-63. The quotation occurs on p. 41.

[63] Delany, *Condition, Elevation, and Destiny,* pp. 179-89.

[64] *National Emigration Convention, 1854,* p. 5.

[65] *Ibid.*, p. 15.

[66] *The Columbian,* January 4, 1854.

The Inevitability of the Douglass-Garrison Conflict

TYRONE TILLERY

Two personalities predominate in the annals of American antislavery thought: William Lloyd Garrison and Frederick Douglass. From 1839, both men worked side by side for the cause of immediate emancipation. Articulating his personal experience as human chattel and his hatred of slavery to audiences both in the United States and abroad, Douglass rapidly ascended as a brilliant thinker and orator in the 1840s, becoming one of the preeminent spokespersons for the abolition movement. By 1847 Douglass's establishment of the North Star, *and the growing rift between him and Garrison, set the stage for Douglass to emerge as an independent leader in the struggle for the freedom of black Americans.*

In chronicling the rise and fall of the relationship between Douglass and Garrison, Tyrone Tillery argues the inevitability of the rupture in their association, delineating the conflict through the ideological differences, as well as the disparate experiences and needs of both men. From Tillery's perspective, Douglass's personal familiarity with the horrors of slavery and his need for independent self-expression in promoting the goals of immediate abolition and full integration of blacks into American society accounted for differences in principles and tactics employed by the two men and placed them on an inevitable collision course. Denounced as an "infidel" by Garrison after 1851, Douglass nevertheless provided a powerful voice for human rights for nearly a half century more.

FROM THE FOUNDING of the American Anti-Slavery Society in 1833 abolitionism was marred by constant intra-group disagreements. Within seven years the movement split itself into two camps, one headed by William Lloyd Garrison and the other commanded by such personalities as the Tappans, James G. Birney, Gerrit Smith and Joshua Leavitt. Ten years later another schism occurred which involved two groups disagreeing on proper tactics to employ in the abolition of slavery. The rupture of 1851 was the sole product of two personalities, William Lloyd Garrison and Frederick Douglass.

Studies of the Douglass-Garrison controversy have attributed the conflict to either the consequence of misunderstood events, beginning with the establishment of Douglass's *North Star* in 1847 and his subsequent betrayal of Garrisonian principles in 1851, or the result of the ambivalence of white abolitionists toward Negroes. For despite the "Clique's public and ardent campaign against overt discrimination, they displayed both a social distaste and an underlying distrust of the individual Negroes they encountered."[1] Both views are correct, but only as contributory factors. Closer examination of the conflict suggests that the split between Garrison and Douglass was inevitable. The conflict developed not from events beginning in 1847, but from circumstances which had created two individuals, each with his own personal needs, ideologies and ambitions.

Frederick Douglass's free life began sometime in September, 1838. But the exultant joy resulting from his new status was short-lived. He soon discovered, upon reaching New York, that even here he was not beyond the power of the slaveholders.[2] Confused and unsure of anything except that "no man would ever have the right to call him slave, or assert mastery over him," Douglass sought refuge in a city where even black people would betray him for a few dollars.[3] Finally, in desperation, Douglass confided in a sailor who put him in touch with David Ruggles, secretary of the New York Vigilance Committee. While hidden in Ruggles' office, Douglass was joined by his future wife, Anna. Twelve days later the two were married and moved to New Bedford, Massachusetts, with only five dollars in his pocket.[4]

But Douglass's financial situation did little to detract from the enthusiasm of being free. The privilege of freedom acted to stimulate Douglass's awareness of becoming his own man. In his words, "you may hurl a man so low, beneath the level of his kind, that he loses all just ideas of his natural position: but elevate him a little, and the clear conception of rights rises to life and power, and leads him onward."[5] Freedom gave Douglass the clear conception he needed and by 1838 he was psychologically ready to become his own master.

Yet, while Douglass may have been psychologically ready to become his own master, in 1838 he had neither the ways nor the means to accomplish it. Still a fugitive, he was in constant danger of being recognized by pro-slavery men. And since slavery demanded the complete ignorance of its chattels for fear knowledge would teach them to throw off their yoke, Douglass had been denied the opportunity of a formal education.[6] Nevertheless, the urgings for self-expression found Douglass seeking membership in the Methodist church. When he found that he could attend white Methodist churches only under humiliating conditions, he joined a small sect of his own race and soon became a leading member.[7] Thus, early in Douglass's free life he learned the shortcomings of working in a white organization, a lesson that would be of immense value in his decision to start a Negro newspaper.

But of all the avenues which afforded Douglass the opportunity to exploit his dormant powers of oratorical and intellectual expression, his introduction to the abolitionist movement *vis-a-vis* the Garrisonian wing was the most fruitful. Six months after reaching New Bedford he became a subscriber to Garrison's paper, and given Douglass's limited achievements in self-expression, the *Liberator* provided him the first opportunity to hear articulated those feelings he held toward the institution of slavery. In the words of Douglass,

> . . . Mr. Garrison, and his paper took a place in my heart second only to the Bible. It detested slavery, and made no truce with the traffickers in the bodies and souls of men. It preached human brotherhood, it exposed hypocrisy and wickedness in high places: it denounced oppression, and with all the solemnity of "Thus saith the Lord," demanded complete emancipation of my race. He seemed to me, an all-sufficient match for every opponent, whether they spoke in the name of the law or the gospel. His words were full of holy fire, and straight to the point.[8]

For seven years following his introduction to Garrison in 1839, Douglass would echo the Garrisonian principles and philosophy. In the capacity of a lecturer, a title which meant little more than the descriptive narration of his life as a slave, Douglass was invited to join the Massachusetts Anti-Slavery Society. As the prize exhibit Douglass traveled with other abolitionists telling the story of his slave experiences. During the first three or four months Douglass's speeches were almost exclusively made up of narrations of his own personal experiences. He was just to give the facts and the white abolitionists would give the philosophy.[9] But Douglass quickly tired of these mechanical maneuvers, for freedom had given him a license to think. As he wrote in his autobiography,

> I could not always follow the injunction, for I was now reading and thinking. New views of the subject were being presented to my mind. It did not entirely satisfy me to narrate wrongs: I felt like denouncing them. I could not always curb my moral indignation for the perpetrators of slaveholding villainy, long enough for a circumstantial statement of the facts, which I felt sure everybody must know. Besides, I was growing, and needed room.[10]

For some time the Garrisonians failed to see that Douglass's talents lay not in his being an escaped slave but in a wide range of abilities. But events rapidly illustrated how seriously he had been underrated. The winter and spring of 1842 found Douglass stumping through eastern and central Massachusetts in the company of Garrison, Samuel J. May, Charles Remond and the Hutchinsons, a musically self-trained family that sang anti-slavery songs.[11] It is significant that on this tour Douglass had not only aroused enthusiasm but made color enviable.[12] Writing to Garrison from Northbridge, a veteran abolitionist observed, "It has been my fortune to hear a great many anti-slavery lecturers and many distinguished speakers on other subjects: but it has rarely been my lot to listen to one whose power over me was greater than Douglass's, and not over me only, but over all who heard him."[13] Apparently, Douglass had already outgrown the limits Garrison had set for him. He no longer merely narrated or imitated Garrison and by 1843 Douglass was criticizing his colleagues when he felt they were not following Garrisonian guidelines.

One such instance occurred while Douglass was accompanying colleagues Charles Remond, Abby Kelley, John Collins, Sidney Gay and George Bradburn on an anti-slavery tour in the West. From the beginning the tour had been hamstrung by a series of difficulties. But none of the difficulties irritated Douglass more than his discovery that John Collins had been using anti-slavery meetings for the promotion of "Fourierism," a peculiar variety of utopian socialism. He criticized Collins for using abolitionism in order to promote his socialism.[14] But upon reporting the incident to the Board of Managers in Massachusetts, Douglass, not Collins, received the reprimand. The reasons given for the reprimand were not primarily the criticizing of a "white" colleague but, as Douglass later admitted ". . . was the use which the Liberty Party papers would make of my seemingly rebellion against the commanders of our Anti-Slavery Army."[15] In the end it was Collins who resigned but the incident had also begun to show Douglass that the "growing room" he needed would be difficult to come by in the Garrisonian wing of the abolitionist party. What Douglass felt as a result of the reprimand is significant in understanding his split with the party later. As Douglass recalled, "This was a strange and distressing revelation to me, and one of which I was not soon relieved."[16]

Douglass' rapid development as a brilliant thinker and orator had caused much concern among his abolitionist friends. Instead of being proud that this former Negro slave had been able in a short time to equal and even surpass many of the white spokesmen against slavery, they were worried by it and even resented it.[17] In a few years Douglass would become fully aware that jealousy, power and envy could take priority over principles.

Despite the resentment on the part of the Boston Garrisonians, Douglass continued to develop his talents, both as an orator and as a writer. With the publication of his *Narrative of the Life of Frederick Douglass* in 1845, Douglass had proven beyond a doubt that here was a man of extraordinary talents.[18] When he departed for his first trip abroad in the same year, people could only echo Wendell Phillips when he said, "If you ever see him, Remember that in my opinion, you see the most remarkable and by far the ablest colored man we have ever had here." It is reported that Phillips told Douglass to be himself and he would succeed; but as Phillip Foner put it, "Not even Phillips dreamed that success would reach such heights. His European visit gave Douglass international reputation. He returned to the States a world figure, a mighty power for freedom."[19]

Barring a few unpleasantries on board the *Cambria*, Douglass's trip to England was an unqualified success. Not only had the reception by the English people been overwhelming, but the stay in England provided Douglass with the intellectual and physical growing room heretofore denied him in America. For the first time Douglass was exposed to a wide range of reform movements. Initially Douglass resisted the lure of the new intellectual freedom, but soon he became convinced that it was impossible to divide the struggle against oppression into separate compartments.[20] In one of Douglass's most prophetic remarks he explained to Garrison,

> . . . though I am more closely connected and identified with one class of outrage, oppressed and enslaved people, I cannot allow myself to be insensible to the wrongs and suffering of any part of the great family of man. I am not only an American slave, but a man, and as such, am bound to use my powers for the welfare of the whole human brotherhood.[21]

Undoubtedly, the spirit of freedom in the British Isles had influenced Douglass's thinking not only on American slavery but also on a variety of other subjects. He was especially impressed in Ireland by what he called "the spirit of freedom that seems to animate all with whom I come in contact—and the entire absence of everything that looked like prejudice against me, on account of the color of my skin—contrasting so strongly with my long and bitter experience in the United States, that I look with wonder and amazement on the transition."[22]

The influence had become evident following a second confrontation with Maria Chapman, leader of the Boston Female Anti-Slavery Society. On this occasion she had impugned Douglass's integrity by cautioning Richard Webb, an Irish abolitionist, to keep an eye on

Douglass, "lest he might be bought up by the London committee."[23] As if symbolic of the changes which had occurred in him, Douglass sharply rebuked Maria Chapman for her insinuations and threatened to leave the Anti-Slavery Society if its members attempted to supervise his activities.[24] For the second time the Boston board had attempted to circumscribe Douglass's activities as an equal in the abolitionist movement. But Douglass had clearly arrived at the level of development where he would not only think for himself on major issues confronting the anti-slavery movement, but would also challenge the abolitionist leaders when he believed they were wrong. This was further illustrated by his sharp criticism of the American temperance movement for failing to include the abolition of slavery within the pale of its activities.[25] The American delegates were furious and the Reverend Samuel Cox delivered a broadside against Douglass. Douglass's rebuttal completely destroyed Cox's argument and his position won him friends on both sides of the Atlantic.[26] Even Garrison issued a statement defending Douglass's reply.[27]

Of all the events that seemed to herald the split between Douglass and Garrison, none could have been more symbolic than the purchase of Douglass's freedom by his English friends late in 1846. Considerable resentment and disappointment was voiced against it by his abolitionist friends, as they had come to believe that the purchase was tacit recognition of the "right to traffic in human beings."[28] Typical of such feelings was a statement by Henry C. Wright in a letter addressed to Douglass:

> I cannot bear to think of you as being a party to such transactions, even by silence. If others will take that paper and keep it as an evidence of your freedom, you cannot prevent them, but I wish you would see it your duty, publicly to disown the deed, and never to recognize that hateful Bill![29]

He also added that if Douglass refused he would never write him again.[30] In vain Douglass tried to explain to his abolitionist friends that his acceptance of the transaction was justified in light of what he termed the distinction between "natural freedom" and "legal freedom." His purchase only satisfied the legal freedom requirement.[31]

Nevertheless, Douglass returned to America a free man. His tour in England had firmly established him not only as the premier speaker for black people, but also as an important spokesman for the abolitionist movement. Before departing, Douglass had been offered a substantial sum of money for the purpose of starting his own paper. But again Douglass met opposition from the Garrisonians. Garrison argued that there were already in existence a number of Negro journals, hence there would be no surprise attached to the appearance of a periodical handled ably by a colored man. Besides, it was doubtful that Douglass would be able to secure enough subscriptions. Garrison also suggested that a venture into journalism would destroy his status as a lecturer.[32] Douglass retreated and temporarily put aside his plans for publication. However, a number of letters poured into the *Liberator* expressing regret that he had decided to postpone his venture. Many letters went so far as to accuse Douglass's opponents of fear. For example, one letter exclaimed, "those who fear Mr. Douglass's editorial duties would withdraw him from the field as a lecturer would do well to remember that the editor of the *Liberator* devoted much time to lecturing in parts of the country, and his editorials are none the less prompt, spirited and plentiful."[33] One letter to Garrison predicted that if published Douglass's paper would "within one year have a greater subscription list than any other anti-slavery paper."[34] And it continued, "is it possible that you and others are fearful that the *Liberator* and the *Standard* will suffer in consequence?"[35]

Douglass published an unconvincing statement denying that he had been coerced by the "Boston Board."[36] But within a month the *Anti-Slavery Standard* announced Douglass would become a permanent columnist for the paper.[37]

Douglass had acquiesced, but not for long; by October rumors spread that he had decided to start his newspaper in Cleveland.[38] However, on November 5, 1847, the *Liberator* announced Douglass was establishing the *North Star* in Rochester.[39] Douglass had decided the time had come for him to rely on his own abilities, proved and potential.[40] Furthermore, he had resolved that a journal excellently managed and edited by a Negro would be a powerful evidence that Negroes were too much men to be chattels.[41] Douglass's reversal of his earlier decision angered many of his abolitionist colleagues; but none was more vexed than Garrison, who considered Douglass's conduct about the paper "highly inconsistent with his decision in Boston."[42] Garrison's accusation seemed based more on fear than on fact. Early in 1847 two incidents aroused his suspicions of Douglass's loyalty. The first happened during his tour with Douglass soon after Douglass returned from Europe. The hardships encountered on the trip, rain, malarial weather, and crowded engagements, had physically drained Garrison. He took ill on September 13, and could not continue with the tour. Douglass offered to remain with his co-worker but Garrison urged he go on with the tour. When learning that Garrison's condition had deteriorated, Douglass reproached himself for leaving him. Slowly Garrison recuperated and accused Douglass of not being concerned about his health, apparently ignoring a letter from Samuel May describing Douglass's sorrow and suspense over his

illness.[43] Perhaps Garrison had become uneasy over the recent sentiments drawn up in a meeting held by black people of Philadelphia
honoring Douglass and Garrison. The sentiment had proclaimed
Douglass "the staunch advocate of Liberty in which time could never
erase the memory of so great a champion." Garrison, on the other
hand, had only been proclaimed the "first to cry hold to the tyrants
of the South."[44]

With the establishment of *The North Star*, Garrison was sure
Douglass's actions reflected "pure infidelity." Undeterred by Garrison's attitude, Douglass continued to publish his paper, and Garrison's disappointment did not prevent him from permitting his paper
to praise the new weekly. In fact, on numerous occasions Garrison's
paper had reprinted articles by Douglass supporting a particular view
on slavery.[45] Douglass kept in contact with Garrison, often lauding
Garrison's achievements to the movement. He and Garrison frequently met at the annual meetings of the American Anti-Slavery Society; but the old camaraderie was gone, and after 1851 the
relationship was in shambles. At that time Douglass publicly announced a fundamental change in his political views.

Since Douglass joined the abolitionist movement he had endorsed the basic theories of the Garrisonian school. One such theory
involved Garrison's view of the Constitution and politics. The Constitution, as Garrison saw it, was a pro-slavery document. And after 1844
the Garrisonians resolved to be non-political and non-voting to insure
"No Union with the Slaveholders."[46] As editor of *The North Star*,
Douglass's views on the subject gradually underwent a change. Being
away from the scrutinizing eyes of the "Boston Board" gave him the
opportunity to observe what other Anti-Slavery men were doing. The
impact of this freedom to independently explore other schools of
thought was reflected in Douglass's ideas on the Constitution. By
March, 1848, Douglass had clearly exhibited signs of confusion and
uncertainty as to the true nature of the Constitution. In the *North
Star* he argued, "that the Constitution of the United States, standing
alone and construed only in the light of its letter without reference
to the opinions of the men who framed and adopted it, or to the
uniform universal and undeviating practice of the nation under it,
from the time of its adoption until now is not a pro-slavery instrument."[47] He did, however, qualify his statement by pointing out that
it did contain features which supported slavery.[48]

Douglass's comments on the Constitution in 1848 were not the
only signs of a radical departure from Garrisonian principles. Frequently Douglass had shown interest in anti-slavery political parties.
In June, 1847, he attended the National Liberty Party convention in

Buffalo and the next year supported it in *The North Star*. He praised the Liberty Party for giving merits to black people.[49] Later that year he also gave credit to the Free Soil Party as a challenge to the slave-holding parties during the Wilmot Proviso escapade.[50] As Douglass saw it: "The intelligence, moral worth and philanthropy and numerical strength assumed by this party makes it our duty to inquire what courses those who stand forth as friends of the slave ought to pursue towards that Party."[51]

Furthermore, Douglass added, the Liberty Party supported many of the same goals as the abolitionists. Like the abolitionists they believed Congress should abolish slavery wherever they possessed the constitutional powers to do so and to free the government from all responsibility for slavery by abolishing all slave trade and declaring no more slave states or slavery in the territories.[52] While Douglass had not relinquished his belief that moral reform should be regarded as the real anti-slavery tactic in favor of anti-slavery political groups,[53] he had arrived at the conclusion that it was his duty to pursue any course which would make anti-slavery advocates, in some degree, a terror to evil-doers.[54]

Step by step Douglass came to believe that the Constitution was not a pro-slavery document and that there was no need to dissolve the Union. He had now substituted Garrison's "No union with slave-holders" for his "No union with slaveholding."[55] At the eighteenth annual meeting of the American Anti-Slavery Society held in Syracuse in May, 1851, Douglass shocked the Garrisonian abolitionists by opposing a proposition not to support any newspaper that did not assume the Constitution to be a pro-slavery document. Douglass protested that the Constitution "might be consistent in its details with the noble purpose avowed in its preamble."[56] Immediately Garrison exclaimed, "there is roguery somewhere," and moved to have *The North Star* stricken from the list; and this was promptly done by the convention. In one instant Douglass had become a heretic.[57]

In vain Douglass denied he had become a renegade. Shortly, accusations that his change in political views was due more to his recent merger with the Liberty Party paper than a sincere conversion came from Garrison's friends. After the initial accusations, issues ceased being the center of the controversy and verbal warfare ensued between Douglass and his opponents. The verbal conflagration reached its height when Garrison insinuated Douglass was having an affair with Julia Griffiths, Douglass's white secretary. Between Douglass and Garrison the die had been cast and the split was now complete.[58]

The split between Douglass and Garrison had finally occurred but the narrative alone fails to completely reveal the complex forces behind it. The events following 1847 were only the symptoms of the disease. For instance, the narrative fails to show that slavery had a profound influence in making the conflict not only probable but inevitable. Slavery had produced certain personality traits in Douglass that would sooner or later cause a collision with Garrison. Contrary to what some historians suggest, Garrison and Douglass were not as similar as they appear; although both men had forceful personalities, and both had come from extremely humble origins, which acted as an impetus to aspire to prominent positions,[59] humble origins and slavery are two very different experiences. In the first place, slavery had provided Douglass with a "sense of the urgency of constant change," the most immediate being the abolition of slavery. And for a change as great as this, a philosophy peculiarly suited for it would have to be found. Such a philosophy could only be found in pragmatism, in which the means justified the ends. Or as Douglass said it, "any measure is vindicated by its results."[60]

It would be hard to believe Douglass had not been influenced by this consideration in his dealings with the Garrisonians. The American Anti-Slavery Society provided Douglass with the most immediate means of achieving his goal, the abolition of slavery. He had adopted Garrison's principles primarily because they seemed at the time to be great and important truths.[61] But as other schools of thought came within his grasp, Douglass was impelled to broaden and even reconsider his views. For Douglass, Garrisonianism necessarily conflicted with his pragmatic nature. Garrisonian abolitionists were narrow and ignored the economic laws and the complexity of social relationships.[62] Their position of undeviating denunciation and negation lacked a permanent appeal to Douglass.[63] Garrison's promiscuous vilification of all individuals, institutions and beliefs he did not agree with made compromise, the necessary corollary to pragmatism, impossible.[64] Through his reading of abolitionist history Douglass had come to the conclusion that Garrison had not begun the movement, or discovered its ideas, nor framed its argument. His only contribution had been the introduction of "immediate emancipation."[65] As Douglass read the history of the abolitionists perhaps he also discovered that there was no historical precedent for the belief that moral suasion could force slaveholders to emancipate their slaves. And in the final outcome it was war and not moral suasion that abolished slavery. In the end Douglass came to regard his affiliation with Garrison as "a dangerous error."[66]

At times Douglass's pragmatism and propensity to change gave the appearance of inconsistency. In 1846 he opposed using force as a means to abolish slavery. To a large peace convention in London he exclaimed, "that nothing can be attained for liberty universally by war, that were I to be asked the question as to whether I would have my emancipation by shedding one single drop of blood my answer would be in the negative."[67] Yet, two years later Douglass was advocating "that slaveholders as a being had forfeited all rights by annihilating all the rights of others. They had no rightful existence on earth."[68] In part Douglass's change was attributed to a visit with John Brown. Brown's argument was that moral suasion would never free slaves and that no people could gain self-respect or be respected who would not fight for their freedom. This was a point too difficult for "common sense" to ignore.[69] Clearly, Douglass's change had been from necessity. No statement better expressed this view than Douglass's article on the wisdom of killing a slaveholder. He commented, "Is it right and wise to kill a Kidnapper. Depends on whether it can be reconciled by showing it not only reasonable but a necessity. Life therefore is but a means to an end. . . ."[70] A similar kind of reasoning had been used in his apparent inconsistency towards the Constitution and the establishment of *The North Star*. What Garrison perceived as an inconsistency was very consistent with Douglass's personality.

If slavery had produced in Douglass's personality a "sense of the need for change," it had also given him the basis for an ideology which again conflicted with Garrison's. Douglass's primary goals had not only been the abolition of slavery but also the integration of black people into the mainstream of American life. Black people should strive to cultivate good character, to be thrifty and industrious, and to acquire as much property as possible.[71] The accumulation of this wealth would be achieved through industrial education of training in mechanical trades. Preferably the schools would be "White institutions, not because they are White but because they afforded a more convenient means of improvement."[72]

Underlying the morals and economic program was the theme of individual and racial self-help that in turn overlapped with an ideology of racial solidarity—of racial cooperation and racial unity.[73] Douglass took pride in being a self-made man. A year after he established *The North Star* he wrote, "Strength comes from contest with difficulties; and although encouragement may be needful to some, obstacles are fine stimulants to others."[74] His belief in racial solidarity had been one of his primary reasons for establishing *The North Star*. As Douglass put it in an article in that publication:

It is scarcely necessary for us to say that our desire to occupy our present position, is neither a reflection on the fidelity, nor the despairment of the ability of our friends and fellow-laborers to assert what "common sense" affirms and only folly denies, that the man to demand redress,—that the man struck is the man to cry out—and that he who had endured the cruel pangs of slavery is the man to advocate liberty.[75]

Douglass knew that "Facts are Facts, White is not Black, and Black is not White. There is neither good sense nor common honesty in trying to forget this distinction."[76] Douglass had also known that blacks were excluded from policy-making decisions in the abolitionist movement. His appointment as temporary president of the American Anti-Slavery Society Convention in 1847 had only been "tokenism."[77] With Douglass's sense of awareness, he obviously knew that many of the white abolitionists subscribed to what Stanley Elkins has labeled the "Sambo" image of Negroes.

This ideology of racial solidarity and the question of whether or not to form separate organizations caused considerable division and argument among articulate nineteenth century Negroes. Even Douglass opposed the idea of separate churches. He felt they only encouraged segregation, increased the feeling of superiority in the minds of white children and encouraged a sense of inferiority in the minds of black children.[78] Unfortunately, many blacks who had lived their entire lives in a white milieu found it impossible to accept any kind of organization entirely Negro. In part this had accounted for Remond's and Purvis's attack on Douglass during the heat of the controversy. Douglass's goals of emancipation and the complete integration of black people into American society at times necessitated the formation of separate organizations or organizations in which black people gave direction.

However, not all of Douglass's impetus came from the desire to abolish slavery and achieve first-class citizenship for blacks; part of it stemmed from an insatiable ambition. Too many historians have failed to realize Douglass was first a man and secondly a Negro. Like any man, Douglass needed recognition and self-esteem, but slavery had given him a stronger need than most men. A man of Douglass's ability would have naturally felt the pains of degradation and humiliation occasioned by slavery much deeper than most. Contrary to the distinguished historian Benjamin Quarles, Douglass did resent many whites and often felt persecuted. Merely because he refused openly to reveal it is not sufficient reason to deny its existence. Slavery had taught black people the necessity of concealing their true feelings. As

Douglass once said about Garrison's unrestrained outbursts, "It is gallant to go forth single-handed, but is it wise."[79]

In the beginning Douglass had realized little of his potential. Insecurity, besides being a fugitive slave, forced him to cling close to Garrison's wing of the abolitionist party. But with the success of an anti-slavery agitator, Douglass was able to realize his own ambitions. His overwhelming reception by the English people in 1845 culminating in the purchase of his freedom and the offering of friends to start his newspaper had given Douglass the means to break away from Garrison. The temporary decision not to publish his paper stemmed from a momentary feeling of insecurity. Or as Douglass subtly put it, "I waited to start my paper due to their superior knowledge, but more importantly I had no means of showing them as unsound."[80] With reassurance from the many people who felt disappointment at his decision, he proceeded to publish the paper. His move to Rochester may have been due less to "motives of peace" than to be free from the stifling influence of the "Boston Board."[81]

Douglass enjoyed his position of preeminence in the abolitionist field. Historians who attempt to cite paternalism as the cause for the conflict should keep in mind that at the time Douglass split with Garrison's party, he occupied a position second only to Garrison in the abolitionist movement. Both the *Liberator* and the *Anti-Slavery Standard* had tried to bribe Douglass with the offer of a permanent column in their paper. Garrison's derisive remarks to Douglass had resulted not from feelings of superiority, but in the words Douglass used to describe Garnet's attack against him, "Vulgar sneers, cowardly insinuations, and impertinent charges, which are the mere outpourings of wounded pride."[82]

At times Douglass's conduct resembled very closely that of Garrison's. On one occasion Douglass had opposed the establishment of a national colored press and urged his readers to make *The North Star* the national organ.[83] Here it is obvious Douglass was reluctant to yield control. Later, he attacked the Reverend William Garnet for proposing to go abroad and advocate moral suasion as a means to overthrow slavery. Since Garnet had been a political abolitionist and had not made a conversion publicly at home, Douglass considered his actions, "the veriest hypocrisy and hollowness."[84] Again, Douglass's ambitions had clouded his mind to the fact that he had undergone constant changes without publicly informing anyone of his conversion. Douglass enjoyed the power which accompanied a position of importance; and on occasion became inflexible and insensitive as on learning that the Reverend Henry Bibb had suggested giving Bibles to slaves. Douglass called the suggestion, "absurd, weak, insipid and powerless."[85] Douglass felt that a slave should first be given "himself" and he would then have the ability as well as the capacity of own a Bible.[86] Furthermore, Douglass pointed out, the majority of slaves could not read. William Garnet, who had entered the argument, accused Douglass of "ambitious designs at the expenses of others," to which Douglass replied by calling him "impertinent."[87] While Douglass's argument against giving Bibles to slaves was much stronger than Bibb's, the tone of his rebuke was wholly unnecessary.

The Douglass-Garrison split aptly illustrated that history rarely operates in black and white contrasts, but in a series of varying grays. The conflict had been the result of not one but a number of subtle causes which neither Douglass nor Garrison could control. It was not only the result of misunderstanding and paternalism, but personality and ideological differences derived from vastly different experiences creating individuals whose needs would eventually run a collision course. The events following 1847 were anti-climactic; the die had been cast years before Douglass and Garrison had met in New Bedford, Massachusetts. Circumstances of birth, of color, of doctrines and philosophy had conspired to make the conflict between Garrison and Douglass inevitable.

Notes

[1] William H. Pease and Jane H. Pease, "Boston Garrisonians and the Problem of Frederick Douglass," *Canadian Journal of History I* (August, 1966), 3.

[2] Frederick Douglass, *Life and Times of Frederick Douglass* (London, 1882), p. 171.

[3] *Ibid.*, pp. 170-71.

[4] Benjamin Quarles, *Frederick Douglass* (Washington D.C., 1948), p. 9.

[5] Frederick Douglass, *My Bondage and My Freedom* (New York, 1968), p. 268.

[6] *Liberator*, January 1, 1831.

[7] Quarles, *op. cit.*, p. 11

[8] Douglass, *Life and Times*, p. 180.

[9] *Ibid.*, p. 185.

[10] *Ibid.*, p. 186.

[11] Phillip Foner, *The Life and Writings of Frederick Douglass* (4 Vols., New York 1950), I, 52.

[12] *Ibid.*

[13] *Liberator*, June 17, 1842. Also quoted in Foner, Vol. I, p. 62.

[14] Douglass, *Life and Times*, p. 197.

[15] *Ibid.*

[16] *Ibid.*

[17] Foner, *Life and Writings*, Vol. I, p. 59.

[18] *Ibid.*, p. 62.

[19] *Ibid.*

[20] *Ibid.*, p. 63.

[21] *Liberator*, September 16, 1845.

[22] *Foner, op. cit.*, p. 64.

[23] *Ibid.*

[24] Pease, *op. cit.*, p. 33.
[25] *Liberator*, January 29, 1847.
[26] *Ibid.*
[27] *Ibid.*, January 1, 1847.
[28] *Foner, op. cit.*, p. 72.
[29] *Liberator*, January 29, 1846.
[30] *Ibid.*
[31] *Ibid.*, January 29, 1847.
[32] Quarles, *op. cit.*, p. 58.
[33] *Liberator*, July 29, 1847. Letter had been sent Garrison in care of the *Liberator*.
[34] *Liberator*, July 16, 1847. Letter to Garrison from Issac Stearns.
[35] *Ibid.*
[36] *Liberator*, July 8, 1847.
[37] *Ibid.*, August 16, 1847.
[38] *Ibid.*, October 1, 1847.
[39] *Ibid.*, November 5, 1847.
[40] Benjamin Quarles, "The Breach Between Douglass and Garrison," *Journal of Negro History*, XXII (April, 1938), 149.
[41] *Ibid.*
[42] *Ibid.*
[43] Pease, *op. cit.*, pp. 35-36.
[44] *Liberator*, September 3, 1847.
[45] *Ibid.* November 17, 1848. Garrison had used Douglass' article on the Free Soil Movement to support his view that political action should never supplant moral suasion as the primary force against slavery.
[46] Quarles, "The Breach," p. 149.
[47] March 16, 1848.
[48] *Ibid.* He specifically pointed out Article 5 Sec. 8, Article 6 Sec. 9, and Article 4 Sec. 2.
[49] *Ibid.*, June 23, 1848.
[50] *Ibid.*, August 18, 1848. Also referred to in the *Emancipation*, September 13, 1848.
[51] *The North Star*, August 18, 1848.
[52] *Ibid.* Not all of Douglass' comments on anti-slavery political parties were complementary.
[53] *Liberator*, November 7, 1848.
[54] *The North Star*, August 18, 1848.
[55] Foner, *op. cit.*, II, 54.
[56] Quarles, "The Breach," p. 149.
[57] Foner, *op. cit.*, 54.
[58] *Ibid.*, p. 62.
[59] Pease, *op. cit.*, p. 29.
[60] Douglass, *Life and Times*, p. 242.
[61] Douglass, *My Bondage and My Freedom*, p. 396.
[62] Quarles, *Frederick Douglass*, p. 16.
[63] *Ibid.*, p. 77.
[64] Gilbert H. Barnes, *The Anti-Slavery Impulse* (New York, 1933), p. 91.
[65] Quarles, *Frederick Douglass*, p. 76.
[66] Douglass, *My Bondage and My Freedom*, p. 396.
[67] *Liberator*, July 3, 1846.
[68] *The North Star*, May 26, 1848.
[69] Douglass, *Life and Times*, p. 238.

[70] *Frederick Douglass Paper*, 1854.

[71] August Meier, "Blueprint for Black People," *Frederick Douglass*, edited by Benjamin Quarles (New Jersey, 1968), pp. 143-144.

[72] *The North Star*, September 29, 1848.

[73] Meier, *op. cit.*, p. 145.

[74] *The North Star*, July 7, 1847.

[75] *The North Star*, December 3, 1847.

[76] *Ibid.*, January 8, 1848.

[77] *Liberator*, June 14, 1848.

[78] *The North Star*, March 10, 1848.

[79] Benjamin Quarles, *Frederick Douglass*, p. 77.

[80] Douglass, *Life and Times*, p. 227.

[81] *Ibid.*

[82] *The North Star*, July 27, 1849.

[83] *Ibid.*, March 10, 1848.

[84] *Ibid.*, June 27, 1849.

[85] *Ibid.*, June 25, 1849.

[86] *Ibid.*

[87] *Ibid.*

Part Three

FREEDOM'S PEOPLE: AFRICAN AMERICANS DURING THE POSTBELLUM RECONSTRUCTION ERA

Exodus [to Kansas in 1879] was a form of action which could be undertaken by uneducated and illiterate people without extensive training or elaborate organizations. Permanently degraded in their Southern environment, the Negroes in an assertion of their self-respect and pride pulled up stakes and left.

Higgins,
Negro Thought and the Exodus of 1879

Slavery Revisited: Peonage in the South

N. GORDON CARPER

Early twentieth-century crusaders cut a wide path in their efforts to change America. Throughout the Progressive era, these reform-minded men and women worked for social justice as well as educational, legal, and political reforms. All manner of persons, from immigrant children to African Americans, and all manner of societal institutions, from the convict-lease system to political patronage, became subjects of the era's crusading zeal. For example, journalist Upton Sinclair's novel The Jungle *(1906), exposed unsanitary and dangerous working conditions in the meat-packing industry, leading to the passage of the Meat Inspection Act and the Pure Food and Drug Act. The establishment of the National Association for the Advancement of Colored People (NAACP) in 1909 by Progressive reformer W. E. B. DuBois and others provided an organizational approach to achieve social and political justice for blacks. Similarly, the crusading efforts of Fred Cubberly, the United States Commissioner in Florida, led to national exposure and condemnation of the convict-lease and debt peonage systems as twin forms of twentieth-century black slavery.*

Gordon Carper's essay traces an important, albeit painful, story of modern slavery. The author explores the dynamics of how racism, industrialization, and materialism in the postbellum South forced thousands of black men and perhaps hundreds of black women into involuntary servitude in the phosphate mines, lumber camps, and turpentine plantations. Carper relies on U.S. Department of Justice records, periodicals, and judicial opinions to document this history of Progressive era crusaders seeking justice for victimized African Americans.

THE HUMANITARIAN SPIRIT of the nineteenth century helped bring about the downfall of slavery. As chattel slavery was abolished, however, the former slave-holding states enacted a series of labor laws aimed exclusively at the freed slaves, which created a new system of forced labor known as peonage.[1]

By definition, *peonage* is a form of involuntary servitude based on alleged debt or indebtedness. As of 1915 at least six former slave-holding states had statutes which made it possible to compel men to labor for others against their will. Both the turpentine and cotton belts of Florida, Georgia, Mississippi and Alabama proved to be fertile areas where white entrepreneurs held lower-class Americans in conditions of involuntary servitude.[2] In many cases corrupt sheriffs and judges in conjunction with the monied interests placed men in conditions of peonage with no official judicial proceedings whatsoever. But then most peons were black and few Southern white entrepreneurs had any inclination toward equal justice for all.[3]

The origins of peonage are as varied as they are complex. Through law, custom and racism as well as the political, economic and social chaos resulting from the Civil War-Reconstruction era, men were shackled physically and spiritually and compelled to labor for those who constituted the "Establishment." Historians will never know how many people were victimized by this institution. The institution was widespread throughout the South, however, and during the Progressive era there were limitless numbers of peons who suffered indignities generally unheard of in modern America. During a five-month period in one town on the southern coast of Florida, zealous local officials placed hundreds of men in conditions of peonage.[4]

Although there were several laws which created conditions of peonage throughout the South, the "Black Codes" and the contract labor laws were the most popularly used instruments. Florida's Black Code of 1865 stipulated that anyone who did not pay a fine should be hired out "at public outcry to any person who will take him or her for the shortest time and pay the fine, forfeiture and penalty imposed, and cost of prosecution." Such punishment resulted from convictions of assault, misdemeanors, malicious mischief, assault and battery, vagrancy and "all offenses against Religion, Chastity, Morality and Decency."[5]

Of all the Black Codes, that section dealing with vagrancy was applied most often to freed Negroes. And few convicted of vagrancy were able to pay their fines and court costs. As a result they took the second alternative, one to six months as a county convict. At this point they were usually leased to the highest bidder and privileged to participate in another peculiarly Southern institution, the convict-lease system. Frequently, the convicts were detained beyond the term of sentence. When this happened a condition of peonage existed.[6]

Throughout the South the convict-lease system directly led to and brought about peonage. According to Charles W. Russell, Assistant Attorney General of the United States, there was a positive relationship between peonage and convict leasing. He pointed out that convicts were leased and subleased and not allowed to depart upon the expiration of their sentences. "In other words," said Russell, "after the law has finished with him he is held in involuntary servitude by the man who has leased him . . . . The State gets no pay for the months he is thus detained, and the lessee gets his labor without having to pay anything."[7]

Although enforcement of the Black Codes, particularly that section dealing with vagrancy, produced widespread conditions of peonage in the South, an equally compelling origin evolved during 1900 and 1901, when numerous laborers were arrested under the contract labor laws governing "false pretenses." In northern Florida arrests were made by local sheriffs for labor contractors who charged that laborers had acquired "goods and money" under false promises to labor. However, none of these early peonage cases was brought to trial. Rather, the contractor worked out compromises with the laborers, whereby they agreed to work out the alleged debt and costs of arrest. Later on labor contractors "dispensed with the services of the sheriff and his deputies and were making arrests on their own account and holding their own courts."[8]

Both the Black Codes and the contract labor laws supported the tendency in the South to weave about ignorant black laborers a legal system which would guarantee not only second-class citizenship for blacks but which would force them into complete economic dependence upon the will of the white land owners and employers.[9] Peonage in the South was not, however, restricted to black men. White immigrant laborers were actively recruited to work on Southern railroads, in the turpentine forests, and at other enterprising activities. Throughout the Progressive era immigrants received inducements to migrate south where while attempting to work off transportation costs they were driven deeper into debt via the renowned commissary system.[10]

The climate of opinion which fostered peonage in the South and which made it a predominantly black institution resulted from a series of historical events. The antebellum South was dominated by a plantation economy. A characteristic of the plantation economy was slavery—a system which resulted in the social, political and economic domination of white over black. Early in its history, therefore, whites in the South developed the habit of exploiting the labor of less fortunates. Although the Civil War-Reconstruction era saw the "peculiar institution" abolished and blacks win fundamental political rights, for the South that same era produced more problems than it solved. State treasuries were empty, institutions of political, economic and social control were destroyed—the South experienced complete chaos. Suddenly a new labor system had to be devised in a section of the country where there was no capital. Sharecropping, convict leasing and ultimately peonage seemed to fit the vicissitudes of the time. Moreover, the liberators from the North brought with them their newly developed concepts of an industrial capitalistic society in which labor, regardless of race, was exploited. This, combined with Southern slave standards and race hatred and intensified by the passions of war and reconstruction, made the South a fertile field for the exploitation of peonage. Add to this the fact that the majority of peons in Southern states were Negroes who were accustomed to working for Southern whites under a system of forced labor, and one can see why peonage was accepted more readily in the South than elsewhere in the United States.[11]

During the Progressive era the escalating number of peonage violations attracted the attention of Fred Cubberly, United States Commissioner for the Northern District of Florida. Cubberly's decision to investigate resulted in the first peonage cases tried in the United States courts under the peonage statutes of 1867 which outlawed debt slavery in all states and territories.[12] The case prosecuted by Cubberly involved S. M. Clyatt, a wealthy turpentine operator from Tifton, Georgia. In early 1901, J. R. Deen, a Florida naval stores operator, told Cubberly about a group of armed men who had arrested illegally several laborers at Deen's camp.[13] Cubberly investigated Deen's charge and uncovered the following peonage case.

S. M. Clyatt and two other armed men went to Florida as "man hunters." Before leaving Georgia, Clyatt secured warrants for five Negro laborers who had worked for him but later went to Florida and secured employment at Deen's turpentine farm. The warrants charged the laborers with gambling. Upon arrival at Deen's farm, Clyatt turned over the Georgia warrants to the Bronson deputy sheriff, "who did not read them, but arrested two men whom Clyatt pointed out." Clyatt placed irons on the two Negroes, Mose Ridley and Will Gordon, and proceeded to take them back to Georgia. The Negroes were taken to Georgia with no Florida court proceedings. Later, when officials tried to locate the men as witnesses in the Clyatt peonage case, they could not be found. Several secret service men were sent to find the black laborers but to no avail.[14]

As Clyatt's case went to court, it created considerable interest throughout Florida.[15] Clyatt and his friends raised large sums of money to aid him in his defense. At the trial no evidence was produced in contradiction to the United States Government's case. The evidence substantiated the charge that Clyatt had unlawfully taken Ridley and Gordon to his turpentine farm near Waterloo, Georgia. The Negroes were held and forced to work for Clyatt until the alleged debt was paid. After hearing the evidence, a jury in the United

States court at Tallahassee, Florida, returned a verdict of guilty. Clyatt had violated the peonage laws of the United States and the court had upheld the constitutionality of the 1867 peonage statute.[16]

Cubberly's work in the Clyatt case created a sensation throughout much of the nation. The New York *Independent*, a muckraking journal, induced Cubberly to write a story on peonage using the Clyatt case as the major theme.[17] In 1903, an article appeared in *Outlook* which was largely an exposé of peonage in the South.[18] The latter article pointed out that Southerners guilty of peonage violations argued that compulsory labor was an economic necessity. In the name of "economic necessity" turpentine operators induced justices of the peace and local policemen to enslave American citizens. But in almost every peonage case tested, the evidence suggested that the "machinery of the law was used corruptly for the purpose of enslaving freemen. . . ."[19]

In February, 1904, the *Independent* published an article titled "The New Slavery in the South—An Autobiography." The article related the life story of a Negro peon who had been hired out to a peonage camp captain at the age of ten. The peon's story was pathetic:

> In many cases it is very evident that the court officials are in collusion with the proprietors or agents, and that they divide the 'graft' among themselves. As an example of this dickering among the whites, every year many convicts were brought to the Senator's camp from a certain county . . . way down in the turpentine district. The majority of these men were charged with adultery . . . Upon inquiry I learned that down in that country a number of negro lewd women were employed by certain white men to entice negro men into their houses; and then, on certain nights, at a given signal, when all was in readiness, raids would be made by the officers upon these houses, and the men would be arrested and charged with living in adultery. Nine out of ten of these men, . . . would find their way ultimately to some convict camp. . . . The low-down women were never punished in any way.[20]

Florida's turpentine operators constantly violated the peonage laws. The laborers in the turpentine business were generally Negroes who were forced to buy their supplies from the camp commissaries. When a laborer's debt at the store exceeded his ability to pay, he was enslaved for as many as twenty years. This condition prompted one Florida newspaper reporter to write: "Were they white men the sympathy of the state would be aroused in behalf of the laborers, but being negroes, in the language of Chimmie Fadden, 'what d'ell,' will be the general comment, 'Tisn't right'. "[21]

Cubberly, in his drive to prosecute peonage violations in Florida, discovered that employers, in order to secure laborers, would

"advance wages, pay railroad fares and even provide men with funds
to go out and 'recruit' hands." This situation made it easy for a Negro laborer "to 'jump' his contract with his advance in his pocket,
and go to the next white man, who [would] almost . . . surely give
him another advance and no questions asked . . . ." The labor contractor naturally desired to get even, which resulted in peonage violations. "If the system of advances of money and goods was abolished,"
wrote Cubberly, "there would be but few peonage cases."[22]

Cubberly's advice was ignored and the problem of peonage continued to plague the South. In 1906, there was concern over alleged
cases of peonage in southern Florida. A woman informed President
Theodore Roosevelt that hundreds of men in Florida, "both white
and negroes are held in virtual slavery."[23] The men responsible for
this condition, however, were Northern capitalists who had invested
in Southern industries such as phosphate mining and turpentine
processing. The female informant alleged that law officers of southern Florida were "parties to the enslaving of negroes in the
phosphate mines, turpentine farms and lumber mills."[24] Although the
woman neglected to report the practice of peonage on the Florida
East Coast Railway, it was this situation which stirred the President,
the press, and Florida's Governor into action.[25]

Henry Flagler, a wealthy Floridian, built the Florida East Coast
Railway. During 1905 Flagler employed laborers in the construction of
the Key West extension of his road. A Florida labor agency operating
in New York induced Northern men to work for Flagler. But the
agency frequently gave the prospective laborers false information concerning the employment.[26]

Cries of peonage violations in south Florida had sounded for
years. But few people in Florida, or elsewhere for that matter, were
interested in making the effort necessary to insure the civil liberties
of America's less fortunate black and white citizens. By 1906, however,
a number of Flagler's laborers had returned to New York and reported their experiences to John N. Bogart, Commissioner of Li-
censes for the city of New York. Bogart listened to their grievances
and was convinced that Flagler and other leading Florida citizens
were holding thousands of migrant workers in peonage.[27] Bogart
stated that the men who came to his office were in poor physical
condition and often quite young. Because of the treatment they endured at Flagler's camp, the Commissioner argued that the men were
incapable of continuing hard work.[28]

As Bogart's investigation continued he learned how the laborers
had become victims of debt slavery. Flagler paid the migrant laborers'
transportation charges to Florida and in return the men contracted

to work until the railroad company was reimbursed. The pathetic physical condition of some of the men, however, made it impossible for them to work until their debt was paid in full. If they attempted to leave Flagler's camp, the workmen were subject to Florida's laws governing debt and to the possibility of becoming peons.[29] When arrested they frequently were given the choice of continuing to work for Flagler, work which they physically could no longer perform, or serving time in the convict-lease system. Given the harsh realities of Flagler's labor camps, some volunteered to risk their lives in the equally burdensome convict-lease system. Others who violated their labor contracts attempted to escape but to little avail. They usually were caught because Florida's local constables had good reason to be zealous in their duties.

According to an editorial in the *Florida Times-Union*, Flagler and the state needed laborers and were not concerned about the means used to get them. The article suggested that when Flagler's laborers broke their contract, local law officials received substantial commissions for each arrest and conviction. Every conviction meant another laborer and so zealous were the officials "that in one town in five months 334 convictions were obtained" on charges varying in seriousness from vagrancy to violation of labor contract and upward.[30]

After a vain search for the source of the cry of peonage in the railroad camps it became apparent where and how that cry arose. Northern laborers attracted south by Flagler's agents found conditions in the South radically different from those at home. When the constables finished their work, men who originally labored for Flagler found themselves working in state and county convict camps where they were frequently detained beyond the term of sentence. Others went back to work for Flagler and often found themselves in perpetual indebtedness.[31] Whether Florida's methods of dealing with labor contract violations and vagrancy were better than the methods used in the North is open to question. But according to one correspondent, one thing was certain: as long as Florida continued to lease its vagrants and convicts to private interests, "whose only object is to get all the work possible out of them without considering their feelings, protests against these conditions are sure to continue" and the cries of peonage would not cease.[32]

Peonage charges were brought against David E. Harley, agent for Flagler, and the trial took place in November, 1908. The government argued that several thousand men were forced to work on Flagler's railroad. "These men," said the attorney, "were held in slavery." After hearing all the argument, Judge Hough in the United States Circuit Court ordered the jury to bring in a verdict of not guilty in the cases of David E. Harley and three employment agents accused of conspiracy to hold workmen in peonage and slavery. The judge reasoned that the prosecution had failed to prove "an agreement of minds with evil intent to conspire."[33]

According to the United States Department of Justice, a verdict of not guilty was expected. The *Florida Times-Union* sought to drive federal officials out of the state "by suppressing and misrepresenting the truth."[34] As the press attempted to influence juries and public opinion, other forces worked against the United States officials who prosecuted Flagler and his agents. Flagler, the Florida Turpentine Association, the United Groceries concern, and the newspapers which relied upon the *Times-Union* for their material all used their influence to get Flagler and his agents acquitted.[35]

The outcome of the Flagler case did not deter Cubberly and the United States Department of Justice from their efforts to halt peonage in the South. Alexander Irvine, a writer for *Appleton's Magazine*, praised Cubberly for his work in prosecuting violators of peonage laws. Irvine told Cubberly that more work had to be done and that he, Irvine, was going to investigate alleged peonage cases in Florida and write a book on the subject.[36]

Alexander Irvine finally went South and worked as a teamster in the lumber camps of the Jackson Lumber Company. Largely as a result of the work of Irvine and Cubberly, a number of peonage cases were tried against the company, which had induced Northern laborers to work in the Florida lumber camps through methods which violated the peonage laws. When the story came to light, twenty-eight indictments were brought against the company and a number of convictions resulted.[37]

Irvine was so impressed with Cubberly's role in the peonage cases that he wrote President Theodore Roosevelt on Cubberly's behalf. In his letter Irvine stated that all of the "government activity . . . in prosecuting violators of the Anti-Peonage Laws was due . . . to Cubberly's activity."[38] Irvine reminded the President that there was an opening for the position of district attorney for the northern district of Florida. In view of Cubberly's excellent record, Irvine hoped that the President would grant him the appointment. Responding to Irvine's letter, the President commended Cubberly for his work; he pointed out, however, that the incumbent of the position referred to in Irvine's letter had done an excellent job and probably would be retained. Lamenting that it was difficult to find the right position for a man with Cubberly's outstanding service record, Roosevelt stated: "I am all the while being reminded of the Russian proverb: 'Once in ten years you can help a man.' The chance does not seem to come much more often."[39]

While Cubberly, Irvine and others worked zealously to prosecute peonage violations in Florida, other national leaders labored to curtail the incidence of debt slavery in Alabama. Of the peonage cases prosecuted in Alabama during the Progressive era, that of Alonzo Bailey, which began in 1908 and culminated in a 1911 Supreme Court ruling, proved to be the most significant.[40]

Bailey was a black farm laborer who contracted to work for the Riverside Company of Montgomery, Alabama. In his contract Bailey received a $15 advance which he was to repay at $1.25 a month for the duration of his contractual obligation. After completing about one month's service, Bailey left the farm and apparently did not repay the money. At this juncture he was subject to Alabama's contract labor law which merely necessitated that the prosecution prove that Bailey intended to defraud his employer.

Alabama's contract labor law disturbed Booker T. Washington as well as other less known but equally interested citizens and leaders in the country. Bailey's dilemma gave these men the test case they needed to get a United States Supreme Court ruling on the constitutionality of existing contract labor laws in Alabama as well as in other Southern states.

With great speed, Bailey's case went before the Alabama Supreme Court, which ruled that he was guilty of fraud and that the contract labor law was constitutional since its purpose was to punish those guilty of fraud and not "the mere failure to pay a debt."[41] But when Bailey's attorney, Edward S. Watts, attempted to take the case to the United States Supreme Court, the judicial process bogged down. After considerable legal and political haggling, however, the court agreed to review the case. Justice Charles Evans Hughes delivered the majority opinion in January, 1911. The Court ruled that involuntary servitude could be imposed by a state only as punishment for a crime. But no state could "compel one man to labor for another in payment of debt, by punishing him as a criminal if he does not perform the service or pay the debt."[42] The argument closed on a very important note by stating that the contract labor law in question violated Bailey's civil rights as constituted under the Thirteenth Amendment.[43]

With the ruling in the Bailey case much of the legal structure which gave impetus to peonage in the South had been declared unconstitutional. United States Assistant Attorney General Charles Russell argued that in a technical sense the Bailey decision rendered null and void all state laws, such as the contract labor laws and vagrancy, which created conditions of peonage.[44] In a legal sense then peonage was no more. Yet, in fact, peonage violations continued down to the present day. Although legal slavery in the United States no longer existed after the Thirteenth Amendment and subsequent Supreme Court rulings, debt slavery continued to exist in the opinions, sentiments and practices of the American people. Obviously the forces of racism and an expanding capitalism with its concomitant need for labor were stronger than the law of the land. Those who fought for the abolition of peonage with limited success during the decade from 1901 to 1911 continued their efforts.

By far the majority of peonage incidents in the South occurred as a result of county rather than state activity. Local constables and sheriffs constantly aided the labor contractors in acquiring labor. Once the contractor induced a man to work at his camp, the laborer was caught. If the worker attempted to leave, the employer would have him arrested and sentenced to serve time in the convict-lease system. Many times a laborer worked first as a convict, then as a peon for the same employer.[45] The grounds for arrest often were not valid, but few seemed to care whether the men confined in peonage and convict camps were given equal justice or treated in a humane manner.

Nowhere were peonage abuses worse than at Captain Alston Brown's turpentine camp located in Dixie County, near Cross City, Florida. Most of the men who processed the pine forests for Brown were Negroes.[46] The majority of the laborers were "recruited" by Brown through the county convict-lease system or peonage. Dixie County Judge W. H. Matthis immeasurably aided Brown in his recruiting process.[47] Through their illegal practices, a number of innocent men and women were kept in a condition of involuntary servitude. The testimony which the Negro peons gave to federal investigators uncovered one of the most inhuman labor systems ever devised by man.

In an interview with Rosa Whitlock, a female peon at Brown's camp, special agent John Bonyne uncovered some incredible facts. Mrs. Whitlock's husband had worked for two years on Brown's turpentine farm. After spending two weeks visiting her husband in February, 1921, Mrs. Whitlock asked him for money for her return trip home. He told her "that he could not furnish her with money because he was in debt to Captain Brown for $50.00, and Capt. Brown would not let him have the money . . . ." Later, Brown told Mrs. Whitlock that she could not leave the camp. The rule at Brown's camp was "that no negro could leave his camp without his consent." Mrs. Whitlock devised a scheme by which she could get away and later tell her story to agent Bonyne. She testified that she saw men, women and children who had been unable to leave the camp for a period of years. If a camp convict or peon died he was buried in the camp cemetery and Brown did not notify relatives or friends of the death. Mrs. Whitlock concluded that people who had worked for Brown for fifteen years never saw an outsider and they were not allowed to leave the camp. If they had any money, "they had to buy everything at Capt. Brown's store."[48]

Special agent Howard P. Wright interviewed Mrs. Georgia Jones whose son, sixteen-year-old James Jones, was recruited by an agent to work on Brown's turpentine farm. Mrs. Jones stated that she received a letter from her son asking that she send him some money. She promptly forwarded $4.00 to her son, who apparently never received the money. Later Mrs. Jones discovered that whenever Brown took on a Negro laborer, he was "kept in debt and never allowed to leave."[49]

The letter written by James Jones indicated the severity of the work at Brown's camp as well as the methods used by Brown to keep the laborers on his farm. The boy wrote:

> Been down here working in water for four days and now my feet have done got water poison and I aint been able hardly to walk—an Willie is gone I dont know where he is. I am sick from wading in this water. I want to leave here and I want you Ma to try and send me two dollars . . . so I can leave from this place, that is the only way that I can get away from here is walk. They will put me in jail, so try to get $2.00 for me.[50]

Brown brutally punished his laborers and forced the women to suffer terrible indignities. According to Lizzie Rush, if a good looking woman came to Brown's camp and one of the laborers told the Captain that he "wanted" her, Brown would order the husband of the woman to other quarters while the wife stayed with the stranger.[51] Frequently Brown took $2.50 from the men for allowing them the privilege of sleeping with the camp women.[52] Miss Rush added that if a Negro woman refused to obey Brown's order, he would give her fifty lashes. The testimony of other female laborers at Brown's camp substantiated Rush's statement.[53]

Vina Lee Wright stated that as a little girl she worked for Brown's cook. When the girl was only thirteen years old, Brown entered the child's room "and made her do what he wanted; that she had a baby girl by Capt. Brown, and that Capt. Brown told her to say nothing about it to any one at any time."[54] According to Miss Wright's testimony, her sister, Lillie Johnson, had the same experience with Brown.[55]

Convict Will Jeffrey was sentenced to six months hard labor at Brown's Blue Creek Camp. After keeping Jeffrey for seven months, Brown told the prisoner he was free. Before Jeffrey left, Brown sent him to the commissary to get a pair of trousers. The following morning Jeffrey was ordered to go to work pulling boxes to pay for the trousers. Eight years later, Jeffrey was informed that he still owed Brown "$148.50, which he would have to work out."[56]

Brown beat his laborers unmercifully. On several occasions his nephew, Mose Brown, whipped the laborers so severely that they died. Peon Will Anderson told a special agent that laborer Wash Menner was beaten so badly by Mose Brown that blood ran from Menner's nose and mouth. "Mose Brown helped Menner in to a wagon and took him back to the camp and put him in the stockade; Menner died within a week from the effects of the beating."[57] After Menner died, Brown informed the laborers that he would kill any man who told how Menner had died.

As the testimony against Alston and Mose Brown continued to mount, Cubberly informed special agent Howard Wright that a warrant was issued for the arrest of the two men on charges on peonage. Wright told Cubberly that everything was in order and that special agent M. J. Cronin obtained information from Judge Matthis's records which indicated that the Judge was involved in the Brown case. Wright informed Cubberly that the records suggested that a number of black people were arrested on the basis of warrants secured by Mose Brown and tried by Judge Matthis on charges of "violation of labor contract,' which according to the judge's own statement, means 'a debt that they owed the company for which they worked.' " Unable to pay the assessed fine, the Negro laborers were placed in peonage camps. Wright closed his letter to Cubberly by observing that in all the peonage cases related to Brown and Judge Matthis the laborers were charged with "assault and battery" as well as "violation of labor contract." This was done "to hold these negroes in the event the violations of labor contract failed."[58]

Matthis's interpretation of what constituted a violation of a labor contract resulted in convictions which were "direct violations of the Peonage laws."[59] When the Federal Bureau of Investigation indicated Matthis's role in the Brown peonage case to the United States Attorney General's office, Cubberly was advised to prosecute Matthis along with Mose and Alston Brown.[60] Rush Holland, Assistant Attorney General of the United States, told Cubberly that the evidence in the Brown case was conclusive. Holland was interested "particularly in the part played by Judge W. H. Matthis, County Judge, especially where his records confirmed his participation in one of the most horrible peonage cases ever brought to [his] attention."[61]

As the grand jury hearing on Brown's case approached, the federal officers prepared to take their star witnesses to Gainesville, Florida, in preparation for the trial. George Finch, one of the prosecution's star witnesses, was on his way to Gainesville when Deputy Sheriff Noah Green shot at him five times. Later Green told Finch that if he did not surrender he would be killed.[62] Supporters of Alston and Mose Brown used threats and force in an attempt to intimidate other prosecution witnesses.[63] Through the work of agent Charles Jordan, however, the witnesses were assembled for judgment day.

The grand jury hearing at Gainesville brought to light conclusive evidence against Judge Matthis, Mose Brown and Alston Brown. The three men had violated the peonage laws of the United States by holding laborers in a condition of involuntary servitude for alleged debts. The trial decision was based on testimony given by both Negroes and whites. A Putnam Lumber Company accountant, Charles B. Davis, testified that Brown held Negroes for debts. He testified that Brown often took money rightfully belonging to the laborers. Concluding his testimony, Davis stated that Brown severely whipped the peons; he forced the Negro women to work as prostitutes; and he illegally kept the laborers in debt.[64] Witnesses James Fisher, John Herilhy, Edward Scruggs, and McEnd Wade, all white public officials and professional people, substantiated Davis's testimony.

To students of history interested in peonage, the Brown case holds unusual significance on two counts. First, no other case analyzed in contemporary scholarship better illustrates the sordid abuses of the system, particularly as they relate to the role of women. But more important, of all the published material on peonage nowhere is the relationship between peonage and the convict-lease system more clearly evidenced. Brown worked peons and convicts at the same tasks and housed them in the same camps. If a peon tried to leave he was placed back into the system as a convict. If a convict served out his sentence, he found himself in debt to Brown via the commissary system and forced back into the system as a peon. One might as well ask: How did the laborer manage to successfully leave the system? For many the answer was only through death. In essence there was no way out of the system.

Cubberly, Irvine, Russell, Washington and many other reform minded citizens had fought valiantly for over twenty years to abolish peonage. The abolitionists through the Clyatt case of 1902 saw the Supreme Cout uphold the constitutionality of the 1867 peonage statute. But peonage violations continued as the economic and political leaders in the South found new ways to use old laws as the Black Codes and the contract labor laws. Then in 1911 the Supreme Court ruled in the Bailey case that all state laws which compel a man to labor for another in payment of a debt are unconstitutional. The legal fabric which supported peonage was destroyed. Yet the Establishment continued to subvert the intent of the law and to violate the civil liberties of America's less fortunates.

When the abuses of peonage erupted to volcanic proportions as evidenced in the Brown case, the reform troops of the Progressive era were called upon once more. If peonage and convict leasing were inextricably related, then the legal base of not one but both must be abolished. By 1922 the peonage and convict-lease abolitionists had combined forces and managed to focus national attention on the death of Martin Tabert, who had fallen prey to Florida's county convict-lease system.[65] While serving a ninety-day sentence on a charge of vagrancy, Tabert was leased to the Putnam Lumber Company of Dixie County, Florida. He was brutally beaten and died in early 1922.[66] A nationally publicized investigation of Tabert's death uncovered unbelievable brutalities in both convict and peonage camps.[67] Early in the case, Samuel D. McCoy, correspondent for the New York *World*, and Amos Pinchot, a New York attorney and brother of the national politician, Gifford Pinchot, became the leaders in the abolitionist crusade against the lease system.[68] Both men emphasized the need to abolish convict leasing, which in turn would reduce significantly the incidence of peonage. Pinchot reminded the abolitionists, however, that "the lumber, turpentine and similar interests" would have to be checked or "peonage and corporal punishment will not be abolished, though certain motions may be gone through in order to appease public opinion . . . ."[69] He concluded his letter stating that he simply would not visit Florida "as long as peonage survives in the beautiful state, which has been so deeply wronged by men careless of its honor and contemptuous of the sanctity of the human body and the dignity of human life."[70] Later, in a letter to the editor of McCoy's paper, Pinchot stated that he had seen peonage and the lease system in operation and he knew about the brutal conditions which McCoy and the New York *World* hoped to end.[71] He hoped that his letter on the peonage cases would aid the abolitionists in their cause.[72]

McCoy's work was truly significant. Largely due to his work, newspapers throughout the country ran editorials demanding that the Florida legislature abolish the lease system.[73] In Florida alone, at least fifty newspapers attacked the lease system as well as peonage and demanded that they be abolished.[74]

By April, 1923, the sentiment of the nation was openly against the lease system. Public opinion demanded that it be abolished. Cubberly, Pinchot, McCoy and many others had done their jobs well. On May 25, 1923, Governor Carey Hardee signed a bill which abolished the convict-lease system.[75] One more impetus to peonage had been removed. One more step had been taken toward equal justice for all.

Unfortunately, the abolitionists would have their spirits dampened again. While the sordid details of the Tabert case were still fresh in everyone's mind, disclosures of peonage violations continued to make the headlines.[76] Yet the legal base which for generations had buttressed peonage was destroyed, and by 1925, all Southern states had abolished the convict-lease system. What else could be done? All that remained was the need to change the ethic of a nation. In the last analysis if one expected man's behavior to change, then the root cause of peonage must be altered through a humanitarian, equilitarian educational campaign. Although the Black Codes, the contract labor laws and racism helped explain why peonage persisted in the South, these were not adequate explanations. Rather they were and are symbolic of a more basic cause, the American ethic. America not only experienced the expanding capitalism of the nineteenth century, but she also experienced the development of concomitant conservative-social Darwinist ethic. The expanding industrial society created a labor demand which exceeded the supply, and the conservative-social Darwinist ethic saw every institution of social control lend its authority to those who would exploit their fellowmen for profit. What chance did America's poor have in a society which argued that the rich were godly and the poor were sinners? How would one expect peonage to disappear when the highest court in the land subverted the intent of the Fourteenth Amendment by ignoring black men and by defining corporations as legal persons? Peonage violations would continue as long as America continued to define a man's worth by his material possessions. On the other hand, if the American people ever decided to pay more than lip service to the proposition of the dignity and equality of all men, perhaps then peonage and other similar practices would end.

Notes

[1] Lafayette M. Hernshaw, *Peonage*, Occasional Papers No. 15 (Washington, D.C.: The American Negro Academy, 1915), p. 5.

[2] *Ibid.*, p. 7. See also Pete Daniel, *The Shadow of Slavery: Peonage in the South 1901-1969* (Chicago, 1972), pp. 19-42.

[3] Theodore B. Wilson, "The Black Codes of the South" (Doctoral dissertation, Department of History, University of Florida, 1962), p. 192.

[4] Jacksonville *Florida Times-Union*, April 21, 1907.

[5] Florida *Acts and Resolutions*, 1865, c. 1465, pp. 20-22.

[6] N. Gordon Carper, "The Convict-Lease System in Florida, 1866-1923" (Doctoral dissertation, Department of History, Florida State University, 1964), 304-29. In his book, *The Shadow of Slavery: Peonage in the South, 1901-1969*, Professor Daniel dismisses the relationship between peonage and convict-leasing. Although he refers to an unpublished master's thesis completed in 1964, titled "The Convict-Lease System in the Post-Civil War South," he fails to examine two doctoral dissertations which demonstrate that the convict-lease system clearly functioned as an origin for peonage. See Carper, *ibid.*, and Hilda J. Zimmerman, "Penal Systems and Penal Reforms in the South Since the Civil War" (Doctoral dissertation, Department of History, University of North Carolina, 1947).

[7] U.S. Department of Justice, Report on Peonage, by Charles W. Russell, Assistant Attorney General (Washington, D.C., 1908), p. 17.

[8] Fred Cubberly Papers, Letter from Fred Cubberly to Richard Barry, August 17, 1906. P. K. Yonge Library of Florida History, University of Florida.

[9] Pete Daniel, "Up From Slavery," *Journal of American History*, LVII (December, 1970), 656.

[10] *Crescent City News*, September 5, 1901. See also U.S. Department of Justice, 1908a. Report on Peonage by Charles W. Russell, Assistant Attorney General, February 14, 1907, p. 4.

[11] Blake McKelvey, "Penal Slavery and Southern Reconstruction," *The Journal of Negro History*, XX (1935), 153-79.

[12] Cubberly Papers, Letter from Fred Cubberly to Richard Barry, August 17, 1906. In his study on Peonage in the South, Daniel correctly portrays Cubberly as one of the first government officials in the Progressive era who devoted his energy to the abolition of peonage. Yet ironically Daniel did not consult the Cubberly papers.

[13] Cubberly Papers, Letter from Fred Cubberly to Charles Russell, December 18, 1906; see also *Jasper News*, April 4, 1902.

[14] *Ibid.*, Letter from Fred Cubberly to Richard Barry, August 17, 1906; *Ibid.*, Letter from Fred Cubberly to Charles Russell, December 18, 1906.

[15] *Jasper News*, April 4, 1902; see also Jacksonville *Florida Times-Union*, March 27, 1902.

[16] *Ibid.* Cubberly stated that most of the $90,000 raised by the turpentine operators of Florida and Georgia to defend Clyatt was used to impeach Judge Swayne because he allowed a verdict of guilty. See Cubberly Papers, Letter from Fred Cubberly to R. L. Anderson. August 17, 1906.

[17] Fred Cubberly, "Peonage in the South," *Independent*, LV (July 9, 1903), 1616-18.

[18] "Peonage," *Outlook*, LXXIV (July 18, 1903), 687-88.

[19] *Ibid.*

[20] "The New Slavery in the South," *Independent* (February 18, 1904), 413.

[21] *Crescent City News*, September 5, 1901.

[22] Cubberly Papers, Letter from Fred Cubberly to Richard Barry, August 17, 1906.

[23] Live Oak *Daily Democrat*, October 13, 1906; see also Fernandina *News*, October 18, 1906; U.S. Department of Justice, *Report on Peonage*, p. 1.

[24] *Ibid.*

[25] U.S. Department of Justice, *Report on Peonage*, p. 1.

[26] Jacksonville *Florida Times-Union*, April 21 and May 12, 1907; see also *Tallahassee Sun*, March 30, 1907.

[27] U.S. Department of Justice, 1908a, p. 4.

[28] Jacksonville *Florida Times-Union*, May 12, 1907; see also Clarissa Olds Keeler, *The Crime of Crimes or the Convict System Unmasked* (Washington, D.C.; Pentecostal Era Co., 1907), p. 25. Keeler suggests that hundreds of youth ranging in age from 7 to 20 were enslaved in peonage and convict camps.

[29] Jacksonville *Florida Times-Union*, May 12, 1907.

[30] *Ibid.*, April 21, 1907.

[31] *Ibid.*

[32] *Ibid.*

[33] *Tampa Tribune*, November 11, 1908. See also United States vs. Sabbia, Triay and others, accused of peonage. Report of Official Court Stenographer, 1909, Library of Congress.

[34] U.S. Department of Justice, *Report on Peonage*, p. 5.

[35] *Ibid.* The foreman of the jury was the President of the United Groceries Company, which supplied the commissary stores at turpentine peonage camps. The commissaries, through exorbitant prices "kept the laborers in debt and, as a consequence, in peonage." U.S. Deparment of Justice, 1908a, p. 4.

[36] Cubberly Papers, Letters from Alexander Irvine to Fred Cubberly, January 28 and March 13, 1907.

[37] *Tallahassee Sun*, November 9, 1907; see also Keeler, *ibid.*, p. 17.

[38] Cubberly Papers, Letter from Alexander Irvine to President Theodore Roosevelt, December 1, 1908.

[39] *Ibid.*, Letter from President Theodore Roosevelt to Alexander Irvine, December 2, 1908.

[40] Daniel, "Up From Slavery," 654-70.

[41] Bailey vs. State, 158. Alabama 18 (1908).

[42] Bailey vs. Alabama, 219 U.S. 244 (1911).

[43] *Ibid.*, 245.

[44] Hernshaw, *ibid.*, p. 12.

[45] Carper, *ibid.*, pp. 304-29.

[46] Cubberly Papers, Letter from Howard Wright to Fred Cubberly, June 9, 1922.

[47] *Ibid.*; see also Cubberly Papers, Letter from Howard Wright to Fred Cubberly, May 26, 1922.

[48] *Ibid.*, Report on Peonage Violations by Special Agent John Bonyne, June 10, 1921.

[49] *Ibid.*, Report on Peonage Violations by Special Agent Howard Wright, September 9, 1921.

[50] *Ibid.*

[51] Cubberly Papers, Report on Peonage Violations by Special Agent John Bonyne, November 11, 1921.

[52] *Ibid.*, April 24-30, 1922.

[53] *Ibid.*

[54] *Ibid.*

[55] *Ibid.*

[56] *Ibid.* One can only speculate that Jeffrey purchased a very costly pair of trousers.

[57] *Ibid.*

[58] *Ibid.*, Letter from Howard Wright to Fred Cubberly, May 26, 1922.

[59] *Ibid.*, Report on Peonage Violations by Special Agent M. J. Cronin, May 25, 1922.

[60] *Ibid.*, Letter from Rush P. Holland to Fred Cubberly, June 19, 1922.

[61] *Ibid.*

[62] *Ibid.*, Letter from Charles Jordan to Howard Wright, July 9, 1922.

[63] *Ibid.*

[64] *Ibid.*, Grand Jury Testimony given by Charles Davis, July 24, 1922.

65 Carter, *ibid.*, pp. 330-80.

66 Samuel D. McCoy Papers, Letter from Glen Thompson to Mr. Tabert, August 25, 1922, Florida State Library, Tallahassee, Florida.

67 Minutes of the Joint Committee in Committee Room in Behalf of the Senate and the House of Representatives Appointed to Investigate the Death of Martin Tabert, Senator Stokes, Chairman, Monday, April 17, 1923, Office of the Secretary of State, Capitol Building, Tallahassee, Florida.

68 Carper, *ibid.*, pp. 370-80.

69 Amos Pinchot Papers, Letter from Amos Pinchot to Elizabeth Skinner and Mrs. W. S. Jennings, April 16, 1923, Library of Congress. This letter may also be found in the McCoy Papers.

70 *Ibid.*

71 Pinchot Papers, Letter from Amos Pinchot to editor of New York *World*, April 16, 1923.

72 *Ibid.*

73 McCoy Papers, Letter from August Rehan to Samuel McCoy, April 24, 1923.

74 *Ibid.*, "Abolish the Lash and the Lease" editorials.

75 Jacksonville *Florida Times-Union*, May 24 and May 25, 1923; see also Tallahassee *Daily Democrat*, May 24 and 25, 1923; New York *World*, May 25, 1923; *Acts and Resolutions*, 1923, c. 9332, pp. 412-413, and c. 9202, p. 231.

76 While the Brown and Tabert cases were in the news, Florida's Governor Sidney J. Catts was indicted for peonage violations. Although the federal government had a strong case against Catts, ultimately the Governor was acquitted. For a detailed discussion on this case, consult Carper, *ibid.*, pp. 325-29.

Some Notes on the Role of Negroes in the Establishment of Public Schools in South Carolina

EDWARD F. SWEAT

Francis Louis Cardoza, A. J. Ransier, and other African American delegates to South Carolina's constitutional convention in 1868 used their new-found political power to create a model educational system. Meeting in the city of Charleston, the African American delegates agreed that education was an essential tool for achieving first class citizenship. Nullifying almost a century of laws and customs designed to deny poor whites and enslaved blacks even the rudiments of an education, conventioneers, led by black delegates, ultimately authorized a tax-supported, universal school system for all South Carolinians.

Writing in the early 1960s at the vortex of Southern defiance against African American demands for civil rights and equality, Edward Sweat's essay contextualizes the struggle for universal education. Sweat argues that the United States Supreme Court's 1955 decrees favoring school desegregation reflect only the most recent battles in the ideological war to educate African American children. Even though African Americans, like the 1868 South Carolina delegates, created the blueprints for a public education system worthy of the American democratic ideals, their vision had not been realized.

IF THE IMPENDING public school crisis in the South can be said to result from the efforts of Negroes to get the decision of the United States Supreme Court implemented in the face of determined opposition from white political leaders,[1] it can also be affirmed that Negroes played a positive and decisive role in laying the foundations for the region's public school system of free, tax-supported schools. Over a half century ago, William E. B. DuBois flatly asserted that the thirst of the Negro for knowledge—a thirst that was to prove persistent and durable—was responsible for the birth of the public free school system of the Southern states.[2] As a matter of record, "A universal, well-established system dates from the day the black man got political power."[3] Earlier than that, Thomas Miller, one of the six Negro delegates to the South Carolina constitutional convention of 1895,[4] listed as one benefit derived by the state from Reconstruction government the building and maintaining of school houses.[5] That the establishment of the public school system represents one of the lasting benefits and positive accomplishments of governments organized under the Congressional plan of Reconstruction has been attested to by a number of reputable scholars of the period.[6]

The circumstances associated with the creation of a system of tax-supported public schools in the state of South Carolina are illustrative.[7] When the all white ultra-conservative architects of the first post-Civil War government erected in the state ignored the principle that the rights and duties of the freedmen had to be recognized in the state rebuilding process, their actions met with resistance from Congress and were criticized by Negroes of the state themselves. A group of Negroes assembled in Charleston to denounce the cavalier action of the state legislature in excluding them from the rights of citizenship "cheerfully accorded strangers, but denied us who were born and reared in your midst."[8] Their concern for education can be seen in their pledge to support "every measure calculated to elevate us to the rank of a wise, enlightened and Christian people," and in their expression of appreciation and gratitude for the "noble and self sacrificing spirit manifested by the various philanthropic and Christian associations . . . in providing teachers and establishing schools among us." Significantly, a resolution was adopted insisting upon good schools and the thorough education of their children throughout the state.[9]

The state government, which was the object of their censure, was eventually overthrown by Congress and the machinery for the establishment of a new one set in motion by the same branch of the national government. In this process the role of the Negro was that of an actual participant. The presence of seventy-six Negro delegates among the one hundred twenty-four elected to the South Carolina constitutional convention of 1868 meant that "for the first time in the history of the state the Negro was represented in an official body."[10] This convention has been referred to as "the first experiment in this country of working out a government based on the co-operation of the two races."[11] The individuals who composed the membership of the convention as a whole were men of varied character, attainments, and background. It seems hardly necessary to observe that, since about half of the Negro members had been slaves, one of their more distinguishing characteristics was their illiteracy. It should be noted, however, that the participation of this group in the proceedings of the body was limited in the main to voting under the direction of their leaders. This latter group included men who were far from being either illiterate or ignorant and who were doubtless as "learned as the leaders of any similar body which met in the Southern states since 1865."[12] Indeed, one of the local papers felt that "Beyond all question, the best men in the convention are the Colored members."[13]

Among the Negro delegates to the constitutional convention of 1868 was Francis Louis Cardoza.[14] This formally trained, intelligent, and articulate native of the state had been born in Charleston, reared in the North and educated abroad.[15] Prior to his entrance into politics he had served as pastor of a New Haven, Connecticut, church and on two separate occasions had founded and efficiently administered successful schools erected for Negroes in postbellum Charleston.[16] He was honored by his colleagues in the convention by being selected to serve as chairman of the important committee on education. Thus it was that a Negro of superior intellect and cultivation became the principal architect of South Carolina's first free, tax-supported school system. There is no question that educational opportunities of sorts had existed in the state before the Civil War. But there could be found no universal system of public schools financed by taxes levied on all citizens of the state. As early as the eighteenth century South Carolina had undertaken to establish county systems of schools, but the cost of operating such schools was not borne by direct taxation for that purpose.[17]

An 1811 act of the South Carolina legislature established free schools, but such institutions became in reality pauper schools for orphans and children of indigent parents. Even this measure came to be bitterly opposed by those elements of the population who conceived education to be the individual parent's responsibility and not that of the state, and who were congenitally opposed to taxation of all kinds.[18] The really fundamental problem of establishing free common schools, on the basis of direct taxation, was not solved by the state prior to the period of Congressional Reconstruction. As for Negroes, schools seemed not to have existed outside of Charleston. Schools which were organized in that city were neither state administered nor state supported. One such example can be found in the efforts of free people of color of Charleston who organized the "Minor Society" in 1810 to found a school for the training of their orphan children.[19] With the passage of stringent laws which made it illegal to teach any Negro, slave or free, it became increasingly difficult for people of color to obtain formal training. The fact that some schools for Negroes continued to operate in Charleston, despite the law, was both a testimonial to certain liberal whites and the ability of the antebellum Southerner to wink at the violation of the law when it served his purpose. For the majority of the Negro population, such instruction as they secured was of a clandestine nature often stimulated by the desire of certain whites to teach slaves religion.[20] Efforts to provide for the education of the colored race evoked strong resentment from a majority of the whites to whom the idea of attempting to educate the group was "the height of absurdity and folly." The South Carolinian, who paid extemely light taxes, had no wish to assume the burden of educating the children of poor whites, much less that of educating the children of a people regarded by him as inferior and uneducable. As a result, the provision of the state constitutional convention of 1868 for a tax-supported system of universal education was one of revolutionary import.

The committee on education of the constitutional convention of 1868 was composed of three white men and five Negroes, one of the whites subsequently serving as Superintendent of Public Instruction for South Carolina.[21] This report, laden as it is with historical significance, is reproduced in part below:

> Whereas, we hold these statements as axioms: that education is knowledge; that knowledge is power; that knowledge rightly applied is the best and highest kind of power; that the general and universal diffusion of education and intelligence among the people is the surest guarantee of the enhancement, increase, purity and preservation of the great principles of republican liberty; therefore it shall be the duty of the general assemblies, in all future periods of this commonwealth, to establish, provide for, and to perpetuate a liberal system of free public schools, to cherish the interests of literature and the sciences . . . to encourage private and public institutions, rewards, and immunities for the promotion of agriculture, arts, commerce, trades, manufactures, and natural history of the country; to countenance and inculcate the principles of humanity and general benevolence, public and private charity, industry and economy, honesty and punctuality, sincerity, sobriety, and all social affections among the people.[22]

The report's significance lies in its being adopted as a part of the new constitution. This meant that for the first time in its history the state of South Carolina provided constitutional and legal sanction for a tax-supported school system open to all. The committee's report contained provisions for a state superintendent of instruction and the manner in which he was to be elected. The general assembly was empowered to provide for a system of free public schools which should be kept open for at least six months annually. Section five of the report significantly broke with the antebellum past in its provision for the application of a "general capitation tax" and the assessment of a poll tax for the financial support of the public schools of the state.

Consideration of the committee's handiwork really got under way with a rather heated discussion centering around the fourth section of the report which recommended compulsory attendance at school for all children. Among the Negro delegates who favored compulsory education was A. J. Ransier, who was to become one of the two Negroes to serve as Lieutenant Governor of South Carolina during the Reconstruction period. He urged that the compulsory feature would compel neglectful parents to send their children to school, a stand based on his conviction that intelligence, education, and the progress of the people were necessary for the success of a republican government.[23]

As arguments for and against the compulsory section became more acrimonious, there developed a tendency to confuse the subject with the provision that all public schools should be free and open to all children. Certain elements within the convention argued that the adoption of the compulsory section would compel attendance of both white and colored in the same school. This line of argument evoked from Cardoza the sharp statement that the assertion by these delegates that the committee on education "would compel white and colored to go together in these schools" was both "ungentlemanly" and "untrue."[24] He called attention to the fact that the report simply provided that all children should be educated; whether in a public or private school would be a decision for the parents to make. It was made clear that at no point, the eleventh section included, was it said that there should not be separate schools, even though the report did not specifically call for separate schools.[25] Later attempts to educate Negroes and whites in the same schools would suggest, however, that some members of the convention were fairly certain that ultimately the children of both races would attend integrated schools.[26]

On the matter of taxation, there were those among the delegates who felt that failure to pay the poll tax should be grounds for depriving a person of the right to vote. After noting that the committee on education had included both a tax upon property and the poll tax, chairman Cardoza expressed his willingness to "receive amendments and suggestions" that would forever deny the legislature the power to deprive any person of the right to vote. It is of more than passing interest to observe that the amendment adopted by the convention that "no person shall ever be deprived the right of suffrage for the non-payment of said tax," was offered by a Negro delegate.[27] With the adoption by the convention of the committee's report and the subsequent ratification of the constitution, South Carolina at long last had authorization for a free, universal school system supported by tax money.

Despite the acerbity with which many South Carolinians of this day attack events of the Reconstruction era,[28] the cold fact is that the return of "home rule" to the state did not quite mean the return to everything antebellum. Since no new constitutional convention was called in the state until 1895, the Reconstruction constitution with its provision for universal education remained as the state's basic law. A school law based on these provisions was formulated in 1878, and with some modifications was retained. When it was felt necessary to draw up a new constitution the provision for public education originally found in the 1868 constitution was not essentially altered.[29]

Unfortunately, the complete implementation of the provision for true universal education was not to approach fulfillment until the twentieth century. In the organized movement toward fulfillment, universal education in the South came to mean education for the benefit of the white majority of the population. This is particularly evident in the realm of state appropriations for public schools. For, despite the actions of such foundations as the Slater and Jeanes funds, and the efforts of Julius Rosenwald in supplementing meager state appropriations, there still existed a marked disparity between state funds for white schools and those for Negro schools. This did violence to the principle of universal tax-supported education as visualized by the makers of the Reconstruction constitutions. The doctrine of "separate but equal" as established by the United States Supreme Court in *Plessy v. Ferguson,* for many years gave constitutional sanction to state laws requiring separate educational facilities. That these facilities were far from being equal is a fact that requires no documentation. State governmental leaders, for the most part, could comfort themselves with the propositions (widely accepted by the dominant group) that (1) Negroes received in facilities and services more than they paid in tax money, and (2) Negroes were being provided as many educational opportunities as they either desired or could absorb.

More fundamental, perhaps, was the inability of the separate Negro school to provide the basic service of promoting cultural equality. A respected student of the South and its institutions in speaking of this weakness in 1951, had this to say: "The fact that the school was forced to separate the races in its classrooms meant to the black child denial of opportunities for cultural contacts with members of the supposedly superior white race."[30]

The unanimous decision of the Supreme Court in 1954 which held that the doctrine of "separate but equal" had no place in public education points to the eventual implementation of the promise of true universal education as envisaged by the makers of the state constitutions of 1868. That this is unpleasant reality and that it came as a rude shock to many white Southerners, there is no doubt. But it is also true that there will come, perhaps gradually, the time when they must face up to the inevitableness of the situation.[31] When that day does come, then the dream of the Negroes who did so much during the Reconstruction to give to the South its first effective free public school system will be realized.

Notes

[1] For a recent analysis of the situation in one state written for the general reader, see Douglas Kiker, "The Coming Battle of Atlanta," *Look,* June 21, 1960, pp. 53-56.

[2] William E. B. DuBois, "Reconstruction and Its Benefits," *American Historical Review,* XV (July, 1910), 781-99.

[3] *Ibid.,* p. 797.

[4] A convention to revise the handiwork of the 1868 constitutional convention, which was composed of Negroes and whites, was not called until 1895, despite the fact that native white South Carolinians had regained control of the state government by 1877.

[5] *The Occasional Papers of the American Negro Academy,* No. 6 (Washington, D.C., 1899), p. 13.

[6] Howard K. Beale, "On Rewriting Reconstruction History," *American Historical Review,* XLV (July, 1940), 807-27; Francis B. Simkins, "New Viewpoints of Southern Reconstruction," *Journal of Southern History,* V (February, 1939), 49-61; Bernard A. Weisberger, "The Dark and Bloody Ground of Reconstruction Historiography," *Journal of Southern History,* XXV (November, 1959), 427-47.

[7] For a detailed examination of the activities of another Southern state, see Horace Mann Bond, *Negro Education in Alabama: A Study in Cotton and Steel* (Washington, D.C., 1939), especially pp. 87-94.

[8] *Proceedings of the Colored People's Convention of the State of South Carolina Held in Zion Church, Charleston, November 1865* (Charleston, 1865), pp. 9ff.

[9] *Ibid.,* p. 10.

[10] Francis B. Simkins and Robert H. Woody, *South Carolina During Reconstruction* (Chapel Hill, 1932), p. 91.

[11] A. A. Taylor, "The Negro in South Carolina During the Reconstruction," *Journal of Negro History,* IX (October, 1924), 383.

[12] Simkins and Woody, *op. cit.,* pp. 91-92.

[13] Charleston *Daily News,* January 31, 1868.

[14] *Proceedings of the Constitutional Convention of South Carolina, 1868* (Charleston, 1868), p. 1. Hereinafter referred to as *Proceedings.*

[15] Cardoza entered school in Charleston in 1842 and attended until he was twelve years old; his higher education was obtained at the University of Glasgow and at the Presbyterian Seminaries in Edinburgh and London. This man served in the state government of South Carolina as Secretary of State and later as State Treasurer. The most adequate biographical sketch of Cardoza is found in William J. Simmons, *Men of Mark, Eminent, Progressive, and Rising* (Cleveland, 1887); Clerk of the Senate, University of Glasgow to writer; Statistician, Public Schools of the District of Columbia to writer.

[16] Records of the War Department, Bureau of Refugees, Freedmen, and Abandoned Lands. From the Synopsis of School Reports, The National Archives, Washington, D.C.; *The American Missionary,* X (April, 1866), 270-71.

[17] Edgar W. Knight (ed.), *A Documentary History of Education in the South Before 1860* (5 vols., Chapel Hill, 1949), I, 671, 676.

[18] Charles W. Dabney, *Universal Education in the South* (2 vols., Chapel Hill, 1936), I, 226-27.

[19] Carter G. Woodson, *The Education of the Negro Prior to 1861* (Washington, D.C., 1919), p. 129.

[20] *Ibid.*, pp. 212, 220, *passim.*

[21] Edgar W. Knight, "Reconstruction and Education in South Carolina," *South Atlantic Quarterly*, XVIII (October, 1919), 354.

[22] *Proceedings*, p. 264.

[23] *Ibid.*, pp. 688-89.

[24] *Ibid.*, p. 704.

[25] *Ibid.*, p. 706.

[26] Dabney, *op. cit.*, p. 234.

[27] *Proceedings*, pp. 711-13, 738.

[28] For example, see editorial, "Root of Trouble" in the Columbia (S. C.) *State,* June 16, 1960. In this editorial the expression "a reign of mad dogs" is used to sweepingly characterize the period.

[29] Dabney, *op. cit.*, p. 237.

[30] Francis Butler Simkins, *The South Old and New: A History 1820-1947* (New York, 1951), p. 280.

[31] For a perceptive analysis of the situation see editorials by Ralph McGill in the *Atlanta Constitution*, September 15, 1958; February 14, 1960.

The Negro and the Democratic Party, 1875-1915

AUGUST MEIER

Less well known in the story of Reconstruction era politics is the African American struggle, in both the North and South, to use the ballot wisely, to forge political alliances, and to negotiate compromises. While the Republican Party, as the party of Lincoln, retained the loyalty of African Americans throughout the period, some blacks found it politically expedient to join the Democratic Party, to advocate a third party, or to take an independent stance.

August Meier's essay chronicles the complexity of black political thought and strategy during the period under review. The author argues that since the political stakes were high, translating into patronage, favorable legislation, and economic opportunity, blacks learned quickly to maneuver in political waters. By the early 1880s, just a decade after ratification of the Fifteenth Amendment, African Americans demonstrated considerable political sophistication. Many black leaders cautioned that blind loyalty to one party could mean political race suicide. Like their white counterparts, blacks attempted to use the ballot and political party affiliations as vehicles for progress, a progress that more often than not, however, remained unrealized.

UNTIL THE TIME OF Franklin Roosevelt and the New Deal, the great majority of Negroes consistently maintained their allegiance to the Republican party. Nevertheless, at least twice between the end of Reconstruction and the First World War—once in the 1880s and again between 1908 and 1912—distinguished persons in the Negro community attempted or advised cooperation with the Democratic party.

On the other hand, there were always some Negroes who supported the Democrats. Even during Reconstruction a number had done so for a variety of reasons—sympathy, cajolery, ambition, or intimidation. Certain antebellum free Negroes who had been attached to upper class whites by virtue of their occupational roles as barbers or skilled artisans, and some of the antebellum house servant slave group, who identified their interests with those of their former masters, voted for the Democrats out of conviction.[1]

Then, too, during Reconstruction, rumblings of dissatisfaction were heard within Republican ranks. A few men, like the minister J. Sella Martin, followed Sumner into the ranks of the Liberal Republicans in 1872. Senator Hiram Revels went so far as to leave the party in 1875, charging that because of corruption and dishonesty it had lost all right to political power.[2] Senator Blanche K. Bruce in 1876 criticized the party because of P. B. S. Pinchback's exclusion from the Senate, and he and Pinchback (formerly acting governor of Louisiana) advised Negroes to divide their vote in order to obtain the best political advantage. Both, however, soon became loyal Republicans again.[3] Congressman John R. Lynch, speaking in 1876, probably expressed some Negroes' viewpoint well enough when he said that the ideal situation would be for Negroes to be "independent" in politics, but that the attitude of Southern whites forced a political division along racial lines.[4]

The story of Negroes and the Democratic party in the South after Reconstruction is soon told. As suffrage declined, support of the Democrats did also. Those who did stand with the Democrats tended to be the old servant class or successful, conservative businessmen.

Nor were Negro Republican leaders always averse to working with the Democrats. White Republicans of Mississippi complained, during the Arthur administration, of secret arrangements between Democrats and Negro Republicans, permitting Negroes the crumbs of Federal patronage, in return for unpublicized support of Democrats in state and local elections.[5] Moreover, in the black counties of both Mississippi and South Carolina there appeared the practice known as "fusion"—of dividing up the offices between Negro Republicans and white Democrats so that the former held a seat or so in the legislature and a share of the less important local positions. This compromise appeared in six or eight Mississippi counties in the 1880s, and in Georgetown, Beaufort, and Berkeley in South Carolina during the eighties and early nineties.[6]

During the eighties and nineties Southern Negroes participated to some extent in the reform or "independent" and agrarian political movements; and in the party warfare that followed, many sided with the Democrats. In Virginia most Negroes at first supported the Readjustors in the late seventies and early eighties; later the Conservatives made serious inroads into the Negro vote.[7] In Georgia in 1889 many refused to support the Independent candidate espoused by white Republicans, because of his anti-Negro sentiments, and a number voted the Democratic ticket.[8] The Populist Movement also resulted in large numbers of Negroes "voting" Democratic, as the result of economic pressure, intimidation and fraud. In some cases Negroes voluntarily supported the Democrats against the Populists. In Georgia, for example, Democrats appealed to Negroes by nominating William J. Northen for governor. In Atlanta and in Augusta Negroes formed Democratic Northen clubs, and in the latter town registered Negro votes for Watson's rival for the senate.[9] One observer claimed that while Negroes voted on both sides, "of the State as a whole it may be said the Populism was defeated by the Colored voters espousing the Democratic side."[10]

While the majority of Negroes remained loyal to the Republicans, significant criticism and even some defections were evident during the eighties in the North. From ardent championship of the Negroes' cause, the party had shifted first to compromise and then to complaisant acceptance of the Southern race system. The Compromise of 1877 frankly symbolized what actually had been the underlying trend for several years—that the Republican party was simply unwilling to enforce the Reconstruction legislation in the South. President Arthur's administration courted anti-Negro white "independent" political groups in the South, in an attempt to increase party strength. Not only did Republicans fail to halt outrages and disfranchisement, but it was a Republican Supreme Court that in 1883 declared the Civil Rights Act unconstitutional; and it was a Republican Congress that in 1890 repudiated its campaign pledges by failing to pass the Lodge Federal Elections Bill and the Blair Federal Aid to Education Bill, which would have protected Negro political rights and improved Negro schooling in the South. Republican presidents grew increasingly silent on Negro rights, while the lily-white faction of the party made its appearance. The success of the Democrats in 1884 and 1892, if anything, hastened Republican desertion of the Negroes' cause. On the other hand Negroes were impressed by Cleveland's moderate policy in regard to colored officeholders, and by the favorable actions of certain Northern Democratic state machines like those in New York and Massachusetts. Consequently Northern Negroes were brought to criticism and disillusionment, and in some cases even withdrawal from the Republican party.

Suggestions either of outright espousal of the Democrats, or of urging division of the Negro vote and "independence" in politics, were heard in the late 1870s, and rose to a crescendo during the early 1880s. Among the voices raised in behalf of this point of view were those of former abolitionist leaders Peter H. Clark and George T. Downing. A Republican since 1856, Cincinnati high school principal Clark had joined the Liberal Republicans in 1872, and thereafter worked with the Democrats, except in 1878 when he was a candidate for state school commissioner on the Workingmen's ticket. He insisted that his support for the Democrats was not at variance with his desire for full citizenship rights for Negroes.[11] In 1885 he stated his political credo:

> I have never thought it wise for the colored vote to be concentrated in one party, thus antagonizing the other great party and tempting it to do against us as Republicans what they would have hesitated to do against us as Negroes. Whenever colored men find themselves in accord with Democrats in local or national issues they should vote with them and thus disarm much of the malevolence that is born of political rather than racial antagonism. . . . The welfare of the Negro is my controlling political motive, and I supported Mr. Cleveland because I thought his election would promote that welfare.[12]

Downing, a wealthy caterer of New York and Newport, and one of the most distinguished American Negroes both before and after the Civil War, was in the forefront of those agitating for equal rights. As early as 1869 he had thought Negroes entitled to more consideration from the party which emancipated them; in 1871 he and Frederick Douglass engaged in a spirited controversy over the virtues of the party.[13] But it was not until 1883, that he finally broke with the Republicans,[14] after assuring himself that leading Democrats in Northern states favored racial justice. At that time, he declared himself in favor of "a division of the colored vote, because I believe it will be better to have more than one party anxious, concerned, and cherishing the hope that at least a part of that vote may be obtained; because division would result in an increased support from all quarters."[15]

By 1883, in fact, considerable disaffection had appeared. In Pennsylvania a Colored Independent Party included noted men like the abolitionist Robert Purvis and William Still of Underground Railroad fame.[16] In South Carolina the politician and lawyer D. Augustus Straker espoused the cause of "colored Independents." Negroes, he said, "are shaking off the waist-strings which politically and otherwise attach us to others who lead us as cattle."[17] A national convention of colored men at Louisville in September heard Frederick Douglass call himself "an uneasy Republican," and urge Negroes to "follow no party blindly. If the Republican party cannot stand a demand for justice and fair play it ought to go down."[18] Later in the year, the Georgia politician and editor Colonel W. A. Pledger, chairman of the convention's executive committee, hoped that body would adopt a policy that would either bring recognition by both parties and a division of the vote, or else recognition by one party to which Negroes could then adhere.[19] In Massachusetts James M. Trotter broke with the party and resigned his post as assistant superintendant of the registered letter department in Boston—a political appointment he had held for eighteen years. About the same time Democratic Governor Benjamin F. Butler, who had received a substantial Negro vote on the basis of his war record, appointed the lawyer-politician George L. Ruffin judge of city court for Charleston—making him the first Negro judge in the North. From then on the number of Negro "independents" in Massachusetts gradually increased.[20] Two years later the Massachusetts Colored League was formed with Ruffin as president. At its first meeting it called attention to the favorable actions of the Democrats, and declared that since the Republican party was no longer what it was in Sumner's day, Negroes should support the party that offered them most.[21]

Two leading newspaper editors during the 1880s, W. Calvin Chase of the Washington *Bee* and T. Thomas Fortune of the New York *Freeman, Globe* and *Age*, were both highly critical of the Republicans and espoused a division of the vote, though political realities and perhaps campaign subsidies kept them in the Republican column at election times. To Chase it seemed in 1883 that Negroes had been loyal to a party that had "deserted, disowned, and frowned upon the colored people of the South in 1876," and that thereafter had "steadily ignored the cardinal principles" of its campaign platforms. "We unhesitatingly charge that the present managed Republican party is a little, if anything, better than the hide-bound slaveholding Democratic party."[22] A few months later, however, he regarded "the action of the Democratic party . . . a sufficient evidence to convince the Negro that it is dangerous . . . to make any concession whatever with the party."[23] While in the spring of 1884 he regarded Negroes as "the balance of power in the coming political contest," by September he was enthusiastically supporting Blaine and accusing "the so-called Negro Democrat" of attempting "to mislead an oppressed race of people." But scarcely was Cleveland elected than he urged Southern Negroes to divide their votes, and added that "the time has now come for the Negro . . . to be an independent in the body politic. It is the folly of the Republican party which will necessarily compel us to be independents."[24] Chase's erratic course, symptomatic of Negro discouragement in the face of growing Republican indifference, continued into the next century.

Far abler was Timothy Thomas Fortune, the leading Negro journalist between the middle eighties and 1907, when he sold the *Age* to Fred R. Moore and Booker Washington. In the early eighties he argued that Negroes must be less "clannish" in politics, for "the idea of political unanimity had been tried and found wanting." He "arraign[ed]" the "selfish" Republican party for its disastrous Reconstruction policy of "revolting peculation and crime . . . bankrupting and terrorizing" the South, and for its "base ingratitude, subterfuge and hypocrisy to its black partisan allies," whom it left to the mercy of their enemies. Because the party had "degenerated into an ignoble scramble for place and power," had "made slaves freemen and freemen slaves in the same breath by conferring the franchise and withholding the guarantees to insure its exercise," had "betrayed its trust in permitting thousands of innocent men to be slaughtered," and in failing to protect Negro political rights in the South, he did "not deem it binding upon colored men further to support the Republican party when other advantageous affiliations can be formed." While nothing but evil existed in the "bourbon Democratic party," still a Negro could be "an independent, a progressive Democrat. . . . The hour has come when thoughtful colored men should cease to put their faith upon broken straws; when they should cease to be the willing tools of a treacherous and corrupt policy."[25]

"Give us a new party," Fortune exclaimed editorially on February 3, 1883. Colored Republicans in New York City, he said, had been quick to accept office from the Democrats,

> and if they will allow us to insinuate, all the recognition they ever will get will be outside of the Republican party. . . . The colored men of the North may 'kick' against the independence of *The Globe* all they want to, but, until they acquire some of the backbone which we have all along told them they need, they will be used to pile up high majorities for the Republican machine and be squelched after the election just as if they were so many mushrooms.

After the Civil Rights decision, he bitterly denounced the Republican Party, not only for it, but also for "the infamous barter and treachery" of the Compromise of 1877, and "the effeminate, the puerile, the nerveless policy pursued by Mr. R. B. Hayes." "We do not," he added, "ask the corrupt Republican party for sympathy; we shun it with loathing and contempt! Sympathy indeed! . . . We ask for justice, simple justice!"[26] Yet he supported Blaine in 1884, for Democratic policy was even worse than the Republican.[27] During 1885 Fortune was standoffish; the election of Cleveland found him "absolutely indifferent as to the fate of parties because none of them evinced any great concern for our welfare."[28] However, in his book, *The Negro in Politics,* Fortune said Negroes should organize and be active in all parties—in short, "Throw away sentimentality in politics," and act on the motto "*Race first; then party.*"[29] Though the *Age* supported the Republicans in 1888, it afterwards criticized the Harrison administration for the defeat of the Lodge and Blair Bills and the lily-white tendencies in the party. Yet Fortune effectively posed the political dilemma facing Negroes when he asked in 1889:

> But where is the use of dwelling on this question now? The South-
> ern white men have made up their minds to drive the Negro to the
> wall, and the Negro must oppose to the Democrats an unbroken
> front as long as this remains true. As long as the Republican Party
> stands for everything in this respect that the Democratic Party op-
> poses the colored voters will remain in sentiment . . . Republicans as
> solid, as thick and as impenetrable as a Chinese wall. When the
> Democratic party ceases to be a party of unmitigated cussedness the
> discussion of the question of a division of voters in the South will be
> in order.[30]

By and large, though a few organs like the Indianapolis *World* were Democratic sheets, the Negro press remained loyal to, but criti-cal of, the Republican party. Few went even as far as Fortune and Chase in toying with "independency" and support of the Democrats.

While a few older leaders like Clark and Downing openly es-poused the Democratic cause, the chief figures among Negro Demo-crats during the eighties and nineties were J. Milton Turner of Missouri, J. C. Matthews and J. E. W. Thompson of New York state, C. H. J. Taylor of Kansas, H. C. C. Astwood of Louisiana, James M. Trot-ter of Massachusetts, and, though he was not a politician, T. McCants Stewart of Brooklyn. Turner had formerly been an active Republican, serving as minister resident and consul-general in Liberia from 1871 to 1878. J. C. Matthews, an Albany lawyer and former Republican ora-tor, was regarded as the leading Negro Democrat at the opening of Cleveland's first administration. He had joined the Liberal Republi-cans in 1872, and subsequently became a regular Democrat, holding several minor state offices. Cleveland appointed him Recorder of the Deeds for the District of Columbia, the highest post held by Negroes at the time, but he was rejected and replaced by Trotter. J. E. W. Thompson, appointed minister to Haiti, after the Senate had turned down the nomination of historian George Washington Williams, was a leading Catholic layman and a graduate of Yale Medical School in 1883. C. H. J. Taylor, a Kansas lawyer and newspaper editor, served briefly as minister resident and consul general in Liberia briefly in 1887 succeeding another Cleveland appointee, Moses Aaron Hopkins; afterwards he became an attorney in Atlanta. H. C. C. Astwood, a close friend of Taylor's, and sometime editor of Pinchback's *Loui-sianian,* had served as consul to Trinidad under President Arthur, and now became consul to Santo-Domingo. T. McCants Stewart, who had been a South Carolina lawyer and professor before migrating to Liberia, upon his return from Africa in 1885 settled in Brooklyn (where he served as a member of the Board of Education, 1891-1895), and became a supporter of Cleveland, saying "We are neither manly nor politic in clinging to the hem of the garments of the Republican party. . . . We should divide on party questions growing out of silver coinage, the tariff and civil service."[31] He denied that Negroes owed any debt to the Republicans who had abolished slavery as a mere war measure, and claimed that solidity in politics brought hatred from opponents and the contempt of friends.[32]

C. H. J. Taylor's *Whites and Blacks*, 1889, used arguments similar to those of Stewart, and in addition, breathed a spirit of conciliation and friendship for the white South. He urged colored and white taxpayers to vote on the assumption that their interests were one, and told Negroes to cooperate with the best whites. Like Fortune he was highly critical of Radical Reconstruction. Negroes, he said, had "voted in the white political scum they thought to be their dearest friends, but who . . . proved themselves their greatest enemies." "All the trouble between the races," he continued, "originates out of politics, to the detriment and injury of the Negro." If the Negro would show whites that he "understand[s]individual responsibility as a citizen . . . appreciate[s] favors conferred," and no longer exhibits prejudice toward them, "then will come your political emancipation." He did not favor leaving politics, but he did feel that only "the best colored men" should seek political "recognition." If Negroes were so stupid as to vote blindly with the Republicans rather than for the interests of their section, proving themselves "unforgiving" and refusing "the olive branch of political peace offered by Grover Cleveland . . . then by all means disfranchise them, and that speedily."[33]

Most Negro leaders, however, though like Frederick Douglass increasingly critical and even indifferent toward the Republican party, never went so far as to leave it, nor even to urge division of the Negro vote. One important figure, however, did. This was J. C. Price, president of Livingstone College, North Carolina, and one of the top half dozen Negro leaders in the country between 1890 and his premature death in 1894. Price urged "independence" in politics as part of a mildly conciliatory policy toward the South. Writing in the *Independent* in 1891 he predicted Negro "independence" in politics: "The last decade of the century will find him voting for good men and wise measures, rather than for mere partisans as such."[34] Price thought highly of Cleveland and felt that since "the Democrats are the dominant element in the South," Negroes, "as far as is consistent with instincts of manhood . . . would do well to harmonize with that element . . . even at the sacrifice of non-essentials."[35]

Cleveland Democrats continued to be active during Harrison's administration. The platform of the New York State Cleveland League, James C. Matthews, president, in addition to the usual arguments, added a new note—that the Democratic party was the "poor man's party . . . the exponent of labor, which is our lot."[36] A Negro National Democratic League with C. H. J. Taylor as president, and Astwood, Clark, Thompson, Matthews and Turner among its leaders, campaigned for Cleveland in 1892.[37] Confirmation troubles again dogged Cleveland's appointments after his re-election. Taylor, appointed minister to Bolivia, was rejected by the Senate, and it was only with the active lobbying of Douglass among Republican senators that he was approved for Recorder of the Deeds in 1894, having been rejected once for that post also.[38] Astwood, appointed consul to Calais, was also rejected, and angrily turned to the Republican party.[39] The Santo-Domingo post went this time to lawyer Archibald H. Grimke of Boston in 1894, while the Liberian position went to Rev. W. H. Heard, later an emigrationist and bishop in the African Methodist Episcopal Church.

Actually the turn of the decade had marked the high water mark for Negro support of the Democrats before the elections of 1908 and 1912. The rapidly increasing proscription, segregation, and constitutional disfranchisement in the South made it clear that dividing the vote was but an ephemeral hope in spite of Republican indifference. While many might protest at Republican attitudes and praise Cleveland; while even the conservative A. M. E. Church *Review* might say that "When the vote of the colored man in the South becomes worth something his life will be worth something. . . . There is no better way to make his vote valuable than by dividing it,"[40] the idea was chimerical. D. A. Straker had returned to the Republicans by 1888. Downing in 1891 had become critical of the Democrats, though he continued to believe that Negroes should use both parties realistically rather than passively support the Republicans.[41] An important defection was T. McCants Stewart who in 1895, upon being "frozen out" of a job by objecting Democrats, returned to the Republicans.[42] The important Indianapolis *Freeman*, which since its founding in 1888 had supported the Democrats, in 1891 became a Republican paper. Part of the discouragement undoubtedly lay with Democratic appointments, the *Bee* reporting that Matthews would have succeeded John R. Lynch as fourth auditor of the Treasury if Secretary Carlisle had not objected.[43] Perhaps the Cleveland *Gazette* summed up intelligent Negro opinion during the later 1890s when it said: "We have never advocated bolting the [Republican] party, but there are times in its history when it is better to withhold our support and let it suffer an ignominious defeat than perpetuate within its ranks injustice and wrong."[44]

Naturally most of those who supported "independence" or the Democrats were protesting against Republican neglect of Negroes and their rights. Yet as we have observed in a few individuals this policy was associated with the idea of conciliation of Southern whites. Taylor and Price expressed themselves in this fashion. Professor Kelly Miller of Howard University, who had been impressed by Cleveland's attitude toward Negroes,[45] stirred up considerable controversy toward the end of the century by urging "self-effacement" in politics. By this he meant that Negroes, while not giving up their constitutional right to vote, should let the "best class" of whites guide affairs, and should support the Democrats rather than antagonize whites by attempting to be a "controlling factor."[46]

A few distinguished Negroes continued to support the Democrats, usually sporadically as in the case of bishops Abraham Grant and W. B. Derrick of the A. M. E. Church, who voted for Bryan in 1900.[47] So also did the tempestuous Georgia emigrationist, A. M. E. bishop Henry M. Turner, who earlier had worked with Cleveland's Secretary of the Interior Hoke Smith, and as late as 1908 and 1912 was still supporting Bryan and Wilson. Said Turner in 1900:

> I am not a Democrat, never have been one and never expect to be. . . . I dislike Mr. McKinley, and the attitude which he has assumed toward the negro, and I intend to vote for Mr. Bryan in the belief that any change is better than none. . . . For 16 years I have been cooling toward the Republican party.[48]

McKinley had done nothing but make some appointments; Bryan, he was sure, would "use his influence in behalf of right and justice." A good deal of the sentiment leading Negroes to support the Democrats in 1900 seemed to be its anti-imperialist plank. John B. Syphax, a prominent Washingtonian, speaking before the United Colored Democracy in Brooklyn, rang the changes on the treachery of the carpetbaggers and the imperialism of the Republicans and their oppression of colored Filipinos. "Every negro burned at the stake, every negro lynched, ought to be charged to the damnable interference of the Republican party," he was quoted as saying.[49]

An important source of Democratic support in the North was the fact that in many instances Democratic politicians proved more sympathetic to Negro aspirations than did Republicans. Thus, St. Paul lawyer Frederick L. McGhee wrote to Booker Washington on September 14, 1904, explaining that while he was anxious to see Roosevelt re-elected, still he would support the Democrats as he was a member of that party in Minnesota where it was better to Negroes than the

Republicans. In certain Northern cities, moreover, the Democratic machines had begun to court the Negro vote. In Chicago mayors Carter H. Harrison I and II between the early 1890s and 1905 appealed with considerable success to the Negro vote, though the Republican party on the whole remained the choice of Chicago Negroes.[50] A Democratic club had appeared in Boston as early as 1895. The number of Boston Negroes voting Democratic "steadily increased," and in 1905, 1907, and 1909 a substantial number went "independent," "Democratic" or "non-partisan." In 1910 between one third and one half of Boston Negroes voted for the Democratic gubernatorial candidate.[51]

In New York Tammany Hall leader Richard Croker organized the United Colored Democracy to handle Negro patronage—a mere gesture, as almost no Negroes got worthwhile positions.[52] The leaders of the Colored Democracy in New York during the early years of the century were "Chief" Robert E. Lee, who had headed the national Democratic Negro organization in the late nineties; Ralph Langston, son of the noted abolitionist and congressman J. Mercer Langston; and James Curtis.[53] In 1910 a new Democratic state organization with Judge James C. Matthews as chairman, and assistant corporation counsel James D. Carr and street department inspector Robert H. Wood as his chief assistants, was created, rivaling Lee and Langston, and obtaining charge of the state end of the campaign.[54] This campaign was remarkably successful. Internal Revenue Collector Charles W. Anderson reported to Booker Washingon that he had never before "seen so many negroes wearing Democratic badges." It appeared that Matthews, A. M. E. Zion bishop Alexander Walters, and N.A.A.C.P. director of research and publicity W. E. B. DuBois had circularized Negroes, advising them "to vote the Democratic ticket, if they wanted colored policemen and colored firemen in New York City, and a colored regiment of soldiers in the State Guard."[55] By 1913 Carr, DuBois and Wood were quarreling, and Lee had deserted Langston to become Wood's "strongest" supporter.[56] Moreover, the Democratic party proved so disappointing in New York City that by 1915 less than a thousand Negro Democrats remained there.[57]

In addition to the work of Northern Democratic machines, the policies of the national Republican administrations served to lead many to vote Democratic. Only thus can the success of the Democrats in 1910, for example, be explained. Roosevelt's actions alternately pleased and distressed Negroes. His words of commendation for Negro soldiers fighting with the Rough Riders in Cuba were replaced, eighteen months after the event, by charges of cowardice. He received Negroes' praise for inviting Booker Washington to dinner, for closing the Indianola, Mississippi, post office rather than acceding to white demands that he dismiss the Negro woman appointed postmaster, and for doggedly maintaining his efforts to carry the appointment of W. D. Crum as collector of the port of Charleston, South Carolina, in the face of powerful senatorial opposition. Yet meanwhile he was playing a shifty game with lily-white Republicans and Gold Democrats in the South, and by 1905 he was speaking favorably of Southern traditions. In 1906 the impetuous president summarily discharged dishonorably the 25th regiment stationed at Fort Brown, Texas, on unproved charges of rioting in nearby Brownsville. No action of the president hurt and angered Negroes more than this one. Little better was Roosevelt's message to Congress of December, 1906, which blamed Negroes as a whole for the crime of rape, falsely asserted that most lynchings were caused by assaults of Negro men on white women, and urged industrial education as best for Negroes. Taft's pronouncements meanwhile were even less acceptable, indicating as they did that he favored industrial education almost to the exclusion of higher education for Negroes, and that, since the intentions of the framers of the Fourteen and Fifteenth Amendments were unenforceable, he favored ballot restrictions in the South as long as they were consistent with the literal wording of the amendments. Critics also pointed to his connection, as secretary of war, with the president's action in the Brownsville case. While Negroes had been elated over Roosevelt's appointments (forgetting that he appointed far fewer than McKinley), they grew upset over the rapid loss of offices under Taft, and over his frank declaration that he would not appoint Negroes to office in the South where local whites objected. The lily-whites made greater headway than ever, and segregation began to appear in certain federal offices in Washington. By the time of the election of 1912 Negroes were faced with a sorry choice indeed: a Democratic candidate, Wilson, born in the South, who would make only the vaguest concessions to Negroes in his campaign promises; Taft, who had thoroughly alienated Negroes during his administration; and Roosevelt, who, while appealing to Negro voters in the North, refused to seat Negro delegates from the South at the Progressive party convention. Under the circumstances most Negroes voted for Roosevelt.

Another factor that served to crystallize the hostility of a certain group of Negroes toward Roosevelt and Taft was their association with Booker T. Washington. Those "radical" Negroes like Monroe Trotter (son of James M. Trotter), editor of the Boston *Guardian*, and the noted W.E.B. DuBois, men who criticized Washington for his conciliatory tone, his policy of gradualism, his acceptance of segregation, and his soft-pedaling of the franchise and higher education, were also resentful of the control he exercised as arbiter of federal appointments for Negroes under Roosevelt and Taft—a power that he used to enhance his personal position and undercut his critics. Their dislike of Washington combined with other factors we have mentioned to make their attack on the two presidents and the Republicans especially bitter. And it was this group of "anti-Bookerites" that was to play the most important role in creating sentiment among Negroes for the Democrats between 1908 and 1912.

The Negro press reflected the growing dissatisfaction with Republican policies. Even organs close to and subsidized by Booker Washington roundly berated Roosevelt for his stand on Brownsville and his message to Congress in December 1906, and certain of them were lukewarm toward Taft in 1908. Fortune, whose *Age* was subsidized by Washington, though he had given up ideas of political "independency" during the 1890s after Brownsville, spoke of the "party treachery" and recalled the misdeeds of the Republicans since 1877.[58] In succeeding years the *Age*, edited by another Washington protégé, Fred R. Moore, criticized Taft throughout most of his administration, and boomed local Democratic politicos in New York City. Editor George L. Knox of the Indianapolis *Freeman*, who had been irked in 1904 by Washington's insistence that he not run for Congress so as not to jeopardize Roosevelt's chances in Indiana, critcized the Negro's gullibility in politics, and in 1908 displayed an indifferent air, declaring that race was not an issue in the campaign, that Repubicans did not care about Negroes, that Negroes should vote for the friendliest men, and that—to be frank—local Democrats were pretty good.[59]

By 1908, moreover, substantial elements of the Niagara Movement, the protest organization launched in 1905 to combat the Washington "heresies" and to agitate for equal rights, had come out definitely in support of the Democrats. As early as 1907 the Niagarite orator Rev. Reverdy C. Ransom had expressed delight at signs of Negro political independence.[60] At a stormy convention in Philadelphia in April 1908, called by Monroe Trotter on behalf of the Constitution Colored League,[61] "radicals" Alexander Walters, Trotter, and Revs. S. L. Carothers and J. Milton Waldron of Washington emerged as the group that came to be the backbone National Negro American Political League formally organized in Chicago in June. This league was reported to consist of representatives of groups like the Afro-American Council (formerly the leading rights organizations among Negroes, and between 1902 and 1907 controlled by Booker Washington, but now on its decline), the Niagara Movement and the Constitu-

tional League (an interracial precursor of the National Association
for the Advancement of Colored People), all of which were in the
anti-Bookerite camp. Waldron became its president, and it took a
strong stand against Roosevelt's policies.[62] During the summer Bishop
Walters asserted, in his characteristically bumbling manner, that
Bryan had assured him that he would reinstate the Brownsville
soldiers and work against disfranchisement; Bryan promptly denied
making the latter promise.[63] The New England Suffrage League, led
by Trotter, in October declared that "neither Mr. Bryan nor any
other Northern Democrat could be more pro-southern in feeling
than President Roosevelt."[64] In fact, a significant segment of thoughtful Negroes did support Bryan in 1908. The Cleveland *Gazette* followed the other "radical" leaders in deserting "Mr. Disfranchisement,
Jim Crow Car' Taft"; it urged Negroes to vote for anyone else in fact,
and thus "preserve your self-respect, manhood, and race-respect."[65]

It was, however, DuBois who gave the best rationale for the position of the "radical" anti-Bookerites who attempted cooperation
with the Democrats in 1908. Like some other Niagarites DuBois
merged his disgust with Roosevelt and Taft and his opposition to
Washington with his proclivities toward the labor movement and the
socialization of property, and believed that the Democratic party
might well move toward both racial and economic justice. At first he
was lukewarm. In February 1908 he called the Socialists "the only
party which treats the Negroes as men," and urged Negroes to do
their best to defeat Taft in the nominating convention, to "uproot
Rooseveltism if it snaps heart strings." At that time he had thought
Bryan as bad as Taft, but a month later he viewed Bryan's silence on
the Negro problem as "infinitely better" than the statements of the
"coward of Brownsville."[66] Reactionary Northern Republicans had
sided with Southern Democrats to deprive Negroes of their rights,
and if this "wing of the Republicans triumph, we are in grave danger" of being "sentenced for a century to Jim Crow cars, peonage,
and disfranchisement." Deserted by the Republicans, Negroes should
"punish the party that insults and neglects us." Southern Democrats
were not fools, and if Bryan should win by virtue of Negro votes in
the twelve states where they formed a "balance of power," the Democrats would no longer "flout" them.[67]

By the summer DuBois was asserting that Negroes should support the Democrats aside from purely racial considerations, for "the
Democratic party today stands for the strict regulation of corporate
wealth, for the freedom and independence of brown and black men
in the West Indies and the Philippines, for the right of labor to strive
for higher wages and better working conditions, for a low tariff, and

for the abolition of all special privileges." As laborers, as colored men, and as consumers, Negroes would benefit from a Democratic victory.[68] Whether or not Bryan would appoint Negroes to office was relatively unimportant; Negroes should vote for justice for all Americans, for the party whose economic policies would benefit them in the long run.[69] By the fall he declared that Negroes had the opportunity of splitting the Northern and Southern wings of the party, making it truly the party of the masses; of ending "the impossible alliance of radical socialistic Democracy at the North with an aristocratic caste party at the South . . . [which] does not believe in free trade and . . . does believe in Imperialism, caste privilege, and a free hand to corporate wealth." The "solid" Southern Democratic vote and the solid Negro Republican vote were equally illogical. *"The Negro voter, today therefore, has in his hand the tremendous power of emancipating the Democratic party from its enslavement to the reactionary South."* Moreover since Northern Democrats treated Negroes "better" than Northern Republicans, Negroes should at least give the Democrats a chance.[70]

After the election the Colored Democratic organization continued to be active, at first under the presidency of Waldron who also became chairman of the Niagara Movement's Suffrage Department.[71] It met in May 1909 at Columbus, and at Atlantic City in 1910, by which time the name had been changed to the National Independent Political League. At this meeting Walters, the only African Methodist Episcopal Zion bishop to vote Democratic in 1908, became president and Trotter corresponding secretary.[72] This group achieved some success in the elections of 1910 as we have seen. It claimed to have had over forty campaign speakers at work, with headquarters in New York, cooperating with Trotter's New England Suffrage League, and carrying on vigorous campaigns in New Jersey, Massachusetts, New York, Ohio, Illinois, Indiana, and Missouri.[73]

The same group joined heartily in the 1912 campaign, though Walters was by then trying to cultivate friendly relations with Booker Washington. As Arthur S. Link has pointed out, most Negroes still feared the Democrats and were skeptical of Wilson.[74] Link makes a great deal of the influence of Oswald Garrison Villard in swinging the Negro "radicals" of the N.A.A.C.P. (the Niagara Movement having disappeared when most of its members joined the new organization formed in 1909-1910), behind Wilson,[75] though as we have seen, this group actually had been supporting the Democrats since 1908. They swallowed Wilson because of their hostility to Roosevelt, Taft, and Washington. The National Independent Political League, whose president was now the former Niagarite Byron Gunner,[76] worked closely with the Colored National Democratic League, of which Walters was president.[77] The former organization published a series of pamphlets and broadsides, which urged that "A good Democrat is as good as a good Republican. . . . Governor Wilson is a good man. He has never harmed our race. He is a Christian gentleman," reviewed the treacherous Republican past, and pointed to the growing segregation in the federal offices at Washington.[78] The N.A.A.C.P. organ, the *Crisis*, edited by DuBois, had from the beginning urged "independence" in voting, and supported the Democrats. After toying with the idea of working with the Progressives, DuBois withdrew from the Socialist Party which he had joined in 1911 in order to support Wilson.[79] He rationalized his action:

> As to Mr. Wilson, there are, one must confess, disquieting facts; he was born in Virginia and he was long president of a college which did not admit Negro students and yet was not honest enough to say so. . . . On the whole, we do not believe that Woodrow Wilson admires Negroes. . . . Notwithstanding such possible preferences, Woodrow Wilson is a cultivated scholar and has brains. . . . We have, therefore, a conviction that Mr. Wilson will treat black men and their interests with far-sighted fairness. He will not be our friend, but he will not belong to the gang of which Tillman, Vardaman, Hoke Smith and Blease are the brilliant expositors. He will not advance the cause of the oligarchy in the South, he will not seek further means of 'Jim Crow' insult, he will not dismiss black men wholesale from office and he will remember that the Negro in the United States has a right to be heard and considered; and if he becomes President by the grace of the black man's vote, his Democratic successors may be more willing to pay the black man's price of decent travel, free labor, votes, and education.[80]

Debs may have been the ideal candidate, but Wilson the only realistic choice.

There were some difficult moments, as when Waldron misstated some of Wilson's views, making them appear more favorable to Negroes than they really were, but in the end the anti-Roosevelt, anti-Taft, anti-Tuskegee group swallowed Wilson upon his own profession of being a Christian gentleman, and his promise, given in general terms, of fair dealing, even though he refused to make a forthright statement on Negro rights.[81] Walters of course was primarily interested in playing politics and later burnt his fingers. Only a minority went along with the Walters-DuBois-Trotter-Waldron group. The Cleveland *Gazette*, for example, thought it was decidedly a "radical" anti-Bookerite organ, felt that Taft was the least of the three evils that had a chance of winning.[82] Yet, though not all the "radicals" supported Wilson, outside of the professional Democrats it was among this group that the party found its chief support. Though the majority voted for Roosevelt, Negro Democrats claimed thirty percent of the Negro vote.[83]

After the inauguration disillusionment with Wilson set in quickly enough. Walters, who was feted as the successful leader of the Colored Democracy at a banquet attended by almost three hundred of the cream of Washington society and of the Booker Washington political coterie,[84] soon found himself in deep water due to his inept political maneuvering, and the president's evident intention not to appoint many Negroes to office. Wilson failed to keep his promise of awarding the posts of minister to Haiti and the Recorder of the Deeds—both traditionally Negro offices—to Negroes. Walters himself turned down the Liberian post, which was finally given to James L. Curtis on Walters' recommendation.[85] He did succeed in obtaining a few minor appointments, such as a place for Langston in the internal revenue service,[86] but a large number of both major and minor officeholders were turned out and replaced by whites.

Another important issue was the matter of segregation in the Federal offices, a policy greatly broadened under Wilson. Walters expressed surprise. "Believe me," he said, when informed that the Secretary of the Treasury had indicated that Walters approved the segregation as long as the objectionable signs were removed, "when I tell you that I have never in any way, shape, or form indorsed segregation by the administration and never will."[87] He remained hopeful, however. In October 1914, in reply to an inquiry by editor Reverdy Ransom of the A.M.E. Church *Review* as to what he planned to do in view of the open segregation of personnel and the "wholesale dismissal of Negro Federal office holders and Civil Service employees," despite campaign promises, Walters defended his course. He still hoped that Northern and Western Democrats would restore the ballot and that motivated by practical politics, the Democrats would respect Negro rights. He reiterated his stand against segregation and the loss of offices, but recalled that these policies had begun under Republican auspices. He said that he would urge the president to keep his promises, and Negroes to divide the vote. If such steps did not "effect a cure," he would urge a Negro political party.[88]

A few months later things came to a head when a delegation headed by Trotter obtained an audience with the president on the segregation matter. The conference closed quickly and unpleasantly when the president ordered the obstreperous editor out of his office for what he deemed insulting language.[89] Thus by at least tacit approval to the " 'Jim Crow' insult," by "dimiss[ing] black men wholesale from office," and by seemingly failing "to remember that the Negro . . . has a right to be heard and considered," Wilson had almost step by step refuted DuBois' campaign estimate of him. And so ended the honeymoon between the "radical" Negroes and the Democrats. The paradoxical union of officeseekers and anti-Bookerites, disillusioned Republicans and economic radicals, was unable to weather the chilling realities of the Wilson administration. The National "Independent" Political League soon sank into oblivion. And naturally so, for it is difficult to see how those who criticized Booker Washington for toadying to Southern whites could long remain wedded to a party largely dominated by that same element.

Thus twice in little more than a generation Negro efforts at cooperating with the Democratic Party, of attempting to use the vote of the race as a "balance of power" between the major parties in order to gain concessions from both, had failed. Only when the Democratic party changed its national policy and courted the Negro vote, did DuBois' vision of a union of black and white workers in a party dedicated to the welfare of the common man seem to achieve even partial realization.

Notes

[1] Alrutheus A. Taylor, *The Negro in the Reconstruction of Virginia*, (Washington, 1926), 542, 193, 222, 254; A. A. Taylor, *The Negro in South Carolina During Reconstruction* (Washington, 1924), 7, 12, 193-6, 205, 207-11, 242; Vernon Lane Wharton, *The Negro in Mississippi, 1865-1890* (Chapel Hill, 1947), 165-7; Ella Lonn, *Reconstruction in Louisiana after 1868* (New York, 1918): Francis Butler Simkins and Robert Hilliard Woody, *South Carolina During Reconstruction* (Chapel Hill, 1932), 448, 465-6, 511, 513.

[2] Samuel Denny Smith, *The Negro in Congress* (Chapel Hill, 1940), 24.

[3] *Ibid.*, p. 28; Sadie Daniel St. Clair, "The Public Career of Blanche K. Bruce," Unpublished Ph.D., dissertation, (New York University, 1947); Blanche K. Bruce Papers, Howard University, 1876-1877.

[4] *Congressional Record*, 44th Congress, 1st session, 3782-3.

[5] Willie D. Halsell, ed., "Republican Factionalism in Mississippi, 1882-1884," *Journal of Southern History*, VII, 1 (February, 1941), 84-101.

[6] Wharton, *op. cit.*, pp. 202-3; George B. Tindall, *South Carolina Negroes, 1877-1900*, (Columbia, S.C., 1952), 62-4.

[7] Taylor, *The Negro in the Reconstruction of Virginia*, 268-74.

[8] Julian C. Ward, "The Republican Party in Bourbon, Georgia, 1872-1890," *Journal of Southern History*, IX, 2 (May, 1943), 200.

[9] Jamie Lawson Reddick, "The Negro and the Populist Movement in Georgia" (unpublished M.A. thesis, Atlanta University, 1937), 49-50.

[10] John Hope, "Negro Suffrage in the States Whose Constitutions Have Not Been Specifically Revised," *American Negro Academy*, Occasional Papers, #11, *The Negro and the Elective Franchise*, 1905, 53.

[11] Washington *New National Era and Citizen*, December 18, 1873.

[12] Washington *Bee*, March 14, 1885.

[13] *Proceedings of the Colored National Labor Convention . . . 1869* (Washington, 1870), 3; Washington *New National Era*, (July 13, 1871).

[14] S.A.M. Washington, *George Thomas Downing* (Newport, 1910), p. 19.

[15] New York *Globe*, May 12, 1883.

[16] Washington *Bee*, February 10, 1883.

[17] New York *Globe*, September 1, 1883.

[18] Alexandria *People's Advocate*, October 6, 1883; New York *Globe*, September 29, 1883.

[19] Washington *Bee*, December 1, 1883.

[20] John Daniels, *In Freedom's Birthplace* (Boston, 1911), 110, 112, 119, 120, 454.

[21] New York *Freeman*, December 12, 1885.

[22] Washington *Bee*, April 14, 1883.

[23] *Ibid.*, June 23, 1883.

[24] *Ibid.*, April 5, September 6, November 22, 1884.

[25] T. Thomas Fortune, *Black and White* (New York, 1884), 95, 99, 104, 117-8, 124, 126, 127-8.

[26] New York *Globe*, October 27, 1883.

[27] *Ibid.*, July 26, 1884.

[28] New York *Freeman*, February 7, 1885.

[29] T. Thomas Fortune, *The Negro in Politics* (New York: Ogilvie & Rowntree, 1886), 58-9, 38.

[30] New York *Age*, July 20, 1889.

[31] New York *Freeman*, April 4, 1883.

[32] New York *Age*, November 19, 1887.

[33] C. H. J. Taylor, *Whites and Blacks* (Atlanta, 1889), 43-50, 17, 21, 27, 41.

[34] J. C. Price, "The Negro in the Last Decade of the Century," *Independent* (January 1, 1891), 5.

[35] William J. Walls, *Joseph Charles Price* (Boston, 1943). According to Walls Price declined Cleveland's offer of the Liberian post in 1888. The Cleveland *Gazette*, December 17, 1886, had reported that Price was actively soliciting the position.

[36] *Proceedings of the Convention of the New York State Cleveland League . . . 1892* (Brooklyn, [1892]), 12.

[37] Letterhead of letter of Nathaniel McKay to Frederick Douglass, July 21, 1893, Douglass Papers.

[38] Washington *Bee*, October 8, 1893; May 26, 1894. For Douglass' role see Taylor to Douglass, May 2, 14, 24, 1894, in Douglass Papers.

[39] Washington *Bee*, September 28, 1894; Cleveland *Gazette*, March 4, 1895.

[40] A.M.E. Church *Review*, XI, 4 (April, 1895), 525-6.

[41] New York *Age*, March 28, October 24, 1891; Indianapolis *Freeman*, November 25, 1893.

[42] Washington *Bee*, August 24, 1895; A.M.E. *Christian Recorder*, October 31, 1895.

[43] Washington *Bee*, August 24, 1895. By 1908 at the very latest, J. Milton Turner had also become a Republican again.

[44] Cleveland *Gazette*, November 12, 1898.

[45] Kelly Miller, "Autobiography" (ms. in possession of Mrs. Mae Miller Sullivan, Washington, D.C.), ch. 16.

[46] Kelly Miller, "The Negro Problem in the South: A Negro's View," *Outlook* (December 31, 1898), 1059-63.

[47] Atlanta *Journal*, September 4, 1900; New York *Sun*, August 31, 1900. Clippings in Hampton Institute Clipping Collection.

[48] Columbia *State*, September 11, 1900, Hampton Institute Clipping Collection. See also Washington *Bee*, September 20, November 3, 1900.

[49] Brooklyn *Citizen*, October 10, 1900, Hampton Institute Clipping Collection.

[50] Horace Cayton and St. Clair Drake, *Black Metropolis* (New York, 1945), 343-5.

[51] Daniels, *op. cit.*, 295-7.

[52] Robert H. Brisbane, Jr., "The Rise of Protest Movements Among Negroes Since 1900" (unpublished Ph.D. dissertation, Harvard University, 1949), 119-120.

[53] Charles W. Anderson to Booker T. Washington, April 4, 1910, Booker T. Washington papers.

[54] Anderson to Washington, October 24, 25, 1910, Washington papers.

[55] Anderson to Washington, November 11, 1910.

[56] Anderson to Washington, November 17, 1913; Anderson to E. J. Scott, April 2, 1913.

[57] Brisbane, *op. cit.*, 120.

[58] New York *Age*, November 8, 1906.

[59] Indianapolis *Freeman*, October 24, 1908.

[60] Reverdy C. Ransom, "The Spirit of John Brown," 1906, in *The Spirit of Freedom and Justice* (Nashville, 1926), 21-2.

[61] New York *Age*, April 18, 1908; Washington *Bee*, April 11, 1908.

[62] New York *Sun*, June 15, 1908, clipping in Washington papers.

[63] Washington *Bee*, July 25, 1908.

[64] Cleveland *Gazette*, October 31, 1908.

[65] *Ibid.*

[66] *Horizon*, III, 2 (February, 1908), 17-18, and III, 3 (March, 1908), 7.

[67] *Ibid.*, III, 4 (April, 1908), 4-6.

[68] *Ibid.*, IV, 1 (July, 1908), 5-7.

[69] *Ibid.*, IV, 2 (August, 1908), 2-4.

[70] *Ibid.*, IV, 3 (September, 1908), 4-6. Undoubtedly much of the appeal Democrats made to Northern working-class Negroes was along economic and class lines, but we have no available information as to just why the rank and file Negro Democrats voted as they did.

[71] *Ibid.*, IV, 5-6 (November-December, 1908), 12.

[72] Cleveland *Gazette*, May 22, 1909; Washington *Bee*, July 2, September 10, 1910.

[73] Washington *Bee*, November 26, 1910.

[74] Arthur S. Link, *Wilson: The Road to the White House* (Princeton, 1947), 501-2.

[75] *Ibid.*, 502-3.

[76] J. Milton Waldron and J. D. Harkless, *The Political Situation in a Nutshell* (Washington, [1912]), 30, Waldron was national organizer and chairman of the campaign committee.

[77] *The New Era* (Democratic campaign sheet), I, 5 and 12, March 22, May 10, 1912.

[78] National Independent Political League, *Pamphlet #3*, [1912], n.p. and *Questions and Answers* (broadside), 1912.

[79] Waldron and Harkless, *op. cit.*, 11, 16, 17.

[80] *Crisis*, IV, 4 (August, 1912), 181.

[81] Link, *op. cit.*, 504-5.

[82] Cleveland *Gazette*, September 28, 1912.

[83] Washington *Bee*, April 5, 1913.

[84] Washington *Bee*, March 8, 1913.

[85] Alexander Walters, *My Life and Work*, (New York, 1917), 192-7.

[86] Anderson to Washington, September 11, 29, 1913. Washington papers.

[87] Washington *Bee*, September 20, 1913.

[88] A.M.E. Church *Review*, XXXI, 1 (July, 1914), 73-5; and XXXI, 2 (October, 1914), 208-211.

[89] Washington *Bee*, November 21, 1914; A.M.E. Church *Review*, XXXI, 3 (January, 1915), 309-318; *Crisis*, IX, 3 (January, 1915), 12-13.

Black Participation in the Centennial of 1876

PHILIP S. FONER

*As Americans prepared to celebrate the hundredth anni-
versary of the nation's founding, racial prejudice curtailed
meaningful participation by blacks. In spite of the valiant efforts of African Americans to showcase black contributions to
American life and culture, the Centennial Exhibition in Philadelphia in 1876, with a few minor exceptions, ignored blacks.
Only a sculpture by African American Edmonia Lewis commissioned for the Exhibition and the speeches by African Americans Lewis Hayden, George Washington Williams, and a few
others provide a glimpse of what a full-scale black involvement
in the Centennial might have been.*

*Through the prism of the Centennial Exhibition, Philip
Foner's essay lays bare the widespread racial animosity that
characterized the post-Civil War generation. While the vast majority of blacks, both in the North and the South, expected inclusion into American society, most whites of that era typically
were either hostile to blacks or simply chose to ignore the existence of the African American population. Foner's analysis of
the 1876 Centennial provides a specific, revealing perspective
for understanding the decades of racial strife at the end of the
nineteenth century.*

SO LONG AS SLAVERY EXISTED, most blacks refused to participate
in a celebration of the Fourth of July on July 4th, setting aside July
5th for the purpose. In the July 5, 1832, address in the African
Church, New Haven, Connecticut, Peter Osbore declared: "Fellow
Citizens: On account of the misfortune of our color, our fourth of
July comes on the fifth; but I hope and trust that when the Declaration of Independence is finally executed, which declares that all men
without respect to person, were born free and equal, we may then
have our fourth of July on the fourth." Frederick Douglass, the ex-
slave and black abolitionist, summed it up succinctly in his great
speech, "The Meaning of July Fourth for the American Negro," delivered in Rochester, New York, July 5, 1852: "I am not included within
the pale of this glorious anniversary! . . . This Fourth of July is *yours*,
not mine. You may rejoice, I must mourn . . .".[1]

Twenty-four years later, on May 10, 1876, marking the opening
of the long-awaited Centennial Exhibition in Philadelphia, Frederick

Douglass was one of the dignitaries seated on the main platform in the company of President Ulysses S. Grant, Secretary of State Hamilton Fish, members of Congress, governors, and ministers of foreign countries. But it was only by a miracle that the gray-headed Douglass was there. The police of Philadelphia had refused him admittance, unable to conceive that a Negro—they used a more pejorative term— would be allowed entrance to this august company on this august occasion. In vain, Douglass had remonstrated, showing his ticket of admission to the platform. "It was feared he might have gone out with the crushed and fainting," said the New York *Herald* correspondent, "if Senator Conkling had not seen him, and vouching for his right to be present, enabled him to pass the line. As he reached the platform, he was loudly cheered."[2]

There would undoubtedly have been many more cheers had Douglass been one of the many speakers. But the greatest orator in the nation, whom Abraham Lincoln has said was the "most remarkable man" he had ever met,[3] had not been invited to be heard—only to be seen. Yet even this, as we shall see, was more than was typical of the general nature of black participation in the Centennial of 1876.

As the nation throbbed with preparations to celebrate its one hundredth birthday, there were not a few Americans who viewed the forthcoming celebration as "an overgrown and spread-eagle Fourth of July," "a gigantic fraud to enrich some people," an opportunity for "mindless patriotism and commercial exploitation." With millions unemployed as a result of the business depression that had started in 1873, with the scandals of the Grant administration coming to light, and revelations of corruption in government and business increasing steadily, the argument was that there was little indeed for Americans to celebrate. Better, far better, that the funds to be spent on the Centennial Exhibition be used to provide food, clothing, and shelter for the starving and homeless.[4]

Such bitter thoughts, inspired by the approaching Centennial, seem not to have been shared by most blacks. For one thing, a number of black spokesmen felt that the Centennial offered an opportunity to show the American people the contributions of black Americans to the creation and building of the nation, a subject ignored in nearly all history books then in use in the schools and colleges. "We have been hypocrites and liars with respect to our real history long enough," insisted Robert Purvis, veteran black abolitionist and civil rights leader of Philadelphia in May, 1873, as he called for making the truth available "on the 4th of July, 1876." This truth "would reveal that it was an incontestable fact that the blood of a negro was the first shed for liberty in the Revolution, and that blacks had taken an active part in the War of 1812 and in our late civil war for freedom." Perhaps, Purvis argued, white Americans, made aware of these contributions, would use the Centennial as the occasion to eliminate whatever remained of color prejudice. In that event, Negroes, having defended the flag on the battlefield, "would have one to glory in at the Centennial."[5]

Speaking in the House of Representatives on May 7, 1874, on the bill calling for Congress to appropriate $3,000,000 in aid of the Centennial celebration,[6] black Congressman Josiah T. Walls of Florida criticized those who sneered at the approaching celebration. On behalf of himself and a people who had lived to witness "the tardy but in the end full and complete vindication of the sublime simple announcements of the Declaration of Independence," Congressman Walls urged the swift adoption of the bill. He argued that the Centennial would bring the nation together for the first time since the Civil War, and "discourage and extinguish all feelings of sectionalism." Moreover, it would help eliminate the "remaining bitterness" still rankling in the breasts of those Southern "irreconcilables" who regretted the abolition of slavery, and refused to accept Negroes as full-fledged American citizens. Walls closed on a note of exultation and prophecy as he predicted that the Centennial celebration would become the occasion for "a common and patriotic demonstration of a hundred years of popular government for the political necessities of the races." It would be the occasion, too, for the expression of "the spontaneous joy of a free people at their unbroken Union and the restored unity of their nationality." And none would "hail the glorious old banner—the Stars and Stripes—with more joy than the men of the South."[7]

The *New National Era*, a black weekly published in the nation's capital hailed Congressman Wall's speech as proving "that colored Congressmen are alive to everything tending to promote the general welfare of the country." It urged blacks throughout the nation to mobilize their forces to assure that Negroes were at least as well represented at the Philadelphia Exhibition as they were in the halls of Congress where there were seven, six in the House and one in the Senate. To be sure, all of course were from the South, but the black weekly argued that it was not outside the realm of reason to hope that the Centennial celebration, by helping, in Congressman Wall's words, to "extinguish all feelings of sectionalism," would usher in an era when many states in the North and West would send blacks to the halls of Congress.[8]

Spurred by such optimistic outlooks, the Convention of Colored Newspaper Men, meeting in Cincinnati in August of 1875, adopted an ambitious Centennial program. It envisaged the publication of eighteen volumes "to be known as the 'Centennial Tribute to the Negro,'" which would serve "to let the coming generations know our true history." The first three volumes would trace the history of the Negro people from their "Ancient Glory" in Africa to their introduction to the New World. These would be followed by the fourteen volumes covering such themes as "One Hundred Years with the Negro in Battle," "One Hundred Years with the Negro in the Schoolhouse, or as an Educator," "One Hundred Years with the Negro in the Pulpit," "One Hundred Years with the Negro Lawyers and Doctors," "One Hundred Years with the Negroes' Muse," "One Hundred Years with the Negroes' Pen, and Scissors and Press," "One Hundred Years with the Negro in Business," "One Hundred Years with the Negro as a Farmer and Mechanic," and "One Hundred Years with the Negro Statesman or Politician." The final volume was to be simply entitled, "Negro Martyrs."

The black newspapermen also appointed a committee to be known as the Centennial Committee, whose duty it would be to correspond with the Centennial Commissioner, and urge upon him "the necessity of having the productions of the colored race represented at the Centennial Exposition," and, in particular, to make certain that the "religious, literary, educational and mechanical interests of the Negro would be fully represented." The committee was also empowered to procure a statue from Edmonia Lewis, the famous black sculptress then residing in Rome, and arrange to have the work exhibited at the Centennial Celebration, "in the name of the colored women of America." Following the Exposition, this work of art would be placed permanently in some public building or park in the city of Washington.[9]

The question of financing such an ambitious project was left vague. All that was suggested was that the Centennial Committee organize a movement "among our ladies" to carry the program into being.[10] Needless to say, with such loose provision, not much of the project could be realized. With the assistance of the African Methodist Episcopal Church, funds were raised for works of art by Edmonia Lewis.[11] But the project for the eighteen-volume "Centennial Tribute to the Negro" never got off the ground.

A few blacks served on the local committees which every state, almost every large city, and many smaller ones set up to prepare their exhibit. Unfortunately, we know very little about this aspect of the Centennial of 1876 since few white newspapers reported such activity; few black newspapers of the period have survived, and the Centennial Commission Papers in the Archives of the City of Philadelphia contain nothing about the role of blacks in the preparations for the celebration.[12] One clue is the following sentence in the *People's Advocate* of Washington, D.C., one of the few black weeklies which has survived: "Colored men were appointed to the several local committees created by the Centennial Commission, prior to the opening of the Exhibition, with the same authority to act as their white *confreres*." But this is distressingly indefinite; it mentions "local committees," but gives no names, no places, and no working details.[13] We may conclude that the appointments, if they occurred at all, probably took place in a Southern area, still in Republican hands, or in an area, North or South, with a strong black school system, such as Cincinnati or Philadelphia.

We do know something of the participation of Negro women. The Women's Pavilion at the Philadelphia Exposition was the creation of the Women's Centennial Committee, originally a group of thirteen appointed in 1873 by the planners of the Exhibition. Subcommittees were organized in all the states and large cities of the country to raise funds for the Pavilion.[14] In this connection, black women were invited to participate on the Philadelphia subcommittee. However, it was made clear to these women that they were to operate as a separate committee, and solicit subscriptions among blacks only; that they had "no right to work among white people," and the "whole work of the group be confined to colored people alone." When the black women objected, charging that this was nothing less than segregation by color, they were informed by a representative of the Women's Central Committee that this was in keeping with the laws of the land, and if they did not approve of them, they could emigrate to Africa. At this the black women resigned from the committee, and drew up a set of resolutions denouncing the Women's Centennial Committee for attempting a "revival of the bitterest colored prejudices."[15]

The incident was widely publicized in the Philadelphia press and in the *New National Era*, and the Women's Centennial Committee, somewhat startled by the publicity, beat a hasty retreat. An apology was delivered to the black women, in the form of resolutions assuring them that no "distinction" would be made between races in the raising of funds, and urging them to continue to serve. The apology was accepted, and the Philadelphia sub-committee of the Women's Centennial Committee functioned with black women represented. But it had taken a struggle and considerable publicity for these women even to win the right to serve on the basis of equality.[16]

The reluctance to allow blacks to participate as equals to whites was evidenced again in Philadelphia a year later. To help raise funds for the Centennial Exhibit, the police of Philadelphia sponsored a benefit at the Arch Street Theatre on the night of April 16, 1874. The event was widely publicized, and all Philadelphians were urged to purchase tickets and attend. Evidently forgetting that the City of Brotherly Love was the most racist city in the North,[17] Pusey A. Peer and his wife, a black couple, decided to attend. They purchased tickets, but when they presented themselves at the theatre, the policemen sponsoring the event insisted that they would not have the "Centennial Benefit" stained by "nigger money." Mr. Peer vehemently insisted on his right to attend. "Throw the niggers out," was the response, and the black couple was forcibly ejected from the theatre. In the process, both sustained severe bodily injuries. In addition, Mrs. Peer was robbed of her fur cape and her husband of his watch. Not a single Philadelphia paper rebuked the people responsible for this vicious conduct, or pointed out that it made a mockery of the "Centennial Benefit."[18]

It came as no surprise, then, that the Philadelphia Exhibition, during its construction and operation, showed also how restricted were the opportunities for black workers. Nearly two hundred Centennial buildings were constructed between May, 1875, and the opening the following year. (One, the Memorial building, was said to be the largest building in the world, occupying over 21 acres.)[19] But not a single black worker appears to have been employed during this huge construction at a time when perhaps seventy percent of the blacks of Philadelphia were unemployed.[20] On the eve of the opening of the Exhibition, Robert Lowry of Iowa, a Vice President of the Centennial Commission, called upon the body at least to allow Negroes to have positions as guards. Nothing came of the suggestion.[21]

Visiting the Centennial city after the Exhibition opened, a black Georgian wrote that he "could not discover among all that mass of people one single Negro in the discharge of any duty save as restaurant waiters and barbers in the hotels."[22] The fact that this observation was criticized because it did not mention that "a few black messengers, janitors, etc., are now employed in the Memorial building," only added weight to the black visitor's discouraging comment.[23]

The paucity of Negro exhibits also discouraged black visitors. In the entire exhibition, one wrote, he could find only one exhibit devoted to American Negroes—the statue of "The Freed Slave" in Memorial Hall, a heroic figure of a male black holding aloft the parchment of the Emancipation Proclamation with broken chains at his feet.[24] But this was not even the work of a black artist. Indeed, apart from the trinkets and other artifacts in the exhibits of the Gold Coast, West Africa, Liberia, and South African Orange Free States, only one work of art by a black artist was in the entire exhibition— Edmonia Lewis' sculpture, "Death of Cleopatra."[25]

A number of newspaper editorials argued that nothing else could be expected since Negroes had too recently shed their shackles to show proficiency in the arts and sciences.[26] But Colonel J. W. Forney, Philadelphia's leading journalist, was more to the point when he voiced regret on the eve of the Fourth of July:

> . . . that the great show of the American people's industry and independence will close with the one link in the chain of its complete history left out. Although the chains of slavery have been broken from the limbs of an entire race in the blaze and fire of our advancement, and the negro stands before the law a freeman, covered with the habiliments of citizenship, yet, the prejudice against him, the results of his previous condition, have prevented him from taking any part or having a prominent part of this marvellous undertaking in celebration of one hundred years of American independence, save that of a menial, the water-drawers and hat-takers, to the assembled races now to be found there.[27]

Shocked by this observation, Pennsylvania Judge William D. Kelley, a long-time champion of civil rights, pleaded with the Centennial Commission to fill this serious gap in the Exhibition by inviting Frederick Douglass to read the Emancipation Proclamation after the Declaration of Independence was read on the Fourth of July. Later that same day, he should deliver an address from the platform of Memorial Hall, portraying the contributions of black Americans in the War for Independence and for the preservation of the Union during the Civil War.[28]

As might be expected, nothing came of this suggestion. Instead, Reverend J. W. Jenifer, minister at the St. John's African Methodist Episcopal Church, Pine Bluff, Arkansas, was invited to deliver an address on July 4th on the occasion of laying the base of the Richard Allen Monument. The monument itself was being completed by Edmonia Lewis in Rome, and was scheduled to be unveiled in the Centennial grounds on September 23, the anniversary of the issuing of the preliminary Emancipation Proclamation by President Lincoln—in short, just before the Centennial Exhibition closed.[29]

While Reverend Jenifer did not fulfill the role Judge Kelley had had in mind, not mentioning the American Revolution or the Civil War and black participation in these conflicts,[30] he struck what must have been a strange note at an Exhibition, a major theme of which was the new harmonious relations between North and South. For he

referred to the "outrages and murders" committed against Negroes
in the South by the "Klu Klux Klan and White Leagues," charged
that they were "the fruits of wanton prejudice, hatred and hellish passions," and accused the federal government of "weakness" in yielding
to the lawless foes of black Americans. Calling upon the government
to spend as much money to provide education for the Freedmen of
the South as they did for internal improvements and military appropriations,[31] he predicted that if this were done, the blacks, along with
the immigrants and the capitalists, would make their contribution to
transforming the South into a "land of peace and plenty."[32]

None of the white speakers at the Centennial Exhibition on
July 4, 1876, mentioned Negroes, and very few outside of Philadelphia did in the orations delivered that day throughout the nation.
One, however, did, and his reference is an interesting index of the
viewpoint among sections of the white population. In the course of
his centennial oration at Covington, Kentucky, Hon. W. E. Arthur
told Negroes in the United States how fortunate they were that their
ancestors had been taken from Africa into slavery in this country. But
for that, they would be living in a continent with "scarce any society
superior to that of the gorilla and the monkey," existing on the edge
of "the dividing line between man and brute," practicing "the lowest
vices of both," and spending their lives in "chaos without change."
Thus black Americans had a special reason to celebrate the one hundredth anniversary of a nation which had rescued them from all this
horror and permitted them to partake of the fruits of civilization.[33]

While the vast majority of American communities were deprived
of the opportunity to hear any oration outlining the contributions of
Negroes to the creation of the nation, some were not. In Boston, the
distinguished black abolitionist and civil rights spokesman, Lewis Hayden, delivered an historical paper before the Colored Ladies Centennial Club; in Portsmouth, Virginia, Professor John M. Langston of
Howard University delivered an historical address before the Banneker Lyceum; and in Avondale, Ohio, the future black historian,
George Washington Williams, delivered an oration entitled, *The American Negro from 1776 to 1876.*

In his address Langston paid tribute to Crispus Attucks, and
Benjamin Banneker. Black Americans, he pointed out, should celebrate not only the Declaration of Independence, but also a man like
Crispus Attucks "brave and courageous who gave up his life one hundred years ago on the sacred soil of Massachusetts in order to make
the Independence we now celebrate possible." Nor should they forget that it was America's first black man of science, Benjamin Banneker, who had played so important a role in the creation of the city

of Washington, D.C., the nation's capital.[34] A distinguished teacher himself, Langston hailed the state of Virginia for having established a common school system, and not allowing her sons and daughters, as in the days of slavery, to grow up "in ignorance, to a heritage of crime and degradation. . . ." Today, he noted, "your schools, a double system, white and black, are better than none. But I trust the day is not distant when they will be one—a common school, standing open for all regardless of race or color."[35]

Langston's speech in Portsmouth, Virginia, July 4, 1876, has the distinction of being the only oration by a black American included in the nearly 900-page *Orations, Addresses and Poems, Delivered on the Fourth of July, 1876, in the Several States of the Union.* Unfortunately, the volume, published in 1877 and edited by Frederick Saunders, contains not a single clue as to who Langston was.

The orations of Lewis Hayden and George Washington Williams covered a larger canvas. Hayden dealt not only with Crispus Attucks, but with Peter Salem, Salem Poor, and other blacks who had fought with the patriots in the War for Independence. He went on to depict the contributions of the black Massachusetts 54th and 55th Regiments during the Civil War, describing the heroism of black soldiers at the battles of Port Hudson, Milliken's Bend, and Fort Wagner. Unfortunately, Hayden noted sadly, slavery and racism had "closed the eyes of this nation to its indebtedness to the colored race."[36]

It had closed its eyes to black women as well as men. Black women, Hayden emphasized, had not been idle during the American Revolution. For one thing, there was Deborah Gannett, the black female soldier who fought in the Continental Army disguised as a man under the name of Robert Shurtleff.[37] After describing other contributions of black women to the American nation, Hayden said to the members of the Colored Ladies Centennial Club:

> E'er another Centennial rolls around, may you be possessed of these rights for which your sisters during and after the War for Independence fought to achieve not alone for men, but for women as well. Since it is written, "There is no rest for the wicked, saith my God," who can doubt that ere another century shall spread its pages before the world, even *this* wrong will be repaired, and that our country will stand forth triumphantly as the living exponent of the principles of self government, liberty, justice, and humanity for all its people—women as well as men![38]

George Washington Williams began his Fourth of July Centennial oration with the statement: "If any class of people in our composite nationality have claims upon the Union, if any class of people, after the Puritan, can justly claim a part in establishing the colonies as independent states, it is the American Negro." He then proceeded to prove his assertion, citing the role of Crispus Attucks, Salem Poor, Peter Salem, the Black Regiment of Rhode Island, and other blacks who fought in both the Continental Army and Continental Navy during the War for Independence. Moving on to the War of 1812 and Civil War, Williams urged the Republic to remember that "its most precious stones were cemented by the blood of her negro soldiers, whose devotion to the flag was deathless and whose fame will never fade." He also called upon Americans to remember that when almost 200,000 blacks fought in the Union Army to preserve the Union—the vast majority of them fugitive slaves—they, in the process, became their own liberators from slavery, so that it was not just the Emancipation Proclamation but the black slaves themselves that broke the chains of slavery. "The American negro," Williams cried, "deserves the admiration of the civilized world for melting off his chains in the fires of rebellion, and for helping to establish a free government without a single slave under the fold of its flag."

If the blacks in Colonial America helped to create the first Republic in the New World, Williams noted, it was the black slaves of the French West Indies who built the second Republic. Haiti was brought into being "on the ruins of slavery, and it was the slaves themselves who ratified its benign and humane principles with their own blood." Slavery, he observed, was overthrown in the French West Indies by the military efforts of the slaves. "This is the negro's place in history—his own deliverer," Williams insisted. Continuing, he observed:

> Daniel O'Connell said to Ireland, "Hereditary bondsmen know ye not, that he would himself be free, must first strike the blow?" The French West Indian negro anticipated O'Connell, and when he rose he made even the mighty Napoleon tremble!

In closing Williams pointed to Phillis Wheatley, poet; Benjamin Banneker, scientist; Charles L. Reason, mathematician; James McCune Smith, physician; Peter H. Clark, teacher; Henry Highland Garnet, Alexander Crummel, and James W. C. Pennington, theologians; William C. Nell and William Wells Brown, historians; Charlotte Forten and Frances E. Harper, literary figures; and Frederick Douglass, orator and statesman. He then asked the "negro-haters" whether it was true, as they charged, that "the negro cannot compete with the white races, that he cannot endure the highest forms of civilization; that he cannot master the intricate and subtle problems of the college curriculum!" He ended his great oration with the plea:

> I ask the American people to call to remembrance the valor, military skill, and endurance of the negro in the Wars for Indepen-

dence, of 1812, and the Civil War! I ask the many schools,
academies and colleges open to the race, if the negro has not
shown the largest capacity for the severest culture. I ask the American Congress which has listened to the eloquence of Elliott, Lane,
Lynch, and others, if the negro is a monkey or a man![39]

While the Fourth of July orations delivered by blacks dealt
mainly with the past, the Centennial also was the occasion of a document which concerned itself primarily with the present and future.
This was the "Negro Declaration of Independence" read in Washington, D.C. on the Fourth of July, 1876. This new Declaration of Independence was modeled after the original document drawn up by
Thomas Jefferson. However, rather than George III, the target of specific grievances in the "Negro Declaration of Independence" was the
American government. It was charged with having evaded compliance
with laws necessary for the welfare of Negroes and having imposed
taxes on Negroes without protecting their Constitutional rights. The
document concluded:

> For these and other reasons too numerous for enumeration,
> we feel justified in declaring our independence of all existing politi-
> cal parties, and we hereby pledge to each other our lives, our For-
> tunes, and our sacred Honor that we will, in the future, support
> only those parties whose fidelity to the original Declaration of Inde-
> pendence is unquestioned, and who will make certain that we, the
> negro people, like all other Americans, will in the second century of
> our independence, be assured of FULL AND EQUAL JUSTICE
> BEFORE THE LAW, PROTECTION FOR ALL OUR LIVES AND
> PROPERTY AGAINST LAWLESSNESS AND MOB VIOLENCE, AND
> FULL EQUALITY IN ALL ASPECTS OF AMERICAN LIFE!!!![40]

In the voluminous reports in the contemporary press of events
surrounding the Centennial, not a single white newspaper mentioned
the "Negro Declaration of Independence."[41] The omission suggests
how blind white Americans were toward the grievances of black citizens in their midst as they celebrated their Centennial. As the
Centennial year advanced, fresh evidence of this indifference
emerged. The blody massacres of Negroes in Hamburg and Elton,
South Carolina, which *The Colored Radical*, published in Kansas, called
"the darkest chapters in American history," were accepted as part of
the normal way of life in the America of 1876.[42] By the end of the
Centennial year, the fate of blacks in the South had been sealed in
the nefarious bargain following the disputed election of 1876, by
which the South agreed to give Rutherford B. Hayes the presidency
over Samuel J. Tilden in return for the removal of the remaining
Federal troops and the restoration of home rule—a euphemism for
the right to reduce Negroes to a new form of slavery.[43]

Two years before, in urging Congressional support for the Centennial Exhibition, black Congressman Walls had predicted that this show of national harmony would destroy the power of the few white irreconcilables in the South who refused to accept Negroes as equal citizens. Vain hope! In fact, from the Centennial of 1876, only two positive results for blacks emerged. One was the awarding of $900 as compensation for damages sustained by Pusey A. Peer and his wife, the black couple ejected from the Philadelphia "Centennial Benefit" at the Oak Street Theatre in 1874. The case was finally settled in 1881, and in sustaining the damage award, Judge Sterrett of the Pennsylvania Supreme Court said:

> Whether the tickets conferred merely a license or something more is immaterial. If they gave only a license to enter the theater and remain there during the performance, it is very clear that the agents of the defendant had no right to revoke it as they did; and summarily eject Peer and his wife from the building in such manner as to injure her. We incline to the opinion, however, that as purchasers and holders of tickets for particular seats they had more than mere license. Their right was more in the nature of a lease, entitling them to peaceable ingress and egress, and exclusive possession of the designated seats during the performance on that particular evening.

The case is famous in the history of the enforcement of civil rights in Pennsylvania, and helped break down restrictions against blacks in public facilities of the state.[44]

The other positive result was the influence of the Centennial on the emergence of George Washington Williams as a distinguished black historian. Williams became absorbed in Negro history while doing research on the oration he delivered celebrating the one hundredth anniversary of the Declaration of Independence. After he had delivered the oration, he retired as a minister and lawyer in Cincinnati, in order to devote all his time to writing a general history of Negroes in the United States. After seven years, he published his great work, A History of the Negro Race in America from 1619 to 1880. The work, in two volumes, is divided into nine parts, with a total of sixty chapters encompassing the African background, through the Colonial, Revolutionary era, down to the Civil War and Reconstruction. In each volume several chapters are devoted to social and cultural history.[45]

With the publication of A History of the Negro Race in America from 1619 to 1880, the Centennial of 1876 had produced, even if indirectly and belatedly, what the Negro newspapermen had envisaged in 1875 when they had projected the idea of a multi-volume "Centennial

Tribute to the Negro" which would serve "to let the coming generations know our true history."

Yet even this did not grow out of the official Centennial Exhibition. The story of the participation of blacks in that tremendous,
worldwide exposition was summed up by Colonel Forney, the Philadelphia journalist, when he said: ". . . the prejudice against him, the
results of his previous condition, have prevented him from taking any
part or having a prominent part of this marvellous undertaking in
celebration of one hundred years of American independence, save
that of a menial, the water-drawers and hat-takers, to the assembled
races now to be found there." How completely invisible black Americans were at the Centennial Celebration is illustrated by the fact that
when a delegation of French workers to the Philadelphia Exhibition
submitted a questionnaire to American Socialists on conditions of
workers in this country, both men and women, they did not include
blacks among their queries. Not one of the 34 questions submitted
concerned itself with black workers.[46]

In the historical accounts dealing with the Centennial
Exhibition of 1876, black Americans are also invisible. Three full-
length books, one article in a scholarly journal, and one doctoral dissertation have been written on the Philadelphia Exhibition of 1876.
But in none is there even a mention of the fact that in the preparations for the Exhibition and at the event itself, blacks were discriminated against and kept from making their contributions.[47]

Notes

[1] *The Liberator*, December 1, 1832; Philip S. Foner, *The Life and Writings of Frederick Douglass* (New York, 1950), II, 188-89.

[2] New York *Herald*, May 11, 1876.

[3] Philip S. Foner, *Frederick Douglass: A Biography* (New York, 1964), p. 224.

[4] *Workingman's Advocate*, Chicago, March 6, 1875: Philip S. Foner, *History of the Labor Movement in the United States* (New York, 1947), I, 439-74. Estimates of the number of unemployed varied from 3 to 4 million, or twice the percentage of unemployed in the Great Depression of the 1930s.

[5] *Philadelphia Press*, May 14, 1873. Robert Purvis (1810-1898) was the son of a white South Carolina merchant and a Moorish-Jewish woman whose mother had been a slave. Independently wealthy and so light-skinned that he could have passed for white, he was educated in private schools in Philadelphia, and finished his education at Amherst College. But he left college to devote himself to the anti-slavery movement and at the age of seventeen made his first public speech against slavery. A founder of the American Anti-Slavery Society, Purvis was also a militant fighter against all forms of discrimination against blacks.

[6] In early 1874 President Grant sent Congress a message urging Congressmen to support the Centennial Exhibition. He felt strongly that the failure of the United States to celebrate properly its one hundredth anniversary would be a disgrace. (*New York Times*, February 14, 1874.) Congress did not actually pass a Centennial Appropriation bill un-

til early in 1876, and then as a loan of $1,500,000, not a contribution (*Ibid.*, January 26, 1876; *The Nation*, XXII (February 17, 1876), 105.)

[7] *Congressional Record*, 43rd Congress, 1st Session, Appendix, pp. 250-53.

[8] *New National Era*, May 21, 28, 1874. Two of the black Congressmen were from South Carolina, one each from North Carolina. Florida, Alabama, Mississippi, and Louisiana. In the Senate, former slave Blanche K. Bruce still represented Mississippi.

[9] *Proceedings, Convention of Colored Newspaper Men, Cincinnati, August 4, 1875* (pamphlet in Cincinnati Historical Society), p. 4.

[10] *Ibid.*, p. 5.

[11] The two works of art were the sculpture, "Death of Cleopatra," and the monument of Richard Allen. For the details on the raising of the funds for these works of art, see *The Christian Recorder*, June 15, 1876. *The Christian Recorder*, published in Philadelphia, was the official organ of the African Methodist Episcopal Church.

[12] See United States Centennial Commission Papers (Record Group 230), Archives of the City of Philadelphia.

[13] *People's Advocate*, July 8, 1876.

[14] Dee Brown, *The Year of the Century: 1876* (New York, 1966), p. 139.

[15] *Philadelphia Press*, April 5, 17, 1873; *Philadelphia Times*, April 27, 1873; *New National Era*, May 22, 1873.

[16] "Chairman" of "Colored Centennial Committee," in *New National Era*, June 5, 1873. There are reports of the Women's Centennial Committee of the 2nd, 12th, 15th, 22nd and 27th wards of Philadelphia in the Historical Society of Pennsylvania, but none of them mentions this dispute or the role of black women on the Committee.

[17] See Philip S. Foner, "The Battle to End Discrimination Against Negroes on the Streetcars of Philadelphia, 1859-1867," *Pennsylvania History*, (July and October, 1972), and W.E.B. DuBois, *The Philadelphia Negro* (Philadelphia, 1899).

[18] *Philadelphia Press*, April 13, 17, 1874; Philadelphia *Evening Bulletin*, April 14, 17, 1874; Philadelphia *North American*, April 15, 17, 1874. About $15,000 was realized by the sale of tickets for the Police Centennial Fund (Philadelphia *Evening Star*, April 16-17, 1874).

[19] *Scientific American*, I, No. 9 (February 26, 1876), Supplement; *New York Times*, October 13, 1875; *Philadelphia Ledger*, February 15, 1875.

[20] Philadelphia *Evening Bulletin*, February 15, 1876.

[21] Robert Lowry to United States Centennial Commission, March 12, 1876, United States Centennial Commission Papers, Record Group 230, Archives of the City of Philadelphia; *People's Advocate*, May 27, 1876.

[22] "Red Cloud" in *People's Advocate*, July 1, 1876.

[23] Editorial in response to "Red Cloud" in *ibid.*, July 8, 1876. A study of the Centennial Board of Finance Minutes (Record Group 231, Archives of the City of Philadelphia), which contains the records of the funds disbursed to workers during the construction and operation of the Exhibition is not helpful, since there is no mention of color or race.

[24] A full-page reproduction of the statue of "The Freed Slave" appears in *Frank Leslie's Historical Register of the Centennial Exposition, 1876*, ed. Frank B. Norton (New York, 1877), p. 133.

[25] James J. Johnson in *People's Advocate*, July 1, 8, 1876.

[26] *Philadelphia Press*, June 4, 1876; Philadelphia *North American*, July 12, 1876.

[27] *Philadelphia Press*, reprinted in *People's Advocate*, July 1, 1876.

[28] *People's Advocate.* July 15, 1876.

[29] The monument stood on a granite platform eighteen feet high, with a bust of Richard Allen on it. An effort was made to have the monument placed in Fairmount Park

after the Exhibition closed as a permanent tribute to the blacks of Philadelphia, but the move did not bring any results. (See *The Christian Recorder,* June 15, 22, 29, 1876.) Richard Allen, the first Bishop of the African Methodist Episcopal Church, was the founder of Mother Bethel Church in Philadelphia, and a leading figure in the black community during the years from the 1790s to his death in the early 1830s. He presided at the first National Negro Convention held in the Bethel Church in 1830.

[30] In a "Centennial Sermon: 1876 vs. 1776," which he delivered at his church in Pine Bluff, Arkansas, July 9, 1876, Reverend Jenifer did deal to some extent with the events of the American Revolution and the role of blacks in the creation of the American nation. (See *The Christian Recorder,* August 31, 1876.)

[31] Reverend Jenifer also criticized the fact that the federal government gave "millions to feed and clothe Indians who are too lazy to add one iota to the productive resources of the country." This was unusual, since ordinarily blacks expressed deep sympathy for the Indians and their plight. (See, for example, Philip S. Foner, *The Voice of Black Americans: Major Speeches of Negroes in the United States, 1797-1972* (New York, 1973), pp. 212-13, 224-25.

[32] *The Christian Recorder,* July 8, 1876; *People's Advocate,* July 8, 1876. In inviting capitalists to the South, Reverend Jenifer emphasized a point made popular later by Booker T. Washington: "They will find the affable and strong Negro to welcome them." Reverend Jenifer said. "In him they will find one who is willing and ready to work hard." Washington added that they would find a Negro who shunned labor unions and strikes. Louis R. Harlan, *Booker T. Washington: A Biography* (New York, 1973), I, p. 322.

[33] Frederick Saunders, ed., *Our National Centennial Jubilee, Orations, Addresses and Poems Delivered on the Fourth of July, 1876, in the Several States of the Union* (New York, 1877), pp. 530-31.

[34] Actually, the centennial of the "Boston Massacre" during which Crispus Attucks was one of five killed by the British troops, occurred on March 5, 1870. On Benjamin Banneker, see Silvo A. Bodini, *Life of Benjamin Banneker* (New York, 1972).

[35] *People's Advocate,* July 15, 1876; Saunders, *op. cit.,* pp. 257-69.

[36] Hayden himself had fought long and hard against both slavery and racism. A fugitive slave from Kentucky, he settled in Boston and his home soon became a famous rendezvous for runaway slaves. He was a leader of the Boston Vigilance Committee and many of its meetings were held at his home. During and after the Civil War, he continued to work actively for the cause of equal rights.

[37] Recent research indicates that Deborah Gannett was a white indentured servant. See Julia Ward Stickley, "The Records of Deborah Sampson Gannett. Woman Soldier of the Revolution," *Prologue,* IV (Winter, 1972), 26-42.

[38] *The Christian Recorder,* July 8, 1876. The text of the address was originally published in advance of the Fourth of July in the issues of May 4, 11, 1876, and reprinted following its delivery.

[39] *Centennial. The American Negro. From 1776 to 1876. Oration Delivered July 4, 1876, at Avondale, Ohio, by Rev. George W. Williams* (pamphlet in Cincinnati Historical Society). Williams, a graduate of Howard University and Newton Theological Seminary, served as minister, newspaper editor, and government clerk in New England before moving to Cincinnati, Ohio, where he was a minister and also studied law.

[40] "Negro Declaration of Independence, 1876" (pamphlet in Huntington Library, San Marino, California); *The Christian Recorder,* July 15, 1876.

[41] This conclusion is based on a study of newspapers of July 5-6, 1876, in the newspaper division of the Library of Congress and includes papers from all parts of the country.

[42] *The Colored Radical,* Leavenworth & Lawrence, Kansas, August 24, 1876.

[43] C. Vann Woodward, *Reunion and Reaction: The Compromise of 1877 and the End of Reconstruction* (Boston, 1951).

[44] Drew *vs.* Peer, 12 Norris, 234; *Philadelphia Press*, October 26, 1881; *New York Times*, October 26, 1881.

[45] John Hope Franklin, "George Washington Williams, Historian," *Journal of Negro History*, XXXI (January, 1946), 60-90; Earl E. Thorpe, *Black Historians: A Critique* (New York, 1969), pp. 46-47.

[46] *Vorbote*, Chicago, July 29, 1876. The paper, a weekly organ of the German Socialists, announced in the opening of the article: "The French Workers' Delegation has handed the Socialists gathered in Philadelphia the following questionnaire in the French language."

[47] The books are E. Edgar Trout, *The Story of the Centennial of 1876* (New York, 1929); Dee Brown, *The Year of the Century: 1876* (New York, 1966): William Pierce Randel, *Centennial: American Life in 1876* (New York, 1969); the article is Faith K. Pizor, "Preparations for the Centennial Exhibition of 1876," *Pennsylvania Magazine of History and Biography*, XCIV (April, 1970), 113-32; and the doctoral dissertation is Dorothy E. C. Ditter, "The Cultural Climate of the Centennial City: Philadelphia, 1875-1876" (Unpublished Ph.D. thesis, University of Pennsylvania, 1947).

Negro Thought and the Exodus of 1879

BILLY D. HIGGINS

"We've been working for fourteen long years and we ain't no better off then we was when we commenced." Such sentiments by African American farmers-turned-migrants fueled the short-lived black migration movement from the Southern states to Kansas and Indiana beginning in 1879. With the Compromise of 1877 sounding the death knell of Reconstruction and the prospect of mounting racial conflict, and with crop failures signaling economic ruin for many, thousands of African Americans migrated west. Benjamin "Pap" Singleton, Henry Adams, and others organized groups of black "exodusters" for the trek to what was promised as a new life with better opportunities. Although the migration movement waned by the early 1880s, it serves as an important milestone in the chronicles of African American self-help and racial uplift in the post-Civil War decades.

Employing an intellectual history methodology, Billy Higgins places the 1879 exodus within the various ideologies that framed the migration debate. Similar to the controversy over emigration to Africa and other locales that had occupied black thought for several generations, the migration movement to Kansas had its ardent supporters and detractors. Such luminaries as Frederick Douglass, Richard T. Greener, and Blanche K. Bruce joined a national debate on the migration issue, while white politicians from both ends of the political spectrum also voiced their opinions. Higgins explores the ways in which the African American quest for a promised land prompted intellectual debate and hope as well as consternation and disappointment.

IN THE EARLY MORNING HOURS of March 7, 1879, Captain Lennox wheeled his giant Anchor Line packet, *Grand Tower*, out of her berth in the Port of New Orleans, and turned her north toward St. Louis, 1170 miles up the Mississippi River. A short distance upstream at Delta Ferry Landing, throngs of Negro farmhands packing their "little store of worldly goods" crowded the river bank in anticipation of the steamboat.[1] The next morning, five hundred of these Louisiana blacks paid their passage to St. Louis, and stood casting a farewell look at the familiar sugar and cotton fields from the deck of the *Grand Tower*.[2]

This event was not an isolated episode in the spring of 1879. Similar scenes occurred in many lower Mississippi River landings. In the two weeks that it took the *Grand Tower* to repeat the New Orleans round trip, six sister packets discharged over fifteen hundred Southern Negroes at St. Louis, most of whom transferred straightaway into the westbound boats that plied the Missouri River.[3]

Simultaneously by overland routes, Negroes surged out of Tennessee, Texas, and Arkansas. Their destination was the glorious West, specifically, in this phase, Kansas. To Southern Negroes, the attractions of Kansas seemed as rosy as the repulsions of their birthplace grim. Republican Kansas, they believed, meant forty acre homesteads and the right to vote. To these searching ex-slaves, the abolitionist hero, John Brown, and the present governor, John St. John, who had personally welcomed migrating Southern Negroes into his state, personified a congenial Kansas.[4]

Ultimately, some ten to twenty thousand Negroes participated in the "Exodus of 1879." Estimates of the number of "exodusters" varied greatly from observer to observer since anyone bothering to make an appraisal usually was trying to make a political point. United States Census figures for the Negro populations of 1870 and 1890 are inaccurate. Consequently, extrapolated calculations concerning the geographical redistribution of Negroes in this period are distorted.[5]

Only one fact stands out about the numerical extent of the Exodus: it was relatively small. The general westward expansion, the contemporary European immigration to America, and the great influx of Southern Negroes into Northern cities following World War I all dwarf the Exodus of 1879. Despite dire warnings to the contrary by Southern black politicians and Northern white politicians, the Exodus had spent itself by the next year. After the initial spring frenzy, only a trickle of Southern Negroes continued to drift into Kansas and Indiana. The sensation extended artificially into 1880 because of a congressional hearing into the causes, but, almost as suddenly as it began, the Exodus expired.

Nonetheless, for a brief period it dramatized the discontent that smoldered among many Southern Negroes, and, more importantly, their determination to do something about their situation. Moreover, the controversy that it provoked among black intellectuals, and the attention that it aroused in Southern planters, the national news media, and Congress caused the Exodus to assume a significance far out of proportion to its actual size. This disproportionate impact is related to the circumstances surrounding the end of Reconstruction.

The Exodus came on the heels of the Compromise of 1877, and preceded the gradual shift in Negro thinking from "protest to accommodation."[6] Thrown back upon themselves after the national Republican party dissolved its alliance with Southern Negroes, black leaders were faced with the task of forming new strategies. The Exodus, erupting as it did from the emotions of black masses, caught black leaders unprepared, and the opposing responses to the movement developed into an ideological division. Outwardly, the division concerned the propriety of blacks leaving their traditional home. But the real issue, which was to have repercussions for the next half-century, concerned political orientation. Simply put, it was a question of whether Negroes should rely upon the goodwill and fairness of whites or upon the assertiveness of blacks to achieve the blessings of American society.

During the radical Republican honeymoon, the Southern freedmen, released from bondage without money, possessions, or education, tried valiantly to become an integral part of the economic and political life of their country. Allied with the scattered whites in the South who believed in the Republican party principles, the freedmen, as Booker T. Washington pointed out, "started at the top" of Reconstruction politics. The sight of former slaves in seats of power galled the ex-Confederates, and the vaunted but hollow fellowship between whites and blacks, moulded around paternalism, collapsed under the stress of the new relationship. As animosity grew, rebellious whites in the South turned violence to political advantage.

While the ranks waged a brutal campaign of terrorism, conservative Southern leadership, wiser than the fire-eaters of the fifties, devised a two-pronged strategy. On the one hand, it emphasized unity of purpose with Northern businessmen confident that economic interests would undermine the attack of the radical politicians. At home, by beguiling Southern whites with the romantic image of their past, and by deifying the lost cause, the conservative leaders weakened the ill-constructed Republican alliance that had superficially at least supported the integration of the freedmen into society. As Republican governments in the South sagged, the Compromise of 1877 provided the *coup de grace*, and the nation's white population watched with glee as the Reconstruction house split and slid down the shifting sands of expediency into two separate societies.

Freed from direct federal governmental supervision, Southern redeemers concentrated on eroding the Fourteenth and Fifteenth Amendments to the United States Constitution. Heartened by Northern indifference, Southern whites stifled the aspirations of blacks for political and social equality through local manipulations. Bulldozing, nightriding, voter intimidation, and, an impersonal necessity of the capital-poor South, the crop-lien system, shunted black Southerners back to a way of life more nearly slave than not.[7] Southern whites, with their two hundred years of experience in the science of maintaining dominance, had withstood the brief but furious challenge to their way of life, and were now gaining momentum in their struggle to put down equality of blacks.

The relentless drive toward resurrecting a society based on racial distinctions precluded compromise solutions. Southern Negroes were confronted with the stark options identified by a contemporary observer as either "to withdraw from all participation in . . . political affairs, . . . or to fight, or to migrate."[8]

Many Negroes had felt the impulse to leave the South since that first fugitive slave had set his sight and heart on the North Star. Colonization projects and migratory ambitions were never far from the center of Negro thought in the nineteenth century. Black leaders of all political ideologies carried migration ideas as part of their arsenal. Such diverse personalities as an aristocratic Union Army major, Martin Delany; a fiery African Methodist Episcopal bishop, Henry Turner; and a Louisiana field hand, Henry Adams, held a common conviction that geographical separation was imperative in the solution of racial problems.[9]

As Reconstruction metamorphosed from fact to political epithet, migratory schemes cropped up frequently. The 1864 proposal of Kansas Congressman James Lane to create a Negro state in the Rio Grande region symbolizes the transition in emphasis from colonization abroad to domestic emigration. An 1874 Alabama Negro convention assigned a special committee to investigate the possibility of founding a colony in the western United States as "the best means of ameliorating their condition."[10] Even as this particular committee withered, the impulse was taking another form as small bands of Negro railroad laborers, cowhands, and homesteaders filtered into the West.

Benjamin Singleton, a Nashville, Tennessee, realtor, was instrumental in locating some of these migrants in Kansas.[11] Singleton, nicknamed "Pap" by those whom he helped, was a fugitive slave who returned to his old home after the war and occupied himself in the real estate business. Singleton shared the popular belief that economic independence underwrote political and civil achievement. In his efforts to secure good farms for Tennessee Negroes, however, he was stymied by exorbitant land prices. To this was added Singleton's observation that in the South the whites had too many competitive advantages over the Negroes, and that his race was "coming down, in-

stead of going up."[12] As a result, "Pap" became an emigration advocate impatient to see Negroes move to more bountiful surroundings,
which he initially believed could be found in Kansas. He began his
migration campaign in 1869. For ten years he proclaimed the merits
of moving out of the South. It was this tenaciousness coupled with
his flamboyant testimony before the Congressional investigating committee that captivated contemporary reporters and insured his prominence in the history of the Exodus.[13]

Henry Adams, a Louisiana ex-slave, began organizational work
in 1869 also to determine "whether we could remain in the South
amongst the people who had held us as slaves or not."[14] By 1874, Adams had decided that the answer was negative and began to promote
migration. Indicative of the efficiency and pervasiveness of Adams
and his associates is the membership list of 98,000 Negroes in several
Southern states who affiliated with his colonization council.[15]

Both Singleton and Adams made their appeal to the working
class. Foreshadowing the approaching clash of interests brought
about in the Negro community by the Exodus was the conscious exclusion of certain occupations from the fledgling migratory groups.
To join his movement, Singleton recruited "the men that worked,"
and testified later that "not a political Negro was in it." Singleton implied under questioning by Minnesota Senator William Windom that
those Negroes who owned their homes and who were therefore "in
good circumstances" softpedaled bad conditions and the need to
migrate.[16]

The secret meetings held by the information committees of
Adam's council were composed "of the laboring class." The committees refused to let those that opposed migration speak at these meetings. This was a practical restriction, for most accomplished orators in
the black community were ministers and politicians, whom Adams referred to as "against [the movement] from the beginning."[17]

These organizational activities being carried out among the
black masses structured the existing migratory impulse. The emphasis
on mass participation altered the concept of flight from an individu-
alistic act of protest to a potent expression of group will. Moreover, it
signified the increasing reluctance of many black Americans to depend upon white benevolence to provide better conditions, preferring instead to rely upon their own actions. Specifically, the
migration clubs and co-operatives provided an institutional outlet at
the critical juncture when social unrest gave way to active uprising.
The extensive grass roots efforts facilitated the channeling of frustra-
tions into migratory movements.

Booker T. Washington considered the 1879 Exodus as the "nearest to anything like an uprising of the Negroes in the South since emancipation. . . ."[18] Like most uprisings, the Exodus needed concrete incidents to trigger it. A series of incidents occurred during the winter of 1878-1879. These acted as stimuli powerful enough to mobilize what Frederick Douglass described as "a remarkably home-loving race."[19]

Of prime importance was the crop failure of 1878. This agricultural disaster wrung from many black farmers the last hope of ever escaping indebtedness to merchant-creditors.[20] The pall of futility created by this event yielded to desperation during the lean winter months, and made Negroes susceptible to the proposals of a radical Republican senator, William Windom. In January 1879, concerned with the charges of abrogation of rights of Negroes that drifted steadily into Washington from Republican sources in the South, Windom called for a study on the practicability of a government sponsored relocation plan for those Southern Negroes who were being deprived of their constitutional rights. Without being specific, Windom's reference to receptive territories implied that government lands in the West might be opened up to Negro migrants.[21]

Windom's resolution, which never passed, merely officially articulated ideas already present in the minds of the blacks. Implicit in the resolution was the admission that Congress was no longer willing to interfere in the internal affairs of ex-Confederate states, even to enforce constitutional amendments. Rights of Negroes would be considered, if considered at all, only in the new lands to the West.

While Negroes tended to place Windom's provocative oratory in perspective with the deeper causes, white Democrats were not so objective. Once the Exodus began in earnest, Windom became a convenient scapegoat for them. He was pictured as an agitator set upon stirring up Southern Negroes to further surreptitious political aims. The allusion to free lands was obviously designed to entice Negroes to move north to swell the Republican vote in crucial areas. Although Republicans ridiculed the feasibility of moving enough voters to affect the outcome of a national election, the closeness of the 1876 election detracted from the effectiveness of this argument.[22] A Bourbon Democrat explained the sinister plot: "It's all owing to the radical politicians at the North. . . . They've had their emissaries down here, and deluded the niggers into a very fever of emigration, with the purpose of reducing our basis of representation in Congress and increasing that of the Northern States."[23]

This initial reaction of Democrats hardened into party line as the Exodus controversy assumed national proportions. By insisting upon seeing the Exodus from an exclusively political frame of reference, Democrats, North and South, were unable to discern the profound social significance of the movement, and doomed the ensuing congressional investigation to an exercise in partisan politics.

As easily as some whites read political intrigue into a civil rights resolution by a concerned senator, some blacks detected a conspiracy in a particular political assemblage that convened at about the same time. As was the tendency in Southern states, Louisiana Democrats instigated a constitutional convention as soon as they had regained ascendency in state politics. Satisfied with the Reconstruction constitution, Negroes naturally regarded this revision as an attack upon their rights. Aware of the situation, the convention delegates tried to allay the fears of the Negroes by officially denying any intentions of "restricting the political or religious rights of any class of citizens. . . ." Nonetheless, with or without good cause, the convention induced several hundred "panic stricken" Negroes to set out for Kansas in February 1879.[24]

From this innocuous beginning, the migration, nourished by the circumstances of the time, swelled until it reached a crescendo in May. News of the Exodus, carried on a wave of excitement, swept through black households. "We've been working for fourteen long years," explained a farmer-turned-migrant, "and we ain't no better off then we was when we commenced."[25] Widespread frustration of this kind guaranteed an active response to a mass movement among lower-class Negroes. Exodus was a form of action which could be undertaken by uneducated and illiterate people without extensive training or elaborate organizations. Permanently degraded in their Southern environment, the Negroes in an assertion of their self-respect and pride pulled up stakes and left.

The growing migration inspired Negroes of all classes. Gathering in groups, mass meetings, and conventions, they occupied themselves with the Exodus. They listened to speeches, engaged in debates, cajoled each other, and solicited funds for the movement. Most delegated bodies, including the National Conference for Colored Men, which was held in Nashville, Tennessee, in early May, officially approved of the migration. That this support took the form of flowery resolutions instead of financial underwriting sowed the seeds of failure for the mass migration.

However, the problem of finances assumed a backseat to the deepening ideological split among black leaders. Ironically, it was the white reaction that encouraged optimistic blacks to stand firm in their opposition to the migration. The spontaneity and apparent dimensions of the Exodus caught the white nation off guard. The

New York Times warned its readers that "this is not an ordinary migration," and Negro editors delighted in describing the normally blasé white Southerners as "alarmed."[26] Southern planters were as disturbed by black laborers moving out as Northern Democratic politicians were by black voters moving in. Emotionalism fired crude efforts to prevent Negroes from leaving. Employers threatened to pay Negroes in local scrip. Trumped-up arrests detained would-be migrants. Planters ordered steamers not to pick up "fleeing colored people," and, obediently, "northbound steamboats cruelly ignored" the hailing signals of isolated clusters of Negro exodusters along the river bank.[27]

A gradual return to rationality prompted white planters of the Mississippi Valley to convene in Vicksburg to determine the actual causes of the Exodus. The Vicksburg Convention also included a few Negro planters from the region who were as concerned about the loss of laborers as their white counterparts. After an orderly three day session, the delegates reached a consensus which recognized the validity of complaints by Negroes of political repression and economic disadvantages, and passed a commendable, but toothless, resolution which pledged the participants "to protect the colored race . . . at the polls . . . from fraud, intimidation or 'bulldozing' . . . by whites."[28]

Coming in the first week of May, immediately prior to the opening of the National Conference of Colored Men, which itself was poised to consider the ramifications of the Exodus, the Vicksburg concessions had an appreciable impact on Negro leadership. Indeed, it was this initial reaction by labor-conscious planters that persuaded many Negroes of the willingness of Southerners to barter civil rights for Negro muscle. That white agrarian interests dominated politics in parts of the South was as well-known as their dependence upon Negro labor. Black leaders saw in the Exodus an opportunity to exploit this relationship in order to improve the situation of Southern Negroes. This conservative facet of the movement dominated the thinking of Negroes, and obscured for all but the most perspicacious the radical potential of the Exodus.

Leading Negro politicians, such as Blanche K. Bruce and John R. Lynch, entertained notions of preserving some political strength in the South. Although disturbed by the extralegal disfranchisement of blacks that was being carried out in some parts of the South, the solutions of these political figures did not run toward dissipation of black constituencies through large-scale migrations. Concentrations of protected black votes appeared to them indispensable for black successes. Consequently, they determined the value of the Exodus to be

its threat to the economic life of the South. It was hard political currency to be used at the bargaining table to secure rights for Negroes.[29] Secondarily, the Exodus afforded a dramatic platform from
which Negro spokesmen could assail the sensibilities of Northern
moralists, who, thinking they had ended non-democratic practices in
the South, had turned to other pursuits. Most established Southern
Negroes did not want to go further than this. The reality of migration was to be carefully avoided. P.B.S. Pinchback, who was a former
lieutenant governor of Louisiana, controlled a black New Orleans
newspaper, *The Weekly Louisianian.* Through its pages, he warned his
readers not to fall for migration panaceas, and stressed his point that
"occasional and even violent persecutions . . . do not always justify
nor produce a general abandonment by a people of their homes and
possessions. . . ."[30] *The Weekly Louisianian* walked a delicate line between emphasizing for the benefit of Northern sympathizers the "violence, oppression, and want" suffered by Negroes at the hands of
Southern whites, and urging Negroes not to "cynically condemn" the
sincerity of white planters at the Vicksburg Convention.[31]

Whereas conservative Negro leaders dreaded the specter of a
panicky mass flight spiraling beyond their control, militant Negroes
dwelled on the positive side of the Exodus and urged the movement
on. A prominent Washington, D. C., Negro, O. S. B. Wall, depicted
the Exodus as a "manly and dignified step. . . ." The Honorable John
Mercer Langston, serving as the United States minister to Haiti at the
time, argued that through such action Negroes would lose their "servile psychology," and become "conscious of their own power. . . ."[32]
Negro leaders divided over the different conceptions of the ultimate
purpose of Exodus, and each side sought to crystalize Negro public
opinion behind them. Generally, the pro-Exodus theorists, in
harmony with spontaneous sentiments, held sway. In the end, however, their polemical victory proved to be a Pyrrhic one, for the division itself shattered the solidarity essential for a successful black
migration out of the South.

From the floor of a New Orleans convention hastily assembled
in mid-April of 1879 to consider the situation, Pinchback assailed the
idea of Exodus. Out of the convention's "stormy" and "confused" atmosphere nonetheless came the resolution, enunciated by a less distinguished delegate, that Negroes should "emigrate and settle where
they would be free from shot-guns."[33]

A classic dilemma confronted Bruce and Lynch. Their aversion
to losing large numbers of black voters clashed with their politician's
anathema of swimming against a tide of popular feeling. Bruce admitted that he "studiously avoided giving expression to his views on

. . . the movement of colored people from the South. . . ."[34] Pinned into making a personal statement by an invitation from the prestigious chairman of the Vicksburg Convention, Bruce spoke in such lofty terms that no one could either deny what he was saying or act upon it.[35] After an analysis of his records, Professor Benjamin Quarles concluded that Bruce "took a stand against the movement." It was such evasive behavior that compelled one biographer to charge that although Bruce "defended the rights of the Negro in the Senate, he failed to offer his race positive and forceful leadership."[36]

Indicative of Lynch's studied ambiguity was this assessment of his address before the Nashville conference: "If he had said less, he would have been unfit to represent his people. If he had said more, it might have indicated an unsafe leader." To the approval of this Democratic newspaper editor, Lynch had counseled moderation and reconciliation.[37]

Minor politicians were responsive to local feelings concerning the movement. Often this led to qualified approval of the Exodus by local officials. Mifflin Gibbs, a Little Rock, Arkansas, municipal judge, and James T. Rapier, a former Alabama congressman, were named by Senator Windom to report on the condition of Kansas exodusters. This commission was formed in accordance with a provision of the Nashville conference to investigate the circumstances of the migrants. Gibbs and Rapier traveled at their own expense to Kansas in August, 1879. Most migrants, they reported, were already self-supporting. Some, however, were still dependent upon relief supplied by charitable societies, organized during the heaviest onslaught to help destitute exodusters. At the completion of their junket, the two-man committee advised "the moneyless to avoid the suffering which might lie in wait." Gibb's impressions convinced him that the "gratification of the migratory impulse has in many instances proved disastrous, the yielding to which should be only indulged after every possible effort has been made to remove local obstacles to happiness by uprightness, softening animosities, and by industry accumulate wealth."[38]

Many Northern Negroes endorsed the Exodus at least vocally. Mass meetings were held to generate support for the fleeing Negroes. Frederick Douglass, an opponent of the migration, conceded that "nothing has occurred since the abolition of slavery which has excited a deeper interest among thoughtful men than this Exodus."[39] The *New York Times* exulted over "the largest assemblage of colored people ever seen in this city," which had turned out for an April Exodus rally.[40] For a short time after the contentious New Orleans affair, debate over the merits of the Exodus subsided. Testimonials intended to loosen purse strings replaced objective analysis on the agenda. At such fund-raising rallies, orators sympathetic to the movement would often ridicule opponents of the Exodus. To the accompaniment of his large audience at a New York City gathering, Carlton H. Tandy described his futile effort to "enlist the sympathies of the Honorable Frederick Douglass." A *New York Times* reporter included the crowd's reaction to Mr. Tandy's jibes in his report: "Mr. Douglass disapproved of the emigration [hisses from all quarters of the hall] and did not see exactly what could be done. [hisses] He advised the Negroes to stay where they were. [hisses] I asked him why he did not stay there himself. [laughter]"[41]

Some well-established Northern Negroes, like their Southern counterparts, detected a definite danger in such social convulsions. Isaiah Wears, a prosperous Philadelphia real estate broker, attacked the movement through the pages of the *Christian Recorder*. Although he admitted that there was widespread oppression, he "did not think that the Exodus was the proper remedy." Wears perhaps reveals the precarious foothold of many black businessmen in the North as he insists that Southern Negroes must fight for their liberty in the South, for otherwise, "in any community where the people believe that a little oppression will drive the colored man away they will apply it."[42]

Finding themselves in agreement with the abstract principles of mass migration, Negro intellectuals outside politics and business provided eloquent justification for the Exodus. Professor Richard T. Greener, a Harvard graduate and occupant of the chair of metaphysics at the University of South Carolina until Wade Hampton's return to power, became a leading exponent of the Exodus. Indeed, he and his Howard University colleague, O. S. B. Wall, became so identified with the Exodus that the indignant Negro editor of the *North Carolina Republican* blamed them as the "original promoters of the exodus movement, and on them our righteous indignation and censure should be unsparingly poured." It was through their misrepresentations, the editor continued, that "the seeds of restlessness and discontent have been sowed among our people. . . ."[43]

If Wall did not help sow the seeds of restlessness, he at least by his actions as president of the Emigrant Aid Society, fertilized the fields. Certain that the Exodus would "have an important bearing upon the future material and intellectual development of the race," Wall arranged for the Haitian minister, John M. Langston, to address a Washington, D.C., gathering of the Negro elite. Langston spoke for two hours "in favor of the Exodus." Believing, as did Henry Adams, that there was slight hope of "the permanent elevation of the colored people while they remain in the midst of scenes of their former enslavement," Langston emphasized the psychological and spiritual benefits that this mass action would have for the self-esteem of Negroes. After 245 years of racial stratification, Southern prejudices had hardened beyond easy change, and social discriminations by the ex-master class against the ex-slave would continue, Langston declared, "until, by some manly utterance or courageous deed, the Negro demonstrates his independence. . . ." The problem as succinctly stated by Langston was that the "black man seems to have no rights which the white man is bound to respect." The historical solution to such problems, according to Langston, was the exodus of the persecuted minority.[44]

As the audience clapped and cheered Langston's remarks, the two distinguised guests seated behind him on the speaker's platform stonily ignored occasional calls for rebuttal. Although it was in keeping with Senator Bruce's character to remain silent that night, his companion's refusal to reply to Langston was less predictable, for Frederick Douglass was an outspoken critic of the Exodus. The aging ex-slave had never shied from controversy. As an abolition crusader, he had had sharp ideological disputes with William Lloyd Garrison and Samuel Ringgold Ward. From its very beginnings, braving "opposition from the northern press and the anathemas of the colored people," Douglass had publicly condemned the Exodus and had sought to cool what he considered a rash dislocation by addressing through proxies several of the Exodus conventions, advising Negroes to remain where they were.[45]

Douglass' opposition is especially significant because he was free of the self-interested motives that too frequently inspired many foes of the Exodus. His position as Marshall of the District of Columbia, his financial independence, and his recognition as champion of the rights of Negroes enhanced Douglass' capability to act in the best interests of the Negro race. His stand against the migration must be interpreted therefore as an accurate representation of one branch of contemporary Negro thought as it tried to map out the best strategy to insure the incorporation of Negroes into American society.

Douglass was painfully aware that Negroes were "very badly treated at the South," and was quietly proud that plucky blacks had proved that "Mississippi can originate more than one plan." Yet he was sure that unscrupulous promoters, land speculators, and "northern malignants" were stampeding Negroes just when they were "beginning to accumulate a little property, and to lay the foundation of families."[46]

Since many considered Douglass the foremost spokesman of his race, his arguments naturally attracted substantial interest. The American Social Science Association offered him an opportunity before their national convention to debate Greener on the propriety of the Exodus. Although Douglass did not make the trip to Saratoga Springs, New York, when the conference convened in September, the essay articulating his views which he had written for the occasion was read before the conference by Professor Francis Wayland.[47]

The essence of Douglass' essay was that if the rights of Negroes were not upheld in the South, they would be forever forfeited in the United States, for persecution would inevitably follow Negroes wherever they moved. To advocate exodus was to him a surrender of the right to protection of person and property. "The business of this nation," he firmly believed, "is to protect its citizens where they are, not to transport them where they will not need protection."[48] Essential to this line of reasoning, of course, is an unshakable faith in the ultimate fairness and generosity of the white majority. Douglass depended on progress for the Negroes to come through interracial cooperation. To fortify his optimism, he pointed to what he believed were symptoms of "beneficent reaction" in 1879, and declared the Exodus to be "ill-timed." The nation, he said, stood "at the gateway of a marked and decided change. . . ."[49]

The division in Negro leadership generated from the questionable certitude of this observation. A contradictory assessment compelled South Carolina Congressman Joseph Hayne Rainey to reject the Vicksburg concessions because "white promises could no longer be trusted. . . ."[50] Rainey is a rare example of the Negro politician who by 1879 had come to see the future of Negroes in the South as unpromising. To him, the Exodus had sprung from Southern soil, which was littered with broken promises. Generally faith in interracial cooperation had declined, and many Negroes were searching for substitutes. A rise in race consciousness appeared to parallel the demand for new approaches, and briefly gave additional impetus to all-black endeavors such as the Exodus. Lucius Q. C. Lamar's metaphor captures the essence of this intellectual trend:

> The only mode by which [Negroes] can get rid of their characteristics as a parasite race (sticking on a civilization without partaking of its nature and identity) is to remove it from the structure to which it is attached. If incapable of striking its own roots into the soil, it must die; but in my opinion, it would not die out at the North.[51]

Richard T. Greener's reply to Douglass' essay at the Saratoga Springs debate pointed out the demoralized condition of Southern Negroes, and contended that in the South Negroes were doomed to spend their lives engaged in menial labor, and would "never know [their] own possibilities."[52] John M. Langston agreed that "new scenes and new surroundings seem to me to be absolutely indispensable to render Negroes conscious of their freedom and reponsibilities. . . ."[53]

New scenes and surroundings, however, were restricted to the dreams of the majority of the Southern Negro masses. A black Alabama politician grumbled that 15,000 Negroes from his district alone would migrate the next spring.[54] Such forecasts were common, but migration activity waned in 1880. Singleton, discouraged by increasing hostility in Kansas, diverted the thinning migratory stream toward Indiana. Through his congressional investigating committee, Indiana Democratic Senator Daniel W. Voorhees indignantly sought to expose the Republican conspiracy that was responsible for this unwelcome intrusion into his state. Despite such congressional theatrics and contrary to alarmist publicity, there was only an insignificant influx of Negroes into Indiana.[55]

Ironically, Negro intellectual interest crested as the Exodus itself faded. Just as circumstances conspired to ignite the movement, they conspired to quench it. The Northern welcome iced over as exodusters piled into overcrowded Kansas cities. Kansas land, while not as expensive as that in the South, cost more than most could pay. Counterpropaganda, launched by planters and Northern objectors, which stressed the misery of migrants, began to replace Singleton's circulars. Initial supporters, such as Windom and St. John, somewhat sobered by the potential scale of the migration, moderated their position and sought to control the movement.[56] Negro intellectuals favoring the Exodus seldom came across with substantial financial backing, and a request of the Nashville conference to the United States government to subsidize the move went quietly unheeded. Even local organizers such as Singleton slacked their activities, as they applied themselves to consolidating the newly settled colonies.[57] Finally, with Negroes hopelessly divided, strong central leadership capable of pressing the migratory movement never materialized.

August Meier wrote that the "completed racial system did not develop overnight, but piece by piece. . . ."[58] Certainly the romantic Exodus of 1879 was a key piece. Its failure interrupted efforts of Negroes to achieve common goals through mass social action. Instead, accommodationists arose to insist that uplift must come from individual economic achievement. Deprived of a black power base, leaders depended on the moral indignation of whites to nourish their struggle for political and civil rights. Unfortunately, this proved to be thin and inconsistent soup, hardly able to sustain the vigorous drive required to secure equality for Negroes.

Douglass predicted that the Exodus would "prove a disappointment, a mistake, and a failure." Assuredly, this may have been an inevitability even with the enthusiastic unanimity of Negro leadership. But in retrospect it is certain that by remaining in the South, Negroes conceded political and social inequality.[59] This reality was quickly buried under a deluge of economic exhortations. Douglass urged Negroes to be frugal and build an economic stake. "Put us in Kansas or Africa," he warned in a statement strikingly prophetic of the Tuskegee sage, "and until we learn to save more than we spend, we are sure to sink and perish."[60]

Harsh pragmatism washed away dreams of a black cultural taproot; of a promised land where black values and pride could develop free from cramping white domination. Booker T. Washington hailed the "energetic efforts upon the part of Frederick Douglass and other leaders of the race to prevent the movement assuming larger and more dangerous proportions."[61] Even so, for a while in 1879, the spirit that had sent waves of their blue-coated brothers against the ramparts of Fort Wagner flickered again in the eyes of Negroes.

Notes

[1] *The Weekly Louisianian* (New Orleans), March 15, 1879.

[2] *Ibid.*

[3] *Globe-Democrat* (St. Louis), March 16-31, 1879, as cited in Glen Schwendeman, "St. Louis and the Exodusters of 1879," *Journal of Negro History*, XLVI (January, 1961), 32-34.

[4] Testimony of Dr. J. B. Lamb, "Report and Testimony of the Select Committee of the United States Senate to Investigate the Causes of the Removal of the Negro from the Southern States to the Northern States," *Senate Report* No. 693, 46th Congress, 2nd session, Part 3, 271-73. (Hereinafter referred to as *Senate Report* No. 693.)

[5] John Van Deusen, "The Exodus of 1879," *Journal of Negro History*, XXI (April, 1936), 122; United States Bureau of the Census, *Negro Population in the United States, 1790-1915* (Washington, D. C.: U.S. Government Printing Office, 1918), pp. 28-29.

[6] August Meier and Elliott Rudwick, *From Plantation to Ghetto; an Interpretive History of American Negroes* (New York, 1966), p. 171.

[7] E. L. Godkin, "The Flight of the Negroes," *Nation*, XXVIII (April 10, 1879), 242; Testimony of Henry Adams, *Senate Report* No. 693, Part 2, 101-11.

[8] J. C. Hartzell, "The Negro Exodus," *Methodist Quarterly Review*, LXI (October, 1879), 741.

[9] Martin R. Delany, *et al.*, "Political Destiny of the Colored Race on the American Continent," appended in Frank A. Rollin, *Life and Public Services of Martin R. Delany* (Boston: Lee and Shepard, 1883), pp. 327-67. Turner's nationalistic speeches have been widely reprinted. An example can be found in Herbert Aptheker, *A Documentary History of the Negro People in the United States* (New York, 1951), pp. 757-58.

[10] Testimony of Phillip Joseph, *Senate Report* No. 693, Part 2, 394.

[11] Walter L. Fleming, " 'Pap' Singleton, the Moses of the Colored Exodus," *American Journal of Sociology*, XV (July, 1909), 64-65.

[12] Testimony of Benjamin Singleton, *Senate Report* No. 693, Part 3, p. 380.

[13] *Ibid.*, pp. 379-91.

[14] Testimony of Henry Adams, *Senate Report* No. 693, Part 2, pp. 101-02.

[15] *Ibid.*, p. 110.

[16] Testimony of Benjamin Singleton, *op. cit.*, pp. 380-81.

[17] Testimony of Henry Adams, *op. cit.*, p. 10.

[18] Booker T. Washington, *The Story of the Negro* (New York, 1909), I, 186.

[19] Frederick Douglass, "The Negro Exodus from the Gulf States," reprinted in Carter G. Woodson, *Negro Orators and Their Orations* (Washington: Associated Publishers, 1925), p. 454.

[20] James B. Runnion, "The Negro Exodus," *Atlantic Monthly*, XLIV (August, 1879), 222-24; Testimony of Samuel L. Perry, *Senate Report* No. 693, Part 1, p. 280.

[21] *Congressional Record*, 45th Congress, 3rd session, VIII (December 2, 1878), 483.

[22] *New York Times*, July 12, 1879, p. 4; Rayford Logan, *The Negro in American Life and Thought, 1877-1901* (New York, 1954), pp. 171-72.

[23] Runnion, *op. cit.*, p. 223.

[24] *New York Times*, April 23, 1879, p. 1; *The Weekly Louisianian*, March 15, 1879.

[25] Runnion, *op. cit.*, p. 223.

[26] *New York Times*, April 24, 1879, p. 3; *The Weekly Louisianian*, March 8, 1879.

[27] *Ibid.*, April 23, 1879, p. 4.

[28] The proceedings of the Vicksburg Convention appeared in *The Vicksburg Commercial Daily Advertiser*, May 5, 1879, and are reprinted in *The Journal of Negro History*, IV (January, 1919), 51-54.

[29] Letter from Blanche K. Bruce to Colonel W. L. Nugent, April 13, 1879, cited in *Daily American* (Nashville), May 6, 1879; *ibid.*, May 10, 1879.

[30] *The Weekly Louisianian*, February 1, 1879.

[31] *Ibid.*, February 15, 1879; *ibid.*, May 24, 1879.

[32] Letter from O. S. B. Wall to John Mercer Langston, September 16, 1879, reprinted in *Freedom and Citizenship, Selected Lectures and Addresses of Honorable John Mercer Langston* (Washington: Rufus H. Darby, 1883), p. 232. (Hereinafter referred to as *Freedom and Citizenship*.); John Mercer Langston, "The Exodus," *Freedom and Citizenship*, p. 239.

[33] *New York Times*, April 19, 1879, p. 1; Van Deusen, *op. cit.*, p. 114.

[34] Sadie Daniel St. Clair, "The National Career of Blanche Kelso Bruce" (Unpublished Ph.D. dissertation, New York University, 1947), p. 146.

[35] Letter from Bruce to Nugent, April 18, 1879, reprinted in *Daily American*, May 6, 1879.

[36] St. Clair, *op. cit.*, p. 171.

[37] *Daily American*, May 9, 1879.

[38] Mifflin Gibbs, *Shadow and Light: An Autobiography* (Washington, D. C., 1902), pp. 180-84.

[39] Douglass, *op. cit.*, p. 454.

[40] *New York Times*, April 24, 1879, p. 1.

[41] *Ibid.*

[42] Testimony of Isaiah Wears, *Senate Report* No. 693, Part 3, 151.

[43] Testimony of James H. Harris, *Senate Report* No. 693, Part I, 106.

[44] Letter from Wall to Langston, September 16, 1879, reprinted in *Freedom and Citizenship*, p. 232; *Freedom and Citizenship*, pp. 233-39; *New York Times*, October 1, 1879, p. 1.

[45] *People's Advocate* (Washington, D. C.), October 11, 1879; George W. Williams, *History of the Negro Race in America*, Arno Press-*New York Times* reprint series (New York: Putnam's Sons, 1883), pp. 433-34.

[46] Douglass, *op. cit.*, pp. 459, 453, 467.

[47] *New York Times*, September 13, 1879, p. 2.

[48] Douglass, *op. cit.*, pp. 466-67.

[49] *Ibid.*, p. 465.

[50] Editorial, *Nation*, XXVIII (May 15, 1879), 328.

[51] Letter from L. Q. C. Lamar to Colonel W. B. Montgomery, March 24, 1880, reprinted in Edward Mayes, *Lucius Q. C. Lamar; His Life, Times, and Speeches, 1825-1893* (Nashville: Publishing House of the Methodist Episcopal Church, South, 1896), p. 415.

[52] Richard T. Greener, "The Emigration of Colored Citizens from the Southern States," Woodson, *op. cit.*, p. 477.

[53] *New York Times*, October 1, 1879, p. 1.

[54] Hartzell, *op. cit.*, p. 723.

[55] Emma Lou Thornbrough, *The Negro in Indiana: A Study of a Minority* (Indianapolis: Indiana Historical Bureau, 1957), p. 215.

[56] Testimony of Judge G. W. Carey, *Senate Report* No. 693, Part 3, 391-407.

[57] Fleming, *op. cit.*, pp. 73-74.

[58] August Meier, *Negro Thought in America, 1880-1950* (Ann Arbor, 1963), p. 20.

[59] Douglass, *op. cit.*, p. 468.

[60] Frederick Douglass, *Life and Times of Frederick Douglass* (Hartford, Connecticut: Park Publishing Company, 1882), p. 561.

[61] Washington, *op. cit.*, p. 186.

The Leflore County Massacre and the Demise of the Colored Farmers' Alliance

William F. Holmes

In the aftermath of the Civil War, African Americans labored to carve out an economic foothold for themselves in industry, agriculture, business, and the professions. When racism thwarted their efforts to join forces with whites, blacks formed their own cooperatives, labor unions, and banks. Following the failure of the Freedmen's Bank in 1874, for example, blacks in Richmond, Virginia, formed the Savings Bank of the Grand Fountain United Order of True Reformers in 1888. Discouraged from joining the National Labor Union, a group of black workers from Baltimore, Maryland, organized the National Colored Labor Union in 1869. Similarly, in 1886, the Colored Farmers' Alliance came into existence as a parallel organization to the white Southern Farmers' Alliance.

William Holmes' essay chronicles post-Reconstruction African American unity in the face of violent oppression by whites. In 1889, the leaders and the rank-and-file of the Colored Farmers' Alliance, an economic cooperative, met intimidation and massacre in Leflore County, Mississippi. Drawing from contemporary newspaper accounts, state government records, and census data, Holmes reconstructs an episode of Southern racial violence that led, he argues, to the demise of an organization of African American farmers, and more generally typified a pattern of violence in shaping race relations in the South.

IN EARLY SEPTEMBER 1889 major American newspapers reported that hundreds of Negroes were massing against whites in Leflore County, Mississippi, and that a race war might ensue. Within a few days, however, they reported that all was quiet: National Guardsmen had restored order, in the process killing five blacks.[1] Many Mississippi newspapers denied that the troops killed anyone. "Flying rumors have been received that several negroes have been killed," the Jackson *Clarion-Ledger* announced, "but they lack authenticity."[2] The Natchez *Daily Democrat* warned that the Leflore troubles represented another example of overly emotional reporting by the national press, which in the past had frequently carried false stories of impending race wars.[3] The Raymond *Gazette* admitted that troops went to Leflore

County, but added that, "they were respectfully told that their services were not needed and that the negroes were not in rebellion. My, my how everybody was fooled."[4]

Reports by state and county officials indicated that the trouble had not been too serious. Colonel George S. Green, the officer in charge of the Guardsmen, informed Governor Robert Lowry his troops had arrested some blacks at the scene of the trouble and turned them over to the sheriff. Although he had heard reports that local whites killed four or five "ring leaders," he could not "vouch for this as we did not see any corpses."[5] Sheriff L. T. Baskett of Leflore County explained to the Governor that the riotous blacks had murdered a Negro who refused to join them and that a posse had killed some Negroes who resisted arrest. He did not indicate how many the posse killed. Only the arrival of the troops, Baskett insisted, prevented "a bloody conflict between the races."[6]

Following reports that the troops had restored order, neither national nor Mississippi newspapers gave further attention to the epidsode. Over the next four months, however, reports appeared in black newspapers describing the incident as the "Leflore massacre," in which the whites killed between twenty and a hundred Negroes on the pretext of quelling a rebellion. Some held the guardsmen responsible; others charged that an armed posse roamed the countryside shooting and hanging blacks.[7]

Because the people involved in those events of early September 1889 left no written records and because neither state nor federal authorities investigated the affair, it is difficult to determine fully what happened. Still it is possible to reconstruct a significant portion of the story, for some newspapers secured valuable bits of information, including a few firsthand reports from men who actually witnessed the events. It is worthwhile to discover what happened in Leflore County because that episode well illustrates the role of violence in shaping black history in the post-Reconstruction South. It also helps explain why the Colored Farmers' Alliance, which may have been the largest Negro organization in American history, failed.

The troubles in Leflore County sprang largely from the attempts by blacks to improve themselves financially. At that time the South was overwhelmingly rural, and for many years the farmers of that region had suffered from such problems as rising costs, falling prices, and rural isolation. In the hope of improving their lot, many white farmers joined such organizations as the Grange, the Agricultural Wheel, and the Louisiana Farmers' Union. By the late 1880s the Southern Farmers' Alliance emerged as the region's major agricultural organization and enlisted in its ranks thousands of farmers from throughout the nation. Because the Southern Alliance barred Negroes from membership, blacks formed the Colored Farmers' Alliance and Cooperative Union.[8] Such an organization was sorely needed, for the majority of Southern blacks worked the land and experienced harder times than did most white farmers. While some blacks owned small farms, many more worked as sharecroppers or field hands for white planters. With many of them living at a bare subsistence level, the black farmers, more than any other group in American history, resembled the peasant classes in the poorest European nations of the nineteenth century.

Founded in Houston County, Texas, in 1886, the Colored Alliance soon spread into every Southern state, and at its height in 1891 claimed a membership of over a million. Like other farm clubs of the late nineteenth century, the Colored Alliance was in many respects a conservative organization which urged its members to practice better farming methods, to acquire ownership of their homes, and to improve their level of education. It established exchanges in the ports of Norfolk, Charleston, Mobile, New Orleans, and Houston, through which members bought goods at reduced prices and obtained loans to pay off mortgages. In some areas the Colored Alliance raised funds to provide for longer public school terms, and there are even reports that the Alliance founded academies. Being a fraternal organization, it solicited funds to help sick and disabled members.[9] Certainly there does not appear to have been anything in those goals that should disturb whites, for like many Negro organizations of that era the Colored Alliance urged members to uplift themselves by hard work and sacrifice. It illustrated the philosophy that Booker T. Washington would soon make famous.[10]

Because the Colored Alliance espoused a conservative philosophy and worked for goals similar to other farm organizations, some historians have considered it a mere appendage of the Southern Alliance.[11] There are grounds for taking such a position, for the two alliances agreed on many issues. Both advocated the abolition of the Louisiana Lottery, fearing it might lead some farmers further into debt.[12] In 1889 they joined forces against the Northern Farmers' Alliance by opposing the Conger Lard Bill, a measure that attempted to impose high taxes and strict regulations upon the production of vegetable oil. Northern Alliancemen, many of whom were dairy farmers, supported the Conger Bill, but Southerners, both black and white, wanted to buy vegetable oil at the lowest possible price.[13] In 1890 the Colored Alliance supported the Southern Alliance's subtreasury plan in the hopes that it would provide low-interest loans for farmers as well as higher prices for agricultural produce.[14]

Despite their mutual support of various goals, it would be a mistake to consider the Colored Alliance an adjunct of the Southern Alliance. Sometimes they differed sharply, as they revealed in a clash over the Lodge Election Bill, which proposed federal protection to safeguard voting rights of Negroes in the South. The Southern Alliance unanimously condemned the Lodge Bill, but the Colored Alliance strongly endorsed it.[15] The two Alliances sometimes differed on economic issues: in 1891 officials of the Colored Alliance called for a cotton pickers strike; the Southern Alliance denounced that action.[16] It was, in fact, precisely on those issues where whites used their power to keep blacks in economic and political subjugation that a deep division appeared between the two alliances. Conflicts stemming from those issues contributed to the eventual demise of the Colored Alliance. They gave rise, moreover, to the troubles in Leflore County.

Leflore County, located in the Yazoo-Mississippi Delta, was in one of the last sections of Mississippi to be settled. In the 1880s thousands of Negroes and whites began migrating into the lowland region, clearing forests from vast acres and planting them with cotton. The building of railroads, the beginning of federal flood control programs, and a relative stabilization of cotton prices accounted for the Delta boom of the 1880s.[17] Some hill people wrote off the entire Delta as a swamp, but they were wrong. That sprawling lowland region was blessed with miles and miles of dark, rich soil—soil so rich that its cotton yield per acre exceeded that of all other regions in the United States. As plantations came to dominate the Delta's economy, the whites strove hard to attract Negro laborers to work their lands, and as a result the blacks greatly outnumbered the whites. In Leflore County, for example, in 1890 there were 14,276 blacks and 2,597 whites.[18] By that time, moreover, vast parts of the Delta remained unsettled. Greenwood, with a population of 1,200, was the only village with more than 100 people; the rest of the county consisted of plantations and small trading centers along the Yazoo and Tallahatchee rivers. Dense forests and canebrakes covered much of the land.

It was in the remote parts of Leflore County that Oliver Cromwell began working in the summer of 1889 to organize chapters of the Colored Farmers' Alliance. Cromwell, a black, traveled from plantation to plantation, urging Negroes to join the Colored Alliance. He apparently convinced many to stop trading with local merchants and to do business with a Farmers' Alliance co-operative store in Durant, a town some thirty miles south of Leflore County located along the lines of the Illinois Central Railroad. Although the store was owned by the Southern Alliance, it accepted the business of Colored Alliance members. Cromwell must have made periodic trips to Durant to purchase supplies for his followers. His work alarmed Leflore County merchants, for it caused them to lose business and threatened their control over blacks, many of whom depended upon merchants for advances in credit and supplies. Cromwell not only worked to make Negroes economically self-sufficient, but he also gave a strong example of his personal independence by occasionally delivering bold speeches to rally support for his cause. Those speeches apparently worried the whites as much as did his economic policies. This man truly used the Colored Alliance as a vehicle by which the Delta blacks might lift themselves out of their peasant status.[19]

Around the middle of August 1889 whites began working to undermine Cromwell's activities. At first they circulated reports that Cromwell was an ex-convict who could not be trusted. He had "fleeced" the Colored Alliance, they taunted, by using the membership dues for his own enjoyment. In response to those rumors, many of the Colored Alliancemen met at the village of Shell Mound, where a majority voted to support Cromwell, thereby keeping him at the head of the local chapter. Shortly after that someone sent Cromwell a letter, decorated with skull and cross bones, warning him to leave Leflore County within ten days or face the consequences. Being a man who did not easily cower, Cromwell revealed the warning at another meeting of the Colored Alliance. Again the members supported him. They addressed a note to the whites of Shell Mound, signed "Three Thousand Armed Men," promising to support Cromwell and to defend him should the whites attempt to drive him from the county.[20] After the meeting about seventy-five blacks marched in "regular military style" into Shell Mound and delivered the reply of the Colored Alliance. Convinced that serious trouble would soon follow, many white men in that locale sent their wives and children to Greenwood and other neighboring villages.[21]

In the days immediately following the demonstration by the Colored Alliancemen at Shell Mound, word went out to whites in nearby counties that the blacks were massing for trouble and had collected a huge stockpile of arms. By Saturday, August 31, many armed whites from surrounding areas arrived at Greenwood, where they learned that the blacks had gathered at Minter City, a hamlet twenty-fives miles up the Tallahatchee River. Fearing that a race war might actually erupt, Sheriff Baskett, at ten o'clock that evening, wired Governor Lowry to send troops.[22]

The Governor quickly responded and ordered three companies of the National Guard—the Capital Light Guards of Jackson, the Durant Grays, and Winona Rifles—to proceed immediately to Greenwood. Lowry and several state officials accompanied them. By the following afternoon, September 1, the troops arrived at Greenwood, where the Governor spoke to those who had come from other counties, imploring them to let the guardsmen handle the problem. Many complied and soon left Greenwood for their homes. At eleven o'clock that night the troops boarded the steamer *John Allen* and proceeded up the Tallahatchee to Minter City. Arriving there at eight the next morning, they reported to Sheriff Baskett. Since the previous day the sheriff had been directing a posse of some two hundred men in an unsuccessful search for Cromwell and his followers. When the troops arrived, Baskett ordered them to assist in the search, and during the next six hours the guardsmen arrested about forty blacks and turned them over to the posse. After that the sheriff dismissed the troops and they left Leflore County.[23]

For several days after the troops left, the posse continued to press its search. By September 5 reports circulated that all trouble had subsided. Shortly after that officials in a nearby county captured George Allen, a Negro man who, next to Cromwell, had been a leading force in the local Colored Alliance. What happened to Allen is unknown.[24] Cromwell escaped. He left Leflore County before the serious trouble erupted, for on September 1 a number of people saw him in Jackson; from there, it was believed, he managed to flee the state.[25]

What actually happened in Leflore County between September 1 and 5? Did the whites restore order with as little trouble as Sheriff Baskett's report to the Governor indicated, or were the black newspapers correct in asserting that there had been a massacre? There is strong evidence that the posse killed many. When a correspondent interviewed members of the Capital Light Guard upon their return to Jackson, he found most of them extremely tight-mouthed about what they had seen and done. Some denied that anyone had been killed, but one told of seeing "six dead negroes." Other Guardsmen put the number higher.[26] J. C. Engle, an agent for a New York textile company, was "in and about Greenwood" during the trouble. When he arrived at New Orleans several days later, he told reporters that the Negroes "were shot down like dogs." Members of the posse not only killed people in the swamps, he said, but they even invaded homes and murdered "men, women and children." Engle recalled one act in which a sixteen-year-old white boy "beat out the brains of a little colored girl, while a bigger brother with a gun kept the little one's parents off."[27] Several sources reported that the posse singled out four well-known leaders of the Colored Alliance, Adolph Horton, Scott Morris, Jack Dial, and J. M. Dial, whom they shot and killed.[28] A. C. Chichon, a black resident of Indianapolis, received a letter from a friend in Mississippi telling that after the troops left Minter City the posse hung some of the prisoners.[29] The Detroit *Plaindealer* reported that a "brave colored man" risked his life to investigate the extent of the massacre. He too claimed the whites killed many blacks, but he was sure the whole truth would never be obtained because the Negroes in Leflore County were so terrified "that they dare not speak of the matter, even to each other."[30] The Leavenworth *Advocate* and the *New York Age* claimed that not less than one hundred had been murdered.[31] Although it is impossible to determine exactly how many perished, it seems—based on a survey of all sources consulted—that the whites killed about twenty-five blacks.[32]

It is likely that the posse would have killed more had not some planters restrained the bloody work by protecting Negroes who fled to them. At that time, it must be remembered, the Delta suffered from a shortage of black laborers. While most planters probably did not bemoan the killing and driving away of Colored Alliance leaders, they opposed annihilating people who within a few weeks could pick their cotton.[33]

There is another notable aspect concerning the killings in Leflore County. Despite reports that the Colored Alliancemen had collected a large supply of munitions, it is highly doubtful that many of the blacks were armed. The commander of the National Guardsmen reported that he had not seen a single body of armed blacks during his trip to the Delta.[34] Moreover, some blacks desperately tried to obtain ammunition while fleeing from the posse. On one occasion the whites captured two black men whom they discovered leading mules loaded with rifle cartridges, buckshot, and gunpowder. The men had obtained the supplies in a neighboring county and were attempting to get them to the Colored Alliancemen. On the night of September 3 George Allen led a band of blacks to "Mr. Jamison's" store at Shad's Grove, where they demanded ammunition; Jamison refused and in an ensuing fight they set fire to his store.[35] The most telling evidence of a scarcity of arms among the blacks is the fact that there was not a single report of a white being wounded or killed. Had the blacks been heavily armed, it seems likely that they would have killed some whites in the course of the fight. Apparently the blacks killed one man during the entire melee: George Allen shot a Negro who refused to follow him.[36]

This episode in Leflore County is significant on several counts. For one thing, it presents a startling view of the role of violence in the American South during the late nineteenth century. Although whites killed a sizable number of blacks, the public was almost totally ignorant of what happened; especially did the Mississippi press give little inkling of what transpired in Leflore County. It seems likely that Governor Lowry and other state officials knew something of what happened. Certainly county authorities knew, for Sheriff Baskett directed the posse in its work. Yet neither state nor county officials took any action in response to the mass killings. Such a situation leads one to wonder how many other instances of violence of greater and lesser magnitude occurred in that era and of which nothing is known. Some might argue that the Leflore County massacre represented an unusual event, for it occurred in an isolated frontier section of the South, a section that in some ways resembled the African nations of that era where white minorities used whatever means necessary, including violence, to control black majorities. From what is known of the high number of lynchings and race riots in other parts of the post-Reconstruction South, however, violence was a force that permeated the entire region. The killings in Leflore County illustrate a condition then widespread in the South.[37]

The episode also contributes to our understanding of why the Colored Alliance was such a short-lived movement. Soon after the posse completed its work, many white planters held a meeting in which they adopted resolutions declaring that the Colored Alliance "is being diverted from its . . . supposed purpose and is being used by designing and corrupt Negroes to further their intentions and selfish motives." They then ordered that the Durant Commercial Company, the Alliance store with which many blacks had been doing business, "to desist from selling goods or loaning money to the Colored Alliance or to any of its members." The planters also sent word to the editor of the *Colored Farmers' Alliance Advocate* published at Vaiden, a town in nearby Carroll County, "that the issuances of copies of his paper to subscribers at Shell Mound, McNutt, Sunnyside, Minter City, Graball and Sharkey post offices shall be stopped." Should the editor ignore the warning, he would face the wrath of a "united and outraged community."[38] With so many of the Colored Alliance leaders killed and driven away and with so many of the remaining blacks terrorized, the Colored Alliance movement in Leflore County collapsed.

So long as the Colored Alliance supported the programs of the Southern Alliance, many whites tolerated its existence. But when it tried to solve problems that contributed directly to the plight of Southern blacks, it conflicted with the economic and racial policies of the white South. This was never more clearly illustrated than in Leflore County in 1889 when the blacks pursued policies aimed at bettering their economic conditions and lessening their dependence upon whites. When that happened, the whites suppressed the Alliance, in that instance by mass violence.

Notes

1 *Atlanta Constitution,* September 2, 1889; *New York Times,* September 2, 1889; *New York Tribune,* September 2, 1889.

2 Jackson *Clarion-Ledger,* September 5, 1889.

3 Natchez *Daily Democrat,* September 4, 1889.

4 Raymond *Gazette,* September 7, 1889.

5 *Journal of the House of Representatives of the State of Mississippi at a Regular Session Thereof, Convened in the City of Jackson, January 7, 1890* (Jackson, 1890), p. 597. Hereafter cited as *House Journal.*

6 *Ibid,* pp. 594-96.

7 Washington *Bee,* September 21, 1889; Cleveland *Gazette,* September 21, November 9, 1889; Detroit *Plaindealer,* September 18, 1891; New York *Age,* September 7, 14, December 28, 1889; Leavenworth *Advocate,* September 14, 1889.

8 For able accounts of the plight of Southern farmers during the late nineteenth century see: Theodore Saloutos, *Farmer Movements in the South, 1865-1933* (Berkeley, 1960), pp. 1-101; C. Vann Woodward, *Origins of the New South, 1877-1913* (Baton Rouge, 1951), pp. 175-204.

9 R. M. Humphrey, "History of the Colored Farmers' National Alliance and Co-Operative Union" in N. A. Dunning, *The Farmers' Alliance History and Agricultural Digest* (Washington, 1891), pp. 288-92; Washington National Alliance, May 31, June 7, September 6, November 1, 1890; Raleigh *Progressive Farmer,* December 23, 1890; Houston *Daily Post,* January 3, 4 1889; Richmond *Planet,* August 15, 1891; Kansas City *American Citizen,* July 26, 1889; Jack Abramowitz, "The Negro in the Agrarian Revolt," *Agricultural History,* XXIV (April, 1950), pp. 89-95.

10 August Meier, *Negro Thought in America, 1880-1915: Racial Ideologies in the Age of Booker T. Washington* (Ann Arbor, 1963), pp. 100-18.

11 Saloutos, *op. cit.,* pp. 69-70; John D. Hicks, *The Populist Revolt; A History of the Farmers' Alliance and the People's Party* (Minneapolis, 1931), p. 115.

12 Washington *National Economist,* October 11, 1890; Detroit *Plaindealer,* August 22, 1890; Cleveland *Gazette,* August 30, 1890; Huntsville *Weekley Gazette,* December 9, 1890.

13 Herman Clarence Nixon,"The Cleavage Within the Farmers' Alliance Movement," *Mississippi Valley Historical Review,* XV (June, 1928), pp. 22-23; Raleigh *Progressive Farmer,* January 6, 1892.

14 Washington *National Economist,* June 7, 21, August 23, September 6, December 23, 1890. The subtreasury plan provided that in agricultural regions the federal government would establish warehouses where farmers could deposit their produce when market prices were low and obtain low-interest loans on the commodities they stored. Later, when market prices rose, they could sell their produce—hopefully at a profit. John D. Hicks, "The Subtreasury: A Forgotten Plan for the Relief of Agriculture," *Mississippi Valley Historical Review,* XV (December, 1928), pp. 355-73.

15 Washington, *National Economist,* December 13, 1890; Raleigh *Progressive Farmer,* August 5, 1890, January 27, 1891; St. Paul *Appeal,* December 20, 1890; Leavenworth *Advocate,* December 13, 1890.

16 Abramowitz, *op. cit.,* pp. 92-93.

17 Robert L. Brandfon, *Cotton Kingdom of the New South: A History of the Yazoo Mississippi Delta from Reconstruction to the Twentieth Century* (Cambridge, Mass., 1967), pp. 73-74.

18 *Compendium of the Eleventh Census: 1890,* I, 241.

[19] Jackson *Clarion-Ledger*, September 5, 1889; St. Louis *Post Dispatch*, September 7, 1889; Jackson New Mississippian, September 4, 1889.

[20] Winona *Times*, September 6, 1889; *Atlanta Constitution*, September 2, 1889; New York *Tribune*, September 3, 1889.

[21] St. Louis *Post Dispatch*, September 7, 1889.

[22] *Ibid.*, September 7, 1889; Jackson *New Mississippian*, September 4, 1889.

[23] *House Journal*, pp. 596-97; Natchez *Daily Democrat*, September 4, 1889.

[24] *New York Times*, September 9, 1889.

[25] Raymond *Gazette*, September 14, 1889; *Atlanta Constitution*, September 3, 1889.

[26] *New York Times*, September 4, 1889; *New York Tribune*, September 4, 1889; *Atlanta Constitution*, September 4, 1889.

[27] Cleveland *Gazette*, September 21, 1889.

[28] St Louis *Post Dispatch*, September 4, 1889; *Atlanta Constitution*, September 5, 1889.

[29] Indianapolis *World* quoted in Cleveland *Gazette*, November 9, 1889.

[30] Detroit *Plaindealer*, September 18, 1891.

[31] Leavenworth *Advocate*, September 28, 1889; New York *Age*, December 23, 1889.

[32] Washington *Bee*, September 21, 1889.

[33] St. Louis *Post Dispatch*, September 7, 1889.

[34] *House Journal*, p. 597.

[35] St. Louis *Post Dispatch*, September 5, 1889; *Atlanta Constitution*, September 5, 1889.

[36] St. Louis *Post Dispatch*, September 4, 1889.

[37] Sheldon Hackney, "Southern Violence," *American Historical Review*, LXXIV (February, 1969), pp. 906-25; H. C. Brearley, "The Pattern of Violence," in *Culture in the South*, ed. W. T. Couch (Chapel Hill, 1934), pp. 678-92.

[38] Washington *Bee*, September 21, 1889.

Part Four

FREEDOM DELAYED: SEPARATION AND INEQUALITY IN THE JIM CROW ERA

Criticism by Negroes [Walter White of the NAACP and others]continued to mount against discrimination in the armed forces. . . . A revolution in the racial policies of the services was being called for, but the chiefs of the services soon made it known that they were not revolutionaries.

Dalfiume,
Military Segregation and the 1940 Presidential Election

The Black Movement Against Jim Crow Education in Buffalo, New York, 1800-1900

ARTHUR O. WHITE

The passage of the Civil Rights Act in 1866 gave Buffalo's African American community cause for celebration. Henry Moxley and other prominent black leaders welcomed the Act's provisions guaranteeing citizenship and equal benefits to all as powerful ammunition against the long-standing, racially segregated education system. Similar to the struggle waged by Northern blacks in Boston, Philadelphia, and elsewhere, blacks in Buffalo equated the education issue with antislavery during the antebellum era and with civil rights and first-class citizenship in the postbellum era. Over a century before the United States Supreme Court ruled segregated schools unconstitutional in 1954, the African American community in Buffalo fashioned a variety of organizational and legal strategies in defense of a quality education for their children.

Arthur White provides a revealing glimpse of nineteenth-century American life and culture in this essay that traces a century-long struggle to secure a first-class education for black children. The evidence suggests that racism permeated most aspects of America's Northern communities and Buffalo was no exception. Buffalo's black residents, including skilled tradesmen, professionals, and well-to-do landowners, felt the sting of prejudice; their children, for example, were denied admission to the city's district schools. By examining the legislative and judicial records, White documents the blacks' refusal to accept an inferior education.

IN THE NINETEENTH CENTURY Northern states did not serve as havens of freedom and equality for blacks. Freedmen were forced to use separate churches and schools, and jim crow rode the railroads throughout the "Free States." Almost all Northern states had laws restricting the immigration of Negroes, their right to sit on juries and to give evidence. The expansion of the electorate accomplished during the Jacksonian period resulted in the curbing or denial of the voting rights of Negroes. By 1840, 93 percent of the Northern Negro population lived in states which excluded them from voting.[1] Alexis de Tocqueville, after an extensive tour of the Northern states in 1831, concluded: "Thus the Negro is free but he can share neither the rights nor the pleasures, nor the labor, nor the affections, nor the tombs of him whose equal he has been declared to be; and he cannot meet him upon fair terms in life or in death."[2]

In their struggle for equality blacks gave first place to education. "If we expect to see the influence of prejudice decrease and ourselves respected," a Negro National Convention resolved in 1832, "it must be by blessings of an enlightened education."[3] Peyton Harris, a Negro from Buffalo, saw education as an opportunity to demonstrate equality:

> . . . The education of colored youth . . . has been shamefully contracted. We are bound to put forth for enlarged advantages. When capacity, unbound capacity is exhibited then and then alone, will the contempt and outrages arising from actual or imagined inferiority depart.[4]

In education, blacks faced the same barriers of segregation and discrimination that prevented progress in other phases of society. The method of exclusion from the public schools varied only slightly between states. In New England, local school committees usually assigned Negro children to separate institutions, regardless of the district in which they resided. Pennsylvania and Ohio, although extending public school privileges to children of both races, required separate facilities for black students whenever twenty or more could be accommodated.[5]

In New York State similar conditions prevailed. The state legislature empowered all incorporated cities and villages to establish separate school facilities for Negroes.[6] Most communities sheltering Negro populations chose to segregate: New York city in 1787, Rochester in 1834, Lockport in 1840, and Buffalo in 1842. In Rochester and Lockport the initiative to segregate came from the blacks. In 1834, thirty-two Rochester Negroes, anxious to protect their children from abuse in the common schools, petitioned for an "African School." A committee appointed by the school board to investigate the treatment of blacks in Rochester schools reported:

> . . . Under the present organization our schools are open to all children, and yet it is obvious that in this state the literary and moral interests of the colored scholar can hardly prosper. He is reproached with his color, he is taunted with his origin; and if permitted to mingle with others in the joyous pastimes of youth, it is a favor, not a right. Thus the law which may declare him free is a dead letter. His energies are confined, his mind is in chains, and he is a slave.[7]

In Lockport a similar problem and poor economic conditions kept blacks out of public schools. In 1835 Negroes pleaded publicly for an African school:

> . . . Whereas the colored people of the Village of Lockport, are rapidly increasing in numbers, and consequently aiding in the formation of character, we are desirous that what influence we exert, may tend to some good purpose. Whereas the customs of the county do not permit us—neither indeed do we desire to join in society with those of a different complexion. Therefore, resolved that we hereby constitute ourselves into a society for the promotion of our children's education and our instruction in divine truth. Resolved that we will, if possible raise by subscription $150, to erect a building suitable for a school house and place of public worship. Resolved that we will appeal to the liberality of the citizens of Lockport, for their aid . . . and rely upon the Great Disposer of all human events for its final execution.[8]

In Buffalo, however, the impetus for an African school came from the free school movement. In 1838, a committee of representatives from the city's five wards found that a "trifling tuition charge" prevented "poorer-class children" from attending school and demanded a free system.[9] Most black children, being of the lowest income group, were barred effectively from district schools. With the possibility of free public schools, Nathan Kelsey Hall, law partner to Millard Fillmore and, later United States Postmaster-General, circulated a petition among blacks and whites asking the Common Council "for a free school for blacks."[10] The petition granted, Negro J. C. Wilson opened Buffalo's African school on July 1, 1839.[11]

Both whites and blacks soon discovered the hardships of a segregated school system. The high cost of separate school rendered the education of black children inferior to that of white children. In 1845, when the cost of black education had risen to $10.00 per child while the city average stood at $5.25 per child, Buffalo's school superintendent complained the African school "costs more in proportion than any other in the city, notwithstanding a smaller amount is paid for the salary of the teacher."[12] Thirteen years later the city reduced its average to $5.00 per child while the average for Negroes increased to $10.25.[13] By the time of the school's demise the city was spending $1,000 per year to educate thirty blacks.[14]

Teachers employed by Buffalo's African school received unequal pay and faced high and unstable enrollments. These teachers received from two to three hundred dollars less annually than district school teachers.[15] After 1846 a white male replaced the Negro male teacher and earned a more equitable, but still inferior, salary.[16] Some white teachers, retained under the unequal salary, did not satisfy Negro parents who demanded their removal.[17] In 1867, looking for a cheap but acceptable principal, the city hired a white female who received $600 per annum, less than half the $1,300 paid male principals.[18] The enrollment at the black school averaged one hundred students, of which twenty stayed the academic year. The city average per teacher was fifty students, of which forty usually attended the entire academic year; however, in some years, no black students remained the entire year.[19]

The curriculum and plans of organization offered to blacks stressed only the basic subjects. The curriculum consisted of the beginning aspects of reading, writing, arithmetic, spelling, and grammar. History, geography, and higher branches of the basic subjects taught in district schools were omitted.[20] City ordinances organizing primary schools into two lower departments and one higher department, and later into eight grades, were not applied to the African school.[21] This school began as two departments, later was reduced to one department, and finally to four grades in 1870.[22] Adding to this burden, Negroes were barred from Buffalo's only high school. "It was intended," wrote an alderman in 1847, "to place the school upon the same footing with other schools of the city as to the grade of instruction and to all other privileges and advantages enjoyed by those schools."[23] The high cost of separate but "equal" education made this impracticable.

The physical accommodations of the African school reflected also the hardships of segregation. An 1839 act authorized the city to raise funds by taxes "to purchase a lot and erect . . . a suitable school house for colored children."[24] The school, however, had three locations between 1839 and 1848: a room in a tenement, a Negro church hall, and a basement under a central city market.[25] Late in 1848 the African school was given a discarded district schoolhouse, described by parents of white pupils who had once attended it as "unfit for the public schools."[26] The superintendent in 1844 described the building as "out of repair and built so slightly that it is impossible to write in the upper room on account of the spring of the floor."[27] Frederick Douglass best described an African school as "a low, damp, dark cellar better fit for an ice house."[28] Buffalo's superintendent, however, described the building as "the good effect of the enlightened and liberal policy of the Common Council."[29]

In large cities such as Buffalo, transportation presented the gravest hardship to black students. In 1843, eighty-five black students came from eleven of Buffalo's fifteen school districts, which divided all five city wards.[30] The Negroes in attendance at the African school constituted less than half the two hundred school-age blacks living in the city.[31] In 1865, when thirteen wards divided Buffalo, 90 percent of the 713 Buffalo Negroes lived outside the ward containing the African school.[32]

Superintendents considered poor attendance and transportation the greatest handicaps to the education of Negroes. Buffalo's Superintendent, E. F. Cook, in 1856, connected poor attendance with the transportation problem:

> The irregular attendance of a large portion of the children is a greater evil in this school than in any other in the city. Many families reside at a great distance from the school house which renders the regular attendance of small children difficult.[33]

Superintendent V. M. Rice expressed sorrow for the plight of black students:

> . . . It excites one's pity, to see them in cold stormy weather often thinly clad, wending their way over a wearisome distance. Anyone possessing humane impulses, can but regret that, with all the other burdens which power and prejudice heap upon this people, their children, when so young, are doomed to suffer so much in striving to gain a little light to make their gloomy pathway through life less tedious.[34]

He saw the transportation problem also as a threat to the lives of black children. "There are some who live at a comparatively great distance that at a risk of health if not at the price of life attend this school."[35]

The condition of segregated education for Negroes supported its harshest critics. Peyton Harris, in 1847 as a vice president of a Troy, New York, national Negro convention, denounced the condition of education for Negroes:

> . . . The education of colored youth, up to this time, has been shamefully limited. In very deed it has not reached the dignity and elevation of education. It has been rudimental noting and superficial glancings. To comprehensiveness it has never yet made any pretension; to profundity not the most distant approach.[36]

From Buffalo's neighboring city Rochester, Frederick Douglass spoke of the devastating psychological effects of segregation on black children: "They find themselves excluded from white schools, and they early learn that their complexion is the cause of their exclusion. The consequence is, they are induced to undervalue themselves, and to look upon white children as their oppressors."[37]

He also noted the advantages to the general community of offering blacks integrated education. "To elevate and improve the colored people, is but contributing to the general good of the whole community; and it is evident that colored children will be in a much better position for improvement by sharing the advantages of whites in the common schools."[38]

The clearest indication of the disadvantages of segregated schools for Buffalo black students is illustrated by comparing the illiteracy rates of blacks of school age during segregation with the illiteracy rates of those of school age during integration. Statistics based on the manuscript census of the United States Bureau of Vital Statistics for 1870 and 1880, comparing the educational achievements of blacks and whites in Ward IV, indicate the effects of segregation. Ward IV, in 1870 and 1880, had the largest Negro population (220 in 1870 and 233 in 1880) and contained the African school. It also had a model population composed mainly of laborers and clerks, together with a few skilled workers. When illiteracy is defined as the inability to read or write, 17 percent of the adult blacks exposed during childhood to local school segregation suffered from illiteracy, while only 1.1 percent of the whites in the same period were illiterate. In Ward IV, 85 percent of the white children attended school, compared to 66.7 percent of the black children. Since the Negro population was 17 percent illiterate, it was a case of one illiterate generation raising another. Using similar statistics from the 1880 manuscript census, the sharp increase in the literacy of blacks after only eight years of integration is learned. The illiteracy rate among Negroes aged 15-26 (those of school age after 1872) fell to 6.4 percent, proportionately about three times lower than in 1870 and, in 1880, the percentage of black children attending school increased to 92 percent.[39] These statistics indicate the improved educational opportunities provided Negroes by school integration.

Supported by articulate black leadership and white abolitionists, Buffalo blacks continually protested their inferior education. The highest intensity of protest by Negroes came in the 1840s when Frederick Douglass made his central goal "to battle against all complexional distinctions among men." Buffalo Negro Abner H. Francis, leading member of the integrated Buffalo Anti-Slavery Society, chaired a black convention which recommended "Negroes everywhere use every just effort in getting their children into schools in common with others in the several communities."[41] He used his influence on the local level to encourage protest by blacks. Black public meetings on the subject of education became common occurrences in Buffalo. Black integrationists made their children sit in local schools in defiance of segregation orders, but the school officials humiliated them by refusing them seats and instruction. Sometimes school officials used physical force to drive blacks from the district schools. Negroes withstood these tactics in order to force the hand of city officials,[42] who continually voted for segregation. Most blacks accepted these verdicts and took their children out of the district schools.

Some blacks, however, advocated resistance to segregation orders. Several Buffalo blacks attended a public meeting in 1846 demanding the Common Council to place "resolutions of censure upon some person who had taken part in establishing a school for colored children and excluding them from the district schools." A petition signed by whites and blacks demanded the Common Council to "allow the colored children to attend the district schools and grant them the same privileges that white children enjoy." The Council refused action on the grounds that the state legislature was about to adjourn.[43] The following year, George Weir, 25-year-old African Methodist Episcopal Church trustee, Buffalo merchant and a correspondent with Frederick Douglass, renewed the assault by Negroes on segregated schools. Weir exhorted blacks to action by calling segregation "a violent and unprincipled practice." He informed Negroes that "so long as we as colored people continue to disgrace ourselves by submitting to such vile abuse, just so long will the heel of prejudice bear hard upon our necks."[44] After black children were again ejected from district schools, Weir complained to the Common Council of "the inconvenience and injury Negroes suffered in being restricted to one school."[45] He encouraged blacks "to use all the same means to maintain our rights that our revolutionary forefathers taught us on certain occasions."[46] The Council refused action on the grounds that "in the year 1838 a petition from a respectable portion of the colored inhabitants were [sic] presented to the common council for the establishment of such a school." The Council even insisted "the school has never been in a more flourishing condition" and "few in the city in proportion to the number taught confer greater benefits upon the community."[47]

Already in the 1840s Buffalo had militant white spokesmen who supported black demands for integration. Through a whig newspaper they accused the superintendent of "tyrannically persecuting Negroes by making the complexion of children a test of their right to education." They quoted the city charter as stating that all district schools organized within the city of Buffalo should be public and free to all children under the age of sixteen years residing within said district and accused the superintendent of "acting independent of all law by arbitrarily withholding from them [Negroes] a privilege which is theirs by law and every principle of moral right." They further stated: "It is not necessary, in order to their admittance into district schools, that they shall have long or short noses, that their hair be straight or crisp—or that their skin shall be black, white, copper color or green, only that they be children."[48]

Despite the protesting and the evidence against segregation, city and state officials stubbornly defended segregated education as most appropriate for blacks. In 1841, State Superintendent John Spencer stressed the school board's right to keep black children out of district schools:

> . . . All [children] of a proper age are entitled to admission, as a general rule. There must, however, be some discretion by the Trustees. Persons having infected diseases, idiots—infants incapable of receiving any benefit from the school—and persons over 21 who may be deemed too old—may be excluded. The object of the schools—the most extended instructions—must be considered paramount. The admissions of colored children is in many places so odious that whites will not attend. In such cases the Trustees would be justified in excluding them, and furnishing them a separate room.[49]

In 1846, Alderman O. G. Steele demanded that blacks be ejected from public schools:

> . . . The propriety of separate schools is very apparent. The intermingling of white and black children in our public schools must be productive of great evils. They [the blacks] must be looked upon with aversion and treated with more or less opprobrium and their progress in their studies must be retarded rather than advanced in the public schools.[50]

In 1848, Buffalo School Superintendent Samuel Caldwell physically ejected black children from the public schools, citing racial reasons:

> . . . They require greater patience on the part of the teacher, longer training and severer discipline than are called into existence in the district schools: and generations must elapse before they will possess the vigor of intellect, the power of memory and judgment, that are so early developed in the Anglo-Saxon race. Hence, the importance of a distinct and separate organization of the African school.[51]

His conclusions were supported by a white laborer speaking before the Lockport Board of Education: "There are three niggers in our public schools and I propose therefore that a new school house be built for Whites." This man admitted having two months of formal education.[52] Finally, in 1871, the state superintendent formulated the separate but equal doctrine for New York State:

> . . . Separate schools for colored children . . . shall be supported in the same manner, and to the same extent as the schools . . . for white children, and shall be subject to the same rules and regulations, and be furnished with facilities for instruction equal to those furnished for white schools. Whenever the provisions above have

been complied with, the authorities may insist that colored children shall attend a separate school. . .[53]

During the 1850s a moderate black leadership took over as spokesmen for the Buffalo Negroes and worked to improve the African school. They had previously worked in conflict with black integrationists. City officials used the division to "cite the difference of opinion among the colored people" as the reason for not acting for integration.[54] However, in the 1850s, protest for integration almost ceased and moderate blacks were successful in obtaining a few of their objectives: an evening school and an inferior but large schoolhouse. They also successfully protested the employment of white teachers previously forced out of district schools.[55]

In April, 1866, Congress passed the Civil Rights Act, which stimulated Buffalo blacks to renew their assault on the city's segregated schools. The Act guaranteed to Negroes United States citizenship and "equal benefit of all laws and proceedings for the security of person and property, as enjoyed by white citizens." Violators were guilty of a misdemeanor punishable by a year in jail and/or a fine of one thousand dollars.[56] Buffalo blacks, with legal advisement, assumed this meant that they were "entitled to all the rights, privileges and immunities of all other citizens of the state or the United States." Negroes contended that the city violated this law by withholding from them the privilege to send their children to district schools.[57] This law also persuaded some city officials to support the position of Negroes. In 1867, Alderman August Hager, a Fifth Ward Democrat, admonished the Common Council for continuing segregation: "The Civil Rights Bill," he said, "gave the colored children equal rights with white children, and I want to know if the Common Council of Buffalo or the City Charter is superior to the laws of Congress."[58] But the city refused action, leaving it to the blacks to force a test of the segregated system under the Civil Rights Act.

Henry Moxley soon used this Act to lead the blacks in their most vigorous and sustained effort to force the city to integrate its schools. Born in Virginia in 1808, the son of African slaves, Moxley came to Buffalo in 1832, the year of its incorporation.[59] Upon arrival, he was twenty-four years old and classified as a fugitive slave.[60] A barber by trade, he liked Buffalo and in 1839 found a suitable location for a shop.[61] His shop, which he moved frequently, brought him prosperity and, by 1870, he held almost three thousand dollars in real and personal property.[62] Around 1849 he joined the African Methodist Episcopal Church where he came into contact with the George Weirs, both militant integrationists. In 1850, he served with the younger Weir as a church trustee.[63] Moxley married late in life and, although fifty-eight years old when the Civil Rights Act passed, had four young children, ranging in age from less than one year to six years. Moxley and his wife were literate and through contact with the A.M.E. Church they continued their interest in education.[64] After the passing of the Civil Rights Act, Moxley waited over a year for the city to integrate the schools. Then in June, 1867, Moxley petitioned on his own "to have his children admitted to the school in District 32" where they resided.[65]

On June 24, the Common Council received Moxley's petition and began consideration. Upon its reading, Alderman Hager, of Moxley's ward, proposed an expanded resolution "that the superintendent is hereby directed to admit the children of Henry Moxley, a colored citizen and taxpayer . . . to Public School No. 32, and . . . to admit all colored children to the respective public schools in the boundaries of which school districts their parents reside."[66] Immediately, Democratic Alderman John Auchincole moved to refer the petition and resolution to the Committee on Schools. This move would temporarily prevent the legal admission of black children to the public schools.[67] The resolution to refer passed, 12 to 10, giving the school committee power to make recommendations on admittance of Negroes.[68]

Though closely divided politically, the Council did not vote along party lines. Five Democrats, one "Independent" Democrat, eight Radical Republicans, and eight Union Republicans voted.[69] The Union Republicans locally stood against the radical plan of reconstruction, favoring a more "generous peace."[70] The local Radical Republicans supported the national party. These labels did not determine the vote of the aldermen. The total favoring referral included four Union Republicans, six Radical Republicans, one Democrat, and one Independent Democrat. Those against referral included four Democrats, four Union and two Radical Republicans. The Radicals generally favored referral, the Union Republicans divided evenly, and the Democrats generally favored admission. One Democrat, Alderman C. J. Buchheit, voted to admit the Negro children to the schools because "he was afraid of punishment if admission was refused," and "because the officers of our land say they are our equals."[71] Buchheit's Seventh Ward contained most of the sentiment in the city in favor of increased civil rights for Negroes. In 1886, this ward alone voted for a proposed state amendment to abolish from the New York State Constitution the franchise requirement of $250 for black voters.[72] Joel L. Haberstro, also a Seventh Ward Democrat and a member of the school committee, voted with Buchheit against referral. The other two members of the School Committee, S. S. Guthrie,

Ninth Ward Radical, and Joel Wheeler, Second Ward Radical, voted for referral.

Awaiting final action on his petition, Moxley conferred with other black leaders to increase the scope of his integration drive. In 1861, Moxley became a trustee of the Negro East Presbyterian Church. Here he associated with John Simpson, William Cooper, and Abraham Young, all of whom agreed to work with him.[73] Young, a "whitewasher," had lived in Buffalo since its incorporation and had amassed considerable property, valued at $1,700 in 1870. Married to a German immigrant, he had no children.[74] After securing this support, Moxley next contacted John Dallas and B. C. Taylor, two important black leaders. Both individuals had children of school age. Dallas had two daughters aged thirteen and twelve, and the oldest, Althia, became very important in Moxley's plans.[75] Taylor had five children, three of school age, but he refused to send them to the black school. Taylor, like Abraham Young, had a German-born wife and, next to Moxley, was the most affluent of the group, with property valued at $2,700 in 1870.[76] Taylor, a twenty-year resident, listed his occupation as a "Quack Doctor."[77] Dallas made his living as sexton at the white Universalist Church and by cleaning offices.[78] He arrived from Maryland in 1854 and had considerable property, valued at $2,400 in 1870.[79] Dallas brought two other prominent Negroes to the movement, Lewis Smith and Peyton Harris.[80] A trustee of the Michigan Street Baptist Church, Buffalo's largest Negro church, Harris had long been a well-known integrationist.[81] When vice-president of the 1847 Troy Negro convention, Harris designated its primary objectives as "emerging as soon as possible from all exclusive colored institutions and becoming part of the community." Later, at the same convention, he joined Frederick Douglass in stressing that "the fear of colored children sinking under the weight of prejudice in a white institution is not a conclusive argument against them exercising the right of admission."[82] Harris contributed to the movement by presiding at public meetings called to gain additional support from Negroes. Smith, similar to most of the others, had gained his influence through Negro church leadership, as a trustee for the Vine Street Methodist Episcopal Church.[83] A Buffalonian for fourteen years, Smith, an illiterate, had four children attending the African school and held property valued at $2,000.[84] He donated his church for public meetings.[85] In agreement with Moxley, these prominent blacks and others decided to send their children to the public schools beginning with the September term.

On September 1, 1867, the blacks launched their plan.[86] That day many withdrew their children from the African school and sent them to district schools. Shocked by the presence of black children in their classes, most teachers attempted to remove them. Immediately Negroes threatened suit under the "Civil Rights Bill if anyone interfered with them in this privilege." The school superintendent was soon informed of the threat by the teachers. He later reported that the teachers "preferring to let the city take the responsibility of admitting or rejecting those pupils . . . received them under protest."[87] On September 16, Alderman S. S. Guthrie, School Committee Chairman, announced that "some of our colored citizens" had engaged counsel to prosecute teachers under the Civil Rights Bill. Guthrie "acknowledged" that black "applications for the privilege" of attending the district schools were "common."[88] Eighteen black children had entered the schools and awaited the Council's final ruling.[89] Among them were the children of John Dallas and Henry Moxley. The Dallas girls entered School 11 in the heart of the Fourth Ward.[90] Moxley sent his eldest daughter, aged six, to School 32 in the Fifth Ward. Here she was received amicably by its principal, N. C. Benedict, who appeared to sympathize with the blacks.[91]

After a three-month delay and as a result of the persistence of the blacks, on September 16 the school committee answered Moxley's petition and recommended denial of admission of Negroes. In contrast to pre-Civil War rulings, the report cited only legal reasons. The committeemen, it stated, "are of the opinion that this council has no power to grant the prayer of the petition" becaue the city charter "effectively prohibited the admission of colored children to the public schools" by directing that "the public schools shall be free to all white children . . . and that the Common Council shall provide and maintain one or more free schools for the colored children." The report conceded "that the letter and spirit of the City Charter requires that all children of the city shall have equal opportunities for acquiring an education at the Public Schools" but informed the petitioner, "it is not . . . in the power of your committee to discuss the propriety or expediency of making a change expressly prohibited by the charter and ordinances." The report directed the superintendent to enforce the law by ordering that "the Superintendent of Schools . . . prohibit the admission of any colored child into any of the public schools except the free school provided for said children," and advise the Council if "further action is required for it to offer ample accommodations." The entire school committee, including Joel L. Haberstro, supported the report.[92]

Lively debate among the aldermen followed. John Walls, a Radical, spoke of "such prejudice against colored children on one side of the house at least while the other simply dodged the issue," and complained the "council members were not doing their duty as men in strangling the matter." He challenged the committee "to tell how the colored children are to be educated," arguing it was "hardly fair" to compel blacks to attend one school when they were "scattered all over the city." If they could obtain an education under such circumstances, "it would be a proof of superiority over the Caucasian race." Guthrie replied with a legal argument: "I am not opposed to the colored children attending all public schools for I have been brought up and educated in a school with colored children and was not injured thereby, but the law is laid down." Another alderman inquired of Walls, "Why do you send your children to the segregated Central Schools?" Hager favored integration for the civil good. Although he had "no prejudice against colored children," he opposed "full-grown uneducated niggers going to the polls with me." The majority, preferring the arguments of Guthrie, adopted the report.[93]

Superintendent John S. Fosdick, into whose hands the situation now passed, had been a dedicated teacher most of his adult life. Born in Vermont in 1813, his foremost ambition was to be a teacher. He moved to Buffalo in 1845 and began a teaching career which spanned half a century. His success resulted in his being elected to a two-year term as school superintendent in 1865.[94] Although a "conductor" on the Underground Railroad, Fosdick described the blacks trying to integrate the schools as "mischievous agitators." He also had words for their Negro supporters. "I regret that the colored people have suffered themselves to be misled by men whose object in this affair was a selfish one, because it will embitter the prejudices already existing against them, and cause many who have heretofore been their friends, to withhold their sympathy from them in their future struggle for a higher civilization."[95]

Present at the September 16 Common Council meeting, Fosdick took action immediately. He first inspected the school for blacks and, on September 23, informed the Council that "the building is in good repair, the school rooms are large, well ventilated and very pleasant, there is a good library and there is space for 200 pupils and five teachers while at present only sixty children's names are enrolled in both departments with an average attendance of about forty-five." He found "the order maintained excellent, the teaching thorough" and that "none of our Public Schools are better provided for than this." He only complained: "The progress of the pupils is not as rapid as it would be if they were more regular in attendance and there were fewer cases of tardiness." The Council referred his report to the school committee without comment.[96]

He next contended with the more difficult problem of carrying out the council directive "to prohibit the admission of any colored child into . . . the Public Schools." At the time of his report, blacks for three weeks had defeated every attempt to prevent their children from attending district schools.[97] On September 24, Fosdick began physically expelling blacks from the schools.[98] He first entered the District 11 school where he confronted the daughters of John Dallas.[99] Fosdick "requested" the girls to leave the school, informing them "that they would not be permitted to attend this school."[100] Althia, the eldest, aged thirteen, insisted on remaining and "claimed to have the same right to attend school as white children."[101] According to Fosdick, he then "took hold of her and led her out of the school."[102] A week later, while attempting similar action in School 32 where Moxley's child attended, Fosdick overcame the violent resistance of a "burly Negro and colored troops."[103] On October 8, Fosdick advised the Council of his complete success in expelling Negro children: "I found the number of colored children attending the public schools to be eighteen . . . and these pupils have been directed to attend School 9 [Negro school] and have not attended any of the other schools since they were sent away from them."[104] He later explained that the charter left him no alternative but to expel the children.[105]

Confused and frightened by the swift and severe action of the superintendent, the blacks began losing confidence. Soon after the expulsions, B. C. Taylor called a public meeting in the Vine Street Church and some black parents accused Moxley of "rascality." Taylor informed the assembled blacks that the meeting pertained only to "schools." Unable to resolve the conflict, Chairman Peyton Harris adjourned the meeting with "nothing done."[106]

Still sure of success, Moxley prepared legal action against the city. He retained Albert G. Stevens, a prominent white lawyer, who agreed to "manage the test case without fee." He advised Moxley to prosecute Fosdick "to test the laws of the city as to the admissibility of colored children into the public schools."[107] Although Stevens planned the action under the Civil Rights Act, Fosdick would be prosecuted for "assault and battery."[108] He asked Moxley "to fetch some children" who had been forcibly ejected by Fosdick. He cautioned Moxley that he would incur court costs betwen $100 and $150 "if they get beat." Moxley went to Dallas and Taylor, whose children were involved, and they agreed to let him use their children in the suit. Moxley explained that his own children were too young to "understand the nature of an oath" and could not be used. Dallas had "no objection to the use of his eldest daughter, Althia." Taylor offered "to assume the whole responsibility himself." Moxley declined, promising to "carry it to the Supreme Court of the United States."[109] Later Moxley overcame an attempt by Taylor to gain control of the movement by convincing a public meeting of Negroes that Taylor was a "tricky man to work with."[110] However, presently Stevens interviewed the Taylor and Dallas girls and pronounced Althia Dallas "fittest."[111] Althia told him of being treated brutally by Fosdick. She alleged that Fosdick, "with force and violence . . . did drag her out of her seat and violently shoved, pushed, beat, and struck her, driving her away from the school." She also claimed that he "took away her books."[112] Because of Althia's age, Stevens advised Moxley that he become her guardian. Moxley who had been collecting money from the blacks for the suit, informed Dallas, "he would stand between him and all costs, if he became guardian." Dallas agreed and signed papers making him guardian and liable by law for any judgment brought against Althia.[113] The "test suit" had begun.

Superintendent Fosdick was served with Dallas's summons and complaint on October 11, 1867. Informed city newspapers exclaimed, EJECTION OF COLORED CHILDREN FROM THE PUBLIC SCHOOLS, SUIT AGAINST SUPERINTENDENT.[114] In essence the complaint charged Fosdick with assault and battery for forcibly ejecting the Dallas child from Public School 11 in violation of the Civil Rights Act. It incorporated the Dallas child's testimony and demanded damages of one thousand dollars for the alleged action.[115] Fosdick immediately reported his summons to the Common Council. Since the suit tested the "constitutionality of the Law" under which Fosdick acted, the Council directed City Attorney George S. Wardwell to defend.[116] Wardwell's answer asserted that the "Common Council is authorized to establish and maintain public schools and make such ordinance as they may deem necessary for the good government of said schools." He quoted the City Charter: "All public schools organized in the city of Buffalo shall be free to all white children," and a recently passed ordinance stating, "schools established by the Common Council shall admit all children . . . except colored children." Wardwell defended Fosdick's actions, calling him "the executive-officer of the Common Council" obligated "to carry into effect the charter and orders of the Common Council in respect to Common Schools." Wardwell also asserted Fosdick's right to forcibly eject Althia on the grounds that the charter and the Council failed to specify means of enforcing Council directives. He then concluded that Althia Dallas had violated the charter by attending School 11, causing the superintendent to eject her "in discharge of his duties."[117] Stevens received Wardwell's answer and prepared for trial.

On January 10, 1868, the case of Althia Dallas against John S. Fosdick came for trial before State Supreme Court Justice Charles Daniels. The lawyer's briefs merely restated the complaint and answer. Althia Dallas and Fosdick were not present. Daniels reserved judgment until January 18.[118] Moxley and Dallas expressed confidence that they would win the suit. Moxley told Dallas, "he felt well about it and was sure to win." Dallas replied that if they won, he would "commence another suit in favor of another child."[119] But Daniels, a Republican member of the State Supreme Court since 1863 and later the first Dean of the University of Buffalo Law School, pronounced in favor of defendant Fosdick with costs adjusted at $198.48.[120] Stevens immediately filed an appeal and awaited further direction from Moxley.[121]

After the decision, a nervous John Dallas spoke to Moxley about discontinuing the suit. In their conference Dallas asked him if he was "going on" and added, he "didn't think it was safe." Moxley merely "laughed," calling Dallas "chickenhearted." Moxley made it clear that they would "carry it through from court to court," if necessary, and advised Stevens to proceed with the action.[122]

Stevens broadened the argument in his appeal. He called the state's authorization of the African school "an unauthorized exercise of legislative authority" because the school did not share in either the "Common School Fund" monies or the $25,000 of the "United States Deposit Fund," both guaranteed by statute for the support of the state's common schools. Schools thus partially supported should be open to children of every race because the 1846 School Law "provides that the Common Schools of the state should be free to all children residing within the district, who should be between the ages of five and twenty-one years." Finally, Stevens found: "the provisions of the city charter if . . . construed as to exclude colored children . . . inconsistent with the Civil Rights Bill and therefore inoperative."[123]

Stevens and David Day, the new city attorney, presented their briefs before three State Supreme Court judges on May 4, 1868. Day offered the same arguments as Wardwell. The judges deliberated eleven days. Daniels, who presided, along with Judges Richard Marvin and George Barker, reaffirmed his earlier judgment. Dallas had twenty days to pay the judgment.[124]

The opinion of the majority of the court gave eminence to local ordinances over state and federal laws in matters pertaining to segregated education for Negroes. "But one question is presented for the consideration of this court," Daniels opinioned, "and that is whether a colored child is lawfully entitled to attend a school provided by the city authorities, for the education of white children."

Daniels insisted: "The right to be educated in the Common Schools
. . . is not one of those inherent and paramount rights which the
people by constitutional provision have placed beyond the reach and
control of legislation . . . it has at all times been subject to such restrictions and qualifications the legislature have deemed it proper to
impose." He agreed with Stevens that the 1846 school law "was sufficiently general in its language to include white and colored alike,"
but argued that Section Five of the 1853 City Charter—"all the public
schools organized in the city of Buffalo shall be free to all white children"—required city officials "to organize schools for white children
which they could only do by excluding colored children." Buffalo's
charter was "directly in conflict" with the 1846 school law and, therefore, repealed that previously existing statute for Buffalo. Finally,
Daniels rejected Steven's use of the Civil Rights Act. He admitted the
Act "intended to confer upon the colored people all the substantial
rights of the citizen," but maintained that "the right or privilege of
attending a school provided for white children was not covered by
this act." Althia Dallas did not have "the legal right of attending a
school . . . provided for the education of white children alone," because "she as well as all other colored children were constructively
excluded from attending it." Judge George Barker, a Republican
whose father had been active in the antislavery movement,
dissented.[125]

Although discouraged by this second defeat, Moxley called
blacks to another public meeting to gain support to carry on the suit.
Moxley and Dallas persuaded Stevens to attend. However, those who
attended the meeting decided to discontinue the suit.[126] Moxley's
thirteen-month effort to integrate the Buffalo schools, the last made
by blacks, had been defeated by a two-to-one vote of the State Supreme Court.

In fact, repeated protests by Buffalo blacks never succeeded in
obtaining integration. Instead, integration was the consequence of a
higher social position granted Negroes by the federal Constitution.
After the passing of the Fifteenth Amendment, Superintendent of
Buffalo schools Thomas Lothrope made a plea for integrated schools:

> . . . An increased responsibility is placed upon the community by
> the recent enfranchisement of the colored people. . . . If by being
> deprived of every advantage for the acquisition of the rudiments of
> an education, many of the colored people are incapable of an intel-
> ligent exercise of the rights of citizenship, the duty becomes impera-
> tive to afford them every facility for their education which is
> demanded by the political position they have now assumed.[127]

The Common Council responded with only a few superficial improvements in the school for Negroes. In February, 1872, Lothrope
pleaded again for integrated schools.:

> . . . The colored people, who are owners of taxable property in the
> city, have made frequent application for permission to send their
> children to the graded schools. While the charter plainly provides
> that the city shall maintain separate schools in the abstract the right
> which the colored people claim cannot justly be denied. It is a car-
> dinal principle upon which our free institutions are founded that a
> measure for the support of which the people are taxed they have
> the right to enjoy. The prejudices of many intelligent persons in re-
> gard to the coeducation of the races are so deep-seated that a fair
> and impartial consideration of this important subject is not gener-
> ally entertained. The rights of citizenship together with the privilege
> of the election franchise . . . should entitle the colored people to an
> unbiased consideration.[128]

A month after Lothrope's plea, the Common Council heatedly
debated integration without pressure from blacks. In a report, whose
signers included former city attorney and Fosdick's defender George
Wardwell, a special charter revision committee urged an amendment
to "allow colored children to attend public schools." Immediately,
Republican John Pierce argued that the blacks "had a school" and although his Republicanism might be "doubted," he wanted "the
colored . . . kept separate." Committee chairman Republican F. H.
Sears defended integration. "We could only elevate the colored race
by educating it. At present, many colored children are cut off from
public school advantages." Pierce retorted, "If one colored school is
not enough, let us have another." Democrat George Link insisted
that "if the colored people are citizens, no distinction should be
made." Still unconvinced, Pierce moved to strike the integration
amendment. Republican Joseph Churchyard exploded indignantly in
support of integration:

> . . . It is a relic of barbarism to make distinctions on account of
> color. There is no such thing as a white child. Ninety percent of the
> human kind are colored and all are created by the same almighty
> maker. Children might as well be excluded because they had curly
> hair and red faces. It is a duty we owe the human race to educate
> all alike, and if the charter excludes from the public schools . . . the
> colored children, it does a moral injustice. All such illiberal senti-
> ments as expressed by the word white in the charter are relics of a
> barbaric past. It is time that the prejudice against color is done away
> with.

Turning to Pierce, he admonished, "No man is justified in considering any other class of individuals as unworthy of the same rights that he enjoys."

After Churchyard's remarks, the Council began to move toward integration. Republican John Einsfield offered a compromise that "colored children be allowed to attend such schools as the superintendent should designate." But this compromise did not satisfy Pierce, who condemned all legislation to "compel the association of white children with black ones" because the community was not "yet prepared to receive any such ideas." Although he believed in giving blacks "all the rights and privileges that a fellow creature should enjoy," he was not "for having them in his family, or by his side, or in his society." Pierce then accused Churchyard of saying that "in our churches colored people could be seen sitting by the side of white people," and asked: "In how many churches is it customary?" Churchyard did not know, but said he "had a pew he invited colored people to occupy." Pierce promised to "extend the same privilege if he owned a pew" but to "leave it as soon as the colored man came in." Republican James Van Buren questioned Pierce, "If you were so fortunate as to get a seat in Heaven, would you leave it should a colored person come and sit by you?" Van Buren had attended school "with little black children" and felt "no harm." Democrat John Kelly supported Pierce, and an exasperated Churchyard asked Kelley how he would like it if the Bible read, "Suffer little white children to come unto me." Churchyard felt that discrimination forced "colored children to grow up ignorant little niggers and become bad men and women." "We belong to one great family," Churchyard concluded. The debate ended and the aldermen defeated the Pierce and Einsfield proposals by overwhelming votes, 17-7. An effort by Kelley to postpone action was also defeated. By a "rising" bipartisan vote, the Common Council adopted the report that gave black children the right to attend public schools. Surprisingly, Pierce voted for integration.[129]

Even after integration, schools for Negroes lingered in Buffalo; however, dwindling attendance soon terminated these schools. In 1880, when seventy-five blacks attended sixteen Buffalo public schools and only thirty-five continued at the African school, the superintendent asked for the end of the school:

> . . . For several years the attendance at that school has gradually diminished and is now so small and irregular as to warrant its discontinuance as a separate school. The schools are numerously attended by colored children against whom . . . there seems to exist no prejudice.[130]

His plea heeded, the Buffalo Common Council closed western New York's last African school.[131]

Notes

[1] Leon Litwack, *North of Slavery: The Negro in the Free States 1790-1860* (Chicago, 1961), p. 64.

[2] Alexis de Tocqueville, *Democracy in America*, ed. by Phillip Brady (2 vol.; New York 1945), 1, 373.

[3] *Minutes and Proceedings of the Second Annual Convention For Improvement of the Free People of Color in these United States* (Philadelphia, 1832), p. 132.

[4] *The North Star*, January 21, 1844.

[5] Litwack, *op. cit.*, p. 113.

[6] Fosdick v. Dallas, Appeal Decision, *Howard's Practice Reports*, V. 40 (Albany, 1871), 252, (hereafter cited as Fosdick v. Dallas. Appeal Decision).

[7] *Rochester Daily Advertiser*, March 27, 1850, pp. 2-3.

[8] *Niagara Courier*, September 9, 1835.

[9] *Buffalo Commercial Advertiser*, September 15, 1838.

[10] "Petition of N. K. Hall and Others," December 27, 1838, *Buffalo Common Council Manuscript Minutes*, located in County Clerk's Office, Buffalo City Hall, Buffalo, New York (hereafter cited as BCC MM).

[11] Oliver G. Steele, *Third Annual Report of the Superintendent of Schools*, 1839 (Buffalo, 1840), p. 3, located in the Buffalo and Erie County Historical Society's Files.

[12] Oliver G. Steele, *Ninth Annual Report of the Superintendent of Schools*, 1845 (Buffalo, 1846), p. 12.

[13] E. F. Cook, *Twenty-second Annual Report of the Superintendent of Schools, For 1858* (Buffalo, 1859), p. 13.

[14] Christopher Fox, *Annual Report of the Superintendent of Education for the City of Buffalo for 1880* (Buffalo, 1881), pp. 81-82.

[15] *Annual Report of the Superintendent of Schools for 1840-1868*, Tables *passim*, located in Buffalo and Erie County Historical Society's Files.

[16] Elias Hawley, *Eleventh Annual Report of the Superintendent of Schools for 1847* (Buffalo, 1848), Table E, p. 16.

[17] "Petition of Sundry Colored Citizens," August 17, October 19, 1852; August 21, 1859, *BCC MM*.

[18] John S. Fosdick, *Thirty-first Annual Report of the Superintendent of Schools for 1867* (Buffalo, 1868), pp. 79, 67.

[19] *Annual Report of the Superintendent of Schools for 1840-1848, 1852, 1859* (Buffalo, 1841-49, 1852, 1859).

[20] *Annual Reports of the Superintendent of Schools for 1847-1877* (Buffalo, 1848, 1873), Charts, *passim*.

[21] *Charter of City of Buffalo, 1863* (Ordinances), chap. xxii, Sec. 4 (Buffalo, 1863), p. 91; *Charter of City Buffalo, 1867* (Ordinances), chap. xxiii, Sec. 4 (Buffalo, 1867), pp. 105-06.

[22] *Annual Report of the Superintendent of Schools for 1853, 1863, and 1870* (Buffalo, 1854, 1864, 1871), Table A, p. 81.

[23] Alderman L. H. Burrows, "From the Committee on Schools," April 6, 1847, *BCC MM*.

[24] *Charter of City of Buffalo, 1839, An Act To Amend the Charter*, passed February 14, 1839 (Buffalo, 1839), Sec. 25, p. 85.

[25] *Annual Reports of the Superintendent of Schools for 1839-1848* (Buffalo, 1840-1849), Table I.

[26] Burrows, *op. cit.*, October 19, 1847, *BCC MM*.

[27] Elias Hawley, *Eighth Annual Report of the Superintendent of Schools for 1844* (Buffalo, 1845), p. 16.

[28] *North Star*, November 2, 1849.

[29] Daniel Bowen, *Thirteenth Annual Report of the Superintendent of Schools for 1844* (Buffalo, 1850), p. 14.

[30] Samuel Caldwell, *Seventh Annual Report of the Superintendent of Schools for 1843* (Buffalo, 1844), Table 7.

[31] *Sixth Census of the United States for 1840* (Washington, D.C., 1841), p. 88.

[32] *Census of the State of New York for 1865* (Albany, 1867), p. 5.

[33] E. F. Cook, *Twentieth Annual Report of the Superintendent of Schools for 1856* (Buffalo, 1857), p. 9.

[34] V. M. Rice, *Seventeenth Annual Report of the Superintendent of Schools for 1853* (Buffalo, 1854), p. 29.

[35] *Ibid.*

[36] *North Star* (Rochester), January 31, 1848.

[37] *Ibid.*, August 17, 1849.

[38] *Ibid.*

[39] *Ninth and Tenth Census of the United States for 1870 and 1880, MSS. Schedule I, New York, Erie County, Buffalo, Ward IV*, on microfilm, Lockwood Library, S.U.N.Y. at Buffalo.

[40] *North Star*, August, 1849.

[41] *Minutes of the National Negro Convention at Cleveland*, Resolution 16, September 6, 1848 in *North Star*, September 10.

[42] *Commercial Advertiser*, April 27, 1842.

[43] "Petition of Sundry Colored Citizens and Others, Proceedings and Resolutions of a Public Meeting," March 31, 1846, *BCC MM*; Alderman B. Thompson, "From the Committee on Schools," April 7, 1846, *BCC MM*.

[44] *North Star*, May 12, 1849.

[45] "Petition of Sundry Persons," March 23, 1847, *BCC MM*.

[46] *North Star*, May 12, 1849.

[47] Burrows, *op. cit.*, April 6, 1847, *BCC MM*.

[48] *Democrat Economist*, April 27, 1842.

[49] *Rochester Daily Democrat*, February 20, 1841.

[50] Oliver G. Steele, "From the Committee on Schools," April 26, 1842, *BCC MM*.

[51] Samuel Caldwell, *Seventh Annual Report of the Superintendent of Schools for 1843* (Buffalo, 1844), p. 8.

[52] *Niagara County Intelligence*, December 31, 1862.

[53] *Lockport Daily Journal*, February 27, 1871.

[54] Steele, *op. cit.*, August 1, 1842, *BCC MM*.

[55] "Petition of Sundry Colored Citizens," August 17, September 14, October 19, 1852, "Petition of Sundry Colored Inhabitants," August 21, October 2, 1854, *BCC MM*.

[56] *United States Statutes at Large: 14 Public Laws*, April 9, 1866, chap. xxxi (Washington, D.C., 1866), p. 27.

[57] Fosdick v. Dallas, *Summons and Complaint of Althia Dallas by John L. Dallas, her guardian ad litem, against John B. Fosdick*, Buffalo, October 11, 1867, point 3. Original copy is in the collection of Roy Nagle (Buffalo, New York, October, 1867; hereafter cited as *Complaint of Althia Dallas.*)

[58] *Buffalo Express*, September 17, 1867.

[59] Ninth Census of the United States, MSS, Ward 5. *Buffalo City Directory for 1832* (Buffalo, 1832), p. 120.

[60] Moxley v. Dallas, October 11, 1869, U.S. Circuit Court, Buffalo, New York. (Original copy is in the collection of Roy Nagle, Buffalo, New York.)

[61] *Buffalo City Directory for 1839* (Buffalo, 1839), p. 99.

[62] Ninth Census of the United States, MSS, Ward 5, p. 35.

[63] *Buffalo City Directory for 1849-1850* (Buffalo, 1850), p. 50.

[64] Ninth Census of the United States, MSS, Ward 5, 35. Both Moxley and his wife, according to the 1870 manuscript census, had attended school within the past year.

[65] "Petition of Henry Moxley," *Common Council Proceedings*, June 24, 1867 (Buffalo, 1868), 365. Located in the Buffalo and Erie County Historical Society Files.

[66] "Resolution of Alderman August Hager," in *Common Council Proceedings*, pp. 365-66.

[67] "Motion of Alderman John Auchincole," in *Common Council Proceedings*, p. 366.

[68] "Motion Carried," in *Common Council Proceedings*, p. 366, and *Commercial Advertiser*, June 25, 1867.

[69] *Commercial Advertiser*, November 8, 1865, June 25, 1867.

[70] *Commercial Advertiser*, November 18, 1866.

[71] *Express*, September 17, 1867.

[72] *Express*, November 16, 1866.

[73] *Buffalo City Directory for 1861* (Buffalo, 1861), p. 26.

[74] Ninth Census of the United States, MSS, Ward 5, p. 85.

[75] *Ibid.*, Ward 4, p. 184.

[76] *Ibid.*, Ward 5, p. 163. According to the manuscript census, none of Taylor's children had attended school within the past year.

[77] "Testimony of B. C. Taylor," Moxley v. Dallas, point 8.

[78] *Buffalo City Directory for 1867* (Buffalo, 1867), p. 217.

[79] Ninth Census of the United States, 1870, MSS, Ward 4, p. 184.

[80] "Testimony of Peyton Harris," Moxley v. Dallas, point 12.

[81] *Buffalo City Directory for 1856* (Buffalo, 1856), p. 25. According to the *American Baptist Register*, this church had 93 members in 1852, p. 227.

[82] *North Star*, December 8, 1847.

[83] *Buffalo City Directory for 1862* (Buffalo, 1863), p. 47.

[84] Ninth Census of the United States, MSS, Sixth Ward, p. 34.

[85] "Testimony of Lewis Smith," Moxley v. Dallas, point 18.

[86] *Complaint of Althia Dallas*, October, 1867, point 6.

[87] John S. Fosdick, *Thirty-first Annual Report of the Superintendent of Schools for 1867* (Buffalo, 1868), pp. 12-13.

[88] *Express*, September 17, 1867.

[89] John S. Fosdick, "From the Superintendent of Schools," October 7, 1867, *Common Council Proceedings* (Buffalo, 1868), p. 587.

[90] *Complaint of Althia Dallas, op. cit.*, points 2, 3, and 6.

[91] *Buffalo City Directory for 1867* (Buffalo, 1868), pp. 50, 183; Moxley v. Dallas, point 14; according to Moxley, the entrance of his daughter to School 32 and subsequent three-week attendance went unopposed.

[92] Alderman S. S. Guthrie, "From the Committee on Schools," September 16, 1867, *Common Council Proceedings* (Buffalo, 1868), pp. 537-38.

[93] *Express*, September 17, 1867.

[94] Raymond B. Fosdick, *Chronicle of a Generation* (New York, 1958), p. 2.

[95] *Buffalo Evening News*, November 21, 1905; Fosdick, *Annual Report, 1867, op. cit.*, p. 131.

[96] John S. Fosdick, "From the Superintendent of Schools," *Common Council Proceedings*, September 23, 1867 (Buffalo, 1868), p. 552.

[97] Fosdick, *Annual Report, 1867, op. cit.*, p. 13; Fosdick claimed in his report that prior to ejecting the Negro children from the public school he had "exhausted every other expedient to induce them to attend" the Negro school.

[98] *Complaint of Althia Dallas, op. cit.*, point 6.

[99] Fosdick v. Dallas, *Answer of John S. Fosdick to the Summons and Complaint of Althia Dallas by John L. Dallas, Her Guardian, ad litem*, October, 1867; MS. copy in author's private collection (hereafter cited as *Answer of John S. Fosdick*, October, 1867).

[100] *Ibid.* and Fosdick v. Dallas, "Appeal Decision," p. 251.

[101] *Answer of John S. Fosdick*, October, 1867.

[102] *Ibid.* and Fosdick v. Dallas, "Appeal Decision," 251.

[103] *Express*, October 1, 1867. According to the newspaper. Fosdick was opposed by a burly Negro and colored troops. During the melee that resulted, someone called the police. Alderman Bamler was informed of the incident. He informed the Council of this on September 31. When he was unable to get a confirmation from Alderman Guthrie, the school committee chairman, Bamler, demanded that the sergeant at arms bring in Fosdick. The president of the Council then "decided the question out of order."

[104] John S. Fosdick, "From the Superintendent of Schools," *Common Council Proceedings*, October 7, 1867 (Buffalo, 1868), p. 587.

[105] Fosdick, *Annual Report, 1867, op. cit.*, p. 13.

[106] "Testimony of Peyton Harris," Moxley v. Dallas, point 12.

[107] "Testimony of John Dallas," Moxley v. Dallas, point 3.

[108] Fosdick, *Annual Report, 1867, op. cit.*, p. 12. The term *assault and battery* is used by Fosdick in his report to describe the suit against him.

[109] Moxley v. Dallas, points 2, 9, and 3.

[110] "Testimony of B. C. Taylor," Moxley v. Dallas, point 9. Taylor called a public meeting of the Negroes to decide whether he or Moxley should continue the integration movement, Taylor told the meeting he "would carry on the suit and pay all expenses." Moxley intervened that "he would do all that." Taylor retorted, "I would, I called the first meeting." Chairman Peyton Harris then put the question before the house for discussion and appointed Moxley chairman of a committee of three to raise money. Moxley told the group "if Taylor withdrew he would accept" because "Taylor was a tricky man to work with." Taylor then withdrew, refusing to contribute anything toward the movement.

[111] "Testimony of Albert G. Stevens," Moxley v. Dallas, point 17.

[112] *Complaint of Althia Dallas, op. cit.*, points 6 and 7.

[113] "Testimony of John Dallas," Moxley v. Dallas, points 3, 6 and 7.

[114] Fosdick, "From the Superintendent of Schools," October 21, 1867, *Common Council Proceedings* (Buffalo, 1868), p. 612; though it was received by the Common Council on October 21, his report is dated October 11, 1867; *Commercial Advertiser*, October 22, 1867.

[115] *Complaint of Althia Dallas, op. cit.*

[116] Fosdick, *Annual Report, 1867, op. cit.*, p. 12.

[117] *Answer of John S. Fosdick*, October, 1867.

[118] Fosdick v. Dallas, January 10-18, 1868, Special Term of the State Supreme Court. Eighth Judicial District, Buffalo, New York, MS copy in the author's private collection (hereafter cited as Fosdick v. Dallas).

[119] "Testimony of John Dallas and Henry Moxley," Moxley v. Dallas, points 3 and 15.

[120] Edward Williams, Harry S. Douglass, John T. Horton, *History of North Western New York, I* (New York, 1947), 283; Fosdick v. Dallas, January 10-18, 1868.

[121] Fosdick v. Dallas, *Appeal of Althia Dallas by John L. Dallas, Her Guardian, ad litem*, January 18, 1868.

[122] "Testimony of John Dallas," Moxley v. Dallas, point 7.

[123] Fosdick v. Dallas, "Appeal," The General Term of the State Supreme Court, May 4-15, 1868, MS in Roy Nagle's private collection, Buffalo, New York (hereafter cited as Fosdick v. Dallas, "Appeal"), each point of Steven's argument, especially that concerning the Civil Rights Act, is cited in Fosdick v. Dallas, "Appeal Decision," pp. 252, 253, 256.

[124] Fosdick v. Dallas, "Appeal."

[125] Fosdick v. Dallas, "Appeal Decision," pp. 249-57; Daniels obviously misinterpreted the implications of Section 5 of Buffalo's 1853 Charter ("all public schools organized in the city of Buffalo shall be free to all white children"). Its wording was designed to leave with the Common Council or the superintendent of schools, as the Council should designate, the power to decide on the admission of Negroes. It did not specify the exclusion of Negro children from public schools nor did it require that the schools be organized for white children alone but only that "the schools organized in the city of Buffalo shall be free to all white children." Therefore, by charter provison the Common Council was forbidden to charge white children tuition to attend school. The Common Council or the superintendent of schools still had the power to admit Negro children to the public schools either with or without tuition charge, as Superintendent E. F. Cook did without tuition to public schools of "outside districts" in 1855 and 1857 without legal question. Daniels also in his decision admitted that the revenue of the common school fund and United States Deposit fund had been applied by statute to the support of the common schools but affirmed the "right of a person to attend a public school is nowhere made to depend on the circumstances of its support" nor can objection exist to "creating a public school [Negro school] required to be supported by taxation alone."

[126] "Testimony of John Dallas," Moxley v. Dallas, point 4. Dallas later sued Moxley to recover the judgment against him.

[127] Thomas Lothrope, *Thirty-third Annual Report of the Superintendent of Schools for 1870* (Buffalo, 1871), p. 91.

[128] Thomas Lothrope, *Thirty-third Annual Report of the Superintendent of Schools for 1871* (Buffalo, 1872), p. 131.

[129] *Buffalo Courier* and *Buffalo Express*, March 26, 1872.

[130] Christopher Fox, *Forty-third Annual Report of the Superintendent for 1880* (Buffalo, 1881).

[131] James F. Crooker, *Department of Education Annual Report, 1881* (Buffalo, 1882).

Black Dreams and "Free" Homes:
The Oklahoma Territory, 1891-1894

DANIEL F. LITTLEFIELD, JR. AND LONNIE E. UNDERHILL

Organized as a territory in 1890 and admitted to state-hood in 1907, Oklahoma provided thousands of African Americans with the hope of a promised land. Visionary black entrepreneurs used the settlement of former Native American land to promote racial advancement as well as individual gain. Edward Preston McCabe and James L. Stevens carved out modest fortunes in land speculation while at the same time assisting other African Americans in securing farms or lots in newly formed black towns such as Langston City and Liberty. While McCabe's dream of making Oklahoma a black state with himself as governor quickly faded, the magnitude and sophistication of the migration demonstrate African American determination to create lives of dignity and first-class citizenship.

> *Daniel Littlefield and Lonnie Underhill's essay details a prime example of the black self-help doctrine at the end of the nineteenth century. For many African Americans, migration to Oklahoma proved a viable alternative to the racism and bigotry they faced in the Southern states. Through periodicals and government documents, including county deed books, the authors chronicle the history of blacks who played key roles in settling Western portions of the United States.*

AFTER 1866, THERE WERE CONCERTED EFFORTS on the part of blacks to make the Oklahoma Lands a haven for blacks of the United States and the Indian Territory. However, those efforts met with little success. Nevertheless, blacks of the United States (and especially those of Kansas), refused to give up the idea, and after Oklahoma was opened to settlement on April 22, 1889, there was repeated on a smaller scale an exodus much like that to Kansas a decade before. This time, the efforts of black leaders were directed toward making the new territory a black state.

The dream was especially espoused by Kansas blacks. When it became apparent that Oklahoma would open to settlement, Kansas newspapers such as *The American Citizen* (Topeka) urged every black who wanted 160 acres to prepare and watch diligently for the opening.[1] In July of that year W. L. Eagleson was described as the "prime mover" in a scheme to encourage Southern blacks to emigrate to Oklahoma. He had organized an emigration company, whose purpose it was to establish agents in the major cities of the South. At his headquarters in Topeka, Eagleson estimated that by July of 1890 he would have 100,000 blacks in Oklahoma. He addressed Southern blacks as follows:

> There never was a more favorable time than now for you to secure good homes in a land where you will be free and your rights respected. Oklahoma is now open for settlement. Come in and help make it one of the best states in the union. The soil is rich, the climate favorable, water abundant and there is plenty of timber. Make a new start. Give yourselves and children new chances in a new land, where you will not be molested and where you will be able to think and vote as you please. By settling there you will help open up new avenues of industry, your boys and girls will learn trades and thus be able to do business as other people. Five hundred of the best colored citizens of Topeka have gone there within the last month. They send back word for others to come on, there is room for many more.[2]

Eagleson perfected his organization into the Oklahoma Immigration Organization on July 17 with main headquarters in Topeka and an auxiliary committee in Oklahoma.[3] There were other groups at work during 1889, promoting migration to Oklahoma. Early that year, a black lawyer named S. H. Scott from Fort Smith, Arkansas, had organized and prepared a group of blacks for the run of April 22.[4] At this time was also formed a colony under the direction of the First Colored Real Estate Homestead and Emigration Association of Kansas, led by John Young and D. B. Garrett. Successful in the run, this group established claims in Township 17.[5]

Encouraged by the efforts of such groups, blacks flocked to the new territory in large numbers so that by October the exodus to Oklahoma was compared to that of Kansas a decade earlier. By late that year blacks had established a town called Lincoln near Kingfisher.[6] As blacks rushed to the new territory, whites became fearful that Oklahoma would become a black state. The greatest impetus for the idea of a black state came from Eagleson's group, which had become the Oklahoma Immigration Association. The Association sent letters and circulars to the South and was so successful that by February of 1890 there were seven black settlements in the Territory. In a press release in January, Eagleson said of Oklahoma, "We are determined to take it and make it one of the grandest states in the union."[7]

Much of the black dream depended on the person of Edward Preston McCabe, who had served two terms as State Auditor of Kansas and in 1889 was serving as the Washington agent for the

Oklahoma Immigration Association. Petitions began arriving in Washington from blacks in Kansas and Oklahoma, asking the President to appoint McCabe as Territorial Governor.[8] Throughout March of 1890, McCabe worked unsuccessfully for the position. But by late March, excitement over the prospects of a black state was dying.[9] McCabe gave up the idea of the Governorship and became a candidate for Secretary of the Territory.[10] However, he was disappointed on that count, too. He moved to Oklahoma Territory in April and had been there only briefly when he was appointed the first Treasurer of Logan County.[11] He carried out his duties as Treasurer and ran a real estate office at Guthrie. Although McCabe had evidently given up the idea of a black state, he continued to urge migration of blacks to the Territory, and exerted great influence on their pattern of settlement there.

Throughout McCabe's campaign for the offices of Governor and Secretary of the Territory, the Oklahoma Immigration Association continued its work. It was generally successful and during the early months of 1890 its success added spirit and enthusiasm to McCabe's campaign. R. F. Foster, one of the Association's representatives in the South, reported in April 1890 that on July 1 some 10,000 blacks would leave Alabama for Oklahoma, and that 1,700 had already left Atlanta.[12] In August, a committee of three, representing some 300 blacks from Mississippi, were reportedly going to Oklahoma to investigate the prospects for immigration.[13] And in February of 1891 a delegation of 48 from Arkansas arrived in Guthrie, to be followed by 200 then on their way from Little Rock.[14] By the spring of 1891 blacks from the South arrived in Oklahoma on "almost every train."[15]

By this time, McCabe had emerged as the "prime mover" in the colonization movement and absorbed into his plan of establishing all-black communities many of those men such as W. L. Eagleson, who had managed the Oklahoma Immigration Association. Early in 1891, McCabe affiliated himself with the townsite of Langston City, which he claimed to have founded on October 22, 1890.[16] The town was actually surveyed and platted by a white man, Charles H. Robbins, in August of 1891.[17] Mozell Hill, however, without documentation, claims that McCabe planned the town as a "new Eldorado," and that he bought 160 acres from Robbins in 1890 which he sold in lots. He then supposedly bought another 160 acres and sent agents of the McCabe Town Company, with headquarters in Guthrie, into the Southern states to sell contracts for lots.[18] However, some evidence indicates that McCabe did not own any of the land but was a land speculator, who simply sold lots on the townsite while living in Guthrie.[19] In a like manner, McCabe was labeled a speculator by Paul Jones, a lawyer and one-time secretary of an organization for the relief of the Kansas blacks. Jones, who went with McCabe to Topeka in 1879, claimed that McCabe made large sums of money in land speculation in both Kansas and Oklahoma.[20] However, the *New York Times* says that "it did not take him long to organize a company and secure 320 acres of land on the east line of Oklahoma, where Langston City was laid out."[21] If McCabe did operate through a company, it is unlikely that the titles bore his name, and it would therefore appear that he did not own any land. It may be that McCabe operated through or for Robbins, who had bought the 320 acres he owned on October 11, 1890, and February 6, 1891,[22] about the time when McCabe became associated with Langston. According to Arthur Tolson, McCabe and James B. Robinson simply sold the land and promoted the town.

Regardless of his motives, McCabe did much to promote black immigration to Oklahoma. He advocated a plan of dispossessing whites of political power by organizing colonies of blacks so that a majority of black voters could be situated in each representative and senatorial district.[23] He planned to effect this result by the development of all-black towns such as Langston, to which immigrants could come to wait for lands to be put up for sale or for more Indian lands to be opened.

Through McCabe's efforts, a settlement at Langston was well-established before Robbins platted the town. In April of 1891, it was reported that McCabe had worked for months "through colonization societies . . . to secure population for this new black mecca." He had secured many families and sold lots so that Langston then had a black population of 200, including a doctor, a preacher, and a school teacher; it also had thirty houses and a cooperative garden plot of eighty-three acres.[24]

The *Langston City Herald*, a weekly, began publication on May 2, with W. L. Eagleson as editor. Some sources credit McCabe with establishing the *Herald*,[25] and he did edit it at one time.[26] However, it seems to have been the enterprise of Eagleson who had previously edited and co-edited the Fort Scott, Kansas, *American Citizen* and the *Topeka Kansas Herald*, respectively.[27] He was by trade a newspaper man, whereas McCabe was not, and he seems to have transferred the name of *Herald* to his new area of operation. Nevertheless, it was to become an instrument through which McCabe did his promotional work.

That a settlement called Langston City had been in existence from about the time McCabe claimed to have founded it is evident from the promotional activities of James L. Stevens of Guthrie, who on March 11, 1891, bought what was later known as "College Heights Addition, Langston City."[28] Stevens filed a plat for the addition on April 6.[29] That month, Stevens sent out a flier, addressed to "Everyone who wants a home, where you can be free, equal and independent and enjoy all the rights of American citizens."[30] He described Langston City as a new but prospering community "settled by a good and industrious class of people." He told how hundreds of blacks had come to the new land and found comfortable homes and farms "now worth several thousand dollars, and this at only a few dollars cost to themselves." Many, he said, had taken town lots so that "nearly all our people who had been here any time have their own homes." Stevens's flier further testifies to the earlier existence of Langston City by saying that on December 7, 1890, John M. Langston, for whom the town was named, had written that he expected to raise $25,000 in Washington with which to build a college for blacks at Langston.[31]

Stevens stressed that Oklahoma was the blacks' last chance for land. Then Stevens made his pitch: "To get a farm it is highly necessary for you to buy some of our lots in College Heights Addition, Langston City, as it is the prettiest and best part of the city, and build you a shanty, so you will have a place to stay at until the land opens. Your lots then, no doubt, will be worth twice what you gave for them, and they will be the cause of your getting a good farm."[32] To reassure prospective immigrants, Stevens then described Oklahoma as a land of abundant water, grass, rich farm lands, fish and game, and climate suitable for raising crops so various that it was "almost impossible to have a complete failure in all of them." Stevens's final pitch was as follows: "It is supposed that the colored people who buy in Langston will get the Indian land near to it, which will be a little fortune to any man, because each farm will be worth from $1,600 to $2,000."[33] And in describing the procedure for getting title to the land, Stevens made it appear that getting a home was a foregone conclusion if the people would just come West.

The flier was obviously promotional material for the lots that Stevens was selling, but it was more than that. In a somewhat disorganized fashion, it presented the black man's dream for Oklahoma. He tells how, for years, it was the dream of black leaders to obtain the Oklahoma Territory "for the exclusive use and benefit of the colored people of the South, who were looking with longing eyes to some place where they could enjoy all the God-given rights intended for man by the creator." Having failed that, they hit upon another plan: to organize blacks so that they could obtain great portions of the surplus Indian lands that would be opened to settlement. Langston was founded for the purpose of establishing a rallying point from which blacks would have a chance to get the choice lands. Of current interest to Stevens was the Iowa, Sac and Fox, and Potawatomi lands which were expected to be opened soon; he felt that at least 4,000 people would be needed in Langston in order "to take the country." The idea was to congregate at Langston and enter the land in a body, letting some stay at home and make crops while others filed on the land. Those who remained behind would have the advantage of living in a city that promised to be "one of the great cities of Oklahoma. A negro city for the exclusive use and benefit of our own race."[34] This was appealing, as was his argument against blacks remaining in the South:

> What will you be if you stay in the South? Slaves liable to be killed at any time, and never treated right: but if you come to Oklahoma you have equal chances with the white man, free and independent. Why do southern whites always run down Oklahoma and try to keep the negroes from coming here? Because they want to keep them there and live off their labor. White people are coming here every day.[35]

It does not appear that Stevens was a leader among the Langston group, since he lived in Guthrie, but merely used their arguments to foster immigration, generally, and sell his lots, specifically. In fact, he is so close to them in philosophy that subsequent research may reveal a closer relationship to them than is now apparent,[36] for as Stevens's fliers indicated, the Langston group did indeed have plans for the Sac and Fox, Iowa, and Shawnee-Potawatomi lands which were opened by a run on September 22, 1891. Months earlier, it was rumored among blacks that these lands had either opened or were about to open.[37] The white community became concerned as there continued an influx of blacks intent on being present at the opening.[38] As time for the opening of the new lands approached, whites looked with alarm on a reputedly "secret" organization at Langston that had sent out thousands of letters urging blacks to come to Oklahoma for the opening. If anything about the Langston group were ever "secret," it was certainly not so after August 25, when the group resolved

> . . . that we notify our people, the colored citizens of the south, to be here on the 10th of September, and that those who intend to drive through the Indian country to start at once; and that the 850 Langston Agents throughout the southern states notify the people of the importance of being here by the 10th of September, to join us in securing homes in the new lands.[39]

The *Langston City Herald* also appealed to blacks to come to the opening; a year later, it was to take credit for the success of blacks in the Sac and Fox opening.[40]

Hundreds of blacks had already arrived at Langston and were being cared for until time for the "invasion," as the papers called it. Immigrants arrived daily; thousands more were expected. They were reportedly armed, ready to secure homes "at any price," and were expected "to exclude all but members of their race from securing claims, at least until each negro has found a home."[41] The prime leader in this endeavor was McCabe, who was trying to congregate at least 15,000 of his people at Langston by the day of the opening.[42]

Tension mounted in nearby Guthrie as the day for the run drew near. The arrival of so many blacks was interpreted by Guthrie residents as an intended mass movement into the best of the lands to be opened—the Cimarron Valley, and there were plans on the part of "white settlers" and "cowboys" to preempt claims made by blacks. The Sac and Fox Indians also supposedly resented the presence of blacks in the run. It was claimed that they had sold their lands to the United States with the understanding the lands would be opened to white settlement. They supposedly intimated that they would make it "uncomfortable" for blacks who settled among them.[43]

The question of whether blacks were excluded from the land opening was the cause of excitement in Washington as well. The President's proclamation, setting the date of the opening, had declared that after allotments had been made to the Indians, the remaining lands would be "subject to white settlement." To some white politicians, the wording was such as to exclude blacks. Indignant black leaders in Washington telegraphed Guthrie, instructing blacks there "to join in the rush and secure homesteads, lawfully or otherwise." The matter was clarified, however, when the Secretary of the Interior instructed the Registers and Receivers at the Land Office in Guthrie that

> . . . the words "white settlement," occurring in the Sac and Fox agreement and stated as such in the proclamation of the President on the 18th do not mean and are not construed to mean, to prohibit settlement in that country by other than white men . . . You will receive filings from all duly qualified persons, without distinction of color or other condition than those applicable to other lands, save as to the prices specified. The President concurs in this construction of the law and in these instructions.[44]

Two days before the opening, there were rumors of corruption, as in the opening of the Oklahoma Lands, with "Sooners" already on the lands, preempting the choice claims. The blacks were reported determined to make successful claims to the northern part of the lands.[45] At daybreak on September 21, five hundred blacks from Texas arrived by train at Guthrie and headed for the border of the new lands some nine miles away; half of them went on foot and half by whatever conveyance they could obtain. All were without provisions.[46] During the day, couriers from Langston came into Guthrie, purchased twenty carbines, and returned to "the front." They reported that at Langston the entire townsite was covered with the tents of immigrants and that they were "determined to protect themselves from any attempt on the part of the whites to keep them from the land in the Cimarron Valley."[47]

By this time there were some 2,000 men at Langston; half of them were armed. Determined to succeed, they planned to settle four of their numbers on each quarter section to ensure protection of their claims. On the night of September 21, thirty armed members of the group, headed by "William Eggleston [*sic*] and the postmaster" descended on a camp of whites nearby. The surprised cowboys offered no resistance as the blacks issued a proclamation that the land across the line belonged to them and that they would hold it at all costs. After giving the proclamation they returned to Langston.[48]

On the day of the run, the blacks gathered at the line, many destitute and without food, but all determined to make their bids for new homes. Many of them met with violence. On the northern line, some were intimidated by whites, and they fled to areas where more blacks had gathered. Four miles south of Langston, two blacks became angry when some cowboys indicated their intentions to settle upon a quarter section desired by the blacks. An argument ensued and, as a result, the blacks were badly wounded and did not make the run. McCabe, himself, who went out to see how his people were doing, returned to Guthrie with a report that he had been the object of violence. He had been on the lands a short time when three white men ordered him away. He refused to go, saying that he was an American citizen. One of the men pulled his gun and fired at McCabe, who was unarmed and dodged behind a wagon. The others pulled their six-shooters and fired five or six shots at him; they were almost upon him before he was rescued by a group of blacks who, armed with Winchesters, came to his assistance. In speaking of the white men, McCabe said, "I did not know them, but I believe they belonged to the crowd that threatened to kill all negroes found on the land."[49] In spite of such violence, it was estimated that nearly a thousand black families obtained homes in these reservations.[50]

The next land opening occurred a few months later, when, on April 19, 1892, the Cheyenne-Arapaho lands were opened by a run. Long before that date, however, blacks had their eyes on the Cheyenne country. In 1889, the Oklahoma Immigration Society had looked forward to the opening of these lands and the Cherokee Strip.[51] In the early months of 1890, large numbers of blacks passed through Guthrie on their way to these lands which they thought would open soon.[52] The success of the Langston group had inspired other attempts to do the same kind of work. One such group was the Ethiopian Brotherhood, which incorporated in November of 1891 with a capital stock of $20,000. Its aim was to colonize from 5,000 to 10,000 blacks in the Cheyenne country and the Cherokee Strip.[53]

Thousands of blacks were on hand for the opening of the Cheyenne-Arapaho lands. On the day before the run, large groups of them massed on the sand bars of the Cimarron and along the ninety-eighth meridian south of the river. They carried their children and belongings on their backs. One white promoter had come from Topeka with 200 black homeseekers. Coming to Hennessey by train, they had walked the sixteen miles west to the Cimarron. The promoter boasted that he had collected five dollars apiece from them, promising in return to secure a claim for each.[54] Most of the blacks were afoot, but they did not lose out in the run. They found their way to homesteads which the whites did not consider choice ones in the blackjacks and sandy hills along the North Canadian river, many securing claims along the headwaters of Salt Creek.[55]

Shortly after the Cheyenne-Arapaho opening the *New York Post* predicted that the land would soon be filled with blacks because it was too hilly and unproductive to tempt the more ambitious whites, whereas, it was maintained, blacks were willing to put up with all kinds of hardships if they could secure forty acres and independence. Their homesteading was a cooperative effort: "Those arriving first make a homestead filing, and the land is then divided among others coming later. It is thought that within three years these lands disdainfully left by the whites will be producing good crops of cotton and corn. . . ."[56]

At this time, the Cherokee Strip was still the property of the Cherokee Nation and was not finally made the property of the United States until 1893. It was opened, as were the Tonkawa and Pawnee lands, by a run on September 16. As early as 1890, black politicians such as John L. Waller and some newspapers were urging President Harrison to set aside the Cherokee Strip as a territory within which blacks could establish a state of their own.[57] Blacks had attempted to squat on the Strip in the spring of 1891.[58] Also, McCabe had laid plans to establish two all-black towns near the border of the Outlet to serve in that run as Langston had served in the Sac and Fox opening.[59] Months before the Strip was purchased from the

Cherokees, the *Langston City Herald* had appealed to Southern blacks to "flee the wrath to come" as a result of Democratic victories in the recent national elections: "Oklahoma still invites you. The STRIP will open soon. Come! be here, and take you a claim."[60] The *Herald* warned its subscribers that the Strip would "be about the last chance to secure free homes on government domain."[61]

As the date of the opening approached, the *Herald* continued to send out its appeals: "The strip will hardly be opened before September giving our people good ample time to make it here, and prepare for the all go home race."[62] And, "Everyone that can should go to the strip or the Kickapoo and get a hundred and sixty, all you need as previously announced is a Winchester, a frying pan, and $15.00 to file."[63] The same issue of the *Herald* reported that during the previous week 500 blacks had come into the territory and encamped on the borders of the Kickapoo lands. The *Herald* was misguided in urging blacks to come at this time for the opening of the Kickapoo lands, for that opening did not occur until May of 1895.

There had been earlier predictions that blacks would not come to the opening of the Strip in such numbers as they had come to the Sac and Fox opening. This prediction probably resulted from the fact that these lands were situated a good distance from most of the black population centers. Still, it was thought that two or three "strong" black colonies would be founded in the new land, under the direction of those in the Oklahoma Territory.[64]

Despite predictions, large numbers of blacks ran into the Strip, many securing good claims. And less than two weeks after the run, McCabe had established a new town called Liberty, three miles north of Perry. McCabe had his agents at work in the Southern states, especially in Texas and Mississippi, hoping soon to make Liberty a thriving black community. Meanwhile, the Santa Fe was building a depot there, and McCabe was building a number of "cottages" for occupation by the new arrivals; the houses were to be sold on the installment plan. Territory newspapers had little doubt that McCabe's new town would succeed because, one said, "McCabe rarely takes hold of a matter of this kind without taking good care that the outcome will be satisfactory."[65]

A month later, McCabe was still at his scheme to develop Liberty and, through his agents, was endeavoring as well "to give an impetus to the growth of the old negro town of Langston." Said one paper, "McCabe says Liberty is the coming town on the Strip and he proposes to make a barrel of money out of his scheme."[66] In November, Liberty received a boost when the blacks who were ordered out of the Osage Nation, where they were despised by the Indians, made their way to Perry and McCabe's new town.[67]

After the openings of the Sac and Fox, Iowa, Shawnee-Potawatomi, and Cheyenne-Arapaho lands and, finally, the Cherokee Strip, blacks looked forward to the opening of the Kiowa, Comanche, and Apache lands[68] as well as the Kickapoo lands and even those of the Five Civilized Tribes. One black spokesman said that after all of those openings, "the whole Indian territory will have been swallowed by the white man. Many . . . black men help in the swallowing."[69]

By far, the greatest encouragement to and impetus for black immigration to Oklahoma came from Langston City. Although McCabe's image dominated the scene there were many people involved in its growth and, therefore, its strength. Its growth was generally sponsored by the *Langston City Herald*. For years after its founding, each issue contained a plat of the city that covered three-quarters of a page. At first, the plat carried beside it an advertisement for city lots sold by McCabe. He pointed out that Langston City was a "Negro city," located in a "genial climate" where the land was capable of producing diversified crops. He stressed the value of investing in real estate in a place of "absolute safety, good society, church privileges, and last but not least, absolute political liberty and the enjoyment of every right and privilege every other man enjoys under the constitution of the country." However, he warned blacks not to come unless they were prepared.[70] McCabe operated out of his real estate office in Guthrie, where he resided throughout his career in Oklahoma.

By mid-1893, the plat was still reprinted. However, the lots were no longer advertised by McCabe, but were advertised by the *Langston City Herald* itself, then managed by a Lee J. Meriwether. Meriwether also ran notices to his readers that McCabe, D. J. Wallace, W. L. Eagleson, R. E. Stewart, and B. H. Hooks were "in no wise connected with the *Herald*."[71] All of these men had in some way been associated with the *Herald* and with Langston's promotion. In early 1891, Wallace had been associated with the College Heights Addition to Langston City.[72] In 1892, the Herald Publishing Company had consisted of Clairville Breaux, President, B. H. Hooks, Secretary and Treasurer, D. J. Wallace, Business Manager, and R. E. Stewart, Editor.[73] At the time, Hooks was agent for the College Heights Addition and shared a real estate office with Stewart who was also a lawyer.[74] By mid-1893 Hooks was a deputy sheriff of Logan County and D. J. Wallace was practicing law.[75]

In 1894, Dr. A. J. Alston was editor of the *Herald*, notifying his readers that McCabe, Wallace, Eagleson, Hooks, and, this time, Meriwether were not connected with the *Herald*.[76] The newspaper was still acting as agent for the sale of lots in Langston City as it would do until the plat appeared in its pages for the last time on July 20, 1895.

However, before the *Herald* became a real estate agent, it had operated primarily as an instrument for promotion of immigration to Oklahoma. The "best" of the young men and women were urged to come to "the front," and detailed instructions were given on how to take a homestead, how to file on a claim, how to make final proof, and how to detect fraud. However, it warned prospective homesteaders: "DON'T COME TO THIS COUNTRY UNLESS YOU ARE PREPARED TO SUPPORT YOURSELF AND FAMILY UNTIL SUCH TIME AS YOU CAN RAISE A CROP." Those who were prepared were urged to come to Langston and await the opening of new lands: "If you are doing reasonably well where you are and have employment it will be better for you to stay where you are until late in the winter, but in the meantime you should be making your arrangements, so that when the time comes you will have nothing to interfere with your plans, and remember that this may be your last chance for a free home."[77] Langston was constantly praised through the *Herald's* pages: "Negroes are happier here in Langston and Oklahoma in one hour than they have been in the South for over 250 years, or may hope to be for years to come. . . . The citizens of Langston City eat, walk, sleep, talk, ride, sing, play, work, attend churches and socials, and enjoy the comforts of home, with inestimable amenity and liberty. Yet we want more out here to help the band go sweeter."[78]

As a result of promotional activities, Langston City's growth was rapid and orderly. On September 22, 1891, the day of the Sac and Fox opening, there was held an election which incorporated the city on the Northeast Quarter of Section 24, Township 17 North, Range 1 West of the Indian Meridian.[79] One month later, Langston held its first city election. Elected were as follows: James B. Robinson, First Ward Trustee; A. R. Roberts, Second Ward Trustee; John Allen, Third Ward Trustee; John D. Williams, Marshal; Robert S. Cox, Assessor; F. C. Pollard, Treasurer; Balding H. Hooks, Clerk; and William L. Eagleson, Justice of the Peace.[80]

Langston at this time was only a small cluster of rough buildings. Less than two years later, however, Langston had less the look of a "boomer" town and more of that of a well-established thriving community, containing, among other things, a hotel, dry goods store, drug store, grocery, meat market, livery, cotton gin, and grist mill, as well as a building contractor, a barber, a doctor, and several lawyers and real estate agents.

Thus, by 1893, blacks had established themselves permanently in the Oklahoma Territory. It was true that many were ridden by pov-

erty and suffered a good deal.[81] Most were poor when they arrived. At
Guthrie in 1891, for instance, one reporter found eight families, con-
sisting of 45 persons, living in one storeroom. Many, however, were
given aid by the more fortunate until they could find land and make
a crop or find work.[82] And it is true that blacks became objects of political debate. As early as the summer of 1890, it was reported that
Governor Steele was playing politics with the blacks. In August, an
agent from the Texas cotton belt supposedly came to Guthrie to obtain labor. He offered the blacks 75 cents per hundred pounds and
transportation to Texas. Some fifty agreed to go. But Governor Steele
and his "Republican bosses" supposedly persuaded them to remain,
by "promises of government action and a few dollars," until after the
special election of two members of the Territorial Legislature.[83] Early
the next year, one reporter declared, "Opposition to the negro in
Oklahoma is purely political."[84] It is also true that some blacks were
obviously duped and cheated, such as the colony from Louisiana who
arrived at Guthrie in September, 1893, each holding a ten-dollar cer-
tificate granting him a farm upon arrival.[85] But, finally, it is true that
many who had come had done well. They had established some
thriving communities and well-cultivated farms. The Langston experiment had been the most obvious success, Lincoln was thriving, and
Liberty promised success. Such towns were drawing the better-edu-
cated and monied blacks as well as those professionally trained, who
fostered the dream of becoming a political power and extinguishing
racial prejudice.[86] Many others lived on well-developed farms.

Whites who had seen the arrival of these so-called black locusts
to Oklahoma as an ill omen began to change their minds. One reason was that it appeared that Oklahoma would develop a cotton culture, and blacks had played a role in its development. In the first
three years of Oklahoma's existence, black farmers raised nearly 1,000
bales, netting a cash crop of about $30,000. As the *Arnett Weekly Cou-
rier* put it, "Today ragged colored growers can show money."[87] But
more important, the blacks had faith in themselves as a farming class.
The black men of Kingfisher County, for instance, met in assembly
on February 10, 1894, and passed resolutions recognizing "that Afro-
Americans of the U.S. are by occupation farmers skilled and trained
at that calling," but there were good farming lands to be had in the
counties of Blaine, D, G, Washita, Day, and Roger Mills and in the Ki-
owa-Comanche and Apache reservations, and that it was the duty of
blacks to abandon the South, where they were oppressed.[88]

The Kingfisher group resolved to make their prime object that
of doing all within their power to have their friends and relatives,
"that class of energetic, enthusiastic, frugal, industrious, and hard

working farming talent, to populate and settle this vast, vacant, inval-
uable and productive soil, where they can properly educate their children among an impartial people, build churches and worship God
under their own vine and fig tree—vote their own sentiments and
fear no evil." They therefore recommended the organization of
twenty-five township leagues in the county, directed by the Executive
Board of the Territorial League of Oklahoma. Their duty was to distribute circulars encouraging immigration of the farming class from
the South.[89]

But the great rush of black immigrants into Oklahoma was
over, and any remaining hope of fulfilling McCabe's dream of a black
state was near its end. Flushed by the success of the Langston experiment and the Sac and Fox opening, McCabe had denied that his aim
was to depopulate the South, for such would be a calamity to black
people. However, he optimistically predicted a black population of
100,000 for Oklahoma within two years and, with it, control of political affairs:

> At the present time [1891] we are Republicans, but the time will
> soon come when we will be able to dictate the policy of this Terri-
> tory, or state, and when that time comes we will have a negro state
> governed by negroes. We do not wish to antagonize the whites. They
> are necessary in the development of a new country but they owe my
> race homes, and my race owes to itself a governmental control of
> those homes.[90]

He had spoken of the prospects of Langston's growth. There
was a possibility of securing $25,000 with which to establish a univer-
sity and a training school as well as plans to establish other black
towns in the territory. Finally, he said, "I am not prepared to say just
now what our intentions for the future are, further than that we will
take possession of the land and make ourselves a political power. I
am seeking no office for myself. I am merely using my utmost efforts
for the advancement of my race."[91]

By 1895 nothing was said of McCabe's plan; it had failed. Nevertheless, his promotion of the all-black town set a pattern for other
blacks in the area that was to become Oklahoma, in which more than
a score of such towns were to develop. They included, besides Lincoln, Langston, and Liberty, such towns as Boley, Taft, Rentiesville,
Tatums, Grayson, Summit, Vernon, Redbird, Clearview, and Wybark.[92]
Also, the efforts of McCabe and other promoters had helped a great
many black Americans to become landholders and thus more economically independent citizens. Moreover, McCabe's activities had an
impact on the politics of the Oklahoma Territory, since for the most

part the blacks there remained within the Republican party. As Mc-
Cabe put it, he had made the Territory "safely Republican."[93]

On the other hand, through his promotion, McCabe inadver-
tently misled many blacks. In the *Herald,* he had presented glowing
accounts of Langston's growth as an all-black town. Expecting to find
something more than really existed, many came to Langston and
turned back, disappointed. Others stayed, and like many already
there, were unable to support themselves and had to apply to the
Government for aid.[94] Blame for their suffering was laid to McCabe,
who supposedly had induced them to go there. But McCabe had insisted that he encouraged "only men of means" to Oklahoma, "men
who can care for their families and at the same time improve their
homes."[95] Assessments of McCabe and his motives vary. The latter
may never be known.

Despite the obvious failure of McCabe's plan, many blacks persisted in their optimism. They looked forward to statehood for
Oklahoma.[96] In 1894, it was predicted that Oklahoma would enter the
Union with a larger Afro-American population than any state of its
size and population outside the South. The Memphis *Scimitar* quoted
the following population figures furnished by Peter Flynn Oliver, "a
reputable lawyer at El Reno," who had come to Oklahoma from
South Carolina: 8,566 in Blaine County; 14,000 in Kingfisher County;
8,400 in Lincoln County; 10,000 in Logan County; and a scattering of
others to make up a total of 66,000. These people, Oliver claimed,
held 584,819 acres of land and other property totaling some
$6,353,327. Oliver also pointed out that there were large numbers of
blacks in the Indian Territory, and he predicted that at statehood
Oklahoma would have an Afro-American population of 100,000.[97]
There was obviously something propagandistic and exaggerated in
Oliver's figures for 1894; by 1900 there were only 18,719 blacks in
Oklahoma and 36,965 in the Indian Territory. However, by 1910,
three years after statehood, Oklahoma had 137,612 blacks.[98]

Oliver's optimism came toward the end of the blacks' dream to
make political and economic power a reality in the new land of
Oklahoma. Such power existed only in the all-black or predominantly
black communities. It came also on the eve of a decade of persecution of blacks as they were run out of town after town, and even
counties, in the Oklahoma Territory: Blackwell in 1895 and 1902,
Cloud Chief in 1896, Tecumseh in 1897, Billings in 1899, Lawton in
1902, and Greer County in 1902. Nothing in Oliver's report hinted of
the segregated education which existed in practice at the time and
was given sanction by a law passed by the Territorial Legislature in
1897. Nor did it hint of the attempts to pass separate coach legisla-

tion in 1901. Finally, Oliver's report did not envision the fact that, upon statehood, the first bill introduced in the new State Legislature would be a "jim crow" bill and that the final blow to the black dream for Oklahoma would come only sixteen years later in the "Grandfather Clause" of 1910.

Notes

[1] *The American Citizen*, March 1, 1888, in Martin E. Dann, ed., *The Black Press, 1827-1890* (New York, 1971), p. 288.

[2] "Negroes for Oklahoma," newspaper clipping, Topeka, July 7, 1889, in *Fred S. Barde Collection*, Oklahoma Historical Society Library, Oklahoma City, hereafter cited as *Barde Collection*. That portion of the collection used in this article consists of newspaper clippings, most of which are from St. Louis newspapers; some, however, are not identified.

[3] Newspaper clipping, July 18, 1889, in *Frank A. Root Collection*, Vol I, Indian Archives Division, Oklahoma Historical Society, hereafter cited as *Root Collection*. Root was a Kansas newspaper man; his collection consists mainly of clippings from Kansas newspapers. See also *New York Times*, February 28, 1890, p. 1, c. 5.

[4] See "Negro Going to Oklahoma," Fort Smith, April 12, 1889, in *Barde Collection*.

[5] *The American Citizen*, May 3, 1889, in Dann, ed., *op. cit.*, pp. 288-89.

[6] *Capital* (Topeka), October 18, 1889, in *Root Collection; Norman Transcript*, November 9, 1889, p. 1, c. 2, December 7, 1889, p. 3, c. 6, and December 28, 1889, p. 1, c. 3; "The Negro in Oklahoma," March 19, 1890, in *Root Collection*; "Suffering in Oklahoma," St. Louis, December 25, 1889, in *Barde Collection; New York Times*, April 9, 1891, p. 9, c. 1.

[7] *New York Times*, February 28, 1890, p. 1, c. 5; clipping, January 16, 1890, in *Root Collection*.

[8] *New York Times*, February 28, 1890, p. 1, c. 5; Special to *Globe-Democrat*, February 10, 1890, in *Root Collection*.

[9] "A Negro Commonwealth," Washington, February 13, 1890, in *Barde Collection*; "Oklahoma Colonization," Topeka, March 5, 1890, and clipping, Topeka, February 21, 1890, in *Root Collection; New York Times*, March 1, 1890, p. 4, c. 4; "To Secure Oklahoma," and "Oklahoma Colonization," Washington, March 2, 1890, and Topeka, March 5, 1890, respectively, in *Barde Collection*.

[10] "The Oklahoma Governorship," Washington, March 25, 1890, in *Root Collection*.

[11] Marion Tuttle Rock, *Illustrated History of Oklahoma* (Topeka, 1890), p. 272.

[12] *Indian Chieftain*, April 24, 1890, p. 1, c. 3.

[13] *Ibid.*, August 28, 1890.

[14] *Muskogee Phoenix*, February 12, 1891, p. 9, c. 1.

[15] *New York Times*, April 9, 1891, p. 9, c. 1.

[16] See, *e.g.*, his plat of Langston City in *Langston City Herald*, November 17, 1892, p. 3, c. 1; *Indian Citizen*, (Atoka, I. T.), August 30, 1894, p. 1, c. 4, and *New York Times*, April 9, 1890, p. 9, c. 1, credit McCabe with founding of "inspiring" Langston City.

[17] Arthur Lincoln Tolson, "A History of Langston, Oklahoma, 1890-1950," (unpublished Master's thesis, Oklahoma Agricultural and Mechanical College, 1952), p. 8, citing *Plat Book*, I, 7, Office of the County Clerk, Guthrie, Oklahoma.

[18] Mozell C. Hill, "The All-Negro Communities of Oklahoma: The Natural History of a Social Movement," *Journal of Negro History*, XXXI (July, 1946), 265-66.

[19] Tolson, *op. cit.*, p. 8; Tolson documents his conclusion by an analysis of the public records, particularly deeds, which do not bear McCabe's name. He also supports the conclusion through interviews with early Langston residents. However, Tolson also says

James B. Robinson was a land speculator and owned no land; yet Robinson was elected Trustee of Ward 1 in Langston on October 22, 1891. Nevertheless, Tolson is supported in his conclusions by McCabe's advertisements in the *Langston Herald.*

20 Roy Garvin, "Benjamin, or 'Pap,' Singleton and His Followers," *Journal of Negro History*, XXXIII (January, 1948), 21.
21 *New York Times*, October 10, 1891, p. 10, c. 1.
22 *Warranty Deed Record Book*, No. 1, p. 403, Office of the County Clerk, Guthrie, Oklahoma.
23 Hill, *op. cit.*, p. 261.
24 *New York Times*, April 9, 1891, p. 9.
25 *E.g.*, "Oklahoma as a Negro State," from *New York Post*, 1892, in *Barde Collection.*
26 The *Daily Oklahoma State Capital* (Guthrie), July 17, 1893, p. 4, c. 1, calls him the "erstwhile editor of the Langston Herald."
27 See Dann, *op. cit.*, p. 24.
28 *Warranty Deed Book* "A," p. 2, Office of the County Clerk, Guthrie, Oklahoma.
29 See *College Heights Addition, Langston City, Oklahoma Territory, April 21, A. D. 1891* (Guthrie: State Capital Printing Co., 1891) in Townsite of Langston City, Guthrie Land Office, Oklahoma, National Archives.
30 *Ibid.*, p. 1; see also, Tolson, *op. cit.*, Appendix B, pp. 66-72.
31 *Ibid.*, p. 7.
32 *Ibid.*, p. 4.
33 *Ibid.*, pp. 5-6.
34 *Ibid.*, pp. 4-6; for a discussion of the sociological phenomena behind the establishment of all-black communities in Oklahoma, see Hill's article.
35 *Ibid.*, p. 5.
36 The printed flier which Stevens sent out had been printed by Dr. D. J. Wallace, whose name was scratched out and replaced by that of Stevens. Wallace was a lawyer and real estate man during Langston's early years. He was at one time associated with the *Herald* and later taught school in Langston.
37 *Muskogee Phoenix*, February 19, 1891, p. 1, c. 2.
38 *Norman Transcript*, March 7, 1891, p. 1, c. 2, citing the *Guthrie News.*
39 *Ibid.*, August 29, 1891, p. 2, c. 4. The "letters" referred to here may have been Stevens's fliers which, on page 8, had a section entitled "Agents Wanted." He asked for agents for "all the states and counties in the Union."
40 *Langston City Herald*, November 17, 1892, p. 2, c. 6.
41 *Norman Transcript*, August 29, 1891, p. 2, c. 4.
42 *Kingfisher Free Press*, September 17, 1891, p. 2, c. 1.
43 *New York Times*, September 20, 1891, p. 8, c. 2.
44 *Ibid.*
45 *Ibid.*, September 21, 1891, p. 1, c. 5.
46 *Ibid.*, September 22, 1891, p. 1, c. 4.
47 *Norman Transcript*, September 26, 1891, p. 2, c. 7.
48 *New York Times*, September 20, 1891, p. 1, c. 4; "William L. Eggleston was probably William L. Eagleson, editor of the *Langston City Herald* and the first Justice of the Peace of the incorporated Langston City."
49 *Ibid.*, September 23, 1891, p. 1, c. 5.
50 *Langston City Herald*, November 17, 1892, p. 2, c. 6.
51 Newspaper clipping, July 18, 1889, in *Root Collection.*
52 "Guthrie is Booming," Guthrie, March 13, 1890, in *Ibid.*
53 *Purcell Register*, November 20, 1891, p. 1, c. 3.

[54] Ralph N. Records, "Recollections of April 19, 1892," *Chronicles of Oklahoma*, XXI (Spring, 1943), 19.

[55] *Ibid.*, p. 20.

[56] "Oklahoma as a Negro State," undated, in *Barde Collection*.

[57] "Oklahoma," undated, in *Root Collection*.

[58] *Muskogee Phoenix*, February 19, 1891, p. 1, c. 3.

[59] *New York Times*, October 10, 1891, p. 10, c. 1.

[60] *Langston City Herald*, November 17, 1892, p. 1, c. 1.

[61] *Ibid.*, p. 2, c. 6.

[62] *Ibid.*, June 15, 1893, p. 2, c. 1.

[63] *Ibid.*, p. 4, c. 1.

[64] *New York Times*, February 20, 1893, p. 6, c. 3; this latter prediction did not become reality.

[65] *Daily Oklahoma State Capital*, September 27, 1893, p. 4, c. 3.

[66] *The Daily Leader* (Guthrie), October 18, 1893, p. 3, c. 2.

[67] *Ibid.*, November 8, 1893, p. 3, c. 5.

[68] *Kingfisher Free Press*, February 22, 1894, p. 1, c. 6.

[69] *Indian Citizen*, August 30, 1894, p. 1, c. 4.

[70] *Langston City Herald*, November 17, 1892, p. 3, c. 2.

[71] See *Ibid.*, June 15, 1893, p. 3, c. 3.

[72] *College Heights Addition, Langston City, Oklahoma Territory, April 21, A. D. 1891*, has Wallace's name scratched off of the title page and his name replaced by that of Stevens on page 8.

[73] *Langston City Herald*, November 17, 1892, p. 4, c. 1.

[74] *Ibid.*, p. 4, c. 3 and 6; in 1894 Stewart was elected the Clerk of Logan County.

[75] *Ibid.*, June 15, 1893, p. 4, c. 5-7.

[76] *Ibid.*, August 11, 1894, p. 2, c. 5.

[77] *Ibid.*, November 17, 1892, p. 1, c. 3, and p. 2, c. 6-7.

[78] *Ibid.*, June 15, 1893, p. 2, c. 1.

[79] *Minutes of the Commissioners Court*, No. 1, p. 238, Office of the County Clerk, Guthrie, Oklahoma.

[80] *Ibid.*, p. 272.

[81] *Muskogee Phoenix*, May 14, 1891, p. 1, c. 2; *Lexington Leader*, October 8, 1892, p. 2, c. 2.

[82] *New York Times*, April 9, 1891, p. 9, c. 1.

[83] *Ibid.*, August 16, 1890, p. 1, c. 6; *Indian Journal*, (Eufaula, I. T.) August 21, 1890, p. 4, c. 1. The election of the first legislature was held August 5, but the death of two elected members required the election of replacements.

[84] *New York Times*, April 9, 1891, p. 9, c. 1; see also *Lexington Leader*, October 8, 1892, p. 2, c. 2, and *Norman Transcript*, May 21, 1893, p. 1, c. 3.

[85] *New York Times*, September 15, 1893, p. 5, c. 4.

[86] *Ibid.*, February 20, 1893, p. 6, c. 3.

[87] Cited in *Daily Oklahoma State Capital*, January 13, 1894, p. 3, c. 3. See also, *Kingfisher Free Press*, February 22, 1894, p. 1, c. 6.

[88] *Kingfisher Free Press*, February 22, 1894, p. 1, c. 6.

[89] *Ibid.*

[90] *New York Times*, October 10, 1891, p. 10, c. 1.

[91] *Ibid.* The idea of a university came from John M. Langston; land was donated as early as 1891 for the purpose, but the present Langston University was not established until 1897.

[92] See Hill, *op. cit.*, p. 264. Using Boley as their case study, William E. Bittle and Gilbert L. Geis present the thesis that these towns represented blacks' "visions of self-realization and fulfillment." See their article, "Racial Self-Fulfillment and the Rise of an All-Negro Community in Oklahoma," *Phylon*, XVIII (Third Quarter, 1957), 247-60.

[93] *Edmond Sun-Democrat*, May 24, 1895, p. 2, c. 2.

[94] See *Indian Journal*, August 21, 1890, p. 4, c. 1, and *Edmond Sun-Democrat*, May 24, 1895, p. 2, c. 2.

[95] *New York Times*, October 10, 1891, p. 10, c. 1.

[96] *Kingfisher Free Press*, February 22, 1894, p. 2, c. 2.

[97] Cited in *Indian Citizen*, August 30, 1894, p. 1, c. 4; "A Negro State," undated, in *Barde Collection; Langston City Herald*, October 20, 1894, p. 2, c. 2-3.

[98] *Negro Population in the United States, 1790-1915* (New York, 1968), p. 786.

Struggle for Equality: Fort Des Moines Training Camp for Colored Officers, 1917

HAL S. CHASE

As they had during previous wars, but even more so, African Americans played a substantial role in World War I. According to the noted historian John Hope Franklin, of the two million blacks who registered under the Selective Service Act of 1917, some 367,000 were called into service. Black participation in World War I also included the African Americans' demand for the United States to train black officers for the war effort. A unique coalition, including white liberals and African American college presidents, professors, students, and community activists, pressured government officials until the Fort Des Moines Training Camp for Colored Officers was created.

Working from extensive archival resources of correspondence and periodicals, Hal Chase examines the effort to advance black civil rights and equality through officer training. In 1917 even a segregated camp for the training of black Army officers signaled racial progress. Revisionist in its thrust, Chase's study documents the key roles played by African Americans. Particularly illuminating are the author's details of the youthful energies committed to this project, such as the crucial support for the training camp that emerged with the formation of the Central Committee of Negro College Men.

BLACK AMERICANS have struggled for equality in America for all of its two hundred years, but many of these struggles remain unrecorded.[1] One of the more significant omissions is the absence of an account for the first officers' training camp.[2] The segregated camp was known officially as "The Fort Des Moines Training Camp for Colored Officers," and approximately twelve hundred fifty men attended the camp between June 18 and October 15, 1917. Six hundred twenty-nine men earned commissions ranging in rank from second lieutenant to captain. By their individual and collective effort the men commissioned at Fort Des Moines struck a telling blow for justice and equality.[3]

The history of the camp is an important chapter in the Afro-American protest tradition for several reasons. As noted above, the commissioning of Negro officers at Fort Des Moines seriously contradicted the traditional, discriminatory policy. This is not to say that the movement for Negro officers in World War I was a new demand. Similar protest existed during the Civil War, and following the declaration of war against Spain, John Mitchell, Jr., editor of the Richmond *Planet*, raised the cry of "No Officers, No Fight" which received wide circulation in the black press. The World War I struggle to have Negroes admitted to officer training was a continuation of the movement for full citizenship rights.[4]

The movement for the establishment of a camp was important because it was national in scope, involving Negroes at every level in the community. Black administrators, professors, and students at colleges throughout the country were active in the Central Committee of Negro College Men. The black press hotly debated the issue of a segregated camp and without doubt aroused their readers' interest in the subject. The involvement of white leaders in the National Association for the Advancement of Colored People (NAACP) in the initial phase also contributed to the national scope of the struggle, but most important in this respect was the focusing of protest on the federal government, specifically the War Department and the White House.

In 1917 the White House was occupied by Woodrow Wilson, a Southerner whose earliest memories included the Civil War and Reconstruction. He obviously adopted the white racism and racial prejudice associated with white Southerners, because after his inauguration as President, Wilson acquiesced to the swift increase of racial segregation in federal offices imposed by his Southern, Democratic cabinet members.[5]

White racism was influential in Congress as well. When the issue of universal military service was being debated in 1916, U.S. Senator James K. Vardaman (D.-Miss.) opposed it on clearly racist grounds: "Universal military service means that millions of Negroes who will come under this measure will be armed. I know of no greater menace to the South than this."[6]

Vardaman's efforts and those of like-minded Southern Democratic congressmen failed to exclude Negroes from the enlisted ranks, but they succeeded in barring blacks from the four-week summer reserve officer training camps established by the National Defense Act in 1916. Joel E. Spingarn, an independently wealthy university professor and Chairman of the Board of Directors of the NAACP, attended several of these camps in 1916. In December of the same year he initiated efforts to obtain reserve officer training for Negroes.[7]

Black Americans had made prior attempts to achieve the same end. Some of these, however, involved segregation. In July, 1916, R. R. Wright, Sr., President of Georgia State Normal and Industrial

College in Savannah, wrote President Woodrow Wilson and suggested the establishment of a camp for the training of colored reserve officers. By his own account, George J. Austin, a commodore of cadets at St. Paul's College in Lawrenceville, Virginia, wrote General Leonard Wood, Commander of the Eastern Department, in April, 1916, about a segregated summer camp for college students. General Wood replied that he personally favored the idea, but that practical concerns made it impossible for him to take any action until at least 250 men committed themselves to attending such a camp. After unsuccessfully approaching the War Security League for support, Austin contacted W.E.B. DuBois who refused to support the idea in the *Crisis* because of insufficient time to organize a summer camp for 1916. Austin claims he had a subsequent meeting with DuBois and Spingarn in New York and that he originated the idea for a separate camp.[8]

In any event, Spingarn began his efforts to establish reserve officer training for Negroes in December, 1916. He quickly learned that the Wilson Administration and the Army flatly rejected any racial integration that suggested equality between black and white Americans. Rather than combat such white racism, the Chairman of the NAACP set aside his integrationist principles and began efforts to secure a separate camp.[9]

As a result, General Wood promised to establish a separate camp if the Columbia University professor could obtain two hundred applications from men of "superior character."[10] Consequently, Spingarn sent an open letter entitled "Educated Colored Men" to the New York *Age* which published it in mid-February. The letter explicitly asked black men to accept a segregated camp in order to obtain the more important goal of Negro officers for Negro troops. This appeal sparked a storm of controversy in the black community, and it was a major issue in the black press for several months.[11]

Throughout this period college administrators, young professors and male undergraduates gave Spingarn crucial support. As a group the black collegiate community was the vital force in the struggle to establish a training camp for colored officers. The center of this movement was understandably Howard University. Its location in the nation's capital (where the final decision for the camp would be made) and its prestige in the black academic community were significant factors. Most important, however, was the support of such men as Professor George W. Cook, Secretary of Howard, George E. Brice, president of the student body, and Montgomery Gregory, a young instructor in the English Department.

When Spingarn first solicited Cook's support for a separate camp is unclear, but the Howard administrator was among the first to assume an active role. On February 19, he wrote Spingarn that he had placed the open letter in the Howard University *Journal,* and he added, "I shall see if I can stir up the students and other people. . . ."[12]

In the next three months, Cook worked tirelessly for a separate camp. He made arrangements.for Spingarn's speech at Howard in March, and during the same visit he arranged for the NAACP Chairman to make presentations at Dunbar High School and Armstrong Training School which broadened support for the camp in Washington's black community. Cook aroused additional enthusiasm for the camp by having Sergeant Farrior, a hero of Carrizal, address the Howard student body; but the Howard administrator's most important work was winning support of colleagues such as John Hope, president of Morehouse College, and William A. Joiner, superintendent of Wilberforce University.[13]

Spingarn clearly understood the significance of Cook's support. In early April, the NAACP Chairman wrote New York Congressman Edmund Platt that if he wished more information about the camp movement, he should contact George W. Cook, "who has backed me up in my proposal in opposition to some more radical colored leaders who refuse to make any compromise with the principle of Jim Crowism."[14]

Spingarn received support from other administrators such as William Pickens, Dean of Morgan College, whose efforts paralleled those of Cook; Edward T. Ware, the white President of Atlanta University; and Major Allen Washington, Commandant of Cadets at Hampton Institute.[15] On the other hand, R. R. Moton, Principal of Tuskegee, was noncommittal. In fact, he wrote Spingarn that he did not distribute the application blanks to the camp because "one Trustee [Theodore Roosevelt] has applied to the War Department to recruit a cavalry regiment of colored troops." Fortunately for the camp movement at Tuskegee Spingarn received the support of Julius B. Ramsey, Commandant of Cadets.[16]

The commitment of undergraduate men was equally critical to the success of the officers' training camp. Spingarn needed to obtain two hundred applications to the camp before it could be established. Therefore, he solicited the support of George E. Brice, student body president at Howard. Brice responded affirmatively, and he immediately began seeking applications from his own Omega Psi Phi fraternity brothers and from men who belonged to Alpha Phi Alpha, Kappa Alpha Psi and Phi Beta Sigma, the three other fraternities on campus at that time. The established contacts and communication among fraternity men at various colleges were a significant factor in undergraduate support for the camp.[17]

Alpha Phi Alpha brothers actively recruited for the camp at Cornell and Amherst as well as at Howard. Brice took his efforts beyond Howard by placing a favorable article about the camp in the Baltimore *Afro-American* and by spreading the movement to other black college campuses as a member of the Howard baseball team. In general, he received a favorable response, but his fellow students expressed real concerns as well.[18]

There was a pervasive question whether the proposed camp was for officer training because as Carter W. Wesley, a Fisk student, pointed out to Spingarn, "In the first place your application blank doesn't happen to say officer anywhere." Students also questioned the nature of their commitment and what conditions would be in the camp. Practical concerns also surfaced. George Brice told Spingarn in mid-March that many students did not apply for the summer camp because they needed to work during that time to earn money for their school expenses. Cost of the necessary uniforms was another economic deterrent, but Spingarn mitigated this by offering to pay for the uniforms of one hundred men whose need was certified by their college dean or president.[19]

Even though these concerns had an adverse effect upon applications, Spingarn wrote General Wood on March 28 that he had two hundred thirty-one "bona fide" applications. This almost met the quota of two hundred fifty which the general had revised upward at the beginning of the month. Wood, however, had just been relieved of his command of the Eastern Department, and thus he referred Spingarn to Major Halstead Dorey who was in charge of Civilian Training.[20]

The two men met, and apparently Dorey's suggestion of Ft. Washington, Maryland, as a possible location led the overly eager Spingarn to conclude that the establishment of the camp was imminent. When he heard from Hollis B. Frissel, President of Hampton Institute, on March 31 that forty-six Hampton men had applied, Spingarn concluded prematurely that the struggle for the camp had been won. The same day he wrote Walter R. Brown, Assistant Commandant at Hampton, "I think that the success of the camp is now assured." He also wrote George E. Brice and concluded with the jubilant request: "Please tell the students of Howard that their energy and enthusiasm are as much responsible for this happy result as any one single factor."[21]

On April 7, however, Spingarn's visions of victory were shattered by the declaration of war against Germany. The Chairman of the NAACP was discouraged by the realization that the camp decision would be made in Washington, D.C., rather than on Governor's Island in New York. In this time of crisis, it should be noted, Spingarn turned to the NAACP.[22]

On April 13, Spingarn informed George B. Kelley, secretary of the Afro-American League of Duluth, Minnesota, that "The NAACP has sent its Secretary [Roy Nash] to Washington, D.C. to fight for much more than a separate division." Archibald H. Grimké, President of the NAACP in Washington, D.C., who initially opposed the segregated camp, became personally active at this time. George W. Cook, a vice president of the Washington branch, collaborated in his efforts with his NAACP colleagues. Spingarn and James Weldon Johnson made several trips to the nation's capital.[23]

NAACP members focused their attention upon Representatives, Senators, and officials in the War Department. Their ultimate goal was Secretary of War Newton D. Baker's endorsement of the camp. To obtain this, Roy Nash, NAACP Executive Secretary, motivated U.S. Representative Martin B. Madden of Chicago to write Baker a long letter. The Congressman pointedly asked the Secretary of War if there would be racial discrimination in the bill to raise the national army and if opportunity would be provided for Negroes to become officers. In conclusion, Madden explicitly demanded, "May I assure them that in the present crisis the nation welcomes and will avail itself of the service of all loyal citizens regardless of color?"[24]

On April 17, Roy F. Nash went to the War College and discussed the officer training camp with Major George P. Ahern. When Ahern said he saw no reason why colored men should not be admitted to the four divisional training camps, Archibald H. Grimké quickly wrote Newton D. Baker on NAACP stationery. Grimké reminded the Secretary of War of General Wood's promise, and then claimed that two thousand three hundred twenty-five applications had been received. Grimké added further pressure by asserting that army officers at the War College and the War Department agreed with NAACP officials that an integrated camp was "possible."[25]

The same day Spingarn telegraphed an appeal to Major W. T. Johnston in the War Department and strongly urged an opportunity for colored officer training. Johnston, who later became Adjutant-General, had been placed in charge of the fourteen officer training camps which the War Department announced April 15. These were three-month camps, and candidates who successfully completed the course would receive regular officer commissions in the National

Army. The camps were scheduled to open May 8, and there was no indication in the orders that Negroes would be admitted.[26]

On April 20, Spingarn led a large NAACP delegation to an interview with Newton D. Baker. In addition to Grimké, Cook, and Nash, the group included Moorfield Storey, President of the NAACP. Baker gave "no assurances" to the committee that a separate camp would be established. Spingarn was disappointed and his optimism was shaken further when he learned the following day that Congressman Madden had received no response to his pointed inquiry of the previous week. In fact, Spingarn, perhaps unconsciously, undermined his movement when he revealed to Major Dorey that the three hundred fifty applications which he possessed were to the inoperative four-week summer reserve officer training camps. On April 25, Spingarn heard from Roy Nash that Adjutant General Johnston was "beautifully non-committal." Three days later the Chairman of the NAACP withdrew from the struggle and reported to Madison Barracks, New York, for his own training as an officer.[27]

Spingarn's leadership was quickly assumed by Negroes. In fact, Spingarn encouraged this change. He wrote George E. Brice: "I feel very sanguine that if the colored people will only take up this movement unitedly, they will obtain officers' training for their young men." The same day he wrote a similar letter to George W. Cook. It should be noted, however, that Spingarn referred Brice to Executive Secretary Roy Nash rather than Cook. Furthermore, on April 30, Spingarn gave Nash his complete file concerning the camp, including all the applications and declared, "I think that you had better take charge of the matter hereafter." In a letter to the office secretary, Spingarn authorized the opening of his mail and requested that any correspondence related to the camp be forwarded to Roy Nash. Finally, Spingarn announced his withdrawal to every applicant by means of a printed post card which included the erroneous statement that the camp had been deferred.[28]

Despite such adverse circumstances, Negroes, especially the college community, quickly and effectively reorganized their efforts to obtain the camp. It should be noted that this involved a significantly different commitment for undergraduate men. As Brice wrote Spingarn, "In taking the three month training the greater number of us realize we will have to sacrifice the furtherance of our academic education, but we hope the service of our country and race will more than pay us for the time lost in school and the lives lost in battle."[29]

The vital center of the critical last phase of the struggle was the Central Committee of Negro College Men. The Committee's headquarters were in a dormitory basement room at Howard. Montgomery Gregory, the young drama professor in the English Department mentioned above, was Chairman. C. Benjamin Curley was the secretary. Leaders at other colleges included William Douglas at Lincoln (Pa.), Wiley A. Hall at Virginia Union, Carter W. Wesley at Fisk, Frank Coleman at the University of Chicago and Charles H. Houston at Amherst.[30]

The Committee did not hesitate to act. It held a mass meeting at Howard and raised fifty dollars to send delegates to aid the efforts on other campuses. This resulted from several conferences between Committee members and Congressmen who had promised to act as soon as they were supplied with a list of five hundred volunteers. According to one newspaper account, the Committee had 590 applications in the first week of May. Nevertheless, the Committee felt compelled to print a broadside entitled "Training Camp for Negro Officers" which members personally delivered to Congressmen. In addition, delegations visited the War Department, the Navy Department and Secretary of Interior Franklin K. Lane "with a view," Montgomery Gregory noted, "to having him present our case to the National Defense Council." To arouse support in the black community the Committee printed paper lapel ribbons which read,

I AM
For the Colored
Officers'
Camp.
ARE YOU?[31]

The black community did rally to support the camp, especially in Washington, D.C. A group of prominent citizens joined together to form the Committee of 100. The Reverend J. Milton Waldron, a Baptist minister, was Chairman, but Dr. George W. Cabaniss was the dynamic force. A Committee of Ladies was formed by Mrs. Arthur M. Curtis and Mrs. George W. Cook. Together with the Central Committee of Negro College Men, these two groups petitioned Newton D. Baker.[32]

The Secretary of War was not personally hostile to the rights of Negroes, but white racism was rampant among high ranking army officers. Brigadier General Joseph E. Kuhn, Chief of the War College Division, was especially prejudiced. On May 6 he reported to Chief of Staff Tasker H. Bliss as to the practicality of establishing a camp:

> It is assumed that this question has been raised by the desire of certain colored citizens to attend the Officers' Training Camps. . . .
> The War College Division has no hesitation in recommending that if camps for colored citizens are to be established that they be sepa-

rate from the camps of white citizens. . . . That colored officers should not be assigned to white organizations requires no argument. Whether or not they should be utilized as officers is . . . more of a political than a military question, but in general it is believed that our colored citizens make better soldiers if commanded by white officers than they do under officers of their own race.[33]

Contrary to such racist advice, Newton D. Baker had his personal secretary Ralph A. Hayes inform Howard President Stephen M. Newman on May 12 that "the determination has been made to have a training camp for Colored men." The letter contained no mention of the location or leadership of the camp.[34]

Howard and Hampton seriously contended for the camp but General Kuhn objected to Howard because of the many distractions of the city of Washington. Consequently, President Newman and Secretary Cook supported Kuhn's recommendation of his third choice, Fort Des Moines, Iowa, to prevent the camp being at Hampton.[35]

Chief of Staff Tasker H. Bliss accepted this advice and on May 19 the War Department officially announced that a three-month training camp for colored officers would be conducted at Fort Des Moines. Twelve hundred fifty candidates between the ages of twenty-five and forty would be admitted. They would include two hundred fifty non-commissioned officers from the regular army. Each of the six military departments in the United States had a quota. Department commanders decided the question of state quotas. Accepted candidates would have to pay their transportation to Des Moines, but they would be reimbursed at the rate of three cents per mile. They were to report for training by June 18. No mention was made about the commanding officer, and so the Central Committee of Negro College Men promoted Lieutenant-Colonel Charles E. Young. This move collapsed, however, when the War Department deactivated Young because of high blood pressure. The Central Committee then turned its attention to recruiting applicants.[36]

There was no problem attracting one thousand candidates. Many more than that number presented their credentials and three recommendations to committees located on college campuses, Negro YMCA buildings and army bases. The process was largely self-selective, and the twelve hundred men who reported to the 17th Provisional Training Regiment on June 18 were, in the words of their white commander, "remarkably strong, earnest and well-educated."[37]

The Commander at Fort Des Moines was Colonel Charles C. Ballou, and he set the tone of the camp with these remarks:

I would impress upon each and every one of you the serious reflection on your race that will necessarily follow your failure in this crucial test and the far-reaching results that will flow from your success.[38]

In case any candidate was not already sufficiently impressed with the magnitude of the challenge facing him, Colonel Ballou reemphasized the point most emphatically: "Your race will be on trial with you as its representatives during the existence of this training camp."[39] Moreover, he made it painfully clear that the judge of their trial was not inclined to leniency:

> You may, therefore, expect that no personal sympathy or consideration will deter me from ruthlessly eliminating from the training camp any man that I find falling short of the established standards of honesty, morality and military efficiency.[40]

The schedule was similar to that conducted in other officer training camps; Monday through Saturday morning: Reveille 5:45 a.m., Breakfast 6 a.m., Morning Instruction 7 a.m. to 12 p.m., Dinner 12:15 p.m., Afternoon Instruction 1:30 to 4:30 p.m., Sick call 4:45 p.m., Retreat 5:50 p.m., Supper 6:00 p.m., Study period 7 p.m., Call to quarters 9:30 p.m., Taps 9:45 p.m.

Instruction included infantry drill, physical drill, care of equipment, bayonet and saber drill, signaling and semaphore training, musketry training, regimental organization and trench warfare. Saturday was inspection day. Discipline was enforced by use of "black marks." Accumulation of three "black marks" was grounds for dismissal. The monthly pay was one hundred dollars and it was paid in gold coin.[41]

The camp was officially organized into fourteen companies, but the candidates associated in terms of their college and home city or state. Montgomery Gregory and others established the quasi-social 17th Provisional Training Camp Association. It had about seventy dues-paying members. A Lawyers' Association was also formed. The most significant social institution, however, was the YMCA. Its executive secretary was Robert B. DeFrantz of Kansas City, but its most significant worker and the *paterfamilias* of the camp was Dr. George W. Cabaniss who temporarily gave up his private practice in Washington, D.C., to serve in the camp he had worked so hard to obtain.[42]

From all reports conditions in the camp were good. Montgomery Gregory went so far as to proclaim them "excellent." Edward C. Mickey, a funeral director from Charleston, South Carolina, wrote Archibald H. Grimké that the camp was "very interesting." Mickey may have been referring to the visits of such dignitaries as Colonel Charles E. Young, Tuskegee president Robert Russa Moton, Dean William Pickens of Morgan and Dean Kelly Miller of Howard. Even the Cleveland *Gazette*, which had been the severest critic of the separate camp, printed a letter from a candidate which praised the program, the accommodations and the treatment of the candidates by their white company commanders.[43]

There was some distinction between the veteran, non-commissioned regular army officers and the college graduates who were novices. Unity rather than dissension prevailed among the candidates, however, perhaps because of several incidents of racial discrimination against the candidates in Des Moines. These involved a restaurant, a theatre and one or two drug stores. Colonel Ballou reported to his commanding officer that he resolved the matter "by serving on the one hand the good will, favorable opinion and more tolerant treatment on the part of the townspeople, and on the other hand, by impressing the colored candidates . . . that they could not ram social equality down the throats of the white population, but must *win* it by their modesty, patience, forbearance and character." One wonders whether the twelve hundred trainees won social equality by giving a drill exhibition and singing spirituals before a crowd of fifteen thousand at the White Sparrow Patriotic Services held in Drake University Stadium on Sunday, July 22.[44]

The candidates certainly displayed patience and forbearance in early September when the War Department postponed the commissioning of officers until October. The Baltimore *Afro-American* reported that the order came "like a bolt from a clear sky," but George W. Cook had telegraphed Montgomery Gregory of the postponement possibility on September 8 and had encouraged him to advise the men to be loyal and stick it out. Despite this warning, many of the provisional companies held farewell banquets, and the candidates were disappointed and upset when the deferral order was announced only four days before the scheduled end of the camp.[45]

Various factors contributed to the postponement. As early as July, in a report to Adjutant-General W. T. Johnston, Colonel Ballou unwittingly supported the idea of additional training by asserting, "that the total number of candidates that will develop into officers of more than mediocre efficiency will be relatively small, due to lack of mental potential and the higher qualities of character essential to command and leadership." The need for Negro officers was reduced when the Chief of Engineers and the Quartermaster General resisted efforts to include colored officers in their corps. The Acting Chief of the War College Division suggested that the candidates at Fort Des Moines be commissioned in the Officers' Reserve Corps because as officers in the National Army they would receive pay whether or not they were assigned to actual duty. There was also direct opposition to

the commissioning of any Negro officers in the National Army by
such Negrophobes as U.S. Senator John Sharp Williams (D.-Miss.).[46]

There was never any intention to use Negro officers to command white troops. Hence, the question was what to do with the Fort
Des Moines officers between mid-September and the arrival of Negro
enlisted men at training camps in early November.[47] Nevertheless, the
deferral order was perceived by Negroes as a slur upon the talents of
the candidates and their race. Some thought it was a move to deny
the commissions altogether, but the candidates never gave any serious thought to leaving.[48]

Emmett J. Scott, who had just been appointed Special Assistant
to Secretary of War Newton D. Baker, was the principal speaker at
the commissioning ceremonies held October 10. Six hundred twenty-
nine men received commissions in the National Army: 106 as Captains, 329 as First Lieutenants, and 204 as Second Lieutenants. They
were given two weeks' leave and then ordered to report to seven different camps where they trained Negro enlisted men in separate
units which were combined in France to form the 92nd Division.[49]

Credit for the officers commissioned at Fort Des Moines belongs to black Americans for several reasons. Joel E. Spingarn's efforts for the camp would have failed without the support of George
W. Cook, William Pickens and the endorsement of undergraduates.
Furthermore, the Central Committee of Negro College Men, in conjunction with Dr. George W. Cabaniss and the Committee of 100, succeeded where Spingarn had failed. Furthermore, black NAACP
officials James Weldon Johnson and Archibald H. Grimké contributed
significant efforts. Ultimately, however, the commissioning of six hundred twenty-nine officers at Fort Des Moines was the result of the efforts of the Negro men who attended. But this should not obscure
the larger truth that the success of the Fort Des Moines Training
Camp for Colored Officers was due to the combined efforts of the
old and the young, the college and the community who were strongly
united by a common purpose and a tangible goal.[50]

Notes

[1] Richard J. Stillman II, *Integration of the Negro in the U.S. Armed Forces* (New York,
1968), p. 1. Stillman contends that the issue of equality, defined in political terms of
who should be where, when and how, has created a relationship of conflict between
black Americans and the military. His thesis is substantiated by the history of the Ft.
Des Moines Officers Training Camp.

[2] There are passing references to the Ft. Des Moines camp in numerous works. B.
Joyce Ross, *J. E. Spingarn and the Rise of the NAACP, 1911-1939* (New York, 1972), and
Charles Flint Kellogg, *NAACP, 1909-1920* (Baltimore, 1967) emphasize the efforts to es-
tablish officer training. Brief, factual accounts of the camp are found in Jack D. Foner,

Blacks in the Military in American History (New York, 1974), Kelly Miller, *Kelly Miller's History of the World War for Human Rights* (West Port, 1919), Emmett J. Scott, *Scott's Official History of the American Negro in the World War* (New York, 1969 reprint). John Hope Franklin, *From Slavery to Freedom* (Westminster, 1974), Florette Henri and Richard Stillman, *Bitter Victory: A History of Black Soldiers in W.W.I* (New York, 1970), Arthur E. Barbeau and Florette Henri, *The Unknown Soldiers: Black American Troops in World War I* (Philadelphia, 1974). W. Allison Sweeney, *History of the American Negro in the Great World War* (West Port, 1970 reprint) merely lists the names and rank of those commissioned. The most complete account of the camp experience is John L. Thompson, *History and Views of Colored Officers Training Camp for 1917 at Fort Des Moines, Iowa,* Des Moines: The Bystander, 1917. Thompson was the editor of the local black paper *The Iowa Bystander* and for the most part his rare privately published book contains brief biographical sketches of some five hundred candidates obtained by use of a printed questionnaire. Marvin Fletcher, *The Black Soldier and Officer in the United States Army, 1891-1917* (Columbia, 1974) does not consider the Ft. Des Moines camp and actually concludes with a treatment of the Brownsville affair.

³ The change resulting from the establishment of Ft. Des Moines was significant but not categorical. "For a good many years the Federal Government has made it possible for young Negroes to get the necessary training for officers in the military department of Wilberforce under the instruction of regular army officers." [*e.g.,* Charles Young and Benjamin O. Davis, Sr.] William A. Joiner (Superintendent, Wilberforce University) to George W. Cook, April 9, 1917. Joel E. Spingarn Papers, Moorland-Spingarn Research Center, Howard University, Washington, D.C. (N.B.—Hereafter all references to Joel E. Spingarn are designated by his initials JES. All references to data in his papers are those in the Moorland-Spingarn Research Center at Howard and are designated simply JES Papers.)

⁴ Lawrence D. Reddick, "The Negro Policy of the U.S. Army, 1775-1945," *Journal of Negro History* XXXIV (January, 1949), 9-29. George P. Marks III, *The Black Press Views American Imperialism, 1898-1900* (New York, 1971), pp. 33-50 reveals that Mitchell's "No Officers, No Fight" campaign received wide support in the black press.

⁵ Nancy J. Weiss, "The Negro and the New Freedom: Fighting Wilsonian Segregation," *Political Science Quarterly,* LXXXIV (March, 1969), 61-79. Kathleen L. Woglemuth, "Woodrow Wilson and Federal Segregation," *Journal of Negro History,* XLIV (April, 1959), 158-73, and "Woodrow Wilson's Appointment Policy and the Negro," *Journal of Southern History,* XXIV (November, 1958), 457-71.

⁶ Washington *Bee,* April 7, 1917, p. 4. Newspaper Room, Library of Congress, Washington, D.C. (N.B. Hereafter all references to newspapers are to microfilm copies available at the Newspaper Room, Library of Congress unless stated otherwise).

⁷ Ross, *op. cit.,* pp. 3-15, 85. Kellogg, *op. cit.,* p. 25. Stephen R. Fox, *The Guardian of Boston: William Monroe Trotter* (New York, 1971), pp. 217-18, presents an erroneous chronology not substantiated by his sources.

⁸ R. R. Wright, Jr. to JES, April 3, 1917, and R. McCants Andrews to JES, March 3, 1917, JES Papers. James A. Lightfoot to JES, February 22, 1917 and Giles B. Jackson to JES, March 22, 1917, JES Papers. George J. Austin to JES, January 4, 8 and 24, 1917; JES to George W. Cook, May 2, 1917, JES Papers. New York *Amsterdam News,* April 4, 1917. Clipping in NAACP Papers, Box C-376. Library of Congress.

⁹ Ross, *op. cit.,* p. 85.

¹⁰ DeLancey K. Jay to JES, December 22, 1916, JES Papers. W. E. B. DuBois memo to JES, September 7, 1916. One of the five items listed was, "I have written Maj.-Gen. Wood." JES to George W. Cook, May 2, 1917. General Leonard Wood to JES, January 9, 1917, JES Papers.

[11] New York *Age,* February 21, 1917, p. 1. Baltimore *Afro-American,* February 24, 1917, p. 4. Cleveland *Gazette,* March 3 through July 7, 1917, page varies. *Gazette,* March 3, 1917, p. 1. *Gazette,* March 10, 1917, p. 1 and March 24, 1917, p. 2. Gilchrist Stewart to JES March 10, 1917, JES Papers. New York *Age,* March 1, 15 and 29, 1917, p. 4. Boston *Guardian* as reprinted in the Cleveland *Gazette,* May 19, 1917. St. Paul *Appeal* as cited in *Gazette,* April 14, 1917, J. Q. Adams to JES, prior to May 16, 1917. JES Papers. "Bruce Grit" in letter to the editor, New York *News,* March 8, 1917.

[12] George W. Cook to JES, February 19, 1917. JES Papers.

[13] George E. Brice to JES, April 3 and 26, 1917. Cook also wrote Edward T. Ware, the white president of Atlanta University. Myron W. Adams to George W. Cook, May 6, 1917, JES Papers.

[14] JES to Edmond Platt, April 7, 1917. JES Papers.

[15] William Pickens to JES, February 27, March 12, March 28, and April 13, 1917. William Pickens to George W. Smith, April 7, 1917. Joseph Fletcher to William Pickens, April 9, 1917, JES Papers. Myron W. Adams to JES, March 27, 1917. Major Allen Washington to JES, March 2, 1917. R. R. Wright, Jr. to JES, April 3, 1917. Grover Harden to JES, March 19, 1917. JES Papers.

[16] Robert Russa Moton to JES, April 16, 1917. Julius B. Ramsey to JES, February 10, 1917. JES Papers.

[17] L. D. Reddick, ed., *Thirty-five Years of Sigma* [Phi Beta Sigma] (1949) contains brief biographical sketches of several men who attended Ft. Des Moines. Robert L. Gill, *The Omega Psi Phi and the Men Who Made Its History* (1963), pp. 5-6. Charles H. Wesley, *The History of Alpha Phi Alpha: A Development in College Life, 1906-1960* (Washington, D.C., 1961), pp. 155-57. Victor R. Daly November 7, 1975 stated that his interest in the camp was initiated by a letter from Howard H. Long, the president of his fraternity, Alpha Phi Alpha. Elder W. Diggs, founder and Grand Polemarch of Kappa Alpha Psi, actively participated in the struggle for officer training and earned a commission at Ft. Des Moines. J. Jerome Peters, C. Roger Wilson and William L. Crump, *The Story of Kappa Alpha Psi, 1911-1961* (Philadelphia, 1967), pp. 35-6.

[18] George E. Brice to JES, March 14, 16 and 24, and April 3, 1911. Hollis B. Frissel to JES, March 20, 1917. Carter W. Wesley to JES, April 7, 1917. R. R. Wright, Jr. to JES, April 18, 1917. William A. Joiner to JES, April 9, 1917. There was also support from undergraduate women. Hallie E. Queen (Chairwoman, Howard University Red Cross Auxiliary) to JES, April 9, 1917, JES Papers.

[19] Carter W. Wesley to JES, April 9, 1917. George E. Brice to JES, March 8, 1917. Edward M. Beasley (Fisk) to JES, April 3, 1917.

[20] Hollis B. Frissel to JES, March 30, 1917. JES to General Wood, March 28, 1917. Seventy-five of the total were from Howard alone, George E. Brice to JES, March 8, 1917. General Wood to JES, March 8, 1917. Application blank in Thomas Montgomery Gregory Papers, Central Committee of Negro College Men folder. Moorland-Spingarn Research Center, Howard University. When General Wood increased the necessary number of applications from 200 to 250, Spingarn had only 69. *The Branch Bulletin,* March, 1917, p. 31. General Wood to JES, March 29, 1917. Leonard B. Wood Papers. Library of Congress.

[21] Hollis B. Frissel to JES, March 30, 1917. JES to Walter R. Brown, March 31, 1917. JES to George E. Brice, March 31, 1917. Ironically, Spingarn's premature optimism appeared in the Afro-American press the following week when it was no longer operative. *Afro-American,* April 7, 1917, p. 1. *Bee.* April 21, 1917, p. 1.

[22] As late as April 6, 1917, Spingarn implied to Brice that only the place and date of the camp remained in doubt. JES to George E. Brice, April 6, 1917. JES to U.S. Repre-

sentative Edmund Platt, April 7 and 8, 1917. JES to Major Allen Washington, April 17, 1917. JES Papers.

23 JES to George B. Kelley, April 13, 1917. Roy Nash to G. H. Sturdin, April 12, 1917. JES Papers, Copy of Martin B. Madden to Newton D. Baker, April 13, 1917 in Archibald H. Grimké Papers. Moorland-Spingarn Research Center. Howard University JES to George W. Cook, April 7, 1917.

24 Martin B. Madden to Newton D. Baker, April 13, 1917 (copy), A. H. Grimké Papers.

25 A. H. Grimké to Newton D. Baker, April 19, 1917. Grimké's concluding appeal was made for the "10,000,000 loyal Americans for whom this Association speaks." A. H. Grimké Papers.

26 JES to Major Johnston, April 19, 1917. JES to Major Halstead Dorey, April 20, 1917. JES Papers. War Department to General Wood, telegram, April 17, 1917, Leonard B. Wood Papers.

27 News release, April 28, 1917. JES Papers. *Afro-American*, May 5, 1917, p. 1, *re* Moorfield Storey, JES to George E. Brice, April 28, 1917. Martin B. Madden to JES, April 21, 1917. JES to Major Halstead Dorey, April 20, 1917. Roy Nash to JES, April 24, 1917, JES Papers.

28 George W. Cook to JES, April 25, 1917. JES to Brice, April 28, 1917. JES to George W. Cook, April 28, 1917. His own statements to the contrary, the *Afro-American* stated editorially that JES was "greatly discouraged." May 5, 1917, p. 1. See also letter from George C. Sutton to Harry C. Smith, dated Washington, D.C., April 28, 1917 printed in the *Gazette*, May 5, 1917, p. 2. JES to Roy Nash, April 30, 1917. JES to Miss R. G. Randolph, April 30, 1917. JES Papers. New York *Globe*, May 14, 1917, clipping cites the "failure of the recent efforts by the president of the NAACP [Spingarn] to establish a camp at Plattsburg." NAACP Papers, Administrative files, Box C-376 Manuscript Division, Library of Congress, Washington, D.C. See open letter addressed, "Dear Brother" signed "Central Committee of Negro College Men" in Atlanta *Independent*, May 24, 1917. JES Papers.

29 George E. Brice to JES, April 26, 1917. JES Papers.

30 Montgomery Gregory to JES, May 2, 1917. JES Papers. List of undergraduate leaders, Thomas Montgomery Gregory Papers.

31 Montgomery Gregory to JES, May 2, 1917. JES Papers, *Afro-American*, May 5, 1917, pp. 1, 4. See also pledge lists, no date, Central Committee of Negro College Men folder. Thomas Montgomery Gregory Papers. Scott, *Scott's Official History of the American Negro in the World War* (New York reprint), 1969, p. 84.

32 *Iowa Bystander*, August 31, 1917, p. 2. State Museum and Archives, Des Moines, Iowa. George W. Cook to JES, May 4, 1917, C. Benjamin Curley to JES, May 17, 1917. JES Papers, Stephen M. Newman (the white President of Howard University) to Ralph A. Hayes (private secretary to Newton D. Baker), May 11, 1917. R.G. 94, Records of the Adjutant-General's Office, 1780-1917. National Archives, Washington, D.C. The Reverend J. Milton Waldron to Newton D. Baker, May 11, 1917, copy in Thomas Montgomery Gregory Papers. Gregory claimed authorship of this letter.

33 Brigadier-General Joseph E. Kuhn to Major-General Tasker H. Bliss, May 6, 1917, R.G. 94. Records of the Adjutant-General's Office, National Archives.

34 Ralph A. Hayes to Stephen M. Newman, May 12, 1917, copy in JES Papers. Kellogg, *op. cit.*, p. 256 states that the resolution was passed before the decision was made. James B. Morris, November 4, 1974 made an unsolicited reference to a possible March on Washington if officer training was not established. Frederic J. Haskin, New York *Globe*, May 14, 1917, cited the possibility that the movement at Howard to establish officer training could receive a "great impulse in June at the Fiftieth Commencement"

which would attract a great number of distinguished Howard alumni from around the country. NAACP Papers, Box C-376.

[35] Brigadier-General Joseph E. Kuhn to Major-General Tasker H. Bliss, May 15, 1917. R.G. 94. Records of Adjutant General's Office, National Archives. Stephen M. Newman to Newton D. Baker, May 11, 1917. Major Allen Washington to Montgomery Gregory, May 17, 1917.

[36] *Iowa Bystander,* May 25, 1917, p. 2. Scott, *op. cit.,* p. 85. *Afro-American,* June 2, 16, 1917, p. 1. Colonel Young to Montgomery Gregory, May 14, 1917. Thomas Montgomery Gregory Papers. *Afro-American,* May 26, 1917, p. 4. See copy of open letter to "Dear Brother." In Scott, *op. cit.,* pp. 88-9.

[37] The author wishes to thank James B. Morris and James W. Mitchell of Des Moines, Louis R. Mehlinger, Victor R. Daly, Louis H. Russell, James B. Lomack and Major Peter L. Robinson for accepting a request for a taped interview. The tapes have been given to the Moorland-Spingarn Research Center at Howard University and are hereafter cited by name and date of the interview. Louis R. Mehlinger, October 25, 1975, Louis H. Russell and Major Peter L. Robinson, November 22, 1975, stated they were examined at Howard. Victor R. Daly, November 7, 1975, said he went to the YMCA in New York City. James B. Morris and James W. Mitchell, November 4, 1974 were examined at Ft. Des Moines and Ft. McPherson (Ga.) respectively.

[38] *Iowa Bystander,* June 29, 1917, p. 2.

[39] *Ibid.*

[40] *Bee,* July 14, 1917, pp. 4, 6.

[41] *Iowa Bystander,* June 22, 1917, p. 1. *Leslie's Weekly,* October 13, 1917, pp. 512, 520. *Afro-American,* July 7, 1917, p. 1. Lucy F. Pierce, "Training Colored Officers," *Review of Reviews* LVI (December, 1917), p. 640. Interview with James B. Morris and James W. Mitchell, November 4, 1974.

[42] All the men interviewed cited persons from their home towns as their closest friends. Company 5 was known familiarly as the "Washington Company" because many of its members either lived there or had attended Howard University. Louis R. Mehlinger, October, 1975, Louis H. Russell and Major Peter L. Robinson, November 22, 1975, James B. Lomack, December 7, 1975.

[43] All those interviewed reported that camp conditions were good and their recollections are supported by primary sources. Montgomery Gregory to JES, August 11, 1917. JES Papers. Edward C. Mickey to A. H. Grimké, September 4, 1917. A. H. Grimké Papers. *Gazette,* June 30, 1917, p. 2. Colonel C. C. Ballou to Adjutant-General W. T. Johnston, July 10, 1917, pp. 2-3. General T. H. Barry to W. T. Johnston, July 13, 1917. R.G. 407. Records of Adjutant-General Office, National Archives. Mickey may have had in mind the visits of such dignitaries as Colonel Charles Young, Tuskegee president R. R. Moton, Dean William Pickens of Morgan and Dean Kelly Miller of Howard. *Iowa Bystander,* July 20, 1917, p. 1; August 24, 31, 1917, p. 2. *Afro-American,* August 18, 1917, p. 1.

[44] All interviewees except Major Peter L. Robinson noted the difference in the educational level of the regular army men and the college candidates. Ralph W. Tyler to George A. Myers, September 2, 1917, reel 7. George A. Myers Papers. Western Reserve Historical Society, Cleveland, Ohio. *Afro-American,* June 30, and July 14, 1917, p. 1. Colonel C. C. Ballou to W. T. Johnston, July 10, 1917, p. 3. R.G. 407. Records of Adjutant-General Office, National Archives, *Iowa Bystander,* July 27, 1917, pp. 2, 3.

[45] George W. Cook to Montgomery Gregory, September 8, 1917. Thomas Montgomery Gregory Papers, *Afro-American,* September 22, 1917, p. 1. Tasker H. Bliss to W. T. Johnston, September 11, 1917. R.G. 165, Records of the War Department, General and Special Staffs, National Archives.

[46] C. C. Ballou to W. T. Johnston, July 10, 1917, p. 5. R.G. 407, Records of the Adjutant-General Office. Colonel P. D. Lochridge to Tasker H. Bliss, August 31, 1917. R.G. 165. Records of War Department, General and Special Staffs. Joseph E. Kuhn to Tasker H. Bliss, July 31, 1917, p. 2. R.G. 407. Records of Adjutant-General Office. Montgomery Gregory to Emmett J. Scott, September 26, 1917. Thomas Montgomery Gregory Papers. W. T. Johnston to Newton D. Baker, September 4, 1917. R.G. 165. Records of War Department, General and Special Staffs. No evidence has been found which links the postponement of commissions at Ft. Des Moines to the so-called Houston riot of August 1917.

[47] C. C. Ballou to George W. Cabaniss, September 14, 1917 as reprinted in the *Bee*, October 6, 1917, p. 2. Ballou's view is supported by an article in the New York *Age* entitled, "Camp Arrangements for Negro Conscripts Undecided," June 12, 1917, p. 1, and by another article published September 27, 1917, p. 4.

[48] James W. Johnston to Montgomery Gregory, September 18, 1917. George W. Cook to Montgomery Gregory, September 18, 1917. George W. Cook to Montgomery Gregory, September 21, 1917. Thomas Montgomery Gregory Papers. *Bee*, October 6, 1917, p. 2. *Age*, October 4, 1917, p. 1. Telegrams from W. E. B. DuBois and James W. Johnson urging the candidates to stay in *Iowa Bystander*, September 21, 1917, p. 1.

[49] *Iowa Bystander*, October 12, 1917, p. 2. Franklin, *op. cit.*, (3rd ed., New York, 1969), p. 457. *Iowa Bystander* October 26, 1917, p. 1. Scott, *Scott's Official History*, p. 9. All other divisions were trained as units in separate camps in the U.S.

[50] Joel E. Spingarn receives exclusive credit for the establishment of the Ft. Des Moines camp in Kellogg, *op. cit.*, 256. Ross, *op. cit.*, p. 88, declares that Spingarn virtually ensured the establishment of the camp. Franklin, *op. cit.*, p. 456 cites efforts of students and the Committee of 100 as well as those of Spingarn. For credit to Spingarn for his "initial" and "preliminary" efforts see Kelly Miller to JES, November 17, 1917, and William Pickens to JES, May 13, 1917. JES Papers. The *Gazette* gave primary credit for the establishment of the camp to the "pluck" of Howard students, June 9, 1917, p. 1. The *Afro-American*, May 19, 1917, p. 1, expressed a similar view. JES to A. H. Grimké, April 3, 1917. JES to Mrs. M. C. Simpson, April 25, 1917. A. C. McIntyre (President of the NAACP Louisville, Kentucky branch) to Roy Nash, April 8, 1917. Henry A. Hunt (Principal of Ft. Valley High and Industrial School, Ft. Valley, Ga.) to Roy Nash, April 13, 1917. JES Papers.

The Afro-American Response to the Occupation of Haiti, 1915-1934

BRENDA GAYLE PLUMMER

Issued in 1904, President Theodore Roosevelt's Corollary to the Monroe Doctrine provided the ideological framework for securing United States hegemony in Latin America and for curbing European imperialistic designs in the Western Hemisphere. During the first two decades of the twentieth century, the United States, the self-proclaimed international police power, sent its troops into Cuba, Nicaragua, the Dominican Republic, Panama, Mexico, and Haiti. While United States officials claimed these foreign interventions were humanitarian in purpose, critics argued that financial gain formed the true basis of the government's actions. The United States occupation of Haiti is a case in point. The occupation, lasting nearly two decades, raised the ire of the African Americans who recognized that American racism and materialism had been exported to Haiti.

Brenda Plummer's essay provides a context for examining the origins of a Diaspora consciousness within the African American community. Black acquiescence to United States propaganda that the occupation was a "civilizing" mission faded when African Americans compared the Haitians' plight to their own struggle for first-class citizenship. Plummer argues that as black Americans gained a heightened political maturity as well as an international awareness, their sympathies toward their Haitian brethren increased. As a result, black Americans used various political, organizational, and journalistic measures to end what they viewed as American imperialism in Haiti.

IN 1915 THE UNITED STATES began a military occupation of Haiti which lasted two decades. Citing widespread violence, actual anarchy, and imminent danger to foreigners' lives and property, the federal government ordered Marines landed at Port-au-Prince. The United States rarely enjoyed harmonious relations with the Caribbean nations in the early twentieth century, and the Haitian occupation was unprecedented in both its duration and the extreme racism that characterized American behavior in the black republic. Historians have examined many facets of the United States' control of Haiti from 1915 to 1934, including reaction to the occupation from the American press.[1] Scant attention, however, has been paid to the black American response to events in Haiti, and the role blacks played in opposing the occupation has been neglected.

The reaction of black Americans to the Haitian occupation is significant because it reflects the great change during this era in blacks' self-assessment, and in their view of kindred peoples of African descent in other parts of the world. Well-known race leaders led the way in responding to the Haitian controversy, but once it became familiar to the public, ordinary black Americans reacted to the racial injustices they believed were occurring in Haiti. They wrote letters to the State Department, to the black press, and to the President of the United States; they attempted to use their leverage as Republican voters; and they agitated for participation in policymaking that affected Haiti.

The landing of Marines in Haiti in the summer of 1915 made little initial impression on blacks. Like that of most Americans, their attention focused primarily on the war in Europe, and they were at first indifferent to the Haitians' plight. Such spokesmen as Booker T. Washington believed the Haitians a backward people in need of discipline and enlightenment. Unimpressed by the refinement of the Haitian élite, Washington felt that the Caribbean nation's economic stagnation and political violence owed much to its neglect of sound industrial education.[2] Aside from the handful of intellectuals who gloried in Haiti's revolutionary past and in the unique culture of its people, most blacks looked upon the occupation as a logical consequence of that country's chronic political turbulence.[3] Others shuddered at the lurid accounts of voodoo that frequently appeared in the popular press. Texas educator E. L. Blackshear condemned both the civil disorder and the religious heresy and in 1912 urged the formation of an international peace-keeping force to occupy Haiti.[4]

These evaluations by black Americans shifted in the years after World War I. The decline of the accommodationist outlook, the greater prominence of civil rights organizations, and resurgent black nationalism helped to create a sympathetic climate among blacks for small, embattled Haiti. The new mood strengthened protest against the occupation and forced policymakers to temper the roughshod manner in which the United States' business in Haiti was conducted.

The chronicle of this episode in Afro-American history properly belongs to the growing store of knowledge about the relationship of black Americans to world affairs: their interest in international relations, and their role as brokers in matters that concern other peoples of color. Black Americans exhibited a persistent interest in their government's activities in Haiti. They placed Haitian needs on their own political agendas. Through contacts with informed Haitians, they maintained surveillance of the United States administration in Port-au-Prince. American blacks did not possess sufficient clout to bring the occupation to a speedy conclusion, but through continued watchfulness and protest, they were able to set limits to the blatancy of coercion in the black republic.

Interest of black Americans in Haiti began in the nineteenth century. Before the general abolition of slavery in 1865, anti-slavery advocates viewed the island nation as concrete proof that blacks could rule themselves. Yet, not everyone was pleased by the quality of Haitian public life. Critics condemned Haiti's incessant changes of government, voodoo, and the parasitism of the ruling elite. The black emigrationist James Theodore Holly, for example, though committed to the country's independence, desired fundamental changes in the way it managed its affairs. In the 1850s, Holly developed an ideology designed to transform Haiti's Franco-African mores into "Anglo-African" ones. He wanted to send "Black Anglo-Saxon" missionaries to Haiti who would spread the message of Protestantism, industrial habits, and the English language.[5] Holly perceived black Americans as intermediaries between two societies—one white, advanced, and Christian, and the other black, benighted, and in need of salvation.

Holly's evangelical, redemptionist viewpoint still prevailed in the early twentieth century. Leading spokesmen felt that only outside influence could raise the productivity and living standards of Haitians to the level of United States citizens because of the irresponsibility of Haitian rulers. Such evidence of anarchy as the Haitian civil wars at the turn of the century, for example, repelled prominent journalist Timothy Thomas Fortune.[6] The "radical" publication *Voice of the Negro*, while militantly pro-black in domestic matters, regarded Haiti as an international reprobate.[7] Some commentators, because they wanted Haiti to serve as a shining example of what blacks could achieve, felt betrayed by that country's weakness. "We long to see Haiti demonstrate to the world the capacity of the Negro for self-government and self-improvement," the *New York Age* editorialized during the first days of the occupation, "and each time that she suffers from revolution and lawlessness we experience a feeling of almost personal disappointment over it."[8]

The *Age's* disappointment rested on the notion that Haiti had an obligation to blacks everywhere to prove that people of African descent were politically mature. In the context of the racist social science of the early 1900s, this burden of proof was especially onerous.[9]

Yet, some blacks made their peace with Social Darwinist ideas about the relative efficiency and worth of respective races. While claiming that blacks must progress slowly and lag behind whites, Booker T. Washington, for instance, had become the most powerful race leader in the United States. Ironically, Washington expressed strong doubts about America's course of action in Haiti. With characteristic shrewdness, he perceived the limitations of military rule and the adverse effects of racism. Haiti should be civilized, but not at gunpoint, he maintained. Haitians needed public education, particularly agricultural and industrial schooling. Care should be taken to send them no negrophobes, the Alabaman warned.[10]

Black Americans' sentiments toward Haiti from the nineteenth century through the early years of the occupation thus swung between the poles of expectation, pride, and missionary zeal on the one hand, and embarrassment, despair, and irritation on the other. Their ambivalence rested chiefly on the instability of Haitian politics in an age in which the quality of government was considered to reflect racial capacity.[11] Once black Americans stopped accepting racist views of themselves, however, they were increasingly able to break free of the apologetics that had shaped their outlook on Haiti. The American military occupation provided a test of this changing thought as post-World War I society set the stage for questioning the old beliefs about race.

The United States' desire to play a regulatory role in Haiti originated in 1913. In that year the State Department replaced Henry Watson Furniss, the American minister to Haiti and a fifteen-year employee, with an inexperienced, white former congressman from Missouri. New administrations often made ministerial changes, especially if the incumbent represented a different party. Moreover, President Woodrow Wilson and his Secretary of State, William Jennings Bryan, planned major modifications within the State Department. Furniss' dismissal was nevertheless significant because the Haitian post traditionally had been awarded to a black.[12] Bryan did not intend to take the Haitian post from blacks permanently. He thought a white man should be appointed only "until affairs there could be straightened out."[13] Bryan's statement suggested that a black minister might make the Wilson administration's contemplated policies in Haiti more difficult to execute.

The dismissal of Furniss coincided with the national displacement of black officeholders during the Wilson years. Wilson also incurred black resentment by intensifying segregation in federal bureaus and departments.[14] After his election victory, Wilson reneged on private, verbal promises apparently made to blacks during his campaign. In August 1913, William Frank Powell, a former minister to Haiti, accused Wilson of steering the ship of state "upon the rocks of unredeemed pledges" to Afro-American voters.[15]

Wilson's new minister to Haiti stayed at his post for less than a year. Another white, Arthur Bailly Blanchard, replaced him. Blanchard did not evince great enthusiasm for Haiti, and was not even in the country when the Marines landed. As a result, no respected diplomat remained to work with the occupation forces to neutralize the more authoritarian aspects of their military presence, and cooperate with the Haitian government. Racism permitted the rationalization of violent acts, which gradually came to the attention of blacks in the United States.

This violence was most extreme during the "bandit-suppression" campaigns in the countryside. Haitians resented what they considered an American invasion, and in 1915 and 1918-1919, peasants rose in arms to repel the Marine patrols. The military responded by launching counterinsurgency strikes against these guerrillas. The Marines razed settlements and shot those whom they believed to be rebels and bandits. Americans officially acknowledged the deaths of over three thousand persons in these conflicts.[16] Haitian residents of urban areas also experienced aggression. Soldiers inflicted assaults, harassment, and verbal abuse on individuals of all social classes. This mistreatment took on a particularly racial character. Americans insisted on segregation and introduced jim crow into hotels, restaurants, and clubs in the cities.[17]

Other American policies irked the Haitians. They detested forced labor, called the *corvée*, which required peasants to work on road gangs far from their homes under the supervision of armed soldiers. The pay was nominal and food and lodging frequently inadequate. The prisoners of war, taken in the counterinsurgency campaigns, suffered the most. Made to construct airstrips and other facilities, they were worked relentlessly. In his memoirs, General Lewis B. Puller considered one of these forced labor projects reminiscent of "the building of the pyramids." As commander of a project that utilized prisoners of war, Puller recalled his feelings of guilt when the men collapsed and died. "I may go to hell for this," he confided to a visitor.[18]

Physical abuse did not constitute the sum of Haitian grievances. Many profoundly disliked governmental policies which they felt had been forced on them. American guns propped up an unpopular regime and safeguarded a national bank owned by foreigners and operated only for their benefit. The national constitution was suspended and the legislature permanently adjourned. The salaries of a large bureaucracy of white officials bled the modest Haitian treasury, while native functionaries were paid much less for the same work. A treaty, signed under duress, guaranteed all these inequities. Curfews, press censorship, and intensive surveillance made Haitian dissidence extremely risky.[19]

The severity of American policies can be understood only if the low evaluation accorded Haitians by leading United States officials is appreciated. General John B. Russell, for many years High Commissioner, the most powerful administrator in the "treaty government," held publicly that the average Haitian had a mental age of seven.[20] Robert Lansing, who succeeded Bryan as Secretary of State, had little faith in the Haitians' capacity to establish a sound government without American assistance. He believed they shared their "inherent tendency to revert to savagery" with Liberians and Afro-Americans alike. This degeneracy, he added, "makes the negro problem practically unsolvable" in the United States.[21] Other State Department personnel agreed. The Haitians "are not even children in the sense that we use the word," one of them wrote, "since they have had no ancestry of intelligence as a foundation."[22] American military officers were quicker to use racial epithets and to make sweeping statements. Some leading officers expressed their bitter contempt for Haitians in their correspondence as "wretched people," "damned liars," "grasping niggers," and "miserable cockroaches."[23]

A social climate which held coercion to be an acceptable and often necessary means of controlling blacks deeply influenced white American officials' attitudes. The era of 1915-1934 witnessed the persistence of lynching, debt peonage, and the exploitation of prison labor in the Southern United States, where most black Americans then lived. In the North, repression took the form of white vigilante assaults on urban ghettoes and widespread police brutality. Popular literature and the nascent film industry supported the stereotypes that helped whites justify their violent behavior.[24] American forces also had the benefit of relative anonymity in their actions in Haiti; public attention dwelled on the war in Europe. Few whites or blacks knew or cared, at first, what was happening on the small Caribbean island. Open and repeated injustice, however, fed uneasy rumors about events in the black republic.

Resident missionaries were the first outspoken critics of American policy in Haiti. S. E. Churchstone Lord, who worked for the African Methodist Episcopal Church, complained about the brutality and depravity of the Marines. He criticized the sluggishness of American reform efforts, and recommended the introduction of Protestant social workers, both black and white. Lord advocated the establishment of industrial schools patterned on Tuskegee Institute, and staffed by black American teachers.[25] Another evangelist, the Welsh-born L. Ton Evans, shared Lord's views.[26] Evans, however, received a stern rebuke from a conservative lay leader of his organization, the Lott Carey Mission Society. This layman, A. M. Moore, an executive of the black-owned North Carolina Mutual Insurance Company, disapproved of Evans' outspoken protests. "We want you to understand that the American Negro stands loyally behind the President and his action in shaping the destiny of Haiti," Moore asserted. The missionary was to say no more on the subject, "as it is clearly not in the minds of the American Negroes to undertake to shape the political policy of an independent country of which they know little."[27] Blacks did not widely agree with Moore, however, and their criticism of the occupation continued to mount.

The National Association for the Advancement of Colored People (NAACP) was the first major black organization to oppose the occupation. Its publication, *The Crisis,* edited by W. E. B. DuBois, had condemned intervention from the beginning. Haiti had suffered from bad leadership in the past, the journal conceded, but the federal government ought to "help Haiti rid herself of thieves and not try to fasten American thieves on her."[28] The NAACP field secretary, James Weldon Johnson, did not immediately share DuBois' disapproval. "He disliked Woodrow Wilson intensely," according to his biographer, but Johnson continued to think that the United States' strategic interests in the Caribbean necessitated the intervention. By 1918, however, when the State Department forced the Haitians to accept an unpopular constitution, Johnson changed his mind, and he would thereafter contribute to altering the opinions of others.[29]

The spirit of the times made Haiti an important issue to blacks. The timing of the occupation was especially significant. The Bloody Summers of 1918 and 1919, the agitation for a federal anti-lynching bill, and the rise of militant nationalism put racial matters at the forefront.[30] Black Americans perceived the Haitians as related to themselves, and increasingly admired the Haitian tradition of resistance to servitude and fierce independence. It is therefore not surprising that the Haitian issue was featured prominently by the NAACP.

In 1918 the NAACP grew uneasy at reports of violations of due process in Haiti, and considered launching an investigation of the occupation. NAACP officials consulted prominent Republicans Theodore Roosevelt and Hamilton Fish, Jr. as to the value of such an undertaking, which Field Secretary Johnson would execute. Roosevelt and Fish, probably motivated by partisan interests, endorsed the idea, but Johnson did not go to Haiti until 1920, an election year. The G.O.P. supplied his traveling expenses, and the NAACP helped the Republicans develop a campaign issue with the understanding that the Haitians' condition would improve under a Republican administration.[31]

Johnson was eminently appropriate as the NAACP's investigator. Partly of West Indian origin, he spoke French, had prior diplomatic experience in Central America, and was one of the most influential Afro-American leaders. On arriving in Port-au-Prince, Johnson interviewed a cross-section of the Haitian and American communities. He also traveled in rural areas during his two-week sojourn.[32] Johnson made two major contributions to the liberation of Haiti. He intensively publicized the Haitians' plight in the United States and assisted them in organizing the Patriotic Union, a protest group consciously modeled after the NAACP and committed to agitation within the confines of the law.[33]

In the course of his inquiry, Johnson became convinced that American banking interests had played a large part in the decision to send in the Marines. "The main object of the Occupation is to get a strangle hold on the economic life of the country," he wrote in his notebook. Having persuaded the United States to intervene, the banks were "now sucking the milk from the cocoanut[sic]."[34] Johnson also condemned the behavior of some American residents: the habitual drunkenness of some of his compatriots, their recklessness, and their general arrogance distressed him. The NAACP field secretary reported interviews with Marines who gleefully admitted committing shocking crimes. "Many of the things which the Haitians rightfully consider cruel and brutal, American marines consider, I might say funny."[35]

Once back in New York, Johnson wrote a series of articles on the occupation for the liberal journal *Nation*.[36] The pieces were indignant exposés publicizing the failings of American policy. Intent on exploiting the political possibilities of the Haitian question, Johnson corresponded with President Wilson's foes. Well-known Republicans Henry Cabot Lodge, Medill McCormick, and Warren G. Harding received communications from Johnson on Haiti.[37]

The efforts of Johnson and the NAACP did not end with Republican leaders. In an attempt to broadcast the Haitian issue to a large black audience, Johnson wrote a surprising, little-known letter to Marcus Garvey in September 1920, which urged Garvey to denounce the occupation. The letter informed the black nationalist that "it was exceedingly necessary that the colored people of America unite with their brothers in Haiti" to effect the restoration of Haitian sovereignty. Much has been made of the mutual antagonism between the NAACP leadership and Garvey, but the desire to create public awareness of the Haitians' situation overrode the strategic and tactical differences between the NAACP and Garvey's Universal Negro Improvement Association (UNIA).[38]

In the months ahead, the NAACP took the lead in keeping alive American interest in Haiti. To involve whites, it entered into a coalition with the Popular Government League and the Foreign Policy Association to oppose the intervention. The Foreign Policy Association comprised numerous influential persons interested in American foreign relations. The Popular Government League's membership included trade unionists, intellectuals, civic leaders, government officials, and former functionaries.[39] Together, these organizations emphasized the coercive nature of the occupation. With the help of the white attorney and NAACP activist Moorfield Storey, Johnson also founded the Haiti-Santo Domingo Independence Society, comprised of liberals prominent in the civil rights, civil liberties, and urban reform movements of the time,[40] and dedicated to the withdrawal of American troops from both those countries.

The Wilson administration proved sensitive to the unfavorable publicity and made a cabinet-level decision to respond to the criticism. The Secretary of the Navy sent a commission of inquiry to Haiti in October 1920, and the Marines conducted a separate investigation. Neither found anything substantively wrong with the occupation. They acknowledged individual cases of wrongdoing by military personnel, but regarded them as exceptional. The military investigators pointed to certain courtmartials which had already taken place.[41] Despite the political capital that Republicans made of the occupation, administration officials insisted that the weakness and degeneracy of the Haitians necessitated continued American control.[42]

Johnson profited from his intransigence. He drew candidate Warren G. Harding's attention to the Haitian question, and gave him another weapon with which to assail the Democrats. After Harding's victory at the polls, the NAACP, the Foreign Policy Association, and the Popular Government League pressured the President-elect to start a new investigation which, unlike those of the Wilson administration, would not attempt to cover up American misconduct.[43] Recognizing his debt to political creditors, Harding announced in 1921 that a new commission of inquiry would be appointed.[44]

The Haitians greeted Harding's election with elation, believing a new party in power would result in a change of policy and expecting much of the NAACP's publicity campaign. Johnson encouraged this faith; he urged his correspondents in Port-au-Prince to avoid any

factional differences or disorders which would delay a Republican solution to the problem.[45]

As Harding had used the Haitian issue to appeal to black voters
for support, many blacks believed that he would democratize decision
making on Haiti to allow them to participate in running that country.
Robert Russa Moton, Washington's successor as president of Tuskegee
Institute, wanted blacks included on Harding's investigative body, declaring that he could "suggest colored men who would in no way embarrass the administration." Moton believed that the ideas of
Washington and other racial conservatives could solve Haiti's
problems.[46] The State Department, however, still proved unwilling to
send nonwhites on an official Haitian mission.

To the disappointment of blacks, the Wilsonian pattern of segregation continued in the Harding years. The new president was ill-
informed on issues of interest to blacks, and reluctant to address
them explicitly. A February 1921 conference between Harding, Johnson, and others revealed that the President knew nothing about black
education and had never even heard of Moton.[47] The State Department nevertheless informally solicited Moton for an independent trip
to Haiti the following year. When Moton could not go, W. T. B Williams, dean at Tuskegee, was chosen to replace him and report on
Haitian education. Williams, however, had no authority to inquire
into the political or military aspects of the occupation.[48] An all-white
Senate commission of inquiry late in 1921, like the 1920 military commissions before it, recommended that intervention, though in need
of reform, be continued.[49]

Blacks continued their agitation for inclusion on an investigative commission. J. Finley Wilson, president of the National Negro
Press Association and editor of the Washington Eagle, wrote to Harding about this matter in February 1922. The Association claimed to
represent some four hundred black periodicals across the country,
and Wilson wanted a member of it named to any new commission of
inquiry the government might designate.[50]

Meanwhile, the NAACP's efforts to publicize injustices in Haiti
bore fruit by 1922. Disapproval of the occupation among blacks was
not limited to leaders and intellectuals. The American-Haitian Benevolent Club, which represented Haitians descended from black American emigrants of the 1850s and 1860s,[51] condemned martial law and
the seeming unanimity of both the Democratic and Republican parties on the harsh treatment of blacks. The Club did not question the
basic assumption that Haiti needed regulation by a strong, neighboring country; it did, however, request that only black troops occupy
the country.[52]

To mollify blacks, the Harding administration named one black clerk to the Port-au-Prince legation. The appointment had little pacificatory impact. Black voters would not be fooled by it, *The Crisis* fumed. "The Republican Party cannot find a dozen respectable Negroes who will wash its dirty linen in Haiti," DuBois wagered. In Port-au-Prince, the clerk, Napoleon Marshall, found himself the target of suspicion and mistrust on the part of his superiors. Isolated and socially ostracized by his countrymen, he developed lasting friendships with sympathetic Haitians and later became a vocal opponent of the occupation.[53] The State Department's attempt at token representation of black Americans in the treaty administration had backfired.

The Marshall case illustrated Washington's failure to halt black opposition. It also exemplified the government's scant commitment to racially integrating its personnel in Haiti. American policymakers opposed in principle to the official presence of blacks there justified their opinion by presenting it as Haitian preference. The State Department's view of W. T. B. Williams' educational fact-finding tour demonstrates this clearly. According to Assistant Secretary of State William Phillips, the Haitians drew a color line between blacks and mulattoes.[54] Phillips asserted that Haitian mulattoes disliked being termed black, and cited the Haitian minister in Washington as one who thought that black Americans would not be accorded the same respect in Haiti as whites. Phillips recalled the experience of Williams, who was treated cordially by the Haitian president and his retinue, but with apparent "restraint." He added that "other officials of the Government did not show a whole-hearted desire to cooperate with Doctor Williams in his work." It is not clear from Phillips' remarks, however, how much of this coolness derived from xenophobia, or how much of it was due to Haitian distaste for the Tuskegee educational philosophy. At any rate, the State Department did not deem it wise to send any more blacks to Haiti at that time.[55]

The Secretary of State himself, then Charles Evans Hughes, reiterated Phillips' views. Hughes felt that any bad experience suffered by black Americans in Haiti would not alter their negative opinion of the occupation. He did believe, however, that it would make Haitian-American relations more difficult, as Haitian prejudices were not being respected.[56] In an earlier memorandum, the State Department's Division of Latin American Affairs opined that a black commissioner to Haiti who did not return with a favorable impression of the occupation would "defeat one of the principal objects of sending him—that is, to obtain the support of negro public opinion."[57]

Washington officials never succeeded in winning over black Americans to a pro-occupation position. The government's cavalier attitude toward participation by blacks simply underscored the racism that lay at the base of its Haitian policies in general. President Harding's administration civilianized the occupation, ended the more flagrant abuses of power, and reduced the prominence of the military in Haiti. However, the colonial features of the "Haitian protectorate" persisted, as did the objections of black Americans.

Black critics of America's Haitian policy included Lemuel Livingston, a career consul and a former schoolmate of James Weldon Johnson. In 1921 Livingston confessed that in his 32 years as consul in Cap Haitien, he had failed to persuade the Haitians to make political reforms. When the Marines landed, he depicted them as benefactors. Now Livingston believed he had been mistaken. He deplored treaty officials' lack of statesmanship, and noted that they often worked without instructions from Washington. Haiti had been treated like a conquered nation, he observed.[58] Other protesters spoke with greater feeling than experience. Lillian Bermudez of Brooklyn, whose merchant seaman son had witnessed American brutality while in Haitian ports, protested bitterly to the Secretary of State. Her letter linked the troubles in Haiti to American racism and imperialism in the Caribbean.[59]

Church groups were particularly vocal in their concern about Haitian conditions. In July 1924, the National Sunday School and Baptist Youth Progressive Union Congress, the foremost black Baptist youth group, wrote to President Coolidge to request an end to military rule in Haiti and the restoration of its civil government. The Harlem Refuge Church of Christ called attention to the suppression of civil liberties in Haiti in a 1925 letter to Coolidge. The letter demanded release of political prisoners, restoration of the constitution, and withdrawal of American troops.[60]

Black political groups protested the occupation. The 1924 National Colored Republican Conference meeting at Atlantic City voted nine resolutions against the occupation.[61] American policy also drew fire from the left. The pro-Communist American Negro Labor Conference prominently featured Haiti at its 1925 meeting. A. Phillip Randolph's socialist *Messenger* represented much of the radical thought on the question, "Santo Domingo and Haiti are the Ireland of America," it declared. It claimed that an imperialist drive for raw materials prompted the United States' desire to control Latin America.[62]

These examples indicate the variety of black persons and groups which addressed the Haitian issue and the nature of their objections to American policy. Protesters included both prominent and obscure men and women. The interest of church groups and religious organizations is especially significant, because clergymen and lay representatives did not often take a strong stand on foreign policy matters.

Agitation by blacks did not stop at registering protest. Efforts were made to lend material support to the Haitians. One such effort culminated in the Overseas Navigation and Overseas Trading Company, designed to ship goods between Haiti and American ports. Sponsored by the prominent West Virginia banker Charles E. Mitchell, the company planned to make all of its transactions through black American banks, which would assist in underwriting its ventures.[63] Strictly charitable activities also played a part. Harriet Gibbs Marshall, the wife of the black legation clerk, worked on a clothing drive for needy Haitian children, She, Addie Hunton, and other black clubwomen established a women's social service organization, L'Oeuvre des Femmes Haitiennes pour l'Organisation du Travail, in Haiti. Mary McLeod Bethune served on its advisory committee, and its Haitian membership included the wives of distinguished Haitian scholars and statesmen.[64]

This international cooperation was affected by the influx of West Indian immigrants to the Eastern United States during the 1920s. Between 1910 and 1920, Caribbean newcomers arrived at the rate of five thousand a year. Race-proud, independent, and ambitious, many of the immigrants joined UNIA,[65] which kept abreast of events in Haiti. The *Negro World*, its official organ, reported frequently on Haiti. Timothy Thomas Fortune, who had thought little of the black republic at the turn of the century, now championed its cause on its editorial page. Fortune reiterated Garvey's sentiment that the occupation was a "farce and a lie."[66]

A small Haitian community emerged among the West Indians. By 1930, 500 Haitians lived in New York City. Most were students and skilled workers who had more freedom of political expression in New York than in Port-au-Prince.[67] Some agitated tirelessly for Haitian independence. These included Joseph Mirault, New York correspondent for the Patriotic Union's *Le Courier Haïtien*, who supported his desk through work as a Pullman porter; Jean-Joseph Adam, a prominent Garveyite and frequent columnist for the *Negro World*; and Theodora Holly, daughter of the famous emigrationist, who came to the United States at the invitation of Booker T. Washington's widow. For a brief period in 1925, Holly edited the French page of the *Negro World*.[68] These Haitians contributed to the growth of black American consciousness of the Haitian issue. As nationalists promoting a nationalist cause, they fired the imagination of those who saw Haiti as part of a larger African world which must be redeemed from white control.

The Haitian community in the United States worked with other blacks to publicize and attack the American policy. It staged a hostile demonstration when Haitian president Louis Borno in 1925 visited the United States. It organized an informational trip to Haiti for a black Republican clubwoman. It produced theatricals to make the Afro-American community more aware of Haitian culture and Haiti's current problems.[69] The connection between the Haitian situation and the plight of all blacks was delineated by Bishop John R. Hurst, an American-educated Haitian who led the Protestant Episcopal Church in Port-au-Prince. In a statement in *The Crisis*, Hurst wrote that the Haitian problem "is but the Negro question in a new form." The efforts of Haitians "to assist in the rehabilitation of the Negro race," a task assigned them by Providence, had been "violently arrested." The American intervention was thus an attack on the progress of all blacks.[70]

The pages of *The Crisis* and the facilities of the NAACP were readily available to defenders of Haitian independence. While visiting the United States, Haitian nationalist Sténio Vincent regularly used the NAACP offices as a headquarters for the Patriotic Union.[71] By the late 1920s, however, the NAACP had ceased assuming vigorous leadership in the Haitian controversy. Its growth in membership and revenues had slowed appreciably in 1927, and it lacked the resources to energetically continue the struggle.[72] The Haitian occupation had become a long-term affair: the federal government eliminated some of its most noxious features in order to preserve political and economic domination more securely. An entrenched bureaucracy controlled the island republic, and if it was less impetuous than the Marines had been, it was no less stubborn. A campaign of organized opposition to the occupation in mid-decade necessitated a sustained effort.

Despite limited resources, the NAACP employed *The Crisis* to keep the issue before its readers. *The Crisis* followed Haitian news, published Haitian poetry, and reviewed books about the black republic.[73] Other groups continued to lobby for the restoration of Haitian sovereignty. In 1927 the Empire State Federation of Colored Women's Clubs declared to Washington: "The Negroes of the United States are keenly interested in the actions of the American government in Haiti, and hope those actions will be such that we can support them with our approval and votes."[74]

Black churches and the press continued to rally around the Haitian cause. The Abyssinian Baptist Church in Harlem, one of the strongest institutions in the New York community, directed a mass petition drive against the occupation early in April 1929. At the same time, the editor of the *American and West Indian News* a Harlem-based periodical, wrote an open letter to President Hoover condemning the length of the continued American presence in Haiti.[75]

Napoleon Marshall, the black legation clerk, served at his post from 1922 to 1928. He formally declared his opposition to the occupation in 1929. In a *New York World* article of February 10, 1929, Marshall blasted the treaty government, denouncing its badly conceived and poorly executed reforms, and its rude, aggressive functionaries.[76] Wanting to make the occupation once again a campaign issue, he arranged contacts between Haitian dissidents and persons close to philanthropist Julius Rosenwald who, as the Haitian newspaper *Le Nouvelliste* pointed out, had been a significant contributor to Hoover's successful presidential campaign.[77]

Opposition by blacks to the occupation remained consistent. Haiti was not always front page news, but it continued to create negative comment among blacks. Washington policymakers, however, placed Haiti on the back burner after 1922. The government kept a low profile on matters concerning Haiti, responded courteously to letters of petition and protest, created a largely ceremonial post for a black American, and—went on with business as usual.

The occupation might have continued in this manner but for an outbreak of violence in 1929. By the end of the 1920s, Haiti's problems included burdensome taxes, student dissatisfaction with the American operated agricultural schools, the unpopularity of President Borno, falling coffee prices, the restriction of immigration to Cuba, and unrest among the employees of the customs service.[78] The detonation of this potentially explosive situation came in the town of Aux Cayes on December 6 when a group of 1,500 peasants entered the city intent on presenting their grievances to local authorities. They encountered a Marine patrol of twenty men who were unnerved by the large size of the crowd confronting them. The Marines shot seventy-five people, killing at least twenty-five.[79] Despite officials' efforts at suppression, the news reached the United States, and banner headlines about Haiti reappeared. That violence provoked an atmosphere of crisis which gave anti-occupation groups the momentum they needed to launch yet another assault on American control of the black republic.

Respondents to the crisis included the Communist Party of the United States, which sent press releases on the Aux Cayes incident to black newspapers throughout the country. Among less radical protesters, the Foreign Policy Association and the NAACP held lectures and public debates on Haiti. Disapproval of the occupation even extended to the Urban League, which traditionally took little interest in foreign policy matters. Its organ, *Opportunity*, had mildly disapproved of governmental actions in Haiti in the past. As a result of the latest crisis, its objections intensified, and the journal decided that Aux Cayes was "no trivial matter." *Opportunity* endorsed the Foreign Policy Association's recommendation that a black be placed on a new commission of investigation. President Hoover, it argued, must come to realize that "ruthless militarism in Haiti" would contradict his Good Neighbor Policy of reconciliation.[80] Though quiescent for years, the problem of the occupation still festered. "Like Banquo's ghost, the Haitian question will not down," the *Amsterdam News* commented. "Though buried under volumes of official reports of American benefits to Haiti—order established, roads built, public works undertaken, great loans secured from Wall Street, and other deodorizers—the rottenness of the American occupation of Haiti still sends forth its stench."[81]

On December 6, President Hoover designated yet another commission of inquiry. The question of the propriety of selecting a black commissioner again arose. This time, the Haitian chargé d'affaires in Washington, acting on Borno's orders, specifically requested that a black American be named to the proposed body. Borno realized that denying membership to a black American would allow his opponents to call the selection process undemocratic.[82]

Hoover appointed a five-man, all-white commission headed by Cameron Forbes, a former New Jersey governor. He selected a separate group of blacks to study the progress of education in Haiti. Robert Russa Moton led this group. Moton was accompanied by the presidents of Howard University and Georgia State Industrial College; by W. T. B. Williams; and by two journalists, Carl Murphy of the *Afro-American*, and T. F. Prattis of the Associated Negro Press.[83]

This investment of responsibility in Moton did not satisfy everyone. *The Crisis* opposed Moton's acceptance of what it considered a "subordinative appointment." Moton was not charged with a comprehensive review of policy; he could report solely on the progress of education. As the treaty administration directly controlled only the agricultural schools, Moton's criticisms would be levied against the Haitian government, and not against white American administrators.[84]

The commission's report reflected changes that had taken place in pedagogy employed by blacks as well as in the view blacks held of the occupation. The report contested the separation of agricultural and industrial education from the rest of the country's school system, and reproved the Haitian government for its long-term failure to provide mass education.[85]

Whatever the merits of Moton's findings, *The Crisis* accurately assessed his status in Haiti as second-class. He and his colleagues received separate and unequal treatment when their work was completed. The Forbes commission had been allotted $50,000 to conduct its research; the manner of its travel and lodging in Haiti fitted its dignity and high purpose. The Moton group, however, was temporarily stranded in Port-Au-Prince because United States Navy ships refused to accommodate black passengers, even when they were official agents of the federal government.[86]

After Aux Cayes, the Hoover administration decided to gradually withdraw from Haiti as part of a general review of United States Latin American policy. During an economically depressed era, expensive military interventions were burdensome.[87] The new Good Neighbor policy of rapprochement with Latin states cleared the path to presidential succession in 1930 of Haitian nationalist Sténio Vincent. Vincent had worked closely in the 1920s with the NAACP and other pro-independence support groups in the United States.

The effect of Afro-American public opinion on United States foreign policy in Haiti had been pervasive and complex. The Wilson administration ignored demands of blacks for participation in the treaty regime. Harding, who used the occupation issue to campaign successfully among blacks, yielded to their pressure to initiate an investigation and send a black specialist to Haiti. Calvin Coolidge was the least responsive to dissident voices. Yet, during the mid-1920s, opposition to American control had become so well established that the State Department felt compelled to minimize its visibility in the island republic. The Hoover administration acquiesced to a demand for another black commission, but handled it in a manner similar to that employed by Harding. State Department officials, upset by the Haitian uprising of 1929, were highly sensitive to criticism and attempted elaborate and futile defenses of the occupation.[88]

In the course of the 1915-1934 intervention era, opinion among black Americans remained disapproving, but underwent some change. Increasing numbers of blacks abandoned the notion of participation in the regime as they came to see it as undemocratic, racist, and unproductive. They foreswore the belief that Haitians could profit from accommodationism, as they likewise rejected this formula for themselves.

Militancy among blacks in the 1920s underlined the Afro-American response to the Haitian question. The somewhat chastened atmosphere of the depressed 1930s did not, however, neutralize the opposition of blacks to prevailing policies. In 1931 *The Crisis* opined that the following campaign year would determine Haiti's fate.

"Franklin Roosevelt and Herbert Hoover must answer to Black America and answer with great frankness if they expect Negro votes," the journal asserted.[89] Ultimately, the effect of the election on the Haitian issue was negligible, for Roosevelt continued the program of retrenchment and nonconfrontation in Latin America begun by his predecessor.[90]

The United States returned sovereignty to Haiti in 1934, two years before its treaty with that country expired. The political pressure that blacks generated in the early 1920s led the American government to rule Haiti with more circumspection. Protest and agitation by blacks were instrumental in bringing Washington to a realization that its Haitian policies had failed. Economic depression did the rest. Haitian president Sténio Vincent acknowledged the significance of the black American contribution in a letter of *The Crisis*. Vincent expressed

> my personal gratitude, that of the Government and of the People of Haiti, to all those American friends, colored or white, who, so willingly and so courageously have taken part, on our side, in the long and hard struggle of which the day of last August 21st marked the crowning victory, and who, by their prayers, by their efforts, and by their great publicity campaign have in such a large measure contributed to the freedom of my country.[91]

Vincent's tribute underscored black Americans' ready identification of racial injustice when it occurred as a concomitant of foreign policy. Their opposition to the occupation reflected an understanding of the similarities between their own condition and that of the Haitians, as it attested to their growing political maturity in the interwar years.

Notes

[1] Hans Schmidt, *The United States Occupation of Haiti, 1915-1934* (New Jersey, 1971); David Healey, *Gunboat Diplomacy in the Wilson Era: The United States Navy in Haiti, 1915-1916* (Madison, 1976); John W. Blassingame, "The Press and American Intervention in Haiti and the Dominican Republic, 1904-1920," *Caribbean Studies* 9 (July 1969): 27-43.

[2] Booker T. Washington, "Haiti and the United States," *Outlook* 111 (November 17, 1915): 681; Washington to John S. Durham, April 10, 1905; Richard W. Thompson to Emmett Jay Scott, December 2, 1905, both in Louis Harlan and Raymond W. Smock, eds., *The Booker T. Washington Papers*, vol. 8 (Urbana, 1979).

[3] Among the cognoscenti one may include the nineteenth century emigrationists James Theodore Holly and Dennis Harris, whose pro-Haitian writings have been collected by Howard H. Bell, ed., *Black Separatism and the Caribbean, 1860* (Ann Arbor, 1970); Frederick Douglass, *Life and Times of Frederick Douglass, 1892* ed. (New York, 1962), pp. 599-620; and Reverend T. G. Steward, "Life in a Negro Republic," *Independent* 56 (March 3, 1904): 477-79.

[4] E. L. Blackshear to the Secretary of State, May 13, 1912, Records of the Department of State Relating to the Internal Affairs of Haiti, 1910-1929 (hereinafter referred to as the Decimal File), 838.404.

⁵ Holly's beliefs are elaborated in James Theodore Holly, *A Vindication of the Capacity of the Negro Race for Self-Government and Civilized Progress*, in Bell, op. cit.

⁶ T. Thomas Fortune, "Haytian Revolution," *Voice of Negro* 1 (April 1904): 138-42.

⁷ Strong criticism of Haiti was reflected in such *Voice* articles as Fortune's "Haytian Revolutions," cited above; John S. Durham, "The Hidden Wealth of Haiti," vol. 1 (April 1904): 142-46. See also Arthur Schomburg, "Is Hayti Decadent?" *Unique Advertiser* (August 1904): 8-11.

⁸ *New York Age*, August 5, 1915.

⁹ George M. Fredrickson, *The Black Image in the White Mind: The Debate on Afro-American Character and Destiny, 1817-1914* (New York, 1971), pp. 54, 69, 259.

¹⁰ Washington, "Haiti and the United States," p. 681.

¹¹ For a general discussion of the impact of Comtian positivism and a racist international milieu on the Haitian intelligentsia, see Patrick Bellegarde-Smith, "Haitian Social Thought in the Nineteenth Century: Class Formation and Westernization," *Caribbean Studies* 20 (March 1980): 5-33.

¹² Elihu Root to Edward Everett Hale, November 9, 1908, Elihu Root Papers, Library of Congress, Washington, D.C. Woodrow Wilson let it be known that he would make no appointments of blacks in the face of white opposition, *New York Age*, April 17, 1913. 1:1. See also James A. Padgett, "Diplomats to Haiti and Their Diplomacy," *Journal of Negro History* 25 (July 1940): 265-330.

¹³ Bryan to Wilson, Woodrow Wilson Papers, Library of Congress, Washington, D.C.

¹⁴ On the Furniss dismissal and criticism by blacks of Wilson's appointment policy, see William Monroe Trotter to Josephus Daniels, August 22, 1913, Josephus Daniels Papers, Library of Congress.

¹⁵ Powell to Wilson, August 25, 1913, in Arthur Link, ed., *The Papers of Woodrow Wilson*, vol. 28 (Princeton, 1966-), pp. 221-23. For segregation in federal employment during the Wilson years, and the decimation in the black ranks of the civil service, Kathleen L. Wolgemuth, "Woodrow Wilson's Appointment Policy and the Negro," *Journal of Southern History* 24 (November 1958): 457-71, and her "Woodrow Wilson and Federal Segregation," *Journal of Negro History* 44 (April 1959): 158-73.

¹⁶ Admiral H. S. Knapp to the Secretary of the Navy, October 2, 1920, Decimal File, 838.00/1704; Schmidt, p. 103, 103n; Brenda Gayle Plummer, "Black and White in the Caribbean: Haitian-American Relations, 1902-1934," (Ph.D. dissertation, Cornell University, 1981), pp. 465-71.

¹⁷ Schmidt, op. cit., pp. 100-07, 130-33; Plummer, op. cit., pp. 647-49.

¹⁸ Burke E. Davis, *Marine! The Life of Lt. Gen. Lewis B. (Chesty) Puller, USMC, (Ret.)* (Boston, 1962), pp. 41, 45. The corvée was abolished in 1918, but continued illegally in some areas until the end of 1919.

¹⁹ Georges Sylvain to James Weldon Johnson, November 26, 1920, James Weldon Johnson Collection, Yale University, New Haven, Connecticut; J. Price-Mars to Walter White, March 28, 1934, Papers of the National Association for the Advancement of Colored People, Library of Congress, Washington, D. C.

²⁰ John B. Russell, "A Marine Looks Back on Haiti," typescript in the United States Marine Corps Historical Museum, Personal Papers Collection, Washington, D. C.

²¹ Robert Lansing to J. H. Oliver, January 30, 1918, quoted in Rayford W. Logan, *Haiti and the Dominican Republic* (New York, 1968), p. 126.

²² H. M. to William Phillips, October 31, 1918, Decimal File, 838.00/1547.

²³ Littleton D. Waller to John A. Lejeune, September 5, 1915; October 13, 1915; and June 11, 1916, John A. Lejeune Papers, Library of Congress, Washington, D. C. Smedley D. Butler to Col. Waller, July 13, 1916; to Butler Wright, October 13, 1916; to

Thomas S. Butler, July 5, 1916, Smedley Darlington Butler Papers, United States Marine Corps Historical Museum, Personal Papers Collection.

[24] See Fredrickson, *op. cit.*, for a study of the racial attitudes of the era. Also, Paul Murphy, "Sources and Nature of Intolerance in the 1920's," *Journal of American History* 51 (June 1964): 60-76.

[25] S. E. Churchstone Lord to the Secretary of State, October 28, 1915, Decimal File, 838.42/3.

[26] L. Ton Evans' testimony in United States Senate Inquiry into the Occupation and Administration of Haiti and Santo Domingo, *Hearings Before a Select Committee on Haiti and Santo Domingo*, 3 vols., 67th Congress, 1st and 2nd sess. (Washington, D. C., 1922).

[27] A. M. Moore to L. Ton Evans, August 2, 1918, Decimal File, 838.00/1552; Emmett Scott to Bainbridge Colby, April 22, 1920, Decimal File, 838.00/1629.

[28] *The Crisis* 10 (September 1915): 232; ibid. 11 (November 1915): 30-32.

[29] Eugene Levy, *James Weldon Johnson Black Leader, Black Voice* (Chicago, 1973), pp. 202-04.

[30] Of the abundant literature concerning racial friction and exploitation during this period, some representative examples are Murphy, "Sources of Intolerance"; Elliott M. Rudwick, *Race Riot at East St. Louis, July 2, 1917* (Carbondale, Ill., 1964); Kenneth T. Jackson, *The Ku Klux Klan in the City, 1915-1930* (New York, 1967); Pete Daniel, *The Shadow of Slavery: Peonage in the South, 1901-1969* (Urbana 1972); NAACP, *Thirty Years of Lynching in the United States, 1889-1918* (New York: 1919, rep. New York, 1969).

[31] Levy, op. cit., pp. 202-04.

[32] James Weldon Johnson, *Along This Way* (New York, 1933), pp. 344-53; Rayford W. Logan, "James Weldon Johnson and Haiti," *Phylon* 32 (Winter 1971), pp. 396-402.

[33] Johnson, op. cit., pp. 347-48.

[34] Notebook 1, Haiti, Johnson Collection; Johnson, p. 349.

[35] Special Report of the (NAACP) Field Secretary on His Visit to Haiti, Johnson Collection.

[36] James Weldon Johnson, "Self-Determining Haiti," *Nation* 111, 4 parts, (August 28-September 25, 1920).

[37] This correspondence is in the files of the NAACP Papers, Library of Congress.

[38] The Assistant Secretary to Marcus Garvey, September 22, 1920, NAACP Papers.

[39] National Popular Government League to the Secretary of State, April 27, 1922, Decimal File, 838.00/1867; William B. Hixson, Jr., *Moorfield Storey and the Abolitionist Tradition* (New York, 1972), p. 73; *The Crisis* 22 (October 1921): 273.

[40] Hixson, op. cit., 272; Medill McCormick to Charles Evans Hughes, October 6, 1922, Decimal File, 838.00/1911. Noted white personalities in the anti-occupation groups included publisher Lewis S. Gannett, Felix Adler of the Ethical Cultural Movement; clergyman Henry Sloane Coffin; Ernest Gruening, editor of the *Nation*; and prominent NAACP members Mary White Ovington, Arthur B. Spingarn and Oswald Garrison Villard.

[41] Robert B. Asprey, *Once a Marine: The Memoirs of General A. A. Vandegrift* (New York, 1964), p. 57; General Lejeune, Report of the Military Situation in Haiti, October 4, 1920, and Lejeune to the Secretary of the Navy, September 8, 1920, both in the Josephus Daniels Papers.

[42] E. David Cronon, ed., *The Cabinet Diaries of Josephus Daniels* (Lincoln, Nebraska, 1963), pp. 553, 590, 591, 546.

[43] Hixson, op. cit., p. 73.

[44] R. R. Moton to Henry P. Fletcher, October 7, 1921, Decimal File, 838.00P81/10.

[45] See the correspondence in series I, folder 543 of the Johnson Collection.

[46] Ibid., Moton to S. G. Inman, October 6, 1921, Decimal File, 838.00P81/10.

47 Richard B. Sherman, "The Harding Administration and the Negro: An Opportunity Lost," *Journal of Negro History* 49 (October 1964): 156.

48 Decimal File, 838.4237/11to, n. d.

49 Senate, *Inquiry*, Schmidt, p. 123.

50 J. Finley Wilson to President Harding, February 9, 1922, and Robert Woods Bliss to Wilson, March 1, 1922. Records of the Department of State Relating to Political Relations Between United States and Haiti, 1910-1929, 711.88/157.

51 For information about this emigration, see Floyd W. Miller, *The Search for a Black Nationality* (Urbana, 1975), pp. 232-49.

52 The American-Haitian Benevolent Club to Charles Evans Hughes, January 25, 1922, Decimal File, 838.00/1826.

53 Marshall was barred from the segregated American Club, patronized by military brass and civilian treaty officials. Personal MSS, Napoleon Marshall File, Howard University Moorland-Spingarn Research Center, Manuscript Division, Washington Conservatory of Music Papers.

54 William Phillips to Medill McCormick, July 13, 1923, Decimal File, 838.00/1950.

55 Ibid.

56 Ibid., Charles Evans Hughes to McCormick, February 6, 1924.

57 Dana Munro's memorandum, January 14, 1924, Decimal File, 838.00/2007.

58 Lemuel Livingston to the President of the United States, May 18, 1921, Decimal File, 838.00/1775. Biographical information on Livingston from the State Department Biographic Register, and Roger Gaillard, *Les Cent-Jours de Rosalvo Bobo, ou une mise à mort politique* (Port-au-Prince: Presses Nationales, 1973), p. 18, n. 12.

59 Lillian Bermudez to Charles Evans Hughes, February 14, 1922, Decimal File, 838.00P81/13.

60 National Sunday School and B. Y. P. U. Congress of America to Calvin Coolidge, July 2, 1924, Decimal File, 838.00/2030; R. C. Lawson to Calvin Coolidge, December 14, 1925, Decimal File, 838.00/2178.

61 *New York Times*, July 5, 1924, 13:1.

62 Harry Curran Wilbur to Edwin T. Clark, April 30, 1926, Decimal File, 838.00/2243; *Messenger* 3 (August 1921): 226.

63 *The Crisis* 25 (December 1922): 77.

64 Harriet Gibbs Marshall to Hughes, March 22, 1924, Decimal File 838.40/orig.; Addie Hunton to Mrs. Marshall, June 19, 1926, Washington Conservatory of Music Papers, Save Haiti League membership files. This women's group also established an industrial school in Port-au-Prince sustained by charitable activity in that city and in New York. *Amsterdam News*, February 15, 1928, 8:5.

65 "The Rise of the West Indian," *The Crisis* 20 (September 1920): 214-15.

66 Fortune wrote the editorial page of the *Negro World* from 1922 to his death in 1928. See obituary, June 9, 1928, p. 4.

67 Joseph Nivarel to the President of the United States, July 1, 1921, Decimal File, 838.00P81/8. Ira DeA. Reid, *The Negro Immigrant, His Background, Characteristics and Social Adjustment, 1898-1937* (New York, Columbia University Faculty of Political Science, Studies in History, Economics and Public Law, no. 449, AMS Press, 1939).

68 *Negro World*, April 28, 1923, p. 1; July 7, 1923, p. 8; February 7, 1925, p. 7.

69 *Amsterdam News*, June 16, 1925, p. 1, 3; February 15, 1928, p. 8; September 1920, p. 8; July 21, 1925, p. 1.

70 *The Crisis* 20 (May 1920): 34.

71 Walter White, *A Man Called White: The Autobiography of Walter White* (New York, 1948), p. 116.

72 James Weldon Johnson to C. Austin Burrows, December 8, 1927, NAACP Papers.

[73] *The Crisis* 35 (July 1928): 230-31; (August 1928): 267; vol. 37 (January 1930): 18, 32.

[74] Layle Lane to the Secretary of State, December 17, 1927, Decimal File, 838.00/2424.

[75] *The American and West Indian News*, April 13, 1929; A. Merral Willis to Herbert Hoover, April 12, 1929, Decimal File, 838.00/2513.

[76] *New York World*, February 10, 1929; John B. Russell, "General Conditions in Haiti," April 17, 1929; Dana Munro to Francis White, April 19, 1929, both Decimal File, 838.00/2523.

[77] *Le Nouvelliste*, in Russell to the Secretary of State, note enclosed with Russell's dispatch of March 5, 1929, Decimal File, 838.00/General Conditions/15.

[78] Schmidt, op. cit., pp. 196-200; Plummer, op. cit., pp. 669-71.

[79] Schmidt, pp. 199-200; Plummer, p. 670.

[80] *Opportunity* 8 (January 1930): 7.

[81] *Amsterdam News*, December 11, 1929, p. 30.

[82] Stimson to Russell, November 11, 1929, Decimal File, 838.00/2604; Russell to the Secretary of State, December 30, 1929, 838.00/Commission of Investigation, Personnel, *Amsterdam News*, December 11, 1929, p. 1: December 13, 1929, p. 1ff; February 12, 1930, p. 1; March 5, 1930, p. 3.

[83] Journal of Cameron Forbes, vol. III, W. Cameron Forbes Papers, Library of Congress, Washington, D. C.: *Amsterdam News*, December 11, 1929, p. 1; December 18 p. 1ff; February 12, 1930, p. 1; March 5, 1930, p. 3.

[84] *The Crisis* 37 (April 1930): 137.

[85] Raymond Wolters has described the changes in educational attitudes among blacks in *The New Negro on Campus: Black College Rebellions of the 1920s* (Princeton, 1975). See also Kenneth James King, *PanAfricanism and Education: A Study of Race, Philanthropy and Education in the Southern States of America and East Africa* (Oxford, 1971). For Moton's activities, see the *Amsterdam News*, December 11, 1929 p. 1ff; February 12, 1929, p. 1; March 5, 1930, p. 3; Francis Whiite to the Secretary of State, February 19, 1931. Francis White Papers, National Archieves, Washington, D. C.

[86] Schmidt, op. cit., p. 185.

[87] Bryce Wood, *The Making of the Good Neighbor Policy* (New York, 1967), pp. 123-25.

[88] Donald B. Cooper, "The Withdrawal of the United States from Haiti, 1928-1934," *Journal of Inter-American Studies* 5 (January 1963): 84-5.

[89] *The Crisis* 38 (November 1931): 372.

[90] Sumner Welles, *The Time for Decision* (New York, 1944), pp. 185-241.

[91] Sténio Vincent to Roy Wilkins, September 16, 1934, in *The Crisis* 41 (October 1934): 292.

The Black Press and the Drive for Integrated Graduate and Professional Schools

BILL WEAVER AND OSCAR C. PAGE

Even as the numbers of African Americans seeking a graduate education steadily increased in the 1930s, white Southerners clung to the Plessey v. Ferguson *"separate but equal" doctrine. To maintain segregation, Southern states resorted to a variety of schemes, including paying the out-of-state tuition fees for black graduate students to attend Northern schools. While information detailing the NAACP's legal challenges to integrate American education is generally known, historians have largely neglected the role of the black press in presenting the legal struggle to its readership. Apart from reporting the facts, collectively the black press did yeomen's work, researching the pertinent legal issues, evaluating the lawyers' strategies, and interpreting the judicial outcomes. In the final analysis, the black press, through its insightful and informed reporting, deserves credit for preparing the African American community for the hard-fought legal challenges ahead.*

Authors Bill Weaver and Oscar Page chronicle two important interrelated histories: the history of the NAACP's legal battle to integrate graduate and professional schools, and the role of the black press as an important source of informed community consciousness during the desegregation struggle. Combined, these histories document the degree of racial unity and African American organizational skills brought to bear on the jim crow educational system in the South.

IN 1954 THE UNITED STATES SUPREME COURT in *Brown v. Board of Education* handed down the latest in a long sequence of achievements leading to an end to legally sanctioned second-class education for blacks in this country. Between the mid-1930s and 1954, several court cases having a direct bearing on the struggle to end segregated education were decided. The purpose of this study is to analyze the reaction in the black press to the breakthroughs accomplished in these cases.[1]

In the 1930s the National Association for the Advancement of Colored People chose a legal staff and identified target areas for legal attacks on segregation. One of the areas selected was graduate and professional education, chosen because no state institution for blacks provided such training. It was thought that the courts therefore could breach the walls of segregation without ruling on the validity of the separate-but-equal concept.[2]

In the mid-thirties several states enacted provisions whereby scholarship aid (usually equivalent to the out-of-state portion of one's tuition) was offered to blacks who agreed to attend a graduate or professional institution in another state. The requirement of being exported to another state for training, however, appealed to few blacks desiring advanced education. The first case to challenge this policy was that of Donald Murray, a resident of Maryland, who was denied admission to the University of Maryland Law School solely on the basis of race. The decision handed down from the Maryland Court of Appeals answered two critical questions. The court determined that an offer of out-of-state tuition did not compensate for the requirement that one leave the state to obtain advanced degrees and that it was inadequate for the state to maintain a separate law school for blacks. The University of Maryland therefore was ordered to admit Murray to its Law School.

Shortly after the *Murray* decision was announced, a suit was filed in Missouri in the hope of invalidating the out-of-state scholarship there. The NAACP legal staff publicized the *Murray* decision and informed branch offices of its desire to challenge the out-of-state scholarship in other states. The St. Louis branch of the NAACP expressed an interest in seeing the matter tested in Missouri,[3] and, apparently, several students volunteered. Lloyd Lionel Gaines, a black St. Louis youth and a graduate of Lincoln University in Jefferson City, Missouri, was selected, and he applied in 1936 for admission to the University of Missouri Law School. Two significant factors worked in favor of Gaines' selection: (1) he was an honor graduate of Lincoln University, and (2) he was a product of a Missouri segregated school. For the state to claim that this honor graduate was inadequately prepared for admission to the University of Missouri would have been an indictment of the segregated school system that the state was attempting to defend.[4]

In March, 1936, the University of Missouri denied Gaines' request for admission. The NAACP immediately petitioned the state court to require his admission on the grounds that only through admission to the Law School at the University of Missouri could the University be in compliance with the Fourteenth Amendment. Attorneys for the University, on the other hand, argued that the University had no choice but to obey the state law requiring separation of the races, and added that, as a state institution, Lincoln University had been empowered to open new schools (graduate and professional) as the need arose.

The state court upheld the denial of admission, and the NAACP appealed the case to the Missouri Supreme Court. Before this Court, Gaines' counsel argued that Lincoln University's authority to establish schools when sufficient need arose was inapplicable, for Gaines' rights were individual rights and thus the exercise of them must not depend upon securing enough interested students to justify creation of a separate law school. Furthermore, his attorney charged, irreparable damage would be done to other qualified blacks because of the delay in their legal training while they awaited the establishment of a law school at Lincoln University. The arguments of the plaintiff notwithstanding, the Missouri Supreme Court sustained the decision of the lower court.

The NAACP immediately petitioned the United States Supreme Court to hear the case. The Court agreed, heard arguments, and on December 12, 1938, rendered a 5 to 2 verdict in favor of Gaines.[5] The nation's highest tribunal remanded the case to the Missouri Supreme Court with the requirement that Gaines be admitted to the University of Missouri Law School, in the absence of other means that would provide him equal treatment within the State. Thus, the Supreme Court of Missouri, which previously had rendered a decision against Gaines, was permitted to determine what constituted an equal opportunity for a legal education and what means could be used to provide that opportunity.

The immediate reaction of the black press to the Supreme Court's decision was one of moderate elation. New York's *Amsterdam News* called the ruling comparable to the Bill of Rights and the Emancipation Proclamation; the Pittsburgh *Courier* called it "the greatest decision in the court since the grandfather clause was declared unconstitutional," adding that "the vast robbery of Negro youth through discriminatory schooling nears its end"; and the Indianapolis *Recorder* viewed the decision as setting the stage for the "funeral march of hatred."[6]

Most of the black press viewed the decision as merely opening the door for a lot of hard, tedious work in an effort to realize equal opportunity. The Cleveland *Gazette* saw the decision as a "body-blow to the South's jim crow laws," and predicted that little by little the South would be forced to recognize that "our people have some rights that even they must respect."[7] Cautioning blacks against unfounded optimism, the Chicago *Defender* characterized the Supreme Court decision as "one of limited character and effect," which had not abolished the jim crow system in Missouri, and which, in effect, had reaffirmed the doctrine established in the *Plessy* decision.[8] Charging that the *Gaines* decision did not mean any fundamental change in the educational system for black Americans and recognizing the limitations of the decision and the distance yet to be covered, the *Defender* dourly predicted that:

> there is no hope for the black man until through death, resignation and political pressure justices are appointed to the Supreme Court who will directly overrule the Jim Crow theory adhered to by the Court and interpret the 14th and 15th Amendments to the Constitution in a manner which will accomplish the intentions of the Congress and of the people at the time of their passage.

Despite the absence of apparent success in the *Gaines* decision, the NAACP's Roy Wilkins, optimistically predicted that "the inequitable distribution of federal funds for education, the pitiable elementary schools, the lack of high schools, and the wide variation in salaries for teachers can now be brought into court with brighter chances of victory."[9] The *Courier* expressed the belief that the decision would put states that maintained separate school systems on the defensive; and Charles Houston, one of the NAACP attorneys, saw the decision as having a wider implication which would accord blacks equal facilities in hospitals, playgrounds, parks, and in every type of public institutions where the policy of a state insists upon separation of the races.[10] The *Amsterdam News* prophetically interpreted the decision as only a beginning and added that "Negro leaders all over the country are girding themselves for a smashing attack upon the citadels of prejudice and discrimination in the Southern States. . . ."[11] All in all, the *Courier* most accurately captured the sentiment of the black press in general when it termed the decision "a practical though not idealistic victory."[12]

The black press applauded the Supreme Court's decision to put constitutional rights on an individual basis whereby enjoyment of them was not dependent upon volume of demand. The *Courier* elaborated upon this point by asserting that the *Gaines* decision had:

> established beyond doubt that tax-supported educational systems cannot get around doing their duty by pleading paucity of Negro students, by advancing the argument of the exorbitant expense of identical biracial systems, nor by inviting Negro applicants to go outside the South for advanced courses.[13]

The black community may have derived some hope regarding future cases before the Supreme Court because of the apparent reversal of racial attitudes demonstrated by Justice Hugo Black. Though a southerner and former Ku Klux Klan member whose confirmation the NAACP had bitterly opposed, Black had voted with the majority in the case. *The Crisis*, noting its previous opposition to Black's confirmation, complimented the southern jurist for "sticking to the clear meaning of the Constitution."[14]

Optimism in the black press also derived from confidence in the talent and clever legal action of the NAACP legal staff. The *Courier*, speaking of the legal success, observed that "discrimination can be successfully attacked if our case is well prepared and vigorously and persistently prosecuted."[15] Walter White, Executive Secretary of the NAACP, noted the special burden on NAACP attorneys to produce a flawless case, for, in his words, "there were many cases where a misplaced comma or a not altogether perfect preparation in the handling of the case in the courts below had permitted the court to throw cases out because of minor defects."[16]

To leave no hero unheralded, the *Amsterdam News* reminded its readers that "too much credit cannot be given to young Gaines for his courage to stick to his guns. . . ."[17] Similarly, at a banquet in St. Louis shortly after the decision, attorneys associated with the case pointed out that Gaines had lost three good years during which he could have completed his law course elsewhere. "He has sacrificed for all the people," said one of the attorneys, "and his sacrifice must not be in vain."[18]

The *Gaines* decision, the *Courier* insisted, was "the entering wedge in a campaign to improve the education of Negroes in the South all down the line to the smallest rural school."[19] Realizing the importance of extending the principles enunciated by the Court in the *Gaines* case, *The Crisis* inaccurately predicted, however, that its legal staff would move quickly to apply the principles to elementary and secondary schools.[20] Apparently the editor of *The Crisis* was not fully aware of the plan of attack drawn up by the NAACP's legal department. At that point, not enough groundwork had been completed to risk attacking unequal educational opportunities in a level of education where a dual system already existed.

The black press was noticeably concerned over the extent to which the Missouri Supreme Court would comply with the spirit of the Supreme Court decision. The *Courier* concluded that the American reaction to the decision would be "the acid test of the sincerity of its [United States'] efforts to practice the race tolerance and racial goodwill it is preaching to the Germans."[21] With no apparent regard for the international implications of the situation, the South predictably was negative to the *Gaines* decision. The southern response was an admixture of hostility toward the NAACP and quandry as to the most effective means of circumventing the Supreme Court's ruling.[22]

Whether the *Gaines* decision had improved higher educational opportunities appreciably for black Americans only time would tell. The Supreme Court had reaffirmed the Maryland court decision that out-of-state scholarships did not constitute equality of educational opportunity. Unfortunately for higher education for blacks, the Court had stricken down only the out-of-state scholarship plan; and in leaving the case to the Missouri Supreme Court to determine what constituted a proper remedy, it had opened the door to abuse. Missouri established under state court approval a law school affiliated with Lincoln University but located in St. Louis, and several southern states followed Missouri's lead in circumventing the principles established in the *Gaines* decision. The extent to which state officials were committed to absolute subterfuge became obvious throughout the next decade as facilities in southern states for graduate and professional training for blacks existed to a much greater degree on paper than in reality.[23]

Nowhere was the full impact of the *Gaines* decision more thoroughly understood than in the black press. Guarded optimism prevailed throughout the black press as to the significance of the decision, as to the chances of enforcing the spirit of the decision, and as to extending the principle to areas other than graduate and professional training. The black press cautioned its readers not to expect too much from the Court's decision. It astutely measured the depth of Southern resistance and accurately predicted the means by which the segregationist South would resist the decision. The black press believed the *Gaines* decision to be a good starting place, and it advised black Americans to recognize the decision as a victory for correct principle, achieved through the determined efforts of blacks themselves.

Sadly, Lloyd Gaines never attended the University of Missouri, for he mysteriously disappeared before enrolling and was never seen again. Progress in graduate and professional education for blacks in Missouri after the *Gaines* decision occurred very slowly. A law school was established at Lincoln University, and, opening in St. Louis amid protests, it lasted only four years. The journalism school, also established at Lincoln University, achieved educational respectability, partly because of the instructional contributions of the journalism faculty of the University of Missouri. Although the *Gaines* decision was circumvented more frequently than it was applied in good faith, its significance lies in the fact that it supplied the legal basis for other legal decisions regarding desegregation of graduate and professional schools after World War II.

For almost a decade after the *Gaines* decision in 1938, little significant progress was made in the war against racially segregated educational institutions. Two major factors retarded the drive: (1) a preoccupation with the war effort,[24] and (2) a severe shortage of funds to support NAACP legal efforts. However, with the out-of-state scholarships invalidated, after the war the NAACP resumed its attack on inequality of educational facilities. The integrationists' position in higher education received a considerable boost in 1947 when President Truman's Committee on Civil Rights made its recommendations, documenting how the separate but equal doctrine had failed.[25]

In January, 1946, Ada Lois Sipuel, a twenty-two year old honor graduate of Langston University, applied for admission to the College of Law of the University of Oklahoma. Her request for admission was denied, and, with the assistance of the NAACP[26] she followed the same line of appeal, with the same results, in the Oklahoma courts as Gaines had done in Missouri. The United States Supreme Court reversed the Oklahoma decision; but only five days afterward,[27] the Oklahoma Supreme Court issued an interpretive ruling that the *Sipuel* decision had no effect on the segregation statutes in Oklahoma, indicating that the spirit of the *Sipuel* decision could be fulfilled by the establishment of a law school for blacks within the state.

The black press received the news of the Supreme Court's *Sipuel* decision with understandable caution.[28] Roy Wilkins prophetically commented that the *Sipuel* decision might crack open professional and graduate schools in some Southern states but was unlikely to do so in others.[29] The *Defender* cautioned that while the *Sipuel* decision was a step forward, it did not "sound the death knell of Jim-Crow higher education in Dixie."[30] Admitting that the Southern states "may still beat the rap by improvising segregated schools," the *Defender* proudly announced that "the props of Jim-Crow are buckling." The St. Louis *Argus*, interested in widening the coverage of the decision, immediately urged the NAACP or some other organization to sponsor a case for the admission of a black to the Missouri Medical School and the Rolla School of Mines.[31] The *Argus* then followed up its request by comparing facilities at Lincoln University with those at State teachers' colleges and found them grossly unequal.[32]

Most black newspapers were troubled over the Oklahoma Supreme Court's interpretation and considered it a blatant means of undermining the *Sipuel* decision. They were also troubled over the efforts in the State legislature to establish a separate law school at Langston University. The Philadelphia *Tribune*, commenting upon the Oklahoma court's interpretation, lamented that "every time the enlightened people of America have reason to believe that the people of the South are gaining wisdom, an incident of this kind happens to prove their continued stupidity."[33]

The Oklahoma legislature moved quickly to establish a law school, and it brought a chorus of negative comments from the black community. Thurgood Marshall of the NAACP announced that there was no such thing as separate but equal facilities; and George M. Johnson, Dean of the Howard University School of Law, tersely commented that "it takes more than brick and mortar to provide separate but equal educational facilities."[34] The *Michigan Chronicle* scored heavily with the criticism that "in one breath intolerant whites charge that Negroes are ignoramuses and in the next they denounce attempts to provide Negroes with adequate educational opportunities. They want to keep us ignorant and then hold us responsible for it."[35] And the black press rejected outright a proposal by five Southern governors that funds from Southern states be given to Meharry Medical College in Nashville to establish a graduate school for black students from Southern states.[36] The *Amsterdam News* admitted that an expansion of educational facilities for blacks in the South was needed, but concluded that as the proposed effort was "to establish Jim Crow on a more solid and permanent foundation, any such project, so far as it upholds the separation of the races, should be vigorously opposed."[37] The same New York newspaper, characterizing the effort as "an unvarnished subterfuge," saw the proposal as "a solution by the South to solve the problem in its own nefarious Jim Crow way before it is too late to keep the sunlight of democracy from coming over the horizon of the Southland." The *Atlanta Daily World*, cautioning Meharry against accepting funds proposed by the Southern governors, asserted that it could see no reason for anyone to work at cross purposes with the black leaders and organizations spearheading the fight for educational opportunities. The *Daily World* argued that regional colleges were not the answer to equal education between blacks and whites, and labeled it "the plainest type of folly to indulge Southerners in the thought that Negroes will be satisfied with this arrangement. . . ."[38] The same newspaper pointedly remarked that equal opportunities could be delayed indefinitely by "heads of Negro institutions holding forth phony mediums of escape to those southerners who are grappling with the problems."

Chicago's *Defender* commented that the Southern governors realize that "the time has come when they must either give ground to democracy or pull a rabbit out of a hat," and the *Defender* assuredly added that "no matter how big a rabbit they pulled out of a hat, the trick is not going to fool anybody."[39] The same newspaper reminded black America that no matter how practical jim crow schools might appear to be in some areas, it must be remembered that "they are monuments to racial discrimination which has no place in a democracy dedicated to freedom and equality." The first steps toward decency in the South, according to the *Defender*, should start in the schoolrooms, where "the youth of Dixie would have a chance to grow out of the reach of the racist mythology which has poisoned the minds of their fathers." Accelerating the barrage against the plans of the Southern governors, the *Courier* issued an emotional appeal:

> Men of Meharry, sons of Meharry, protest against this treachery! The proud tradition of Meharry, the honor of Meharry is at stake. Surely there are enough red-blooded fighting graduates who revere and treasure the memory of the Hubbard brothers to fight against any idea that will use this honored institution as a cat's paw to pull the chestnuts out of the fire in order to aid damnable Southern desires to evade the law and the high court of our land.[40]

From his official position, Walter White served notice that the NAACP would legally challenge any such effort to evade the "clear mandate" of the Supreme Court in the *Gaines* and *Sipuel* cases. The NAACP, White said, "has fought too long and difficult and expensive a fight for decent education for the nine million Negroes of the South to permit any board of trustees or any aggregation of Southern governors to foul the victory."[41] Continuing the theme, the *Argus* urged its readers to "accept no make-shifts," for "the criterion of the Supreme Court is low enough."[42]

While the Southern governors were developing their abortive plan and the black press was denouncing it, Ada Lois Sipuel Fisher[43] announced that she would not enroll in the dubious law school established at Langston University. Instead, she applied again for admission to the University of Oklahoma, where she was again rejected. Marshall petitioned the Supreme Court to require the University of Oklahoma to admit her, but the Court denied the request on two dubious bases: (1) the plaintiff had argued the petition on a different point from that upon which the original *Sipuel* decision had been made, and (2) it was the District Court's responsibility to determine whether or not the mandate had been obeyed.[44]

The refusal of the Supreme Court to order Ada Fisher's admission to the University of Oklahoma provoked bitter disappointment in the black press. The Los Angeles *Sentinel*, in an editorial entitled "Supreme Court Turns Tail," complained of the Court's taking refuge behind technicalities.[45] The Indianapolis *Recorder* viewed the decision as "a desperate effort to corral the black vote in Northern states for the fall election, while at the same time hanging on to the Solid

South."[46] The depth of the *Recorder's* despair was registered in its argument that organizations promoting black Americans' rights switch their attacks from the judicial to the political arena.

The failure of the Supreme Court to order Fisher's admission to the University of Oklahoma in February, 1948, did not terminate the issue for the NAACP in behalf of Fisher. Yet, suddenly, Ada Fisher ceased to be the focus of the NAACP drive, for in January, six other blacks had applied for admission to various graduate and professional programs at the University. They were denied admission; but one of them, George McLaurin, appealed his case, ultimately won and, in October, 1948, became the first black to enroll at the University of Oklahoma.

Eight months after McLaurin was admitted to a graduate program in Education, less than two weeks before the Langston University Law School closed operations, and three years and five months after originally applying for admission, Ada Fisher was admitted to the Law School of the University of Oklahoma. By the time this long-awaited event occurred, the attention of the black community had been diverted to two other cases, one of which involved McLaurin at the University of Oklahoma. A tribute which had been offered in the Philadelphia *Tribune* immediately after the Supreme Court had handed down the *Sipuel* decision was even more deserved after almost three and a half years of legal hassle:

> Many years hence, when the silly prejudices which made the *Sipuel* decision necessary have been eradicated, colored graduate students will go about their studies taking their admission to southern colleges as a matter of course. Only the historians will remember Ada Lois Sipuel who bearded the lion of prejudice in his den and wrested from him a decision which, as it is implemented by action, will be a new day in education for colored Americans.[47]

Nowhere were the gains and losses in these cases more thoroughly understood than in the black press, which always displayed a cautious optimism throughout the judicial struggles. Editors of black newspapers recognized the efforts of Southern governors as last-ditch stands against the drive for equal opportunity, and they opposed them with unflinching determination.

Although George W. McLaurin was admitted to the University of Oklahoma School of Education, the University segregated him in the classroom, library and cafeteria.[48] Less than a month after being admitted, McLaurin returned to court to challenge the University's right to segregate him within its facilities. The District Court denied McLaurin's contention that isolation placed upon him a "badge of inferiority" and asserted that McLaurin was being offered an equal educational opportunity. Thurgood Marshall, who had argued the case, appealed the issue to the Supreme Court.

On June 5, 1950, the same day that the Supreme Court handed down two other significant civil rights decisions,[49] the court unanimously decided that "such restrictions impair and inhibit the ability to study, to engage in discussions and exchange views with other students, and, in general, to learn his profession."[50] Commenting upon the defense's contention that if such restrictions were removed there would still be no mixing of the races, the Court pointed out that there is an important difference "between restrictions imposed by the state which prohibit intellectual commingling of students, and the refusal of individuals to commingle where the state presents no such bar." In the *McLaurin* decision, the Supreme Court had impaired the separate-but-equal principle in that once blacks were admitted to graduate and professional schools, they must be accorded the same treatment—not equal or substantially equal treatment—as that accorded whites.

The black community was understandably elated over the *McLaurin* decision, but the euphoria was magnified by the fact that another important decision regarding higher education was announced the same day. The *Sweatt* decision combined with that in the *McLaurin* case to provide a dramatic success on that June day in 1950.

The case of Heman Marion Sweatt, a black resident of Houston, is similar to that of Lloyd Gaines of a dozen years before.[51] Sweatt was denied admission to the Law School of the University of Texas, and he took the case to the Federal District Court. Although the Court ruled in Sweatt's favor, it granted the University of Texas six months to establish a law school for blacks. A one-roomed, two professional law school was established in Houston, and the Court inexplicably interpreted it as offering equal facilities for legal training. Sweatt appealed the case, and the lower court's previous decision was set aside and the case was returned to the lower court for a full trial. By the time of this trial, the Houston law school had been replaced by another located in a basement room of a building adjacent to the State Capitol in Austin. The issue became exactly what the NAACP had chipped away at in the *Gaines* and *Sipuel/Fisher* cases—the validity of separate-but-equal principle.

Despite the persuasive testimonies of nationally distinguished legal educators, the court decided that Sweatt was being granted an equal opportunity for legal training. The NAACP appealed the decision to the Supreme Court, where an attempt was made by NAACP attorneys to prevent the Court from sidestepping the separate-but-

equal doctrine. In addition to the argument regarding grossly unequal legal education facilities, plaintiff's counsel insisted that there
was a special need for legal training to be conducted in an integrated
classroom, a microcosm of an integrated society. Speaking for a unanimous court, Chief Justice Fred M. Vinson declared:

> The law school, the proving ground of legal learning and practice,
> cannot be effective in isolation from the individuals and institutions
> with which the law interacts. Few students and no one who has prac-
> ticed law would choose to study in an academic vacuum, removed
> from the interplay of ideas and the exchange of views with which
> the law is concerned. The law school to which Texas is willing to ad-
> mit petitioner excludes from its student body members of the racial
> groups which number 85% of the population of the State and in-
> clude most of the lawyers, witnesses, jurors, judges, and other offi-
> cials with whom petitioner will inevitably be dealing when he
> becomes a member of the Texas Bar. With such a substantial and
> significant segment of society excluded, we cannot conclude that
> the education offered petitioner is substantially equal to that which
> he would receive if admitted to the University of Texas Law
> School. . ."[52]

To the disappointment of anxious blacks, the Supreme Court
added that it saw no reason to reexamine the doctrine established in
Plessy v. Ferguson. However, the handwriting on the wall was that the
Court was ready to inquire into specific situations to determine
whether or not the separate-but-equal doctrine was applicable to the
facts of a particular case. The *Plessy* decision was no longer an impen-
etrable shield of armor to protect all segregation laws against successful attack. No separate law school could meet the test of equality laid
down in the *Sweatt* case, and most graduate and professional schools
would have encountered similar difficulties.[53]

The reaction of the black community to the *Sweatt* and *McLaurin* decisions can be described as optimistic, though not ecstatic. The
Pittsburgh *Courier* carried the complete text of the decisions and accompanied them with a page of lurid photographs depicting the
types of discrimination that had been outlawed.[54] Several black newspapers concentrated on what the Court did not do rather than on
what it did. The Boston *Chronicle* soberly commented that within the
next decade "less than a hundred Negroes out of the millions in the
region which the Court's ruling directly affects will benefit immediately from the decision."[55] The Baltimore *Afro-American*, referring to
the Court's refusal to review the doctrine of separate-but-equal,
charged that the Court "pruned a noxious weed instead of pulling it
out by the roots."[56] The Indianapolis *Recorder* characterized the
Court's procedure as smacking of "hand-washing in the face of dan-

gers that threaten American democracy and the very survival of the nation."[57] The Chicago *Defender* confidently predicted that "if the learned justices wish to skin the cat of Jim Crow a little at a time instead of ending the business with one dramatic flourish, our enjoyment of full citizenship may be delayed but it will not be denied."[58] The *Defender* urged its readers to "look to see where the acorns are comin' from and pitch in our two-buck membership to the NAACP . . . ."

The *Crisis*, the official organ of the NAACP, cautioned blacks in America that the fight was not over, commenting that they had won "a strategic victory in a flanking battle, but the war itself is yet to be won."[59] The Los Angeles *Sentinel,* urging its readers to lay plans for still further tests of segregation and discrimination, reminded them that "the price of liberty is unceasing vigilance."[60] The St. Louis *Argus* expressed the feeling of many when it said:

> Understandable joy over these decisions unfortunately must be tempered by the mere fact that civilized men were forced to the highest court in the land to obtain what is less than ordinary human courtesy. It speaks ill of the whole nation that in the 20th century the primitive customs which shielded the naked greed of the slaveholder still curse the land.[61]

The defense argument that such decisions would intensify racial hatred in the South and the pronouncements of Governor Herman Talmadge of Georgia and gubernatorial candidate M. E. Thompson that they would personally secure white schools against intrusion by blacks, prompted widespread criticism in the black press. The *Sentinel* echoed the comments of numerous other black newspapers when it predicted that no amount of non-violent racial integration would prevent the "prophets of doom" from their phobic reactions, and the Los Angeles newspaper confidently added: "It is plain as can be the nation as a whole has outgrown the Jim Crow system."[62]

It has been a common practice for black newspapers to instruct their readers on how to behave while using their newly acquired rights. The Philadelphia *Tribune* did just that when it cautioned its readers that

> . . . it now becomes more imperative than ever before that Negroes prepare themselves for this new freedom. As the bar falls down. Negroes have responsibilities and duties greater than ever before. Things which were excusable under Jim Crow laws and practices are no longer permitted. . . .The danger is that the change may catch Negroes unprepared. So many Negroes have suffered from persecution that they do not realize what is happening. Then, too, there are others who have lost all faith in the democratic principles of their government and have accepted their inferior status as perma-

nent. The leadership which has fought so brilliantly for equality of opportunity must now engage in the herculean effort of getting Negroes prepared for its enjoyment.[63]

The decisions of 1950 represented limited progress earnestly desired and diligently pursued.[64] The black press should share much of the credit for progress toward integrated graduate and professional education. It correctly interpreted the individual steps along the way, and it kept its readers from excessive elation over small accomplishments and excessive elation over small accomplishments and excessive depression over delays. Throughout the dozen years between the *Gaines* decision and the *McLaurin* and *Sweatt* decisions, the black press never waivered, and it produced a surprisingly united front regarding where blacks were, where they wanted to be, and what the difference was between the two.

Notes

[1] The cases under consideration are the *Gaines* Case (1938), *Sipuel/Fisher* Case (1948), the *McLaurin* Case (1950), and the *Sweatt* Case (1950). The black press reviewed in the study is *The Crisis* and eleven black newspapers; Atlanta *Daily World*, Baltimore *Afro-American*, Chicago *Defender*, Cleveland *Gazette*, Detroit *Michigan Chronicle*, Indianapolis *Recorder*, Los Angeles *Sentinel*, New York *Amsterdam News*, Philadelphia *Tribune*, Pittsburgh *Courier*, and St. Louis *Argus*.

[2] The NAACP lawyers believed that the Supreme Court was not ready to strike down "separate-but-equal" and therefore chose to have the Court destroy the underpinnings of "separate-but-equal" without actually issuing an opinion on the *Plessy* principle. See William H. Hastie, "Toward an Equalitarian Legal Order, 1930-1950," *Annals of the American Academy of Political and Social Science*, 407 (May 1973).

[3] For a detailed description of the case, see Daniel T. Kelleher, "The Case of Lloyd Lionel Gaines: The Demise of the Separate But Equal Doctrine," *Journal of Negro History*, 56 (October 1971): 262-71.

[4] Ibid., p. 264.

[5] *Missouri ex. rel. Gaines v. Canada*, 305 U.S. 337.

[6] New York *Amsterdam News*, December 24, 1938: Pittsburgh *Courier*, December 24, 1938: Indianapolis *Recorder*, December 31, 1938.

[7] Cleveland *Gazette*, December 17, 1938.

[8] Chicago *Defender*, December 24, 1938.

[9] *The Crisis* (January 1939): 17.

[10] *Courier*, December 17, 24, 1938.

[11] *Amsterdam News*, December 17, 1938.

[12] *Courier*, December 24, 1938.

[13] Ibid.

[14] *The Crisis*, op. cit.

[15] *Courier*, December 24, 1938.

[16] *Amsterdam New*, December 17, 1938. *The Crisis* pointed out that the NAACP had been successful in attacking unequal salary scales prevailing in Maryland and that the Maryland attack had served as a guide to black teachers who launched similar attacks in Virginia, Florida, and Alabama. *The Crisis*, op. cit., p. 10.

To bolster its argument as well as to provide direction for its goals, the NAACP prepared a 24-page pamphlet entitled "Racial Inequalities in Education," which revealed that: (1) in the South, 252.5 percent more money was spent on education for white children than for Negro children, (2) Southern and Border states diverted federal funds from black land-grant colleges, (3) black taxpayers were required to support schools to which their children were denied admission, (4) black teachers lost thousands of dollars every year because of salaries inferior to those of white teachers, and (5) Southern and Border states denied blacks an equitable share of Public Works Administration and Federal Emergency Relief Administration funds for building schools and transporting pupils to classes.

[17] *Amsterdam News*, December 17, 1938.

[18] *Courier*, January 14, 1939.

[19] *Courier*, December 24, 1938.

[20] *The Crisis*, op. cit., p. 10.

[21] Ibid. This statement was an obvious reference to American objections to German expansion at the expense of what the German government called "inferior," non-German people.

[22] Dean Ira P. Hildebrand of the University of Texas Law School urged immediate establishment of legal training at Prairie View Normal College for Negroes, thus permitting continued exclusion of Negroes from the University of Texas without violation of the Court's ruling. Reported in *Amsterdam News*, January 7, 1939.

Only a few days after the *Gaines* decision, South Carolina initiated legislation to establish a law school at South Carolina A and M. North Carolina Governor Clyde Hoey urged the State Legislature to establish Negro graduate and professional school, adding that although North Carolina would not tolerate mixed schools for the races, North Carolinians "do believe in equality of opportunity in their respective fields of service. . . ." Governor Hoey asserted that "the white race cannot afford to do less than simple justice to the Negro," though he never defined "simple justice." *Courier*, January 28, 14, 1939.

To their credit, administrators of black colleges, though desperately in need of funds, refused to aid segregationist white officials by offering to establish separate graduate and professional schools at their own institutions. The lone exception was Dr. John M. Gandy, President of Virginia State College, who no doubt had the future of his own institution in mind when he suggested that several states combine their financial resources in the creation of professional schools for black Americans. *Recorder*, December 31, 1938. This idea was permitted to die by blacks because of its similarity to the out-of-state scholarship program and by whites because it would require investing state funds in facilities in other states. This plan was eagerly embraced after the *Sipuel* decision ten years later by several governors who tried to effectuate it by proposing to subsidize Meharry Medical College.

Only one small crack appeared in the solid wall of black press opinion, and it surfaced in the Atlanta *Daily World*'s comment that it was not "sensible to think that coeducation of both groups could be immediately injected into our complex society. . . ." adding "perhaps the scholarship arrangement is the best suggestion, after all." Atlanta *Daily World*, December 19, 1938.

[23] The black law school established in Texas and attacked in the *Sweatt* case in 1950 was a classic example of this subterfuge.

[24] Shortly after Pearl Harbor there was a meeting of Negro newspaper editors with government officials in which the editors were asked to "ease up" on cries of discrimination. When they refused, federal officials watched the black press very carefully during the war. George Scuyler, "Our Press," *Courier*, June 17, 1950.

[25] *To Secure These Results* (Report of the President's Committee on Civil Rights), 1947. In a report by the President's Commission on Higher Education, entitled "Higher Education for American Democracy," six volumes of material attested to inequality of educational opportunity. The Atlanta *Daily World* pointed out that in Louisiana none of the 137 public and private black schools was accredited, while 466 white public and private schools were accredited. *Daily World*, January 3, 1948.

[26] Amos T. Hall, eminent black attorney from Tulsa represented the plaintiff.

[27] Attorneys for the state of Oklahoma admitted before the Supreme Court that in the two years since Sipuel's request for admission the state had done nothing whatsoever to provide a law school for Negroes, *The Crisis* (February 1948).

Walter White said that "Southern arrogance, nurtured on generations of riding rough-shod over Negroes, was never more patent than in the admission by one of the Oklahoma attorneys that precisely nothing had been done to comply with the Federal Constitution's insistence that there be no discrimination." *Defender*, January 31, 1948.

[28] Most of the Negro newspapers did not appear until after the Oklahoma Supreme Court had offered its interpretation of the decision and in so doing had indicated the attitude of the South.

[29] He thought it likely in Texas, Arkansas, Kentucky, Missouri, North Carolina, and Virginia, but unlikely in Mississippi, South Carolina, Florida, Alabama, and Georgia. Detroit *Michigan Chronicle*, January 24, 1948.

Under the sanction of the State's highest court, Oklahoma legislators launched an effort to establish a separate law school at Langston University. Similar efforts were begun in several other Southern states, while the governors of several of those states made plans to circumvent the *Sipuel* decision by cooperatively establishing a regional graduate and professional school for blacks.

Dr. Sherman D. Scruggs, president of Lincoln University, capitalized on the State of Missouri's intentions and asked for a $291,000 increase over the previous year's budget. Smiting the state with its own sword, Scruggs said, "Lincoln University is constantly faced with the mandate to offer a quality of administrative and instructional services that are equally comparable with that of the University of Missouri in all the offerings it provides." He added: "Separate schools for Negroes are maintained in Missouri by law. You have within your power to provide otherwise, but until you do, I know you will want to provide adequate facilities for the education of our Negro children." St. Louis *Argus*, January 30, 1948.

[30] *Defender*, January 24, 1948.

[31] *Argus*, January 16, 1948.

[32] Ibid., January 23, 1948.

[33] Philadelphia *Tribune*, January 20, 1948.

[34] *Daily World*, January 21, 1948.

[35] *Michigan Chronicle*, January 31, 1948.

[36] The governors were: Thompson of Georgia, McCord of Tennessee, Lane of Maryland, Tuck of Virginia, and Caldwell of Florida. On February 25, 1948, they presented their proposal to Congress in Washington, but no action was taken.

[37] *Amsterdam News*, February 28, 1948. *The Argus* agreed, February 6, 1948.

[38] *Daily World*, January 21, 1948.

[39] *Defender*, January 31, 1948.

[40] *Courier*, January 31, 1948.

[41] *Defender*, February 7, 1948.

[42] *Argus*, February 13, 1948.

[43] She had married since the case was decided by the Supreme Court.

[44] The original argument had been based on the fact that there was no law school in Oklahoma except that at the University of Oklahoma, whereas the second argument was based upon the contention that, although there were two law schools in the state, that at Langston University was grossly inferior. See, *Fisher v. Hurst*, 333 U.S. 147.

[45] Los Angeles *Sentinel*, February 26, 1948.

[46] *Recorder*, February 28, 1948.

[47] *Tribune*, January 17, 1948.

[48] John T. Hubbell points out that the University spent quite a bit of time preparing "colored only" sections of its facilities. Hubbell, "The Desegregation of the University of Oklahoma," op. cit.

[49] They were: *Sweatt v. Painter*, involving separate educational facilities, and *Henderson v. United States*, involving segregation dining facilities in interstate travel.

[50] *McLaurin v. Oklahoma State Regents* 339, U. S. 853.

[51] For a complete, though biased, contemporary account of the early stages of the case and of the evidence presented by the plaintiff, see Charles H. Thompson, "Separate But Not Equal: The Sweatt Case," *Southwest Review* 33 (Spring 1948).

[52] *Sweatt v. Painter* 339 U.S., 849-50.

[53] G. Loren Miller, *The Petitioners: The Story of the Supreme Court of the United States and the Negro* (New York, 1966), pp. 340-41.

[54] *Courier*, June 17, 1950.

[55] *Chronicle*, June 10, 1950.

[56] *Afro-American*, June 10, 1950.

[57] *Recorder*, June 17, 1950.

[58] *Defender*, June 17, 1950.

[59] *The Crisis*, July, 1950, 443.

[60] *Sentinel*, June 15, 1950. Ironically, this editorial appeared on the same page as chapter 15 of Booker T. Washington's *The Story of My Life and Work* which was running in weekly installments.

[61] *Argus*, June 9, 1950.

[62] *Sentinel*, June 22, 1950.

[63] *Tribune*, June 10, 1950.

[64] Unfortunately, the *Sweatt* and *McLaurin* cases were not class action suits, and as a result, many Southern states devised means by which blacks were prevented from enrolling in white graduate and professional schools. See, Miller, *Petitioners*, p. 341.

Military Segregation and the 1940 Presidential Election

*On the eve of the United States entry into World War II,
the American Armed Forces mirrored the rest of the nation in
its racial patterns and practices. Typically, racial segregation
or in other instances, racial exclusion, characterized both the
military and the defense industry. African Americans protested
such treatment. The long-standing military segregation particularly vexed many African Americans who viewed equality in
the armed services as an important aspect of first-class citizenship. With the approaching presidential election in 1940, key
African American leaders seized the opportunity to pressure the
Roosevelt administration into integrating blacks throughout the
military. The ensuing battle of opposing wits and counter
strategies pitted civil rights giants Walter White and A. Philip
Randolph against the President and his recalcitrant Secretary
of War and Secretary of the Navy. Importantly, the efforts to
end military segregation in 1940 continued and allowed the
nation to inch its way toward societal integration in the postwar era.*

*Writing at the height of the Vietnam War, historian
Richard Dalfiume begins his essay by juxtaposing African
Americans' reluctance to fight in Southeast Asia in the 1960s
with the earlier crusade to integrate the American military in
the late 1930s and early 1940s. Each epoch in a different way
provides a signpost to measure the black struggle for equality
as full-fledged American citizens.*

TODAY THE MILITANT SEGMENT of the civil rights movement de-
plores the use of colored troops in a war against the colored people
of Asia. The Student Nonviolent Coordinating Committee has labeled
these soldiers "black mercenaries" fighting an imperialist war. The
left-wing Negro protest goes further, also opposing the draft because
low-income Negroes are disproportionately represented among the
draftees. This means that a larger percentage of black Americans are
serving throughout the combat units in Viet Nam than their percentage of the total population. Ironically, it was only a generation ago
that the most militant Negroes were fighting to overcome discrimina-

tory restrictions on their service in the armed forces. Then the cry was "the right to fight." An examination of earlier efforts to integrate the armed forces—in 1940—sheds some light on the goals and tactics of the civil rights movement of yesteryear, as well as the response of the federal government to such protests.

The cover of the July, 1940, issue of the magazine of the National Association for the Advancement of Colored People, *The Crisis*, depicts Air Force planes flying over an aircraft factory turning out rows of new planes. FOR WHITES ONLY is the caption across the picture, and at the bottom of the page is written: "Negro Americans may not help build them, repair them, or fly them." The major issues for Negro Americans during World War II are graphically illustrated on this periodical cover. The war in Europe had resulted in an expanding American defense industry; white unemployment was being reduced while employment discrimination meant a continuation of the Depression for Negroes.[1] Defense preparations also meant an expansion of the armed forces in which Negroes were anxious to serve. However, black Americans were determined to prevent what they regarded as the wholesale segregation and discrimination to which their soldiers had been subjected in World War I.[2] The forthcoming presidential election of 1940 meant that Negroes would have a chance to wield some of their new national political power to achieve their ends. War in Europe and an election at home made the racial policies of the armed forces a political issue for Negroes.

Black Americans were restricted to a minimal role and rigidly segregated in those branches of the armed forces where they were allowed to serve in the 1930s. In the Navy, Negroes could enlist only in the all-Negro messman's branch. The Marine Corps and the Army Air Corps excluded them entirely. In the Army, Negroes were prevented from enlisting except for the few vacancies in the four Regular Army Negro units that had been created shortly after the Civil War, and the strength of these had been reduced drastically in the 1920s and 1930s. The restrictive attitude of the various armed services was the result of a racist stereotype of Negro servicemen that had been fully developed during World War I and perpetuated thereafter. The basis of the stereotype was the belief that as soldiers Negroes were inferior to whites: they were inherent cowards and therefore unsuited for combat roles; they lacked mechanical ability and were therefore unsuited for technical roles. On the other hand, Negroes were thought to be "peculiarly suited" for labor and service duties. Segregation was a necessity, the armed forces reasoned, because separation was the general rule throughout American society. Because of these attitudes, the commanding officers of most of the branches of the armed services wanted as few Negroes as possible. When it was not possible to restrict them completely, Negroes were assigned mainly to labor duties.[3]

Although the most important bread and butter issue for Negroes in the late 1930s and early 1940s was employment discrimination, their position in the armed forces was an important symbol. If one could not participate fully in the defense of one's country, one could not lay claim to the rights of a full-fledged citizen. *The Crisis* expressed this in its demand for unrestricted participation in the armed forces: "this is no fight merely to wear a uniform. This is a struggle for status, a struggle to take democracy off of parchment and give it life."[4] Herbert Garfinkel, a recent student of discriminatory employment practices during this period, points out that "in many respects, the discriminatory practices against Negroes which characterized the military programs . . . cut deeper into Negro feelings than did employment discrimination."[5]

The increasing possibility of war led to a rapidly expanding correspondence with the War Department concerning Negro soldiers in the late 1930s. This was also due, in part, to the *Pittsburgh Courier,* an influential Negro newspaper, which, together with a group of World War I Negro officers, in 1938 formed a Committee for Participation of Negroes in the National Defense. The impetus behind the formation of this group was expressed in a letter from the editor and publisher to President Roosevelt:

> I feel, and my people feel, that this is the psychological moment to strike for our rightful place in our National Defense. I need not tell you that we are expecting a more dignified place in our armed forces during the next war than we occupied during the World War.[6]

Roy Wilkins, the editor of *The Crisis,* wrote the Secretary of War that he knew "of no other single issue—except possibly lynching—upon which there is a unanimity of opinion among all classes in all sections of the country." And as a reminder that a presidential election was due soon, the Secretary was told that the administration which broke down the restrictions against Negroes serving in the armed forces "is certain to receive the gratitude of Negro voters in a substantial manner."[7]

Much of the stimulus behind the concern of Negroes over their position in the armed forces was the memory of what had happened to them in World War I. Charles H. Houston, a noted Negro civil rights lawyer, related in the Negro press his experiences as a young officer in 1917-1918. His bitter memories were recounted, he said, "so that our white fellow citizens may learn they must treat Negroes as equals, and that this generation of Negro boys may have their eyes opened to what is ahead of them."[8] Other former Negro soldiers recalled their experiences for a new generation, and the Negro press was full of general articles reopening the old wounds of the World War.[9]

Concern that Negro soldiers would be denied combat roles and confined to labor units in any future war, also a legacy of the First World War, was widespread. Suspicion on this matter was aroused by frequent reports in the Negro press that the remnants of the four Regular Army Negro regiments had been reduced to orderlies for white officers, gardeners, and "flunkies."[10] The Associated Negro Press brought together a group of black leaders to discuss the position of Negroes in national defense in September, 1939. While they were divided over whether or not Negroes should demand a segregated Army division and how Negroes would be affected by a future war, these leaders were unanimous in their determination to resist any attempt to restrict black soldiers to labor battalions.[11]

The result of this agitation was that Negro organizations and individuals began to ask for a greater role in the armed forces. The National Bar Association created a committee to end the exclusion of Negroes from the National Guard of most states. The National Negro Insurance Association adopted a resolution against the restrictions on Negroes in the Army and Navy. A black American Legion post in Memphis, Tennessee, organized a group to seek a Negro National Guard unit for that state. In Michigan, a Negro state senator proclaimed that black people should refuse to fight in a future war unless admitted to the armed forces in time to train properly. A Negro newspaper editorialized this line of argument. "It is better to insist on training now . . . than wait until the conflict begins and be rushed as raw recruits into a slaughter that will kill us by the thousands before we learn to protect ourselves."[12]

The efforts of Negroes to broaden the opportunities available to them were first directed at legislation, and to the Air Corps in particular. Since the First World War, Negroes had attempted to get into the Air Corps, but the answer had always been that no Negro units existed in this branch of the service to which they could be assigned. In 1939, Congress passed a law authorizing the use of civilian aviation schools for the basic training of military pilots. This training was to be administered by the War Department, and Air Corps personnel were to supervise it. Pressure by Negroes had resulted in an amendment specifying that one of these schools would be designated "for the training of any Negro air pilot." Although the intent of the amendment was to get Negroes into the Air Corps, the War Department took the position that this law did not direct the enlistment of Negroes into this branch of the Army. One school was designated for pilot training for Negroes, but, unlike schools for whites, it was run by civilians instead of the Air Corps. Furthermore, its graduates were not taken into the Air Corps as were the whites because the War Department claimed there were no Negro units to which they could be assigned. In short, Negro air units could never exist because Negroes were not allowed to enlist, and Negroes could not enlist because there were no Negro Air Corps units.[13]

The Air Corps was not the only branch of the service to antagonize Negro voters in an election year. Bitterness of Negroes toward the Navy was particularly evident in 1940. This service was the most outspoken in its racial policy; the fact that it saw fit to allow black sailors to serve only in the menial capacity of messmen insulted Negroes. In practically every issue of the major Negro newspapers during 1940 there were articles and editorials condemning Navy racial policy. And the Navy appeared to do nothing to lessen this animosity. The Naval Academy refused to allow a Negro Harvard lacrosse player to participate against the Navy team. In 1940 the Navy gave "undesirable" discharges to thirteen Negro messmen who wrote a letter to a Negro newspaper criticizing their working conditions.[14] When a member of the Committee on Participation of Negroes in the National Defense Program conferred with Navy officials in November, 1940, the Navy issued the following statement: "After many years of experience, the policy of not enlisting men of the colored race for any branch of the naval service, except the messman's branch, was adopted to meet the best interests of general ship efficiency."[15]

Remembering their experience with the Air Corps, Negroes and their allies in Congress fought to secure more specific amendments to legislation in the summer and fall of 1940. One such piece of legislation was H.R. 9850, "An Act to Expedite the Strengthening of the National Defense." The Committee on Participation of Negroes in the National Defense arranged to have Senators Sherman Minton of Indiana and Harry H. Schwartz of Wyoming, both Democrats, introduce an amendment providing that "no person shall be excluded from any branch of the military establishment on account of race, creed, or color." The Army General Staff objected strenuously to the amendment. Secretary of War Woodring wrote congressmen that the amendment might result in the enlistment of a large number of Negroes; this would "demoralize and weaken the effect of military units by mixing colored and white soldiers in closely related units, or even in the same units." In the end, an amendment that made no change in the situation was substituted: "that no Negro because of race shall be excluded from enlistment in the Army for service with colored military units now organized or to be organized for such service."[16]

The Selective Training and Service Act passed in September, 1940, was the occasion for the most intense effort by Negroes to amend legislation concerning the armed forces. Senator Robert F. Wagner, Democrat of New York, introduced an amendment that no one, on the basis of creed or color, should be denied the right to volunteer for the armed services. Although Southerners in Congress objected to this amendment, it was included in the bill but with a "joker," so Negroes thought: any person could volunteer provided that "he is acceptable to the land or naval forces for such training and service." The services were still free to refuse Negro volunteers. Representative Hamilton Fish, Republican of New York, managed to attach another amendment to the Selective Service Act, providing that draftees would be selected in "an impartial manner," and their selection and training would be without discrimination "on account of race or color." As with other legislation, Negroes were to find that the intent of such amendments could be changed by their administration.[17]

The failure of Negroes to achieve a breakthrough against discrimination and segregation in the armed forces made this a major political issue for them in the 1940 presidential election. As early as 1939, the *Pittsburgh Courier* was editorially "demanding" that "the color bar be abolished in the armed forces"; its readers were reminded that "there will be a hard-fought Presidential election campaign within the twelve month, and our vote will be solicited."[18] By mid-1940, Charles H. Houston, legal counsel for the NAACP, was telling Negroes to let their Congressmen know that discrimination in the armed forces was an issue in the election. Walter White, executive secretary of the NAACP, made it known at his organization's annual meeting that this matter was the major issue: "Any candidate for President meriting the colored support must stand first for elimination of the color line from the armed services. . . ." Negro Democrats were supporting a third term nomination for President Roosevelt, but they wanted him to see that Negroes were admitted to every branch of the armed services.[19]

President Roosevelt and his Administration's New Deal had had a profound impact on Negro Americans. Years after Roosevelt's death, the Negro rank and file ranked him second to President Kennedy as the President who had done most for the rights of Negroes. Negro leaders ranked him third behind Presidents Kennedy and Truman.[20] In 1940, a Negro editor described the most important contribution of the New Deal to the Negro masses as being "its doctrine that Negroes are a part of the country and must be considered in any program for the country as a whole."[21] This attention, together with the alienation of black voters from the Republican Party, had led in 1936 to a majority of the Negro vote going to the Democratic party for the first time.[22] But 1940 marked the beginning of a period when Negroes would no longer be satisfied with recognition only.

Although black Americans, as the most economically depressed group in the population, did profit from New Deal relief programs, Roosevelt personally did little for the cause of civil rights. Arthur Schlesinger, Jr. has stated that civil rights for Negroes were not in President Roosevelt's "own first order of priorities."[23] Frank Freidel has found that Roosevelt's attitude toward segregation is "not clear," but that he "seemed ready to leave well enough alone in questions that involved white supremacy."

> Roosevelt did not stand in the path of those who were endeavoring to obtain greater civil rights for Negroes, but neither would he fight in their behalf. . . . At the most his was a position of benevolent neutrality—he was disposed to capitulate when they could muster sufficient force.[24]

No doubt Roosevelt's attitude on the rights of Negroes was influenced by the importance of the South in his party, but he also appears to have had a conservative attitude on race relations, believing that steps on behalf of Negroes must be slow and made one at a time.[25] This belief in a slow pace on behalf of the rights of blacks probably explains his privately expressed dislike of the NAACP.[26]

In 1940 the Republicans, anxious to get the Negro vote back into the fold, recognized the emotional impact upon Negroes of discrimination in the armed forces. Senator Robert Taft, a Republican hopeful, was telling black audiences that he stood for proportional representation of Negroes in all branches of the armed services.[27] The Republican Party platform on the rights of Negroes gave its nominee, Wendell L. Willkie, known as an exponent of equal rights for Negroes, a liberal plank on which to run:

> We pledge that our American citizens of Negro descent shall be given a square deal in the economic and political life of the nation. Discrimination in the civil service, the Army and the Navy and all other branches of the government must cease.[28]

The *Pittsburgh Courier* gave the statement front page treatment and called it "the strongest plank in the history" of the Republican Party for the abolition of discrimination against Negroes. Underneath this story, the *Courier* printed a letter from Roosevelt's secretary to Robert L. Vann, publisher of the *Courier* and prominent Roosevelt supporter in 1932 and 1936, stating that the President did not have time to meet and discuss the problem of discrimination in the armed services.[29]

Indicative of the importance of the Northern Negro vote to the Democratic coalition is the fact that the Democratic platform in 1940 mentioned Negroes by name for the first time in history.[30] In contrast to the Republican platform, however, the Democratic platform contained a general statement of what had been done for the Negroes in the past. In addition, it pledged that the party would "continue to strive for complete legislative safeguards against discrimination in government service and benefits, and in the national defense forces."[31]

By the middle of 1940, there was evidence that the majorities Negro voters had given the Democrats in 1936 were endangered by defections. Charges of discrimination in some of the relief agencies and in defense matters became more frequent. The apparent sincerity of Willkie's stand on civil rights issues also played a part. In August, 1940, the *Pittsburgh Courier,* which had been one of the strongest supporters of F.D.R. in 1932 and 1936, came out in support of Willkie for President.[32] A Gallup Poll reported that the Democrats still had a majority of the Negro vote, but there had been a considerable shift to the Republicans since 1936.[33]

Black Democrats were worried and voiced their concern to the White House. A Negro Democratic state senator from Michigan wrote that Negroes were very much concerned over their lack of participation in national defense. As an example, he pointed out that the Michigan legislature had appropriated the necessary money to form a black unit in the National Guard, but the War Department had stated that it would refuse to recognize such a unit if formed.[34] Mrs. Mary McLeod Bethune, Negro adviser in the National Youth Administration, warned the White House that "there is grave apprehension among Negroes lest the existing inadequate representation and training of colored persons may lead to the creation of labor battalions and other forms of discrimination against them in event of war." Mrs. Bethune reported that Negroes were urging the appointment of a Negro adviser to the Secretary of War to help in correcting this situation.[35]

As time for the election came closer, some Negro newspapers stepped up their criticism of the Roosevelt Administration on matters concerning Negroes. For example, the Baltimore *Afro-American's* editor expressed his bitterness over the continued restriction of enlistments of Negroes in the armed services at a time when these services were begging for volunteers: "In this regard, President Roosevelt not only forgot us but he neglected us, deserted and abandoned us to our enemies."[36] This paper printed article after article disclosing segregation and discrimination in New Deal agencies and departments such as the Civilian Conservation Corps and the Agriculture Department. Even Roosevelt's Warm Springs, Georgia, hospital for polio patients came under attack as a reporter found only one Negro patient there, and this one segregated in the basement. Willkie's statement in campaign speeches that he would do something about discrimination in the armed forces was headlined: "Willkie Says He'll End Jim Crow in Service Units." Finally, the *Afro-American*, a Negro newspaper that had not supported a Republican candidate for President since 1924, endorsed Willkie. And high on its list of reasons for doing so was Roosevelt's toleration of discrimination against Negroes in the armed forces.[37]

Roosevelt was concerned over Negro criticism on this matter. On September 5, 1940, the White House directed the War Department to prepare and hold a statement to the effect that "colored men will have equal opportunity with white men in all departments of the Army."[38] In a cabinet meeting on September 13, 1940, Roosevelt said that he was "troubled by representations of the Negroes that their race under the draft was limited to labor battalions." The Army informed the President that it planned to have 10 percent of its strength composed of Negroes. Roosevelt then suggested that the War Department publicize this fact. After this meeting, Secretary of War Stimson told the Army General Staff that he wanted "an exact statement of the facts in the case, and . . . how far we can go in the matter."[39] This first of a series of White House statements designed to reassure Negroes on the eve of the election was issued on September 16, 1940. This announcement stated that 36,000 out of the first 400,000 men drafted by the military under the new Selective Service Act would be Negroes, and that the Army was making a start in developing Negro air units.[40]

Criticism by Negroes continued to mount against discrimination in the armed forces. Walter White asked Mrs. Roosevelt to arrange a meeting between the President and a delegation of Negroes to discuss this matter. Mrs. Roosevelt characterized the conference as "important and immediate"; the President agreed to such a meeting on September 27, 1940, to include representatives of the Army and Navy.[41] Walter White of the NAACP, T. Arnold Hill, adviser on Negro affairs in the National Youth Administration, and A. Philip Randolph, head of the Brotherhood of Sleeping Car Porters, were the three Negro leaders to confer at the White House.

On the morning of the conference these three met and put their demands concerning Negroes in national defense in the form

of a memorandum to the President. The main points in this memorandum were that Negro officers and enlisted men should be used
throughout the services, with the only restrictions being their individual ability. One of the major demands was that "existing units of the
army and units to be established should be required to accept and select officers and enlisted personnel without regard to race." This
meant abandoning segregated units and integrating Negroes throughout the services as individuals. A revolution in the racial policies of
the services was being called for, but the chiefs of the services soon
made it known that they were not revolutionaries.[42]

Present at the meeting with the three Negro leaders were the
President, Secretary of the Navy Frank Knox, and Assistant Secretary
of War Robert P. Patterson. The President announced that Negro
units would be organized in all branches of the Army, and that he
would look into the ways by which discrimination in the services
could be lessened. Assistant Secretary Patterson stated that the War
Department planned to call Negro reserve officers to active duty, but
that the date had not been decided upon. The Navy indicated that it
was not willing to make any concessions in its policy. Secretary Knox
stated that he felt that the problem in his service was almost impossible because of the close living conditions on board ship. "Southern"
and "Northern" ships in the Navy were impossible, Knox said. At the
close of the meeting, Roosevelt promised to write or talk to the Negro leaders again after conferring with government officials. But the
next thing the leaders heard was a White House press release an-
nouncing a decision that had been made.[43]

On October 8, 1940, the Assistant Secretary of War submitted to
the President a full statement of policy already approved by the Secretary of War and the Army Chief of Staff, and Roosevelt initialed his
"O.K."[44] Revealing ignorance of the feeling of Negroes, the press secretary for the President, Stephen Early, quickly sent the statement to
the Democratic National Committee for full publicity. "You are at liberty to use it in the colored press and to have it given the widest possible distribution among colored organizations through the country,"
Early said.[45]

The policy stated by the War Department and initialed by
Roosevelt was not new, and therefore made no concessions to the demands of Negroes. It contained the main points of a policy adopted,
but not announced, by the War Department in 1937: the proportion
of Negroes in the Army would be the same as the proportion of Negroes in the country's population; Negro units would be established
in each branch of the Army, combatant as well as noncombatant; Negro reserve officers would serve only in Negro units officered by Ne-

gro personnel; Negroes would be given the opportunity to attend officer candidate schools when they were established; Negro pilots were being trained, and Negro aviation units were to be formed as soon as the necessary personnel was available; Negro civilians were being given an equal opportunity for employment at Army arsenals and installations. The statement concluded:

> The policy of the War Department is not to intermingle colored and white enlisted personnel in the same regimental organizations. This policy has proven satisfactory over a long period of years, and to make changes would produce situations destructive to morale and detrimental to the preparation for national defense. For similar reasons the department does not contemplate assigning colored reserve officers other than those of the Medical Corps and chaplains to existing Negro combat units of the Regular Army.[46]

Within the War Department, as long as this policy remained in effect, this statement was referred to as the President's "directive," or as Presidential "sanction" for the Army's policy, or "the President's policy of segregation of the races."[47]

In releasing this policy statement to the press, Early had implied that it had the approval of the Negro leaders who had met with the President on September 27. This resulted in charges that White, Hill and Randolph had "sold out" Negroes by agreeing to segregation in the armed forces.[48] To defend themselves, these three charged that the White House statement was a "trick," denied they had approved of such a policy, and printed the memorandum that they had given to the President to indicate that they had opposed continued segregation in the armed services. Roosevelt and the War Department policy received bitter criticism in the Negro press. It was pointed out that the assignment of Negro officers only to Negro units already officered by Negroes meant that they could be assigned to only two National Guard regiments. Contrary to the policy statement, not one Negro was receiving military pilot training and as recently as October 1, the Adjutant General had written that "applications from colored persons for flying cadet appointment or for enlistment in the Air Corps are not being accepted." Negroes everywhere denied the contention that the Army's policy of segregation had proven satisfactory in the past, and they recalled the First World War.[49]

The Republicans seized this issue and used it in their appeals to black voters. One full-page newspaper advertisement pointed out that one hundred white colonels had been promoted over the highest ranking Negro officer in the Army, Colonel Benjamin O. Davis. Another was headed: "Roosevelt, as Commander-in-Chief, permits Jim Crow in the U.S. Navy."[50] Negro Democratic Party workers were worried over the effect of the War Department policy statement on the Negro vote. One suggested a move by the White House that Negro newspapers had advocated for several months. This party worker felt that the "greatest stroke of the year" would be the promotion of Colonel Davis to general, making him the first Negro to hold this rank. Another party worker suggested that Negro voters would be soothed by the appointment of Negro assistants to the Director of Selective Service and the Secretary of War.[51]

Will Alexander, an adviser to the Administration on racial matters, recalled the deep concern in the White House about the Negro vote. Alexander received an urgent call from one of F.D.R.'s chief aides, Harry Hopkins, just before the 1940 election. Hopkins told Alexander that Roosevelt had done more for Negroes than anyone since Lincoln. Now it looked as though the Negro vote was going to go against him in the election. Hopkins wanted Alexander to tell him what could be done to keep the Negro vote Democratic.[52] From talks with Negroes, Alexander knew what they wanted—the promotion of Colonel Davis to general and a Negro assistant to the Secretary of War.

The White House began making a series of announcements in the few weeks before the election in an effort to mend fences with the Negro voters. To discount assertations of Negroes to the contrary, the War Department announced on October 16 that Negro aviation units would indeed be formed. Then there came announcements that new Negro combat units were being formed in the Army. Walter White had complained since the October 9 White House release that his position as a Negro leader had "been seriously impaired" by the implication that he had agreed to Army segregation. Stephen Early, the White House press secretary, was reluctant to correct this impression publicly, but, apparently under pressure from Roosevelt, he did so about a week before the election. The President himself wrote to White, Hill and Randolph on October 25, 1940, expressing regret that the statement had been misinterpreted, and pledging that Negroes would serve in all branches of the service. Roosevelt pointed out that this would be a "very substantial advance" over past policy, and concluded by telling the three Negroes that "you may rest assured that further developments of policy will be forthcoming to insure that Negroes are given fair treatment on a nondiscriminatory basis."[53]

The "further developments" came in the week before the election. Colonel Davis was promoted to the rank of general. General Davis had served as a first lieutenant in the Eighth United States Volunteer Infantry during the Spanish-American War. In 1899 he enlisted as a private in the Regular Army all-Negro Ninth Cavalry and was commissioned a second lieutenant in 1901. By 1930 Davis had been promoted to colonel, and for many years had served as an instructor of military science in Negro colleges. The Negro press had been hinting that, similar to Colonel Charles Young of World War I fame, he would be retired rather than promoted.[54]

Roosevelt also accepted the suggestion that a Negro assistant to the Secretary of War should be appointed, and he persuaded Secretary Stimson to make such an appointment. "The Negroes are taking advantage of this period just before [the] election to try to get everything they can in the way of recognition from the Army," Stimson complained in his diary.[55] The man announced to fill this position was William H. Hastie, a graduate of Harvard Law School. He had served as an assistant solicitor in the Department of Interior; he had been the first Negro appointed to the federal bench; he had served as chairman of the National Legal Committee of the NAACP; and just before his appointment as Civilian Aide to the Secretary of War, he was Dean of the Howard University Law School. The NAACP persuaded Supreme Court Justice Felix Frankfurter, a former professor of Hastie's, to recommend him to Stimson. During his service as Civilian Aide, Hastie would be considered within the War Department as an "NAACP man."[56]

Before the election, Roosevelt made one more significant appointment—a Negro adviser to the Director of Selective Service, Colonel Campbell C. Johnson.

In general, the Negro press praised these appointments, but their political significance did not go unnoticed. Negro Republicans charged that the appointments were a "political trick," and the *Pittsburgh Courier* warned that they "should not deceive any self-respecting Negro."[57] On the other hand, a Negro newspaper supporting Roosevelt looked upon these appointments as evidence of the President's "determination to bring about greater integration of colored citizens into the fundamental activities of government."[58]

Apparently the appointments and announcements by the White House were enough, if they were needed at all, because the majority of the Negro vote went to Roosevelt again in 1940. Although some Negro leaders began to defect from the Administration, the masses who received the benefits remained convinced that it was in their interest. However, the Negro majority was reduced over the 1936 total.[59] The NAACP was certainly pleased with Roosevelt's actions regarding the armed forces: "We have worked night and day during recent weeks to take personally to the people the things you did and wrote," and "I am certain tomorrow will reveal that Negroes know the truth,"

Walter White had written to the President on election eve.[60] Inexperienced in wielding their new national political power, and apparently feeling that half a loaf was a victory, Negro leaders felt that they gained as much as could be expected.

What did Negroes gain in regard to the armed forces, except the appointment of a Negro general and two Negro advisers? Most vocal Negroes, including the three leaders who presented their demands to the President, were asking for the end of segregation in the armed forces. The Navy refused to lift its restrictions on accepting Negroes only for the messman's branch; the Army said there would be Negro aviation units and that Negroes would serve in all of its branches. But both of these services, and the White House policy statement of October 9, 1940, steadfastly refused to abandon the principle of segregation. One Negro newspaper saw the point: "We asked Mr. Roosevelt to change the rules of the game and he counters by giving us some new uniforms. That is what it amounts to and we have called it appeasement."[61]

Defense preparations and the politics of an election year had stimulated agitation against the racial policies of the armed services, but the agitation had not ended segregation. The emotional impact of this issue would grow during World War II. The hypocrisy involved in fighting with a segregated military force against aggression by an enemy preaching a master race ideology was too obvious for Negroes. The end of military segregation had to await a new President, Harry S. Truman, and the rise of civil rights to a national political issue.[62] Eventually the armed forces would become one of the most integrated institutions in American life, so much so that militant civil rights advocates would consider the services "too integrated."

Notes

[1] For the extent of unemployment among Negroes in the 1930s and discrimination in defense industry, see E. Franklin Frazier, *The Negro in the United States* (New York, 1957), pp. 599-606; Robert C. Weaver, "Racial Employment Trends in National Defense," *Phylon*, II (Winter, 1941), 337-58; Louis C. Kesselman, *The Social Politics of FEPC* (Chapel Hill, 1948), pp. 6-7.

[2] The discrimination against Negro soldiers during World War I and the lasting bitterness that resulted are discussed in: Richard M. Dalfiume, "Desegregation of the United States Armed Forces, 1939-1953" (Unpublished Ph.D. dissertation, University of Missouri, 1966), pp. 4-25; Emmett J. Scott, *The American Negro in the World War* (n.p., 1919); W. E. B. DuBois, "The Black Man in the Revolution of 1914-1918," *The Crisis*, XVII (March, 1919), 218-23, "An Essay Toward a History of the Black Man in the Great War," *The Crisis*, XVIII (June, 1919), 63-87, and "The Negro Soldier in the Service Abroad During the First World War," *Journal of Negro Education*, XII (Summer, 1943), 324-34; John hope Franklin, *From Slavery to Freedom* (2nd ed. rev.; New York, 1956), pp. 447-77; Gunnar Myrdal, *An American Dilemma* (New York, 1944), p. 745.

[3] For the prevalence of this stereotype in World War I and its perpetuation to the World War II years and after, see "The Colored Soldier in the U.S. Army: Prepared in the Historical Section, Army War College, May, 1942" (Typewritten manuscript in the Office of the Chief of Military History), pp. 57-128; General Robert Lee Bullard, *Personalities and Reminiscences of the War* (Garden City, 1925), pp. 294-98; Ulysses G. Lee, Jr., *The United States Army in World War II: Special Studies:* The Employment of Negro Troops (Washington, D.C.: Government Printing Office, 1966), chaps. 1-2. Dalfiume, *op. cit.,* pp. 10-22, 25-29, 60-62, 72-75, 82-83, 274-75; William H. Hastie, "Negro Officers in Two World Wars," *Journal of Negro Education,* XII (Summer, 1943), 316-23.

[4] "For Manhood in National Defense," *The Crisis,* XLVII (December, 1940), 375.

[5] Herbert Garfinkel, *When Negroes March: The March on Washington Movement in the Organizational Politics for FEPC* (Glencoe, 1959), p. 20.

[6] Robert L. Vann to Roosevelt, January 19, 1939, OF 93A, Franklin D. Roosevelt Library (hereafter referred to as FDRL).

[7] Roy Wilkins to Secretary of War Harry H. Woodring, March 9, 1939, OF 93A, FDRL.

[8] *Pittsburgh Courier,* July 20, 1940. Houston's memoirs ran for a number of issues: July 27, 1940; August 10, 1940; September 7, 14, 28, 1940; October 5, 12, 1940.

[9] See the series of articles by a Negro veteran in the Baltimore *Afro-American,* December 9, 30, 1939. Examples of articles recalling the discrimination of World War I are *Pittsburgh Courier,* October 7, 14, 1939; Walter Wilson, "Old Jim Crow in Uniform," *The Crisis,* XLVI (February, 1939), 42-44, and (March, 1939), 71-73, 82, 93.

[10] See for example, the Baltimore *Afro-American,* October 14, 1939; *Pittsburgh Courier,* April 13 and June 8, 1940.

[11] *Pittsburgh Courier,* September 16, 1939.

[12] *Ibid.,* October 28, 1939, July 6, 1940, October 19, 1940; *Norfolk Journal and Guide,* July 6, 1940; Baltimore *Afro-American,* October 21, 1939.

[13] Lawrence J. Paszek, "Negroes and the Air Force, 1939-1949" (Unpublished paper read at the Southern Historical Association meeting, November 12, 1964), pp. 2-3; Lee, *op. cit.,* pp. 55-63; W. J. Trent, Jr., Adviser on Negro Affairs in the Office of the Secretary of the Interior, to M. H. McIntyre, Secretary to the President, January 31, 1939, OF 93, FDRL; James L. H. Peck, "When Do We Fly?" *The Crisis,* XLVII (December, 1940), 376-78, 388. It was not until January, 1941, that Negroes were made a part of the Air Corps and this occurred only because of White House pressure. See Florence Murray (ed.), *The Negro Handbook,* 1942 (New York, 1942), pp. 78, 81-82.

[14] *Pittsburgh Courier,* October 5, November 23, 1940; Baltimore *Afro-American,* December 21, 1940; Anonymous, "The Negro in the United States Navy," *The Crisis,* XLVII (July, 1940), 200-01, 210.

[15] *Pittsburgh Courier,* November 23, 1940.

[16] *Ibid.,* June 22, 29, 1940; Lee, *op. cit.,* pp. 68-69.

[17] Lee, *op. cit.,* pp. 71-74; Selective Service System, *Special Groups: Special Monograph No. 10* (Washington, D.C., Government Printing Office, 1953), pp. 3, 42-45.

[18] October 7, 1939.

[19] Baltimore *Afro-American,* June 22, 29, 1940; *Pittsburgh Courier,* June 29, 1940.

[20] William Brink and Louis Harris, *The Negro Revolution in America* (New York, 1964), pp. 90, 214.

[21] "The Roosevelt Record," *The Crisis,* XLVII (September, 1940), 343.

[22] Elbert Lee Tatum, *The Changed Political Thought of the Negro, 1915-1940* (New York, 1951), pp. 139, 147-61, 180-81; Franklin, *op. cit.,* pp. 512-28; Walter Johnson, *1600 Pennsylvania Avenue* (Boston, 1960), pp. 81-82.

[23] Arthur M. Schlesinger, Jr., *The Age of Roosevelt: The Politics of Upheaval* (Boston, 1960), p. 431.

[24] Frank Freidel, *F.D.R. and the South* (Baton Rouge, 1965), pp. 73, 81, 97.

[25] This is the impression conveyed by the memoirs of a prominent Negro New Dealer. See Mary McLeod Bethune, "My Secret Talks with F.D.R.," *Ebony*, IV (April, 1949), 42-51.

[26] Roosevelt's private opinion of the NAACP is found on a note attached to a letter to Arthur B. Spingarn, President of the NAACP, October 1, 1943, PPF 1336, FDRL. Spingarn had written a letter to Roosevelt asking him to write a letter recognizing the twenty-five years of service by Walter White to the NAACP. The note reads: "Miss Tully brought this in. Says the President doesn't think too much of this organization—not to be to[o] fullsome—tone it down a bit." For Roosevelt's toleration of segregation and discrimination in New Deal programs, see John A. Salmond, "The Civilian Conservation Corps and the Negro," *Journal of American History*, LII (June, 1965), 75-88; Allen Francis Kifer, "The Negro Under the New Deal, 1933-1941" (Unpublished Ph.D. dissertation, University of Wisconsin, 1961).

[27] *Pittsburgh Courier,* June 8, 1940.

[28] *New York Times,* June 27, 1940. The Republican platform also supported legislation to guarantee the franchise to Southern Negroes and legislation against lynching, two important items that the Roosevelt Administration was reluctant to support.

[29] July 6, 1940.

[30] Johnson, *op. cit.,* p. 82.

[31] *New York Times,* July 18, 1940.

[32] August 24, 1940.

[33] *New York Times,* February 4, 1940; Franklin, *op. cit.,* p. 517.

[34] Charles C. Diggs to Stephen Early, July 1, 1940, OF 93, FDRL.

[35] "Memorandum on Negro Participation in the Armed Forces," n.d. (around August, 1940), OF 93, FDRL. This memorandum appears to have been written by Robert C. Weaver. See Weaver, Administrative Assistant to the Advisory Commission to the Council of National Defense, to Oscar Chapman, July 12, 1940, Chapman papers, Harry S. Truman Library.

[36] August 31, 1940.

[37] August 17, 24, 1940; September 7, 14, 21, 1940; October 19, 1940.

[38] Memorandum to G-1 and G-3 from the Chief of Staff, September 5, 1940, quoted in Lee, *op. cit.,* p. 75.

[39] Memorandum to G-1 from General George C. Marshall, Chief of Staff, September 14, 1940, quoted in *ibid.*

[40] *Pittsburgh Courier,* September 21, 1940.

[41] Memorandum by S.T.E. for General Watson, September 19, 1940, OF 2538, FDRL; Walter White, *A Man Called White* (New York, 1948), p. 186.

[42] The complete text of this memorandum is contained in an NAACP press release, October 5, 1940, in OF 93, FDRL.

[43] *Ibid.,* White, *op. cit.,* pp. 186-87.

[44] Stephen Early to Robert P. Patterson, Assistant Secretary of War, n.d., AG 291.21, Army General Staff papers, National Archives Record Group 319.

[45] Memorandum to Charlie Michelson from Stephen Early, teletyped to Democratic National Committee, October 9, 1940, OF 93, FDRL.

[46] *Ibid.*

[47] Lee, *op. cit.,* p. 76.

[48] Most bitter in its denunciation of the three Negro leaders was the *Chicago Defender,* October 19, 1940.

[49] "White House Blesses Jim Crow," *The Crisis*, XLVII (November, 1940), 350-51, 357; the reaction of the Negro press to the statement is summarized in "The Problem," *Time*, October 28, 1940, p. 19.

[50] Baltimore *Afro-American*, October 12, 19, 26, 1940.

[51] Bishop R. R. Wright, Jr., Chairman, Colored Division, National Democratic Headquarters, Midwestern Region, to Stephen Early, October 16, 1940, OF 93, FDRL; Summary of Memorandum to the President from James Rowe, October 18, 1940, OF 2538, FDRL.

[52] Will W. Alexander, "The Reminiscences of Will W. Alexander" (Oral History Research Office, Columbia University), p. 360.

[53] *New York Times*, October 16, 1940; Stephen Early to Walter White, October 18, 1940; White to Early, October 21, 1940; Early to White, October 25, 1940; Franklin D. Roosevelt to White, Randolph, and Hill, October 25, 1940, all in OF 93, FDRL.

[54] Richard Bardolph, *The Negro Vanguard* (New York, 1959), pp. 449-51.

[55] Henry L. Stimson, "Stimson Diary" (Typewritten manuscript in the Yale University Library), October 22, 1940.

[56] *Ibid.*; Bardolph, *op. cit.*, pp. 360-61; Interview with James C. Evans, Department of Defense, July, 1964.

[57] *Pittsburgh Courier*, November 2, 1940.

[58] *Norfolk Journal and Guide*, November 2, 1940.

[59] Franklin, *op. cit.*, p. 517.

[60] Walter White to the President, November 4, 1940, PPF 1336, FDRL.

[61] Baltimore *Afro-American*, November 2, 1940.

[62] Although the Navy began to formulate a policy of integration at the end of World War II segregation in the military did not begin to crumble rapidly until President Truman issued Executive Order 9981 in July, 1948. This order stated that it was the policy of the President that there should be "equality of treatment and opportunity" for all persons in the armed services without regard to race. The President's Committee on Equality of Treatment and Opportunity in the Armed Services, popularly known as the Fahy Committee, was established to implement the order.

The Black Press and the Assault on Professional Baseball's "Color Line," October 1945–April 1947

BILL L. WEAVER

Between the end of World War II in 1945 and the passage of the Civil Rights Act in 1964, key institutions within the black community facilitated the transition from racial segregation to integration. Most notably, the black church and church leaders championed the causes of black freedom and integration. But like the black church, the black press also provided valuable institutional leadership in the struggle for first-class citizenship. The manner in which the black press covered Jackie Robinson's entry into major league baseball is a case in point. Black newspapers and their editors not only reported the high-spirited events and attitudes surrounding the Robinson milestone; they also chronicled the various stages of the saga and analyzed its overall significance. For many people, Robinson became a symbol for all African Americans who hoped to enter the American mainstream. With so much at stake, the black press took great pains to capture the true essence of Robinson's story for their communities and for all of America.

Bill Weaver's essay gives us a glimpse of the African American mind-set in the postwar decade. Having fought World War II for the double "V," victory at home and victory abroad, African Americans deeply resented what appeared to be a return to the prewar racial status quo. Consequently, for many people the news of Jackie Robinson's having been signed by a major league baseball team signaled racial progress and high hopes for the future. Weaver surveys a wealth of black newspapers and highlights a distinguished group of African American journalists who were eager to welcome Robinson as the advance guard of a new millennium in race relations and opportunities for blacks.

ONE NEED ONLY TO LOOK at a major league baseball game to witness the progress in race relations made in that professional sport since 1945. The color line—admittedly imaginary but no less real—was broken by Jackie Robinson over a period of seventeen months (November 1945–April 1947). During that crucial period the American Negro press provided a valuable service in contributing to the integration of the sport.

The black press has served traditionally as both an organ of protest and an instrument of race unity.[1] E. Franklin Frazier's contention that the Negro press "creates and perpetuates the world of make-believe for the black bourgeoisie"[2] seems inaccurate and unjust. An investigation of the roles played by black newspapers on several issues reveals those newspapers to have been acutely perceptive and remarkably capable of assessing the importance of racial advances in the context of what the race ultimately hoped to achieve. Many people agreed with one writer's 1945 assessment that no single group in America had a greater responsibility in the postwar years than did the Negro press.[3] The extent to which it understood and met its responsibility can be observed in its handling of the assault on professional baseball's "color line."

Jack Roosevelt Robinson is a classic example of human achievement under adverse circumstances. Born to Georgia sharecroppers, abandoned by his father, and moved to California as a small child, Jackie Robinson rose to athletic prominence at Muir Technical High School in Pasadena, at Pasadena Junior College, and at the University of California at Los Angeles. Adversity in the form of blatant racial discrimination stalked his term of military duty. Capitalizing upon his athletic reputation from UCLA, Robinson quickly acquired a college coaching position, but after a short while, he abandoned coaching in favor of professional baseball. Inasmuch as the major leagues barred Negroes, Robinson's only opportunity was to sign a contract with the Kansas City Monarchs of the Negro Leagues. Composed of several teams owned by white businessmen, the Negro Leagues operated on a very limited budget and were tarnished by widespread gambling involving club owners. Many people viewed the Negro Leagues as a poor outlet for Negroes' baseball skills, and from time to time rumors circulated that owners of major league clubs planned to "clean up" the Negro Leagues either through purchase or by establishing a competing league composed of Negro players. From all outward appearances, no thought had been given to the idea of admitting Negroes to the major leagues.

Although there was no indication that professional baseball's "color line" was under consideration, aroused hopes for racial equality emerged from World War II, and legislative enactments and federal orders in the immediate postwar years did much to convert the aroused hopes into positive results. On a more materialistic level, the supply of white baseball talent had been depleted during the war, and the wealth of black talent became more noticeable to at least one major league owner. The "Double V" campaign, launched by the National Association for the Advancement of Colored People (NAACP) during the war with the expressed desire for a civil rights victory at home to accompany a military victory abroad,[4] precipitated the establishment of the Fair Employment Practices Commission and ultimately influenced the passage of Fair Employment Practices laws in some states. Passage of the New York FEPC law in 1945 was quickly followed by efforts by Negroes to apply the new statute to professional baseball.[5] Despite the fact that Branch Rickey, president and chief stockholder of the Brooklyn Dodgers, minimized the influence of the FEPC law,[6] it obviously fortified his position.[7] Probably, as Carl Rowan has suggested, both New York Governor Thomas E. Dewey and New York City Mayor Fiorello LaGuardia measured the issue of professional baseball integration in terms of the black votes it would attract in return.[8]

Integration of major league baseball was not altogether unprecedented, but it had occurred either very long ago (in the 1870s and 1880s) or had been camouflaged by a player claiming to be of another nationality.[9] There would be, of course, no breakthrough for the race as long as integration could be accomplished only by employing subterfuge.

In an address delivered at Wilberforce University in 1948, Rickey mentioned that he had spent $25,000 in 1945 scouting "colored players."[10] Three scouts in the Dodger organization had combed the Negro Leagues in search of talent for Rickey, whom they thought to be establishing another Negro league to utilize existing ballparks while home teams were out of town.[11] Rickey's selection process included more than on-the-field activities, and Jackie Robinson was brought to Brooklyn for a gruelling session designed to demonstrate his ability to cope with intense racial opposition.

On August 28, 1945, Branch Rickey signed Jackie Robinson to a contract but asked that no announcement be made until December.[12] However, on October 29, 1945, Rickey called a press conference, ostensibly to denounce the management of the Negro Leagues, and almost as an afterthought, he announced that Brooklyn had signed Jackie Robinson to a contract and had assigned him to the Montreal minor league club. That news hit the Negro press like a bombshell. The Pittsburgh *Courier* carried an exhaustive account of the event, and, with the exception of the Atlanta *Daily World* and the Birmingham *World*, most black newspapers gave thorough treatment to the breakthrough.

Negro newspaper responses seemed to fall into four categories: (1) comments on the significance of the breakthrough, (2) expressions of appreciation for Rickey's actions, (3) expressions of racial hopes pinned on Robinson, and (4) analyses of the intense pressure placed on Robinson and expressions of cautious optimism regarding the outcome of Robinson's efforts. The New York *Amsterdam News* called the event "just the drop of water in the drought that keeps faith alive in American institutions."[13]

Detroit's *Michigan Chronicle* commented that

> The clubs which insist on drawing the color line have been pushed out on a limb. Sooner or later they will meet the censure of the American public which, despite the popularity of color prejudice, has an ingrained sense of true sportsmanship. Joe Louis would never have won the hearts of Americans if this were not so.

The same paper carried Roy Wilkin's regular column in which Wilkins pointed out that the signing of Robinson

> means that in a new and dramatic fashion the fact that the Negro is a citizen with talents and rights is being heralded to the nation. The people who go to baseball games do not, in the main, go to lectures on race relations, nor do they read pamphlets about goodwill. The millions who read box scores very likely have never heard of George Washington Carver. But Jackie Robinson, if he makes the grade, will be doing a missionary work with these people that Carver could never do. He will be saying to them that his people should have their rights, should have jobs, decent homes and education, freedom from insult, and equality of opportunity to achieve.[14]

Guarding against overemphasis on the signing of the black player, the *Amsterdam News* reminded its readers that Negroes

> fought a war for four years to rid the world of vicious racial theories, racial and religious discrimination and segregation. Yet, the fact that Jackie Robinson, a young Negro who is intellectually, culturally and physically superior to most white baseball players, has signed a contract to play in a minor league has caused a national sensation.[15]

Much emphasis was placed in the Negro press on the role of Rickey in achieving this racial breakthrough. The Boston *Chronicle* urged its readers to write Rickey and express gratitude for his actions. The euphoria of the moment prompted one writer of a letter to the editor to suggest that a campaign be begun to boost Branch Rickey for President, Frank Sinatra for Vice President, Dr. Mary Mcleod Bethune for Secretary of State, and Mrs. Eleanor Roosevelt for Secretary of the Interior.[16] Rickey was characterized in *The Crisis* in December, 1945, as "a deeply religious man with the fire of the crusader burning in his breast," and labeled as the "John Brown of baseball."[17] The

Courier opined that "when Branch Rickey stood up and defied a baseball world he knew would be rebellious, . . . he was motivated by a
firm conviction within that he was doing the right thing." Continuing, the *Courier* claimed that Rickey signed Robinson because he believed the Negro shortstop was a great prospect and because "his
conscience would not permit him to wallow in the mire of racial discrimination."[18] On the other hand, the Indianapolis *Recorder,* without
attempting to denigrate Rickey, reminded its readers not to neglect
what it called "the real factor behind the scenes," Governor Thomas
E. Dewey, and suggested that "only by the actions of such Americans
in high places can this nation hope to 'win the peace.' "[19]

Negro newspapers were careful to point out the racial responsibility that had come to Robinson as a result of his selection. Robinson, according to the *Courier,* carried "the hopes, aspirations and
ambitions of thirteen million black Americans heaped on his broad,
sturdy shoulders."[20] *The Crisis* called him the "symbol of hope of millions of colored people in this country and elsewhere," and pointed
out that upon Robinson was "pinned the hopes of millions of fair-
minded whites who want to see every American get a chance regardless of race, creed, or color."[21] The *Amsterdam News* cautioned that
"the weight of knowing how much race pride and how much the future of youngsters hangs in the balance can be an oppressive although challenging load."[22] The Philadelphia *Tribune* optimistically
asserted that the signing of Robinson was "but the forerunner of the
days when practically every team—even the Athletics in our city—will
have one or more colored players on their teams, solely on their ability to play their positions and on their value to the team."[23] To this
optimistic note the *Courier* added another by commenting that there
was "every reason to believe that he [Rickey] will continue to scout
Negro players and if he finds one capable of making the grade won't
hesitate to sign him." Encouragingly, the *Courier* added that he is
"not limiting Robinson to the confines of the International
League."[24]

Soon after signing Robinson, Rickey signed Johnny Wright, a
Negro pitcher, and assigned him to the Montreal club.[25] Wright spent
the 1946 season in Montreal, but early in 1947 he was released by the
Dodger organization. By the time that Wright had received his release, two other Negroes, Roy Campanella and Donald Newcombe,
had signed Dodger contracts and were performing for another of the
club's minor league teams.

The extent to which Robinson was aware of his unique position
became clear in an interview with Wendell Smith of the *Courier* in
which he promised that "If I make the team I will not forget that I

am representing a whole race of people who are pulling for me."
Continuing, Robinson said "I am some sort of a guinea pig in this
thing," whereupon he promised to be "the best guinea pig that ever
lived, both on the field and off." He concluded the interview with
the promise to "try to do as good a job as Joe Louis," who, he said,
had "done a great deal for us and I will try to carry on."[26]

Several sources expressed confidence that Robinson would succeed in baseball, but at the same time cautioned fans against celebrating racial victories too quickly. The *Amsterdam News* exuded
confidence in the success of this experiment when it said that

> As in all competitive fields, where merit has a chance to show, base-
> ball, along with boxing and track, will discover the best man will al-
> ways win the plaudits of the great American audience. The bulk of
> American people are willing to give homage and praise to accom-
> plishments—without looking for a color label.[27]

The *Courier,* enraged by a comment in the New York *Daily News* pre-
dicting that Robinson was only a 1,000 to 1 shot to make the grade,
predicted success for Robinson, but urged blacks not to "work up a
lather until he's actually on the ball club and making a name for
himself."[28] The Indianapolis *Recorder,* issuing the same caution, reminded fans of a situation in 1923 when the entry of a Jew was bal-
lyhooed only to find later that the player failed to meet the
expectations which his people had for him.[29]

Except for a few instances, such as opposition from the Negro
Leagues, opposition from Washington Senators owner Clark Griffith,
and rumors of opposition from some Dodger players, the response
from the baseball community was a favorable one.[30] Rickey obviously
expected some opposition from other owners, and though he apparently received it, there are conflicting reports on the form that opposition took.[31] Rickey's terse comment regarding the alleged
opposition of some Dodger players (particularly one—Dixie Walker)
was "we pay those players to play ball. The job of picking players is
my job."[32]

The black press expressed concern over those who opposed the
move toward integration. *The Crisis* lamented the fact that Rickey
must fight some of Robinson's own people [the Negro Leagues] on a
matter which "benefits them most."[33] In response to the players who
had allegedly expressed reservations about playing against a Negro,
the *Michigan Chronicle* stated that "the southern white boys who may
be shocked will recover in due time," and added that "a good democratic shock in the right place might do them a lot of good." The
same paper viewed all those who opposed the move as "warped-
headed bigots," to whom it offered its "complete contempt."[34]

The 1946 season, as expected, proved to be extremely important in the move to integrate major league baseball. Prior to having played a game in the minor leagues, Jackie had been cast as the hero of a new comic book which traced his career to date. Obviously, black Americans needed another Negro athletic hero; the "Brown Bomber," Joe Louis, was not enough. Beginning with spring training in Florida, the Negro press followed Robinson's successes on the field and lamented his difficulties off the field.[35] The *Courier* took pride in dispatching its sports editor to Florida to cover Robinson's spring training experiences. At first, the *Courier's* reporter, Wendell Smith, was moved by the favorable reception which Robinson received in the South, causing him to conclude after one warm reception that "it definitely proved that baseball fans, whether in North or South, appreciate talent and will not hesitate to give credit where credit is due." Smith was equally impressed with writers of Southern papers whom he claimed to have been "eminently and conspicuously fair."[36] But as time wore on, he became more and more concerned with the racial discrimination that emerged. He and other reporters noticed that attendance by blacks at ball parks in the South was frequently limited because of the restriction in the number of seats constructed in the segregated portion of the park.

The reporters acquired renewed admiration for Branch Rickey when he moved his teams, Brooklyn and Montreal, from Sanford, Florida, to Daytona Beach because of the racial policies in the former city.[37] They admired Rickey even more when he refused to play games in which Robinson and Johnny Wright would not be free to participate.[38] The *Courier* applauded Rickey's answer, "without Robinson and Wright, there'll be no games," and added that the "stirring declaration pierced the usually impregnable armour of public office holders" in those Southern cities. Such action, according to the *Courier,* "left a scar that will become more prominent and discernable each day as the world looks down with startled curiosity at the part of its anatomy that is being gnawed by the parasite of racial discrimination!"[39]

In November, 1945, Robinson had declared that his efforts were aimed at racial as well as personal gain. Certainly his convictions were deepened by the racial discrimination which he and his wife, Rachel, encountered in route to spring training in 1946. They had been removed from an airplane in favor of white passengers, and finally found themselves forced to ride a bus to Sanford. Robinson commented later that he realized as they bounced up and down on the back seat of that bus that there was "much more at stake here than just my pride."[40] Rather than serving as a detriment to his career, incidents like these probably spurred him to greater effort, and ultimately, to greater success.

In an effort to prove that baseball club owners who took a chance on Negro players would be well rewarded, black writers pointed out that such clubs would not only draw the Negro patrons, who had been passive about organized baseball for years because of the ban against their players, but also thousands of white fans who come out of "sheer curiosity or because they, too, approve of Negro players in organized baseball."[41] At the end of the 1946 season *The Crisis* proudly reported that "on his own account he [Robinson] is responsible for at least 50,000 additional paid admissions. . . ."[42]

Initial success on the playing field elicited a chorus of gleeful comments in the black press. Wendell Smith's colorful report of Robinson's home run in his first minor league game indicates the ecstasy which he must have experienced. "The ball," he reported, "glistened brilliantly in the afternoon sun as it went hurtling high and far over the left field fence." Robert L. Vann, editor of the *Courier,* writing in the same issue, offered the timely reminder that more than opportunity was needed in order to achieve success like that of Robinson; "one must," he said, "equip himself to succeed when opportunity is opened to him."[43] To Wendell Smith, Robinson's initial success proved that "class tells in the stretch." Confident that Robinson would succeed, the *Courier* assessed the value of what his early efforts had accomplished:

> Many other doors are going to be opened from now on in America to young colored men and women, and it is to be fervently hoped that all those who get the opportunity to enter hitherto untrodden fields will be as well qualified to deliver the goods as these young athletes who have defied tradition and won.[44]

Despite many successful days on the field, Robinson experienced some equally unsuccessful ones. Sam Lacy, sports editor of the Baltimore *Afro-American,* took one such opportunity to address an open letter to Robinson's Montreal manager, Clay Hooper:

> With your club this year is Jackie Robinson, the first lad of his race to win a trial with an organized minor or major league team. He is human regardless of the color of his skin. And, being human, he'll have "good" days and "bad" days.
>
> He'll have moments like that triumphant opening when he became a hero before 30,000 patrons and won smiles and pats on the back from you. But he'll also have moments like Sunday's in Baltimore, where 25,000 fans saw him boot away the [sic] your second game with the Orioles of that city.

You, like Jackie, are on the spot, if for no reason than that you come from a section of the country that is generally regarded as hostile to Robinson's people. . . . Another player would have been "bawled out" by you immediately after the game was over, and I am hopeful you didn't "bend over backwards" in this case simply because it was Jackie.

If you didn't give him hell, you should have. Jackie's people don't want him treated any different from the rest.[45]

Not many such letters were needed during the 1946 season, as Robinson had very few bad days.

The behavior of black fans proved to be a major concern in the Negro press. Wendell Smith warned of the dangers inherent in lack of discretion on the part of over-enthusiastic fans, and he added:

The guy who is so stimulated by the appearance of Robinson and Wright in Montreal uniforms that he stands and rants and raves, yells and screams, before they have even so much as picked up a ball, is the guy who will be cheering them out of Organized Baseball rather than in.

The guy who makes himself conspicuous by going into convulsions whenever Robinson swings at a ball, or Wright throws one, is not going to help the situation, but, rather, put more pressure on them.

Now that they have made the team and are set for the long pennant grind, the Negro can help by taking some of the pressure off them. Cheering is all right at the proper time, but it is unnecessary before something has happened.

Drinking in the stands and rowdy deportment will only embarrass Robinson and Wright and hamper their efforts to reach the big leagues.[46]

Joseph D. Bibb, syndicated columnist, also urged self-restraint, reminding his readers that "if Jackie and Johnny make good, they will be heralded by the white sporting fraternity, notwithstanding. Remember Joe Louis."[47]

During the 1946 season fans came from far and near to see Robinson and Wright play,[48] and their trips were richly rewarded, for Robinson finished the season as the top hitter in the league, as the best-fielding second baseman, in a tie for most runs scored, and second in the league in stolen bases. To cap off an outstanding season, he led the Montreal Royals to the International League championship and thus to the Little World Series against the American Association champion Louisville Colonels. In the Little World Series Robinson performed well despite racial difficulties encountered in Louisville, where the attendance of Negroes was carefully regulated, thus leaving outside the ball park many disappointed and resentful

blacks. The 1946 season had clearly shown the world that Jackie
Robinson could play baseball and could weather the racial
difficulties.

Spring training in 1947 would help determine whether Jackie
could be elevated to the major leagues. After the 1946 season, the
Courier assured its readers that Robinson would join the Brooklyn
team in 1947 and commented that "in most minds, the names
'Robinson' and 'Brooklyn' are synonymous."[49]

In an obvious effort to prevent a repeat in 1947 of the racial
problems encountered in Florida in 1946, Rickey conducted spring
training in Cuba. Both the *Chronicle* and the *Courier* made a special effort to compliment Rickey for expending the extra money necessary
to give the Negro player a better opportunity to show his abilities un-
molested by outsiders. As spring training proceeded, and as Robinson
proved to be up to form, the *Courier* kept before its readers the subject of Robinson's chances of elevation to the major leagues. On one
occasion the *Courier* predicted:

> If Robinson fails to make the grade, it will be many years before a
> Negro makes the grade. This is IT! If Jackie Robinson is turned
> down this week, then you can look for another period of years
> before the question ever arises officially again.[50]

Although the announcement that Jackie Robinson would join
the Dodgers surprised few people, it unleashed a flurry of pent-up
words from the Negro writers. The St. Louis *Argus* expressed its
thanks to Rickey and commented: "We, as Negroes have so long and
so many times found ourselves impotent, lying as it were, at the pool,
with no one to 'dip us when the water was troubled.' "[51] The *Chronicle's* headline, "TRIUMPH OF WHOLE RACE SEEN IN JACKIE'S DE-
BUT IN MAJOR-LEAGUE BALL," was followed by the comment that

> the discrimination in this field has always been felt keenly; more
> keenly because of the predominance of colored participants in
> more lines of sports, and the fact that in the colored baseball
> leagues were players who when they met white big-league players in
> off-season competition, frequently came out on top.

Continuing, the *Chronicle* gave credit to the New York Communist newspaper, the *Daily Worker*, which, according to the *Chronicle*,
was largely responsible for getting the crusade for integration of major league baseball started. The *Chronicle* concluded with a compliment and a question:

> A tree of progress grows in Brooklyn now. Will similar trees grow in
> the rest of the big league cities, such as Boston, to which Jackie will
> come next Sunday for the Dodgers-Braves game?[52]

A cartoon, appearing in the Birmingham *World,* showed Jackie sliding in safely at home, enabled by "qualifications" and "fair play" to beat the late throw which was labeled "Jim Crow."[53] Both the *World* and the Atlanta *Daily World* carried an editorial, notable for its placing achievements in proper perspective.

> Achievement is not a matter of race and color. It is a matter of environment and opportunity. Human beings grow and develop much alike, both modern science and Christianity affirm this biological truth. But if a Negro turns out to be a bad actor; if he jostles a white passenger in his haste to secure a seat, or if he commits some outrageous crime, almost always, American prejudice charges it up to race.
>
> That is why Negro Americans may take pardonable pride in the field or [of] sports, in the arts and sciences, in business or the professions. They have got to make the grade, or else it is going to be written off as a racial and color weakness.

"America," continued the two Southern newspapers,

> can gain another important lesson. That the names of Jackie Robinson, Joe Louis, George Washington Carver and hundreds upon hundreds of others, didn't just happen; that in spite of the barriers of race and color, distinguished achievement, industry and manliness are traits which must eventually be recognized under any skin.[54]

The *Michigan Chronicle* saw the move as totally consistent with American claims of democracy and commented that "the closed door in major league baseball was a symbol of intolerance and of bigotry which put us to shame all over the world."[55] Roy Wilkins elatedly said, "Well, our boy, Jackie Robinson made it. If you give our folks a fair chance some of them will always make it."[56]

The *Courier* carried two photographs of Robinson, one in his Brooklyn uniform, under which were placed the words, "Man of Destiny," and the other showing Robinson standing outside the Dodger clubhouse door containing a sign "Keep out." Under this photograph the *Courier* said:

> This is the door—that Rickey has finally opened. The keep out sign doesn't mean Jackie, or any other colored player who can make the grade. The great American pastime has really become American at last.[57]

The *Amsterdam News* sought to emphasize the accomplishment as only a small portion of the total movement for equality and reminded its readers that

> Although everyone is pleased that Jackie Robinson was rightfully promoted from the Montreal team to the Brooklyn Dodgers, democracy still marches at a snail's pace. For in the year 1946 A.D., the fact that a qualified ball player who happened to be colored was

signed by a major league baseball club (at a notoriously low salary) was looked upon as earth shaking. . . .

The big point to all this is, until it ceases to be news when colored Americans are expected in positions from which they have been hitherto barred without so much ballyhoo, it cannot be said that America has become of age and is accepting the colored man or woman on merit. Unfortunately, Jackie Robinson is still a Negro ball player first and a big leaguer second. This is only because it is most unusual for a colored man to play in the big leagues and because he has not yet been accepted as a ball player first and a colored man second.

Furthermore, it is not likely that any other Negro ball player will be signed by any big league team in the near future, in spite of the fact that the racial bar has been smashed. In fact, one or two Negroes work in many positions in business and other organizations for generations, yet no other Negroes, though even more qualified, are not [sic] hired. These handful of colored people working in what is described as "unusual positions" are singled out and pointed to with pride as being examples of racial progress.

In truth, the few Negroes employed in positions rarely held by other members of that race only emphasizes how deep rooted is discrimination in this country.

In conclusion, the *Amsterdam News* expressed pleasure that Robinson had been given his deserved chance, but lamented that it had not come earlier. "While it is something to crow about," commented the New York paper, "it is also something to impress upon us that discrimination and segregation are still rampant and basic in the U.S.A."[58]

The Crisis saw Robinson's selection by Brooklyn as a wise move because that city seemed most likely to greet him with minimum reservations and to give him an even chance to make good on his merits. *The Crisis* also cautioned fans, Negro and white, against regarding Robinson as a "a miracle man," for he "is not hired to solve the race problem, but to play baseball."[59]

Negro baseball fans were as pleased with the success of their hero as were the reporters. They turned out in great numbers in all National League cities to see him play. The *Afro-American* conducted a sports quiz in which the winner got an all-expense-paid trip to Brooklyn to see Jackie play. The *World* announced the chartering of a special train that would carry fans from Memphis to St. Louis to see Robinson on his first trip to that city. The *Amsterdam News* announced that a Jackie Robinson Booster Club had been formed by 500 citizens of Harlem, each of whom had agreed to purchase two tickets to each of Brooklyn's home games.

Again, as the Negro press had done in the spring of 1946, it cautioned Negro fans to be on their best behavior. "The Negro fan," charged the *Defender*, "has been the 'hot potato' dodged by managers who would have taken a chance by signing a Negro player."[60] The *Courier* urged Negroes to "take this tremendous victory in stride." Continuing, the *Courier* issued the

> challenge to keep our mouths closed and give Jackie the chance to PROVE he's major league calibre! The challenge to conduct ourselves at these ball games in the recognized American way! The challenge to NOT recognize the appearance of Jackie Robinson as the signal for a Roman holiday, with the Bacchanalian orgy complex! The challenge to leave whiskey bottles at home or on the shelves of the liquor store . . . and to leave our loud talking, obscene language and indecent dress on the outside of the ball parks. The challenge to learn something about the game . . . in order that we will know what's going on out on the ball field, and won't humiliate Jackie by our lack of knowledge![61]

In the same spirit the *Defender* urged that "above all, let us not hold up the game—in a ludicrous ceremony—to present him with a box of southern fried chicken," and in his regular column in the *Defender*, Walter White pleaded with Negro fans to behave, reminding them that whether or not club officials began to give opportunities to other Negroes would depend partly on how Negro fans behaved.[62]

The *Argus* asked its readers to "act like human beings and not like a tribe of cannibals," when attending ball games. Pointing out racial difficulties that would be encountered at ball parks, the *Argus* added that there would be times when "people of the other race will say things about him but remember they are IGNORANT and you will only show your IGNORANCE by saying something to them."[63] Emphasizing the importance of good behavior, Roy Wilkins reminded Negro baseball fans that Robinson had been hired to play baseball and should not be expected to be a "battering ram against prejudice." Wilkins added that good ball-playing would enable Robinson to do his part in the "larger fight."[64]

Some Negro newspapers suggested restraint on the part of Negro fans on the grounds that elevation of a Negro to the major leagues was long overdue and, therefore, should not be viewed as a benevolent gift. The *Courier* pointed out that since Negroes "contend rightly for equality of opportunity, with all being on the same basis, let us be civilized enough to accept this evidence of American progress and fair play as what is expected."[65] The *Afro-American* asked that Robinson be treated "as just another ballplayer, not as a phenomenon," and the *Amsterdam News* concluded that when fans went to Ebbets field to cheer for Jackie, they were "only giving expression to their long period of starvation for recognition of their race."[66]

The *Crisis* charged that Negro newspapers, themselves, had a duty to perform in accurate reporting. Criticizing Negro newspaper reports that left the impression that "Jackie was the whole show," the *Crisis* argued that "this kind of reporting and editing can do as much damage as a drunken, loud-mouthed fan."[67]

Despite the reports that illuminated Robinson's good qualities, he endured a considerable amount of abuse during the first season. In September, 1947, *Ebony* claimed that Jackie, "with his quiet, modest, yet assured manner is winning many, many friends and proving himself the exact opposite of all the stereotypes about ball players and about Negroes."[68] At the same time, he acquired numerous enemies, many nameless, who constantly bombarded him through the mails with vicious threats. To play ball successfully amidst such an atmosphere of fear required a phenomenal degree of courage. The *Chronicle* succinctly phrased it when that paper said that "as a pioneer Jackie Robinson comes to bat with myriad eyes, not all friendly, focused upon him."[69]

Racial difficulties within the ranks of professional baseball emerged during the early part of the season when the Philadelphia Phillies employed an umbridled use of racial slurs and when rumors circulated that the St. Louis Cardinals planned to strike rather than play against Robinson. Both incidents were handled firmly, with Commissioner Chandler ordering a halt to racial slurs, and National League president Ford Frick issuing a forceful statement that strikers would face stiff penalties.

By mid-season, Robinson was doing so well that any attempt to mount an attack on him would have been extremely difficult. By season's end, Robinson had led the league in stolen bases, had batted a respectable .296, and had figured in numerous ways in Dodger victories which brought the National League pennant to Brooklyn for the first time in many years. He had established his credentials in major league baseball in which he was to have a notable but sometimes stormy career. Beyond doubt, the Negro newspapers that followed his career day to day, and repeatedly pictured him as a symbol of opportunity to black youth, played an important part in his successful assault upon professional baseball's "color line."

Notes

[1] Lewis H. Fenderson, "The Negro Press as a Social Instrument," *Journal of Negro Education*, XX (Spring, 1951), 181-83.

2 E. Franklin Frazier, *Black Bourgeoisie* (Glencoe, Ill., 1957), p. 174. 3 Harry McAlpin, "The Postwar Responsibility of the Negro Press," *Opportunity*, XXIII (April-June, 1945), 70.

4 Negroes found it difficult to believe that the United States could crusade abroad against Nazi racism and brutality while condoning racism, brutality, and oppression at home. See, for example, Donald McCoy and Richard Ruetten, "The Civil Rights Movement, 1940-1954," *Midwest Quarterly* (October, 1969), 17.

5 In an effort to speed application of the New York law to major league baseball, the "End Jim Crow in Baseball Committee" was formed in New York, and through street meetings, picketing of ballparks, etc., it achieved some valuable publicity. Shortly after the passage of the law, two Negro ballplayers forced a tryout with the Dodgers, but nothing came of their efforts.

6 In defense against the charge that he had signed Robinson to avert trouble with the New York anti-discrimination law, Rickey said that "it wasn't on my mind when I signed Robinson. I've been checking on Negro ballplayers for more than three years, long before the bill ever came up." Interview with Wendell Smith, Pittsburgh *Courier*, November 3, 1945.

Al Campanis, who was playing for the Dodgers' Montreal club at the time says that Rickey mentioned the newly enacted law as he explained his move to his players. (Letter: Al Campanis to Author, February 2, 1976).

7 The Chicago *Defender* viewed Rickey's action as an outgrowth of a December 3, 1943, meeting of representatives of the Negro Newspaper Publishers' Association with Commissioner K. M. Landis and representatives of the National and American leagues. (Chicago *Defender*, November 3, 1945). Don Dodson, who was executive director of the Mayor's Committee on Unity of New York City and advisor to Branch Rickey on the problem of baseball integration, concludes that the law was a factor in Rickey's consideration, although he admits that Rickey had scouted Negro players well before the law's introduction in the legislature. See Don Dodson, "Integration of Negroes in Baseball," *Journal of Educational Sociology*, XXVIII (October, 1954), 78.

8 Carl T. Rowan (with Jackie Robinson), *Wait Till Next Year: The Life Story of Jackie Robinson* (New York, 1960), p. 102.

9 The most recent well-documented case had occurred in 1907 when Charlie Grant played with the New York Giants, and things went well until a group of his Negro friends in Chicago got together to give him gifts, whereupon it was confirmed that he was a Negro. There have been rumors since that persons passing themselves off as whites or of another nationality were, in fact, Negroes.

10 In this address on February 23, 1948, Rickey created an uproar among baseball club owners by charging that in 1945 a report containing a malicious charge that "however well intentioned, the use of Negro players would hazard all of the physical properties of baseball." The remarks, reported in all Negro newspapers and in *Sporting News*, elicited bitter denials from other owners.

11 See Clyde Sukeforth's story in Donald Honig, *Baseball When the Grass was Real* (New York, 1975).

12 Dodson claims to have influenced the timing of the announcement which was designed to occur before contract-signing time in order that players would understand the prospects for 1946 when they signed their contracts. (Dodson, op. cit., p. 78).

13 New York *Amsterdam News*, November 3, 1945.

14 Detroit *Michigan Chronicle*, November 3, 1945.

15 *Amsterdam News*, November 3, 1945.

16 Pittsburgh *Courier*, November 24, 1945.

17 Dan Burley, "What's Ahead for Robinson?" *The Crisis*, LII (December, 1945), 364.

[18] *Courier*, November 3, 1945.
[19] Indianapolis *Recorder*, November 10, 1945.
[20] *Courier*, December 29, 1945.
[21] Burley, op. cit., p. 364.
[22] *Amsterdam News*, November 3, 1945.
[23] Philadelphia *Tribune*, April 27, 1946.
[24] *Courier*, November 3. 1945.
[25] The Chicago *Defender* found it ironic that "America, supposedly the cradle of democracy, is forced to send its first two Negroes in baseball to Canada in order for them to be accepted." (April 13, 1946).
[26] Ibid.
[27] *Amsterdam News*, November 3, 1945.
[28] *Courier*, November 3, 1945.
[29] *Recorder*, November 10, 1945.
[30] Bob Feller, the great Cleveland Indians pitcher, created some flak by commenting that Robinson had "football shoulders" which would inhibit his batting and by asserting that if Robinson had been a white man, he probably would not have been considered big league material.
[31] Just what happened in the inner councils of major league baseball on this issue has not been established, although it appears that most owners were reluctant to integrate baseball but were unwilling to publicly state that position.
[32] *Courier*, November 3, 1945.
[33] Burley, op. cit., p. 364.
[34] Michigan *Chronicle*, November 3, 1945.
[35] One allusion to Robinson's off-the-field problems appeared in the Birmingham *World* in the form of a cartoon showing Robinson fielding a ball while ominous faces labeled "threatening letters" and "racial slurs" watched him intently. *(World*, May 20, 1946).
[36] *Courier*, March 23, 1946.
[37] A delegation of Sanford, Florida, citizens visited Rickey early in spring training and asked that Robinson and Wright be ousted from the camp. The *Courier* refrained from publicizing the Sanford visit for fear that "the power of suggestion might create a similar development elsewhere. . . . "*(Courier*, April 13, 1946).
[38] As a result, games were cancelled at West Palm Beach, Jacksonville, Sanford, and DeLand, Florida; Savannah, Georgia; and Richmond, Virginia.
[39] *Courier*, April 13, 1946.
[40] Interview conducted by Sam Lacy, sports editor, Baltimore *Afro-American*, March 15, 1947.
[41] *Courier*, May 4, 1946.
[42] *The Crisis*, October, 1946.
[43] *Courier*, April 27, 1946.
[44] Ibid.
[45] *Afro-American*, May 4, 1946.
[46] *Courier*, April 20, 1946.
[47] Ibid., April 27, 1946.
[48] At some point during the season another Negro, Roy Partlow, was added to the Montreal team, but newspapers said little of it.
[49] *Courier*, February 22, 1947.
[50] Ibid., April 12, 1947.
[51] St. Louis *Argus*, April 18, 1947.
[52] Boston *Chronicle*, April 19, 1947.

53 Birmingham *World*, April 25, 1947.
54 Atlanta *Daily World*, April 16, 1947: *World*, April 18, 1947.
55 *Michigan Chronicle*, April 19, 1947.
56 Ibid., April 26, 1947.
57 *Courier*, April 19, 1947.
58 *Amsterdam News*, April 19, 1947.
59 *The Crisis*, LIV (May, 1947).
60 *Defender*, April 19, 1947.
61 *Courier*, April 19, 1947.
62 *Defender*, April 26, 1947.
63 *Argus*, April 25, 1947.
64 *Michigan Chronicle*, April 26, 1947.
65 *Courier*, April 26, 1947.
66 *Afro-American*, April 19, 1947; *Amsterdam News*, April 19, 1947.
67 *The Crisis*, LIV (May, 1947).
68 "Family Man Jackie Robinson," *Ebony*, September, 1947, p. 15.
69 *Chronicle*, April 19, 1947.

Part Five

FREEDOM'S CHAMPIONS: RACE LEADERSHIP AND ORGANIZATIONAL EFFORTS

Miss [Ida B.] Wells deserves more credit than any other individual [for] having brought [lynching] before the eyes of the world and, in so doing, having accelerated the establishment of law and decency in the American South.

Tucker,
Miss Ida B. Wells and Memphis Lynching

Writing from his Birmingham jail cell, [Martin Luther] King revealed that the purpose of nonviolent direct action was "to create such a crisis and foster such a tension that a community which has constantly refused to negotiate is forced to confront the issue. It seeks to so dramatize the issue that it can no longer be ignored."

Colaiaco,
Martin Luther King, Jr., and the Paradox of Nonviolent Direct Action

Booker T. Washington and the Ulrich Affair

*Catapulted to national prominence in 1895 by his At-
lanta Exposition address, Booker T. Washington became the
most influential black leader since Frederick Douglass. Aligning his public positions with the racist views of many whites,
Washington espoused a program of racial uplift that emphasized industrial education, economic assimilation, and political
and social accommodation in a hostile Southern environment.
Urged upon African Americans as the best path toward race
advancement and peaceable relations between the races, Washington's formula alarmed a portion of the black population
and met vigorous opposition from some black leaders, perhaps
most notably W.E.B. DuBois. The resistance to Washington,
much of which was embodied after 1910 in the National Association for the Advancement of Colored People (NAACP),
turned on the hotly contested issues of education, disfranchisement, segregation, lynching, and other evils in which Washington's critics saw the threat of new forms of slavery.*

*In 1911 Washington's influence on the national scene
came under scrutiny in a much publicized event resulting from
a physical attack on Washington by white American Henry Albert Ulrich, the ensuing investigation, and Ulrich's subsequent
trial. In the following essay, Willard Gatewood unravels the
incident to reveal a great deal about racial prejudices in both
the North and South as well as the magnitude of the gulf between Washington's supporters and detractors. According to
Gatewood, some NAACP officials viewed the controversy surrounding Washington as an opportunity for reconciliation between the two sides. This rapprochement was short-lived,
however, and the Ulrich affair provided reinforcement for the
more militant supporters of full citizenship for African
Americans.*

THE FAMOUS ADDRESS delivered by Booker T. Washington, principal of Tuskegee Institute, at the opening of the Atlanta Exposition in
1895, marked his rather sudden emergence as the acknowledged
leader of Negroes in the United States. In this speech he set forth his
philosophy of race relations, known as the Atlanta Compromise,

which subordinated the civil rights of Negroes as a group to their economic advancement as individuals. In propagating his policy of accommodation, he displayed a rare talent for "manipulating the symbols and myths dear to the majority of Americans."[1] Within a few years after his Atlanta address, Washington had become a figure of national importance who counted among his friends wealthy industrialists, prominent editors and even presidents of the United States as well as a network of strategically placed individuals within the Negro community. A complex and sometimes authoritarian personality, he sustained his claims to race leadership through the perfection of what his critics termed the "Tuskegee Machine." But by 1911 his power and influence had been significantly eroded, especially by the activities of W.E.B. DuBois, Monroe Trotter and other Negroes of the "talented tenth" who were in fundamental disagreement with his tactics rather than his ultimate goals. In particular Washington viewed the National Association for the Advancement of Colored People, organized in 1909, as a direct challenge to his leadership. He rejected the overtures of Oswald Garrison Villard and other white leaders of the NAACP who sought to enlist his cooperation. Suspicious of their motives and convinced that the NAACP, especially its one Negro official, DuBois, represented "the enemy," Washington attempted to prevent defections among his own followers and mobilized the "Tuskegee Machine," including its subsidized press and various organizations among Negroes, in an effort to contain the new association.[2] Then, rather abruptly early in 1911 a note of unprecedented harmony came to dominate the relations between the NAACP and Washington's forces. This rapprochement resulted largely from a much publicized physical attack upon Washington during a visit to New York City. The incident itself indicated the dimensions of racial prejudice in the Progressive Era while Washington's handling of it revealed much about his methods and the nature of his "organization."

There was nothing extraordinary about Washington's trip to New York in mid-March, 1911. He often visited the city to plead the cause of Tuskegee Institute before various groups and individuals and to discuss the affairs of the school with the chairman of Tuskegee's board of trustees, Seth Low, who had been president of Columbia University and mayor of New York. While in the city, Washington usually conferred with Charles W. Anderson, his most trusted lieutenant among Negroes in the area, and with the editors of the New York *Age,* a leading Negro newspaper which he subsidized. When Washington arrived in the city on Saturday, March 18, 1911, following engagements in Chicago and Detroit, he went directly to the Manhattan Hotel where he customarily stayed. The following day he delivered an address at Mount Olivet Church in the morning and another at the Church of the Pilgrims in Brooklyn in the afternoon. That evening, following dinner at the hotel, he decided to attempt to locate Daniel C. Smith, a public accountant with offices in New York, who served as the auditor for Tuskegee. When Washington left Alabama, Smith was there concluding an audit of the school's financial records. A letter from Emmett J. Scott, Washington's secretary and confidant, had indicated that Smith would probably be in New York by March 19. Scott was aware that Washington desired to confer with Smith and Low "in reference to a projected change in the accounting of the farm work at the Institute." His letter either reached Washington in Chicago or was waiting for him upon his arrival at the Manhattan Hotel. At any rate, Washington either misplaced or destroyed it and, as he recalled the contents, Scott had written that Smith could be reached at the home of friends, the McCrarys, at $11^{1/2}$ West Sixty-third Street. Relying on his memory, Washington set out about nine o'clock on the evening of March 19 to find the McCrary residence.[3]

Arriving at the address, he found an "apartment house occupied by different families on different floors, whose names appear with bells on an index" in the vestibule. When no one responded to the bell he rang, Washington left the building and strolled around the neighborhood in the hope that the occupants would soon return home. He returned twice to the apartment hallway. The third time, after he had put on his glasses and while he was pressing the bell marked "Cleary," a man leaped from the shadows and shouted: "What are you doing here? You have been hanging around here for four or five weeks. Get out of here!" When Washington tried to explain, the man struck him and the two men struggled briefly in the hallway. Pursued by his assailant, the Negro educator fled into the street where another, unidentified person attacked him with a club. In his flight Washington stumbled several times and was kicked by others who joined the pursuit. Fortunately for him, a detective and a policeman noticed the disturbance. They dispersed the menacing crowd and escorted Washington and his first assailant to the Sixty-eighth Street Police Station, where Washington finally convinced the precinct officials of his true identity. After charging his assailant with felonious assault, Washington entered Flower Hospital to be treated for ugly lacerations of the face and scalp.[4]

The man who had attacked Washington was Henry Albert Ulrich, described as "a big German," who resided in the apartment house on West Sixty-third Street. Ulrich was a part-time carpenter and "a dealer in animals." As the manager of the Westside Dog Exchange, he had been charged earlier in the year with the theft of a prize Pomeranian dog. The version of the affray provided by Ulrich and the woman whom reporters presumed to be his wife was wholly different from that given by Washington. According to their accounts, "Mrs. Ulrich" had noticed "a Negro loitering on the sidewalk outside their apartment." When she went out on an errand, he asked her a question "unrelated to any search for a Mr. Smith," and followed her for some distance. Finding the man still loitering near the apartment upon her return, she informed her "husband" of his presence, whereupon Ulrich hid in the shadows of a nearby doorway. The Negro, they said, first tried to "peep into the flat between the shade and the window sill." Then, when he went inside the building, Ulrich followed him and caught him in the act of "looking into the keyhole" of an apartment occupied by Frank J. Revette. At this point, according to Ulrich's testimony, he struck Washington and chased him into the street. Infuriated because the police refused to charge Washington with illegal entry, Ulrich promised to fight what he termed "this mockery of justice." Friends and neighbors rallied to Ulrich and pledged him financial assistance in securing competent legal counsel.

Upon the request of Washington's physician, the formal arraignment of Ulrich, scheduled for Monday morning, March 20, in the Westside Magistrates' Court, was postponed until that afternoon. Wilford H. Smith, a Negro attorney engaged by Washington, assured the court that his client would be able to attend the afternoon session. Smith had previously handled cases against disfranchisement and segregation, secretly inspired or supported by Washington. Representing Ulrich was James R. Moore, an attorney retained by his friends, one of whom posted his bail of $1,500. While his attorney was securing a postponement of the arraignment, Washington remained closeted with Seth Low in his room at the Manhattan Hotel. At the conclusion of their conference Low issued a lengthy statement of "the facts in the case" which in effect exonerated Washington of any misconduct or wrongdoing. "The trustees of Tuskegee Institute have absolute confidence in Dr. Washington," Low concluded, "and they will give him whatever support and aid he needs."

At two o'clock on the afternoon of March 20, Washington, his head swathed in bandages, appeared at the Westside Court accompanied by P. B. S. Pinchback, the well-known Negro political figure and former Lieutenant Governor of Louisiana. A large crowd of spectators, predominantly Negroes, jammed the courtroom and overflowed into the street. Through agreement of counsel for both sides, the charge of felonious assault against Ulrich was reduced to simple assault, a move which Washington approved following consultation with Low and other friends. Ulrich waived examination and was bound over to the Court of Special Sessions, which presumably would hear the case later in the spring. So great was the throng by the end of the brief court proceeding that Washington and Pinchback, flanked by a borough president and a deputy police commissioner, had considerable difficulty in reaching their automobile. Ultimately it was necessary to call out police reserves to clear the street of a crowd obviously sympathetic to Washington. According to the *New York Herald*, the police also began "to exercise special surveillance over the colored quarters" of the city in order "to guard against . . . race riots resulting from the recent troubles of Booker T. Washington."[5]

A mysterious woman whom Washington's lawyer had been prepared to call as a witness was present at the afternoon session. She was the real Mrs. Ulrich, who, along with two children, had been deserted by her husband. One of Washington's friends in Orange, New Jersey, had secured from an official of the Children's Aid and Protective Society there documentary evidence to prove that Ulrich had not only abandoned his family and defied a court order to contribute to their support but also that he was leading "a double life." The woman with whom he lived at the West Sixty-third Street address was actually Laura Page Alverez, the estranged wife of a Spaniard. Further investigation revealed that Mrs. Alvarez had retained custody of their child over the strong objections of her husband. With the aid of a Negro companion Alverez had attempted to kidnap the child in mid-February, 1911. Already anxious about the safety of her daughter, Mrs. Alverez, as some suggested at the time, may have jumped to the conclusion that the Negro in the apartment building on the night of March 19 had been sent by her husband to kidnap the little girl.[6]

Beginning on March 20, the story of the assault upon Washington and subsequent developments in the case made the front pages of newspapers throughout the country. Concerned about the possibility of unfavorable publicity, Washington had telephoned the Associated Press from his hospital room on the night of the attack in an attempt to "belittle" the incident and to secure the assistance of the wire service in minimizing its coverage. But his efforts were in vain. The whole episode became hopelessly garbled in a tangled web of fact and fiction, most of which ultimately found its way into print. Washington himself apparently contributed to the confusion by holding several press conferences to elaborate upon the details of the assault and to explain why he had gone to the West Sixty-third address in the first place. The result was a phethora of news stories which pointed up certain discrepancies in his various versions of the affair. Perhaps, as some observers suggested, the discrepancies between his original account of the affair given to the police on the night of the attack and his later versions resulted in part from his dazed condition at the time the former statement was given. At any rate, it appeared that the more Washington talked with reporters the more damage he did his own cause.[7] An Indiana editor voiced the perplexity of many journalists when he remarked: "The real mystery is found in the fact that a man of Booker Washington's wisdom, knowing the prejudice against his race, should have sought a friend in strange quarters at a late hour of night."[8]

Much of the confusion centered around the letter which Washington received from his secretary, Emmett J. Scott, regarding the arrival of the auditor, Daniel Smith, in New York. At one point the wire services quoted Washington as denying that he had ever received any such communication. The denial immediately prompted speculations as to why Washington had gone to $11^1/_2$ West Sixty-third Street. Then, as if to make matters worse, Smith disclaimed any knowledge of Washington's desire to meet him and denied that he had any friends living in or near the address on the West Side. He accused Scott of committing "a careless blunder." Some reporters intimated that Washington's trek to West Sixty-third Street was all the more strange in view of the fact that Smith had an office at 32 Broadway and a residence in Montclair, New Jersey, both of which apparently had telephones. Rumors circulated to the effect that Washington was drunk and had been assaulted by Ulrich because he had addressed Mrs. Alverez as "Sweetheart." In his original version of the affair, Ulrich claimed he had mistaken Washington for a burglar; later he declared that he had attacked him for insulting his wife. Washington repeatedly denied such allegations. "There is not the slightest basis," he declared, "for any statement that I have ever accosted or insulted a woman, black or white. . . ." Finally, in an effort to forestall further complications, Scott hastened to New York, assumed full responsibility for suggesting the possibility of Smith's presence at the West Side address, and prevented Washington from having further encounters with reporters. In fact, neither Scott nor Washington released any more public statements on the affair.[9]

Despite the physical and emotional strain of the ordeal, Washington filled his speaking engagements in New Jersey and Pennsylvania before returning to Tuskegee. Everywhere his reception was more cordial than usual. Within a week after the assault he had received expressions of sympathy and support from hundreds of Americans of both races.[10] Of all the messages to Washington none provoked as much comment as the one from President William Howard Taft. The letter, written in the President's own hand and dated March 21, read:

I am greatly distressed at your misfortune and I hasten to write you of my sympathy, my hope that you will soon recover from the wounds inflicted by insane suspicion or viciousness, and of my confidence in you, in your integrity and morality of character and in your highest usefulness to your race and to all the people of this country.

It would be a nation's loss if this untoward incident in any way impaired your great power for good in the solution of one of the most difficult problems before us.

I want you to know that your friends are standing by you in every trial, and that I am proud to subscribe myself one.[11]

Taft's letter, printed verbatim in many newspapers, produced far more than an expression of profound gratitude from Washington. It probably prompted more applause from Negroes in general than any other public gesture that Taft made as President.

In view of the political predicament of Taft and the Regular Republicans in 1911, it was not surprising that some observers interpreted his message as an attempt to cultivate support among Negroes. But whatever the motive that prompted such a forthright endorsement of Washington, the President's letter assisted "Tuskegee Politicians" in their attempt to placate Negroes disturbed by the steady advance of lily-whitism during his administration. Whitefield McKinlay, Washington's closest friend in the District of Columbia and a Taft appointee, headed a delegation of Negroes who called upon the President to express the gratitude of the local Negro community for his generous letter. Charles W. Anderson of New York, whose appointment as collector of internal revenue in 1905 had been arranged by Washington, assured Taft that Negroes "would never cease to love the President who was great enough to stand by their race . . . in the hour of its greatest need." As soon as he learned of the President's message to Washington, Anderson telephoned Fred R. Moore, editor of the New York *Age*, to remind him that Taft "was the best friend the Negroes have ever had in the presidential chair." According to Anderson, Moore admitted that the anti-Taft position of his paper in the past had been "wrong . . . and promised to turn over a new leaf."[12]

Despite the compliments heaped upon the President by white citizens sympathetic with "the great work of Dr. Washington" and by such members of the "Tuskegee Machine" as McKinlay and Anderson, Taft's letter was by no means an object of universal praise. It is doubtful whether the gesture effected any change in the hostile attitude which DuBois, Trotter and other anti-Washington spokesmen displayed toward Taft. And certainly there were whites disturbed by what they interpreted as a change in his acquiescence in lily-white Republicanism. For example, an influential Republican in Missouri was utterly shocked that the President "would take the trouble to volunteer such a letter to this Negro" [Washington]. He was convinced that the message would cost Taft "thousands of Republican votes" in that state. An editor in Rome, Georgia, assured the President that his "testimonial to 'dear Dr. Washington'" weakened rather than strengthened his political position, while a newspaper in Illinois reminded Washington that earlier Taft had written a letter expressing confidence in his Secretary of the Interior, Richard Ballinger. "Where is Ballinger now?" it asked.[13] But none of the criticism was as devastating as that by Thomas Dixon, the well-known novelist and lecturer on racial themes. Although Dixon admitted that it seemed "incredible" that Washington could have committed the crime of which Ulrich accused him, he found it even more incredible that Taft would "rush off a letter to the Negro educator" without awaiting the outcome of the trial. If Washington was guilty, Dixon declared, he should pay the penalty without the President using "his mighty office to whitewash him." He insisted that the white man surely had "some rights in court [which] a Negro and his friends must respect." In short, Dixon felt that "the curious and suspicious" circumstances surrounding the whole Ulrich-Washington affair should have promoted more discretion on the part of the President.[14]

In contrast to the implications of Dixon's references to the incident, most editors expressed their confidence in Washington's innocence. Some journals, such as *Harper's Weekly*, dismissed the affair as a case of mistaken identity which would in no way damage Washington's reputation. The lesson to be learned from this disgraceful assault upon "one of the really great educators of his time," according to *The Outlook*, was that "too many Americans are prone to take the law into their own hands." But the editors were quick to point out that if Ulrich was to be held accountable for his error, "the city should see to it that he can have recourse to a police that he can trust." In effect, then, Washington's experience provided *The Outlook* with an opportunity to castigate the municipal administration of New York for its failure to insure residents of a trustworthy police force sufficient to "maintain law and order."[15] For other editors, the assault on Washington involved far more than the demoralized condition of the New York police, a case of mistaken identity, or questions of law and order. It was "a singularly noteworthy instance of reckless passion engendered by racial prejudice and hatred." Simply because of the color of his skin, Washington had been attacked under circumstances in which a white man would have gone unnoticed. The Sacramento

Union and the Butte, Montana, *Inter-Mountain*, agreed that racists would seize upon the incident as evidence to support their "leopard spots theory" regarding Negroes; in fact, some were already citing the affair to prove that no amount of enlightenment "could overcome the Negro's brute instinct." Although editors who emphasized racial prejudice as the most significant aspect of the affair disagreed about its ultimate effect upon Washington's career, a substantial number believed that his "power for good," especially in the South, would be seriously impaired.[16]

Although Washington himself claimed to see only an attitude of friendliness and generosity in the comments of the Southern press, its editorials actually expressed little more than passing interest in his welfare or the future of his work. Most Southern journalists were preoccupied with rejoicing over the fact that the attack on Washington had occurred in the North rather than in the South. James Calvin Hemphill, editor of the Richmond *Times-Dispatch*, treated the incident in a semicomic manner, urging "Booker" to stay in the South among his "true friends." Feeling that his "first duty" was to acknowledge "such a magnificent and generous editorial," Washington hastened to assure Hemphill that indeed if he were to be lynched, he preferred to be lynched in the South "by my friends and not by strangers."[17] Delighted that Yankees could not describe the affair as another "southern outrage," the *Atlanta Constitution* concluded: "it all goes to show that human nature is pretty much the same the world over; red blood boils at the same affront—whether real of imaginary—in every part of the civilized world." Other journals in the South, following a similar approach, were more explicit in suggesting that Washington might well have been guilty of some "shady" activity on the night of the attack.[18] Writing in the Saint Louis *Mirror*, Marion Reedy suggested that the real import of Washington's mishap in the South, though largely "voiceless in the southern press," was to vindicate the racist demagogues. He explained:

> The conduct which is alleged against Washington is too closely related to the horror and terror of the South to be in any fashion minimized. Anything but that hint of familiarity with a white woman might have been forgiven. . . . It fits in so aptly with the South's dictum that the Negro cannot . . . restrain the impulse of the servile class to sexual relations with the whites.[19]

Reedy's analysis was not altogether irrelevant. Beginning in Greenville, Alabama, and spreading to other parts of the South, campaigns were initiated by whites to raise funds for Ulrich's legal expenses. Donations to the fund were to be considered contributions to the cause of protecting white womanhood.[20] The pronouncements of well-known Southern Negrophobes served to encourage such efforts. Thomas Dixon, for example, told his audiences: "If I should catch any Negro, educated or uneducated, messing around my door in a suspicious way, when defenseless women were behind that door, I should certainly attempt to kill him."[21] Senator Benjamin Tillman of South Carolina described Washington as "a humbug" whom a German was forced to chastize because he "had made goo-goo eyes" at his wife. In Mississippi, the Washington-Ulrich affair caused at least one lynching and figured in the rhetoric of the political campaign of 1911. In a small delta town an argument between a Negro man and a white man over the guilt or innocence of Washington led to a fight in which the Negro man shot the white man. Shortly thereafter a mob lynched the Negro. During the summer, as James K. Vardaman campaigned for the Senate, he incorporated into his standard fare on the depravity of Negroes a denunciation of "Booker Washington for peeping through a keyhole at a New York prostitute." Vardaman assured white Mississippians that Washington "should have been killed" for his offense.[22] But neither Tillman nor Vardaman equalled the crudity of Thomas E. Watson of Georgia, who described "Booker's escapade in New York" as evidence that Washington occasionally "laid aside the irksome robes of conventional propriety" to indulge his "inherited appetites." It was merely the "recrudescence of nigger" which prompted him to address Ulrich's mistress as "sweetheart" and took him "to the white woman's bed-room door." Watson was certain of Washington's guilt because the odor of liquor had been found on his breath and he had "fled like a guilty man who did not want his identity revealed." Hopefully, according to Watson, the incident would induce those "who have slopped over in praise" of Washington to recognize him at last for what he really was—"a commonplace schoolteacher, an ordinary lecturer, an inferior book-writer and a blundering 'masher.' "[23]

Busy "watching and gauging public sentiment," Washington obviously was well aware of such outbursts. A month after the incident, he reported that notwithstanding the expected abuse from Watson and Vardaman, the "best people" within the white community continued to stand by him and his school.[24] Of equal, if not greater, interest to him at this particular juncture was the reaction to the incident among Negroes and its effect upon his position as their spokesman. He could scarcely have been disappointed by the displays of affection in so many quarters at a time when the challenge to his leadership appeared to be reaching a climax. The Negro press was virtually unanimous in condemning "the outrageous and unjustifiable" attack upon him. Even such persistent editorial critics as Harry Smith of the

Cleveland *Gazette* and Monroe Trotter of the Boston *Guardian*, while not effusive by any means, were relatively generous in their comments. Similar to other Negro journals, the *Chicago Defender* took special care to refute "the wicked insinuations" made regarding his mission to the West Side apartment house. The editor of the *Defender* attached particular significance to the report that Mrs. Alverez was a native of Georgia where "she and her kind have done the eagle scream before and the poor Negro who should be under the sound of her gloats would swing from a tree before she could finish."[25] And while the Negro press eulogized Washington, Negroes in various cities of the North and Midwest convened mass meetings to reaffirm their confidence in his leadership. In some instances, Washington's lieutenants, with his full knowledge, staged these meetings with the obvious purpose of taking advantage of the situation to bolster his declining influence and prestige.

In New York Charles W. Anderson arranged the most widely publicized of these mass meetings, which was held in the Bethel African Methodist Episcopal Church, the church of the anti-Bookerite clergyman Reverdy Ransom.[26] Anderson carefully prepared a program which included addresses by Negroes representing all shades of opinion toward Washington. "I talked brass tacks to each speaker before the opening of the meeting," he wrote Washington, "and cautioned them against any intemperance of language." In addition to Anderson himself, the speakers included Fred R. Moore of the New York *Age*, Ransom, Reverend Adam Clayton Powell, whose past activities placed him among the anti-Bookerites, James L. Curtis, a friend of Trotter and a champion of civil rights for Negroes, and Edward E. Lee, an important member of the New York Democratic organization. Fearful lest Curtis and Lee "cause trouble," Anderson scheduled their addresses so that they spoke after the newspaper reporters had departed. Moore, Ransom and Powell delivered "conservative" speeches in which they emphasized how the attack upon Washington pointed up the sad plight of Negroes in the "land of the free." Employing effusive language, Anderson first eulogized Washington, then spoke extravagantly of Taft's letter as the most important document "in furthering the Square Deal for the colored race since the Emancipation Proclamation." Lee and Curtis, on the other hand, refused to abide by the rules prescribed by Anderson. They used the occasion to speak "intemperately" about lynching and other manifestations of prejudice and to praise the militant tactics of Trotter. The meeting concluded with the adoption of a series of resolutions pledging "unshaken faith" in the integrity and leadership ability of Washington. By preventing Curtis and Lee "from getting their jackassical diatribes in print," Anderson insured that the press coverage of the meeting would convey the impression of complete harmony. Washington, impressed by his skillful handling of the meeting, assured him that the newspaper accounts were "all that we could expect."[27]

While Washington's allies were busy preserving his image, Oswald Garrison Villard was accelerating his efforts to bring about an *entente cordiale* between the Tuskegeean and the NAACP. Apparently Villard believed that the circumstances created by the Ulrich-Washington episode favored the achievement of his goal. Washington obviously desired to receive all the support he could get, while a friendly gesture toward the NAACP by him well might ease the organization's financial crisis.[28] Both Washington and Seth Low conferred with Villard shortly after the incident. Following these conversations, Villard continued to press the matter of unity in correspondence. Washington agreed that the time had come "when we should lay aside personal differences and personal bickerings." He also complied with Villard's request for an exchange of fraternal delegates between the NAACP and his own organization, the National Negro Business League.[29] Villard, in turn, secured the passage of a resolution by the NAACP on March 21, 1911, which read: "Resolved that we put on record our profound regret at the recent assault on Dr. Booker T. Washington in New York City in which the Association finds renewed evidence of race discrimination and increased necessity for the awakening of the public conscience."[30] Hopeful that the resolution marked "the beginning of friendly relations" between the NAACP and the Tuskegee forces, Villard was convinced that Washington must make the next move by toning down the "villainous" criticism of the NAACP which regularly appeared in the pro-Washington press. He urged Robert R. Moton of Hampton Institute, an experienced mediator between the Bookerites and anti-Bookerites, to prevail upon Washington to pass the word to those Negro newspapers, especially the New York *Age*, which he controlled. Moton contacted Washington who, ever cautious about revealing the extent of his influence over the Negro press, protested that Villard "overestimated" his power, but who nonetheless did advise Moore, editor of the *Age*, "to assume a more friendly spirit toward the Association for the Advancement of Colored People."[31]

The so-called reconciliation between Washington and his critics which followed the Ulrich affair proved to be of short duration. From the beginning it was more illusory than real. In spite of the impression conveyed by mass meetings such as that arranged by Anderson or the promise of the apparent *rapprochement* between Washington and the NAACP, the basic causes for the existence of a cleavage within the Negro community remained unchanged. Neither Ulrich's attack nor the testimonials of faith in Washington's leadership had softened the attitude of the most effective anti-Bookerite, DuBois. Other key figures in the NAACP, while willing for the organization to express its sympathy, were opposed to any resolution of endorsement. Several lawyers within the organization either considered Washington's explanations of his encounter with Ulrich as legally weak or as "pure invention." In fact, Albert E. Pillsbury of Boston, a member of the original executive committee of the NAACP, appeared to be as dubious of Washington's version of the incident as some of the more outspoken racists of the South. Under the circumstances, then, the most that Villard could get in the way of a resolution was a mild expression of regret and sympathy.[32] At the same time the magnanimity of such well-known editorial critics of the Tuskegee approach as Harry Smith and Monroe Trotter had stopped far short of anything resembling endorsement of Washington. For their part, Washington and his allies continued to remain skeptical of "the enemy." Charles Anderson expressed the attitude of suspicion common among Bookerite spokesmen in replying to Washington's request for advice regarding the Villard proposal. "I think we ought to show a desire to get together," he wrote, "and let any refusal to do so come from the other side. For us to decline the olive branch would be to expose us to the charge of being narrow, and it would give the scoundrels on the other side an excuse for wielding the dirty weapons, which they know so well how to use."[33] It was scarcely a genuine commitment to unity which motivated his approval of the plan for an exchange of delegates between the NAACP and the National Negro Business League.

If Ulrich's attack on Washington figured in what appeared to be a "love feast" between the contending forces in the spring of 1911, Washington's handling of the case and the delay in bringing Ulrich to trial did nothing to prolong it. From the outset Washington had remained in constant touch with Seth Low on how to proceed against Ulrich. Both preferred to avoid a full-fledged courtroom drama; they first considered a plan whereby Ulrich would issue a statement retracting his accusations against Washington at the same time that he pleaded guilty to the assault charge. Presumably Low would then arrange to have Ulrich's sentence suspended.[34] On April 8, 1911, Washington wrote Low:

> . . . Personally I do not desire to prosecute Ulrich. I feel nothing would be gained for myself or the interests of the school, if I were to appear as cherishing a vindictive spirit toward him. I am sure that not only he, but others, will be less likely in the future . . . to think

that because a man is a Negro, he is therefore presumed to be an
intruder or a criminal.

The only thing that deters me in dropping the case . . . is the
statement made by the woman who posed as his wife. If there was
some way of disposing finally and forever of those statements, without going to court, I should personally feel that is the best way of
getting rid of the whole matter.[35]

Emmett Scott, who actually prepared the statement of retraction that
Ulrich was supposed to sign, cautioned his attorney, Wilford Smith,
against action that would place Washington in the position "of buy-
ing anybody off." But the recalcitrance of Ulrich and the inclination
of Assistant District Attorney John C. Smith, who was in charge of the
case, to dismiss the charge against him precluded the immediate implementation of the plan devised by Washington and Low. When the
Court of Special Sessions convened on April 3, 1911, Ulrich pleaded
not guilty and "the case was adjourned without date." Although
Washington was still committed to the original procedure for dealing
with Ulrich, he became increasingly skeptical of its prospects for
success.[36]

When the case continued to be postponed, both friends and
critics of Washington became impatient. His friends promised financial aid for additional counsel, while critics denounced Washington
for his failure to press for a settlement of the matter in a public trial.
Harry Smith, in the Cleveland *Gazette*, came to the conclusion that
the Ulrich-Washington case was "one of the most peculiar" that he
had ever encountered. "If Washington does nothing," he said, "people must draw their own conclusions."[37] When the case was not
scheduled for the July term of the court, Washington's critics became
frankly indignant at what they considered his obvious reluctance to
press for a showdown. Although Washington seemed particularly disturbed by the editorials of Trotter in the Boston *Guardian*, Smith's paper was scarcely less severe in its arraignment of him. The *Gazette*
maintained that Negroes were entitled to know whether the man who
claimed to speak for them was really innocent of "questionable intentions in being in that 'free and easy' section of New York at that time
of night. . . ."[38] This reference to the unsavory reputation of the
neighborhood in which Washington was assaulted merely put into
print rumors that had been widely circulated ever since the occurrence. Convinced that such insinuations were "calculated to do us
great harm," Washington concluded that despite friendly gestures immediately after the mishap, there had been no fundamental change
in the attitude of his critics. But more disturbing to him was what he
interpreted as the tendency among Negro editors, once friendly to

his cause, to follow the lead of Trotter and Smith in questioning his handling of the Ulrich case.[39]

Contrary to the impression created by his critics, Washington had not been idle regarding the matter. Rather he had been pursuing it in his own peculiarly indirect way with the aid of Low, Scott and Anderson as well as his attorney. While his attorney was collecting evidence about Ulrich "in reference to his dog stealing and . . . improper living," Washington himself was securing proof to refute the rumors that impugned his own character and conduct. The surgeon at Flower Hospital who treated him on the night of the attack certified that Washington was entirely sober and displayed only "the true and courteous character" for which he was well known. When the detective who had intervened to save Washington from further beating by Ulrich and possibly mob action, agreed to testify in his defense, especially in regard to the falsity of Mrs. Alverez's charges, Washington was sufficiently grateful to urge Anderson to use his influence in obtaining some kind of official reward or promotion for him.[40] But Anderson had more pressing chores to perform. For example, Washington wanted him to secure a statement from the mayor's office which would confirm his contention that the West Sixty-third Street area was a reputable neighborhood and the particular apartment house was "a decent house." Washington also requested Anderson to find a way "to get a close personal hold" upon the district attorney "without bringing up my case at all." "I wish in some way you could not only find out who is the backer of the District Attorney," Washington wrote, "but also in your own way to get in close personal touch with him something in the same way you are with the other officials." Apparently his purpose was to insure a friendly attitude on the part of the district attorney and his subordinates.[41] Whether because of Anderson's success or some other reason, the assistant district attorney in charge of the case rather suddenly became cooperative and even assured Washington that he "had it in his power" to force a retraction from Ulrich. But much to Washington's disappointment, Ulrich still refused to retract his original testimony and the assistant district attorney suggested that the case be held over for the fall term of the court. Finally convinced that Ulrich would not relent and worried by the mounting criticism of his handling of the affair, Washington became reconciled to the ordeal of a public trial. By mid-July he was writing his attorney: "If we can get Ulrich where we want him, I think we could arrange to have the matter brought up in court at any time and settled." He was, in fact, ready "to fight this case to the bitter end."[42]

On November 6, 1911, the Ulrich case was tried in the Court of Special Sessions in New York City. A three-judge panel heard testimony from a parade of witnesses including Ulrich, Mrs. Alverez and Washington. No evidence was introduced which had not already been thoroughly aired in the press. Mrs. Alverez described in detail her encounter with Washington, who, she testified, had been caught "peeping through the keyhole of her apartment" as well as that of the Revettes and had greeted her as "sweetheart." One of the justices who questioned Washington closely on his reason for visiting that particular apartment house appeared to be dissatisfied with his answers. Perhaps the least convincing part of Washington's testimony was his attempt to explain why he persisted in ringing the bell marked Cleary when the name of the family with whom the Tuskegee auditor was supposed to be staying was McCrary. Although the court dismissed the charge against Ulrich, one justice delivered a strong dissenting opinion. News stories, headlined "Ulrich's acquittal," gave the impression that the court considered his attack "provoked and justifiable," when in fact the majority opinion was that the charge of assault was not proved beyond a reasonable doubt. Whatever the technical differences, Ulrich was freed of the assault charge. But, in large part because of Anderson's diligence, he was immediately arrested again and extradited to New Jersey to stand trial for deserting his wife and family.[43]

Negroes, especially Washington's supporters, were profoundly disturbed by the verdict. Roscoe Conkling Bruce, son of the Negro senator from Mississippi during Reconstruction, summed up a prevalent attitude when he wrote: "if the courts accept the testimony of a dog-fancier and wife-deserter as conclusive against that of the greatest educator and publicist of our race, of what avail is the testimony of a black mechanic or farmer, however industrious and honest, as against the most worthless white man?"[44] Washington himself admitted that "such decisions . . . do not tend to increase one's respect for law and order, as administered in some quarters."[45] Even Harry Smith of the Cleveland *Gazette* conceded that "justice went visiting" during Ulrich's trial.[46] Without being specific, some Negroes predicted that the verdict would have dire political repercussions. Charles Anderson, more concerned about the political past than the future, was certain that if the court's decision had been rendered a week earlier the Democrats would not have carried the Borough of Manhattan in the November elections. Professor Kelly Miller of Howard University wanted to call a conference of Negro leaders to protest the verdict, but was persuaded against such a move by Whitefield McKinlay who, like Anderson, assumed that "the best way to treat such incidents is to allow them to be forgotten."[47]

Whatever may have been the proper course, the Ulrich case was not forgotten, least of all by Washington. Shortly after the assault, Low suggested that Washington should have a companion to accompany him constantly in the future. Washington quickly made such arrangements because his experience with Ulrich had "demonstrated how easy it would be for anyone not only to assault me but also to entrap me into a scheme to be greatly to my damage."[48] Always sensitive to public reaction, he was undoubtedly pained by the repercussions of the incident and the renewed gossip prompted by the outcome of the trial. It was particularly disheartening to encounter rebuffs from the very elements of the white South which he had so long attempted to placate, at least overtly, by his philosophy of accommodation. He could expect racist demagogues to persist in casting him in the role of a lascivious black beast. But more distateful was the action by the Texas legislature in refusing to allow him the use of the House of Representatives for an address and the criticism of him as a worthy spokesman of Negroes by a respected political figure in Alabama.[49] Such rebuffs were all the more cause for anguish because they coincided with the decline of his political power and the resumption of attacks by his opponents within the Negro community. Already exhausted by his long years of strenuous activities, Washington suffered from the incident far more than either he or Emmett Scott was willing to admit publicly. Privately, Washington confessed that his "unfortunate experience in New York" and the events which followed it had left him "in a rather collapsed condition." Some of those close to him claimed that he never fully recovered from the psychological and physical strain.[50]

Some observers of the American scene in 1911 attached a significance to the Ulrich affair which went far beyond any personal injury to Washington. Commentators in Europe, even more emphatically than those in the United States, interpreted the incident as evidence of "a dangerous rise in racial tensions." For example, the British press generally agreed that the attack on Washington pointed up "one of the gravest social problems on the American continent" and offered proof that "the segregating sentiment" was no longer confined to the Southern states.[51] Tragic though observers considered the implications of the Ulrich-Washington affair, they were scarcely less impressed with the irony of the episode. The motive which presumably prompted Ulrich to attack the most distinguished Negro in America as well as the geographical setting of the assault contributed to the ironic note: suspected of committing the "unpardonable" of-

fense, the most eloquent spokesman of the philosophy of accommodation among Negroes was not only beaten by Ulrich and another
white man, but was also threatened by an angry mob of whites, not in
the South, but in New York City. Washington frankly admitted that
"the most hurtful part of the whole experience" was the accusation
that he had made improper advances to a white female. Clearly, he
regarded as national in scope what Marion Reedy described as "the
South's dictum that the Negro cannot be trusted to restrain the sexual impulse of the servile race. . . ." In commenting upon the Washington-Ulrich affair, one Negro journalist reminded his readers that
in matters of prejudice and discrimination the South excelled the
North by "a half degree and a half degree only."[52] Any effect that the
"excruciating experience" in New York may have had upon Washington's attitude or tactics was not immediately discernible. But it could
scarcely have done other than strengthen the determination of the
anti-Washington forces in their efforts to achieve full citizenship
rights for Negroes. In a sense, the incident justified their opposition
to Washington's accommodating philosophy.

Notes

[1] August Meier, *Negro Thought in America, 1880-1915: Racial Ideologies in the Age of
Booker T. Washington* (Ann Arbor, 1963), pp. 101-02.

[2] See Charles F. Kellogg, *NAACP: A History of the National Association for the Advancement of Colored People,* Vol. I: *1909-1920* (Baltimore, 1967), 67-83; *Booker T. Washington
and His Critics: The Problem of Negro Leadership.* Edited with Introduction by Hugh Haw-
kins (Boston, 1962); Arna Bontemps, *100 Years of Freedom* (New York, 1962), pp. 175-
200; Elliott M. Rudwick, "Booker T. Washington's Relations With the National Association for the Advancement of Colored People," *Journal of Negro Education,* XXIX
(Spring, 1960), 134-44.

[3] *New York Times,* March 20, 21, 1911; *New York Age,* March 23, 1911.

[4] *New York Times, op. cit.; Philadelphia Tribune,* March 25, 1911; New York *Age, op. cit.;*
Bontemps, *op. cit.,* p. 214.

[5] *New York Times, op. cit.;* Norfolk *Virginian Pilot,* March 23, 1911; *New York Herald,*
March 25, 1911; see also a scrapbook of newspaper clippings marked "Attack on
B.T.W.," Hampton Institute Library, Hampton, Virginia.

[6] *New York Times,* March 22, 1911.

[7] *New York Times,* March 20, 21, 1911.

[8] Lafayette (Indiana) *Journal,* March 22, 1911.

[9] *Atlanta Journal,* March 22, 1911; *New York Times,* March 22, 1911; Atlanta *Georgian and
News,* March 25, 1911; letter from B. T. Washington to J. C. Hemphill, March 28, 1911
(James C. Hemphill Papers, Duke University Library); Bontemps, *op. cit.,* p. 215; *Chi-
cago Defender,* October 21, 1911.

[10] Such expressions of sympathy and support are found in abundance in the Booker T.
Washington Papers (Manuscript Division, Library of Congress).

[11] Letter from W. H. Taft to B. T. Washington, March 21, 1911 (William Howard Taft
Papers, Manuscript Division, Library of Congress).

[12] *New York Times*, March 24, 1911; W. Anderson to W. H. Taft, March 24, 1911 (Taft Papers).

[13] Letter from A. W. Gray to W. H. Taft, March 23, 1911 (Taft Papers); Rome (Georgia) *Tribune-Herald*, April 2, 1911; Bloomington (Illinois) *Bulletin*, March 23, 1911.

[14] *Kansas City Post*, March 28, 1911.

[15] *Harper's Weekly*, LV (April, 1911), 5; *The Outlook*, XCVII (April 1, 1911), 707-08.

[16] Sacramento (California) *Union*, March 24, 1911; Butte (Montana) *Inter-Mountain*, March 22, 1911; see also press clippings in the Washington Papers; "The Attack on Booker Washington," *The Literary Digest*, XLII (April 3, 1911), 664-65.

[17] Richmond *Times-Dispatch*, March 21, 1911; letter from B. T. Washington to J. C. Hemphill, March 23, 1911 (Hemphill Papers).

[18] *Atlanta Constitution*, March 23, 1911; *Lynchburg News*, March 23, 1911; Vicksburg (Mississippi) *Herald*, March 21, 1911; Bontemps, *op. cit.*, pp. 214-15.

[19] Quoted in the *Salt Lake City Weekly*, April 1, 1911, and *The Literary Digest*, *op. cit.*, 664.

[20] New York *Sun*, March 21, 1911.

[21] *Kansas City Post, op. cit.*

[22] Francis B. Simkins, *Pitchkins Ben Tillman: South Carolinian* (Baton Rouge, 1944), p. 400; Vicksburg *Herald*, May 13, 1911; New York *Journal*, March 27, 1911; letter from B. T. Washington to Seth Low, April 19, 1911 (Washington Papers).

[23] "Was the Learned Doctor Drunk?" *The Jeffersonian* (March 30, 1911), 8.

[24] Letter from B. T. Washington to Seth Low, April 19, 1911 (Washington Papers); B. T. Washington to W. H. Taft, March ?, 1911 (Taft Papers).

[25] *Chicago Defender*, March 25, 1911; for Negro press reaction see New York *Age*, March 30, 1911; *Metropolitan Monthly* (Dallas, Texas), May 11, 1911; Cleveland *Gazette*, March 23, 1911.

[26] For an account of the meeting see New York *Age*, March 30, 1911.

[27] Letters from C. W. Anderson to B. T. Washington, March 28, 1911, Anderson to Washington, March 29, 1911, Washington to Anderson, April 3, 1911 (Washington Papers).

[28] Kellogg, *op. cit.*, p. 80.

[29] Letters from O. G. Villard to B. T. Washington, March 27, 1911, Washington to Villard, March 30, 1911, Washington to Villard, April 19, 1911 (Washington Papers); Kellogg, *op. cit.*, pp. 81-82; Samuel R. Spencer, Jr., *Booker T. Washington and the Negro's Place in American Life* (Boston, 1955), pp. 176-77.

[30] Letter from O. G. Villard to B. T. Washington, March 31, 1911 (Washington Papers).

[31] Letter from O. G. Villard to R. R. Moton, April 5, 1911, B. T. Washington to R. R. Moton, April 10, 1911, B. T. Washington to O. G. Villard, April 19, 1911 (Washington Papers).

[32] Kellogg, *op. cit.*, pp. 81-83.

[33] Letter from C. W. Anderson to B. T. Washington, March 29, 1911 (Washington Papers).

[34] Letters from Seth Low to B. T. Washington, March 27, 1911, Washington to Low, April 8, 1911 (Washington Papers).

[35] Letter from B. T. Washington to Seth Low, April 8, 1911 (Washington Papers).

[36] *New York Times*, April 4, 1911; letters J. Scott to W. H. Smith, April 6, 1911, B. T. Washington to W. H. Smith, May 15, 1911, Smith to Washington, May 25, 1911 (Washington Papers); *Chicago Defender* (October 21, 1911) maintained that Ulrich, though quick to plead not guilty, had been responsible for the delay in bringing the case to trial. He apparently hoped that Washington would drop the charges.

[37] Cleveland *Gazette*, April 1, May 6, 1911; Boston *Guardian* quoted in *ibid.*, May 6, 1911.

[38] *Ibid.*, July 22, 1911; *Chicago Defender*, July 29, 1911.

[39] Letters from B. T. Washington to W. H. Smith, July 22, 1911, Washington to Smith, August 2, 1911 (Washington Papers).

[40] Letters from J. W. Reed to B. T. Washington, April 12, 1911, B. T. Washington to C. W. Anderson, May 2, 1911 (Washington Papers).

[41] Letters from B. T. Washington to C. W. Anderson, May 5, 1911, Washington to Anderson, April 16, 1911 (Washington Papers).

[42] Letters from B. T. Washington to W. H. Smith, July 14, 1911, Washington to Smith, July 22, 1911 (Washington Papers).

[43] *New York Times*, November 7, 1911; Washington *Evening Star*, November 6, 7, 1911; letters from W. H. Lewis to J. Scott, November 13, 1911, C. W. Anderson to J. Scott, December 5, 1911 (Washington Papers).

[44] Letter from R. C. Bruce to B. T. Washington, November 7, 1911 (Washington Papers).

[45] Letter from B. T. Washington to W. H. Lewis, November 20, 1911 (Washington Papers).

[46] Cleveland *Gazette*, November 11, 1911.

[47] Letters from C. W. Anderson to B. T. Washington, November 16, 1911, Whitefield McKinlay to B. T. Washington, November 11, 1911, Kelly Miller to B. T. Washington, November 15, 1911 (Washington Papers).

[48] Letter from B. T. Washington to Seth Low, April, 1911 (Washington Papers).

[49] Cleveland *Gazette*, August 19, 1911; *Journal of the House of Representatives of the Thirty Second Legislature of Texas, First Called Session*, 1911, I, 132, 142-43; Bontemps, *op. cit.*, p. 216.

[50] Letter from B. T. Washington to Seth Low, April 3, 1911 (Washington Papers); Bontemps, *op. cit.*, p. 216.

[51] For British reaction see *The Times* (London), March 22, 1911; *Yorkshire Post*, March 22, 1911; *Yorkshire Daily Observer*, March 22, 1911; *Irish Times* (Dublin), March 22, 1911; *Leeds Mercury*, March 22, 1911; *Daily Sketch* (Manchester), March 22, 1911; *The Free Press* (Aberdeen), March 23, 1911.

[52] Chicago *Defender*, March 25, 1911.

Miss Ida B. Wells and Memphis Lynching

David M. Tucker

In the 1890s, violence by whites against African Americans, manifested in race riots and lynchings of black men and women, became a constant throughout the South. By 1904, the average number of blacks lynched annually exceeded one hundred, becoming in some communities a perverse form of entertainment for white families. Among black leaders protesting the violence and terrorism of the era were black women, such as Mississippi native Ida B. Wells. Wells' earliest attacks on lynching occurred in Memphis, Tennessee, where as a young journalist her candid and forceful condemnations of atrocities against blacks resulted in her having to flee Memphis for the North. Continuing her campaign there, Wells became a well-known antilynching and militant journalist, supported by black intellectuals and women's groups such as the National Association of Colored Women. Invited on at least two occasions to lecture abroad, Wells communicated the horrors of lynch law to an international audience. Her 1892 publication, A Red Record, Tabulated Statistics and Alleged Causes of Lynching in the United States, *provided the earliest analysis of lynching available to African American leaders.*

David Tucker presents Wells as a convincing and powerful advocate for the end of mob violence and for social justice for African Americans. Writing before the publication of Wells' autobiography, Crusade for Justice *(1970), Tucker makes excellent use of contemporary press accounts to support the contention that Wells' crusade in England and the subsequent denunciations of lynching in the British press weakened mob law in Memphis. He concludes that Wells' activities forced a new outlook upon the city's leadership that resulted in a cessation of lynchings for more than two decades.*

HISTORY, AS IT HAS BEEN WRITTEN, is largely the story of men: the women have been confined to the home and to the local society page. Certainly nothing but this venerable tradition could have kept American historians, who have rarely published articles about any individual woman, from recognizing the significance of a black woman, Miss Ida B. Wells. For in the long struggle against lynching in the South, Miss Wells deserves more credit than any other individual, having brought this practice before the eyes of the world and, in so doing, having accelerated the establishment of law and decency in the American South.[1]

Born in 1862, the daughter of house servants in Holly Springs, Mississippi, Miss Wells became a school teacher in her early teens in order to finance her own education. She first attended the local Rust College, and later enrolled for summer sessions at Fisk University. Then, like thousands of other Mississippi Negroes, this little brown woman moved north to Memphis, the striving commercial center of the mid-South. There she taught at Kortecht Public School, became the star of local literary circles, and won admittance to Memphis black society, an aristocracy based on complexion, education, and talent.[2]

Black society bitterly resented racial discrimination in Memphis and applauded Miss Wells for her record of vigorous protest against the system. As a young teacher she had paid first-class fare in order to assert her right to ride in the railroad's ladies' car; and at being forced to leave, she had fought to the point of taking the Chesapeake, Ohio, & Southwestern to court in 1884. She had even won the local decision, though it was later reversed by the Supreme Court of Tennessee.[3] After publishing an account of her struggles in the local Negro press, Miss Wells won such applause that she begun to write regularly, using the pen name "Iola," for the Negro press throughout the country. At the 1887 National Afro-American Press Convention she was named assistant secretary for the group and was acclaimed the most prominent correspondent for the American black press.[4]

While all agreed that Miss Wells could handle a goose-quill as easily as any man in the newspaper world, her feminine beauty was a subject of some controversy in the Afro-American press. Reproducing a woodcut engraving of Miss Wells, which revealed a young woman with distinctly Negroid features, the Cleveland *Gazette* apologized, "the picture, though an accurate likeness, hardly does her justice,"[5] to which the Memphis *Free Speech* added, "Iola will never get a husband so long as she lets these editors make her so hideous."[6] The Indianapolis *Freeman*, however, maintained that the picture "flattered her" and told its readers, "Iola makes the mistake of trying to be pretty as well as smart. She should remember that beauty and genius are not always companions. George Eliot, George Sand, Harriet Beecher Stowe and many other bright minds of that sex were not paragons by any means."[7]

As a serious journalist, Miss Wells purchased a third interest in the most militant Memphis journal, *Free Speech and Headlight*. The editorial offices of *Free Speech* were in the Beale Street Baptist Church under the nominal editorship of the Reverend Taylor Nightingale. Since the duties of ministering to the congregation and presiding over the University of Western Tennessee, which was housed at the time within the Beale Street Church, prevented Nightingale from do-ing more for the weekly paper than sell it from his pulpit on Sun-days, the real editorial work fell to Miss Wells and to J. L. Fleming. A native of Arkansas, Fleming had received a grammar school educa-tion in Memphis before launching his own weekly, *The Marion Head-light*, in Crittenden County, Arkansas. The paper ran successfully until 1888, when more than a hundred Winchester-carrying whites rode into town and liberated their county from Negro rule by informing their county judge and eight other black politicians, two preachers, and one newspaper editor that the town was no longer large enough for black leaders and white Crittenden Countians.[8] Fleming had re-treated east to join forces with Taylor Nightingale and Miss Ida B. Wells.

The new *Free Speech and Headlight* soon found itself facing a ra-cial crisis in Memphis. While for almost a quarter of a century Mem-phis Negroes had been able to vote, hold public office, and serve on the city police force, a new generation of young Memphians were now launching a campaign to end participation by Negroes in politics and to reestablish white supremacy. "The older men have been con-templating the situation for, lo, these many years," the young white editor of the Memphis *Weekly Avalanche* declared. "They've been say-ing, 'If the North will let us alone, we'll work this out in time.' The time for that sort of talk has gone by. The young men of today say, 'We are going to work this out, and do it right now . . . and the North can do all the howling it wants to.' "[9]

The determination of young white racists to overthrow Recon-struction was met by militant opposition from the Negro community, and *Free Speech and Headlight* was the voice of this black protest against white back-lash in the late eighteen-eighties:

> The dailies of our city say that the whites must rule this coun-try. But that is an expression without a thought. It must be borne in mind that the Lord is going to have something to say about this and all other government. It may be expected that the black man will press his claim 'till Shiloh comes.'
>
> The old Southern voice that was once heard and made the Negroes jump and run like rats to their holes is 'shut up,' or might well be, for the Negro of today is not the same as Negroes were thirty years ago, and it can't be expected that the Negro of today will take what was forced upon him thirty years back. So it is no use to be talking now about Negroes ought to be kept at the bottom

where God intended for them to stay; the Negro is not expected to
stay at the bottom.[10]

The *Free Speech* editorials were entirely defensive, and yet they
were taken as evidence of the folly of educating black men and held
up as proof of the perfidy of black ministers. Since the newspaper
was edited and sold in the oldest and most elegant black church in
Memphis, white Memphians assumed the Reverend Nightingale was
instilling the doctrine of hate rather than the gospel of love in the
minds of the rising generation of blacks. The whites were particularly
outraged by a *Free Speech* editorial supporting retaliatory violence:

> Those Georgetown, Ky., Negroes who set fire to the town last
> week because a Negro named Dudley had been lynched, show some
> of the true spark of manhood by their resentment. We had begun
> to think the Negroes of Jackson and Tullahoma, Tenn., of Forest
> City, Ark., and nearly the whole state of Mississippi, where lynching
> of Negroes has become the sport and pastime of unknown (?) white
> citizens, hadn't manhood enough in them to wriggle and crawl out
> of the way, much less protect and defend themselves. Of one thing
> we may be assured, so long as we permit ourselves to be trampled
> upon, so long we will have to endure it. Not until the Negro rises in
> his might and takes a hand in resenting such cold-blooded murders,
> if he has to burn up whole towns, will a halt be called in wholesale
> lynching.[11]

In reply, the outraged white Memphis press penned a justification of lynching. Though lynching was in violation of the written law,
the *Appeal-Avalanche* pointed out, "Rev. Nightingale should reflect
that there is a higher law" which provided that "the rapist must pay
the penalty with his life." This higher legislation superseded all other
because the people willed it and "at such times they, the law-makers,
rise above all law."[12] After the white press had set the Reverend
Nightingale straight on the legitimacy of lynching and rigorously condemned him for publishing such a "vile, incendiary and murder-ap-
plauding article," the civil authorities stepped in to force the minister
out of the community. By exploiting a feud within Nightingale's
church in which thirteen ousted members of the Beale Street Church
had brought assault and battery charges against the Reverend, the
Memphis authorities were able to convict the preacher in the criminal court. Nightingale was sentenced to eighty days in the county
workhouse, and rather than serve the sentence he fled at once to
Oklahoma.[13] But expelling the Reverend hardly affected the city's
militant black journalism, since it had been Fleming and Miss Wells
who had written and would continue to write the paper's protest
columns.

It was Miss Wells's editorials against the Memphis lynchings of 1892 which first brought her to the national attention of white America. It all began in South Memphis, on the curve of Walker Avenue and Mississippi Boulevard, where a joint stock grocery store had been organized by some of the city's most prominent black capitalists and socialites. The Peoples' Grocery Store, as it was called, entered competition with a white merchant, W. H. Barret, who operated a grocery just across the street. Relations between the two businesses were never friendly, and friction was eventually followed by physical violence. After several incidents, which Barret seems to have instigated himself, the white man persuaded a Shelby County grand jury to indict the officials of Peoples' Grocery for maintaining a nuisance. Enraged, the black community held a meeting where certain speakers reportedly called for cleaning out the "damned white trash" with dynamite. At this point Barret appealed to Shelby County's criminal court Judge DuBose, charging his competitors with conspiring against whites, and securing warrants for the arrest of two of them who had spoken out at the meeting. Barret then, it seems, had the Peoples' Grocery informed that a white mob was planning to assault their store, so that when nine deputy sheriffs dressed in civilian clothing converged on the grocery after dark in order to deliver their arrest warrants, they were taken for a mob and fired upon.[14]

After brief firing, in which three deputies were shot down with head and face wounds, most of the Negroes ran while the deputies rushed in and arrested Calvin McDowell, the grocery clerk, and Will Stewart, a stockholder. The cry of race riot was given and the whole of Memphis became a walking arsenal. Armed white men and boys helped the deputies round up and arrest thirty more accused rioters, among them Tom Moss, the mail carrier and Methodist Sunday school teacher who served as president of the store. Not content with arresting all accused rioters, Judge DuBose took illegal action to disarm the black community, and ordered that the arms of the Tennessee Rifles, a Negro state militia company, be confiscated. The Negro armory was forcibly entered and the rifles carried to the sheriff's office. When neither local authorities nor the state militia commander protested the breach of law, Negro officials chose to announce the disbandment of their company in a bitter press release: "To wear the livery of a commonwealth that regards us with distrust and suspicion, a commonwealth that extracts an oath from us to defend its laws and then fails to protect us in the rights it guarantees, is an insult to our intelligence and manhood."[15]

At three o'clock on Wednesday morning, four days after the shoot-out on the Curve, nine white men, apparently deputy sheriffs, entered the county jail, seized Tom Moss, Calvin McDowell, and Will Stewart, who were regarded as the leaders of the Peoples' Grocery, took the prisoners a mile north of the jail, and shot them in cold blood on a vacant lot next to the Chesapeake and Ohio tracks.[16] Thus three men were lynched in a city of over 85,000 and without the remotest chance that the murderers would ever be brought to trial.

Appalled by this, the worst atrocity against blacks since the Memphis police riot of 1866, the black community turned out by the thousands for the largest funeral procession ever to have taken place in Memphis. Resolutions condemning the lynchings and recommending emigration were adopted at a black town meeting; and the cries of "On to Oklahoma," which had already been heard for several years, sent entire church congregations west, across the Mississippi, and over the Old Military Road. As many as two thousand black Memphians may have fled the city not only in search of freedom for their children, but with the vague hope that depopulating the area would cause the whites to regret their violent oppression of black people.[17]

In the weeks following the lynching, Miss Wells's angry editorials demanded the trial and conviction of the murderers in the name of God and justice.

> The good colored citizens of Memphis who have been interested in and worked for the prosperity and success of the city; who stood by the white people when the plague of '78 and '79 threatened to sweep the town from the face of the earth, demand that the murderers of Calvin McDowell, Will Stewart and Tom Moss be brought to justice. We ask this in the name of God and in the name of the law we have always obeyed and upheld and intend to uphold and obey in the future.[18]

The journalist took the train out to Oklahoma herself to assess the territorial advantages for future Negro immigration; and at home she participated in the black community's boycott of the Memphis city street cars.[19] The first threats on Miss Wells's life, however, came only after a *Free Speech* editorial of May 21, in which she disputed the old rationalization of the whites for lynching by intimating that Southern white women were sexually attracted to black men. In the article, which responded to the lynching of eight more Negroes that week, Miss Wells dared to comment that "Nobody in this section of the country believes the old threadbare lies that Negro men rape white women. If Southern white men are not careful they will over-reach themselves and public sentiment will have a reaction, or a conclusion will be reached which will be very damaging to the moral reputation of their women."[20]

At this, the Memphis *Scimitar*, assuming that the article was Fleming's, threatened that, "unless the Negroes promptly applied the remedy it would be the duty of the whites to tie the author to a stake, brand him on the forehead and perform a surgical operation on him with a pair of shears."[21] The Memphis *Commercial* agreed: "There are some things the Southern white man will not tolerate, and the obscene intimations of the foregoing have brought the writer to the outermost limit of public patience."[22] The white city leaders called an urgent meeting at the Merchants Exchange and voted to attempt to head off yet another lynching by sending a delegation to warn the *Free Speech* never to repeat such ideas or "suffer the consequences." Not surprisingly, editors Fleming and Wells were not there to receive the committee, having chosen already to leave the Bluff City for the relative safety of the North; and the Memphis sheriff put a final end to *Free Speech*, selling the newspaper office and paying off the creditors.

The former co-editors went their separate ways in the North: Fleming launched a Chicago *Free Speech* while Miss Wells joined the staffs of the *New York Age* and the Chicago *Conservator*. Relations were less than cordial between the two as Ida referred to Fleming as her former "business manager" and took credit herself for all of *Free Speech*'s past militancy.[23] Whether Miss Wells had, in fact, wielded the more forceful pen is less than clear, but certainly after 1892 she alone launched the crusade against lynching in the South which gained the nation's attention. Lynch law had reached its highest level in history and Miss Wells determined to bring the matter before the public eye. Not content with merely telling her story in the Afro-American press, she sought to present her case before an international audience. By securing the support of none less than the eminent Frederick Douglass, she wrote and financed an anti-lynching pamphlet for distribution at the 1893 World's Columbian Exposition in Chicago. And when the British editor of *Anti-Caste* asked her to speak in England, Miss Wells departed for Europe immediately.[24]

In speeches and in a pamphlet, *United States Atrocities* (London, 1893), Miss Wells indicted lynching as the latest attempt to preserve white supremacy at any cost. The American press and pulpit were afraid to resist lynching, she contended, because they had swallowed the Southern myths about black men raping white women. The chastity of white women was perfectly safe among black men, Miss Wells stressed: "White men lynch the offending Afro-American not because he is a despoiler of virtue, but because he succumbs to the smiles of

white women."[25] She supported her claim by presenting recent items
from the press about white women in Memphis who had seduced or
voluntarily submitted to black men. Further to silence the Southern
fiction that lynch law was only used to check the "bestial propensities
of black men," she cited statistics from the *Chicago Tribune* which
showed that during the past nine months only one third of the men
who were lynched had even been charged with rape.

The newspaper woman made Memphis her prime target. Not
only had she an account to settle with the white community there,
but the city was an excellent example of the white South's barbarity
in general. On July 22, 1893, three thousand Memphians watched as
a Saturday night crowd broke into the Shelby County jail and seized
Lee Walker, an accused rapist. The mob stripped the man of his
clothing, cut his throat, hanged him on a telegraph pole outside the
jail, and then burned his body, all without a shot ever being fired in
defense of the prisoner by Sheriff McLendon. Nor would the lynchers ever be tried, for as the *Appeal-Avalanche* argued, "Walker was
guilty—not of murder, or arson or forgery, but of rape, a crime
which, whenever and wherever committed, calls for reprisal at the
hands of the citizenship of the particular community."[26]

But even Memphis had her Achilles heel: her fear for her reputation and commercial prosperity; and to the horror of the city's
Chamber of Commerce, Miss Wells went to work on this weak spot,
holding up the Bluff City's sins for the world to view during two lecture trips to England in 1893 and 1894. The black American journalist had been invited to the British isles by Catherine Impey, editor of
Anti-Caste in Aberdeen, Scotland, who explained in a letter of March,
1893: "We want you to come over and help us begin the organization
of an anti-slavery movement."[27] Miss Impey, a reformer who hoped
that lectures on lynching would arouse moral sentiment for racial
equality in the American South and throughout the British empire,
guaranteed that all of Miss Wells's expenses would be paid. The
American journalist accepted the offer, began with a lecture in the
Music Hall at Aberdeen, and told her story in more than a dozen cities in Scotland and England. Through lectures that were praised as
lucid, cultured, and effective, Englishmen were given their first opportunity to hear and applaud the Afro-American opposition to lynch
law. "Her quiet, refined manner," the *Manchester Guardian* observed,
"her intelligence and earnestness, her avoidance of all oratorical
tricks, and her dependence upon the simple eloquence of facts
makes her a powerful and convincing advocate. . . . "[28]

British audiences were so sympathetic that Miss Wells returned
again the next spring for a longer trip, which she confined in the

main to London; and there she visited all the journals which influenced English opinion and spoke to more than a hundred nonconformist churches, clubs, drawing room gatherings, and dinner parties. Among her successes was a large breakfast reception for members of Parliament and their wives at the Westminster Palace Hotel, where she informed her audience of the increased frequency and barbarity of lynchings in the Southern states and the failure of either local officials or Northern opinion to insist that legal due process replace mob violence. Miss Wells then asked for and received the promise that English public opinion would endorse the basic right of a fair trial for every Southern Negro accused of a crime.[29]

Lectures produced more than applause and petitions to the American Ambassador; they won for Miss Wells special interviews with the *Daily Chronicle, Christian World, Westminster Gazette, London Sun,* and the *Labor Leader.* News clippings of these interviews soon flooded in through the mails to the white Memphis press, along with letters which asked, for example, if the city were really so brutal and heartless as they had been told in the article, "The Bitter Cry of Black America—A New Uncle Tom's Cabin." The Memphis editors must have winced on discovering what sort of articles were published in the *London Sun:*

> Miss Ida B. Wells is a negress, a young lady of little more than twenty years of age, a graceful, sweet-faced, intelligent, courageous girl. She hails from Memphis, Tenn. She is not going back there just now, because the white people are anxious to hang her up by the neck in the market place, and burn the soles of her feet, and gouge her beautiful dark eyes out with red-hot irons. This is what the Southern American white man does with a Negro or negress for preference, when he wants a holiday sensation; and when he finds a charming victim, such as this sweet girl would make, the mayor of the town orders the schools to be closed, and the little scholars turn out in holiday ribbons, and their parents don the Sunday go-to-meeting best, and lead the youngsters out by the hand. They all go out to see the fun, and have their photographs taken at the scene of martyrdom, and there is much rejoicing over the black sinner that repenteth not.[30]

The "red record" of Southern whites had been so terrible, the English press reported, that Miss Wells took more pride in her black blood than in her white. "If Christianity is to be the test," she said, "then I may well be prouder to belong to the dark race that is the most practically Christian known to history. . . ."[31] While Southern whites had shown themselves savage and unchristian, Negroes had shown themselves meek in spirit; for centuries they had turned the left cheek when smitten on the right; they had blessed them that persecuted them; and they had prayed for those that despitefully used them. The alleged propensity of black men for raping white women, Miss Wells said, was a myth created to protect the sexual pride of white men. She said:

> You see, the white man has never allowed his women to hold the sentiment 'black but comely,' on which he has so freely acted himself. Libertinism apart, white men constantly express an open preference for the society of black women. But it is a sacred convention that white women can never feel passion of any sort, high or low, for a black man. Unfortunately facts don't always square with the convention; and then, if the guilty pair are found out, the thing is christened an outrage at once and the woman is practically forced to join in hounding down the partner of her shame.[32]

By quietly relating her own Memphis experiences and presenting her statistics from the *Chicago Tribune*, Miss Wells easily convinced her audiences of the shameful operation of Southern lynch law and of the moral obligation of English sentiment, which had once aided in the destruction of chattel slavery, to help complete the work of emancipation of American blacks. The London *Daily Chronicle* instructed England's religious leaders to arouse the moral indignation of Christians in America.[33] The *Westminster Gazette* said, "if a tithe of the ghastly tales she tells are true, it is well-nigh incredible that this sympathy should be denied by any civilized human soul upon God's earth, in America or out of it."[34] The *London Sun* had little doubt that Miss Wells's charges were true. "If her pleasant face is not an absolute guarantee of absolute truthfulness, there is no truth in existence."[35] Ida B. Wells thus returned from her second European tour with America and especially a certain New South city smarting under British criticism.

Miss Wells's lectures were a smashing success. For one thing, they inspired the English to form an anti-lynching league with a treasury of five thousand pounds for the purpose of investigating and publicizing the persecution of Southern Negroes in America.[36] Naturally the merchants back in Memphis were alarmed at the impact of Ida Wells's lectures; for being among the largest cotton exporters in the world, they depended upon the English textile industry for much of their business. It was no surprise, then, that those Chamber of Commerce capitalists who owned the local white press felt compelled to reprint certain British reports of Miss Wells's lectures abroad in order to refute their charges against the Bluff City. The Memphis *Commercial Appeal* accused her of gross exaggeration and insisted that Memphis was really a decent place for blacks to live. But significantly, in this effort to repair the city's damaged reputation, newspaper editors at last condemned lynching unequivocally and even tried to make their position retroactive by insisting they had never approved mob law.

When the leading authority on nineteenth century lynch law, James E. Cutler, suggested that Miss Wells's English efforts were largely futile,[37] he failed to assess the impact of English opinion on Memphis civic leaders. Influence is difficult to measure, to be sure; but when the Memphis lynching of 1894 occurred shortly after Miss Wells's return from England (six accused barn burners were shot while being brought to the Shelby County jail), white business leaders immediately took conspicuous steps to condemn the crime publicly. Businessmen called a public meeting in the Merchant's Exchange where they adopted resolutions censuring the "wicked, fiendish and inexcusable massacre," demanded the "arrest and conviction of the murderers," and raised one fund for apprehending "the criminals" and another for the benefit of the widows and orphans of the "murdered men."[38] Never before had the white citizens made such a forthright condemnation of racial lynching. It was time indeed, the *Commercial Appeal* explained, to rise up in opposition to barbarism and murder because "if this crime goes unpunished," the paper warned, "every friend of Memphis must be dumb before the accusations of its enemies, for silence will be our only refuge from the pitiless fire of denunciation that will be heaped upon us."[39]

A Shelby County grand jury promptly indicted thirteen white men for murder, went on record as being appalled by the outrage, and announced their hope for conviction and the death penalty. "We cannot close this report," the grand jury said, "without expressing our horror of the cold-blooded, brutal butchery of these six defenseless men, the cruelty of which would cause even a savage to hang his head in shame."[40] And although the city never succeeded in convicting the band of lynchers,[41] the practical need to end lynching, and the new philosophy which it forced on the city's leadership, seem to have put an end to the crime in the Bluff City for more than two decades.[42] For this, Miss Ida B. Wells deserves the lion's share of the credit; for it was she who had held the sins of the city up for the whole world to see and had thus shamed white Memphians into doing at last what decency and equality of law had always demanded.[43]

Notes

[1] Brief sketches of Miss Wells may be found in: Arna Bontemps and Jack Conroy, *Anyplace but Here* (New York, 1966); Allan H. Spear, *Black Chicago* (Chicago, 1967); Langston Hughes, *Famous Negro Heroes of America* (New York, 1958).

[2] Cleveland *Gazette*, April 4, 1885, March 26, 1887, July 6, 1889; Henry Davenport Northrop, *The College of Life* (Chicago, 1895), pp. 99-101.

[3] Chesapeake, Ohio & Southwestern Railroad Co. v. Wells, 85 Tenn 613 (1887).

[4] New Orleans *Weekly Pelican*, August 13, 1887.

[5] Cleveland *Gazette*, July 6, 1889.

[6] *New York Age*, August 24, 1889.

[7] Indianapolis *Freeman*, August 24, 1889.

[8] Cleveland *Gazette*, August 4, 1888.

[9] Memphis *Weekly Avalanche*, July 11, 1889.

[10] *Free Speech* reprinted in Memphis *Weekly Avalanche*, July 13, 1889: rather than inserting *sic* after every failure of the white press to capitalize *Negro*, I have capitalized the word in all quotations; copies of *Free Speech*, like twenty-five other black newspapers published in Memphis, were never preserved for the historian. Memphis public libraries did not even subscribe to Negro newspapers prior to 1966. See Armistead Scott Pride, "A Register and History of Negro Newspapers in the United States, 1827-1950" (Unpublished Ph.D. dissertation, Northwestern University, 1950), pp. 359-60, for a listing of the black Memphis papers.

[11] Memphis *Appeal-Avalanche*, September 6, 1891.

[12] *Ibid.*

[13] *Ibid.*, September 10, 11, 13, 1891; Memphis *Public Ledger*, November 2, 1891; *Langston City Herald*, January 5, 1893.

[14] Fred L. Hutchins, *What Happened in Memphis* (Memphis, 1965), pp. 36-40; Nashville *Daily American*, March 7, 1892; Memphis *Weekly Appeal-Avalanche*, March 16, 1892; the most persuasive statement of facts was assembled by five Memphis Negro ministers and published in the St. Paul *Appeal*, March 26, 1892.

[15] Cleveland *Gazette*, March 26, 1892.

[16] The first reports (*Weekly Appeal-Avalanche*, March 16, 1892) carried the jailer's story that seventy-five masked men had entered the jail, but by the end of the month even the white press no longer believed the lynching party to have been more than ten men (Nashville *Daily American*, March 30, 1892).

[17] Kansas City *American Citizen*, April 1, 1892; Cleveland *Gazette*, April 2, May 28, 1892; *Washington Bee*, April 2, 1892; the Reverend W. A. Brinkley, editor of the Memphis *Living Way* and pastor of the Washington Street Baptist Church, sold his church to the local Jewish community and moved his congregation west. At least three other ministers—W. F. H. Morgan, J. L. Lee, and R. N. Countee—also moved west.

[18] *Free Speech* reprinted in Kansas City *American Citizen*, April 1, 1892.

[19] *Langston City Herald*, April 16, 1892; Indianapolis *Freeman*, April 23, 1892; Ida B. Wells, *United States Atrocities* (London, 1893), p. 15.

[20] Kansas City *American Citizen*, July 1, 1892; Nashville *Daily American*, May 26, 1892.

[21] *Ibid.*

[22] Kansas City *American Citizen*, July 1, 1892.

[23] *Ibid.*; Indianapolis *Freeman*, July 21, 28, 1894.

[24] Catherine Impey to Ida B. Wells, March 19, 1893, reprinted in Topeka *Call*, April 15, 1893.

[25] Wells, *op. cit.*, p. 3.

[26] Memphis *Appeal-Avalanche*, July 23, July 28, August 3, 1893.

[27] Topeka *Call*, April 15, 1893.

[28] *Manchester Guardian*, May 9, 1893.

[29] *The Times*, June 7, 1894.

[30] *London Sun* reprinted in Memphis *Appeal-Avalanche*, June 12, 1894.

[31] *Westminister Gazette* reprinted in Memphis *Appeal-Avalanche*, May 29, 1894.

32 *Ibid.*

33 *New York Times,* April 29, 1894.

34 *Westminster Gazette* reprinted in Memphis *Appeal-Avalanche,* June 12, 1894.

35 *London Sun* reprinted in Memphis *Appeal-Avalanche,* June 12, 1894.

36 *Cyclopedic Review of Current History,* IV (1894), 647; Miss Wells's lecture points are summarized in: Ida B. Wells, *A Red Record* (Chicago, 1894).

37 James Elbert Cutler, *Lynch Law: An Investigation into the History of Lynching in the United States* (New York, 1905), pp. 229-30.

38 Memphis *Commercial Appeal,* September 8, 1894.

39 *Ibid.,* September 17, 1894.

40 *New York Times,* September 16, 1894.

41 Memphis *Commercial Appeal,* December 15, 1894.

42 The Memphis press never again condoned lynch law and no lynching occurred until 1917, when Ell Person, an accused axe-murderer, was lynched just outside the Memphis city limits.

43 On June 27, 1895, Miss Wells married Ferdinand L. Barnett, a Chicago Negro attorney, journalist, and president of the Illinois Anti-Lynching League. Until her death in 1931, Mrs. Wells-Barnett continued to be an outspoken foe of lynching. The major source on Miss Wells now is her diary. Alfreda M. Duster, ed., *Crusader for Justice: The Autobiography of Ida B. Wells* (Chicago, 1970), which was published after this article was written.

Only for the Bourgeois?
James Weldon Johnson and the NAACP,
1916-1930

BERNARD EISENBERG

The arduous task of making a living became even more burdensome for African Americans as industrialization continued to shape the economy of the United States after World War I. For black workers in both the North and South, the move into urban communities brought unfavorable contact with organized labor. Excluded from membership by most of the trade unions that monopolized employment, black workers could make little headway in the industrial arena. For them, membership in unions existed only in segregated locals or independent African American labor associations.

 Bernard Eisenberg's study explores the labor policies of the National Association for the Advancement of Colored People (NAACP) during the tenure of James Weldon Johnson, the organization's first African American Executive Secretary. While some scholars have criticized the organization's labor record, Eisenberg argues that the NAACP demonstrated deep commitment to black workers during its early years, despite the anti-union sentiment of some of its members and supporters. The author offers as evidence the favorable opinion of unions expressed by Johnson and other NAACP officials, the numerous examples of aid to black workers, the joint lobbying efforts of the NAACP with the American Federation of Labor to end racial discrimination, and the endorsement of the Brotherhood of Sleeping Car Porters.

THE NATIONAL ASSOCIATION FOR THE ADVANCEMENT OF COLORED PEOPLE has often been labeled a conservative organization, concerned mainly with courtroom victories for its middle-class membership. Particularly in the 1960s, younger and more militant civil rights advocates found the Association irrelevant to the broad political, cultural, and economic needs of the black community. In the process of criticism and doubt, however, many forgot, or never realized, that the early NAACP, in fact, was considered a radical organization. Especially under the leadership of James Weldon Johnson, its first black Executive Secretary, the Association developed a broad range of ideas for coping with a racist environment. Much more than a vehicle for abstract judicial victories, the NAACP used its tiny annual budget, which today would barely pay the salary for one full-time executive, to criticize United States foreign policy, lobby for anti-lynching legislation, campaign in congressional elections, encourage cultural achievement by race artists, and help organize black workingmen. This paper is concerned with Johnson's role in shaping the economic orientation of the early NAACP, an aspect that the present-minded tend to ignore.[1]

Johnson came to the Association in 1916, after a varied and often distinguished career as educator, lawyer, lyricist, consul, poet, and writer. Born forty-five years earlier in Jacksonville, Florida, he later recalled that his childhood years were pleasant and "free from undue fear of or esteem for white people as a race." Not until his student days at Atlanta University did he begin to experience the suffocating impact of America's caste system. Color penetrated every aspect of the school: students rode segregated trains to the University, saw their teachers ostracized by the white community, and charged their debates with the issue. After graduating from Atlanta in 1894, Johnson became principal of his former grade school in Jacksonville. He was just twenty-three years old. In addition to being an educator, Johnson developed other interests: publishing his own newspaper, studying for the bar, and writing the words for "Lift Every Voice and Sing," later called the Negro National Anthem and still sung in schools throughout the nation. Around the turn of the century, however, opportunities for blacks in the South became increasingly limited. Armed with many talents, Johnson set out for New York in the summer of 1899, determined to write lyrics for the theater. Joined by his brother Rosamond and Bob Cole, a versatile showman, Johnson composed the words for scores of humorous and lilting tunes that were produced in New York and London. The trio caught the fancy of the public. In 1904, when Marie Cahill sang their "Congo Love Song," one admirer remembered it as "the most popular song in New York and throughout the country." It grossed $13,000 in royalties.[2]

After several years of success, however, the routine of writing lyrics and jokes on schedule became burdensome. Johnson wanted to do more serious writing, and when an opportunity came in 1906 to serve as U. S. Consul in Puerto Cabello, Venezuela, he saw it as a chance to escape the feverish pace of Manhattan. Once established in Latin America, Johnson sent verse to the *Century Magazine* and *The Independent,* and began work on a novel, *The Autobiography of an Ex-Colored Man,* which was published anonymously several years later. Although he was promoted in 1909 to the new consulate in Corinto, Nicaragua, Johnson decided to abandon the diplomatic corps four years later, after Woodrow Wilson and the Democrats swept into office. Corinto had been a hot, miserable town without social amenities, and the new powers in Washington had no intention of advancing black Republicans when so many white Democrats hankered after office. Johnson returned to Manhattan and, with characteristic courage and confidence, began yet another career, as columnist for *The New York Age*, one of the oldest and most influential race newspapers in the country. His weekly editorial, widely syndicated, dealt with almost every aspect of black life in America. He warned of hostile bills in Congress, refuted the theory of white supremacy, and contrasted unfavorably the hundreds of federal agents enforcing the Prohibition Amendment with the negligible number backing the Fourteenth. His writings reflected the wide range of activities in his life, and just as he later broadened the scope of the NAACP, he widened the perspective of his readers. He discussed the Irish question, world disarmament, and classical music, as well as lighter subjects like the art of tipping and the length of women's skirts. Since newspaper work neither exhausted his time nor paid well, Johnson continued to write songs (with Jerome Kern, Will Marion Cook, and Harry Burleigh) and publish poetry. Then, late in 1916, he accepted an offer to work for the NAACP, established just seven years before. His entire life, Johnson later wrote, had been preparation for this new task.[3]

The Association was still a fledgling organization when Johnson arrived to assume the post of Field Secretary. The national organization had but two office rooms on Fifth Avenue and a staff of four: Johnson, the Executive Secretary, a stenographer, and a bookkeeper. Dr. William E. B. DuBois, editor of *The Crisis*, had a separate staff of fewer than ten. Conceived in 1909, the Association had grown slowly, mainly in the North, and always in the towns and cities: Ohio in 1916 had more branches than the entire Old South. Such retarded development meant that the biracial group lacked not only an impressive membership for successful lobbying, but also funds to carry out its essential program of immediate and complete civil rights. "It was my idea," Johnson recalled in his autobiography, "that the South could furnish numbers and resources to make the Association a power." The NAACP had not only to address white America, but awaken black America, particularly in the Dixie region where most of the race lived and where only three of the 68 branches operated. Johnson threw himself wholeheartedly into the job. He prepared a pamphlet on how to form a branch (which was used for many years by prospective members) and became, as his title suggested, active in the field. His Southern birth, upbringing, and contacts made him an ideal instrument for penetrating the Mason-Dixon line. Appointed in December, Johnson was on the road by mid-January, touring from Richmond to Tampa, including Norfolk, Raleigh, Augusta, Savannah, and his own Jacksonville. He addressed some 6,000 persons, left branches in 13 cities, and secured more than 700 new members. The field work, of course, extended beyond the Southland. During a three-month period in 1918, for example, Johnson visited locals and addressed large groups in Boston, Providence, New Haven, East Orange, Philadelphia, and Baltimore. He then went on to Pittsburgh and Cleveland to meet with several church audiences. He spoke at the Young Men's Christian Association in Gary; to black soldiers in Rockford, Illinois; to social workers in Kansas city; at the A. and M. College in Tallahassee, and finally ended his campaign with a speech at Mother Zion A. M. E. Church in Harlem.[4]

During his four years as Field Secretary (1916-1920), Johnson supervised a significant growth that resulted in the forming of 274 new branches and the adherence of 90,000 new members. Since each local was required to list the names and occupations of all subscribers, it is possible to determine with some precision the economic class attracted to the early NAACP. Some branches were negligent, and some records have been lost, but enough information is available for generalization. If one examines the Southern locals that Johnson directly helped organize in 1917, one notes the involvement of large numbers of clergymen, professionals, and businessmen. Of 345 members in nine branches, 46 were teachers or professors; 43, doctors or dentists; 35, clergymen; and 15, undertakers (almost every local had one). Another 44 persons listed themselves in either the insurance or real estate business. However, 27 artisans, 18 workingmen, and nine servants also joined, and two of these became local officers. In ten other Southern branches, not directly organized by Johnson, the middle class was again prominent. Among 416 members, 151 were educators, clergymen, doctors, or businessmen, who filled 15 of the 31 officer positions. But workingmen, servants, and artisans were not negligible: there were sixty-six. In six Northern locals examined, a much smaller proportion of the bourgeois appeared, possibly because the northward migration of blacks during and after the First World War attracted mostly those who were not well-established economically. With 313 subscribers, these branches contained 91 workingmen, 48 servants, and 21 artisans; in addition, half of the officers came from this group. Farmers—whether tenants, sharecroppers, or proprietors—did not constitute more than 5 percent of the total membership in any section of the nation. Obviously, the middle class was important to the early NAACP, but a sizeable and surprising number of recruits came from the urban working class. Moreover, locals did not follow any clear bourgeois program. The Atlanta branch, one of the most strongly middle class, in leadership and membership, led the fight to defeat a city bond proposal that ignored black school children, aided a blind mother whose husband was in prison, assisted a man searching for his sister, cared for one woman (with seven children) whose husband had mysteriously disappeared, and gave money to a man "to get his wife away from" the county.[5]

It is ironic that the NAACP, created and supported by avowed socialists like William E. Walling, Mary White Ovington, Charles E. Russell, and William E. B. DuBois, gained the reputation for being conservatively oriented toward the middle class. The evidence is abundant, however, that the Association was deeply committed to the black worker, and that this commitment persisted through the 1920s after Johnson became the first black Executive Secretary (1920-1930) of the NAACP. This is not to deny the existence of dissent within the organization, even in the upper echelons. In 1917, Executive Secretary John R. Shillady wrote that many liberal friends of the organization were anti-union and laissez-faire adherents. "Mr. [Oswald Garrison] Villard and, I think, Mr. [Moorfield] Storey," were two Board Directors mentioned by Shillady. The socialist Walling more than once complained about such men. He described the " 'bad' element in the NAACP" to fellow trade unionist John R. Frey, and warned Johnson to beware of such "pseudo-liberals." Villard's *Nation*, Walling wrote, was "unspeakable" and even DuBois was "N.G." (no good). Walter White later recalled that many members of the NAACP supported Capital rather than Labor.[6]

Lack of enthusiasm for the labor movement after World War One was not suprising—even whites were losing interest. Union membership, concentrated in only a few industries, had fallen precipitously from more than five million in 1920 to less than three and one-half million by 1929. Union leadership, tied to an obsolescent craft structure, largely ignored great segments of the labor force in new fields like autos and chemicals. Jurisdictional disputes, ideological conflicts with communists, ethnic hostilities, unfriendly courts issuing injunctions, company unions and welfare capitalism—all helped to lessen workers' loyalty to the movement. Logically, black workers should have sided with the unions. Their dilemma, however, was that while most worked with their hands, they were not accepted as brothers by fellow white laborers. When blacks became strikebreakers in order to eat, this only encouraged further prejudice and resistance.

As a result, conservative blacks in the NAACP, like Dean Kelly Miller of Howard University, advised the race to support the employer, not the employee. Such examples of anti-union sentiment within the Association, naturally, were interpreted to discredit the entire organization. Marxist William Z. Foster complained that prominent left-wingers among the Association founders acted more like liberals than socialists: "there were no trade unionists among this group." *The Messenger,* a pro-union black publication, edited by A. Philip Randolph and Chandler Owen, accused the NAACP (and the National Urban League) of lacking sympathy for the working masses:

> Both are bourgeois organizations supported by the dilettante of both races and "good" white people, who get a thrill by chasing around the country holding conferences and "viewing with alarm" the condition of the "deah workers." Neither organization has a single union worker in its offices nor has any real effort been made to organize them and thus get a group of intelligent young Negroes into the labor force.[7]

However, the evidence to the contrary is more impressive. In 1919, a year that witnessed intense industrial and racial strife, the annual NAACP convention took a strong stand in favor of labor unions. An earnest appeal was made by the delegates to all black laborers to accept the advantages of organization within the American Federation of Labor. In 1923, Mary White Ovington, Chairman of the national Board of Directors, inquired of the president of the Shreveport branch what "such an organization as ours could do in the South to help labor union conditions." Two years later, Johnson gladly assisted Frank Crosswaith, Executive Secretary of the Trade Union Committee for Organizing Negro Workers. "I think this movement is all right," Johnson wrote, and then helped secure $500 from the Garland Fund, of which he was a trustee. In 1926, Robert Bagnall and William Pickens, two officers of the Association, clearly stated their positions in favor of the labor movement. Bagnall wrote that unions helped emancipate workers from "serfdom," while Pickens believed that even if whites discriminate, blacks should establish their own unions until organized labor finally realized that it could not succeed without biracial support. More to the point, Johnson and the Association played a significant role in establishing the Brotherhood of Sleeping Car Porters, the first black labor union in America.[8]

When the organizers of the proposed Pullman Porters' union met in September 1925, Johnson appeared as a representative of the NAACP, along with Hugh Frayne from the American Federation of Labor. To one black observer, collaboration between the Executive Secretary of the Association, the AF of L, and black workers was "incomprehensible." James H. Hogans, a conservative columnist for the *New York Age*, asserted that the labor federation had been more hostile to the race than even the Ku Klux Klan, and that the NAACP worked strictly for social and legal ends. "Don't forget," he warned the porters, "that most of the important Negro men who are endorsing and advocating your acceptance of unionism are not men of your sphere. They live in an entirely different atmosphere, socially and intellectually." A. Philip Randolph, general organizer of the Brotherhood, whose journal had earlier branded the NAACP as "bourgeois," quickly rebuked Hogan, and characterized both the AF of L and Johnson's Association as "fighting organizations." He even defended as proper the NAACP's reputed emphasis on social and constitutional rights: higher wages, fewer hours, improved labor conditions "are the most important aspects of our social rights . . . because we must first be before we can be anything."[9]

As the struggle over union recognition continued, it forced race leaders to line up with either the Pullman Company or the workers. Johnson was entreated to counter the influence of conservative blacks like Perry Howard, special assistant to the U.S. Attorney General and Republican Negro National Committeeman from Mississippi, who supposedly had "gone on the payroll of the company to break the union." Randolph wrote to Johnson about company threats and bribes, and asked for public support. "It will be of tremendous moral value to the movement and the men will appreciate it." Johnson's response forthrightly supported the brotherhood. Before a large audience in Chicago, he demanded the removal of Howard from the Department of Justice, and in a letter to Roy Lancaster, Secretary-Treasurer of the union, he expressed approval of the organizing efforts. Johnson wrote that opposition from the company and its allies was expected, "but it is despicable when it comes from colored men professing to be working in the interests of the Pullman car porters." He urged the workers to be neither cautious nor fearful, but to determine what was best for themselves. Directly referring to Perry Howard, a persistent adversary, Johnson said that "only a man ignorant of present day conditions, or a hypocrite, could advise the Pullman porters that it is an unwise step for them to take to form themselves into a brotherhood. He argued that if the railway engineers, conductors, firemen, brakemen, and others can organize, then why not those who are "perhaps the hardest worked, and certainly the poorest paid" on the roads. Randolph thanked Johnson for his "vigorous and militant letter," and Lancaster noted the good it would do in furthering unionization. "Only yesterday," Lancaster wrote, "I converted a porter who has spent more than 42 years in the service,

by privileging him to read it." "Permit me to say," he added, "that
from personal observation, I find that our group . . . has a well
founded as well as deserved confidence in you and your work, and
your personal endorsement as well as official, has meant much to us
in this movement."[10]

Throughout 1926, the friendly cooperation between the two
groups continued. In March, Branch Director Bagnall informed local
NAACP officials in Michigan, Ohio, Pennsylvania, and other industrial states that the Brotherhood "has the hearty endorsement of the
National Association for the Advancement of Colored People." In
April, Chandler Owen appealed to Johnson for legal assistance in a li-
bel suit involving *The Whip,* a black newspaper published in Chicago.
Owen and his associate Randolph had accused the paper of transfer-
ring 55 percent of its stock to an attorney of the Pullman Company.
Although Owen sensed that the NAACP did not want to involve itself
in a dispute between two black parties, he believed that the case was
an exception. "We are confronted," he told Johnson, with "venal and
corrupt Negroes who serve to conceal the hand of more unscrupulous whites in the background." Since the NAACP was an ally, the
union expected defense funds to counter such "covert attacks." The
financially hard-pressed Association gave the matter serious thought,
but, as Johnson pointed out, the question was beyond its scope. Johnson, however, through his influence with the Garland Fund, did secure by November 1929 more than $19,000 for the Brotherhood. This
sum enabled Randolph and Owen to continue printing *The Messenger*
and the *Black Worker,* the union's official organ.[11]

Randolph went still further in his request for support. In June
1926, he asked Johnson, Walter White, Pickens, and Bagnall to secure
an official endorsement of the union at the annual convention of the
Association meeting that year in Chicago, the very headquarters of
the Pullman Company. Such an approval would "hearten other Negro organizations to take a similar position, especially those organizations that are quite encrusted with conservatism." The militant labor
leader described the NAACP as "the biggest and most important organization among Negroes today," "unequivocally on the side of the
Negro workers." The Association did not fail him. Randolph was invited to address the convention, which he enjoyed "hugely," and was
deeply impressed by the action taken. Encouraged by Johnson,
White, Pickens, and Bagnall, the convention sanctioned the work of
the union and expressed satisfaction that two aims of the NAACP—
organization of black workers and their acceptance into the ranks of
white unions—had been advanced by the Pullman porters. Later in
the year, White continued the efforts on behalf of the union with a

"militant and brilliant presentation" (Randolph's description) before the Congregational Church Convention, which afterwards endorsed the Brotherhood. Randolph congratulated White for his "fearless and constructive criticism of Negro preachers," who so often fought union efforts. The NAACP also awarded its Spingarn Medal to the Pullman porter leader, and the union reciprocated by inviting Johnson, as Executive Secretary of the Association, to its "first birthday," along with such noted trade unionists as Norman Thomas, Elizabeth Gurley Flynn, Hugh Frayne, and Morris Hillquit.[12]

In 1927, the NAACP was instrumental in forming a biracial Citizens' Committee of One Hundred to support the Brotherhood. A substantial number of backers came from the Association, including Johnson, White, DuBois, Villard, Bagnall, Spingarn, John Haynes Holmes, John E. Nail, and Lillian Wald. The Committee sent out circulars to all porters and maids urging them to join the union, sought to free the Brotherhood from a jurisdictional dispute with another AF of L union, and pressed the U.S. Mediation Board to resolve the issue between the workers and the Pullman Company.[13]

Such an abiding concern for black workingmen was not unusual for the NAACP. The records of the early Association are replete with examples of active support by Shillady, White, Ovington, and others. Shortly before the Armistice in 1918, for example, the NAACP tried to aid a number of brick masons who had been hired in Cleveland and sent to work at the Air Nitrates Corporation at Muscle Shoals, Alabama. When the men, all union workers, including two members of the Cleveland NAACP, arrived, they were refused work and sent home after six days without compensation. Corporation and labor officials were not consistent in explaining the incident. At first, the company asserted that the men had shirked their jobs. William Dobson, General Secretary of the Bricklayers International, agreed that refusal to work rather than prejudice was the issue. Dobson wrote that the men lacked "the right spirit" in wanting "to force themselves" on the same scaffold with the white men, rather than work by themselves. But the real reason for the company's action was evident in a letter sent by its hiring agent to Shillady. The agent stated "that it would be impossible to employ this type of labor with the white labor used here" for fear of friction between the two races. With this clear admission of discrimination, Shillady immediately protested to the corporation, the AF of L, and the U.S. Department of Labor. "A result we of this Association would greatly deprecate," he wrote to Frank Morrison, Secretary of the AF of L, "would be a growth of the feeling now too prevalent among educated workmen as well as the less educated among them, that organized workmen are

distinctly hostile to them." Racial antagonism would not benefit labor, "but rather those who seek to exploit both whites and blacks."
The bricklayers' union replied coldly that the blacks should have realized what the situation was in Alabama, and unless they wanted to
make trouble, should not have left Cleveland.[14]

In November 1919, a more serious labor disturbance developed
in the South. Again, the NAACP showed no hesitation in defending
the workmen involved. The incident occurred in Bogalusa, Louisiana:
four black and white members of the local carpenters' and joiners'
union were murdered in broad daylight in the office of the Central
Labor Union. The president of the NAACP branch in New Orleans
reported that the people of Bogalusa had been warned to avoid the
union. At least one old black man had his hand broken after refusing
to tear up his union card. Others were intimidated, bribed, or arrested on specious charges. It was useless, the branch pointed out, to
appeal to city officials because the mayor of the town was also vice
president and general manager of the lumber company that had employed the slain men. Miss Ovington, chairman of the Association's
Board of Directors, took a special interest in the case. Impressed that
white union men had been murdered protecting a black labor
leader, she offered the assistance of the NAACP in the hope that
such biracial efforts, rarely seen since the days of the Populists, would
mark a turning point in the history of Southern labor.[15]

The hope, however, was premature. The United States after
World War One faced a period of intense racial hostility and strife.
Again and again, the Association received reports of discrimination
and violence. While the national railroads were still under federal
wartime control, one of the government's regional directors advised
the operating companies not to hire blacks for any job category in
which they had not been employed previously. The NAACP protested
to William G. McAdoo, Director General of the Railroads, and asked
that such sweeping and flagrant discrimination be repudiated. The
order was thereafter withdrawn. One year later, the Association again
successfully complained to the Railroad Administration that black
brakemen, conductors, and others were being classified as porters in
order to deny them appropriate pay. At the request of the Association of Colored Railroad Trainmen, the NAACP appealed the decision, and gained a wage increase for the workers affected. In 1921, a
violent challenge appeared on the Yazoo and Mississippi Valley Railroad. White workers in Arkansas, Mississippi, and Tennessee had sent
threatening letters (signed "Zulus") to black trainmen. Those who refused to be intimidated were dragged from the cars, severely beaten
or whipped, and in some cases shot to death. One man was found in

Mississippi with seventeen bullet holes in his head and body. For almost fifty years black railroad workers had been a common sight in the South, but after the attacks and assassinations, only few remained. J. H. Eiland, Grand President of the Association of Colored Railroad Trainmen, asked his old friend Walter White for support. The NAACP sent appeals to the U.S. Attorney General and to the Interstate Commerce Commission, but the federal authorities refrained from assuming jurisdiction. The Illinois Central Railroad, however, allied to the Yazoo and Mississippi, took action. Special secret agents of the road began an investigation that uncovered a plot by white men to kill black trainmen in order to get their jobs. The Superintendent of the Illinois Central promised to protect the threatened men, and several whites were arrested. Walter White expressed pleasure with these "tangible" results, and Eiland conveyed the gratitude of his workers to the NAACP.[16]

Numerous appeals came to the Association directly from workers—postal and customs employees, railroad porters, domestics—who were mostly concerned with cases of alleged prejudice in employment, promotion, and dismissal procedures. Walter White, Assistant Secretary of the NAACP in the 1920s, usually handled such cases, but Johnson also responded to the petitioners. Although the NAACP generally did not think that job recruitment was within its purview—it lacked an employment department and referred many appeals to the National Urban League—it did not entirely ignore the problem. At times, NAACP executives asked personal acquaintances to find suitable work for able blacks, as when Walter White wrote to his friend Dr. George E. Haynes, Director of the Bureau of Negro Economics, to find employment for two candidates. The Association also used its press releases to indicate openings for black workers in various Northern industrial centers. One such notice appeared in 1925, when the American Tube and Stamping Company of Bridgeport, Connecticut, had places for forty laborers and helpers.[17]

Although the Association declared itself to be non-partisan, it made definite overtures in 1924 to the Progressive Party, and in the process indicated the economic leanings of its leadership. Led by Senator Robert M. LaFollette, the Progressive coalition of farm and labor reformers had one of the most liberal platforms in United States history, including the abolition of child labor, federal ownership of railroads, collective bargaining for workers, and popular election for judges. But, despite an official endorsement by the NAACP, the Third Party offered not one word for blacks, preferring instead to attract Southern white voters. Keenly disappointed, Johnson sent a special appeal to the LaFollette camp, linking the emancipation of black people to

> . . . the same problems of labor and wage, of monopoly and privilege, of effective industrial democracy, which face all laboring classes the world over. . . . It is this widespread and determined race discrimination that is alienating the Negro vote from the progressive liberal and labor vote, and is furnishing the capitalist free of charge not only cheap and increasingly efficient and non-union and union-hating labor, but also a large and growing vote in the main industrial centers of the country.

With no encouragement coming from LaFollette, the Association took great pains to deny that it ever sanctioned the Party. In a stream of letters and press releases, NAACP officers tried to correct the "misapprehension." Although DuBois, Pickens, and White continued to speak for the Progressives, Johnson, a committed Republican since early manhood, decided to vote for John W. Davis, the Democratic Presidential candidate. But, however diverse its political directions, the NAACP remained steady in its economic aims.[18]

One of the major problems in black-labor relations in the 1920s was with the American Federation of Labor. It was not that the Federation openly favored racial exclusion; indeed, its constitution and annual conventions clearly spoke against discrimination. Almost 190 affiliated locals consisted exclusively of blacks, while only eight of the 110 autonomous internationals expressly barred Negroes. However, many others rationalized the dearth of race members by citing employer hostility, the long period of apprenticeship, or the absence of black workmen in the trade. The crux was that entry into a union affiliated with the AF of L required membership in a local that was subordinate to an autonomous international. The Federation consisted of these independent units and had no power over them. Again and again, AF of L annual conventions denounced race prejudice, prompting men like Villard to prophesy, prematurely, the crumbling of the color line. But, upon examination, one discovered that only recommendations, not commands, had been made. Federation leaders sent numerous assurances to the NAACP declaring that they were doing their "level best to organize all workers irrespective of color, creed, or politics," but when Johnson asked for definite implementation, the reply was vague.[19]

In 1928, William English Walling, "the millionaire Socialist," attempted to play the role of middleman between the labor Federation and the NAACP, which he had helped found. Writing to William Green, AF of L leader, Walling asserted that the Association "has been uniformly pro-labor" and that "colored people are well aware of the fairness of the American Federation of Labor." He urged Green to become "acquainted with that handful of colored men who really constitute the leaders of the race in this country," including Johnson: "there is none more influential." Green exchanged letters with the Executive Secretary, promising to recruit black workers in the next membership drive, and agreeing to convene in Washington a national interracial conference. By December, representatives from labor, government, education, and philanthropy met for several days in what *The Nation* called a "milestone in the progress of the human race." Walter White, more subdued, thought the conference "the most significant gesture ever made in these United States towards solution of the race problem."[20]

The "gesture" soon became, in White's words, "the nadir" of casuistry. The low point, White charged, was when John Frey, Secretary-Treasurer of the Metal Trades Department of the AF of L, sought to justify the exclusion of blacks from the trade unions. Frey claimed that the Federation had done far more for integration than many Christian churches and had done so despite the criticism of Negro leaders who advised the race to shun labor organizations. "The American trade unionist," he added, "is more eager to organize the negro than the negro is to become a member." To Walter White, Frey was defending the Federation by censuring Negroes for their own lack of enthusiasm. Frey read White's critique "with utter amazement," and complained to Walling about its "viciously inaccurate" remarks. But others besides White criticized Frey. Miss Ovington wrote to Walling that "it was a great disappointment to all of us interested in the Federation of Labor and the Negro worker. Mr. Frey showed us conditions, but he had no constructive program." Several attempts were made to heal the rift, particularly since White did not oppose unions and Frey did not reject black members. Mary Van Kleeck, Director of the Russell Sage Foundation and Chairman of the conference, told Frey that his frank statement was useful, but unless his words were coupled with positive moves, Negroes would not be impressed. The Federation made no moves, however, while Johnson remained Secretary. Nonetheless, the NAACP hoped for them, and friendship for labor continued despite union activity.[21]

Because of the abundant evidence available, it is difficult to accept the thesis of scholars like Elliot M. Rudwick, Sterling D. Spero, Abram L. Harris, and others that the NAACP did not wish to engage in union activities, nor did it believe that unionism came within its scope. The thesis is accurate if it means that the Association *per se* did not organize workers. But it is misleading to imply that the Association did not encourage or directly aid unionization by others.

Rudwick, Spero, and Harris write that DuBois was the exception to
their generalization. Actually, support for the labor movement came
from all of the national officers, including Johnson, White, Ovington,
Pickens, and Bagnall.[22]

Yet, however sympathetic the NAACP was towards unions, it was
not doctrinaire. Class was subordinate to race whenever the Association detected discrimination by trade unionists. In 1923, for example,
the Indiana Foundry Corporation informed the National Office that
the molders' union in Muncie was picketing the company and intimidating the workers, most of whom were nonunion blacks. The corporation supported the open shop principle, but was "the only local
foundry that has ever tried to employ colored men on skilled work."
The union, on the other hand, favored a closed shop and was expected to replace the race workers once this had been achieved. De-
ploring the efforts of the Muncie molders while expressing the
"highest appreciation" to the company, Johnson urged local NAACP
officers in nearby cities to aid the foundry. He believed it essential
that black workers who had migrated northward not lose their jobs
and return to the South; otherwise "they will be set further back than
they were before."[23]

Despite an enduring sympathy for black workingmen and the
labor movement, the NAACP never considered unionization a pan-
acea. In fact, toward the end of Johnson's tenure as Secretary, as the
Great Depression deepened over the land, the manifold nature of
the race problem and the limited resources of the Association compelled even him to stress the legal path. In revealing reports prepared in 1929 and 1930 for the Garland Fund by Johnson and other
members of its Committee on Negro Work, a grant of $100,000 was
requested for a legal assault to secure political and civil rights for the
race. The reports were hardly briefs for bourgeois economics: "propaganda must clearly and consistently preach the doctrine of organized
labor, of socially owned and controlled capital, and of a rational distribution of wealth. . . ." But more fundamental needs, best fulfilled
by victories in the courts, first had to be met. These included a series
of suits to investigate incidents of lynching, open juries to blacks,
challenge residential segregation, regain the suffrage, force equality
of services on railroads and in the schools. With 300 branches
throughout the country, hundreds of correspondents who could submit test cases, and a list of 123 lawyers in 33 states who were ready to
serve at less than their usual fees, the NAACP had the machinery,
personnel, experience, and technique to carry out such a campaign.
Despite formal opposition within the Fund—Grace Burnham, of the
radical Labor Research Association, feared that "liberals" led by the

NAACP were out to "divert the Negro masses from the left wing organizations"—Johnson's request prevailed. In May 1930, the Fund released $100,000 for the massive campaign. Legal tactics had always been part of the Association's program. Now, for the first time, it had the wherewithal to employ the tool effectively.[24]

The emphasis on court procedures, which began at the end of Johnson's secretaryship, has often been construed as a policy to benefit the Negro middle class while ignoring the masses. This interpretation is advanced today as it was in the 1930s. Louis Lomax has written that before 1958 "Negro writers, clergymen, schoolteachers, lawyers, social workers" publicly supported the NAACP's commitment to legalism, although many "felt that the desegregation fight should take on a broader base." Actually, the Association arrived at its judicial emphasis only after attempting other methods and concluding that the courts offered the most tangible results. Moreover, many thousands of dollars had been spent defending those clearly outside the professional and business classes: soldiers of the Twenty-fourth Infantry, an all-black unit of the regular army; and impoverished sharecroppers in Elaine, Arkansas. In the latter case, involving 79 farmers accused of conspiracy to murder whites, the NAACP spent more than $30,000 in a series of appeals that eventually reached the U.S. Supreme Court, which set all the men free. The Association announced that the Arkansas Peonage Cases "served notice on the entire South that no Negro can be so ignorant, poor or helpless that he can be done to death without our doing our best to prevent it—so long as the N.A.A.C.P. lives." Unfortunately, the concentration of the NAACP's limited resources on court litigation, at a time when the nation was in the midst of depression and when the race expected the Association to champion every phase of the race problem, led to confusion, frustration, and mistrust. The evidence suggests, however, that if Johnson and the National Office became narrow in their methods, they had been broad in their aims.[25]

Notes

[1] Robert L. Allen, *Black Awakening in Capitalist America* (Garden City, 1969), pp. 66, 97, 106-07; Bernard Eisenberg, "James Weldon Johnson and the NAACP, 1916-1934" (Doctoral dissertation, Columbia, University, 1963), *passim.*

[2] James Weldon Johnson, *Along This Way* (New York, 1933), pp. 4-18, 45-78, 103-57, 175-213: Wayne Francis, "Lift Every Voice and Sing," *The Crisis* 32 (September 1926): 234-36; Louis E. Lomax: *The Negro Revolt* (New York, 1962), pp. 48-50; Isaac Goldberg, *Tin Pan Alley* (New York, 1930, 1961 ed.), p. 150; Mary White Ovington, *Portraits in Color* (New York, 1927), pp. 1, 7; Eugene Levy, *James Weldon Johnson* (Chicago, 1973), pp. 75-98.

[3] Johnson, op. cit., pp. 218-38, 251-69, 289-309; Levy, op. cit., pp. 99-147; Ludlow W. Werner, "The New York Age: Lusty Veteran," *The Crisis* 45 (March 1938): 75; Johnson's first column, entitled "Views and Reviews," appeared in the *Age*, October 15, 1914; see also January 13, April 8, May 13, 1915; January 13, March 2, 1916; January 24, April 24, 1920; January 8, August 20, December 10, 1921; January 14, March 25, September 16, October 21, 1922; June 16, 1922; hereafter referred to as Views.

[4] Charles F. Kellogg, *NAACP, a History of the National Association for the Advancement of Colored People* (Baltimore, 1967), *passim*; NAACP, *The Branch Bulletin*, December 1916, January and July 1917, July 1917, July 1919, March 1920, hereafter referred to as BB; James Weldon Johnson, *How to Form a Branch of the NAACP* (New York [1916?] 1925 ed.); Board of Director Minutes, March 12, 1917; July 9, 1918; December 8, 1919, NAACP Collection. Library of Congress, hereafter referred to as BODM; Views, June 20, 1920.

[5] *Fourteenth Annual Report of the NAACP for the Year 1923* (New York, 1924), 45; BB, October 1919, December 1921, February 1922; see applications for charter from Atlanta, Athens, Augusta, Charleston, Jacksonville, Norfolk, Raleigh, Richmond, and Tampa in Branch Files, NAACP Collection, Library of Congress, hereafter BF; other branches used were Jackson, Memphis, Portsmouth (Va.), Mobile, San Antonio, Houston, Petersburg, Charleston (W. Va.), Wilmington, Greensboro, Gary, East Chicago, Anderson, Adrian, Ann Arbor, and Battle Creek, ibid.: Annual Report for the Atlanta branch, 1920, ibid.

[6] Shillady remarks in Labor File, 1917 folder, NAACP Collection, Library of Congress, hereafter LF; Walling to Frey [January 1929], Frey Papers, Library of Congress, hereafter FP; Walling to Johnson, August 11, 1922, Walling file, NAACP Collection, Library of Congress; White, *A Man Called White* (New York, 1948), 214.

[7] Irving Bernstein, *The Lean Years* (Cambridge, Mass., 1960), pp. 84-90; Johnson *Along This Way*, pp. 45-6; Kelly Miller, "The Negro as a Workingman," *American Mercury* 6 (November 1925): 313; Bernard Eisenberg, "Kelly Miller: The Negro Leader as a Marginal Man," *The Journal of Negro History* 45 (July 1960): 190, hereafter JNH; see warning of the A. M. E. Zion Church *Chicago Defender*, May 12, 1934; William Z. Foster, *The Negro People in American History* (New York, 1954), p. 429; *The Messenger* 7 (October-November 1925): 346.

[8] Sherman C. Kingsley, "A Militant Negro Conference," *The Survey* 42 (July 12, 1919): 579-80; Ovington to Dr. H. C. Hudson, June 5, 1923, BF (Shreveport); all citations from LF: Crosswaith to Johnson, July 25, 1925; Johnson to Crosswaith, July 27, 1925; Johnson to Mrs. Florence Kelley, October 1, 1925; Bagnall to Thomas Dabney, November 22, 1926; Pickens to Dabney, November 13, 1926.

[9] Hogans, *The Age*, October 3, 1925; Randolph quoted in ibid., October 24, 1925.

[10] The Federated Press release, November 27, 1925, LF; all correspondence in ibid., dated 1925: Randolph to Johnson, November 13; Johnson to Lancaster, November 20; Lancaster to Johnson, November 25; Randolph to Johnson, December 26; *Age*, November 7 and October 24, 1925.

[11] All correspondence in LF, dated 1926: Robert Bagnall to Mrs. C. J. Jones, March 12; Bagnall, "Extracts from Minutes," March 19; Owen and Randolph to Walter White, April 7; Johnson to Owen, April 12: Owen to Johnson, April 21; Saunders Redding, *The Lonesome Road* (New York, 1958), pp. 261-62; Miscellaneous Correspondence, 1922-1941. I. 215, American Fund for Public Service (Garland Fund), New York Public Library, hereafter AFPS.

[12] All correspondence in LF, dated 1926; Randolph to Johnson, June 22, and similar letters to White, Pickens, and Bagnall; Randolph to Johnson, July 1, and similar letters to White, Pickens, and Bagnall; Randolph to White, September 15; Frank R. Crosswaith

to Johnson, August 18; The Federated Press release, August 21; *Seventeenth Annual Report of the NAACP for the Year 1926* (New York, 1927) 32; Redding, op. cit., p. 262.

¹³ All citations from LF: Federated Press release, February 27, [1927]; Randolph to Editor, January 19, 1927; Johnson messages to President Calvin Coolidge and U.S. Mediation Board in *New York World* and *New York Herald*, June 8, 1928; on jurisdictional dispute, see William Green to Rienzi B. Lemus, March 31, 1926; Lemus to Green, May 18, 1926; Lemus to T. Arnold Hill, January 29, 1926.

¹⁴ All correspondence from LF, dated 1918: Arthur Moore, et al. to William Dobson, July 6; William Laskie to J. J. Marsh, July 17; Dobson to Frank Morrison, September 25; A. A. Reimer to Shillady, August 18; Shillady to Morrison, September 9; Shillady to George A. Haynes, October 19; Rev. S. A. Brown to Shillady [November]; Shillady to Morrison, October 14; Shillady to Brown, October 19.

¹⁵ See LF, 1920: General Executive Board to the District Councils, January 9; Ovington, "Bogalusa", reprint from *The Liberator*, January 1920; T. J. Green, "Report on the Situation at Bogalosa;" Ovington to Frank Morrison, February 7.

¹⁶ *Report of the NAACP for the Years 1917 and 1918* (New York, 1919), p. 45; Shillady to McAdoo, November 29, 1918, Storey Papers, Library of Congress; Johnson, Report of the Secretary, August 15, 1921, ibid., *New York Tribune* and *New York World*, August 1, 1921, clippings in LF; Eiland to White, June 13, 1921, ibid.

¹⁷ All citations in LF; Johnson to Mrs. M. E. Worrell, March 12, 1925; White to Isaac Webber, July 12, 1923; James S. Joseph to White, December 18, 1924; White to Haynes, October 11, 1918; White to Lucious J. Jordan, February, 1920; White to Clarence C. Kittrell, February 18, 1920; NAACP press release, October 30, 1925.

¹⁸ *The New York Times*, July 1, 1924, 3:4: *Crisis* 28 (September 1924): 22, and 29 (November 1924): 13; all citations from Political File, dated 1924, NAACP Collection, Library of Congress: NAACP press release, July 3, 11, and 25: White to LaFollette, July 25; Johnson to Walter Bilder, July 11; Bilder to Johnson, July 8; Johnson to Editor, *New York World*, July 14; Johnson to Ernest Gruening, September 17 and October 17; Pickens to A. P. Randolph, August 5.

¹⁹ Sterling D. Spero and Abram L. Harris, *The Black Worker* (New York, 1931, 1969 ed.) pp. 87, 144-45, 463-4: *The Social Bulletin*, December [1922], XI, LF; "Labor Unions Excluding the Negro," [1921], ibid.: convention declarations in FP; Villard, "Crumbling Color Line," *Harper's Magazine* 159 (July 1929): 156-167; Frank Morrison to Johnson, July 22, 28, and 30, 1924, LF; Johnson to Morrison, July 2 and 28, 1924, ibid.; Eliot M. Rudwick, "W. E. B. DuBois: in the Role of Crisis," JNH 43 (July 1958): 233; *Fifteenth Annual Report of the NAACP for the Year 1924* (New York, 1925): 48-9.

²⁰ All correspondence from LF: Walling to Green, May 29; Green to Walling, May 31; NAACP press release, November 19 and 30: Johnson telegram to Green, November 19: Green to Johnson, November 20; Editorial, *The Nation* 128 (January 9, 1929): 31; White, "Solving America's Race Problem," ibid., 42.

²¹ Ibid., 42: Frey, "Attempts to Organize Negro Workers," *American Federationist* 36 (March 1929): 297-98, 304-05; all correspondence in LF: Frey to Walling, January 10; Frey to Van Kleeck, January 10; Ovington to Walling, April 27; White to Walling, January 18; Frey to Ovington, May 8; Frey to Walling, May 8; Walling to White, n. d.: Van Kleeck to Frey, January 15.

²² Spero and Harris, op. cit., pp. 463-64; Rudwick, op. cit., p. 233; Jervis Anderson, *A. Philip Randolph* (New York, 1972) writes that prominent blacks like Kelly Miller and Perry Howard opposed The Brotherhood, but nowhere does the author show any NAACP support.

²³ H. B. Harvey to NAACP, August 21, 1923, LF: Johnson to Harvey, September 17, 1923, ibid.

[24] All citations from AFPS, Board of Directors, 1934-1941, II, Report of the Committee on Negro Work, October 18, 1929, 4-9; Memorandum, Committee on Negro Work, (1930), 30-48; Burnham to Roger Baldwin, January 20, 1930, p. 28; Baldwin *et al.*, to Board of Directors, February 24, 1930, p. 29.

[25] Louis Lomax, op. cit., pp. 78-9, 120; Johnson, *Along This Way*, pp. 321-25, 342; Johnson, *Black Manhattan* (New York, 1930), pp. 239-41; Johnson, "The Militant N.A.A.C.P.," *The Southern Workman* 57 (July 1928): 247-48; Johnson Memorandum, May 15, 1924, Miscellaneous Correspondence, 1923-1933, p. 3, AFPS; *Moore vs. Dempsey* 261 U.S. 86; *The New York Times*, January 10, 1923, 12:2; BB, March and April 1923; Views, June 30, 1923; [Arthur Spingarn] to William F. Fuerst, November 14, 1925, James Weldon Johnson Memorial Collection, Yale University.

Negro Leaders, the Republican Party, and the Election of 1932

Charles H. Martin

When he took the oath of office on March 4, 1933, newly elected President Franklin D. Roosevelt could not claim any significant popularity among black voters. Although Roosevelt, who captured 22.8 million popular votes, easily beat incumbent Herbert Hoover, with only 15.8 million votes, the vast majority of the African American electorate had remained loyal to the Republican Party. This traditional African American loyalty to the party of Lincoln was in spite of rampant economic despair in the black community as well as a rigorous campaign by many black leaders who favored the Democratic ticket. Taking a "wait and see" posture, African Americans were inclined to judge Roosevelt by his actions, rather than his campaign promises.

Through the prism of a presidential election, Charles Martin gauges the political climate among African Americans at the beginning of the Great Depression Era. Adversely impacted by the nationwide economic downturn, the black community found itself caught between the proverbial rock and a hard place. The choices proved to be more complex than merely choosing a presidential candidate. For the African American electorate in 1932, party loyalty, political integrity, and economic survival all hung in the balance. Martin's essay goes far toward analyzing the key personalities and issues in this political drama.

THE YEAR 1929 did not mark the start of the Great Depression for Negro Americans. As early as 1927 Negroes began to be discharged by industry, and by 1929 some 300,000 Negro industrial workers were estimated to be unemployed.[1] As of 1930, 65 percent of the working black population was employed in either agriculture or domestic and personal service, two occupational groups which suffered severely from the depression. This factor caused the unemployment rate for Negroes to run much higher than the rate for whites and forced Negroes to seek public relief in disproportionate numbers. Black women were particularly hard hit because of their predominance in household service.[2] Quite naturally, Negroes looked to President Herbert Hoover and the Republican Party for solutions.

The failure of the Hoover Administration to convince Negroes that it was encouraging the return of prosperity added economic grievances to a growing list of political complaints.

As early as 1924, several prominent black leaders deserted the GOP. In the presidential campaign of 1928 this trend continued. Negro voting clubs for the Democratic candidate, Alfred E. Smith, were organized in Georgia, Florida, Kentucky, Virginia, Massachusetts, New York, Ohio, Illinois, New Jersey, Pennsylvania, and fifteen other states. Several respected Negro newspapers supported Smith, marking "the first time in history that the colored press has supported in such large numbers a Democratic aspirant for the Presidency."[3]

The dissatisfaction of Negroes with Hoover and his policies continued after he took office, particularly since the depression intensified their suffering. Negroes shared with other Americans the feelings expressed by A. Napoleon Fields:

> Hoover blew the whistle,
>   Mellon rang the bell;
> Wall Street gave the signal,
>   And the country went to h—!

Hoover's failure to aid Negroes earned him Walter White's biting epithet of "the man in the lily-White House."[4] *The Crisis* suggested a fitting slogan for the seeming helplessness of Hoover and the government—"Millions for Defense but not one cent for Starvation"—and scorned Hoover's worries about a sound financial system: "Sound Money! Yes, but most of us have forgotten how money sounds."[5] As the Administration proved unable to solve the economic crisis, critics finally began to challenge the system itself. Columnist George Schuyler's acid indictment was typical: "Only the misinformed and weakminded can place much dependence in the capitalistic enterprise after the lessons of the past ten years."[6]

The Reconstruction Finance Corporation also came under considerable fire from Negro spokesmen. *The Crisis* led the attack:

> O, by the bye, that financial reconstruction is getting on famously. A breadline of 858 banks, 18 insurance companies, 8 mortgage loan companies, 16 railways and a few other miscellaneous beggars have been relieved of their immediate necessities to the tune of 200 million and some odd cents. They are now hoping to totter on until the administration can slip them a few more doles from the taxpayers' money. Meantime, the unemployed are—unemployed; which we admit is not exactly playing the game.[7]

In October, 1932, it declared, "No wonder the RFC did not want the nation [to know] that its chief charity was relieving banks, which had already relieved a million or so depositors of their hard earned savings."[8] The Pittsburgh *Courier* challenged certain features of Hoover's recovery program too: "We are not in sympathy with any program intended to give the bankers more money with which to retrieve their lost fortunes scattered all over Europe. We are interested, however, in the rehabilitation of American industries, the small fellow, the little business man, the farmer."[9] *The Crisis* dismissed the plight of farmers, though, when compared to that of Negroes—"The farmers have been starving for less than twenty years. Why should they complain? Let us colored people tell them something about long distance starvation."[10]

Some black leaders especially resented the president's efforts to extend relief to banks instead of people. W. E. B. DuBois criticized Hoover: "Yet, we Negroes were the first and severest sufferers from depression and the last to be relieved."[11] Like Hoover and other people, however, Negroes sometimes expressed an optimism not merited by the facts; even the Pittsburgh *Courier* could state, "We do believe that within a few months the shadow of depression will disappear and the sunlight of good times will shine again."[12] Negro leaders were rarely so hopeful except in moments of escapism. A sentiment far more common was that expressed by Sonnyboy Sam, the easy-going comic-strip character in the *Courier*. When asked a question concerning how much longer the depression would last, he replied, "There's one thing certain, Hoover can't live forever!"[13]

The presidential election of 1932 well illustrated the Republican Party's loss of support among Negro leaders and newspapers. Initially most black newspapers concentrated their fire on Hoover. A long list of political skeletons was hauled out of the closet. Negroes were reminded of Hoover's lily-white tactics in 1928, his nomination of Judge John J. Parker to the United States Supreme Court, a decline in patronage for black Republicans, segregation of the Gold Star mothers, and Hoover's failure to pose with Negro Republican delegations. Citing these complaints and others, Walter White told the concluding meeting of the annual convention of the National Association for the Advancement of Colored People in May that the Negro vote would come into its own as an independent force that year since the "old practice of handing out a few dollars to a group of discredited and powerless white and Negro politicians is futile." White blasted Hoover's record for its failures but cautioned that neither party's leading candidate "stirs the blood" of black voters.[14]

The Republican Party convention in June failed to halt the party's sagging image among Negro spokesmen. A proposal by the NAACP for a forthright denunciation in the convention platform of discrimination, lynching, and the lily-white movement was rejected in favor of a traditional expression of friendship for Negroes, a sham which Walter White labeled mere "flapdoodle." White went on to warn that "no one familiar with the Republican Party's recent record with regard to the Negro can take this plank seriously." Privately he confided to Claude A. Barnett of the Associated Negro Press that while the platform adopted was poor, he shuddered to think how much worse it might have been without the efforts of the NAACP.[15]

Postconvention campaigning likewise failed to excite the black community and even some Negro Republican leaders. The Pittsburgh *Courier,* upset by Hoover's evasiveness and indifference toward Negro delegations, claimed that the president treated fish on a fishing trip better than he had representatives from any black group.[16] Letters and editorials also appeared in print emphasizing the lack of interest of the GOP "general staff" in Negroes—"If Frederick Douglass were alive today he would not close his eyes to everything he could easily see."[17] In August, 1932, *The Crisis* commented: "Mr. Hoover's record on the Negro problem is not clear and in that respect it resembles his record on everything else."[18]

A few black Republicans attempted to defend the party, repeating the traditional praises of the party of emancipation, but without much enthusiasm. Jefferson S. Coage, Recorder of Deeds for the District of Columbia, reminded the public that the GOP had "made it possible for the laborer to enjoy a five day week and a six hour [*sic*]day."[19] In deference to increasing protest from Negro Republicans, Hoover belatedly agreed to meet and pose with a delegation of Negro Republicans on October 1 at the White House. A worried group of 110 party stalwarts assembled there to ask affirmation of the traditional Republican stand for rights and freedoms for Negroes. Roscoe Conklin Simmons, flamboyant orator and party hack, warned the president that black voters were being told that "our party has deserted the old faith" and begged Hoover to reassert the historic policies. Thanking the delegates for coming, Hoover recounted past acts of friendship toward Negroes by the GOP and promised, "You may be assured that our party will not abandon or depart from its traditional duty toward the American Negro."[20] The Cleveland *Gazette,* one of the few remaining Negro newspapers supporting the GOP, reacted favorably to the meeting and suggested that "the thing to do in November is to overwhelmingly defeat southern Democracy and its candidates, Roosevelt and Garner, and continue the Republican party in control of the government for the good and welfare of all the people, particularly our people."[21] Most other newspapers were less impressed, with the general consensus being quite critical. The Baltimore *Afro-American* warned readers in a front page editorial not to be fooled by this "gesture of despair," while the *Louisiana Weekly* stressed the point that action, not "rosy promises," was what Negroes really needed.[22]

Early comment by Negroes on Hoover's opponent and his policies was not favorable either. Two issues were of considerable importance in the initial opposition to Franklin D. Roosevelt, the first being his frequent trips to Warm Springs, Georgia, and his apparent enjoyment of southern living. *The Crisis* was ready, as usual, with an acerbic commentary:

> FDR has spent six months out of every twelve as Governor of New York and the rest swimming in a Georgia mudhole. If he is elected president, we shall have to move the White House to Warm Springs and use Washington for his occasional vacations.[23]

The second issue was Roosevelt's role in the drawing up of the "ruthless" Haitian Constitution. As early as 1929 DuBois had used this charge to attack Roosevelt, and it was repeated with frequency during the early part of the campaign.[24] The pro-Republican Cleveland *Gazette* gave the story great play, quoting the *New York Times* of August 19, 1920, which reported that Roosevelt had said, "The facts are, I wrote Haiti's constitution myself, and if I do say it, I think it is a pretty good constitution." The *Gazette* disagreed with the latter part of Roosevelt's statement, saying, "As a matter of fact, the enforcement of the Roosevelt Haitian Constitution has occasioned the *bloodiest chapter in all the history of Haiti.*"[25]

To some members of the Negro press, FDR was a "shifty politician" who was customarily vague—"Mr. Roosevelt's record on the Negro problem is clear. He hasn't any."[26] *The Crisis* was especially hostile to Roosevelt's early candidacy:

> Governor Roosevelt of New York has just swapped as sheriff one Tammany ward leader for another, and thus gathered up the plaudits of the unco guid with one hand, and the New York delegation to Chicago with the other. Which we call statesmanship of a high order![27]

Shortly after Roosevelt's nomination, the Chicago *Defender* posed some questions vital to Negroes:

> Mr. Roosevelt has been nominated on a platform of many promises. Has he the inclination to yield to the opportunities which are now his? . . . Mr. Roosevelt comes of a preferred class of America's body politic. Will he be able to sense the social and economic needs of the man farthest down?[28]

As the campaign wore on, Roosevelt began to gain ground. His trip to Chicago to address the Democratic Convention convinced the Norfolk *Journal and Guide* that he was "a man of action."[29] Various

Negro organizations and prominent individuals publicly endorsed Roosevelt. Robert L. Vann, editor of the Pittsburgh *Courier*, told a Cleveland audience in September, "I see millions of our people turning the picture of Abraham Lincoln to the wall."[30] The Democratic Party expanded its organizational efforts to win the black vote. A Negro "Big Four" was organized to coordinate these efforts. Members of this group were Vann; Dr. Joseph L. Johnson of Columbus, Ohio; Dr. William J. Tompkins of Kansas City; and Julian D. Rainey.

Black Republicans increased their public criticism of the GOP leadership and some even defected to the Democrats. W. J. Yerby, a veteran of twenty-six years in the Foreign Service and a former consul in Sierra Leone, announced for Roosevelt, as did other lifelong Republicans.[31] Several Negro classmates of Roosevelt openly endorsed the Democratic nominee. Such news was usually featured in Negro newspapers. Former classmate G. D. Houston told the Baltimore *Afro-American* that FDR was "true blue" and that his slogan of the "forgotten man" was "sober realism."[32]

Probably the most successful strategy employed by Roosevelt to win the support of Negroes was his usual straightforward approach to problems and his friendliness and openness. This technique was most successful when Negro newspapermen overcame their initial suspicion of him and began to ask for interviews. Reporter E. W. Wilkins gained an important story for the Baltimore *Afro-American* when he approached FDR at Topeka, Kansas, in late September. Wilkins informed *Afro-American* readers of the results of the interview in this manner:

> "Your forgotten man has become a famous symbol, Governor Roosevelt. Is the Negro included in the plan you have to aid the plight of that mass of people?"
>
> "Absolutely and impartially," he stated with vigor. His voice carried plainly to the circle of white people surrounding us.[33]

This statement was repeated widely by Democrats and paraphrased in an advertisement in *The Crisis*.[34]

The growing public support for the Democratic nominee spread even to his running mate, John Nance Garner of Texas. Negroes had originally been frightened by Garner's presence on the ballot, particularly because the question of Roosevelt's health increased the significance of the vice-presidential candidate. Congressman Oscar DePriest illustrated Republican efforts to use the issue to scare Negroes into remaining loyal when he told a Cleveland audience, "If Roosevelt gets into the White House, it will be only a short time before Garner will be president."[35] The Norfolk *Journal and Guide* was one of the first black newspapers to look upon Garner's candidacy with leniency. On July 9 it assured its readers, "If colored Americans have any misgivings because of Mr. Garner's rise they may rest assured that if he becomes vice president he could serve them no worse than has Mr. Curtis; and, if fate should name him President, he could serve them no worse than has Mr. Hoover."[36] Others echoed the *Journal and Guide*, including the Reverend Marshall Shepard, secretary of the National Baptist Convention, who stated that "Garner could do not worse" than Hoover if he became president.[37] Negro Democrats naturally endeavored to spread such sentiments too.[38]

Moreover, Garner seemed willing to make at least minimal efforts to reassure black voters. The same Baltimore *Afro-American* reporter who interviewed Roosevelt in Topeka also cornered Garner there. In the ensuing conversation he made the following statements:

"I believe in a fair deal for the submerged part of the population and you know that the Negro belongs to that class.

"I am for absolute equality for all men before the law.

"I am not in favor of specific legislation for the Negro. No intelligent Negro wants that and it would be wrong."[39]

This statement and other comparable ones caused the Chicago *Defender* to wonder if this was the same John Nance Garner who hailed from Uvalde, Texas. The *Defender* felt that Garner might have changed but commented, "We do not believe that the candidate for vice president on the Democratic ticket possesses requisite qualifications to carry on the great responsibilities incident to the running of the American government."[40] Garner's statement on "absolute equality of all men before the law" was circulated and later appeared in an advertisement in *The Crisis*.[41] A reporter for the Pittsburgh *Courier*, after a private interview with Garner, came away impressed with his "humanitarian and democratic principles."[42] While Negroes were never won over to warm support for Garner, at least they began to regard less fearfully his presence on the ballot.

Roosevelt's hard campaigning evidenced itself as Negro leaders continued to turn against Hoover. Historian Rayford Logan, then a youthful Socialist, told West Coast voters that "no self-respecting Negro can vote for Herbert Hoover," although he cautioned that "a vote for Roosevelt means merely a protest against Hoover."[43] Vicious attacks on Hoover's personal life were circulated telling of his cruel treatment of nonwhites in China and South Africa.[44] The Pittsburgh *Courier* urged Negroes to "help their white fellow citizens eliminate Hoover, Hooverism, and the GOP permanently from our national capital."[45] The *Louisiana Weekly* turned its editorial voice to national politics for a change, suggesting that "Hoover for ex-president is not a bad idea."[46] On October 22, the Pittsburgh *Courier* reported that two local Hoover meetings had failed miserably, while huge crowds greeted Roosevelt. One of the Hoover meetings had evidently turned into a farce, as one of the speakers, a Negro preacher, told the small crowd that it was "time for Negroes to desert the Republican Party."[47] Columnist Kelly Miller defended FDR by pointing out that the GOP had operated under FDR's "ruthless constitution" for Haiti and that Senate Republicans had done more to kill the Dyer Anti-lynching Bill than had Garner.[48]

The Crisis summed up many of the complaints against Hoover in its November issue by alleging, "No one in our day has helped disfranchisement and race hatred more than Herbert Hoover by his 'Lily-White' policy, his appointments to office, and his failure to recognize or appreciate the plight of the Forgotten Black Man."[49] The Reverend Marshall Shepard spoke for most black leaders when he called upon "all Negroes who have the future of the race at heart to forsake the lily-white party of Hoover and put in the White House another Roosevelt."[50]

As election day neared, most Negro newspapers urged their readers to reject Hoover, the "Pilot of Shipwreck," and support FDR. The Norfolk *Journal and Guide* announced that it was supporting Roosevelt because "it believes that Mr. Roosevelt is vastly superior to Mr. Hoover in political stature and humanitarian qualities. . . ." It astutely interpreted the election campaign, realizing that "unless the recent liberal trends in the Democratic party have been misinterpreted, its ascendancy to national power should favorably affect the political and economic status of the American Negro."[51] The Pittsburgh *Courier* urged its readers to vote for Roosevelt, pointing out that FDR had said what freedom-loving Negroes had wanted to hear.[52]

The Baltimore *Afro-American* endorsed Roosevelt, saying that what the country needed in the White House was a great humanitarian—FDR.[53] Roosevelt had recently affirmed to another *Afro-American* reporter his interest in Negroes by promising, if elected President, to "accord colored citizens of this country as full a measure of citizenship in every detail of my administrative power as [is] accorded citizens of any other race or group."[54] Kelly Miller surveyed the opinions of the Negro press in his weekly newspaper column. He found eight newspapers which gave FDR some form of support—the Norfolk *Journal and Guide*, the Louisville *News*, the Houston *Informer*, the Kansas City *Call*, the Baltimore *Afro-American*, the Pittsburgh *Courier*, the New York *Age*, and the Washington *Tribune*. The New York *Amsterdam News* and the Philadelphia *Tribune* were the only papers he found still clinging weakly to the GOP.[55] The name of the Cleveland *Gazette* should also be added to the latter group. Two newspapers, the Chicago *Defender* and the Savannah *Tribune*, failed to endorse either candidate.[56] Clearly FDR had the support of the largest and most respected Negro newspapers, although several were not overly enthusiastic about their choice.

Yet despite the hardships of the depression, the urgings of Negro leaders, and the endorsements of Negro newspapers, black voters in 1932 remained surprisingly loyal to the Republican Party and Herbert Hoover. Some Negro leaders simply claimed that along with other Americans, they had rejected Hoover overwhelmingly. Their claims, added to the heavy endorsement of FDR by Negro leaders, have misled writers concerning the amount of black support for Roosevelt.[57] Nonetheless, what facts there are decidedly show that FDR did not receive a majority of black votes in 1932. In Chicago, where a pro-Negro Republican machine had built up a considerable following, Hoover gained 76.6 percent of the total black vote.[58] Negro areas in Cleveland and Philadelphia also went solidly Republican, with Hoover gaining over 70 percent of the Negro vote in each city.[59] In Baltimore, the Negro vote for Roosevelt was put at 46 percent; in Columbus, Ohio, it was set at 25 percent; and in Pittsburgh the figure was 53 percent.[60] Roosevelt ran strongest in New York City, where he received close to 60 percent of the black vote.[61] While such statistics may not tell the whole story, they indicate that FDR received a surprisingly small amount of voting support from Negroes in 1932, although the total Negro Democratic vote represented a significant increase from that of earlier years.[62]

But this is not to say that the black masses necessarily supported Hoover. Those Negroes who voted in the 1932 presidential election and earlier elections tended to be more pro-GOP than those who did not vote. A survey conducted at the first of September by the Baltimore *Afro-American* found 1,381 readers supporting Hoover and 1,357 backing Roosevelt. Of those supporting Hoover, 954 were registered voters, while only 268 of the 1,357 backing FDR had registered.[63] While too much can be made of this one example, it shows that Negro voters tended to be considerably more Republican oriented than Negro non-voters. Ironically, despite the stand of Negro leaders and newspapers, black voters remained loyal to the GOP in 1932. Negro leaders had no such sympathy for Hoover, however, and most shared the sentiment of *The Crisis* when Hoover left office—"Well, Mr. Hoover, here's hoping a long rest. The longer the better."[64]

Notes

[1] Charles S. Johnson, "Incidence Upon the Negroes," *The American Journal of Sociology*, XL (May, 1935), 737.

[2] "Washington Conference on the Economic Status of the Negro," *Monthly Labor Review*, XXXVII (July, 1933), 43.

[3] Monroe N. Work, *Negro Year Book, 1931-1932* (Negro Year Book Publishing Co.: Tuskegee, Alabama, 1931), p. 87.

[4] Walter White, *A Man Called White* (New York, 1948), p. 104. An account of complaints by Negroes against Hoover can be found in Dewey H. Palmer, "Republican Presidents and the Negro Voters, 1920-1932," unpublished paper read before the Southwestern Social Science Convention, April 8, 1966.

[5] *The Crisis*, XXXIX (March, 1932), 80; and XL (April, 1933), 77.

[6] Pittsburgh *Courier*, January 30, 1932, p. 10.

[7] *The Crisis*, XXXIX (May, 1932), 150.

[8] *Ibid.* (October, 1932), 310.

[9] Pittsburgh *Courier*, January 30, 1932, p. 10.

[10] *The Crisis*, XL (December, 1933), 269.

[11] W. E. B. DuBois, "Postscript," *The Crisis*, XXXIX (November, 1932), 362-63.

[12] Pittsburgh *Courier*, January 16, 1932, p. 8.

[13] *Ibid.*, April 30, 1932, II, p. 3.

[14] *New York Times*, May 23, 1932, p. 33.

[15] NAACP press release and Walter White to Claude A. Barnett, June 28, 1932, NAACP Papers, Library of Congress.

[16] Pittsburgh *Courier*, May 28, 1932, p. 10.

[17] Chicago *Defender*, July 9, 1932, p. 12; and Savannah *Tribune*, June 16, 1932, p. 4.

[18] *The Crisis*, XXXIX (August, 1932), 246.

[19] *Ibid.* (October, 1932), 314.

[20] *New York Times*, October 2, 1932, p. 32.

[21] Cleveland *Gazette*, October 15, 1932, p. 2.

[22] Baltimore *Afro-American*, October 8, 1932, p. 1; *Louisiana Weekly*, October 15, 1932, p. 8; Pittsburgh *Courier*, October 8, 1932, p. 10; and Norfolk *Journal and Guide*, October 8, 1932, p. 6.

[23] *The Crisis*, XXXIX (July, 1932), 214.

[24] Chicago *Defender*, September 10, 1932, p. 14; *The Crisis*, XXXVI (January, 1929), 5; and Cleveland *Gazette*, September 17, 1932, p. 1, and October 29, 1932, p. 2.

[25] Cleveland *Gazette*, September 24, 1932, p. 2.

[26] *The Crisis*, XXXIX (August, 1932), 246.

[27] *Ibid.* (April, 1932), 116.

[28] Chicago *Defender*, July 9, 1932, p. 12.

[29] Norfolk *Journal and Guide*, July 9, 1932, p. 6.

[30] Cleveland *Gazette*, September 17, 1932, p. 1.

[31] Baltimore *Afro-American*, October 8, 1932, p. 13; Norfolk *Journal and Guide*, July 9, 1932, p. 1; *Louisiana Weekly*, July 9, 1932, p. 6; and Pittsburgh *Courier*, October 8, 1932, II, p. 2.

[32] Baltimore *Afro-American*, October 22, 1932, p. 1, and October 29, 1932, p. 1.

[33] *Ibid.*, September 24, 1932, p. 1.

[34] *The Crisis*, XXXIX (November, 1932), 366; and Norfolk *Journal and Guide*, September 24, 1932, p. 1.

[35] Cleveland *Gazette*, September 17, 1932, p. 1; and *Louisiana Weekly*, July 30, 1932, p. 4.

[36] Norfolk *Journal and Guide*, July 9, 1932, p. 6.

[37] Pittsburgh *Courier*, October 15, 1932, p. 3.

[38] Baltimore *Afro-American*, October 22, 1932, p. 21.

[39] *Ibid.*, September 24, 1932, p. 1.

[40] Chicago *Defender*, September 3, 1932, p. 14.

[41] *The Crisis*, XXXIX (November, 1932), 366; Pittsburgh *Courier*, October 22, 1932, p. 1; and Norfolk *Journal and Guide*, November 5, 1932, p. 1.

[42] Pittsburgh *Courier*, November 5, 1932, p. 4.

[43] Baltimore *Afro-American*, October 22, 1932, p. 21.

[44] Pittsburgh *Courier*, October 15, 1932, p. 10; Baltimore *Afro-American*, October 8, 1932, p. 19; and October 15, 1932, p. 9.

[45] Pittsburgh *Courier*, October 8, 1932, p. 10.

[46] *Louisiana Weekly*, October 8, 1932, p. 8.

[47] Pittsburgh *Courier*, October 22, 1932, p. 1.

[48] Baltimore *Afro-American*, October 15, 1932, p. 1; *Louisiana Weekly*, October 15, 1932, p. 8; and October 29, 1932, p. 8.

[49] *The Crisis*, XXXIX (November, 1932), 362-63.

[50] Pittsburgh *Courier*, October 15, 1932, p. 3.

[51] Norfolk *Journal and Guide*, October 29, 1932, p. 6; and November 19, 1932, p. 6.

[52] Pittsburgh *Courier*, October 22, 1932, p. 10.

[53] Baltimore *Afro-American*, October 29, 1932, p. 6.

[54] *Ibid.*

[55] *Ibid.*, October 22, 1932, p. 6.

[56] Chicago *Defender*, November 5, 1932, p. 14; and Savannah *Tribune*, November 3, 1932, p. 4.

[57] Benjamin Quarles, *The Negro in the Making of America* (New York, 1964), p. 208. Monroe N. Work, *Negro Year Book, 1937-1938*, p. 97, commented, "they [Negroes] constituted a considerable part of the land slide for Roosevelt." Arthur Krock, "Did the Negro Revolt?" *Opportunity*, XI (January, 1933), 19 and 28, likewise overestimated the black vote for Roosevelt.

[58] Elmer William Henderson, *A Study of the Basic Factors Involved in the Change in the Party Alignment of Negroes in Chicago, 1932-1938* (Unpublished master's thesis, The University of Chicago, 1939), p. 19.

[59] Samuel Lubell, *White and Black: Test of a Nation* (New York, 1964), p. 57.

[60] Gunnar Myrdal, *An American Dilemma* (New York, 1962), pp. 495-96.

[61] Lubell, *op. cit.*, p. 57.

[62] Pittsburgh *Courier*, November 26, 1932, II, p. 9.

[63] Baltimore *Afro-American*, September 3, 1932, p. 1. The prizewinning letter in the poll was that of Bernice Thomas of Philadelphia, who said that the Republicans and Democrats had had their chance and now it was the Communists' turn, since "they certainly can't do any worse."

[64] *The Crisis*, XL (April, 1933), 77.

Walter White and the American Negro Soldier in World War II: A Diplomatic Dilemma for Britain

Thomas Hachey

Nearly one million African Americans served in the United States armed forces during World War II, with almost half of them engaging in service in foreign theaters. Despite several pronouncements against discrimination and some significant promotions of African Americans to the higher military echelons, unequal and exclusionary treatment remained a troubling aspect of black participation in the war. Racial bigotry and prejudicial policies led to racial clashes both on and off military bases in the United States and abroad and caused dissatisfaction to soar among black military personnel. Furthermore, African Americans were troubled by the difficulty of reconciling the global fight for freedom with their racial plight in America.

Thomas Hachey's essay examines the 1943 visit to England by NAACP Executive Secretary Walter White to investigate the treatment of African Americans in the armed forces. Using declassified government archival records, Hachey unveils the confidential concerns and precautions undertaken by foreign officials in conjunction with White's historic visit to the British war front. The author credits the efforts of Walter White and the NAACP for the accelerated military desegregation during the Truman Administration.

WORLD WAR II is more frequently viewed by the Western World as a struggle which liberated millions from fascist or Nazi tyranny than as a war which hastened the emancipation of the colored races from the oppression of a Caucasian-dominated world. Since that emancipation has been an evolving consequence of the Second World War rather than one of the principal Allied objectives, the real significance of that epic conflict for the nonwhites of the world was not immediately apparent in the post-war years. In retrospect, it can be seen that the callous or indifferent attitudes of American and British authorities, both military and political, further exacerbated frictions in the multi-racial societies and in the territories governed by a white, imperialist elite. The plight which black Americans shared with colored peoples in other parts of the globe was typified by the indignities suffered by Negroes serving in the United States Army during World War II. The arrival of black American troops in England during 1942 produced problems which were invariably the result of racial bigotry on the part of white officers and soldiers, principally from the American armed forces, against blacks in their own army. British government and military authorities supplemented the overtly prejudicial policies of the United States Army with a more covert bias and attitude of condescension toward Negro American troops.[1] When, in 1943, Walter White, the vocal and militant Executive Secretary of the National Association for the Advancement of Colored People (NAACP), announced his intention to investigate the treatment accorded Negroes serving with U.S. armed forces in England, and to visit other war theatres, including British colonial territories in Africa and Asia, he caused reverberations in London which were felt in nearly every office in Whitehall.[2]

British authorities were well aware that Walter White was not to be dismissed as a person of little consequence. It was this same man who, together with A. Philip Randolph, had organized a march on Washington to protest discrimination in war industries. President Roosevelt succeeded in prevailing upon the Negro leaders to cancel their march, but only after promising to issue an executive order against job discrimination. The story of how White did indeed visit war fronts in Europe and the Far East to investigate cases of discrimination against black soldiers, as well as foreign victims of racial prejudice, is best recalled in his 1948 autobiography *A Man Called White*.[3] What remained unknown until recently, however, is the degree to which his travels concerned the British Government, and the confidential precautions which were undertaken, some of them in conjunction with American authorities, to insure that White's travels and investigations would not embarrass or prove troublesome to either ally. The telegrams, dispatches and memoranda of the London war-time ministries provide that account. Documents such as these would have remained closed to public view for many more years had it not been for the reduced restrictions of the Public Records Act of 1967 and a subsequent parliamentary ruling in 1971 which authorized the opening of government archives through the year 1945.[4] These heretofore unavailable archival sources were accordingly declassified, arranged by subject headings, and made available at the London Public Record Office for the first time in 1972.[5] The value of these documents for those interested in the black American experience, apart from their significance for students of Anglo-American relations, lies in the unique perspective which they render, as the confidential observations of professionally skilled foreign observers, on Mr. White's historic journey.

Since succeeding James Weldon Johnson as Executive Secretary of the NAACP in 1929, Walter White had taken an activist role. His determination to redress the injustices suffered by black Americans was extended overseas when the military demands of the Second World War resulted in the assignment of tens of thousands of blacks to foreign posts.[6] Despite the war-time censorship in the United States, there were occasional cryptic press reports from abroad of clashes between white and Negro American soldiers as early as 1942. It was primarily for the purpose of investigating these stories that Walter White applied to the War Department for permission to travel overseas.

He was also interested in gathering material for a book on "Global War in Terms of Race-Relations," however, and it was this latter quest and his expressed desire to visit military theatres in Asia and Africa which caused the London Government rather considerable concern. When the Foreign Office received a communication from Ambassador Halifax in Washington outlining the projected travel plans as White had represented them at the Embassy, London responded with an urgent telegram reflecting His Majesty's Government's grave misgivings over specific parts of White's proposal. The Foreign Office told Halifax that it had no objection to the first part of White's itinerary, in which he planned to visit United States armed forces stationed in England. But his proposal to visit India and to meet with nationalist leaders Mohandas Gandhi and Jawaharlal Nehru was quite another matter since both men had been interned by British authorities for seditious activities which were not without racial overtones. Moreover, the Foreign Office reasoned, Wendell Wilkie had been denied access to those same leaders when he had undertaken a similar world tour in 1941-42 and any special consideration for White might be viewed as discriminatory by Wilkie. The Foreign Office instructed Ambassador Halifax to determine whether President Franklin Roosevelt supported White's request to visit India and remarked that Secretary for India Leopold Amery would be glad to see him but that he should be under no illusion as to the prospects of being permitted to see Gandhi.[7]

Doubtlessly preoccupied with many other urgencies of the moment, the British Embassy in Washington failed to inform London of White's departure for England on January 3, 1944. Nevile Butler of the Foreign Office received a telephone call on January 11 from an irate Robin Cruikshank of the Ministry of Information, the man whose responsibility it was to deal with foreign correspondents, demanding to know why the Embassy had not alerted anyone to White's arrival. Since Viscount Halifax had known that the NAACP leader's trip was imminent, Cruikshank thought the Embassy should be reproached for its negligence. He reminded the Foreign Office that the Colonial Office was anxious "to deflect" Mr. White from some of his intended plans, but added that Amery would be happy to receive the visitor. Cruikshank also cited Herbert Agar[8] as his source in describing Walter White's status as that of a war correspondent attached to several publications, including the *Saturday Evening Post, Time,* and *Fortune,* and whose expenses were being funded by the NAACP.[9]

Butler promised to give the matter his immediate attention and, a few days later, sent a memorandum to both the Colonial Office and the India Office in which he represented White as war correspondent for *Life* magazine "whose London bureau are said to be not too pleased at his coming." White was also described as being potentially troublesome and, as evidence of this, Butler cited an article from the *Chicago Defender,* a Negro newspaper, in which White had described the moderates in India, saying, "It appears that Negroes are not the only ones who are cursed with Uncle Toms."[10]

If White's arrival in England seemed to catch British officials by surprise, the American Embassy and military authorities in London appeared to be fully informed. In his autobiography, White conjectured that it probably had been the War Department in Washington which had sent word of his coming and had warned that he be "handled carefully." He sensed that American military officers were making elaborate efforts to prevent him from visiting certain areas and troops. But he also found Major General John C.H. Lee to be exceptionally candid and cooperative. At a dinner hosted by General Lee, the NAACP leader was introduced to the top-ranking officers of the Service of Supply. Lee conceded to White that frictions between Negro and white American soldiers were creating problems for the United States Army both in its relations with the British and in its preparations for the invasion of France. The General then assigned one of his officers to act as White's guide, and provided him with a staff car and chauffeur. He also directed commanding officers of areas and base sections to permit White to see whatever he wished under any circumstances of his choosing. White was also pleased to find at General Lee's dinner party, "my old friend Jock Lawrence, whom I had known in Hollywood, who had just been made Chief of Army Public Relations."[11]

It would seem that the Americans, at least up to this point, kept the London Government better informed on Mr. White's whereabouts and activities than did the British Embassy in Washington. On January 24, a Foreign Office official wrote a minute for that ministry's internal circulation which read in part: "Herbert Agar and Jock Lawrence (P.R.O. to Eisenhower) think they can keep WW in order, according to Lawrence—they are going to see everything he writes. . . . " It went on to state that Lawrence was in favor of letting White go to India and had told his British colleagues that White had a personal letter from FDR to Stalin. The minute concludes: "With the Negro and liberal vote so important in the [upcoming 1944 presidential] election this solicitude for WW is not surprising."[12]

At the Ministry of Information on Mallet Street in London, Robin Cruikshank was by this time in close contact with White and the latter's activities were reported to the Foreign Office in some detail. Since Cruikshank's letter of January 18, 1944, to his colleagues at the Foreign Office reveals at least as much about official British attitudes toward the visiting American journalist as it does about Walter White himself, the letter is included here in its entirety:

> Walter White, the Negro Secretary of the National Association for the Advancement of the Coloured People, has gone on a fortnight's tour of U.S. Army camps in this country.
>
> He came to see me again on Saturday and told me that General Lee and his staff entertained him to dinner to discuss the position of the coloured troops, and that Mr. [John G.] Winant [United States Ambassador to Britain] had also had a long talk with him.
>
> White went on to say that he hoped to see Mr. [Anthony] Eden [Foreign Secretary], the Prime Minister [Winston Churchill] and Mr. [Leopold] Amery. He described several conversations he had had with Lord Halifax. He has an introduction to [British Ambassador to Moscow] Sir Stafford and Lady Cripps from Madame Chiang and the Generalissimo [Chiang Kai-shek] promised to see him in Chunking.
>
> White's two preoccupations are "the resentment of the coloured troops at race discrimination" and the position of India. He has some interesting stories to tell of the way in which Berlin and Tokio radio play on the race theme.
>
> One small but significant touch. Since he has been in London White has heard two Air Raid alerts, accompanied by a very moderate amount of gun fire, but this has impressed him quite beyond expectation. "Ah," said he, shaking his silver head, "that brings home the terrible reality of war in a way you could never know in New York." I think there is a key to the solving of the White problem here: he is an imaginative and impressionable character, and if our people can show him stirring and remarkable things when he goes about the Empire it will do much more good than arguing over his race theories. We have a hard nut to crack, but he is well worth tak-

ing a lot of trouble over, for by so doing we may be able to soften some of the preconceptions which are going to subserve that famous book on "Global War in Terms of Race." I did my best with him, and he is going to call on me again when he comes back to town.

By the way I don't know if I explained that he is as white as his name, and does not appear to possess a chemical trace of coloured blood. His accent is only very faintly Southern American. (He was born in Georgia). He is a cultured and intelligent man; has great charm of manner; and it is difficult to believe that he is as inflexible in his outlook as he really is.

Yours ever,
R. J. Cruikshank[13]

Ambassador Halifax sent a telegram to the London Foreign Office on January 22 in reply to a telegram received by the British Embassy in Washington from that Ministry only a few days before. London had instructed its Ambassador to ascertain whether or not the United States Government would take the initiative in preventing Walter White from journeying to other war theatres following his visit in England. Halifax could only respond that the War Department, which had accredited White as a war correspondent to the British Isles only, was disinclined to accredit him to any other theatre. But the Ambassador thought that the United States Government probably would be unwilling to prevent White's journeying elsewhere because of the bad publicity it would engender amongst the black community in America. "If we want to keep him out of India or the Colonies," continued the Ambassador, "we shall have to do so ourselves by refusing him a visa." Halifax thought that it might be best to tell White that London was prepared to let him go anywhere the United States War Department agreed to accredit him. "This would place the onus of opposition on the United States authorities."[14]

Meanwhile, White undertook a tour of American military bases throughout England during which he interviewed Negro soldiers about their treatment by the United States Army. Commanding officers, White recalls, were often less than cooperative until he insisted upon the prerogatives promised him by General Lee. Thereafter, he was usually able to speak with the black troops in mess halls, or in barracks, and without the intimidating presence of their superiors. White deemed this experience to be "no credit to America." An appalling number of men put their prejudices above their patriotism and actively conspired to make the lot of the Negro soldiers as unpleasant as possible. The same tactics were also employed against white officers and enlisted men who had the temerity to oppose such mistreatment and humiliation. Furthermore, there were innumerable instances where Negro soldiers were courtmartialed, convicted, and sentenced to long terms for minor offenses while white soldiers who had committed far more grievous crimes were either acquitted or punished lightly.[15] Upon returning from his investigative trip, White ensconced himself at the Cumberland Hotel on the outskirts of London and immediately began to write a report on his findings.

On January 28, Nevile Butler sent a confidential letter to Robin Cruikshank at the Ministry of Information thanking him for keeping the Foreign Office apprised of Walter White's plans and movements. Inasmuch as White, through Cruikshank, had requested an interview with Secretary for India Leopold Amery, Foreign Secretary Anthony Eden, and Prime Minister Winston Churchill, Butler advised the Ministry of Information that so far as the Prime Minister was concerned, apart from the heavy demands on his time, such an exclusive interview would inevitably create unhappiness among other American journalists who were not accorded the same courtesy. There was, however, no political objection to White's visiting with the Foreign Secretary; but such arrangements normally were made through the American Ambassador to the Court of St. James. Moreover, George Hall, the parliamentary undersecretary of state for foreign affairs, had expressed a strong interest in meeting White and the Foreign Office was equally anxious that he should see Amery at the India Office. The latter wished to impress upon White the fact that he would not be permitted to see interned Indian politicians should he choose to visit that country.[16]

Following Walter White's return to London, he conferred with Robin Cruikshank and informed the latter that he had abandoned his plan of going to Russia and India. He still hoped, however, to visit Africa and said that the United States Army had promised him transportation to that Continent. With an evident sense of relief, Cruikshank reported this latest disclosure to the Foreign Office saying: "His grandiose plans of travelling are gradually diminishing and I am hopeful that he will not cause us as many problems as one time seemed likely."[17] On the following day, February 11, Cruikshank wrote to Angus Malcolm at the Foreign Office subsequent to another visit with White. Cruikshank advised that ministry of White's intention to submit copies of his elaborate report on the treatment of Negro troops in Britain to Generals Dwight D. Eisenhower and John C. H. Lee, as well as to American Ambassador John Winant. Perhaps of greater interest to the Foreign Office was Robin Cruikshank's disclosure that one of the outstanding features of White's document would be a tribute to the kindly way in which the British public had received "the coloured soldiers." It was also noted that Walter White intended to be very condemnatory of certain United States Army officers for their complicity in or indifference toward blatant practices of racial discrimination on bases under their command in England.[18]

White left the United Kingdom for Africa on March 8, 1944, and the London Foreign Office alerted its representatives in Algiers, Casablanca, Brazzaville, Lagos, Accra, Monrovia, and Dakar, of his imminent arrival in those cities. The communication read in part:

He [White] is primarily interested in condition of United States negro troops but is also gathering material for a book on "Global War in terms of Race-Relations." Though strongly anti-imperialist he is personally cultured and agreeable and has been much impressed by things here. Please show him any courtesy that you can.[19]

In his memoirs, White described American Ambassador Winant and Generals Eisenhower and Lee as having been gravely disturbed by the report which he had submitted to them. The NAACP leader remembered Winant actually having requested material which could be used by the Joint Anglo-American Board, of which he was a member, which largely determined both civilian and military life in England. Indeed, White was aware of how various civil and military British agencies had actively and sometimes belligerently resisted, at the outset of the United States' entry into the war, the demands made by some Americans that a rigid color line, which had not existed before the war, be established. He also knew that various and inexorable pressures had changed this initial attitude considerably, especially with respect to contacts between British civilians and Negro American soldiers.[20] Recently released secret British War Cabinet minutes confirm White's suspicions beyond any shadow of a doubt and show him to have been remarkably accurate in his assessment of Anglo-American collusion in the treatment accorded blacks throughout the United Kingdom during World War II.[21]

With unmistakable ebullience, the London Foreign Office's Nevile Butler wrote Sir Ronald Campbell, a subordinate to Ambassador Halifax in Washington, on March 14, 1944:

He [White] has come and gone. . . . What he did not succeed in doing was in getting interviews with the Secretary of State, the Prime Minister or (he even suggested it!) The King. It was felt here that the way in which our public have received the coloured troops has not altogether pleased our Southern friends who think it may lead to trouble for them after the war, and therefore that we might by sticking our necks out rather far if we asked the Secretary of State to see him on his own request alone. It was noted that the President's [Roosevelt's] recommendation was the mildest possible and we therefore asked that his request should be sponsored by [Ambassador] Winant in the proper way. Winant was unwilling, but White was keen. There followed a period of scuffling during which Herbert Agar tried to shoo White away from Winant; the Ambassador stood his ground and, in the end, White went away. He was rather disgruntled, we gather, with Winant and Agar but not, it seems, with us—which is a pleasant surprise. . . .[22]

Before departing England on the global trip which he so ably chronicled in his autobiography, White gave General Eisenhower, as promised, the substance of his findings, together with recommendations. The latter included the establishment of an impartial and biracial board to review the court-martial records of blacks serving in the United States Army; the assignment of white and Negro military police to work in mixed pairs in all areas where troops of both races were garrisoned adjacent to one another; and the termination of discriminatory practices which allowed for "white only" units, such as the medical corps, air and naval units, and the relegating of Negro troops to service and supply branches rather than combat units from which they were totally excluded.[23]

Perhaps there is no real way to determine the measure of influence, if any, which Walter White had upon the plight of colored peoples in other lands either during or following the Second World War. But his achievements in the fight which he waged on behalf of the rights and dignity of black Americans constitute an enduring legacy of considerable significance. Although bigotry and prejudice still contribute occasionally to racial disharmony in the American armed forces, Walter White and the NAACP can claim much of the credit for President Truman's decision to desegregate all branches of the United States military in 1948 which, at the very least, terminated once and for all the disgraceful practice of officially sanctioned discrimination.

Notes

[1] See Thomas E. Hachey, "Jim Crow with a British Accent: Attitudes of London Government Officials Toward American Negro Soldiers in England During World War II," *The Journal of Negro History*, XLIX (January, 1974), 65-77.

[2] In addition to the telegrams, dispatches, and letters, to and from the London Foreign Office, regarding Walter White and his intention to tour different parts of Europe, Africa, and Asia, there exist a substantial number of Foreign Office minutes, as well as communications to and from other ministries in the British Government, which provide still further evidence [not cited herein] of the importance which English officials attached to the journey of the NAACP leader. See the entire volume in F.O. 371/ 38609.

[3] Walter White, *A Man Called White* (New York, 1948). Aside from his autobiography, White's other publications include: *Fire in the Flint* (New York, 1924); *Flight* (New York, 1926); *Rope and Faggot* (New York, 1929); *Rising Wind* (New York, 1945); and a book which was published posthumously entitled *How Far the Promised Land* (New York, 1955).

[4] Access to British Government archives is presently governed by the Public Records Act of 1967, which introduced from January 1, 1958, a "thirty year rule," opening the records then to the end of 1937 and making provision thereafter for the annual advancement of the open date on January 1 of each year. A few papers are closed for fifty years by virtue of the Lord Chancellor's instruments under Section 5(1) of the 1958 Public Records Act.

[5] The suspension of the 1967 Public Records Act was intended to assist scholars engaged in studies which extend over the entire period of World War II. Other than this specific exception, so generously authorized by Parliament, the "thirty year rule" is still in force.

[6] An informative contemporary study of American Negroes in the military is L.D. Reddick, "The Negro Policy of the American Army," *Journal of Negro History*, XXXIV (January, 1949), 9-29.

[7] *Telegram* No. 8207, London Foreign Office to the British Embassy, 27 November, 1943. F.O. 371/38609.

[8] After having edited the *Louisville Courier-Journal* from 1940 to 1942, Herbert Agar, the distinguished author, editor, and publisher had settled in England where he was a frequent consultant to both the American Embassy and the British Foreign Office.

[9] Foreign Office *Minute*, January 11, 1944. F.O. 371/38609.

[10] Foreign Office *Memorandum*, January 14, 1944. F.O. 371/38609.

[11] White, *A Man Called White*, pp. 242-43.

[12] Foreign Office *Minute*, January 12, 1944. F.O. 371/38609.

[13] *Letter*, Robin Cruikshank, Ministry of Information, to Nevile Butler, Foreign Office, January 18, 1944. F.O. 371/38609.

[14] *Telegram* No. 318, British Embassy, Washington, to the London Foreign Office, January 22, 1944. F.O. 371/38609.

[15] White, *A Man Called White*, pp. 243-45.

[16] *Letter*, Nevile Butler, Foreign Office, to Robin Cruikshank, Ministry of Information, January 28, 1944. F.O. 371/38609.

[17] *Letter*, Robin Cruikshank, Ministry of Information, to Nevile Butler, Foreign Office, February 10, 1944. F.O. 371/38609.

[18] *Letter*, Robin Cruikshank, Ministry of Information, to Angus Malcolm, Foreign Office, February 11, 1944. F.O. 371/38609.

[19] *Telegram* No. 235, London Foreign Office to British Ambassador, Algiers (repeated to Casablanca, Brazzaville, Monrovia, and Dakar), March 8, 1944. F.O. 371/38609.

[20] White, *A Man Called White*, p. 267.

[21] See, for example, *Memorandum* by the Lord Privy Seal on United States Troops in the United Kingdom to the War Cabinet, 17 October 1942. Cab. 68/30.

[22] *Letter*, Nevile Butler, Foreign Office, to Sir Ronald Campbell, British Embassy, Washington, March 14, 1944. F.O. 371/38609.

[23] White, *A Man Called White*, pp. 247-48.

The Roosevelt Administration
and Black America:
Federal Surveillance Policy and Civil Rights
During the New Deal and World War II Years

KENNETH O'REILLY

In addition to his efforts to bring a "New Deal" of relief, recovery, and reform to the nation suffering under the throes of the Great Depression, President Franklin D. Roosevelt also extended federal power to control crime. During the 1930s, the Federal Bureau of Investigation (FBI) underwent a metamorphosis of growth and authority under Roosevelt's tutelage to become the administration's solution to the crime crisis. Armed with a host of new federal crimes, including kidnapping and bank robbery, as well as the establishment of a Civil Liberties Unit, the FBI's capacity to fight crime and to protect citizens' rights was greatly enhanced. However, many civil rights advocates criticized the FBI's lack of responsiveness to lynching and other race-related violence. Toward the end of the decade, as the threat of war loomed in Europe, the Bureau directed its attention to a significant number of citizens, including many African Americans, all of whom were suspected of harboring communist or fascist sympathies. Those individuals became targets of the FBI's surveillance techniques.

Kenneth O'Reilly's essay chronicles the development of the FBI as a modern governmental agency, thrust into the vortex of domestic politics, international affairs, and war. The Roosevelt administration's zeal to fight crime and to protect civil liberties was tempered by states' rights politics and the start of World World II. O'Reilly argues that while the FBI had the potential to protect black civil rights, the Bureau's leadership had different priorities and pursued a different agenda throughout the 1930s and 1940s.

THE NATURE OF THE FEDERAL GOVERNMENT'S response to the "Negro problem" during the years 1933-1945 has been the subject of a lively historical debate. For Harvard Sitkoff, the New Deal provided "unprecedented substantive and symbolic aid to blacks" and generally tilled the soil and planted "the seeds that would later bear fruit." Other historians, most notably Nancy J. Weiss, are a bit harder on the

New Deal, contending that blacks bolted the party of Lincoln and voted Democratic because of economic concerns and despite Franklin D. Roosevelt's record on race. Though sympathetic to the plight of black Americans, the President was not prepared to expend any political capital on their behalf or to antagonize Southern Democrats on the race issue.[1]

President Roosevelt's record on the Federal Bureau of Investigation (FBI) is far less ambivalent. FDR brought the New Deal to the FBI's special agents just as surely as he brought it to the nation's farmers, workers, and businessmen. When Roosevelt was first elected, the Bureau had only 266 investigators, 66 accountants, a budget of less than $3 million, and no formal intelligence responsibilities. By the time Roosevelt died in 1945, the FBI had become, in one way, what the New Deal president intended it to be—a thriving bureaucracy with clearly defined missions in the areas of crime control and national security.[2] Like a good many of the Roosevelt-era bureaucracies, the FBI brought the New Deal directly to black America. By the late 1930s the Bureau's domestic intelligence responsibilities included surveillance programs aimed at black men and women. By 1939 the Bureau's criminal jurisdiction had extended far enought to include, at least in theory, most every type of civil rights violation.

This is not to say that the problems facing black Americans were ever more than peripheral concerns for President Roosevelt's New Dealers or FBI Director J. Edgar Hoover's G-men. The administration was far more concerned with the economic crisis and later, as the United States crept toward war, with national security issues. What the New Deal did, to use Sitkoff's metaphor again, was plant seeds that would later bear fruit. President Roosevelt might not have pursued civil rights issues aggressively, but he did put the FBI in the business of investigating civil rights complaints and that task remained a permanent part of the FBI work load despite the persistent efforts of Mr. Hoover to extract his bureaucracy from what he perceived to be a civil rights quagmire. The surveillance of black Americans was also established as a routine part of FBI responsibilities during the Roosevelt years and it would remain so for the next four decades.

From its modest beginnings in 1908, the FBI has been enmeshed in the states' rights controversy. Theories of federalism, with its elaborate systems of deference to state and local authority, historically have confined law enforcement responsibilities to state and local police agencies. The idea of a national police force was alien to American traditions. With the exception of the Espionage and Sedition Acts, which provided, at least in part, a legal basis for its intelligence mission during the World War I era and the postwar Red scare and black scare years, the Bureau's formal criminal jurisdiction was mostly limited to "white slavery" (the Mann Act of 1910), stolen cars (the Dyer Act of 1919), and kidnapping (the so-called Lindbergh Law of 1932 and a companion act). With little to do, the Bureau of Investigation (as the FBI was known until 1935) remained a small and relatively obscure division within the Justice Department.

Franklin Roosevelt changed all that. In most every way the FBI was a creature of the New Deal, one of the alphabet agencies. President Roosevelt and Attorney General Homer S. Cummings promoted the growth of the FBI as part of the administration's broader effort to extend federal power to yet another realm, crime control, once considered to be the exclusive prerogative of state and local government.[3] The decision to expand federal criminal jurisdiction was in part a reflection of the president's concern that the crime problem posed a legitimate threat to "our security." President Roosevelt was equally troubled by the public's "tolerance" of the depression era's flamboyant criminals and the "efforts" of tabloid publicists to "romanticize" the bank-robbing exploits of John Dillinger and dozens of lesser lights.[4]

The Roosevelt solution to the crime crisis was typical New Deal reform, not all that different in form from the Roosevelt solution to the very real industrial and agrarian crises. One way or another, "the strong arm of Government," working through the alphabet agencies and relying on innovative legislation, would solve the nation's problems. In the spring of 1934 the Justice Department drafted and Congress approved, without even taking a record vote, nine anticrime bills. The New Deal crime control package dramatically expanded the FBI's criminal jurisdiction and budget and granted its agents full arrest power and authority to carry any kind of firearm. To counter the public's supposedly romanticized view of Dillinger and the other hoodlums, Attorney General Cummings supplemented the new legislation with an ambitious public relations campaign described privately by White House press secretary Stephen Early as a "plan to publicize and make the G-Men heroes."[5] By the mid-1930s J. Edgar Hoover was box office and his heroic bureaucracy as American as baseball.[6]

The New Dealers invented a number of federal crimes in 1934, but when it came to civil rights violations they lost their nerve. An attempt to include an antilynching bill in the crime control package was killed by the White House. Louis Howe, the President's fixer, thought the lynching bill would "create hostility to [the] other crime bills."[7] Howe was right. For many Southern congressmen, lynching legislation was the most sensitive states' rights issue. It "discrimi-

nated" against specific states and the South as a whole. The other
New Deal crime bills focused on issues that even most conservative
Southern congressmen considered to be national in scope. How
could anyone object to an amendment to the federal bank-robbery
statute extending FBI jurisdiction to all banks insured by the Federal
Deposit Insurance Corporation?

Civil rights people had little enthusiasm for this New Deal-style
war on crime. The National Association for the Advancement of
Colored People (NAACP) picketed one of Cummings' public relations extravaganzas, the National Crime Conference of 1934, to demand the inclusion of a lynching bill. Led by Walter White, the
NAACP tried to convince the Justice Department to use the amended
Lindbergh Law to prosecute members of lynch mobs in cases, such as
the Claude Neal murder, where the victim has been kidnapped and
taken across a state line.[8] The facts in this case were never in doubt.
Abducted in October 1934 from a jail in Brewton, Alabama, Neal was
driven to Florida and lynched. The murder was advertised in local
newspapers and radio broadcasts and thousands of spectators turned
out to watch. The Justice Department, nevertheless, refused to launch
a full-scale investigation or press for prosecution. "The department,"
White said, took "the position that the amended Lindbergh law covered kidnapping for the purposes of gain [ransom], but not for purposes of murder."[9]

The FBI agreed. Persons interested in civil rights continued
throughout the 1930s to contrast the Bureau's high-profile war on
kidnappers and other criminals with the Neal case. When this was
brought to the attention of Walter Winchell, the radio commentator,
newspaper columnist, and Bureau confidant, in a letter that did not
mention Neal by name, Hoover told Winchell that he had no idea
what case he was referring to. The FBI director was more interested
in promoting the crusade against real kidnappers (that is, crooks who
held white folks for ransom), forwarding such items as the following
for Winchell's column:

> The colored boys in Washington who are prone to play hunches in
> the numbers game are reported to have made a killing recently
> when they combined the numbers in connection with the days of
> the month on which the G Men apprehended a number of notori-
> ous kidnappers. Alvin Karpis was apprehended on May 1st; William
> Mahan and Harry Campbell . . . on May 7th, and Thomas H. Robin-
> son, Jr., . . . on May 11th. The colored boys combined the numbers
> 1-7-1 and are said to have cashed in on the hunch.[10]

At a press conference a few days after the Neal lynching, Franklin Roosevelt was asked if he would recommend passage of a pending

lynching bill. The President ducked the question by asking for some time "to check up and see what I did last year. I have forgotten." What Roy Wilkins of the NAACP described as the President's "expedient cowardice," his reluctance to pursue antilynching legislation or to rely on the amended Lindbergh Law, was understandable.[11] The Democratic party had a strong Northern, urban, and liberal base, but it was still, in part, the party of Jefferson Davis. Blacks, ethnics, Catholics, and Jews coexisted with conservative white Southerners. By the late 1930s the tension within the Democratic party had produced congressional rebellion, with Southern Democrats aligning themselves with Republicans in an informal conservative coalition that ground the New Deal to a halt.[12]

Once this coalition hardened, the Roosevelt administration pursued civil rights issues more aggressively. The President had little to lose. After his failed attempt to purge his party of obstructionists, Southern Democrats were about as alienated as they could be. With the coming of the war, there was also less of a need to expand those parts of the New Deal that had been designed to fix a broken economy. On the racial front, in contrast, the war led to pressure on the administration to do more for black citizens. Adolph Hitler's propagandists continually were drawing parallels between the Third Reich's policy toward Jews and the United States government's policy toward blacks.

In 1939 Attorney General Frank Murphy established a special Civil Liberties Unit (renamed the Civil Rights Section two years later) within the Criminal Division of the Department of Justice. Murphy's decision to put the federal government (and the FBI) in the business of protecting civil rights was in part a reflection of his own values. A former NAACP board member, he considered intolerance "the most . . . undemocratic thing in our life today."[13] He was also responding to the demands of organized labor and virtually all civil rights groups that the Roosevelt administration do something about lynching and other violence directed at labor organizers in particular, and blacks in general. Neither Murphy nor Henry A. Schweinhaut, the first chief of the Civil Liberties Unit, however, had a clear conception of the role the unit should play.

The Civil Liberties Unit began slowly, requesting the FBI to investigate only seven civil rights cases in 1939. The public, on the other hand, demonstrated no ambivalence whatsoever and quickly overwhelmed the unit with complaints of civil liberties and civil rights violations. The American people, as Schweinhaut often complained, believed "the Civil Liberties section to be a large . . . arm of the Department of Justice ready to loap [sic] in at a moment's notice to protect civil rights of citizens."[14] The reality was quite different. With a staff of only eight attorneys and with all of the investigative work handled by the FBI, the Civil Liberties Unit did not have the resources to pursue such a mission. Unit attorneys favored mediation of civil rights disputes and urged prosecution of alleged violators only as a last resort.

The type of complaints received by Civil Liberties Unit attorneys covered the entire spectrum. Of this deluge (there were literally thousands of complaints submitted), "only a few," in Schweinhaut's opinion, were "actually within the jurisdiction of the Federal Government." Most of the complaints deemed legitimate had to do with the rights of labor, not the rights of black Americans who suffered under Jim Crow. Even before the formation of the Civil Liberties Unit, the FBI had investigated a few labor intimidation cases under Section 7 of the Wagner Labor Relations Act—the New Deal law that guaranteed employees the right to form unions and bargain collectively.[15]

After the formation of the Civil Liberties Unit the FBI handled hundreds of these investigations. A fairly typical case involved a September 1941 assault on the Congress of Industrial Organizations (CIO) organizers in Helena, Arkansas. When the CIO sent its own investigator, Lucy Randolph Mason, a native Southerner from an old Virginia family, to monitor developments, the Bureau ran a name check. Such interest was routine. FBI policy required the field to "make available to [headquarters] all derogatory information contained in its files regarding the subjects and complainants" in all civil rights cases. On an informal level, this policy extended to anyone showing an interest in such a case. The FBI's name check, in this instance, connected Lucy Mason, a woman whose family tree included John Marshall, the first Chief Justice of the United States Supreme Court, and the Confederate general Robert E. Lee, to the Southern Conference for Human Welfare, the National Negro Congress, and a number of other left-wing groups. She had even signed an International Labor Defense petition protesting the trial and conviction of the Scottsboro boys.[16]

The Civil Liberties Unit did not rely solely on the Wagner Labor Relations Act when seeking to protect the rights of labor to organize. The Wagner Act guaranteed certain civil rights but provided no criminal provision. In order "to put teeth into the Wagner Act," as the FBI put it, the Civil Liberties Unit used two statutes from the Reconstruction era—Sections 51 and 52 of Title 18 of the Federal Criminal Code. These statutes originated in the Enforcement Act of 1870 and the Civil Rights act of 1866 and were intended to guarantee a permanent rights equality and to control Ku Klux Klan terrorism.

Section 51 provided specific criminal sanctions against persons conspiring to deprive "any citizen" of his or her constitutional rights, while Section 52 (commonly referred to as the color-of-law statute) brought local government officials, including police officers, under the umbrella of federal jurisdiction.

For all practical purposes these statutes had been dormant in the twentieth century until Frank Murphy used them to make the civil rights investigation an everyday function of the federal government. If the Civil Liberties Unit was little more than a New Deal "tinker toy," as Richard Kluger, the author of *Simple Justice*, described it, Murphy legitimized, for the first time in the twentieth century, the idea that the government had the right and the duty and the will to investigate, mediate, and if necessary prosecute civil rights violations.

Because Section 51 required proof of conspiracy and Section 52 required specific intent, the statutes raised hard questions about how they were to be enforced and sparked a legal debate that dragged on for decades. And during the war years the Justice Department rejected the description of Section 51 as a "criminal catch-all" offered by one of Murphy's successors, Francis Biddle. The Department adopted a narrow interpretation, concluding that "the ordinary outbreak of ruffian, vigilante activity, not participated in by public officials, whether directed against reds, nazis, negroes, soap-box speakers, or religious groups is not within Section 51."[17] But the government either had to rely on Sections 51 and 52 or to withdraw from the civil rights protection business. In the absence of a New Deal legislative agenda, the Reconstruction era statutes constituted the only available sword.[18]

The Justice Department used Sections 51 and 52 to protect the rights of labor throughout the war years. But the Civil Liberties Unit quickly tilted away from labor and toward civil rights of blacks, as the name change to a Civil Rights Section suggests. By 1941 things were getting better for organized labor. If the world of ops and finks and hooked men so graphically described by the LaFollette Civil Liberties Committee in the late 1930s never quite disappeared, it was fading.[19] Even Henry Ford went along, recognizing the United Automobile Workers in 1941 and firing Harry Bennett and his Service Department thugs four years later. Ford replaced Bennett with John Bugas, former special agent in charge of the Detroit FBI office. Many union organizers were well on their way to becoming union bureaucrats and, like Ford's men, happily trading in their ball bats and steel knuckles for vested suits. When the Civil Liberties Unit established in 1939 the nation was only beginning to wind down from what a task force of the National Commission on the Causes and Prevention of

Violence described thirty years later as "the bloodiest and most violent labor history of any industrial nation in the world."[20]

Most civil rights activists had hoped, all along, that the Justice Department would concentrate on the rights of blacks. "It would warm the cockles of your heart," the NAACP's Walter White wrote Frank Murphy shortly after the formation of the Civil Liberties Unit, "if you knew how great is the satisfaction among colored people all over the United States at your presence in the . . . post of Attorney General."[21] As civil rights complaints poured into the Justice Department, the FBI found itself spending more and more time on police brutality cases and other investigations where blacks were victimized.

A typical case involved Willie Jones of Little Rock. Thirty-nine years old, illiterate, and suffering from syphillis, Jones had been arrested in November 1942 by the sheriff in Bastrop, Louisiana. Held in jail for nearly a month, Jones was never charged with a crime. The FBI noted the facts, forwarded them to the Justice Department, and was advised that no further investigation was necessary. Another case involved a resident of Blytheville, Arkansas, J. S. Baker, who worked in an office building near the local police station and claimed it was a common practice of the constabulary to beat black prisoners. Baker generally ignored the ghoulish sounds coming from the nearby police station, but one morning he stood and listened to the screaming. A group of black residents gathered outside and, with "Bowed heads," told Baker that "the Law [was] beating a poor helpless colored boy." The experience kept Baker up that night and the following morning he wrote the FBI to ask if there was "any Government Agency anywhere in the United States that have [sic] authority to investigate these terrible beatings?"[22]

Whether he intended to be ironic or not, it was no coincidence that Baker directed his letter to the FBI. While the Bureau did all the investigative work for the Civil Rights Section, its efforts during the war years were neither enthusiastic nor effective. In the civil rights field, the FBI was invisible. The classic 1944 study of racism and democracy prepared by Gunnar Myrdal and his small army of collaborators, *An American Dilemma*, did not contain a single reference to the Federal Bureau of Investigation.[23]

On rare occasions, and usually with mixed success, Roosevelt administration officials pressured the FBI to investigate civil rights violations more aggressively. In February 1942, following the lynching of Cleo Wright in Sikeston, Missouri, Attorney General Francis Biddle ordered FBI agents and Civil Rights Section attorneys into the case. In contrast to the other 3,842 recorded lynchings between 1889 and 1941, as one historian of race-related violence has observed, Wright's brutal murder "drew the United States Department of Justice into that area of civil rights for the first time."[24] Biddle also pressured the FBI to investigate more mundane civil rights cases aggressively. Concerned about rumors of black citizens who were arrested, denied access to counsel, and then summarily tried and sentenced during the Detroit riots of 1943, Biddle asked the FBI to determine if this was indeed happening. While the Bureau's Detroit office felt the attorney general's request would "open the door of our investigating certain very important aspects of the riot," the director did not share this assessment.[25]

Hoover's reluctance was not suprising. The FBI was willing to gather intelligence in Detroit. As late as December 29, 1943, more than six months after the riots, the director advised the attorney general that a new wave of violence might be imminent. A racial outbreak was possible in Detroit's Paradise Valley, Biddle learned, as a protest against proceedings brought by a police trial board against two black police officers, Jesse Stewart and Willie M. Williams, charged with conduct unbecoming police officers and failure to prevent a riot.[26] Investigations of alleged civil rights violations, in contrast, were handled in a sporadic and haphazard manner. FBI officials had no intention of investigating local police practices in Detroit or elsewhere and generally resisted pressure from the Justice Department to do so.

For the FBI, and the Roosevelt administration as well, investigation of race-related violence and discrimination was never a central part of the New Deal war on crime. The White House proposed no innovative civil rights legislation and made few attempts to rally public opinion and even fewer efforts to pressure the FBI. The precedent, nevertheless, had been set. Based on administrative discretion, and two very old statutes, the Roosevelt administration expanded the FBI's criminal jurisdiction far enough to encompass most civil rights violations. President Roosevelt and Attorney General Murphy placed the FBI on the firing line in 1939, further enmeshing the Bureau in the states' rights controversy and virtually guaranteeing a major role for J. Edgar Hoover and his bureaucracy in the coming civil rights revolution.

The Roosevelt administration demonstrated far less ambivalence when promoting the growth of the FBI in another area that would effect the civil rights movement in the decades to come. During the New Deal years the FBI opened sweeping domestic intelligence investigations of communist and other radical efforts to influence black Americans. In 1934, with Hitler in Berlin and a number of boisterous and explicitly racist native fascists active on the home front, President

Roosevelt ordered J. Edgar Hoover to investigate "anti-racial" and "anti-American" activities having "any possible connection with official representatives of the German government in the United States."[27] Within two years, and with Franklin Roosevelt's approval, FBI responsibilities expanded to include communist activities. By 1938 the FBI had a special "Negroes" category as part of its domestic communist and native fascist infiltration investigations.

Black Americans were not necessarily singled out for extra-special attention. Other FBI infiltration investigations zeroed in on organized labor, the newspaper field, educational institutions, government agencies, the armed forces, and youth groups.[28] On the other hand, FBI interest in black Americans was at least to some extent unique. The other categories established by the Bureau had more to do with the groups people belonged to or their occupations. The investigations of Negroes, in contrast, were based on color, an entirely different sort of category, and on the assumption that black people posed special loyalty problems for the government. The FBI invariably lumped its wartime reports on "Negro Organizations" with reports on "Communism" and "German, Italian, and Japanese" fifth columnists. But even here Bureau assumptions were paralleled by at least one other government agency, the Office of War Information.[29]

No matter who was being investigated during the New Deal and World War II eras, Hoover and his men as often as not operated according to their own political priorities and thus sometimes created problems for the Roosevelt administration. On at least one occasion in 1942, when relaying President Roosevelt's concern, Attorney General Biddle read the director the riot act. The President felt the FBI was "spending too much time investigating suspected Communists in the Government and out, but particularly in the Government, and ignoring the Fascist minded groups both in the Government and out."[30] Needless to say, Hoover was no fool. He kept most of the FBI's quite extensive record of insubordination and unilateralism tucked safely out of sight. When Franklin Roosevelt looked at the FBI he did not often see a bureaucracy whose agents looked for subversives even in the White House and broke into the offices of the left-wing American Youth Congress to photograph the correspondence of his own wife with Youth Congress leaders.[31] Instead, Roosevelt saw a bureaucracy that appeared to be under control.

Hoover, in fact, sent reports to the White House, some of which the President read personally, detailing what the FBI's agents were doing. They were quite busy, whether compiling "Negro Question" reports on communist-front groups like the National Negro Congress or trying to persuade the non-political Billie Holiday to remove a communist antiwar song, "The Yanks Are Not Coming," from her nightclub repertoire.[32] Other FBI agents approached at least four black-owned newspapers, including the *Pittsburgh Courier*, in an attempt to convince black editors to tone down their "militant crusading."[33] FBI officials described one black paper, the *Chicago Defender*, as "a very strong agitational force among the Negroes, carrying articles inflammatory and sensational in nature." Hoover ordered a report sent to the Justice Department. At the time, the Department was in the midst of a loyalty investigation of the entire black press.[34]

The FBI filed dozens of similar reports with the attorney general and the Roosevelt White House on individuals and groups involved in civil rights activities, from the Southern Conference for Human Welfare to the all-black March on Washington Movement organized in 1941 by A. Philip Randolph. When Randolph's movement threatened to become a reality again in 1942 the FBI escalated its surveillance. Affiliated groups were "checked out" and the most bizarre plots reported. One involved "a one-hour 'blackout' " planned for the south side of Chicago on a night when March organizers were scheduled to be in town for a meeting. Although ultimately the blackout tactic was rejected, the FBI took the opportunity to offer a prediction. "This gesture might possibly result in wholesale looting."

Many of the reports Hoover forwarded to the White House concerning Randolph focused on the efforts of communist and communist-front groups "to counteract inroads made by the March on Washington Movement." The communists assigned this task to a black party member, Ferdinand C. Smith of the National Maritime Union. Smith worked through the Negro Labor Victory Committee and already had lined up a number of prominent speakers, including New York City Councilman Adam Clayton Powell, Jr. The Movement itself, another informant reported, was simply a bluff. In 1942, at least, Randolph and other black leaders had no intention of marching on Washington. They planned to use "the Movement . . . for personal gain and national recognition." Yet another informant expressed the "opinion that Randolph is merely creating a situation, in the hope of being requested by the President, or someone of the White House, to abandon the proposed march." Randolph, in short, sought a concession from the President for calling off a march that he never intended to go through with.[35]

The FBI's informant may have been right on this last point. Randolph's rhetoric about the need for "monster mass meetings" was not translated into practice. The largest of the demonstrations sponsored by the March on Washington Movement in 1942, held after the execution of a sharecropper who had killed his landlord in self-defense, was poorly attended. But the question of whether Franklin Roosevelt (or J. Edgar Hoover or anyone besides the informant) actually believed A. Philip Randolph was playing poker and bluffing is beside the point. Roosevelt wanted all the information he could obtain on Randolph and his nonviolent, direct-action politics. In 1943 the FBI sent over at least six additional reports.[36]

FBI agents had been busy since the summer of 1942 conducting a survey of "foreign inspired agitation among the Negroes," an effort that included the recruitment of black informants in "colored areas and colored neighborhoods," the use of "technical sources" (wiretaps and bugs) on a range of civil rights groups from the procommunist National Negro Congress to the anticommunist NAACP, and a campaign to discover whether domestic servants in Alabama and other Southern states were organizing "Eleanor Clubs." Acting on complaints "that the cause of agitation among the Negroes in this area is largely attributed to the encouragment given Negroes by Mrs. Roosevelt," who had visited Tuskegee Institute in 1941 and "was entertained throughout her visit by Negroes," the FBI made a number of "inquiries." Hoover sympathized with those "white people who found difficulty in retaining their servants as a result of better opportunities offered by various Defense jobs." He wanted to know whether female black domestics really were "demanding their own terms for working" and using the slogan of "A White Woman in the Kitchen by Christmas."[37]

The FBI's agents never did find much foreign-inspired agitation among Negroes. But they kept looking and kept tracking "a definite change in the attitude of some negroes." "A number of them," as the head of the Bureau's Richmond, Virginia, field office mused, "appear to have become more disrespectful, more assertive of their rights and more discontented with their station in life." The net result, in this view, was in line with communist objectives and as well "the Axis aim to create disunity and to cause the Negro to wonder whether he should support our war effort wholeheartedly."[38] Communists and fascists, it would seem, were on the same side during the war years. Within the party itself, the FBI seemed, at times, to be particularly concerned with the efforts of such black communists as Hosea Hudson of Birmingham to conduct "classes in cooperation with the NATIONAL NEGRO CONGRESS for the purpose of teaching negroes how to become qualified voters." The immediate goal of the party's voter registration drive, as the FBI man in Alabama put it, was to insure "the re-election of President ROOSEVELT."[39]

The Roosevelt administration continued to find the FBI's domestic intelligence services useful nonetheless. This was particularly true during the bloody Detroit riot (thirty-four dead citizens) of 1943. Racial disturbances broke out that same year in Beaumont, Texas, Mobile, Alabama, and New York City.[40] For reasons of policy and politics, both the FBI and the Roosevelt administration view of World War II-era racial violence differed sharply from the earlier view of the World War I-era riots offered by the old Bureau of Investigation and the Woodrow Wilson administration. The most pressing issue on the home front during President Wilson's war to end all wars was dissent. Given the widespread opposition to that war it was not surprising that the administration attempted to equate dissent with disloyalty or that the Bureau was recruited for the crusade. To sell the idea that dissent and disloyalty were one and the same, it made sense to raise the specter of foreign agitators and subversives who preached doctrines of global revolution and universal class war.

There was no such need during World War II, when the government saw its principal problem not in building a national consensus but in maintaining one. Even before the United States entered the war, the FBI was clearly committed to countering the alarmists who claimed domestic subversives posed a serious espionage and sabotage threat. "The menace of the situation," as Hoover advised Attorney General Robert Jackson in October 1940, "is in a lot of loose talk and charges and allegations creating a hysterical public viewpoint which breaks down confidence in the constitutional law enforcement agencies."[41] After Pearl Harbor the government's information people did not have to convince Americans of the need to stand against Hitler and Tojo. Because they did not have to sell this war, they could concentrate on more practical problems—for instance, the selling of the Soviet Union as a heroic ally.

Repression of the dissent that did exist never went to the soul of the nation as it had during the First World War. The advocacy prosecutions under the Smith Act of native fascists during World War II clearly forecasted what would come to typify cold war repression. But it would be hard to argue rationally that the government needed the Smith Act during the Second World War in the same sense that the Wilson administration needed the Espionage and Sedition Acts to contain a significant antiwar movement.

When the Detroit riots broke out, then, it was predictable that the Roosevelt administration would attempt to discredit the radical specter. This is not to say that there was no pressure on the administration and the FBI to advance conspiracy theories. From Martin Dies (Democrat, Texas), chairman of the Special House Committee to Investigate Un-American Activities, came the suggestion that the riots were somehow instigated by Japanese agents. If Dies' charges were ridiculous, it should be remembered that the Justice Department had filed sedition charges against at least eighty blacks a year earlier, in 1942, chiefly on the grounds of their so-called transnational racial identification with the Japanese. On the other side, leftists also saw conspiracies. The Detroit FBI office was flooded with telegrams from communists, labor organizers, and civil rights activists demanding an investigation of "pro-Fascist groups," including the Ku Klux Klan, for allegedly instigating the riots. The Communist party blamed the violence in Detroit on the entire spectrum of far-rightists and demanded FBI suveillance of Silver Shirts, Bundists, Klansmen, and other down-home Hitler rooters.

The implications of these conspiracy theories were not lost on the FBI. John Bugas, the head of the local Bureau office, identified the principal radical activity in Detroit as the spreading of propaganda attributing what were clearly "spontaneous racial disturbances" to the "enemies of labor and radical interests." At the same time, a few civil rights leaders blamed the Communist party. National Urban League official Lester Granger said the whole thing was "inspired 'by Communists' " and referred to "an increasing number of attempts by Communists to 'take over' " his organization by forming front organizations with "innocent sounding names."[42]

These conspiracy theories came from all angles and were all rejected by the FBI. Louis B. Nichols, chief of the Bureau's public relations unit, told a number of newspaper reporters that this propaganda played no role in the riots. The Bureau had uncovered "no information," Hoover wrote White House aide Marvin McIntyre, "to substantiate" the charge "that the riot was inspired by foreign elements." The following day another FBI official, Robert C. Hendon, spoke to White House press secretary Stephen Early and reiterated the Bureau's conclusion: "The trouble was of a spontaneous nature," the "result of . . . intense racial feeling between colored and white citizens." Early was relieved. The FBI had confirmed the President's belief that the riot was the outcome of crowded conditions and lack of proper housing.[43]

The Detriot riots offered both opportunity and risk for the Bureau. The most obvious risk involved the states' rights issue and the possibility of criticism being leveled at the FBI for intruding into areas where it did not belong. Bureau officials escaped such criticism, in part, as a result of the Director's highly visible states' rights position. Because riot "matters [were] solely within the jurisdiction of the local authorities," Hoover said, the FBI "had no right or duty to participate." The Roosevelt administration was not as fortunate. Wayne County's antiblack prosecutor William Dowling, for one, was an outspoken critic of Justice Department meddling. Dowling told Francis Biddle's representative in Detroit "to keep his G– D– nose out of Wayne County problems." As Dowling saw it, the riot was caused by the NAACP and the black press! Justice Department intervention was the result of Biddle's attempt "to appease a few strong pressure groups."[44]

On the opportunity side, charges of foreign or subversive influence might justify FBI wiretaps on the leaders of the United Sons of America, the assumed name of the local Klan group then operating in Detroit. These taps, Bugas contended, would "assist the Bureau appreciably in countering the charges being made by certain labor unions and radical interests in Detroit that the riots were Fascist inspired." Bugas's proposal was accepted and several "technical surveillances" were installed. The Detroit FBI office had the telephone of at least one other native fascist, the Reverend Gerald L. K. Smith, tapped since May, 1942, and was picking up some useful items. The FBI learned that Smith and Senator Robert R. Reynolds (Democrat, North Carolina), chairman of the Military Affairs Committee and founder of the far-right American Nationalist party, were trying to persuade the Dies Committee to look into the causes of the riots. Concerned "that 'Reds' in Detroit were trying to blame the riots on good people such as Henry Ford and himself," Smith hoped Dies would emphasize communist responsibility.[45]

Hoover's FBI pursued that issue in a quiet and private way, with an internal report noting the efforts of communist-influenced groups to agitate "militantly among the Negroes in Detroit." Through "inflammatory statements and writing," party leaders were "inciting the feeling of Negroes in the Detroit area."[46] While FBI officials recognized "other contributing factors to the riot" and publicly agreed with the conclusions of independent investigations conducted by the Detroit Urban League, city police, and local newspapers that communist involvement was irrelevant, they did not intend to ignore the party. Even before the riots began, internal FBI reports concluded that most of the demonstrations on behalf of "the Negroes" at the Sojourner Truth Housing Project, a defense tract built for black workers in Detroit, were "Communist-inspired."[47]

Such surveillance was one of two legacies from the New Deal and World War II years that bound the FBI to the struggle of blacks for equality. The other legacy was the administrative decision in 1939 to assign the FBI, a bureaucracy whose director and the men closest to him saw nothing wrong with segregation in "restaurants in New York," the task of investigating all civil rights complaints received by the Justice Department and screened by the Civil Rights Section.[48]

Concerning the surveillance of black men and women, FBI officials pursued their mission enthusiastically and for the most part without much supervision—often going far beyond any authority they may have received from President Roosevelt to conduct domestic intelligence operations. Less enthusiastic about civil rights work, the Bureau adopted a strict legalistic and constitutional posture that contrasted sharply with its extra-legal and unconstitutional surveillance of black Americans. In both areas, the Roosevelt administration had placed the FBI in a position to aid or hinder the gathering civil rights movement. In the years to come movement people would find that a mixed blessing at best.

Notes

[1] Harvard Sitkoff, *A New Deal for Blacks* (New York, 1978); and Nancy J. Weiss, *Farewell to the Party of Lincoln: Black Politics in the Age of FDR* (Princeton, 1983).

[2] Kenneth O'Reilly, "A New Deal for the FBI: The Roosevelt Administration, Crime Control, and National Security," *Journal of American History* 69 (Dec. 1982): 638-58.

[3] Arthur C. Millspaugh, *Crime Control by the National Government* (Washington, D.C., 1937).

[4] Samuel Rosenman, ed., *The Public Papers and Addresses of Franklin D. Roosevelt*, 13 vols. (New York, 1938-1950), vol. 3, pp. 12-13, 242-45, 492-95.

[5] Memo, Stephen Early to the President, July 12, 1940, President's Personal File 2993, Franklin D. Roosevelt Papers, Franklin D. Roosevelt Library, Hyde Park, N.Y.; and memo, Early to Lowell Mellett, July 30, 1940, Official File (OF), 880, ibid.

[6] Richard Gid Powers, *G-Men: Hoover's FBI in American Popular Culture* (Carbondale, Ill., 1983).

[7] William Manchester, *The Glory and the Dream: A Narrative History of America, 1932-1972* (New York, 1975), p. 107.

[8] James R. McGovern, *Anatomy of a Lynching: The Killing of Claude Neal* (Baton Rouge, La., 1982).

[9] Walter White, "U.S. Department of (White) Justice," *Crisis*, October, 1935, p. 310.

[10] Letters, J. Edgar Hoover to Walter Winchell, May 19, 1936, no. 62-31615-42, and July 6, 1938, no. 62-31619-99, Walter Winchell FBI File; and letter, [deleted] to Winchell, June 16, 1938, no. 62-31615-99, ibid.

[11] Weiss, op. cit., p. 199; and Roy Wilkins with Tom Mathews, *Standing Fast: The Autobiography of Roy Wilkins* (New York, 1984), p. 132.

[12] James T. Patterson, *Congressional Conservatism and the New Deal: The Growth of the Conservative Coalition in Congress, 1933-1939* (Lexington, Ky., 1969).

[13] Sidney Fine, *Frank Murphy*, 3 vols. (Ann Arbor, 1975-1984), vol. 3: *The Washington Years*, pp. 79, 82.

[14] Paraphrased in memo, W. Cleon Skousen to [File], Feb. 22, 1940, no. 66-6200-44-2, FBI Civil Rights Policy File.

[15] Memo, K. R. McIntire to Tamm, July 28, 1938, no. 66-6200-44-1, ibid.

[16] Memo, Hoover to Wendell Berge, Nov. 22, 1941, no. 144-9-2, Record Group (RG) 60, Department of Justice Files, National Archives; and memo, Berge to Director, May 21, 1942, no. 144-9-2, ibid.

[17] Department of Justice Circular no. 3356, April 4, 1942, no. 66-6200-44-illegible, FBI Civil Rights Policy File.

[18] Robert K. Carr, *Federal Protection of Civil Rights: Quest for a Sword* (Ithaca, 1947).

[19] Jerold S. Auerbach, *Labor and Liberty: The LaFollette Committee and the New Deal* (Indianapolis, 1966).

[20] Philip Taft and Philip Ross, "American Labor Violence: Its Causes, Character, and Outcome," in *Violence in America: Historical and Comparative Perspectives*, eds. Hugh Davis Graham and Tedd Robert Gurr (New York, 1969), p. 270.

[21] Fine, op. cit., vol. 3 p. 80.

[22] Memo, Hoover to Berge, Oct. 11, 1941, no. 144-9-0, RG60, Department of Justice Files; letter. J. S. Baker to FBI, Sept. 3, 1941, no. 144-9-0, ibid.; memo, Berge to Hoover, Oct. 17, 1941, no. 144-9-0, ibid.; and letter, Fred Hallford to Director, Dec. 28, 1942, no. 144-9-0, ibid.

[23] (New York, 1944).

[24] Dominic J. Capeci, Jr., "The Lynching of Cleo Wright: Federal Protection of Constitutional Rights during World War II," *Journal of American History* 72 (March 1986): 859-87.

[25] Memo, D. Milton Ladd to Tamm, July 22, 1943, no. 44-802-89, FBI Detroit Race Riot File; and memo, Hoover to Attorney General, June 23, 1943, no. 44-802-89, ibid.

[26] Memo, Hoover to Attorney General, Dec. 29, 1943, no. 44-802-171, ibid.

[27] U.S. Congress, Senate, Select Committee to Study Governmental Operations with Respect to Intelligence Activities, *Final Report — Book II, Intelligence Activities and the Rights of Americans*, 94th Cong., 2d sess., 1976, p. 25.

[28] Ibid., p. 32; and idem, *Final Report — Book III, Supplementary Detailed Staff Reports on Intelligence Activities and the Rights of Americans*, 94th Cong., 2d sess., 1976, p. 399.

[29] Clayton R. Koppes and Gregory D. Black, "Blacks, Loyalty, and Motion-Picture Propaganda in World War II," *Journal of American History* 73 (Sept. 1986): 383-406.

[30] Memo, Francis Biddle to Hoover, May 29, 1942, no. 1, Folder 136, J. Edgar Hoover Official and Confidential FBI Files.

[31] See the documents in the American Youth Congress Folder, Nichols Official and Confidential FBI Files.

[32] Mark Naison, *Communists in Harlem during the Depression* (Urbana, 1983), pp. 300-01; and letter, Hoover to Edwin M. Watson, May 31, 1941, FBI Rept. no. 794, OF10-B, Roosevelt Papers.

[33] Jesse T. Moore, Jr., *A Search for Equality: The National Urban League, 1910-1961* (University Park, Penn., 1981), p. 118.

[34] Memo, Ladd to Director, Sept. 23, 1942, FBI File no. 62-116758; and Patrick S. Washburn, *A Question of Sedition: The Federal Government's Investigation of the Black Press during World War II* (New York, 1986).

[35] Letters, Hoover to Watson, June 19, 1941, FBI Rept. no. 835, and June 26, 1942, FBI Rept. no. 2194, OF10-B, Roosevelt Papers; and letter, Hoover to Harry Hopkins, Sept. 4, 1942, FBI Rept. no. 2248-B, ibid.

[36] Letters, Hoover to Hopkins, Feb. 1, 1943, FBI Rept. no. 2304-A, July 3, 1943, FBI Rept. no. 2355-C, July 6, 1943, FBI Rept., no. 2356-A and -B, July 8, 1943, FBI Rept. no. 2357-A, and Sept. 15, 1943, FBI Rept. no. 2416-A, all in OF10-B, ibid.

[37] Memo, Ladd to Director, Sept. 11, 1942, FBI File no. 62-116758; memo, Hoover to SAC Louisville, Aug. 5, 1943, no. 66-6200-44-12, FBI Civil Rights Policy File; memo, E. G. Fitch to Ladd, March 11, 1942, no. 61-6728-220, FBI National Negro Congress File; and memo, Hoover to SAC Philadelphia, n.d. [ca. Dec. 18, 1943], no. 61-3176-178, FBI NAACP File.

[38] Richmond Field Office Rept., Jan. 26, 1943, no. 100-5698-9, FBI Moorish Science Temple of America File.

[39] Birmingham Field Office Rept., Jan. 11, 1945, no. 100-24548-20, Hosea Hudson FBI File.

[40] Harvard Sitkoff, "Racial Militancy and Interracial Violence in the Second World War," *Journal of American History* 58 (Dec. 1971): 661-81.

[41] Memo, Hoover to Attorney General, Oct. 21, 1940, Martin Dies Folder, Hoover Official and Confidential FBI Files. See also Kenneth O'Reilly, "The Roosevelt Administration and Legislative-Executive Conflict: The FBI vs. the Dies Committee," *Congress and the Presidency* 10 (Spring 1983): 79-93.

[42] Memo, Ladd to Director, Sept. 30, 1943, no. 44-802-156, FBI Detroit Race Riot File; and memo, F. L. Welch to Ladd, June 21, 1943, no. 44-802-45, ibid.

[43] Memo, Robert C. Hendon to Tolson, June 24, 1943, no. 44-802-55, ibid.; Hoover to McIntyre, June 23, 1943, no. 44-802-49, ibid.; memo, Nichols to Tolson, June 23, 1943, no. 44-802-8, ibid.; and memo, Hoover to Attorney General, June 25, 1943, no. 44-802-14, ibid.

[44] Memo, John Bugas to Director, July 20, 1943, no. 44-802-92, ibid.; and memo, Tamm to Ladd, June 24, 1943, no. 44-802-11, ibid.

[45] Memos, Welch to Ladd, June 21, 1943, no. 44-802-45, and June 25, 1943, no. 44-802-38, ibid.; and memo, G. Stetter to Ladd, May 21, 1944, no. 62-31615-447, Winchell FBI File.

[46] Memo, Ladd to Director, Sept. 30, 1943, no. 44-802-156, FBI Detroit Race Riot File.

[47] Memo, W. A. Johnson to Ladd, May 17, 1942, no. 62-31615-234, Winchell FBI File.

[48] Memo, Tamm and Tolson to Director, Dec. 12, 1941, Dies Folder, Hoover Official and Confidential FBI Files.

Martin Luther King, Jr. and the Paradox of Nonviolent Direct Action

JAMES A. COLAIACO

By the early 1960s, the slow pace of civil rights reform, the deeply entrenched opposition of white segregationists, and the federal government's lethargy in enforcing civil rights laws all combined to urge African Americans to take more direct actions in bringing about racial equality in American life. The leadership of the Civil Rights Movement, headed by Martin Luther King, Jr., adopted a strategy of mass nonviolent direct action to propel racism upon the national conscience and to force action by the federal government in transforming the social order. King and his lieutenants led demonstrations protesting racial inequalities in public accommodations, schools, jobs, enfranchisement, and other areas. In campaign after campaign in Southern communities, the violence perpetrated upon black protestors, frequently by white law enforcement, dominated the national media prompting the passage of the Civil Rights Act of 1964 and the Voting Rights Act of 1965. Segregationist critics claimed that it was King's challenge of the status quo that provoked violence and disturbed law and order.

James Colaiaco's essay addresses the criticisms leveraged against King and explores the paradox observed by both critics and supporters of nonviolent direct action. Noting King's assertion in the "Letter from Birmingham Jail" that "nonviolent direct action seeks to create such a crisis and foster such a tension that a community that has constantly refused to negotiate is forced to confront the issue," Colaiaco makes clear King's understanding of the coercive value of nonviolent protest in compelling federal action. The strategy, typified in the Birmingham, Selma, and Montgomery campaigns, revealed both intellectual and constitutional underpinnings, and served well as an effective moral force, moving federal action from passive to active engagement in the promotion of civil rights for African Americans, particularly in the South.

I

WHEN THE DEFINITIVE HISTORY of the American civil rights movement is eventually written, one of the central themes will be that Martin Luther King, Jr. ranks among the greatest political strategists of all time. During the decade 1955 to 1965, America was the scene of a social revolution that transformed the politics of the entire nation. King organized an army of nonviolent blacks that succeeded in exposing the evils of white racism and overthrowing the legal system of segregation that had prevailed for generations in the South. King's method of militant nonviolent direct action, inspired by the achievement of Mohandas K. Gandhi in India, disrupted the segregationist order by means of marches, mass demonstrations, sit-ins, boycotts and, whenever necessary, civil disobedience. In the short span of ten years more was accomplished than in the previous one hundred, including the enactment of the Civil Rights Act of 1964 and the Voting Rights Act of 1965. While King was not the first to employ the nonviolent method in an attempt to resolve the race problem in America, he was the most successful in mobilizing masses of blacks to protest nonviolently for the fulfillment of their basic civil rights.

Although dedicated to nonviolence, King drew much criticism because his protest campaigns often were accompanied by violence. In the wake of the successful Birmingham campaign in 1963, journalist Reese Cleghorn wrote that King knew well that "the 'peaceful demonstrations' he organized would bring, at the very least, tough repressive measures by the police. And although he hoped his followers would not respond with violence—he has always stressed a nonviolent philosophy—that was a risk he was prepared to take."[1] Although *Time* magazine chose King as "Man of the Year" in 1964, its feature article contained the following observation: "King preaches endlessly about nonviolence, but his protest movements often lead to violence."[2] When King was awarded the Nobel Peace Prize in December 1964, the *U.S. News & World Report,* in an article entitled "Man of Conflict Wins a Peace Prize," remarked that many Americans believed it "extraordinary that this prize should go to a man whose fame is based upon his battle for civil rights for Negroes—and whose activities often led to violence."[3] In an April 1965 article in the conservative *National Review* entitled "The Violence of Nonviolence," Frank Meyer attacked what he regarded as the "violent essence" of King's method. He charged that King's campaigns depended upon "the provocation of violence" and a "violent assault upon representative, constitutional government."[4]

Such criticism persisted throughout King's public career. In another *National Review* article, published shortly after King announced plans for a spring 1968 Poor People's Campaign, involving massive civil disobedience in the nation's capital, Meyer assailed what he termed King's "insurrectionary methods," and solemnly warned of impending "anarchy."[5] Another critic, Lionel Lokos, in a book assessing King shortly after his assassination in 1968, charged that King's success depended upon both the threat and the provocation of violence, and argued that he left his nation "a legacy of lawlessness."[6] Lokos concluded: "It has often been remarked that while Martin Luther King himself was virtually Nonviolence on a Pedestal, violence somehow never seemed far behind him."[7] Even staunch supporters of King conceded that his success was largely dependent upon the provocation of violence. Civil rights activist Jan Howard, a participant in the Selma voting rights campaign in 1965, maintained that although dedicated to nonviolence as a means of action, the civil rights movement needed violence to sustain it.[8] Historian Howard Zinn also admitted that civil rights were often won at the price of violence, but he contended that the degree of violence resulting from protests was insignificant compared to the justice achieved.[9]

The controversy over King's method arose from the paradox inherent in the strategy of nonviolent protest. Although King repeatedly preached that violence was immoral, his critics were correct in noting that his nonviolent method was most successful when it provoked violence from defenders of the racist order. In a revealing article for the *Saturday Review*, written during the Selma protest, King articulated the strategy of a successful nonviolent direct-action campaign:

1. Nonviolent demonstrators go into the streets to exercise their constitutional rights.
2. Racists resist by unleashing violence against them.
3. Americans of conscience in the name of decency demand federal intervention and legislation.
4. The Administration, under mass pressure, initiates measures of immediate intervention and remedial legislation.[10]

King's critics quoted the above scenario as an example of self-incrimination.[11] They were surprised indeed to find King admitting that nonviolence draws its strength as a technique from the violent reactions of opponents. King and his followers always hoped to achieve their goals peacefully; but since the racist community was usually unyielding, civil rights protesters found that when they used nonviolent soul force, they often were met by physical force. Nevertheless, they were prepared to endure the violence they provoked rather than inflict physical injury upon their opponents. Racists contended that the black protesters should be blamed because their actions precipitated violence and disturbed law and order. Until the protestors arrived, the racists lamented, peace reigned in the community. But this argument rests on the erroneous assumption that the absence of overt conflict in a community means justice is present. The purpose of King's nonviolent direct-action campaigns was to compel racist communities to reveal their injustice and brutality, and to compel the government, whether local or federal, to institute legislative reform.

What King's critics often failed to realize was that nonviolent direct action is not a passive, but a militant and essentially coercive means of bringing about social change. At the beginning of his public career, when King was propelled into international fame by his leadership of the Montgomery bus boycott in 1956, he was inclined to stress the importance of converting his racist opponents by reason and love. But after the wave of student sit-ins throughout the South in 1960, and the Freedom Rides in 1961—which forced Southern communities to comply with federal law—King increasingly perceived the coercive essence of nonviolent direct action. As he developed a more realistic view of humanity and the nature of political power, he saw that more racists were compelled rather than converted. Nonviolent direct action was successful in the South because it exerted political, economic, and moral pressure upon the segregationist order. It was this coercive element in King's nonviolent method that provoked violence from racists.

Critics of King concentrated upon the violence that his method stirred, giving scant consideration to the violence inflicted upon the victims of racist oppression. In almost every instance, it was the racists who committed the violence, while the nonviolent protesters provided the occasion for the racists to reveal their true nature. In effect, the racists said to the blacks: "For the sake of law and order, you must submit to a social system even though you believe it to be unjust. If you protest, however, nonviolently, I will retaliate violently and blame you for provoking me." On the other hand, when the blacks did not protest, their passivity was interpreted to mean that they were content with their subservient condition. For generations, passive blacks had been virtually invisible—to use novelist Ralph Ellison's well-known description. As a result of the nonviolent protests led by Martin Luther King, Jr., blacks were no longer invisible; they literally had thrust themselves upon the national consciousness.

While it is true that the nonviolent protest movement was to a large extent sustained by the violent racist response it generated, one must realize that this violence was intrinsic to the racist social fabric. Such violence was not always apparent. Beneath the calm facade of the segregationist law and order lay the more subtle and often hidden violence of institutional racism. When not overtly subduing its victims with dogs and clubs, a racist society depends upon a latent form of violence, hidden under the guise of law and order. As long as blacks were willing to accept their oppression, they remained victims of a psychological form of violence, one that stripped them of their dignity as human beings. Denied fundamental civil rights, decent housing, and an adequate education, generations of black Americans were broken in spirit by the silent violence of the racist system. But when the nonviolent protesters employed direct action to confront racism, this hidden violence was exposed. King maintained that by resisting, the black man would "force his oppressor to commit his brutality openly—in the light of day—with the rest of the world looking on."[12] The civil rights movement was able to defeat the segregationist order in the South because the violence that it provoked from racists stirred the nation's conscience by making evident the injustice that had always existed, but under the cloak of legitimacy. Each nonviolent protester became a target, magnetizing the hatred of racists and exposing them to public view through the media. Clearly, to blame the nonviolent protesters for the violence that accompanied King's campaigns in the South is a prime example of distorting reality by blaming the victims.

II

An analysis of the history of the civil rights movement in America reveals that blacks most often made significant gains only after they employed nonviolent direct action to disrupt the segregationist order, provoking a crisis. As Charles V. Hamilton has observed correctly: "A politics of crisis is a prominent part of the black political experience."[13] Before the emergence of Martin Luther King, Jr., the dominant means of winning civil rights was the legalism practiced by the National Association for the Advancement of Colored People (NAACP). Since its foundation in 1909, the NAACP had used a combination of public education, legislative lobbying, and court action as means to achieve greater equality for black Americans. Its strategy was to undermine the legal structure of segregation gradually by plodding away case by case through the courts. During the 1940s and 1950s, the Association won a series of impressive victories, climaxed by the Supreme Court decision in *Brown v. Board of Education* on May 17, 1954, declaring segregation in the public schools unconstitutional. But in the years immediately following the *Brown* decision, the great expectation of blacks that segregation was on the verge of defeat

went unfulfilled. Public schools and accommodations remained segregated as the Southern states mounted a strategy of "massive
resistance."[14] White Citizens' Councils were instituted and new life
was breathed into the Klan. Meanwhile the federal government,
adopting a policy of extreme caution, was reluctant to enforce the
Brown decision. Perhaps the most flagrant expression of Southern resistance occurred on March 12, 1956, when 101 Southern members of
Congress signed the "Southern Manifesto," condemning *Brown* as
"contrary to established law and to the Constitution," and appealing
to their states to use "all lawful means to bring about a reversal of
this decision" and to "prevent the use of force in its implementation."[15] Such blatant contempt for the law on the part of the South
had a deplorable consequence. "The true meaning of the Manifesto,"
wrote Anthony Lewis of the *New York Times,* "was to make defiance of
the Supreme Court and the Constitution socially acceptable in the
South—to give resistance to the law the approval of the Southern
Establishment."[16]

In the face of such a deliberate and concerted effort to defy the
law, it became apparent that legislation and court action alone would
be insufficient to achieve full citizenship for black Americans. Obviously, law and court decisions must be enforced in order to be meaningful. The law merely declares and defines rights; it does not fulfill
them. During the 1950s and early 1960s, the Federal Bureau of Investigation and the Justice Department stood by while federal laws were
defied, and civil rights workers were brutally beaten, jailed, and sometimes murdered. Although civil rights laws were enacted in 1957 and
1960, promising greater equality to blacks, these laws were either
poorly enforced or ignored. Hence, a method had to be developed
that would coerce the Southern states to comply with the law of the
land, and induce the President and Congress to be more active in
supporting civil rights. The method, forged in the crucible of the
Montgomery bus boycott and developed into a fine art during King's
Birmingham campaign in 1963, was mass nonviolent direct action.
Under the leadership of Martin Luther King, Jr. and the Southern
Christian Leadership Conference (SCLC)—the organization King
founded in 1957 to coordinate direct-action campaigns—the nonviolent method would revolutionize race relations in the South.

History confirms that the federal government long had been
derelict in its duty to protect the rights of black citizens in the South.
Usually, it enforced civil rights laws only after being compelled to do
so. Although the *Brown* decision outlawed segregation in the public
schools, a crisis was necessary in Little Rock, Arkansas, in 1957, imposing the threat of widespread violence, before President Eisen-

hower dispatched federal troops to enforce a federal district court to desegregate the city's Central High School. Although the Supreme Court had ruled against segregation in interstate travel, first in 1946 in *Morgan v. Virginia*, and again in 1960 in *Boynton v. Virginia*, only after violence was committed against valiant Freedom Riders in 1961 did the Kennedy Administration intervene and the Interstate Commerce Commission (ICC) issue a decree supporting the court decisions. James Farmer, National Director of The Congress on Racial Equality (CORE) at the time and organizer of the Freedom Rides, recalled a strategy of deliberate confrontation: "Our philosophy was simple. We put pressure and create a crisis and then they react. I am absolutely certain that the ICC order wouldn't have been issued were it not for the Freedom Rides."[17] In 1962, President Kennedy sent deputy marshals and federalized the National Guard to quell a riot in which two persons died and 375 were injured, after the University of Mississippi, in defiance of a federal court order, attempted to bar the enrollment of James Meredith.

Martin Luther King, Jr.'s successful nonviolent direct-action campaigns followed a recognizable pattern: the provocation of a crisis—accompanied by racist violence against nonviolent protesters—followed by federal intervention. King's unsuccessful campaign in Albany, Georgia, in 1962, where Chief of Police Laurie Pritchett pursued a strategy of meeting nonviolence with nonviolence and peacefully arrested hundreds of demonstrators, underscored the fact that in order to achieve victory against segregation, the provocation of racist violence was essential. Only after violence was inflicted upon black demonstrators in Birmingham in 1963 was the federal government compelled to intervene and national attention focused upon the evils of racism in the Deep South. During the planning stages of the Birmingham campaign—called Project C (the "C" stood for confrontation)—King's principal SCLC assistant, Wyatt Tee Walker, explained: "We've got to have a crisis to bargain with. To take a moderate approach, hoping to get white help doesn't work. They nail you to the cross. . . . You've got to have a crisis."[18] Writing from his Birmingham jail cell, King revealed that the purpose of nonviolent direct action was "to create such a crisis and foster such a tension that a community which has constantly refused to negotiate is forced to confront the issue. It seeks to so dramatize the issue that it can no longer be ignored."[19] Shortly after King's release from jail, the Birmingham campaign reached a climax when thousands of school children were led in demonstrations that succeeded in bringing the city to its knees. Essential to the success of King in Birmingham was the violent response of Sheriff Eugene "Bull" Connor, who epitomized the worst in Southern racism. King had learned that capturing media attention was necessary for victory in the battle for civil rights. While the demonstrators in Birmingham remained committed to nonviolence, millions of Americans were shocked by scenes on television and in the press, of city police, led by Connor, subjecting blacks to night sticks, high-pressure fire hoses, and attack dogs. After weeks of demonstrations, a settlement was reached, with federal assistance, that met essentially all the blacks' demands. After more violence erupted, not only by whites, but also by blacks who were not part of King's nonviolent army, President Kennedy sent federal troops to the outskirts of Birmingham and announced publicly that the federal government would guarantee the settlement. King's Birmingham campaign succeeded in compelling the federal government to intervene in support of black protesters, and was instrumental in the creation of the bill that would become the Civil Rights Act of 1964. President Kennedy was only partly jesting when he confided to King shortly after the Birmingham settlement: "Our judgment of Bull Connor should not be too harsh. After all, in his way, he has done a good deal for civil rights legislation this year."[20]

In the spring of 1964, King led a campaign to desegregate public accommodations in St. Augustine, Florida, America's oldest city. After weeks of mass meetings and nonviolent marches—which were met by savage white violence—the city sheriff obtained a local court injunction banning night marches. Night marches to the Old Slave Market in St. Augustine's public square had become increasingly effective in dramatizing the contrast between the nonviolent dignity of blacks and the brutality of white racists. Within a few weeks, King and the Southern Christian Leadership Conference (SCLC) were granted a federal court injunction permitting night marches on the grounds that the ban was in violation of First and Fourteenth Amendment rights. Though white racist violence continued, it abated after SCLC lawyers, armed with the recently passed 1964 Civil Rights Act, were successful in securing a federal court order enjoining St. Augustine hotels, motels, and restaurants to desegregate.[21] Although the St. Augustine campaign did not fully achieve its goals, it nevertheless had a national impact. The racist violence it provoked focused attention once again on the grievances of blacks, stimulating federal court action in support of civil rights, and providing publicity that facilitated passage of the 1964 Civil Rights Act by Congress. These achievements, born of a nonviolent protest campaign that kindled a violent response, are a prominent illustration of the benefits derived from the paradox inherent in nonviolent direct action.

The following year, 1965, King and the SCLC launched a voting-rights campaign in Selma, Alabama, which became the climax of the civil rights movement in the South. Here too, King's success depended upon the ability of a nonviolent protest to create a crisis. As he observed: "Demonstrations, experience has shown, are part of the process of stimulating legislation and law enforcement. The federal government reacts to events more quickly when a situation cries out for its intervention."[22] Selma was an ideal place for a nonviolent direct-action campaign. Not only had the vast majority of its black citizens been denied the right to vote, but Sheriff Jim Clark's well-known record of brutality against civil rights workers had made him as much a symbol of white racism as Birmingham's Connor. After weeks of demonstrations and sporadic racist violence, protesters finally were able to provoke a crisis on March 7, "Bloody Sunday," when Alabama state police violently prevented them from marching across the Edmund Pettus Bridge and on to the state capitol in Montgomery to petition Governor George Wallace to enforce voting rights. After further protests, including another tense confrontation on the Edmund Pettus Bridge, President Johnson responded to the growing national outrage on March 15 by issuing an emotional appeal to Congress to support his proposed voting-rights legislation. Within a week, the President dispatched federal troops to Alabama to protect the historic voting-rights march from Selma to Montgomery, culminating in a stirring address to the entire nation by Martin Luther King, Jr. The Selma campaign bore substantial fruit, providing the major stimulus for the passage of the Voting Rights Act of 1965.

In Birmingham, St. Augustine, and Selma, King and the SCLC proved to be consummate masters of the art of crisis politics. They aroused sympathy for the cause of blacks and national anger at the methods used to suppress them. Essential to King's success was his ability to attract media attention to the plight of black Americans and manipulate his opponents into playing directly into his hands. Though King would denounce the immoral practices recommended by Machiavelli for the successful politician, an analysis of his campaigns reveals that while he appeared to be the lamb, in reality his nonviolent method embodied much of the lion and the fox.

III

Citizens of a nation dedicated to the ideals of liberty, justice, and equality are understandably disturbed by the fact that a severe crisis was usually necessary before the federal government would intervene in the states and localities to defend basic civil rights. The frustration of millions of black Americans was articulated by a line in the speech of John Lewis, chairman of the Student Nonviolent Coordinating Committee (SNCC), delivered during the March on Washington on August 28, 1963: "I want to know: which side is the federal government on?"[23] Under the U.S. Constitution, all citizens, regardless of race, color, or creed, are guaranteed the First Amendment rights to speak freely, assemble peacefully, and petition the government for a redress of grievances. The Fourteenth Amendment guarantees the right of equal protection of the laws and prohibits any state from depriving a citizen of life, liberty, or property without due process of law. The Fifteenth Amendment protects the right of all citizens to vote. A democracy seeks to balance two values. On the one hand, law and order must be preserved and violence controlled in order that people's rights will not be endangered. On the other hand, individual citizens must be free to act peacefully to protect their rights. They must be free to dissent, to organize, to demonstrate. The question is: should individuals be prevented from exercising their constitutional rights merely because their actions might provoke violence? In other words, must individuals surrender their right to protest because of the threat of disorder? This is a complex issue, with no easy answer. Of course, the state must preserve order. But if the mere possibility of violence is sufficient to sanction the denial of the constitutional right to protest, all an oppressor must do to prevent the institution of remedial reform is to indicate beforehand that response to protests will be violent. While King's campaigns in the South often stirred racist violence, they did not depart from the requirements of the Constitution. Unlike the racists, who continued to act in defiance of federal law and Supreme Court decisions, King and the SCLC manifested a profound respect for the principle of law and order. They did not seek to destroy the social fabric; they sought instead to make it more just. Hence, whenever their protests involved civil disobedience to what they regarded as unjust segregation laws, they willingly accepted the legal penalty for their principled disobedience.

Despite express constitutional guarantees, blacks in the South frequently were beaten and arrested for picketing and demonstrating peacefully, and deprived of the right to vote. The primary responsibility for the enforcement of the Constitution and the laws of the nation lies with the Executive branch of the federal government. The duty of the President is to "preserve, protect, and defend the Constitution of the United States" (Article II), which is "the supreme law of the land" (Article VI). Nevertheless, the Executive branch, as has been noted, has been reluctant to fulfill its responsibility.

In order to understand why King found it necessary to provoke crises to compel federal intervention on behalf of the rights of black citizens, one must understand certain principles of the American federal system. The issue of enforcing civil rights in the South posed a difficult dilemma for the federal government. The great architects of the U.S. Constitution perceived that since power tends to corrupt, there should be a federal system of government—separating power, in the interest of liberty, between a central national or federal government and individual state governments. Under this system, the states' rights doctrine dictates that police power is reserved first to the local authorities. Consequently, the federal government assumed the authority to intervene in the states—either by court injunction, arrests, or federalizing a state National Guard—only when a federal court order was violated, such as at Little Rock in 1957, or when it was demonstrated that a state could no longer maintain order, such as in Birmingham in 1963 and Selma in 1965. Unless compelled by these criteria, the federal government had refused to intervene in the states to enforce civil rights. But this was no solution for the numerous instances of violence committed against blacks locally in the South. To leave protection entirely in the hands of the state and local authorities, except in cases of intense crisis, was insufficient, for it was often these same authorities who were responsible for the violation of civil rights.

King and the SCLC were counselled on the complexities of federalism by their legal advisors, including members of the NAACP Legal Defense Fund, Inc., seasoned veterans in the struggle for the equality of blacks. Indeed, King learned to take advantage of the dual system of federal-state law that federalism provided. Thus, civil disobedience to state segregation laws was justified on the grounds of an appeal to the higher law of the nation. At the same time, King and his staff understood the importance of maintaining a separation of power between the federal government and the states. But they also perceived that the South long had exploited the states' rights doctrine as a means of protecting its racist policies. During the late 1950s and early 1960s, the repeated demands of civil rights advocates that the federal government pursue a more active policy in enforcing civil rights in the South presented a formidable challenge to the traditional assumptions and rules of federal-state relations.

During the Kennedy Administration, pressure for federal intervention increased as violence against civil rights workers escalated in the Deep South. President Kennedy was determined to proceed with the utmost caution in the field of civil rights.[24] Though black voters had been essential to his slim victory in the election of 1960, he did not want to risk alienating Southern Democrats in Congress, or jeopardize the rest of his ambitious legislative program by calling for the passage of another civil rights act. In response to insistent pleas that the federal government play a stronger role in promoting civil rights, the Administration confined itself largely to supporting a voter registration drive sponsored by the leading civil rights organizations.

The Kennedy Administration sought to explain and justify its caution. Attorney General Robert Kennedy had strong reservations against a civil rights policy that would place what he regarded as too much power in the hands of the Justice Department. In 1963, he requested that the House Judiciary Committee not grant broad injunctive power to the Attorney General in civil rights cases because "one result might be that State and local authorities would abdicate their law enforcement responsibilities, thereby creating a vacuum in authority which could be filled only by Federal force. This in turn—if it is to be faced squarely—would require creation of a national police force."[25] The fullest articulation of the Administration's position was presented by Burke Marshall, Assistant Attorney General and the head of the Civil Rights Division of the Justice Department. In a series of lectures delivered at Columbia University in 1964, published as Federalism and Civil Rights, Marshall echoed Robert Kennedy's fear that effective federal intervention to enforce civil rights would necessitate the institution of a national police force, with dangerous consequences for the federal system. Justice Robert Jackson had warned that "the establishment of the supremacy of the national over the local police authorities" might lead to a totalitarian state.[26] Yale University law professor Alexander Bickel declared that a national police force would be "destructive of the values of a free society." In sum, the Administration's main contention was that more active intervention on its part to enforce civil rights might destroy the delicate balance between the federal and state powers that the Founding Fathers thought essential for the preservation of liberty. In an interview with Anthony Lewis in 1964, Robert Kennedy expressed grave misgivings when asked whether the federal government might assume primary responsibility for law enforcement in the states: "I just wouldn't want that much authority in the hands of either the FBI, or the Department of Justice, or the President of the United States."[27]

Civil rights activists long had pleaded with the federal government to investigate and prosecute cases of racist brutality in the South. According to Marshall, were the federal government to initiate civil rights suits on behalf of private citizens, it would exceed the legitimate limits of its power. The fundamental assumption of the federal system is that constitutional rights are "individual and personal, to be asserted by private citizens as they choose, in court, speaking through their chosen counsel."[28] Moreover, he argued that in order to secure an injunction to protect a citizen's rights, the Justice Department must have specific statutory authority, such as that granted under the Civil Rights Acts of 1957 and 1960 for cases dealing with voting rights.

It was not long before advocates of civil rights subjected the Administration's position to a thorough refutation. Some twenty-nine professors from six of the nation's leading law schools sought to establish a firm legal basis for greater federal intervention in defense of civil rights.[29] Citing the *Debs* case of 1895 as precedent, in which the Supreme Court ruled that the federal government may enforce the law when necessary by injunction in any part of the nation, they argued that the Justice Department could seek injunctions to protect the civil rights of individuals in the Deep South without specific statutory authority.[30] Moreover, they cited Title 10, Section 333 of the United States Code, which reads in part:

> The President, by using the militia or the armed forces, or both, *or by any other means* (italic added), shall take such measures as he considers necessary to suppress, in a State, any domestic violence, unlawful combination, or conspiracy, if it—
>
> (1) so hinders the execution of the laws of that State, and of the United States within the State, that any part or class of its people is deprived of a right, privilege, immunity, or protection named in the Constitution and secured by law, and the constituted authorities of that State are unable, fail, or refuse to protect that right, privilege, or immunity, or to give that protection; or
>
> (2) opposes or obstructs the execution of the laws of the United States or impedes the course of justice under those laws. . . ."[31]

The foregoing section of the U.S. Code was used by the Kennedy Administration to justify sending federal troops to Birmingham in 1963. Moreover, the Supremacy Clause of the U.S. Constitution (Article VI) empowered the federal government to intervene whenever a state failed to protect constitutionally guaranteed rights, such as the rights to vote and to demonstrate. As Haywood Burns has pointed out, the federal government usually justified its refusal to intervene more actively in civil rights matters by blurring the distinction between authority and policy.[32] The Kennedy Administration clearly had the authority to intervene all along; it simply chose not to do so.

As far as a national police force was concerned, civil rights lawyers pointed out that in effect one already existed in the FBI, which was authorized to investigate and arrest criminals who violated federal laws. One of the most persuasive arguments for greater federal intervention was developed by Howard Zinn, who contended that the Fourteenth Amendment had been enacted specifically to place the authority to enforce civil rights in the hands of the federal government whenever a state failed to enforce them.[33] Hence, the federal government had jurisdiction over violations of the Fourteenth Amendment, and its refusal to protect civil rights within the states was an abdication of its legal authority and a violation of the Constitution it was entrusted to uphold. Nevertheless, despite the cogent arguments of civil rights lawyers, the federal government persisted in its policy of intervening directly in the Southern states to uphold civil rights only after a severe crisis arose, such as in Birmingham and Selma. Were it not for these crises, stirred by King's creative strategy of nonviolent direct action, the segregationist system would have been perpetuated for millions of Southern blacks while the national government chose to sacrifice civil rights to a distorted view of federalism.

IV

By 1965, King's method of militant nonviolent direct action had succeeded in arousing the nation to the evils of racism in the South and influencing directly the enactment of historic civil rights legislation. The Civil Rights Act of 1964 and the Voting Rights Act of 1965 transformed the face of the South and exerted a profound effect upon the entire nation. The nonviolent direct-action method enabled oppressed blacks to act constructively towards attaining freedom for themselves and vindicating their dignity as American citizens. Meanwhile, the progress made against segregation in the South had also awakened the blacks of the North. In August 1965, six days of rioting in the Watts section of Los Angeles signalled the end of the era of nonviolence, and served as a grim warning that the problems of the nation's ghettos could no longer be ignored. When King took his nonviolent method to the large Northern ghettos, where the problems were more complex and deeply rooted, he was less effective, for the oppressors were better prepared and more sophisticated, and racism more subtle and intractable. As King and the SCLC learned in Chicago in 1966, it was much easier to desegregate a lunchcounter or a bus station in the South than to eradicate ghetto poverty, unemployment, deplorable housing, and inadequate schools. It was also easier to provoke a crisis in a small Southern city, where nonviolent demonstrations could virtually paralyze a community, than in a vast metropolis like Chicago, where similar demonstrations were readily absorbed and neutralized. Moreover, beginning in 1965, thousands of lower-class ghetto blacks found the violent rhetoric of Black Power more appealing than nonviolence. But once blacks adopted the tactics of violence, they were less successful in exposing the often hidden violence of institutional racism and in compelling the fulfillment of their just demands. King's militant nonviolent method was successful in the South because blacks could be trained in nonviolent tactics that when applied to the racist system created the friction necessary to provoke a crisis and expose the brutality of the oppressors. If Martin Luther King, Jr.'s nonviolent method was paradoxical because it often provoked a violent response, the supporters of the racist system were responsible for the paradox.

Notes

[1] Reese Cleghorn, "Martin Luther King, Jr., Apostle of Crisis," in C. Eric Lincoln, *Martin Luther King, Jr.: A Profile* (New York, 1970), p. 114.

[2] "Man of the Year," *Time*, January 3, 1964, p. 13.

[3] "How Martin Luther King Won the Nobel Peace Prize," *U.S. News & World Report*, February 8, 1965, p. 76.

[4] Frank Meyer, "The Violence of Nonviolence," *National Review*, April 20, 1965, p. 327.

[5] Frank Meyer, "Showdown With Insurrection," *National Review*, January 16, 1968, p. 36.

[6] Lionel Lokos, *The Life and Legacy of Martin Luther King* (New Rochelle, New York, 1968), p. 460.

[7] Ibid., p. 225.

[8] Jan Howard, "The Provocation of Violence: A Civil Rights Tactic?" *Dissent*, 13 (January-February, 1966): 94-9.

[9] Howard Zinn, "The Force of Nonviolence," *The Nation*, March 17, 1962, pp. 227-33.

[10] Martin Luther King, Jr., "Behind the Selma March," *Saturday Review*, 48 (April 3, 1965): 16.

[11] For examples, see Lokos, op. cit., p. 75; and Frank Meyer, op. cit., p. 327.

[12] Martin Luther King, Jr., *Why We Can't Wait* (New York, 1964), p. 27.

[13] Charles V. Hamilton, ed., *The Black Experience in American Politics* (New York, 1973), p. 157.

[14] See Francis M. Wilhoit, *The Politics of Massive Resistance* (New York, 1973).

[15] Ibid., pp. 52-3.

[16] Anthony Lewis, *Portrait of a Decade: The Second American Revolution* (New York, 1964), p. 45.

[17] Quoted in Victor S. Navasky, *Kennedy Justice* (New York, 1971), p. 233.

[18] Quoted in Harvard Sitkoff, *The Struggle for Black Equality, 1954-1980* (New York, 1981), pp. 128-29.

[19] Martin Luther King, Jr., "Letter from Birmingham Jail," *Why We Can't Wait* p. 81; for an analysis of King's famous Letter, see James A. Colaiaco, "The American Dream Unfulfilled: Martin Luther King, Jr. and the Letter From Birmingham Jail," *Phylon*, 45 (March 1984): 1.

[20] King, *Why We Can't Wait*, p. 144.

[21] See Alan F. Westin and Barry Mahoney, *The Trial of Martin Luther King* (New York, 1974), pp. 161-64.

[22] Stephen B. Oates, *Let the Trumpet Sound: The Life of Martin Luther King, Jr.* (New York, 1982), p. 326.

[23] The text of Lewis' speech, which was altered just prior to delivery to mollify its criticism of the federal government, is reprinted in Philip S. Foner, ed., *The Voice of Black America* (New York, 1975) vol. 2, pp. 359-61.

[24] See Carl Brauer, *John F. Kennedy and the Second Reconstruction* (New York, 1977); and Victor Navasky, op. cit.

[25] Arthur M. Schlesinger, Jr., *Robert Kennedy and His Times* (New York, 1979), p. 330.

[26] Ibid., p. 328.

[27] Ibid., p. 329.

[28] Burke Marshall, *Federalism and Civil Rights* (New York, 1964), p. 50.

[29] Haywood Burns, "The Federal Government and Civil Rights," in Leon Friedman, ed., *Southern Justice* (New York, 1965), p. 236.

[30] Howard Zinn, *The Southern Mystique* (New York, 1964), pp. 205-06.

[31] Haywood Burns, op. cit., p. 237.

[32] Ibid., p. 236.

[33] Howard Zinn, op. cit., pp. 207-08.

Appendix

ALPHABETICAL LIST OF AUTHORS WITH CITATIONS

Alphabetical List of Authors with Citations

Bell, Howard H. "The Negro Emigration Movement, 1849-1854: A Phase of Negro Nationalism." *Phylon* 20 (2nd quarter, 1959): 132-142.

Brockington, Lolita G. "Slave Revolt, Slave Debate: A Comparison." *Phylon* 45 (2nd quarter, 1984): 98-110.

Carper, N. Gordon. "Slavery Revisited: Peonage in the South." *Phylon* 37 (1st quarter, 1976): 85-99.

Chase, Hal S. "Struggle for Equality: Fort Des Moines Training Camp for Colored Officers, 1917." *Phylon* 39 (4th quarter, 1978): 297-310.

Colaiaco, James A. "Martin Luther King, Jr. and the Paradox of Nonviolent Direct Action." *Phylon* 47 (1st quarter, 1986): 16-28.

Cornelius, Janet. " 'We Slipped and Learned to Read': Slave Accounts of the Literacy Process, 1830-1865." *Phylon* 44 (3rd quarter, 1983): 171-186.

Dalfiume, Richard M. "Military Segregation and the 1940 Presidential Election." *Phylon* 37 (1st quarter, 1976): 42-55.

Eisenberg, Bernard. "Only for the Bourgeois? James Weldon Johnson and the NAACP, 1916-1930." *Phylon* 43 (2nd quarter, 1982): 110-124.

Foner, Philip S. "Black Participation in the Centennial of 1876." *Phylon* 39 (4th quarter, 1978): 283-296.

Gatewood, Willard B. "Booker T. Washington and the Ulrich Affair." *Phylon* 30 (3rd quarter, 1969): 286-302.

Greene, Lorenzo J. "Mutiny on the Slave Ships." *Phylon* 4 (4th quarter, 1944): 346-354.

Hachey, Thomas. "Walter White and the American Negro Soldier in World War II: A Diplomatic Dilemma for Britain." *Phylon* 39 (3rd quarter, 1978): 241-249.

Higgins, Billy D. "Negro Thought and the Exodus of 1879." *Phylon* 32 (1st quarter, 1971): 39-52.

Holmes, William F. "The Leflore County Massacre and the Demise of the Colored Farmers' Alliance." *Phylon* 34 (3rd quarter, 1973): 267-274.

Kilson, Marion D. de B. "Towards Freedom: An Analysis of Slave Revolts in the United States." *Phylon* 25 (2nd quarter, 1964): 175-187.

Littlefield, Daniel F. Jr. "Black Dreams and 'Free' Homes: The Oklahoma Territory, 1891-1894." *Phylon* 34 (4th quarter, 1973): 342-357.

Martin, Charles H. "Negro Leaders, the Republican Party, and the Election of 1932." *Phylon* 32 (1st quarter, 1971): 85-93.

Meier, August. "The Negro and the Democratic Party, 1875-1915." *Phylon* 17 (2nd quarter, 1956): 173-191.

Mohr, Clarence L. "Slavery in Oglethorpe County, Georgia, 1773-1865." *Phylon* 33 (1st quarter, 1972): 4-21.

O'Reilly, Kenneth. "The Roosevelt Administration and Black America: Federal Surveillance Policy and Civil Rights During the New Deal and World War II Years." *Phylon* 48 (1st quarter, 1987): 12-25.

Page, Oscar C. "The Black Press and the Drive for Integrated Graduate and Professional Schools." *Phylon* 43 (1st quarter, 1982): 15-27.

Plummer, Brenda Gayle. "The Afro-American Response to the Occupation of Haiti, 1915-1934." *Phylon* 43 (2nd quarter, 1982): 125-143.

Sweat, Edward F. "Some Notes on the Role of Negroes in the Establishment of Public Schools in South Carolina." *Phylon* 22 (2nd quarter, 1961): 160-66.

Roper, John Herbert. "Slave Revolt, Slave Debate: A Comparison." *Phylon* 45 (2nd quarter, 1984): 98-110.

Rosen, Bruce. "Abolition and Colonization, the Years of Conflict: 1829-1834." *Phylon* 33 (2nd quarter, 1972): 177-192.

Rury, John L. "Philanthropy, Self Help, and Social Control: The New York Manumission Society and Free Blacks." *Phylon* 46 (3rd quarter, 1985): 231-241.

Tillery, Tyrone. "The Inevitability of the Douglass-Garrison Conflict." *Phylon* 32 (2nd quarter, 1976): 137-149.

Tucker, David M. "Miss Ida B. Wells and Memphis Lynching." *Phylon* 32 (2nd quarter, 1971): 112-122.

Underhill, Lonnie E. "Black Dreams and 'Free' Homes: The Oklahoma Territory, 1891-1894." *Phylon* 34 (4th quarter, 1973): 342-357.

Weaver, Bill L. "The Black Press and the Assault on Professional Baseball's 'Color Line,' October 1945-April 1947." *Phylon* 40 (4th quarter, 1979): 303-317.

Weaver, Bill L. "The Black Press and the Drive for Integrated Graduate and Professional Schools." *Phylon* 43 (1st quarter, 1982): 15-27.

White, Arthur O. "The Black Movement Against Jim Crow Education in Buffalo, New York, 1800-1900." *Phylon* 30 (4th quarter, 1969): 375-393.

INDEX